Web Publisher's Construction Kit with VRML/Live 3D

CREATING 3D WEB WORLDS

DAVID FOX AND PHILIP SHADDOCK

Waite Group Press™
A Division of Sams Publishing
Corte Madera, CA

Publisher: *Mitchell Waite*
Editor-in-Chief: *Charles Drucker*

Acquisitions Editor: *Jill Pisoni*

Editorial Director: *John Crudo*
Managing Editor: *Joel Fugazzotto, LightSpeed Publishing*
Content Editor: *Scott Calamar, LightSpeed Publishing*
Copy Editor: *Jan Jue*

Production Director: *Julianne Ososke*
Production Manager: *Cecile Kaufman*
Production Editor: *Mark Nigara*
Cover Design: *Sestina Quarequio*
Design: *Karen Johnston*
Production: *Christi Fryday, Jude Levinson*

© 1996 by The Waite Group, Inc.® Published by Waite Group Press™, 200 Tamal Plaza, Corte Madera, CA 94925.

Waite Group Press™ is a division of Sams Publishing.

Waite Group Press™ is distributed to bookstores and book wholesalers by Publishers Group West, Box 8843, Emeryville, CA 94662, 1-800-788-3123 (in California 1-510-658-3453).

Printed in the United States of America
96 97 98 99 • 10 9 8 7 6 5 4 3 2 1

Library of Congress Cataloging-in-Publication Data
Fox, David S.
    Web Publisher's Construction Kit with VRML/Live 3D / David S. Fox &
Philip Shaddock.
    p.   cm.
    Includes index.
    ISBN: 1-57169-068-9
    1. Computer Graphics.   2. Three-dimensional display systems.
3. VRML (Document markup language).   4. World Wide Web (Information
retreival system).   I. Shaddock, Phillip.   II. Title.
T385.F684   1996
006--dc20

96-7214
CIP

Dedications

To Emma, in love and squalor.

—David Fox

For my sweetie.

—Philip Shaddock

Message from the
Publisher

WELCOME TO OUR NERVOUS SYSTEM

Some people say that the World Wide Web is a graphical extension of the information superhighway, just a network of humans and machines sending each other long lists of the equivalent of digital junk mail.

I think it is much more than that. To me, the Web is nothing less than the nervous system of the entire planet—not just a collection of computer brains connected together, but more like a billion silicon neurons entangled and recirculating electro-chemical signals of information and data, each contributing to the birth of another CPU and another Web site.

Think of each person's hard disk connected at once to every other hard disk on earth, driven by human navigators searching like Columbus for the New World. Seen this way the Web is more of a super entity, a growing, living thing, controlled by the universal human will to expand, to be more. Yet, unlike a purposeful business plan with rigid rules, the Web expands in a nonlinear, unpredictable, creative way that echoes natural evolution.

We created our Web site not just to extend the reach of our computer book products but to be part of this synaptic neural network, to experience, like a nerve in the body, the flow of ideas and then to pass those ideas up the food chain of the mind. Your mind. Even more, we wanted to pump some of our own creative juices into this rich wine of technology.

TASTE OUR DIGITAL WINE

And so we ask you to taste our wine by visiting the body of our business. Begin by understanding the metaphor we have created for our Web site—a universal learning center, situated in outer space in the form of a space station. A place where you can journey to study any topic from the convenience of your own screen. Right now we are focusing on computer topics, but the stars are the limit on the Web.

If you are interested in discussing this Web site or finding out more about the Waite Group, please send me e-mail with your comments, and I will be happy to respond. Being a programmer myself, I love to talk about technology and find out what our readers are looking for.

Sincerely,

Mitchell Waite

Mitchell Waite, C.E.O. and Publisher

200 Tamal Plaza
Corte Madera, CA 94925
415-924-2575
415-924-2576 fax

Internet e-mail:
Support@waite.com

Website:
http://www.waite.com/waite

CREATING THE HIGHEST QUALITY COMPUTER BOOKS IN THE INDUSTRY

Waite Group Press
Waite Group New Media

Come Visit
WAITE.COM
Waite Group Press
World Wide Web Site

Now find all the latest information on Waite Group books at our new Web site, **http://www.waite.com/waite.** You'll find an online catalog where you can examine and order any title, review upcoming books, and send e-mail to our authors and editors. Our FTP site has all you need to update your book: the latest program listings, errata sheets, most recent versions of Fractint, POV Ray, Polyray, DMorph, and all the programs featured in our books. So download, talk to us, ask questions, on **http://www.waite.com/waite.**

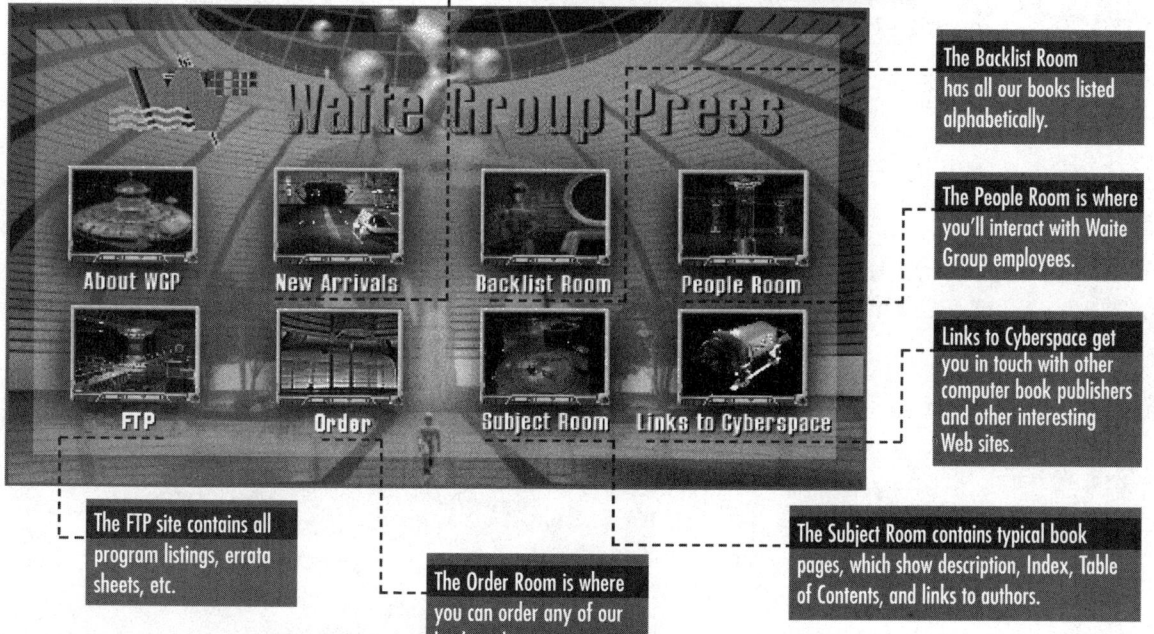

The New Arrivals Room has all our new books listed by month. Just click for a description, Index, Table of Contents, and links to authors.

The Backlist Room has all our books listed alphabetically.

The People Room is where you'll interact with Waite Group employees.

Links to Cyberspace get you in touch with other computer book publishers and other interesting Web sites.

The FTP site contains all program listings, errata sheets, etc.

The Order Room is where you can order any of our books online.

The Subject Room contains typical book pages, which show description, Index, Table of Contents, and links to authors.

World Wide Web:

COME SURF OUR TURF—THE WAITE GROUP WEB

http://www.waite.com/waite
Gopher: gopher.waite.com
FTP: ftp.waite.com

ABOUT THE AUTHORS

David Fox lives in New York City, where he writes novels, screenplays, articles, and technical stuff, depending upon how broke he is. Lately he's been keeping pretty darn busy programming for a major multimedia company. He's the author of several books, including *Love Bytes: The Online Dating Handbook* (Waite Group Press, 1994) and *HTML Web Publisher's Construction Kit* (Waite Group Press, 1995). Reach him at http://found.cs.nyu.edu/dfox.

Philip Shaddock is President of Rage Pictures, a Vancouver-based interactive multimedia production company. His previous Waite Group books are on multimedia programming (*Multimedia Creations*) and 3D modeling (*3D Modeling Lab*); Phil also created the multimedia demo bundled with Waite Group's *Nanotechnology Playhouse*. As a GRASP programmer, he has long been practicing the art of making an elephant dance on the head of a needle. He can be reached at: shaddock@outrage.com.

CONTENTS

TABLE OF CONTENTS

Chapter 12: Applying Surface Attributes and Textures . .275

Acknowledgments

David Fox: Thanks to the VRML community, especially (but not limited to) Gavin Bell, Anthony Parisi, Mita, and Mark Pesce. Thanks to Keith Rule for WCT2POV, an outstanding contribution to 3D graphics. And thanks to McCue and Paper Software for giving the world a world-giver like WebFX and Live3D.

Philip Shaddock: David Fox's enthusiasm was infectious. Thanks to Jill Pisoni for asking me to do the book and John Crudo for ensuring Waite Group's high standards. Scott Calamar edited with kindness, humor, and a sharp eye. Joel Fugazotto did an excellent job of steering the book through its labyrinth. Dan Scherf pulled together a CD out of anarchy. Thanks to the other staff at Waite Group Press, and Mitch Waite, for making book-writing a more pleasurable task than it should be.

Introduction

The first time we saw three-dimensional graphics we were amazed by the beauty, of course, but we were even more wowed by the philosophy. What an idea! Instead of just creating images of the world, as painters and photographers have tried to do for centuries, why not actually try to create the world from the ground up? Instead of protons and electrons, a 3D modeler uses bits and bytes, sculpting vast grids of data that represent exactly what an object looks like in real space.

The first time we saw the World Wide Web, we shared an equal sense of awe. Here were all the major computer networks across the planet, hooked up with a pretty graphical face and talking to each other. And then the idea hit us like a gavel in an old Roadrunner cartoon: What if 3D graphics and the Web were mixed? Not only would you have vast digital worlds, you'd have vast numbers of people coming to visit them and meet in them. The implications were staggering: This wouldn't be a mere alternate world—this would be an entirely different world, where distance, political boundaries, and laws of nature have no reign.

Well, we weren't the only ones with that idea. Dozens of people and companies worked to make this new world a reality. The Virtual Reality Modeling Language (VRML) and Live3D are the first successful attempts to bring widespread 3D graphics to the Internet. This book is for pioneers who want to claim part of the Internet's newest frontier. Conditions are pretty primitive in virtual worlds, and you'll be missing the comforts of more established computer technologies. But if you are the type of person who is adventurous, curious, and loves the freedom of an uncharted, lawless new world, you're going to love VRML.

We have journeyed slightly ahead of you and report wide new vistas just beyond the next ridge. Strange new worlds in lavender, teal, and turquoise. Houses that roll over, twist around, and disappear. Walls that you can pass right through. Checkerboard plains with edges on the swirling abyss. We've packed the tools you'll need to survive and flourish in the brave new world. We've provided tips that help you avoid some of the pitfalls of creating online virtual worlds, and point to many of its facilities and pleasures. You'll learn how to invent your own worlds, define their boundaries, and make them your own.

Here's an itinerary for your exploration:

Part I: Stepping into the Web provides the background you need to begin your three-dimensional foray.

Chapter 1, The World Isn't Flat takes you through the history and ideology of VRML.

Chapter 2, Virtually Amazing is a quick tour through several exciting virtual worlds that already exist.

Chapter 3, Window to the World: WEBFX and Live3D teaches you how to use Netscape's Live3D browser, one of the most advanced and popular VRML browsers in the world.

In case you'd like to try a different viewport, *Chapter 4, Other Exposures* covers all the other major VRML browsers.

Part II: Learning 3D Modeling shows you how to construct 3D worlds suitable for VRML browsers.

Chapter 5, Creating Worlds with 3D Software introduces you to the challenges of transmitting graphics over the Web.

Chapter 6, The Basics of 3D Modeling introduces you to the basics of 3D modeling.

Chapter 7, Using Imagine covers the fantastic Impulse Imagine 3D modeler, which is included with this book.

Chapter 8, Basic Modeling Tools teaches you the basic modeling tools for creating basic objects.

Chapter 9, 3D Modeling Power Tools introduces sophisticated power tools for building more complex shapes.

Chapter 10, Skinning and Deformations covers two of the most popular modeling strategies.

Chapter 11, Coloring and Shading Objects teaches you the art of coloring and shading objects.

Chapter 12, Applying Surface Attributes and Textures shows how to apply surface attributes and textures to objects.

Chapter 13, Creating a Scene in Fountain shows how to assemble objects into scenes, using Caligari's Fountain.

Chapter 14, Trading Worlds: Converting shows you how to take all the exciting stuff you've built and convert it into VRML.

Part III: Programming with VRML reveals the nitty-gritty of this powerful markup language and shows you how to take advantage of it.

Chapter 15, Very, Very VRML gets into the guts of the language, showing you how the format is structured and why.

Chapter 16, Building Blocks: Shaping Nodes shows you how to use shape nodes to create the objects in your virtual world.

Chapter 17, Ganging Up: Groups talks about group nodes, which help you combine shapes to create more advanced shapes.

Chapter 18, You've Got the Look: Properties covers property nodes, which allow you to color, place, or otherwise manipulate your shapes.

Chapter 19, Let There Be Light (and Textures and Cameras) goes into the razzle-dazzle of altering the shading and viewpoint in your virtual worlds.

Chapter 20, Jumping from World to World discusses how to jump across the World Wide Web from one virtual world to another.

Chapter 21, I Want More: Extending VRML teaches you to extend VRML, making it into a more robust language.

Chapter 22, VRML Made-to-Order is a primer in making your virtual worlds interactive. You'll learn how to program detailed instructions for your world to follow.

Part IV: The Nitty-Gritty shows you how to get down and dirty with VRML.

Now that you're ready to dump your virtual worlds on the Web, *Chapter 23, Delivering Reality: Server VRML* can show you how.

Chapter 24, The World's Gears: Client VRML discusses some issues involved in writing your own VRML browser, if you're so inclined.

Finally, *Chapter 25, Making It Really Real: VRML 2.0* is an important and detailed look at VRML 2.0—the future of virtual reality on the Internet.

Part V: Appendixes contains some technical reference information.

Appendix A, Software and Sources shows where you can get information and material on VRML Web construction.

Appendix B, The VRML 1.1 Specification is a printout of the actual design specs for the latest release of VRML.

Appendix C, 3D Modeling Software and Windows 95 explains how to get Impulse's Imagine to run in Windows 95 and overviews a just-released alternative package, Fountain's TrueSpace (Versions of both are included on the CD-ROM).

We're excited by the road ahead, but the trip is not simple, not easy, not without impasses, bugs, and General Protection Faults. So be warned. Don't expect this to be the usual tourist bus into the state park. This ain't no vacation. Your journey into this new world will have its breakdowns, impossible barriers, and dangerous moments. But you wouldn't be in this briefing room if you weren't game for the adventure, now would you?

Almost all the software discussed throughout this book is included on the enclosed CD-ROM. Any examples, scripts, or objects we use are also included. Welcome to VRML. And here's your survival gear: *Web Publisher's Construction Kit with VRML/Live3D.*

ABOUT THE CD

At the back of this book you'll find a CD that contains shareware and evaluation versions of software that you can use to create your own VRML pages. Make sure to check the root directory of the CD-ROM for a README file, which will contain information about any late-breaking updates or additions.

VIEWING THE CD CONTENTS

When you are ready to use the CD, place it in your computer's CD-ROM drive. Click on the Start button, then on Programs to see the Programs menu. Double click on Windows Explorer, and a directory tree appears. Scroll the list on the left side of the screen until you see the icon representing your CD-ROM drive. Double click on the icon, and you'll see a list of the CD's subdirectories, as listed in Table I-1.

Table I-1

Directory	Description
ANIMS	FLC animation files
AUTOSHIP	Demo of Autoship System's 3D NURBS editor
FOUNTAIN	Prerelease demo of Caligari's Fountain VRML generator and browser
IMAG	Impulse Imagine Light 3D modeler for DOS
SOURCE	VRML scripts for projects built in Chapters 15 through 22
TS2TRIAL	Caligari's trueSpace2 3D modeler for Windows
WCVT2POV	WCVT2POV freeware format conversion utility for VRML
WIN32S	Microsoft's Win32s 16-to-32-bit program for Windows 3.1

To go into a specific directory and view its contents, double click on that directory's folder icon. To move elsewhere, click on another directory or drive listed in the tree on the right side of the screen.

Moving Files with Explorer

You can easily copy files while using Explorer. To copy a directory to your hard disk, drag the directory you wish to copy from the file list on the right side of the screen to the appropriate drive and/or directory in the tree on the left.

If you first wish to create a destination directory on the hard disk, click once on the icon in the directory tree representing the preferred hard disk drive. This will make that drive active. Then click on File in the menu bar, then on New in the File menu. Click on Folder to create a new subdirectory, and type in a directory name, such as VRML Kit. You can now drag files and directories from the CD to the new directory using Windows Explorer.

Installation

Most of the products covered here can be installed easily from the CD-ROM. Let's look at each set of tools to see how to install them using Windows Explorer.

Autoship

The directory \AUTOSHIP contains the Autoship 3D NURBS editor. It includes an installation program that sets up Autoship from a CD or floppy. To install Autoship in Explorer, open the \AUTOSHIP directory; then open the \DISK1 subdirectory within \AUTOSHIP. Double click on the file named Instashp to start the install program; then follow the instructions.

Note that this installer is designed for use with floppies and therefore expects you to change disks during the installation. Rather than disks, however, you can simply change directories. When the installer asks for a new disk or directory path, simply replace the name of the current directory with the name of the next sequential \AUTOSHIP subdirectory (that is, \AUTOSHIP\DISK2 and \AUTOSHIP\DISK3). This will point the installer to the next set of files it needs.

FLC Animations

The directory \ANIMS contains FLC animations for multimedia VRML effects. You can move these with a straight copy. In Explorer, you would drag selected files or the entire directory from the CD folder to the desired destination.

Fountain

A sneak preview demo of Caligari's VRML crafting and viewing utility, Fountain, is located in the \FOUNTAIN directory. To install this program, open the \FOUNTAIN directory. Double click on the Setup file to start Caligari's install program; then follow the installer's prompts.

Imagine Lite

A scaled-back version of Impulse's 3D modeler for DOS, Imagine Lite, can be found in the \IMAG directory. You install Imagine Lite with a straight copy. In Explorer, drag the entire directory from the CD folder to the desired destination drive.

Source

You'll find the scripts for the VRML worlds built in Chapters 15 to 22 in the \SOURCE directory. This is another straight copy job. Use Explorer to drag files or the whole directory to a preferred location.

trueSpace2

An evaluation version of Caligari's Windows-based 3D modeler, trueSpace2, is also included on the CD-ROM; once installed, it will provide you with full-featured support for 30 days. When you're ready to install trueSpace2, open the \TS2TRIAL directory on the CD; then double click on the Setup file to start the install program. Follow the installer's prompts.

WCVT2POV

In the \WCVT2POV directory on the CD is a freeware utility that will be useful in converting files for use with your VRML pages. No installation is necessary; just copy the files to a destination. In Explorer, you can drag the entire directory from the CD folder to the desired destination drive.

Win32s

This add-on for Windows 3.1 and Windows for Workgroups 3.11 lets later 16-bit versions of Windows run some 32-bit programs. Win32s, from Microsoft, includes its own installation program. To install it, open the \WIN32S directory; then click on the \DISK1 subdirectory. Click on the file named Setup to start Microsoft's install program; then follow the installer's instructions.

PART I

STEPPING INTO THE WEB

1

THE WORLD
ISN'T FLAT!

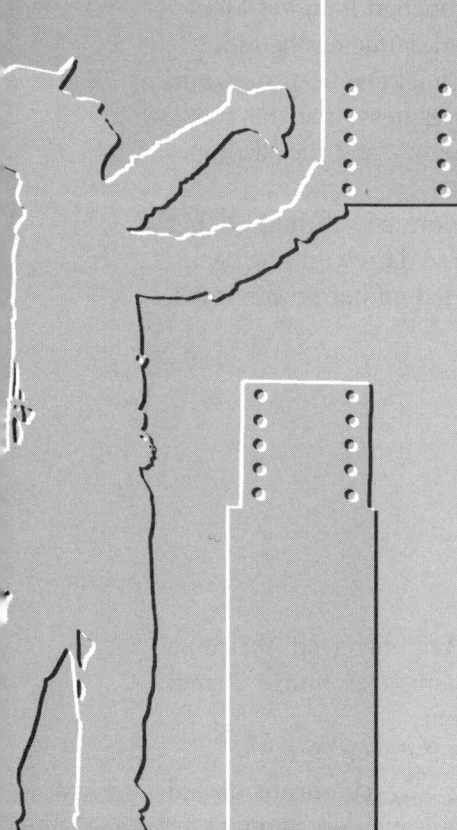

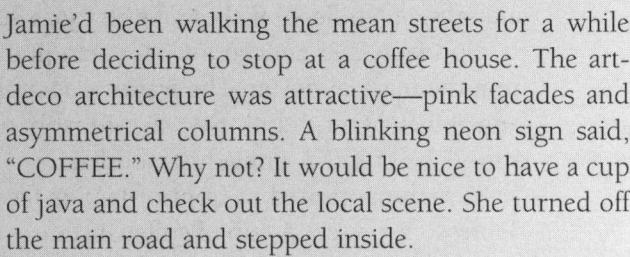

Jamie'd been walking the mean streets for a while before deciding to stop at a coffee house. The art-deco architecture was attractive—pink facades and asymmetrical columns. A blinking neon sign said, "COFFEE." Why not? It would be nice to have a cup of java and check out the local scene. She turned off the main road and stepped inside.

Good choice! The joint was jumpin'. A murmur of conversation came from the back, while '50s juke-box music blared from the side. A trio of weird-looking cats was clustered in one corner, smoking cigs and gesturing wildly. She walked up to one guy, all spiffed-up with slicked-back hair and sunglasses. He had twisty ram horns coming out from the sides of his head and his skin was emerald green.

"Whassup, missy?" the hepcat asked.

"Not much, man, not much," Jamie replied. "Anything going on?"

"Oh yeah, man...like we're having a poetry reading in ten minutes."

Jamie nodded and continued checking the place out. There was some great artwork along the walls— viscous, beatific stuff, like guitars sword-fighting with each other and a spectral sea of eyeballs. One poster in particular caught her eye: HOTTEST NEW JAZZ ACT IN TOWN. She touched the poster and suddenly it came to life, an outta-sight sax-man's notes filled her ears. On the accompanying video, Jamie saw the musician blow his soul into his sax and have it come out ambrosia. She walked further into the poster and a full bio of the artist appeared out of nowhere.

Jamie stepped back and listened to the soul-churning cries of the sax, snapping her fingers. She wondered about jazz's roots, and suddenly a whole documentary about the history of jazz surrounded her. There she was in New Orleans' Preservation Hall, enjoying the first-ever concert. She hung out at the show for a while, but then took control, choosing various artists and eras, an endless jukebox of every jazz song and jazz place in the world.

Suddenly she noticed a waiter standing behind her. Jamie turned away from the magical poster. The waiter was built like a government building—large, efficient, and dull. He was probably not a sentient, but just a bot. "A drink?" he grunted. Jamie just nodded.

A menu appeared in front of Jamie's face. She touched Item #4: Manic-Depresso Espresso. A cup of coffee instantly appeared. Jamie reached for it...

The illusion ended here. Actually having a sip might've been nice but, after all, virtual reality does have *some* limits. The espresso had no smell, taste, or feel. "Give it a few more years," Jamie thought, "and they'll probably figure out a way to brew coffee over the Internet."

Jamie stuck around for the poetry reading before she turned off her World Wide Web browser. Some of the stanzas were so darn wild, she decided to save a copy. She removed her VR goggles, peeled off her powergloves, and ran to the printer:

> *if you exist or not*
> *don't matter to me, baby,*
> *i'll bite your bits,*
> *kiss your pixels,*
> *and when I say I love ya,*
> *it's as true as it always is.*

Groovy.

Now, the preceding scenario is a tad farfetched, but only a tad. Welcome to *networked virtual reality*—groups of humans roaming around a shared world that exists only inside the "mind" of computers.

This is what the Internet was made for, the stuff dreams are made of. Two years ago, the World Wide Web was something only tech-heads played with. Now those *http://* addresses are becoming ubiquitous—showing up on billboards, in small print at the bottom of TV commercials, during *The Simpsons*, and on folks' business cards. Everyone who's anyone has a Web page. It's no wonder the Web took off: it mixes graphics, sound, and text, easily sharing it with computer networks around the world. It's like a living, breathing multimedia magazine. The Web is hot.

Yeah, the Web is pretty great—if you overlook the fact that it's two-dimensional, if you like computers and are comfortable with them, if you've got tons of time on your hands.

Sure, it's fun to click on some text or to type some cryptic Internet address and have volumes of information pop onto the screen. It's even more fun to be able to jump from Web page to Web page like a deranged frog, moving through tangled paths of hypertext. But there's something essential missing. In the real world, people like to walk around bars and check out the wares. They like to push carts down supermarket aisles and grab tempting food. There's something wonderful about roaming through the maze of library stacks and finding that one rare book they've been seeking. Humans touch, see, hear, and even think in more than two dimensions. They like to explore things, walk around them, find horrors or delights hidden in shadowy corners.

Does the Web really compare to real life?

THE VISUAL INTERNET

The Internet—it's the subject of countless courses, books, news stories, and even movies. But what the heck is it, really? The answer depends on your point of view. At its basest level, the Internet is just an inconceivably large bundle of computer data that doesn't even really exist other than as magnetic bits of energy. At its highest level, the Internet is a plane of universal consciousness where people can re-create the world and themselves.

TCP/IP

The Internet began as ARPANET (Advanced Research Projects Agency Network), a network linking U.S. Department of Defense computers across the world. As the cold war thawed, so did military attitudes. Some mainstream universities, companies, and organizations added their small networks to this vast interconnected network. Soon the Internet was born. All the computers on the Internet were able to speak to each other because they used the same *protocol*—an agreed-upon language for communicating. In this case, it was a simple protocol called *TCP/IP* (*Transmission Control Protocol/Internet Protocol*). The Internet was pretty spectacular. If you were on the Internet, you could connect to any other Internet computer and download any information stored there—that is, if you knew where that remote computer was. And there was no easy way of getting to these remote computers, either. Sometimes you'd want to use this funny little program called *Telnet* to actually connect to the remote machine. Other times you'd try to use this thing called *FTP* to turn the remote machine into a vast lending-library of software.

It felt like walking into a huge archive room, thousands of miles long, with rows and rows of papers stacked from floor to ceiling. The Internet was vast, but completely unorganized. Most people had no easy way of finding information.

And then came the Web.

The Web

Here's a wild idea: Organize the Internet. It was 1989 when Tim Berners-Lee and CERN (Center for European Particle Physics) decided to hammer out the details. The Web project began. The idea was to create an easy way for people using any type of computer to retrieve any piece of data. Why not create a common way for folks to see popular types of computerized information and then to move on to other Internet resources? The original Web team decided to use *hypertext* as their means of navigating. When you get to a page on the Web, you can click on special words or pictures and are whisked, at hyper-speed, to another resource. Every part of the Internet would have links to dozens of other parts. Imagine strands of silk stretched between each of the millions of links. The result would be—that's right—a World Wide Web.

Two invaluable acronyms were born during the building of the Web: URL and HTTP. Before they're discussed, it's important to talk about what made the Web usable: *Web browsers*—software that allows you to browse, surf, leap, or tunnel through the Web. In particular, a cute and brilliant little browser known as Mosaic took the world by storm and made the Web a medium for the masses.

Mosaic

The National Center for Supercomputing Applications (NCSA) programmed and distributed Mosaic in 1993. Mosaic could put graphics and different styles of text on the same screen, giving the Web the crisp look of a magazine.

Most likely, you're very familiar with Mosaic-style Web pages as shown in Figure 1-1. Netscape Navigator, Internet Assistant, Quarterdeck, Spry, and other Web browsers are all based on the Mosaic paradigm. Jumping from link to link was as simple as clicking your mouse on a word or picture

Figure 1-1
A typical Web page: pretty but flat. Underlined phrases take you to different screens

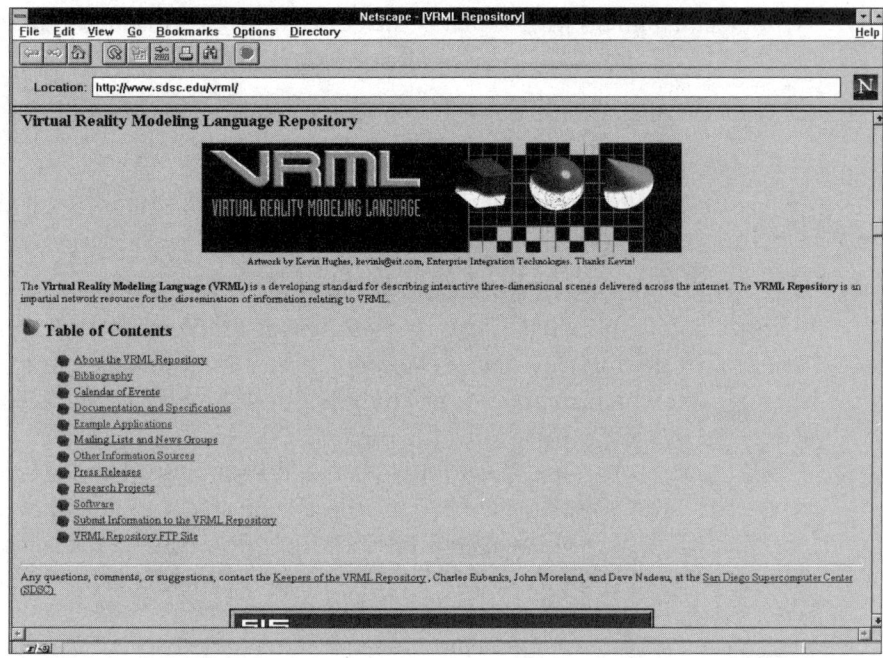

that interested you. Blue words were hyperlinked to new places (linked to further information), black words were not.

But when you jump from place to place, how does the Web browser know where to take you? The answer is URLs.

URLs

A URL is a Uniform Resource Locator. This is an address, like any other address in the world, which can locate anything stored on the Net. URLs can download files using the *File Transfer Protocol* (*FTP*), connect to other machines using Telnet, let you easily view a Usenet newsgroup, help load gopher menus, and even send e-mail. FTP, Telnet, gopher, and Usenet are ways people used to navigate around the Internet in the old days. Now all these tools are combined into one program. All the following are valid URLs:

http://www.anyplace.com/smith/wild.html—Loads a World Wide Web page.

ftp://www.filearchives.com/utilities/cool.zip—Downloads a file called *cool.zip*.

telnet://here.com—Connects to a computer at the *here* company.

⬛ *news:alt.animals.foxes*—Reads the newsgroup postings in a group called *alt.animals.foxes.*

⬛ *gopher://smartpants.edu*—Shows you a menu of information you might want at Smartpants University.

⬛ *mailto:jsmith@smartpants.edu*—Sends electronic mail to jsmith at Smartpants University.

URLs begin with the protocol—the way data should be transferred. Next there's a colon and usually two slashes. This is followed by the name of the computer on which the data is stored. There's another slash, and then the directory in which the data is sleeping is listed. Finally, the URL ends with the name of the file that holds the data.

In other words, a URL simply tells the Web browser how to get to your data. The Web browser connects to the specified computer, moves to the specified directory, and—using the specified protocol—grabs the specified file. You can now easily distribute text, pictures, movies, sounds, software, or any other sort of digital media.

HTTP

The most common type of URL protocol is *HTTP.* This stands for the *HyperText Transfer Protocol* and is the way the Web is woven. Computers that share information over the Internet are known as *Web servers.* A server is like a TV station, radio station, and publishing house mixed into one. Servers use HTTP to send any type of information to any Web browser that asks for it.

Naturally, HTTP is used most often to send hypertext. But HTTP can also be used to send graphics, movies, sounds, or any other digital media—including virtual worlds.

Virtual Reality: Making It Human

The Web, along with Mosaic-inspired browser software, made the Internet easy to explore. But it wasn't quite utopia. If you want to focus on one type of information, you only have two choices: find a list that points to what you're looking for, or surf your brains out. The Web is much like letting your mind wander; you can easily jump from place to place, but if you want to get someplace specific, it's often difficult and involves lots of searching.

The Sticky Web

Since any site can be linked to any other site, there is no linear organization of the World Wide Web. There are millions of ways to find the same place. Many people complain that they browse the Web for hours, tripping over fluff, advertisements, and boring bits of diatribe, and rarely come across worthwhile information. The act of Web surfing is much more interactive than, say, watching TV. But it's still somewhat mindless.

Ever since the Internet began, visionaries were interested in making cyberspace more like the real world. As you move from place to place, the journey should be as interesting and educational as the eventual destination. In a perfect world, your travels around cyberspace would also be *human-centered*—they'd make sense to you from a human perspective. After all, we're not computers. Why should we think like computers? The computer is just a tool. The Web, to be effective, should be a *virtual reality (VR)*. The grand idea behind virtual reality is to get computers to show us things the way we're used to seeing them without computers. As silly as this sounds, this goal is one of the most difficult journeys the human race has ever embarked upon. Virtual reality is not as much about creating artificial reality as it is an alternate reality, a reality as free, as open as the universe itself.

Welcome to VRML, the first step in expressing the Internet in human terms.

Perceptualized Internetworking

The founders of VRML attempted to create a way to achieve *perceptualized internetworks*. This fancy technoterm means the vast Internet should be expressed according to human perspective. It should be a world where people use their innate capabilities to navigate. If they hear laughter and carnival music behind them, they assume they'll see a circus if they turn around. If they smell fat frying, they assume there's a fast-food restaurant ahead. If they see a mall, they either shop till they drop, or run away. If they want a glass of milk, they reach out and grab one.

It's much different to type:

```
HAND ME THE BLUE BOX IN THE BACK RIGHT CORNER OF THE ROOM
```

than to grab the box. The biggest difference is intuition. Children quickly learn that if they want to hold something, they must reach for it. Only people who spend a lot of time with computers can learn the messy commands and routines that allow them to navigate today's Internet.

If you want to visit a friend's home page, you shouldn't need to remember an obscure URL. Instead, you should be able to fly across the planet until you reach your friend's country, descend into his or her neighborhood, and walk around the streets until you find the right house.

Standardizing Reality

For virtual reality to work on a grand scale, everybody must be able to see the same thing, to work with the same tools. VRML is the standard that defines how this new type of perception can be accomplished. It's the blueprint that allows you to create and fly through virtual realities. This is easier said than done. Virtual reality should follow basic laws of nature, yet it should still be limitless, allowing people to build their own ideas. It's no cinch to be God.

How the Internet Is like the Mind

In a way, then, the history of the Internet matches the way the human mind evolves and works. Whenever you come across some data, you remember it. This is similar to the basic TCP/IP Internet—just dropping data in empty space. You then organize it in your mind based on other pieces of information. For example, smelling homemade butter cookies might remind you of your grandmother. This is similar to the Web, where links are drawn between pieces of data, helping you reference them. Finally, you can use these webs of data to create a picture of the world before you. You can then experience things and make sense of them, based on information you've already gathered.

The authors of VRML break down this process into three stages:

- Storage
- Retrieval
- Perceptualization

Just as in the mind, the above stages are not fully developed. As the Internet matures, new ways of storage become popular. New Web browsers make retrieval easier and more beautiful. And attempts at perceptualization have just begun. VRML is the first stage in what will be a never-ending attempt to make sense of the digital world.

Figure 1-2 illustrates the history of the Internet, from storage concept to organized system to perceptualized internetwork. First, various pieces of information are dropped randomly onto the page. Second, these pieces of

Figure 1-2
The evolution
of the Internet,
from disk space
into cyberspace

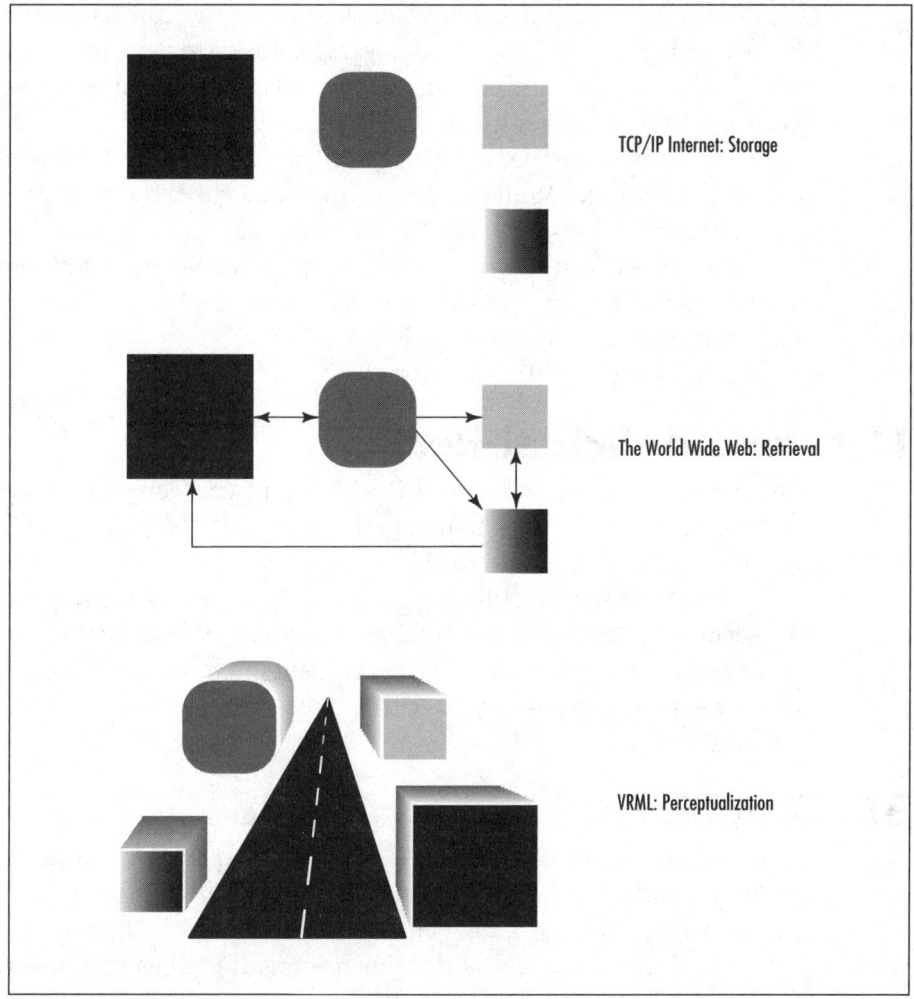

information are connected somewhat logically, so that you can find one piece and have it lead you to the next. Finally, the information is laid out in a way familiar to everyone: like buildings along the sides of a road.

VIRTUAL REALITY? ISN'T REAL REALITY ENOUGH?

Like anything worth pursuing, virtual reality is simultaneously frightening and appealing, perhaps because it implies that there is some sort of demarcated reality to begin with. After all, aren't human senses the virtual reality for the soul?

13

VR can eventually bring any fantasy to life. You can hammer together another reality in the back of your garage. Do what you please. Talk and touch and make love and kill at will, in a place where there are no consequences, rewards, money, pain, or bureaucracy.

An entire alternate landscape could very well render fantasy obsolete. Science fiction writer William Gibson (the same guy who came up with the term "cyberspace") warned that VR might be like "freebasing TV."

Naturally, VR is its own abstract entity—like any art—fresh terrain for pedants, capitalists, and craftspersons alike. But as VR matures, who will be solely responsible for nurturing it?

You will. And VRML is the first step.

Networked Virtual Reality

Virtual reality without a network is a lonely place. Many would agree that the best part of the information superhighway isn't the places you'll go, but the folks you'll meet on the road.

Although artificial intelligence may one day allow us to encounter robots that seem real, this is not one of the main goals of VRML. Rather, the idea is to mix virtual reality with the Internet to yield interesting and beautiful landscapes for people across the world to meet, do business, debate, and be human.

3D Graphics

Sight is probably the sense you use most to interpret the world. Therefore, the key behind virtual reality is three-dimensional graphics. The art and science of 3D graphics has a long and detailed history. The first section of this book introduces you to the third dimension and teaches you how to think, draw, and create three-dimensionally.

Some ferocious programming and cheap hardware have made 3D graphics something most every home computer user can now experience. As 3D objects are arranged into scenes and worlds, a basic virtual reality is constructed. Some VRs are more virtual than others, but the general idea is usually the same: A bunch of 3D shapes are calculated and *rendered* on the screen from a particular point of view. The user can then change his or her point of view, seeming to walk through, fly over, or crawl beneath the objects. Since the objects are, at their core, mathematical, they can be rotated, shifted, or zoomed.

Sound Advice

The latest specification of VRML supports sounds. You use sound to guide you nearly as much as you use sight. You know which sounds scare you and which attract you. Thunder, dogs barking, children laughing, girls giggling, traffic, rock 'n' roll, and millions of other day-to-day sounds paint a landscape as well as any visible object.

The Other Senses

Eventually VRML will be expanded to support touch. Using special *datagloves* or *powergloves,* visitors to virtual realities can reach out to objects and even feel their shapes and textures. Perhaps one day there'll even be the technology for Jamie to smell and taste her coffee. Although VRML is currently visually based, it's important not to neglect your other senses as you build internetworked worlds.

Perhaps the most important sense with regard to virtual reality is the sixth sense—intuition—which guides much of behavior. However virtual worlds are designed, they must be intuitive, with an interface that intrinsically makes sense.

SO WHAT'S VRML, EXACTLY?

It's about time you asked. VRML (pronounced "vermal," like a mix between vermin and thermal—just think of hot rats) is the Virtual Reality Modeling Language. VRML is a format for sending descriptions of virtual worlds back and forth over the Internet. The idea is to build an endless, interconnected, multiuser world. As you walk from scene to scene, the information you'll need to experience your current surroundings will be sent to your home computer.

These virtual worlds are stored on the Internet and linked using the World Wide Web. Like any other World Wide Web resource, virtual worlds are broadcast by Web servers. To see a virtual world, you need a special browser capable of understanding the VRML descriptions and drawing out realistic-looking virtual worlds.

VRML Is Born and Changes Its Name

The basic idea behind VRML has been around since the beginning of computing. VRML itself, however, was first introduced as a realistic possibility at the first annual World Wide Web Conference in 1994. One of the meetings was about virtual reality interfaces for the Web. Many companies, academic researchers, and hobbyists attended, each with their ideas of how virtual worlds should be constructed.

The final consensus was a hazy notion: to create a 3D format that could describe most any scene and that could allow these worlds to be hyperlinked to each other. The term VRML was invented—standing for Virtual Reality Markup Language. This name mimicked VRML's cousin, *HTML*—the *HyperText Markup Language*.

It was soon clear, however, that VRML couldn't just be an extension to HTML. Putting 3D graphics into words was a complicated task. VRML would need to be more than a set of simple tags such as <CIRCLE> and <CUBE>. It would need to be a full-featured format for describing 3D objects. HTML was already well under way and had very little to do with 3D graphics. As the VRML specification puts it, "As a network language, VRML will succeed or fail independent of HTML." And so the official name became *Virtual Reality Modeling Language*.

As you'll learn later in this book, there are many ways to describe 3D graphics. You can break down everything into simple shapes, you can keep track of every point or curve, and you can specify exactly how light will shine onto objects. Many people insisted that their 3D graphic format was the best one to use as the basis for VRML. Others suggested that VRML should be built from scratch, not bogged down by any existing standards.

Somehow, the group agreed that to save time, VRML should be based on a popular, easy-to-use, and full-featured 3D graphic format. The winner of this graphical race was Open Inventor.

Open Inventor: The Format VRML Was Based on

The roots of VRML spring directly from a format known as *Open Inventor* (*OI*) by Silicon Graphics, Inc. (SGI). Open Inventor is a library of graphical routines that C++ programmers can use to easily create realistic graphics. It's also a file format. All in all, OI is pretty cool because it can be used to display nearly any 3D object. The nice thing about OI is how it's endured. Lots of 3D artists and scientists use it, like it, and worked on perfecting it. OI was a great place to base VRML. It has the following features:

- It's object-oriented, which means that it is pretty easy to use and learn.

- There are lots of conversion programs.

- Many people know how to use it.

- Most modeling software can understand or output data in the Open Inventor format.

- It's a simple ASCII file format and can easily be used on any computer platform.

The VRML 1.0 Specification

In late 1994, Tony Parisi and Gavin Bell—two of the world's foremost experts on Open Inventor—drafted the VRML specification based on the input of the thousand-or-so members of the *www-vrml* mailing list.

Mark Pesce, the moderator of the *www-vrml* list and one of the pioneers of perceptualized internetworking, was instrumental in helping to compile the ideas and produce the final VRML specification. Numerous others provided scores of invaluable ideas. On May 26, 1995, the official VRML specification was released.

Starting Simple

Basically, VRML is a stripped-down version of Open Inventor, with a few special World Wide Web functions tacked on. Future versions of VRML will no doubt continue to use ideas and commands from Open Inventor.

Since VRML needed to start simple, it took only the most common aspects of Open Inventor. Namely:

- Basic shapes

- Basic material properties

- Basic transformations

- Basic camera views

- Basic texture-mapping

- Basic lighting

There was very little ability for interaction in the first specification of VRML. The big exception was hyperlinks, which allow you to click on objects and jump from one place to another. The *www-vrml* list drafted a list of what the first version of VRML should include. Some of these features are as follows:

- Renders geometry three-dimensionally

- Works on any type of computer or operating system

- Works relatively fast over low-speed network connections

- Can be extended with additional commands or shapes

Making Space for WebSpace

The first browser that could actually display official VRML worlds was WebSpace. This program was designed by Silicon Graphics (SGI) and TagSystems (TGS), and released free to the Internet community. WebSpace was only available for UNIX computers, but it did a great job. It was destined to become the Mosaic of VRML.

Soon dozens of other browsers hit the market. Intravista released the first Windows VRML browser for the average desktop PC: WorldView. The Web-at-large could now experience VRML.

No two browsers render 3D worlds in exactly the same way. The VRML language suggests—in great detail—how the scene should look. The browser makes a few educated guesses and comes up with a close approximation of the original model. This is similar to how humans see things—one person might be a little nearsighted, and another might be a little color-blind. They can look at the same object and see slightly different things.

VRML Version 1.1

The first version of VRML was a grand experiment. Everybody involved learned lots about 3D graphics and virtual reality. Most importantly, people learned how to send graphics over the World Wide Web so that they wouldn't just be appreciated by people with mainframe workstations and direct Internet connections, but also by the average user with a Windows PC and a 14,400 bps modem.

The *www-vrml* mailing list hammered out the first specification. Toward the end of 1995, the second specification of VRML was drafted. A group of VRML's most active authors formed a group called the *VRML Architecture Group (VAG)*. VAG came up with lots of notions about what VRML 2.0 should do. These are covered in Chapter 25. A full specification should be out by the middle of 1996, with cool browsers following soon after.

Live3D

Netscape Navigator—the world's most popular and expandable Web browser—has recently decided to go 3D and incorporate VRML worlds into their browser. The result is Live3D—an advanced version of VRML which will grow as VRML grows. Live3D has some extensions to standard VRML, allowing animations, rotating objects, streamed video and audio, and other multimedia effects.

WHAT CAN'T VRML DO?

Now that VRML's been hyped as the best thing since Spam, here's some real reality: VRML is the tip of the iceberg, the start of the race, the bottom rung of sea-scum in the evolutionary ladder.

Most people's computers, unfortunately, aren't fast enough to handle complicated 3D graphics too well. Even a simple animation, like a man walking through a forest, is almost impossible to draw real-time with complete realism. Virtual reality is not like a movie—you can't just record several views of the world. You need to actually re-create a world that can be seen from any angle and at any distance. You can read more about some of virtual reality's limitations in Chapter 5.

Virtual Nonreality

The current version of VRML does *not* support:

- Animation—Nothing can move on its own. You won't see birds flying across the top of the screen or cars rolling along a street. Eventually, animation can be as simple as a ball rolling across the screen or as complex as a human who can sit, crouch, shout, wave, and do nearly anything else a real human can do.

- Physics—You can't have objects react according to the laws of nature (no bouncing balls).

- Interactivity—You can't touch objects, move them, or stack them. You can't pick up a cup of coffee and put it on a table. You can't put a quarter into a jukebox. You can't even open doors or type secret codes into panels. Yet.

- Application Programming Interfaces—You can't program your own VRML scenes to do specific things, or work with your computer's specific hardware. You can't write a special routine that will show a movie in the center of a 3D theater.

- Multiusers—You're always alone in the virtual world. Two people can look at the same world at the same time, but cannot see each other.

As VRML matures, all the above scenarios, and more, will become possible.

Life on the Bleeding Edge

VRML, and all VRML products, are bleeding edge. There are bugs, snags, and things that just don't work at all. If you create a simple sphere with VRML, it will look fine on nearly any computer system in the world running any VRML software. If you create a stegosaurus with real lizard-like skin and a photorealistic prehistoric background, you might have some problems. Different browsers draw complex shapes in different ways. Some browsers cannot draw textures, others can only draw certain types of textures. If you don't light your VRML scene, some browsers will light it for you automatically. Others will leave you in the dark.

There are many wrinkles to be ironed out in the VRML specification.

SO WHAT CAN I DO?

Even in its limited form, VRML has some amazing applications. The next chapter takes you on a tour of some of the best VRML worlds, but here are some basic ideas.

Art

Walk through galleries and enjoy an endless selection of paintings. Like real museums, virtual ones can be divided into eras, artists, or styles. Even more importantly, you can stroll around virtual sculptures or statues. Eventually these statues will even be able to move.

Some sites allow you to take shapes and "paint" with them. This acts something like a virtual Lego set.

The nice thing about VRML is no matter where you are, it's always art.

Entertainment

Movie studios can build vast theaters. There can be stage sets, gambling halls, music-listening booths, and pubs where you can stroll around and meet other people. Eventually VRML can be used to create full adventure, action, or video games. You can walk through worlds, solving puzzles and battling trolls. Or visit a version of Disneyland without having to put on those silly mouse-ears.

Sports plays can be replayed in ultra-slow-motion, from any angle.

Fiction can be mixed with VRML. Walk through the Dublin streets as you read *Ulysses*. See every nuance of Wonderland along with Alice. Or you can create a story that changes its plot depending on which direction you move through a scene.

Architecture

The most intricate buildings in the world—or in someone's imagination—can be built down to the last detail. VRML is also a great way to visit buildings or places you otherwise might not see, like the Guggenheim Museum, the Duomo in Florence, a Mayan pyramid, or a prehistoric cave. Build airports, cities, office buildings, luxury condos, or alternate dimensions.

Architectural firms can also build spaces in VRML and have clients and consultants from around the world easily walk through them as a kind of test drive. This can save millions of dollars in development costs.

Science

The possibilities are endless. Here are some of them:

- Biology—You can try an intricate operation by practicing on virtual patients, examine the inner workings of rare plants, dissect frogs without shedding a drop of amphibian blood.

- Chemistry—You can walk around, or inside, the molecular structure of a compound.

- Physics—You can see what happens when two quarks smack into each other. Or you can visit a black hole.

- Psychology—How about a 3D equivalent of a Rorschach test?

History

Time travel is now possible, or at least the illusion of time travel can now be stronger. Visit 1890's New York and stroll through the street of your choice. Or step back some more and visit Rome just before the collapse of its empire. Visit the signing of the Declaration of Independence. Or shuffle through a Civil War battleground.

Since VRML can link to movies, text, or any graphic, a VRML world can become a historical museum with exhibits about any culture, idea, society, event, or locale.

Journalism and Law

Rather than just recount events, virtual reality could help you reenact them. You could browse 3D maps of a warring part of the world, showing battle boundaries, troop movements, and major landmarks. 3D animations were used during the O.J. Simpson trial to show jurors one theory of what occurred.

Business and Marketing

VRML can even make soap ads exciting. It can show the schematic, in all three dimensions, of all your company's latest gizmos. Parts catalogs can be placed online. VRML is a great way for video game companies to preview their wares, or for tourist agencies to preview their lands. If you're a plastic surgeon, you can have people upload their faces and adjust the size of their noses on-the-fly. Your Web site can become a year-round trade show exhibit.

3D graphs of the stock market, and other representations of money or power or time, can help make major decisions much easier.

The next time you buy tickets to Borneo, you'll see a model of the plane you'll be flying. The reserved seats will be red. Click on any other seat to reserve it. Or reserve your seat in a stadium for sporting events and concerts.

 TIP: Since VRML is so new, any site featuring VRML will garner tons of visitors.

Engineering

You can build bridges, planes, or circuits using VRML and share the designs with the world. This can make it easy for engineers to consult with each other, or to teach engineering to students. A French engineer could draft ideas, put them in full 3D on the Web, and allow engineers from other countries to consult on her designs.

Reference

Why pull out an old road atlas when you can actually zoom through the interstates and off-roads of America on a virtual map? Some ambitious companies are even trying to create the whole world using VRML, like a gigantic atlas.

VRML can make researching a whole new experience. For instance, instead of looking up words in dictionaries, you may literally skate over rows of words until you find the one you need. You can use VRML to learn a new language the same way you learned your first language—using real-life examples. For instance, you could go to SpanishLand, click on a house, and see or hear the word *casa*.

Storing files in a 3D environment might wind up being a faster and easier way to organize things. This can combine an intuitive filing cabinet with the speed and search abilities of a computer.

Socializing

Make the world a smaller and better place. Meet friends who enjoy the same things you do. Discuss Communism with a real Communist, hand-gestures and all. Fall in love without buying any drinks. And have the safest sex of your life.

Already, some companies are developing 3D MUDs (Multiple-User Dungeons). This can allow you to form teams with real people and role-play as you trek through strange lands, hunting for treasure and fighting bad guys. Many people are experimenting with *avatars*—representations of themselves in cyberspace. For example, your avatar can be a pink rabbit. You can then hop around virtual worlds, meeting aliens, werewolves, movie stars, chess pieces, and plain ol' people. People will see you, you'll see them, and it'll have the feel of any real-life meeting place, only more unpredictable.

Home Pages

A 3D home page can hold as much information as its 2D counterpart, except it'll usually be a lot easier to make sense of. You can build a gateway to your company, university, or organization, or just custom design your home for other folk to visit.

Education

All of the above scenarios are educational. But VRML can even be used to create entire curriculums of learning. Soon there'll be a VRML site to complement any subject. This can make every day into a field trip.

WHAT DO I NEED?

To start visiting or creating VRML worlds, you'll need the following:

- A computer with a modem. The faster your modem, the better, since some virtual worlds are quite large and can take a while to download. As long as you have a 14,400 bps modem or better you should be okay. However, 28,800 is recommended.

- A World Wide Web–ready account on the Internet. This means you'll either need a direct connection to the Net, or a SLIP/PPP account. If you can run Netscape or Mosaic, then you're all set.

NOTE: Special software, such as the Internet Adapter, can turn a standard Internet account into a SLIP account. Check out a basic Word Wide Web book, such as the Waite Group's *HTML Web Publisher's Construction Kit* (Fox and Downing, 1995) for help and information.

Although you can use this book along with any operating system and any computer, the software on the enclosed disc is for the Microsoft Windows system. When applicable, however, this book will point to places where you can get software for whichever computer platform you're using.

HOW TO CREATE VIRTUAL WORLDS

This book covers the ins and outs of creating internetworked 3D worlds. The basic steps in world creation are

1. Program, model, design, buy, or borrow a set of 3D objects (Part II).

2. Convert these objects to the VRML format (Chapter 14).

3. Arrange everything using VRML commands (Part III).

4. Place everything on an Internet-connected Web server (Part IV).

WHERE THIS BOOK WILL TAKE YOU

Part I of *VRML Construction Kit* shows you to how to connect to the Internet and view virtual worlds. All popular VRML browsers will be covered, including WebSpace, WorldView, and WebFX. You'll also tour some popular VRML worlds already on the Net.

Part II covers the basics of 3D graphics, teaching you how to think in three dimensions. You'll learn what a modeler is and learn how to use the included modeler—Imagine—to create your own 3D objects. Then you'll see how to convert these objects into VRML.

Part III is a complete VRML programming primer. You'll learn the basics of VRML, and how to create shapes, give them properties, group them, arrange them, light them, and hyperlink them.

Part IV shows you how to actually put VRML worlds on the Web and serve them to the world. A chapter even discusses the guts behind VRML, useful for those who are interested in building their own VRML browsers or in authoring software. The next major version of VRML (2.0) will then be previewed, whetting your palate for the near-future of perceptualized inter-networking.

The last part of the book contains the appendixes, which include the official VRML specification, a complete list of VRML sources and places, and a step-by-step look at combining all the techniques you've learned to create your own 3D home page.

All in all, you'll learn how to actually draw useful stuff, arrange it, and put it on the Internet for the world to see. Whether you want to learn about the basics of 3D graphics, get a glimpse of tomorrow's cyberspace, build your own worlds, or even program your own VRML browsers, this book covers it. It's our hope that this book will inspire you to create a wonderful homestead on the frontier of cyberspace. Because cyberspace, along with the future, is immense and wide open.

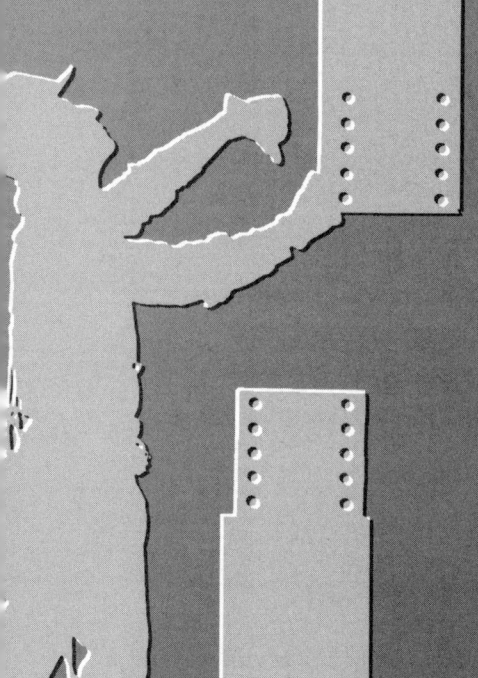

2
VIRTUALLY
AMAZING

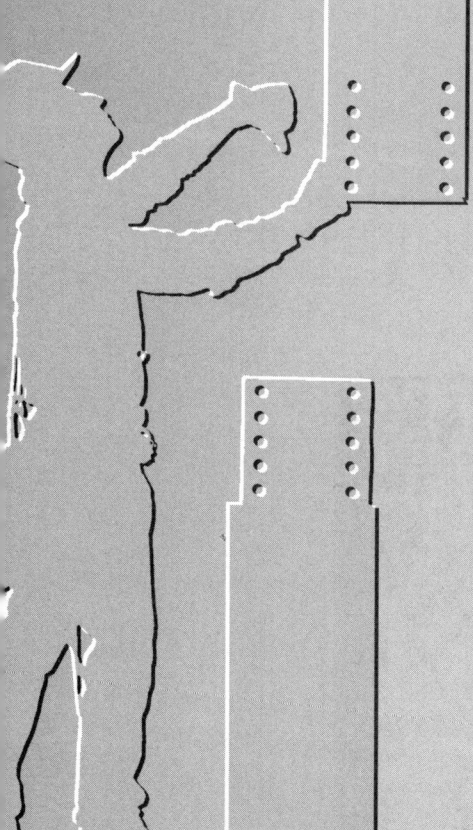

2

Here's the first crop of what Virtual Reality Modeling Language has to offer. Right now, VRML is very young. The sites in this chapter, beautiful and amazing as they may be, are nothing compared to where VRML will take you. They do, however, provide a peek into the future—like seeing the headlights before the train runs you over. This chapter will take you on a tour of some of the world's first 3D World Wide Web pages. The idea is to inspire you, no matter who you are or why you use the Web, to get out there and start creating your own 3D spaces. Read this chapter with an open imagination, and prepare to take virtual worlds to higher levels.

You can view all of the worlds in this chapter as long as you have a VRML and HTML Web browser running on your system. The next two chapters show you how to obtain, install, and use VRML browsers. In most cases, you need to visit the 2D Web page using your standard HTML browser (such as Netscape). This is like reading a pamphlet about a museum before you step inside. You can then click on a VRML link. Your VRML browser will then fire up, load the 3D scene, and launch you into virtuality.

The following categories are completely arbitrary, but a chapter has to have *some* headings.

ART

Several companies and individuals have installed their artwork online. As galleries become established and oft-visited, popular artists will actually vie to have their works on display. Eventually art might even be bought and sold over the Internet.

Abulafia Gallery

http://www.cgrg.ohio-state.edu/~mlewis/Gallery/gallery.html
This is one of the most well-crafted VRML sites. Take a stroll through a spacious art gallery featuring vibrant oil paintings by Matthew Lewis. Several varieties of this gallery are available for various levels of computers—high resolution with textures (see Figure 2-1), medium resolution, and low resolution with no textures.

Interactive Origami

http://www.neuro.sfc.keio.ac.jp/~aly/polygon/vrml/ika/
Use the Net to learn how to make several traditional origami shapes. Start with a plain sheet of paper. Click on it and follow each fold and crease (see Figure 2-2). You can, of course, turn the paper over or look at it from any

Figure 2-1
The Abulafia gallery

Figure 2-2
Interactive
origami

angle, helping you make an exact seam. Continue clicking (and folding) until you create a squid, a bird, or another creature.

E~Scape from New York

http://www.t0.or.at/e~scape/
Explore the beginnings of a full virtual environment at the Institute for New Culture Technologies. You can check out Zero News, the hollow Planet Zero globe, and Synreal City. This wacky world comes complete with bars, libraries, labs, movie theaters, and spaceports. The E~Scape museum (*http://www.t0.or.at/escape/museum/museum.wrl.gz*) is shown in Figure 2-3.

ENTERTAINMENT

Virtual reality isn't gonna last long unless it's downright fun to be in. Luckily, these sites are paving the way to good times.

Virtual Vegas

http://www.virtualvegas.com/vrml/vrml.html
Feel lucky, punk? Although the laws about gambling online with real money have yet to be worked out, you can certainly gamble online with virtual money. Virtual Vegas is just the place.

For now, most of the places in Virtual Vegas (movie theaters, music halls, casinos) are two-dimensional. But if you like, you can try out the 3D slot machine in Figure 2-4. Click on the handle to pull it, and who knows what lady luck will bring?

Figure 2-3
The E~Scape
museum

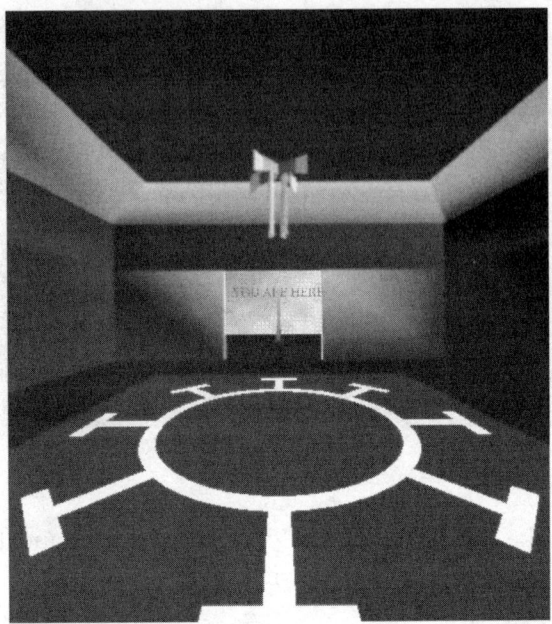

Figure 2-4
Robbing the
one-armed
bandit

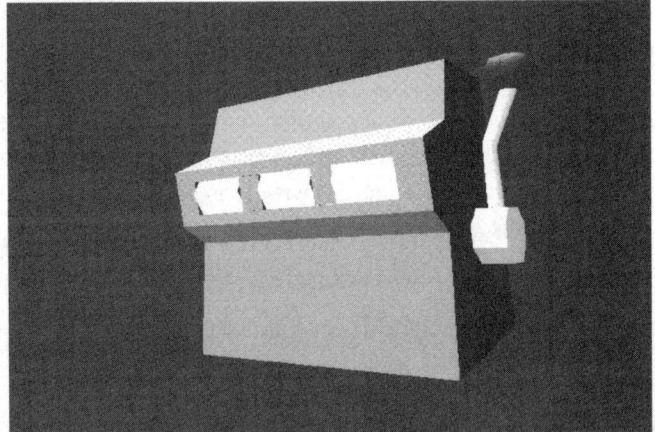

hCAVE

http://jaka.eecs.uic.edu/dave/vrml/CAVE/
http://www.eecs.uic.edu/~mczernus/SKI/Ski.html
hCAVE VR is an advanced virtual reality system. Some of CAVE's applications have been converted to VRML. Start out in a room and open one of the many doors to a fantastic CAVE world. These worlds include

▣ The Aquarium by Mihailo Alic and Dave Adamczyk (see Figure 2-5)—This is an underground world where fish (and fishy things) swim by you.

▣ Crayola Land by Dave Pape (see Figure 2-6)—This is a remarkable 3D world where all the objects are 2D. The effect is like walking through a panorama made from paste and construction paper.

Figure 2-5
The Aquarium

Figure 2-6
Crayola Land

Figure 2-7
Let's Ski!

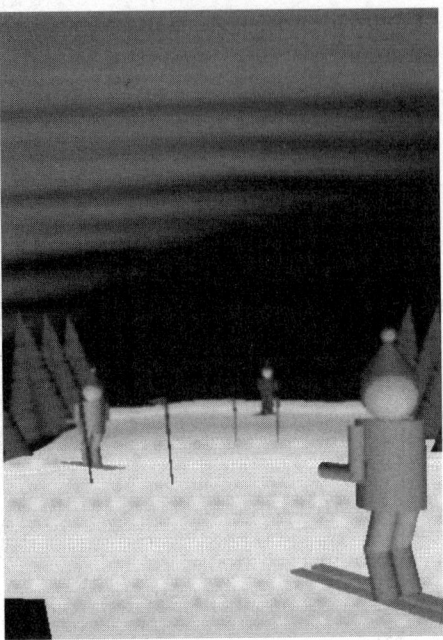

- Let's Ski by Marek Czernuszenko—The original CAVE application lets people compete in the slalom, zipping down the snow and weaving between poles. Figure 2-7 shows a VRML representation of the slopes.

- Snail by George Francis, Glen Chappell, and Chris Hartman—The most beautiful multicolored snail you ever saw.

Star Trek

Star Trek fans may recognize the VRML *Reliant,* shown in Figure 2-8. Eventually entire episodes can be scripted in cyberspace.

IUMA Virtual Reality Lounge

http://www.iuma.com/IUMA-2.0/vrml/new-room.wrl
The Internet Underground Music Archives has long been the place to go to hear songs from the newest, hippest, and most alternative bands. Where you listen to music is sometimes as much a part of the experience as what the music is. Now there's a comfy 3D lounge for you to hang out in, as shown in Figure 2-9. To hear the song of the week, click on the stereo dial.

Figure 2-8
Star Trek
Reliant

Figure 2-9
Chillin' at the
IUMA VRML
lounge

Westworld

http://www.byronpreiss.com/brook/westwld/saloon.wrl
Byron Preiss Multimedia Company allows you to preview what it's like to walk though Westworld—an upcoming 3D action adventure game. You can visit the Saloon, as in Figure 2-10, tilt back your hat, and pour some virtual whiskey.

ARCHITECTURE

Lots of architectural firms, schools, and folks have been drawn to VRML. After all, architecture is what it's all about: building appealing, useful, and beautiful structures.

L.A. Stories

http://www.gsaup.ucla.edu:80/vrml/
The UCLA Department of Architecture and Urban Design offers a couple of highly detailed models of building in the Los Angeles area, including

- The African American Unity Center (see Figure 2-11)

- The UCLA School of Public Policy and Social Research

- The Equitable building

- The Gas building

Figure 2-10
Westworld

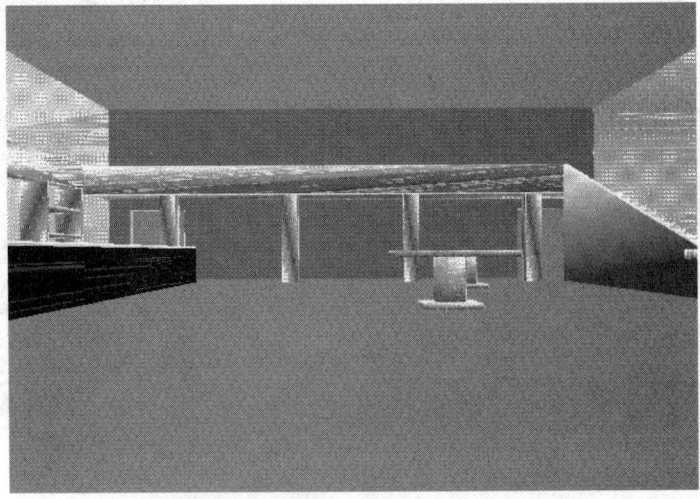

Figure 2-11
The African
American Unity
Center

Churches

http://www.netplace.com/netplace/demo/vrml.html
Netplace Internet Consulting has created an online version of Munich's
Frauenkirche Church (see Figure 2-12).

Figure 2-12
Frauenkirche

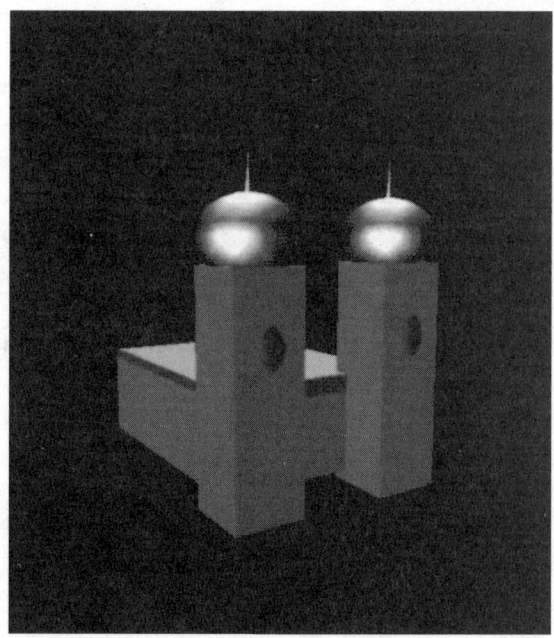

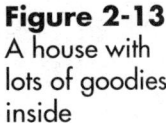
Figure 2-13
A house with
lots of goodies
inside

Houses

You can use VRML to get as detailed as you want. For example, you can walk
through a city, find a building you like, step inside, find a room you like, and
see all the room's furniture in full, as in Figure 2-13. The extent of this detail
is only limited by time, cyberspace imagination, and computing power—all
of which (except time, perhaps) are getting better and better.

The Palladium

http://www.sgi.com/Products/WebFORCE/WebSpace/vrml/Palladio/
Palladium.wrl.gz
The stretch of land known as the Palladium is shown in Figure 2-14, as cre-
ated by SGI.

MATH AND SCIENCE

As much as we hate to admit it, VRML isn't all fun and games. It's also highly useful for scientific visualization, 3D databases, mathematical exploration,
and modeling the behavior of particles.

Figure 2-14
The Palladium

The Eyes Have It

Taking head skull data from Cyberware Laboratory, Inc., Paul Neumann put together this 3D human eye for you to stare back at. This is a complex model, with all of the eye's anatomy modeled in full detail, as shown in Figure 2-15.

Figure 2-15
An eye

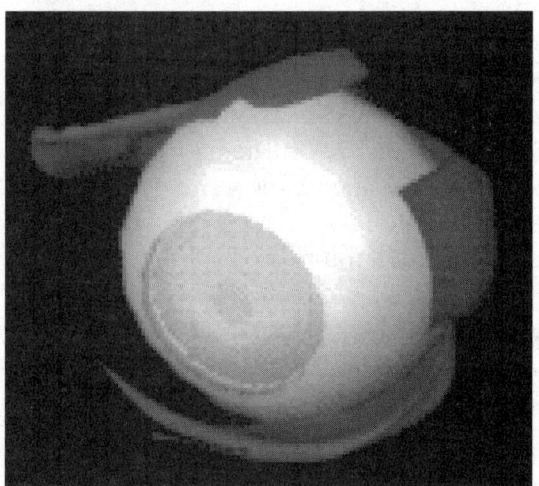

Figure 2-16
Deymier

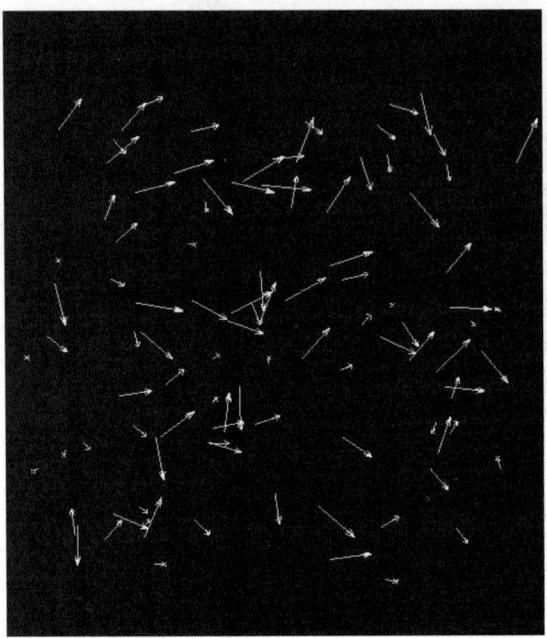

Deymier

http://amber.rc.arizona.edu/vrml/deymier.wrl.gz
The mishmash of arrows in Figure 2-16 represents the Molecular Binding of Ink in an Ink-Jet Printer. As you move around, the arrows change, depending on how close you are to them. This complex model was created by Marvin Landis.

Interactive Membrane Builder

http://bellatrix.pcl.ox.ac.uk/people/alan/WebSpace/builder/form.html
Alan J. Robinson and Barry J. Hardy have created a fully loaded interactive membrane builder. Pick your solute, choose the x and y coordinates for each solute, and then let the computer do its magic. A 3D version of the membrane will appear on your screen for you to study.

Visualize the Impossible

http://www.paperinc.com/worlds/tri.wrl
The famous fractal "sponegtri"—recursively cutting triangles out of a pyramid—can be seen in 3D splendor, as in Figure 2-17. This version was created by DEC's John Danskin.

Figure 2-17
Triangles
within triangles
within...

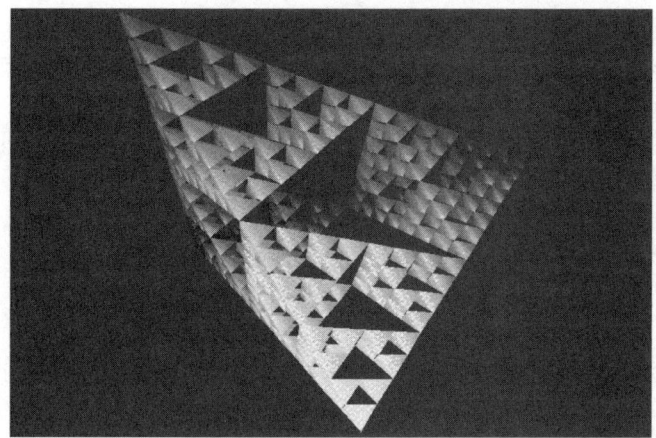

Wave of the Future

http://jean-luc.ncsa.uiuc.edu/Viz/VRML/

The NCSA Relativity and Cosmology Groups have put together some out-of-this-world VRML models. For instance:

- Teukolsky gravity waves (who knows what these are—ask Teukolsky—but they sure look neat) in Figure 2-18.

- The metric from the collision of two black holes in Figure 2-19.

Figure 2-18
Teukolsky waves

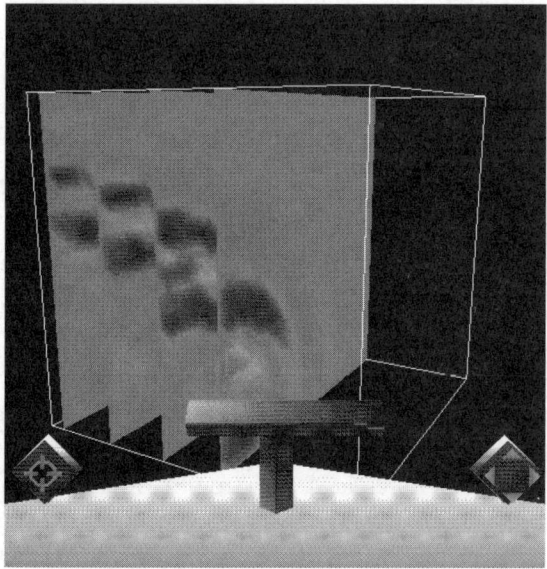

Figure 2-19
Black hole
collisions

Fractals

http://www.sdsc.edu/EnablingTech/Visualization/vrml/tools/fract/index.html
The San Diego Supercomputer Center VRML Fractal Homepage is a collection of several groovy VRML fractals, such as the one in Figure 2-20. Many of these fractals are Lindenmayer systems (L-systems) that use mathematics to create realistic-looking plants.

Nature's Glory

http://kirk.usafa.af.mil:80/~baird/vrml/
Leeomn Baired put up one of the world's first VRML fractal pages. You can load an object and zoom in on it. The closer you zoom in, the more details appear. A beautiful fractaloid tree is in Figure 2-21.

Interactive Abacus

http://speckle.ncsl.nist.gov/greg-bin/abacus
When you run out of fingers and toes, you can turn to the interactive abacus. This is a full working abacus created by Greg Seidman. To slide over some beads, just click on where you want to slide, as in Figure 2-22. A new abacus appears, with the beads positioned exactly where you want them.

Figure 2-20
A fractal

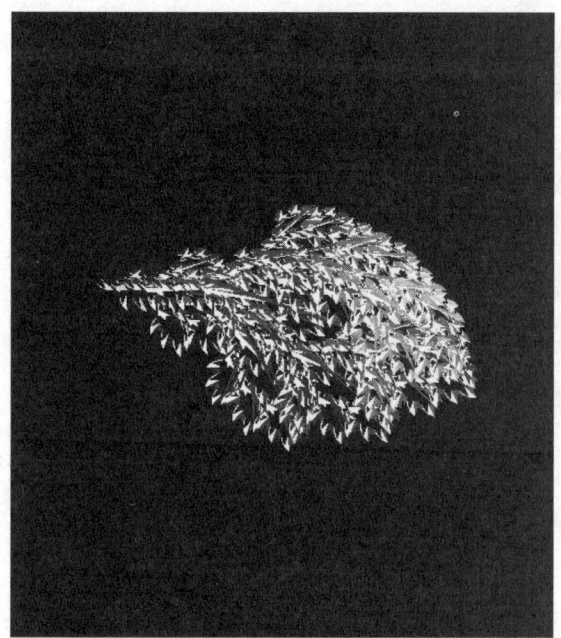

Figure 2-21
A fractal tree
with 256
leaves

Figure 2-22
Abacus

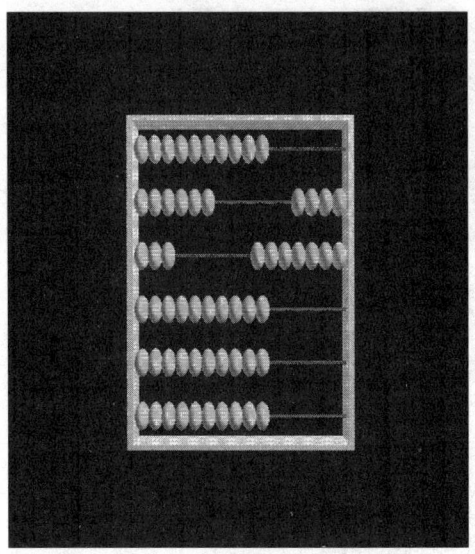

Figure 2-23
Castillo ruins

HISTORY

http://jaka.eecs.uic.edu/dave/vrml/JASON/castillo.wrl.gz
Climb some Mayan ruins from your living room, as in Figure 2-23. This rich
model of the Castillo site seems to have endless nooks and crannies for you
to explore. Another reason for the appeal of VRML is that it allows you to
create long-lost or exotic locations such as this.

BUSINESS AND MARKETING

http://www.sgi.com/Products/WebFORCE/stock1.wrl
SGI's Clay Graham has created a very special room. The moldings along the
floor are not only art-deco, they're information come to life. The tilting of

Figure 2-24
SGI's VRML
stock ticker

the floor and the walls (see Figure 2-24) are based on SGI's current stock trends. Load the room today and it'll look different than it did yesterday.

REFERENCE AND USEFUL PLACES

Find maps of campuses, cities, or planets. Visit libraries filled with every book in the world. Or just discover a new, easier way to sort and deal with day-to-day data like customers' phone numbers, inventory, or bookkeeping. VRML will combine the organizational power of computers with the intuition of real-world storage.

The Earth

http://jaka.eecs.uic.edu/dave/vrml/JASON/TexWorld.wrl
http://www.gwha.com/~jym/VRMLWorld.wrl.gz
There are several projects under way to model the entire planet using VRML, one of which is shown in Figure 2-25. Some globes act as an interface: click on any red dot, and be transported to the appropriate region. Other globes let you zoom into certain areas, from a country to a state to a city down to the buildings and houses in a neighborhood. One project has even created a planet based on live satellite data. You can zoom in on any point on Earth and see what it looks like in *real time*.

Figure 2-25
Planet Earth

Big Person on Campus

Full campuses can easily be put into cyberspace, as in Figure 2-26. You can stroll around, or you can jump directly to buildings such as the reception area, restaurant, administration building, or to certain offices. This is an ideal way for offices, bases, and universities to present themselves online.

Figure 2-26
Walk the
campus

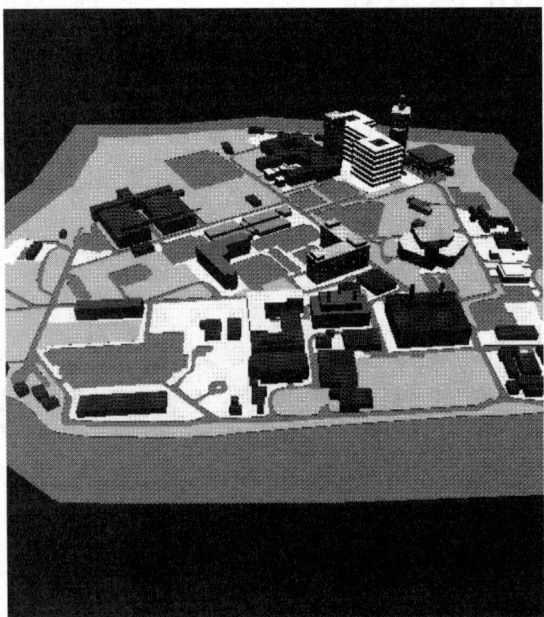

Figure 2-27
A highly
detailed SOMA

Virtual SOMA

http://www.hyperion.com/planet9/vrsoma.htm

One of the most impressive VRML jobs so far is Planet 9 Studio's virtual SOMA (Figure 2-27). San Francisco's SOMA (South Of Market Area) was the first virtual city to go online. The SOMA neighborhood is full of high-tech companies specializing in multimedia, software, Web development, and animation.

As you stroll through SOMA's streets, you will see actual buildings, all to scale. Some buildings will be textured with photographs so you can see *exactly* what the real building looks like. These fancier buildings are links to the company inside. For example, you can walk into WIRED's offices or visit Planet9 Studios. You can even walk into some buildings and wander from office to office.

SOCIALIZING

http://www.virtpark.com/theme/worlds/blacksun.wrl

VRML version 1 does not allow any multiuser interaction. There are many efforts under way, however, to mix the Internet Relay Chat with 3D worlds. Soon, however, you'll be able to walk through virtual worlds and speak with virtual people, culminating in a virtually spectacular social experience.

Some sites are already being developed as common meeting points. For instance, Scott Virtual Theme Parks' Black Sun in Figure 2-28 is a world modeled after Neal Stephenson's *Snow Crash* novel. In the book, the Black Sun is a hangout for the hacker cognoscenti.

It's a very simple world—a black pyramid with the top chopped off.

HOME WORLDS

As with HTML, the biggest allure of VRML will be people who want to place a little piece of themselves onto the Net. Instead of creating a mere home page, you can create a home world. This can be a model of your room or office, your dream house, or any environment where you feel at home (a swamp, inside a volcano, underwater, and so on).

Oz

http://www.oz.is/OZ/Misc/VRML.html
You won't find any lions, tin men, or scarecrows in the Oz world. You will find some quirky houses, however, as in Figure 2-29. You can stroll through these houses and use them to jump to different areas of the Oz Web site. You can find out about Oz's services, products, projects, departments, and staff.

VRMlab

http://www.newcollege.edu/vrmLab/home.wrl
The always changing New College VRMlab is a good example of fine-tuning VRML. The page started off as a simple temple and developed into a full

Figure 2-28
The Black Sun

Figure 2-29
The Oz
animation
house

desert landscape (Figure 2-30). Using tips, complaints, and ideas from the VRML community, this lab was built as an example of what works and what doesn't.

Click on spiders to move to other Web sites, on the pen to send mail to the VRMlab, or on the filing cabinet to visit the VRMlab warehouse of 3D objects.

Ben's Page

http://www.bbcnc.org.uk/bbctv/the_net/ben/vrml.html
Benjamin Wooley has extruded his 2D HTML home page at "The Net" (found at *http://www.bbcnc.org.uk/bbctv/the_net/ben/*) into the third dimension. This

Figure 2-30
VRMlab

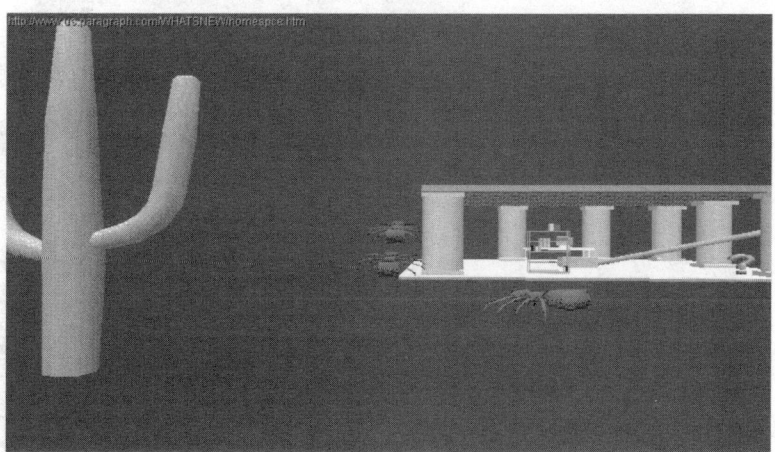

virtual recreation room is homey and fun to hang out in (Figure 2-31). Every object takes you to a different part of Ben's pages.

Robin's Castle

http://reality.sgi.com/employees/robinh/Models/robin1.wrl
SGI's Robin Hayes has created a sleek-lookin' Secret Castle as his home page (Figure 2-32).

EDUCATION

What about VRML *isn't* educational? Many sites strive explicitly to use VRML to augment all sorts of studies.

Jason

http://jaka.eecs.uic.edu/dave/vrml/CAVE/JasonCAVE1.wrl.gz
You can dive beneath the sea from the comfort of your desktop thanks to JASON. The JASON Project is an attempt to take children around the world on virtual field trips to important and exotic scientific expeditions. This year's trip, for instance, carefully recorded and broadcast a journey through

Figure 2-31
Ben's home
page

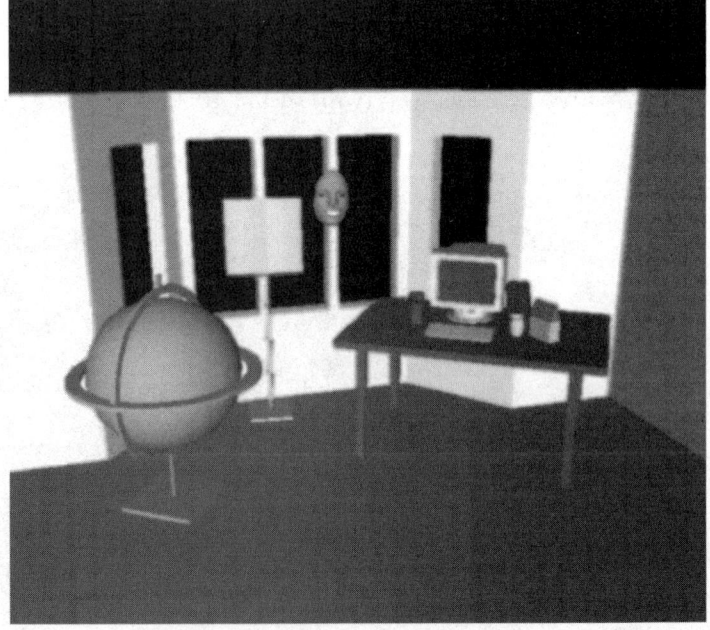

Figure 2-32
Robin's castle

the volcanoes and jungles of Hawaii. Students can learn about techniques, equipment, and the know-how to make exploration possible. Figures 2-33 through 2-35 take you on a virtual tour of an underwater expedition. 3D arrows within the VRML world take you from scene to scene.

Figure 2-33
Start from the
island

Figure 2-34
Jump onto the
ship

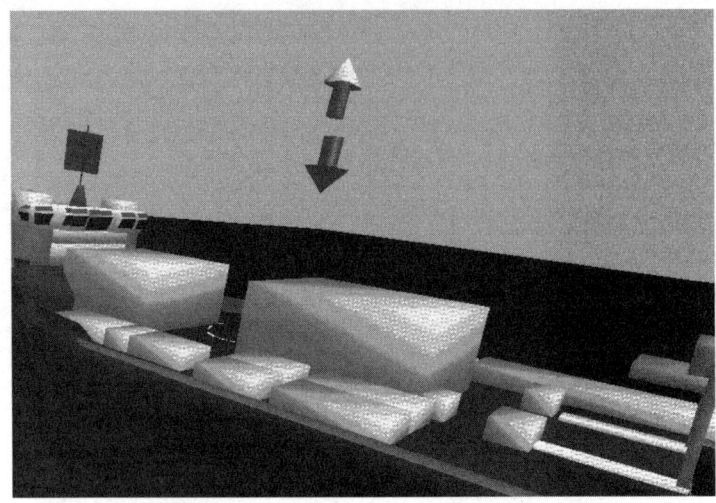

Figure 2-35
Go underwater
with a robotic
submarine

A Real Virtual Forest

http://www.cruz.com/~hughes/tropical_forest.wrl
The EcoSystem program creates a forest model based on user-inputted figures about altitude, rainfall, temperature, and other climate information. Eventually you'll be able to plant your own tree, choosing different species to grow. The EcoSystem uses something called TreeRML to create its forests, as in Figure 2-36.

Figure 2-36
A real virtual
forest

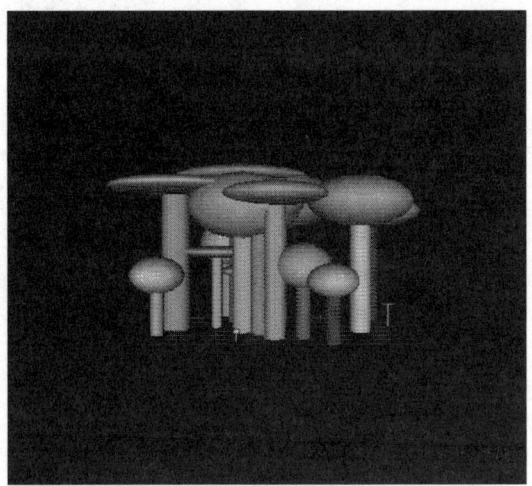

THE END OF THE TOUR

Whenever you take a tour of someplace new and fantastic, you see the most popular sites, learn the most popular history, and are told the most popular anecdotes. But eventually every tour must come to its end. This can be disappointing, but also quite exciting. For now you can wander the foreign land on your own, discovering things with your unique perspective.

Many of the worlds in this chapter lead you to bigger, better, and more distant worlds. Take some time to walk around cyberspace. Get to know the people and the technology. But as you're strolling around, remember: Unlike other distant places, cyberspace is not only easy to visit, it's easy to become a citizen.

There's a big difference between touring a land and knowing it. You can't truly know a land until you've lived there, worked there, and played there. Setting up your own 3D world, then, is more than good fun and good business. It's a way to homestead the vastest frontier ever known. The tour is over. Welcome. Go build!

3
WINDOW TO THE WORLD: WEBFX AND LIVE3D

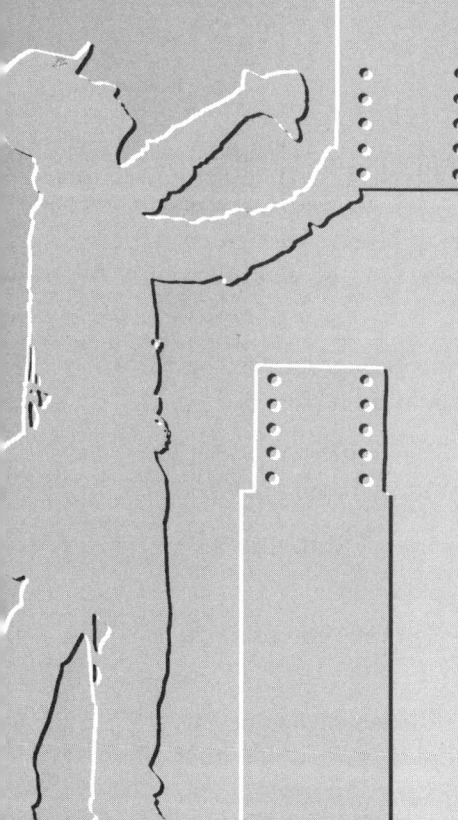

There are four popular VRML browsers competing for your attention, with many more being released every day. The four big ones include

- Paper Software's WebFX/Live3D
- Intervista's WorldView
- SGI and TGS' WebSpace
- NCSA's VRweb

Each of these browsers has its advantages and disadvantages. If you have the disk space and resources, it's a good idea to have *all* these browsers in your software arsenal, depending on the scene you're looking at. Navigation around virtual worlds has a very different feel with each browser. WebSpace is like skimming around with a golf cart, and WebFX is like flying a jet plane. Complicated scenes with fancy lighting and shapes will look best in WebSpace. If you want to move through a scene fast, then WorldView is the ticket you'll need. VRweb best implements *level of detail* (changing an object's shape or complexity based on how close or far you are to it). The next chapter covers all these browsers' pros and cons, and lets you know where you can download or buy the browser of your choice.

By and large, however, this book focuses on Paper Software's WebFX/Live3D. We've bundled WebFX on the enclosed CD-ROM so you can start using it immediately. Although WebFX has its disadvantages, it has many more pluses:

- It runs relatively fast on desktop PCs. Most Internet users use 14,400 baud modems and relatively slow 486 computers. WebFX seems to work the best on these systems.

- It supports all VRML 1.0 nodes, including texture mapping.

- It can handle GIF, JPG, and BMP textures.

- It embeds itself within the most popular Web browser: Netscape Navigator. This makes it a breeze to surf the Web, switching between HTML Web pages and VRML worlds. You can read a 2D Web page, jump to a 3D VRML world, and skip back to a 2D page, all in the same window. You don't even need to configure your Web browser with any special settings. Everything is taken care of for you.

- Navigation is intuitive. It's easy to learn and fun to use.

- Some unique features are added on: Collision detection makes flying through worlds highly realistic—you can't walk through walls or sink beneath floors. Animated textures allow you to wrap objects with video or animations, creating stormy skies, tempest-tossed seas, or other neat effects.

- It supports popular WebSpace extensions allowing background color, background images, and recommended viewpoints to be customized.

- It handles *zipped files,* which is an oft-used way of compressing VRML files. This means it can load and display most any VRML file on the Web.

- It handles common Open Inventor nodes so that even VRML files that aren't strictly legal will still work just fine.

- VRML Live3D extensions let you use 3D animations or rotations to move some parts of a world without moving others.

NOTE: Additional Live3D extensions let you stream in video or audio. This means real-time sound and graphics can fill your virtual worlds. It's free! Which version is for you?

WebFX comes in two flavors:

- Netscape—The Netscape version embeds itself within Netscape Navigator's window. If you use the Netscape Navigator to boogie the Web, try this version. Whenever you come across a VRML site on the Web, WebFX is automatically loaded. This is a handy way to switch between HTML and VRML. This also lets you use Netscape's built-in features such as caching, viewing the VRML's source code, and drag-and-drop loading of Web resources. WebFX/Live3D runs almost seamlessly within Netscape. You can keep bookmarks, view the VRML source, and use all your favorite Netscape functions while flying through a VRML world. The Netscape 2.0 version also has many neat perks, such as VRML frames: This allows you to view a VRML world and HTML page at the same time, within the same window. You can create, for example, a mini-VRML logo within your Web page that people can navigate through.

- WebFX Explorer—This version of WebFX acts as its own browser. It cannot display HTML, but it can load any VRML scene like a whiz. You can use this version along with any other Web browser.

Check out Paper Software's home page at *http://www.paperinc.com* for the latest information or to download the latest version.

INSTALLING IT

WebFX can be found in the WEBFX directory of the enclosed CD-ROM. If you're installing the Netscape version, be sure your Web browser is already installed properly. Each version is in its own subdirectory:

- EXPLORER—The WebFX stand-alone Explorer.

- LIVE3D—The Netscape plug-in.

Simply switch to the directory of your choice. Select the Setup program. If you're using Windows 3.1, select File, Run to run Setup. If you're using Windows 95, just click on the Setup icon. You will then be guided through the installation. You may be asked to specify in which directory Netscape can be found.

To run WebFX, just use your Web browser as usual. Everything else should be taken care of for you.

IMMERSING YOURSELF

It's incredibly easy to start swimming through virtual worlds. You can load worlds stored on your local disk drive, visit worlds on the Internet, or go directly from an HTML Web page into a 3D VRML scene.

Figure 3-1
Loading a
VRML file from
your disk

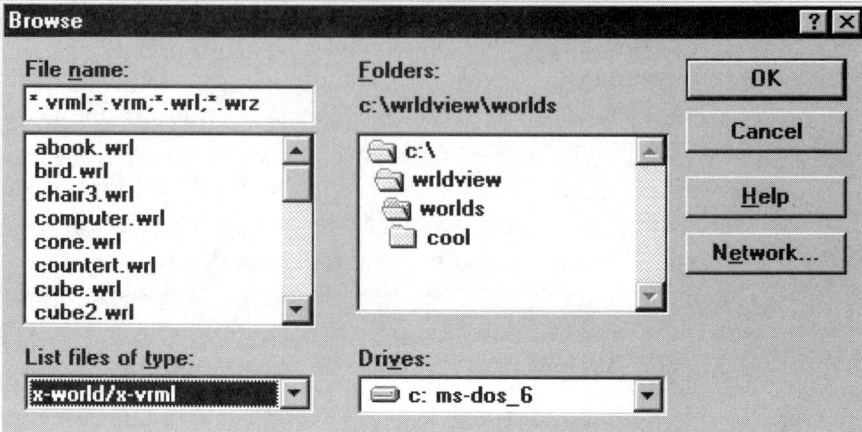

Loading from Disk

If you'd like to open a VRML file that is stored on your disk, simply select File, Open. If you're using Netscape, just find the disk, directory, and file you want and double-click it. Click on the List Files Of Type selection list. Choose the *x-world/x-vrml* type, as in Figure 3-1. Load the WRL file of your choice by double-clicking on it.

The WebFX window will now load. As the graphics are processed, you'll see a green status bar marking the progress. The WebFX interface changes with each new version of the product. The latest interface is shown in Figure 3-2. This interface has the same basic controls no matter which version of WebFX you're using, though sometimes the toolbar is at the top of the screen and sometimes it's at the bottom.

Loading from the Web

If you know the exact URL of the VRML file you wish to view, just type it into the Location box. For example, to load *http://found.cs.nyu.edu/dfox/road.wrl,* just type it in and press ⟨ENTER⟩. The scene will load.

NOTE: VRML scenes often don't stand alone. They may load other WRL files, texture images, or other supplementary files. As these files load, you'll be told so at the bottom of the screen. When the other files load, you can move through the scene if you wish, though it's much faster just to be a little patient and let everything transfer over.

Figure 3-2
A basic WebFX
screen

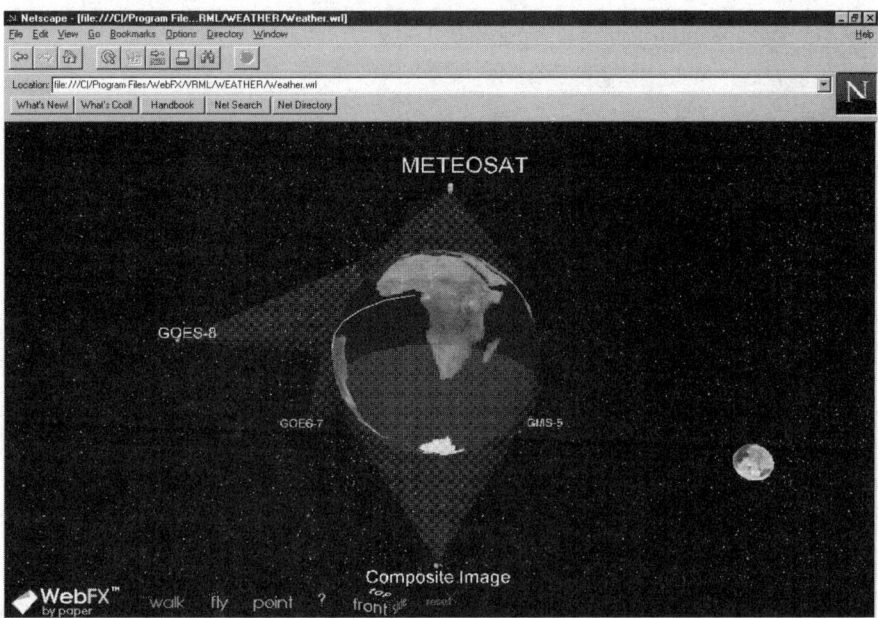

Clicking into a VRML Scene

Many Web pages now have direct links to VRML worlds. If you roll over a 3D link, the cursor arrow will turn into a pointing hand. The URL (the place the link will take you) appears at the top of the screen. Simply click on one of these links, and WebFX will automatically pop up and load the scene you selected. It's that simple.

Other Web pages may have a little window with the HTML screen containing, of all things, a tiny VRML world for you to explore.

WALKING, FLYING, OR MANIPULATING

To begin navigating through a scene, just click anywhere in the WebFX window. At the top of the screen you probably noticed several words or icons. Earlier versions of WebFX will say: Walk, Fly, Author, and Chat. Later versions have the following options: Walk, Fly, Point, ?, Top/Front/Side, Reset, and eventually, Author. Live3D has: Walk, Fly, Point, and Reset. These icons or words correspond to the WebFX modes. Table 3-1 lists all the WebFX navigation commands.

To switch to a mode, just click on it. You can also switch between modes by clicking the *right* mouse button and selecting the Navigation option.

Table 3-1 WebFX navigation commands

Keypress or Mouse Move	Result
Walking	
↑, ↓	Move forward, backward
←, →	Turn left, right
A	Tilt head up
Z	Tilt head down
Left mouse button	Move forward/backward or turn left/right
Right mouse button	Rotate around the entire scene
SHIFT (w/ mouse or keys)	Move faster
ALT (w/ mouse or keys)	Pan left/right or up/down
CTRL (w/ keys)	Automatically walks toward an object
Flying	
↑, ↓	Tilt up, down
←, →	Turn left, right
A	Thrust forward
Z	Thrust backward
Q	Revolve counterclockwise
E	Revolve clockwise
Left mouse button	Tilt up/down or turn left/right
Right mouse button	Rotate about the entire scene
SHIFT (w/ mouse or keys)	Move faster
ALT (w/ mouse or keys)	Pan left/right or up/down
Authoring	
Keyboard	Same as walking
Drag with left mouse button	Move the scene or object
Drag with right mouse button	Rotate the scene or object
Click left mouse button	Select the scene or object
CTRL (w/ left mouse button)	Copy the scene or object
CTRL (w/ right mouse button)	Scale the scene or object
ALT (w/ mouse or keys)	Move scene or object left/right or up/down

NOTE: Eventually WebFX will support even more controls, such as J to jump or the SPACEBAR to open a door or pick up an object.

Walk

Walk allows you to move through a scene as if you're standing on flat ground and taking a stroll. You can move forward or backward using ⬆ and ⬇. You can gradually turn your sight to the left or right by using ➡ and ⬅. If you hold ➡ long enough, for example, you turn a full 360 degrees and wind up right where you started. WebFX uses physics-based navigation. This means the longer you hold down an arrow key, the faster in that direction you will go. When you let go of the arrow, you may even continue walking if you build up enough momentum.

There are several other controls, such as tilting your head up and down or jumping. These movements and their keys are similar to the popular DOOM video game. Check out Table 3-1 for a full list of walk navigation commands. To automatically walk toward an object, just point to it, hold down CTRL and click.

You can also use the mouse to walk through a scene. Just click on the right mouse button and push the mouse forward, away from you. Everything you see will get bigger as you approach, as shown in Figure 3-3. Still holding the button, move the mouse to the right. The world will shift to the left as you turn right, as in Figure 3-4. Now pull the mouse back toward you. Everything gets smaller as you back away (Figure 3-5).

Figure 3-3
Moving closer to the castle

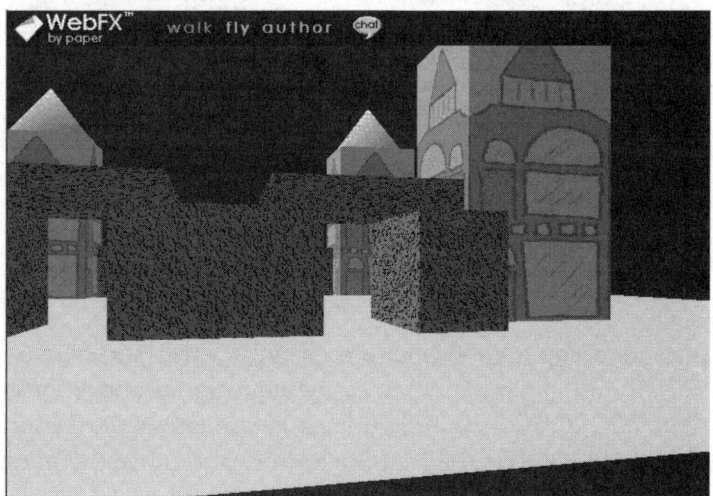

Figure 3-4
Turning to the
right

Figure 3-5
Backing up

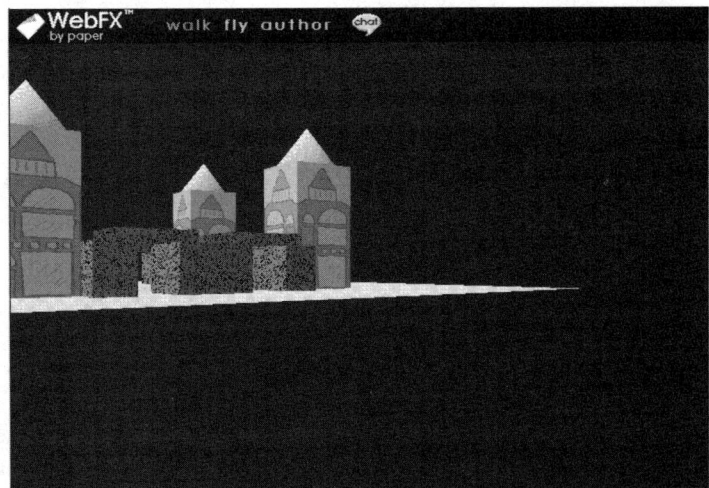

Fly

Flying lets you pretend to be Superman and whisk through a scene at
extreme speeds and angles. You can easily wind up far above, or far below,
a scene, with just a few keypresses. This is similar to the Descent video
game. Simply hold down the left mouse button, and move the mouse in the
direction you want to go. You'll swoop in that direction.

Point

Click on the part of the world you want to zoom in on. You'll be thrust forward toward that point. This is a great way to leap around a complicated world.

?

If you forget which keys or mouse movements do what, just click on the question mark. Navigation hints will appear in the WebFX window. Click on the mark again to remove the hints.

Top/Front/Side

The Top/Front/Side cube is a handy way to quickly change your point of view. To see the world from a bird's-eye view, click Top. Click Side to view it from the side. Click Front to return to the default front view.

Reset

Click on the Reset icon to return to your original camera position. This is useful in case you wander off too far in space and get lost.

Author

This mode is not fully implemented in the current version of WebFX. When and if it works, however, this will be a very important tool. Authoring will allow you to click on any object in the scene and drag it anywhere else. This will make it a snap to throw a bunch of objects into a scene and then arrange them aesthetically. Eventually WebFX will be an indispensable tool for VRML creation. You'll also be able to do simple animations; for instance, you'll be able to move a woman's leg, making her seem to walk.

Chat

This mode, as well, is not fully implemented in the current version of WebFX. Eventually, however, WebFX will be hooked into the *Internet Relay Chat (IRC)*. This will allow you to chat in three dimensions. People will have avatars—3D representations of themselves.

In the very near future you will be able to use VRML and WebFX to walk up to real cyberpeople and type things to them, listening to what they have to say.

ROTATING OR PANNING

What makes VRML different from a video game is that there is no limit to how you can view a world. Walking and flying through a scene usually is not enough. Maybe you want to move up a staircase, or see the back of a building without having to walk all the way around it. WebFX makes it quite easy to check out a scene from any angle, point, or distance. Simply use the right mouse button.

Rotating

At times you'd like to tilt the current VRML scene around to view it from a different perspective. For example, you can easily tilt a 3D biplane. Just hold down the right mouse button, and then spin the airplane in the direction you'd like, as in Figure 3-6. This is similar to walking (or flying) around a sculpture at an art museum. Physics is still in effect. If you spin around an object fast enough, you will continue spinning.

Panning

Sometimes your angle is a little off. You may be too high or low. Or perhaps you've walked into a huge room and want to pan along the front wall without turning. To move the camera (your point of view) straight to the right, left, up, or down, just hold down ALT and use the mouse or arrows to move.

Figure 3-6
Rotating around a VRML world

A CHANGE OF VIEW

To access WebFX's Control menu, press the right mouse button while in the 3D viewing window, as in Figure 3-7. You can use this to set all the WebFX options. Perhaps the most useful option is the Detail item, which gives you the ability to see the same scene a number of different ways:

■ Solid—This makes 3D objects look real, with solid sides.

■ Wireframe—This only shows the important lines used to sketch an object, as in Figure 3-8.

■ Point Cloud—This only shows the vertices (corners) of objects, and looks like a constellation of scattered stars.

Figure 3-7
Making the world simplistic to move around it faster

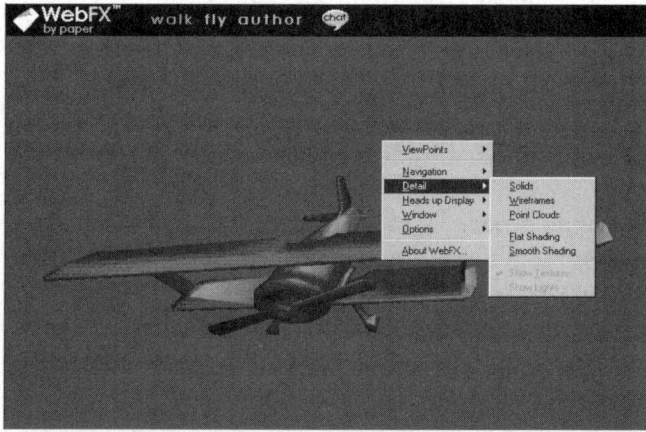

Figure 3-8
The bare bones of a 3D object

Changing detail is an important option in virtual worlds. Since some scenes are awfully complex, moving through them can be excruciatingly slow. If you change a solid world to a wireframe world, then you can whisk through the world much faster. It corresponds to the real world: A finished skyscraper is much harder to move than the girders of an unfinished building.

NOTE: You can also use the Detail menu to change the shading to Flat or Smooth. Flat shading doesn't look as pretty, but objects can be drawn much faster.

VIEWPOINTS

Another useful option in the Control menu is ViewPoints. Many VRML scenes have built-in recommendations of places you should check out. For example, the castle in Figure 3-9 allows you to jump directly to the Threshold, the Courtyard, the Exit, or to a Bird's-Eye view.

When you first load a new VRML world, check out the ViewPoints menu for a quick tour of what the world has to offer.

NOTE: Viewpoints are especially useful if you get lost. Sometimes you'll move so fast through a world that you'll end up on the other side and see only the vast, dark void of empty cyberspace. You might try to turn or pan around, but it may be in vain. You may be thousands of meters away from where you began. You can also return home by selecting the first item in the ViewPoints list.

Figure 3-9
Jumping to some recommended "Kodak-moment" viewpoints

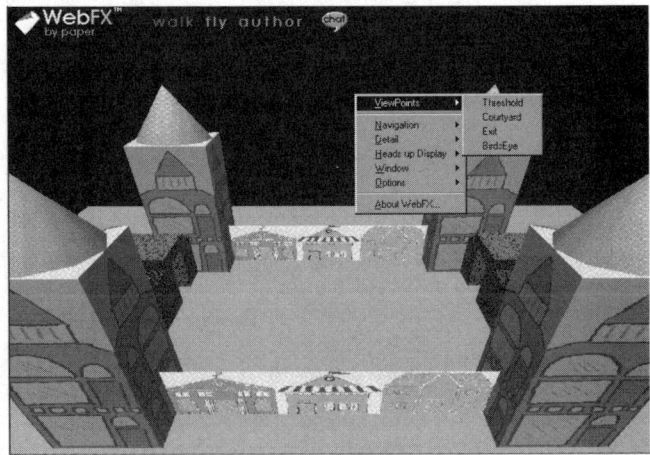

HOTLIST AND BOOKMARKS

A VRML world is basically treated like any other Web page. You can use Netscape's built-in hotlist and bookmark menus to save any VRML location. For instance, select Bookmarks, Add Bookmark.

OTHER OPTIONS

WebFX allows you to customize the look and feel of your 3D experience.

Select the Heads-Up Display option from the control menu to change the look of your WebFX screen. You can toggle a number of options by clicking on them. For example, if you like to have cross hairs in the center of your screen, click Crosshairs. Click Navigation Help if you're a WebFX novice—the commands will be printed right on your screen. Click Download Status if you'd like to be notified of necessary VRML files as they load in.

Select the Option item from the Control menu, and choose Preserve Aspect Ratio if you want to scale everything equally horizontally and vertically. This ensures that a sphere will be perfectly round. If not, the 3D world will be warped, depending on the shape of your WebFX window.

Select the Navigation item to set Collision Detection and Momentum on or off. This way, if you want to become a ghost and walk though a wall, you can.

WEBFX LIMITATIONS

If WebFX comes across a VRML command it doesn't recognize, it'll just ignore it. This may sometimes throw off a scene. WebFX also has some problems with large or complicated files, and may draw things where they don't belong. It can only handle a set amount of colors, and lights are not always drawn the way they should be.

For the most part, however, WebFX does a bang-up job displaying most any VRML world.

FX AND NETSCAPE 2.0

WebFX in combination with Netscape 2.0 is a powerhouse combination. Navigation through 2D pages and 3D worlds is smooth, seamless, and fast. One of the most useful features is the ability to drop small VRML windows onto a Web page, as in Figure 3-10. You can have a 3D company logo, a map of your campus, or any other 3D object lie right atop the HTML page. Simply use the HTML <EMBED> tag.

Figure 3-10
VRML versions of the Netscape, Paper Software, and VRML logos, all within a Web page

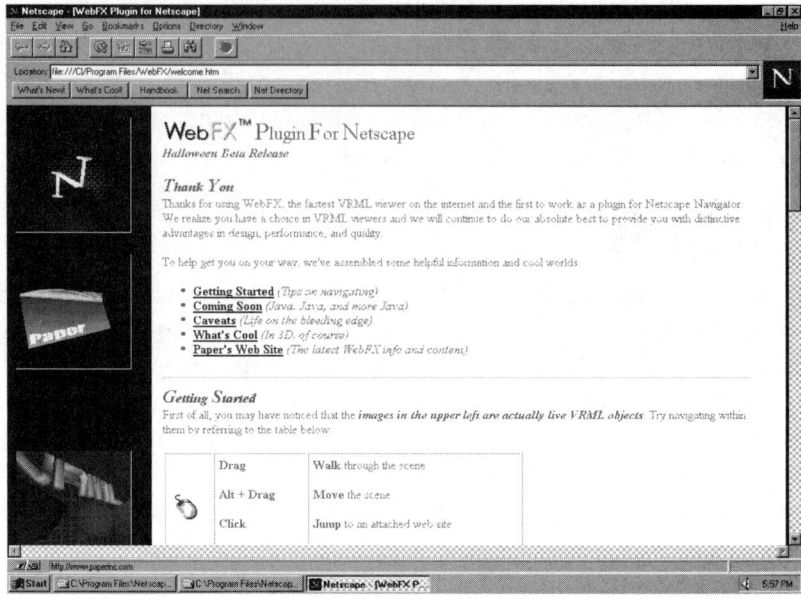

For example, if you have a VRML logo of your company called LOGO.WRL, you can embed it using HTML code similar to the following:

```
<embed src="logo.wrl" border=none align=left width=150 height=150>
```

Borders are optional. You can align the VRML box to the left, center, or right. And you can specify the width and height to be as many pixels as you wish. If you want to learn more about HTML, check out the Waite Group's *HTML Web Publisher's Construction Kit* (Fox and Downing, 1995).

SPECIAL FX

Paper Software is at the forefront of VRML innovation. The next version of WebFX will no doubt be much improved. All VRML 2.0 (Moving Worlds) nodes will most likely be supported. There will even be some extended nodes that allow you to drop movies, animations, and sound directly into the VRML world. Drawing will be faster and more reliable. In addition, WebFX may have a full authoring mode that will allow you to take objects from existing scenes and drag-and-drop them into your own world. A form of 3D chatting will also be available.

Check out the Paper Software Web site at *http://www.paperinc.com* for the latest releases and other updates.

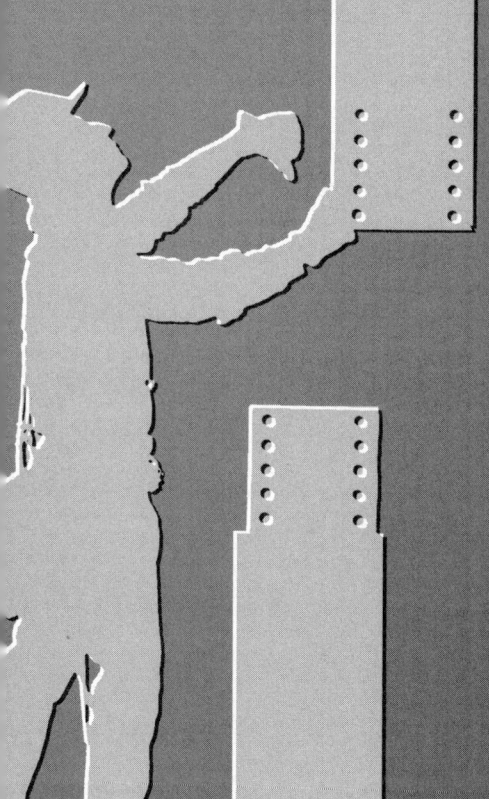

4
OTHER
EXPOSURES

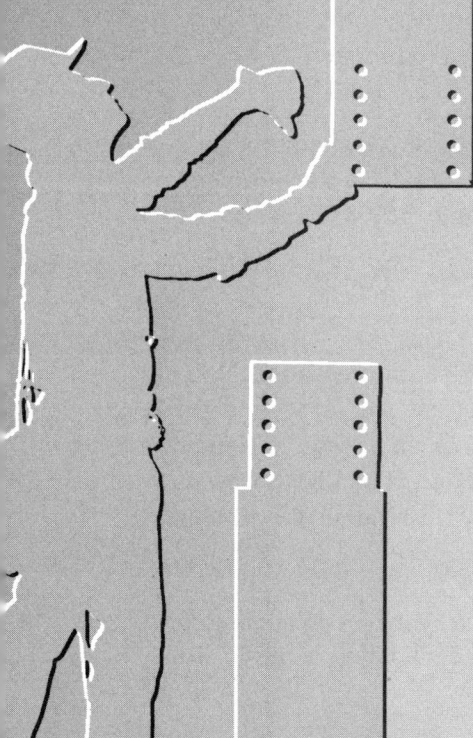

4

Whether you want to call them browsers, viewers, renderers, or Internet-3D thingamajigs, VRML software is flooding the market. There are many VRML browsers and many reasons to use each one. Some browsers load complicated files just fine, while others crash and burn. Some browsers have no problem with JPEG textures; others don't have a clue.

While WebFX seems to be ahead of the pack, this chapter covers three other important VRML browsers:

-  WebSpace
-  WorldView
-  VRweb

There are additional browsers out there, such as VRscout and Fountain. Appendix A shows you how to get hold of alternate browsers. The techniques covered in this chapter, however, should apply to any VRML browser you use.

TALKING TO YOUR WEB BROWSER

The first thing to consider is that there are three categories of VRML browsers:

-  Stand-alone—This is a browser that runs without any other program. It is capable of accessing the Web, loading the WRL file, and rendering the VRML scene. WorldView is a stand-alone browser. You should use a stand-alone browser if all you want to do is see a barrage of VRML files and you don't really care about HTML or other Web goodies.

- ▣ Integrated—This is a browser that runs within a full-featured HTML browser. This is very convenient, allowing you to skip between 2D hypertext and 3D worlds at the click of a link. For example, suppose you're reading a Web page about VRML. If you access a VRML link, the VRML world appears within the same window. WebFX has a version that integrates with QMosaic and Netscape.

- ▣ Helper—This type of browser runs *alongside* an HTML browser. It exploits the HTML browser's capabilities to access the Web and to display HTML pages or deal with any multimedia objects such as sound or video. Whenever a VRML object is loaded, however, the helper takes over and renders the world in its own window. WebSpace is a helper browser.

Integrated browsers are smart enough to automatically talk to your HTML browser (Netscape, Mosaic, and so on). If you're using a stand-alone or helper browser, however, you'll need to configure the Web browser so that it knows what to do with VRML files. It's a necessary but quick process.

Netscape

The easiest way to configure Netscape with VRML is to simply load a VRML file. Try loading one of the scenes in Chapter 2. Netscape will ask you if you want to save the file to disk or configure a helper. Click on Configure Helper App. You can now browse your hard disk until you find your VRML viewer. That's all you need to do. From now on, Netscape will send all VRML files it receives to the program you just selected.

NOTE: The latest versions of Netscape come with the WebFX plug-in already installed. If this is the case, you don't need to do any configuring at all. To see a 3D world, just type its URL in the Location box.

Alternatively, you can manually set up a VRML viewer. Select Options, General (or Option, Preferences in earlier versions of Netscape). Choose the Helper Apps tab or menu item at the top of the window. Click on Create New Type. You'll be asked to enter the MIME Type. Type

`x-world`

Figure 4-1
Setting
Netscape to
understand
VRML

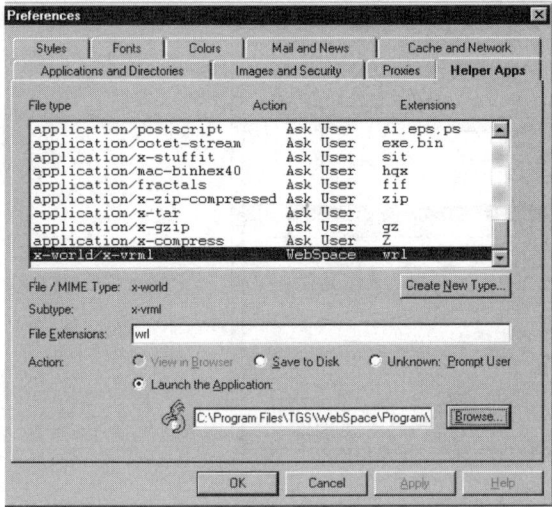

For the MIME Subtype, enter

`x-vrml`

The new MIME type will appear in the helper app list as shown in Figure 4-1. You now need to tell Netscape that VRML files can be distinguished by their .WRL extension. Be sure *x-world/x-vrml* is selected. Click on the File Extension box and type

`wrl`

You now need to tell Netscape which program it should load when it encounters a VRML file. Click on Browse to find your VRML viewer, or type in the full path name of the viewer in the Launch The Application box. For example, if you're using WebSpace with Windows 95, you might use a path similar to

`Files\TGS\WebSpace\Program\WebSpace.exe`

You're done. Click on OK. From now on, any WRL files will be sent over to WebSpace (or whichever VRML viewer you specified).

Spyglass Mosaic

The process is nearly identical for nearly all Mosaic browsers. Try to grab a VRML scene (for example, one of the URLs in Chapter 2). You'll be asked whether you want to save the file to disk or configure a viewer. Click Configure. Click Browse and specify the drive, directory, and file name of the VRML viewer of your choice. Click OK.

Figure 4-2
Setting up a
VRML browser
to work hand-
in-hand with
Quarterdeck
Mosaic

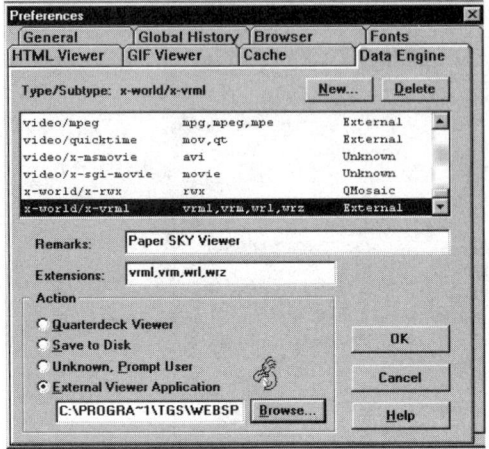

You can also set this up manually. Select Edit, Helpers. Click the Add button. In the Configure File Type area, set the Description to "VRML Scenes." Set the MIME type to *x-world/x-vrml*. The Suffixes box should be set to *.wrl*. Encoding is *Text*. And the Helper App is the full path name of your VRML browser, followed by a space and *%s*, for example:

```
wrldview\wrldview %s
```

Quarterdeck Mosaic

To configure VRML manually with Quarterdeck, select Tools, Preferences, Data Engine. Add the *x-world/x-vrml* MIME type to the list with the *.wrl* extension or suffix, as shown in Figure 4-2. You can then specify a helper app by typing in the full path name and directory of your VRML viewer in the Filename box.

COMPRESSED SCENES

Many VRML files are quite large and would take minutes or even hours to download. Often these files are compressed. A compressed VRML file has the extension .WRL.GZ.

WebFX, WorldView, and WebSpace will automatically decompress any compressed scenes. If you're using a different browser, however, you'll need to decompress the files yourself. To do so, simply download the file and save it to your hard disk. You can then use the GZIP program (on the enclosed CD) to unzip the file. Simply go to the DOS prompt and type the following:

```
gzip -d filename
```

This will create a WRL file. For example, *road.wrl.gz* will become *road.wrl* when you type

```
gzip -d road.wrl.gz
```

You can now load the file as usual using your VRML browser.

LOST IN WEBSPACE

Silicon Graphics' WebSpace was the first commercial VRML browser distributed freely over the World Wide Web. Based on the Open Inventor library, WebSpace still remains a paradigm for how VRML browsers should operate. It offers support for every valid VRML node and does a nearly perfect job of rendering lights, textures, and so on. It hogs lots of memory, however, and runs very slowly on most desktop machines. WebSpace is good if you want to see the intricate details in a pretty scene; it's not so good if you want to navigate through it.

Template Graphics Software has ported several versions of the original WebSpace, which initially ran only on Silicon Graphics workstations. There are versions of WebSpace planned for the following platforms:

- Silicon Graphics workstations

- Sun (Solaris) workstations

- IBM workstations

- Windows NT or 95

- Windows 3.1 (not released yet)

- Macintosh PowerPC (not released yet)

- Digital UNIX (not released yet)

- HP platforms (not released yet)

Getting and Installing It

You can download a version of WebSpace for your computer from the following page:

http://www.tgs.com/

Decompress the file into a temporary directory. It may create three directories: DISK1, DISK2, and DISK3, depending on which WebSpace version you are using. Run the installation program, SETUP.EXE, which may be in the DISK1 directory. All the necessary files will be installed. You can now erase the temporary directory.

WebSpace needs to work hand-in-hand with a Web browser such as Netscape or Spyglass Enhanced Mosaic. It's a good idea to have one of these browsers running in the background each time you use WebSpace.

Seeing a Scene

To use WebSpace to open a WRL file from your hard disk, select File, Open File. Specify the drive, directory, and file name.

NOTE: If you're not attached to the Internet, then any textures or inlined objects will not show up unless you have copies of them on your local hard disk.

To access a scene directly from the Internet, select File, Open Location. You can also click the open location file icon in the toolbar (the arrow-around-the-globe at the top of Figure 4-3). Type in the full URL. WebSpace will use the powers of your HTML browser to download the scene; it'll then use its own powers to display the scene.

VRML and HTML

If your Web browser is configured to work with WebSpace, then clicking on any link to a VRML file will automatically launch the WebSpace program. Likewise, if you roll over some 3D objects, your mouse cursor will change into a target. The URL of this target will appear at the bottom of the screen, in the status line. Click to access the Web page (or sound, movie, or other multimedia resource). If WebSpace can't handle the link, it will launch your HTML browser to take care of business.

Saving

If you've grabbed a virtual world from the Internet and want to store it on your hard disk, select File, Save As VRML. You can then see the scene at any time.

Navigating

WebSpace has two navigation modes:

- Walk viewer—Strolling or flying through a landscape

- Examiner viewer—Rotating or panning your camera around an object

When you load a VRML scene, it tells WebSpace whether it should start up in walk mode or examiner mode. You can change the mode at any time by selecting View, Walk Viewer, or View, Examiner Viewer. As you change your mode, the dashboard at the bottom of the screen changes. The walk mode's dashboard looks like the controls for a golf cart (see Figure 4-3). The examiner's dashboard gives you a trackball to rotate along any axis (see Figure 4-4). You can hide the dashboard if you wish. Simply deselect the Options, Show Dashboard item.

Table 4-1 summarizes all the WebSpace keyboard and mouse controls.

Figure 4-3
Taking a leisurely stroll through a scene using WebSpace

Figure 4-4
Examining a
3D object

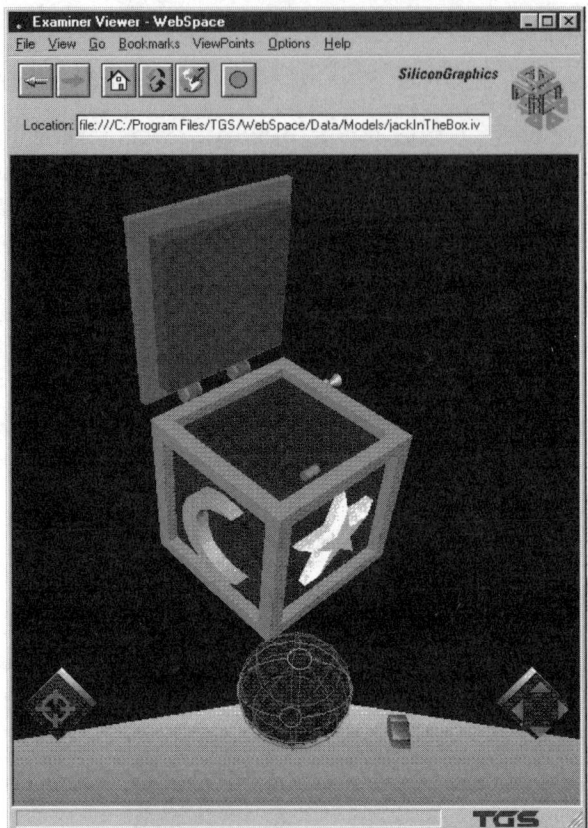

Table 4-1 The WebSpace controls

Function	Mouse (while clicking)	Keyboard
Walk Viewer		
Move forward	CTRL-Push forward	UP ARROW
Move backward	CTRL-Push backward	DOWN ARROW
Turn left	CTRL-Push left	LEFT ARROW
Turn right	CTRL-Push right	RIGHT ARROW
Look left	ALT-Push left	ALT-LEFT ARROW
Look right	ALT-Push right	ALT-RIGHT ARROW
Height up	—	ALT-UP ARROW
Height down	—	ALT-DOWN ARROW
Tilt up	SHIFT-CTRL-Push backward	—
Tilt down	SHIFT-CTRL-Push forward	—

Function	Mouse (while clicking)	Keyboard
Seek	`SHIFT`-Click on area	—
Examiner Viewer		
Tumble/spin	`CTRL`-Move mouse	`UP ARROW`/`DOWN ARROW`/`LEFT ARROW`/`RIGHT ARROW`
Slide Camera	`ALT`-Move mouse	`ALT`-`UP ARROW`/`DOWN ARROW`/`LEFT ARROW`/ `RIGHT ARROW`
Dolly (in/out)	`SHIFT`-`ALT`-Move mouse	`SHIFT`-`ALT`-`UP ARROW`/`DOWN ARROW`

The Golf Cart

Walking through a VRML scene is very intuitive and easy with WebSpace. Just pretend you're sitting behind the wheel of a golf cart or space buggy. To move forward, you can click on the joystick, hold down the mouse button, and push forward; the scene will zoom in toward you. To move faster, push the mouse further upward. As long as you remain clicked on the joystick, you can turn in any direction you wish. The joystick itself will move in the direction you've specified, which helps you understand which way you're actually heading. The cursor will also change into a hand while you're grabbing the stick. To stop moving, just let go of the mouse button.

Yank the throttle to the left (after holding the mouse button down over the joystick) to swivel left without moving forward; the scene will rotate to the right.

Look carefully on the right side of the joystick, and you'll notice a little *tilt knob.* You can use this to tilt the camera angle up, down, left, or right. Just move your cursor over the knob, hold down the mouse button, and move whichever way you want to tilt. This can be handy to look at the floor, or to move your head to the right without changing your orientation.

You might've noticed that you'll always remain level to the ground as you maneuver around with the joystick. You can use the arrow pad to the right of the joystick for height and side-to-side control. To raise the camera, click on the up arrow. To shift the camera over to the right, click on the left arrow. The longer you press on one of the arrows, the further your camera will be shifted. For example, if you're walking toward a door but need to step a bit to the left to enter it, just use the left arrow.

Finally, to the right of the joystick is the target-shaped *seek tool.* This is a unique and incredibly useful WebSpace gizmo that lets you focus on any part of the VRML scene you wish. Simply click on the seek tool. The arrow cursor changes into a target. Click on the part of the scene you wish to approach. You'll automatically be whisked to that part of the scene. This is a very quick and easy way of moving around. For example, if you're looking at a college campus, all you need to do to approach one of the buildings is click on it with the seek tool.

> **NOTE:** If you want to jump immediately to the target, be sure View, Jump Cut is selected. If Jump Cut isn't checked, then you will move smoothly to your seek destination.

You can also use the mouse and keyboard to maneuver. Just be sure the cursor is in the viewing area, and use the shortcuts as listed in Table 4-1.

The Examining Table

WebSpace makes it simple to examine a 3D object. Simply click on the trackball in the center of the control panel. While holding down the mouse button, move the trackball along any axis you wish. The object will rotate accordingly, as in Figure 4-4. This lets you see any side of the current object.

To dolly your camera closer to or farther away from the object, use the thumbwheel, to the right of the trackball. While clicking on the wheel, move it up to zoom in, or move it down to zoom out.

The arrow pad and seek tool work the same as they did in walk mode.

Viewpoints

Some scenes come complete with a list of suggested viewpoints. To see this list, select the ViewPoints menu. There may be a long list of areas to explore. There will also always be an Entry View item, which returns you to the original camera position. This can come in handy if you've wandered too far into a scene and are now lost.

Some versions of WebSpace let you select a useful Undo View function. This will take you to your last position, before you used the joystick or the seek tool.

Rendering Options

Since WebSpace draws graphics so carefully, it often runs quite slowly. The best way to speed things up is to sacrifice some detail. The View menu lets you choose from the following levels of detail:

- Full Detail—All textures, shapes, and colors are drawn as crystal-clear as possible.

- No Textures—Geometry stays the same, but textures will not be shown.

- Low Detail—The scene will be drawn simply, perhaps as a wireframe.

TIP: Choose the Degrade During Moves function under the View menu. This will lower the detail of the scene each time you move, making navigation much faster. When you stop moving, the scene will snap back into full detail.

Each scene that you load has its own default move speed—every time you move forward, you'll jump a certain number of paces. If you want to pump up this move speed, select View, Move Faster. If things are whizzing by too fast, you can also select View, Move Slower.

A BLAST FROM THE PAST: THE HISTORY LIST

WebSpace keeps track of every VRML site you visit during a session. Selecting Go, Back takes you back in time until you reach your home scene (the first scene you looked at). You can then select Go, Forward to cycle back up through your scenes. There are also Back and Forward arrows on the toolbar at the top of the WebSpace screen. Select Go, View History to see a listing of all the sites you've visited. Click on one of the sites to revisit it.

Bookmarks

The history list is only active during your WebSpace session. As soon as you quit WebSpace, all information is lost. If you come across a VRML scene that you *know* you'll want to see again, you can add it to a more permanent list by selecting Add Bookmark from the Bookmarks menu.

To check out your bookmarks at any time, select Bookmarks, View Bookmarks. Select the scene you want, and you'll be whisked there as fast as your CPU and modem can take you there.

Other Options

Finally, the Options menu has a number of additional bells and whistles that make 3D browsing much easier:

- Set Home Scene—You can have your own or your favorite VRML scene automatically load each time you start WebSpace.

- Show Hot Links—Should hyperlinked objects be drawn in a different color than unlinked ones? If so, check this option.

- Show Toolbar—You can hide the toolbar buttons to make the viewing area larger.

▣ Show Location—When you roll over a hyperlink, do you want to see the target location?

When done setting your options, select Save Options from the Options menu.

AROUND THE WORLDVIEW

Intervista's WorldView has been influential in VRML history. It was the first browser available on desktop PCs, and it's the first browser available for Macintoshes. WorldView takes its time planning how to draw a scene, but once the graphics are rendered on the screen, navigating is refreshingly fast. Unlike most browsers, WorldView is designed for humble computer systems (486/50 with 8 MB) with 14.4K-modem connections to the Internet. Graphics are crisp and realistic.

There are versions of WorldView for all Microsoft Windows platforms:

▣ Windows NT

▣ Windows 3.1 or Windows for Workgroups (with Win32s)

▣ Windows 95

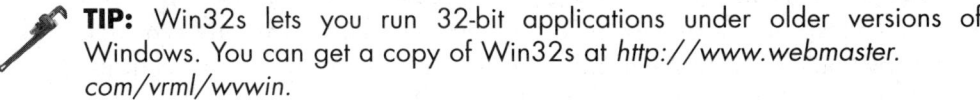

TIP: Win32s lets you run 32-bit applications under older versions of Windows. You can get a copy of Win32s at *http://www.webmaster.com/vrml/wvwin*.

Macintosh versions (for the 68000 and Power PC) are in the works. Check the Intervista home page (*www.webmaster.com*) for the latest release information.

As of this writing, WorldView is in beta release. There are several features not available yet; "yet" is the key word—Intervista plans to support all legal VRML features in its official release version.

Getting and Installing It

Download the WorldView files from:

http://www.webmaster.com/vrml/support

After getting the appropriate version, copy the program to a temporary directory and run it. A bunch of files will be extracted, including the SETUP.EXE program. Run Setup. WorldView will be installed in the directory you specify

(C:\WLDVIEW by default). A WorldView item will then be set up in your Windows Program Manager. You can now erase the temporary directory if you want to save space (and these days, who doesn't?).

The WorldView directory has a WORLDS subdirectory with lots of sample objects and scenes for you to play around with.

Seeing a Scene

To open a .WRL file from the hard disk in WorldView, select File, Open File (or press CTRL-O). Specify the drive, directory, and file name.

NOTE: If you're not attached to the Internet, any inlined objects will not show up unless they're stored on your hard disk along with the WRL file.

WorldView has the power to access the Internet directly. As long as you're connected to the Net (through Winsock or Dial-Up Networking), WorldView is the only program you'll need to view VRML scenes. To access a scene, select File, Open Location (or CTRL-L). Alternatively, click the open book icon in the toolbar at the top of the screen. Type in the full URL.

WorldView reads in the file (it'll say "reading" at the bottom of the screen), spends a good deal of time thinking about it (it'll say "parsing"), and then will draw the scene quite nicely ("rendering").

Navigating

WorldView offers three navigation modes:

- Walk—Walk through the world, as in Figure 4-5.

- Fly—Move in all directions around the world. This mode is similar to walk, but faster and with more freedom. Once you start flying in a certain direction, you will not stop, even when you let go of your mouse.

- Inspect—Rotate or tilt the object on your screen, as in Figure 4-6.

You are given full control via the arrow buttons at the bottom of the WorldView screen. The first set of buttons is the basic Move navigation functions. The second set is the Pitch and Roll arrows. The third set is the Panning functions. Table 4-2 covers how these arrows work within each navigation mode. Navigating takes a bit of getting used to, but once you've gotten it down, you can quickly and easily view the world from any perspective you desire.

Figure 4-5
Moving
through a 3D
Escher
landscape

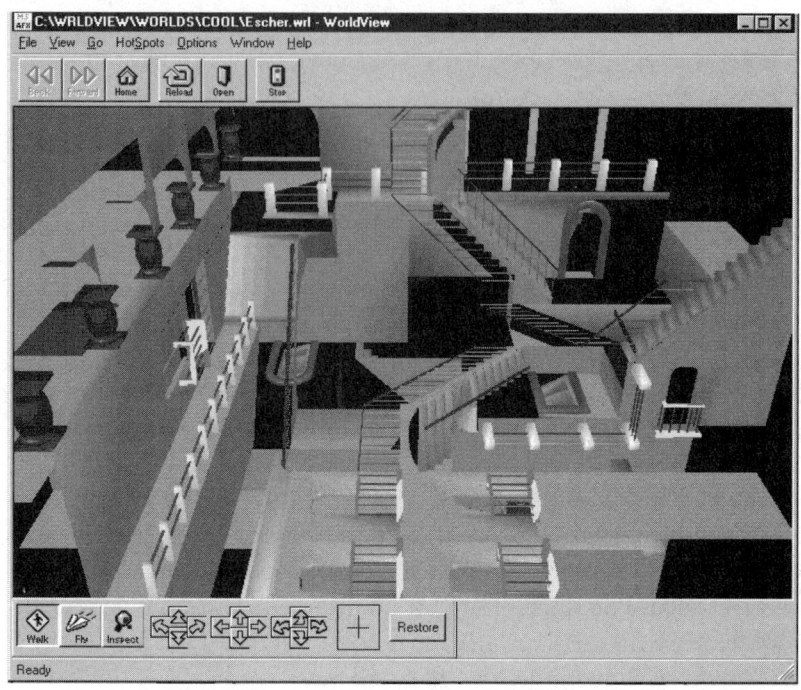

Table 4-2 WorldView navigation

Arrow	Walk or Fly Mode	Inspect Mode
Move		
Up	Move closer	Moves object away
Down	Move away	Moves object closer
Left	Move left	Tilts top of object to the right
Right	Move right	Tilts top of object to the left
Pitch and Roll		
Up	Tilt view up	Tilts top of object toward you
Down	Tilt view down	Tilts top of object away from you
Left	Tilt view right	Tilts top of object to the left
Right	Tilt view left	Tilts top of object to the right
Panning		
Up	Slides up	Moves object up
Down	Slides down	Moves object down
Left	Slides left	Moves object to the left
Right	Slides right	Moves object to the right

Figure 4-6
Tilting, shifting, and walking around an object using inspect mode

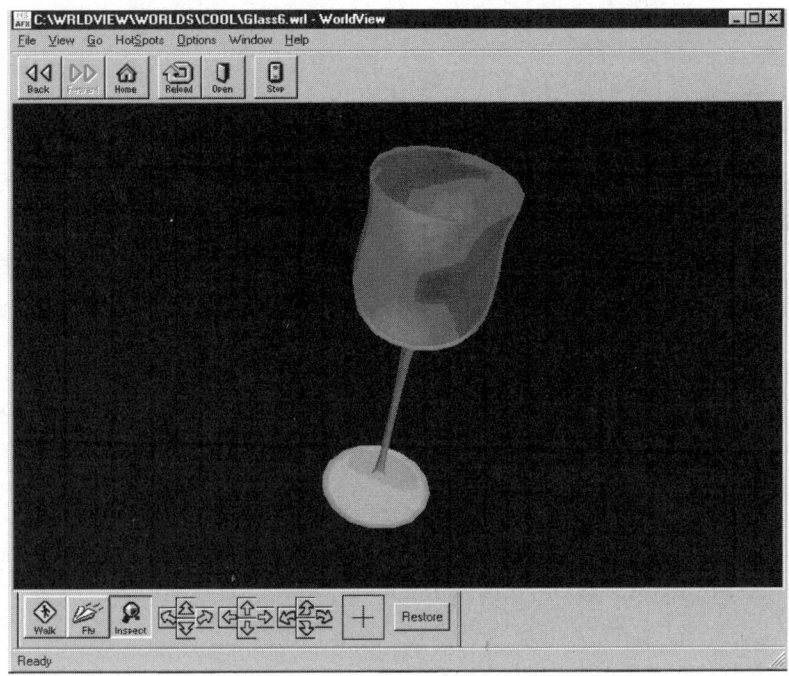

NOTE: Hold down [ALT] or [CTRL] to make many movements faster. This way, instead of just stepping at 10 meters per second (mps), you can step at 20 or 30 mps.

Alternatively, the cross hair to the right of the arrows can be used to navigate. If you click above the cross hair, you'll move forward; click below, and you'll slide backward. Clicking left of the cross hair will rotate you left; clicking right of it will, as you can very well imagine, rotate you right. If you hold down [CTRL] while using the cross hair, you'll perform pitch and roll navigation. Hold down [SHIFT] while clicking on the cross hair to pan across the scene.

Other World Views

In addition, WorldView has a HotSpots menu that lets you add a hotspot (a favorite VRML site) to a list. You can then jump to any of your hotspots with the click of a few menu items.

The View menu lets you choose from several levels of rendering detail: Wireframe, Flat Shading, Gouraud Shading, or the beautiful but time-consuming Phong Shading.

Click the Restore button in the navigation panel to move to the original camera position. You can also set the Restore position anytime you come across an angle you think you'd like to see again by selecting View, Save Viewpoint.

CAUGHT IN VRWEB

VRweb was developed by IICM (Hyper-G team), NCSA (the folks who brought us the original Mosaic), and the Gopher team. It was one of the first browsers to accurately support the Level Of Detail node feature, which changes the look of an object depending on how close you are to it. VRweb is at once very simple and very complex: It has a variety of cool navigation modes, but it doesn't support simple VRML nodes such as WWWAnchor (which makes some objects hyperlinks).

One big plus, however, is that the source code for VRweb (Windows or UNIX versions) is publicly available. This makes it much easier to write your own VRML browser or to understand how browsers work.

VRweb is available for the following computer platforms:

- Windows NT, 3.1, or Win95

- SGI IRIX

- SUN Solaris or SUN OS

- DEC Alpha or DEC ULTRIX

- HP-UX

- IBM AIX

- LINUX

The VRweb team is also working on a Macintosh version.

The Windows versions of VRweb require 32-bit functions. This means you must either be using Windows NT, Windows 95, or Windows 3.1 with Win32s installed. Your machine should also be a 486 with at least 8 MB of memory.

NOTE: You can get a copy of Win32s at *http://www.webmaster. com/vrml/wvwin.*

Getting and Installing It

You can grab VRweb from the Web site

http://www.iicm.tu-graz.ac.at/Cvrweb

Create a VRweb directory. Unzip the version of VRweb you've downloaded into that directory. You may need to go to the DOS prompt and type

`unzip vrw_win`

Replace *vrw_win* with the name of the file you just downloaded. You can now run the VRW_WIN.EXE program.

Seeing a Scene

VRweb does not have any network capabilities. You cannot download a VRML file directly from the Internet; rather, you must save the WRL file to your hard disk and then load it. This does not make viewing faster, though local files will always load much faster than ones in the Internet.

To open a file, click the open folder icon in the toolbar or select File, Open.

Navigating

VRweb has a rich and intuitive navigation interface. Using just the mouse, you can perform most any navigation function you'd ever need. There are five modes:

- **Flip**—This mode is similar to holding an object in your hands; you can easily move it toward you, away from you, to the right or left, or flip it around. Hold down the left mouse button to drag the object. The object will follow your mouse. Hold down the right button to zoom. Push up to move the object farther away, pull the mouse toward you to bring the object closer. Hold down the middle button (or both mouse buttons) to rotate the object. If you move the mouse to the right, the object will spin to the right as shown in Figure 4-7.

- **Walk**—This mode lets you stroll through a scene. Hold down the left mouse button to walk. Push the mouse away from you to walk farther into a scene. Hold down the right mouse button to turn your head. Simply push the mouse right to turn your head that way. Hold down both buttons if you want to shuffle to the left, right, up, or down. For instance, if you move the mouse to the right, the object will slide to the left (see Figure 4-8).

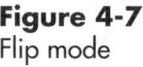 Fly—This mode lets you zip through a scene with much more freedom of movement. You can continuously fly without having to press a button. Up your speed by pressing ⊞, reduce it by pressing ⊟, as in Figure 4-9. The meter to the right of the screen will show you how fast you're going. To start flying, click the left mouse button. Click the button again to stop. While flying, move the mouse in the direction you want to head.

Fly To—Point to a part of a scene, click, and take an express flight directly there. Move the mouse up to move closer to where you've clicked. Move the mouse down to move farther away from that point.

Heads Up—This lets you use all the navigation modes at once. Four icons appear on your screen, each corresponding to one of the modes (as in Figure 4-10). Move your mouse over one of the icons and hold the left button. You can now move the mouse in any direction you wish, either flipping, walking, flying, or flying to.

NOTE: You can speed up navigation by selecting Rendering Interactive, Wireframe. This turns the model into a wireframe every time you move.

Figure 4-7
Flip mode

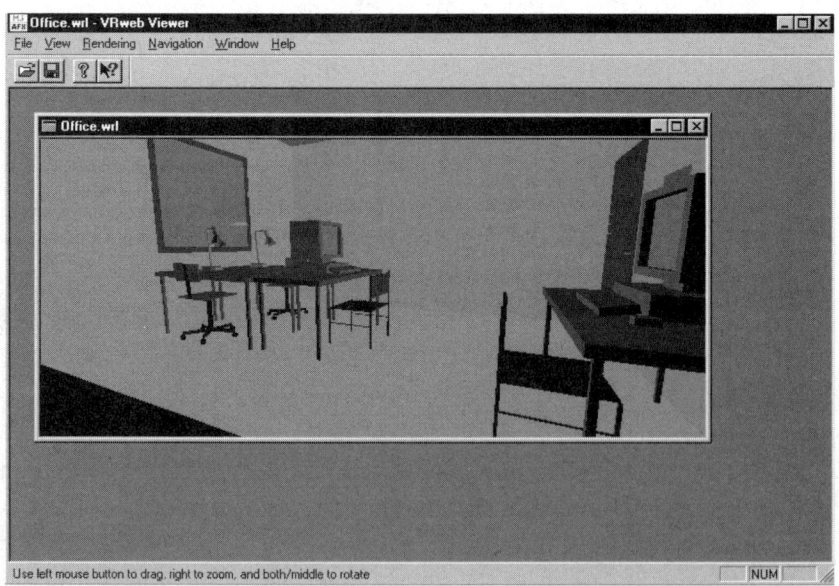

Figure 4-8
Walk mode

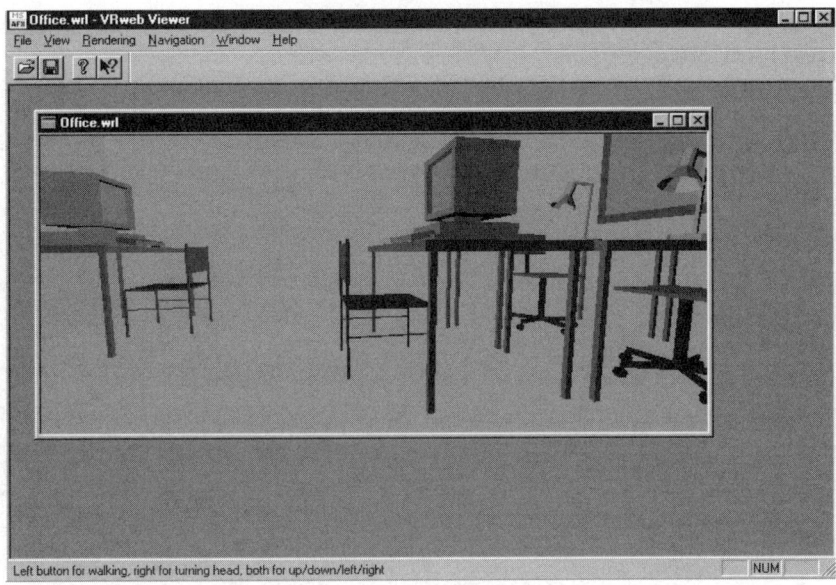

Figure 4-9
Flying

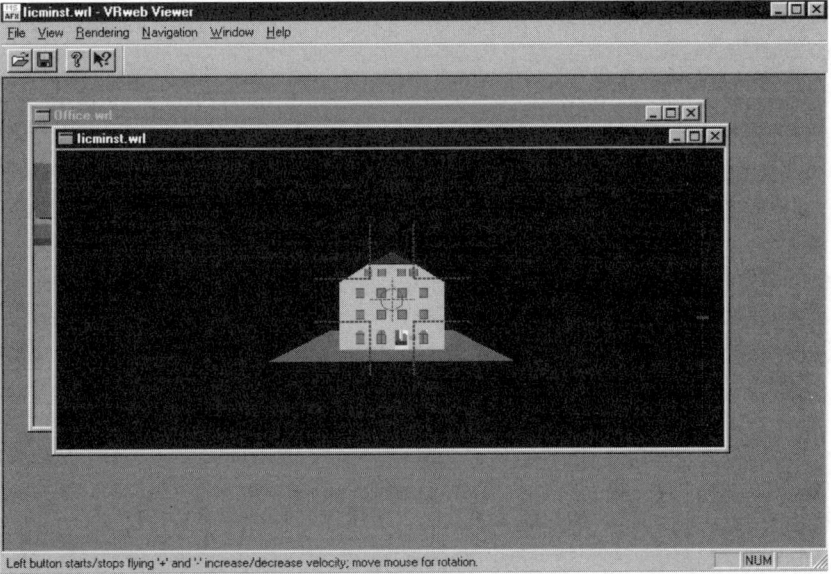

Figure 4-10
Heads up,
dude!

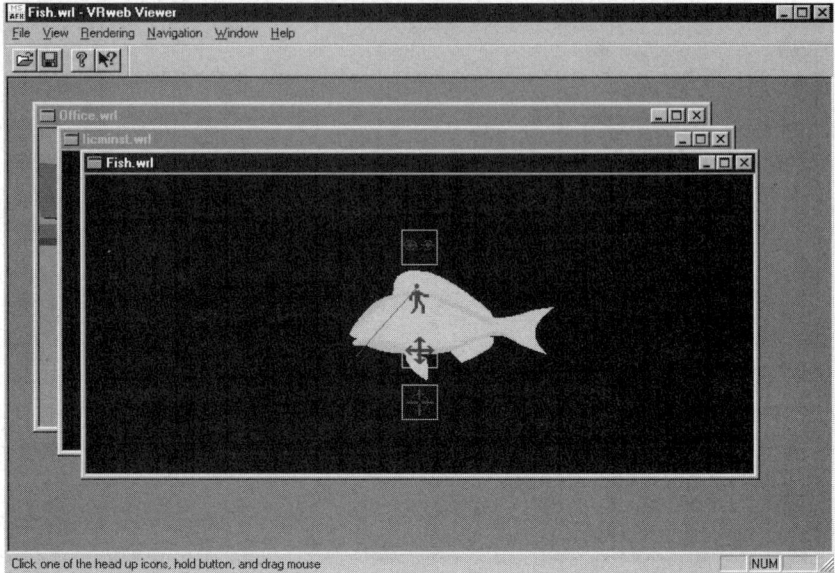

MOVING ON...

Now that you've found your ideal VRML browser, you can flip back to Chapter 2 to see some of the worlds for yourself. More importantly, though, you can use your browser as a base for developing your own 3D worlds.

The rest of this book covers modeling, converting graphics, programming, and serving VRML. As with the real world, seeing what's around you is only the beginning. The next stage is to start creating—adding your unique contribution to society for everyone else to enjoy and use.

PART II
LEARNING 3D MODELING

5

CREATING WORLDS WITH 3D SOFTWARE

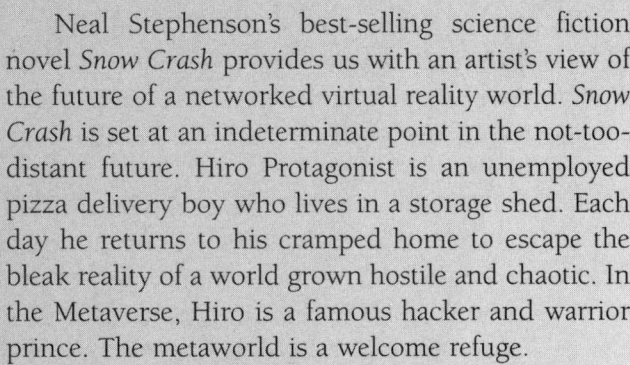

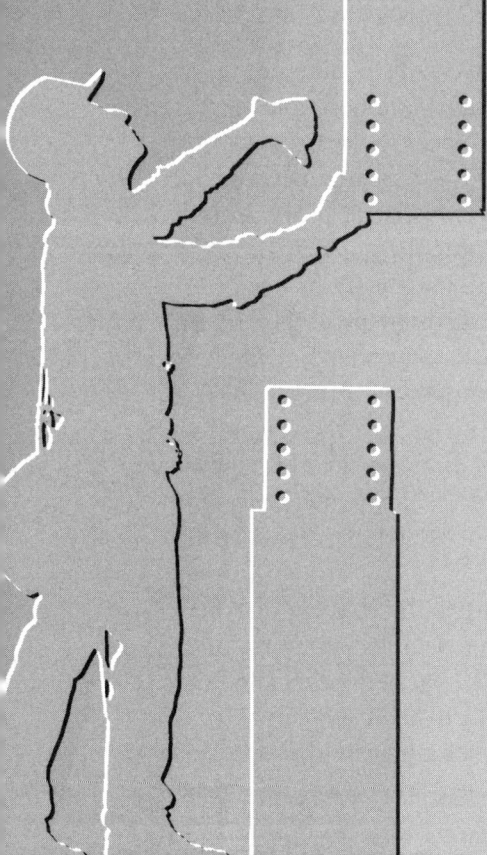

Neal Stephenson's best-selling science fiction novel *Snow Crash* provides us with an artist's view of the future of a networked virtual reality world. *Snow Crash* is set at an indeterminate point in the not-too-distant future. Hiro Protagonist is an unemployed pizza delivery boy who lives in a storage shed. Each day he returns to his cramped home to escape the bleak reality of a world grown hostile and chaotic. In the Metaverse, Hiro is a famous hacker and warrior prince. The metaworld is a welcome refuge.

To those who return to their homes and log onto the Internet to explore its MUDs (Multiple-User Dungeons) and MOOs (MUDs Object-Oriented), the Metaverse bears a striking resemblance to these multiparticipant experiences. In a MUD or MOO the player assumes an identity and does battle online with other human players in a common imaginary world. There are friends and foes. There are creatures and castles. There are rules and levels of privilege that deny or give access to strange worlds. Just like the Metaverse.

Stephenson's description of Hiro and the Metaverse demonstrates a current irony. Science fiction writers need not stray too far into the future to find their themes. Science fiction has begun to hold up a mirror to current, rather than future, reality. Maybe it's even helped shape the present.

In fact, the big difference between the Metaverse and a MUD or MOO is in the interface. While MUDs and MOOs are played at the keyboard, the Metaverse is entered through VR goggles that create the sensory illusion that you are there, not here. In the lingo of virtual reality, worlds that create the impression that you are actually inside another world are called immersive.

IMMERSIVE VR VERSUS DESKTOP VR

Playing back a virtual reality world on the monitor of a computer is called *desktop VR*. Immersive VR depends on a variety of computer peripherals for the illusion of immersion. For example, each of your eyes sees a slightly different view of the world, and these two views are then reconciled by your brain.

The sense of seeing into a world, rather than seeing it played back on the flat surface of the monitor, depends on these two slightly different views of the world. The most common way of presenting the stereoscopic view is through an HMD (head-mounted display), which places the images directly in front of your eyes and blocks out the real world. A steering mechanism, such as a joystick, a dataglove, or a 3D mouse, is required to move around the virtual world. Spatialized, or 3D sound, is required to create the sense that things are happening behind and around you. Some systems even provide a tactile feedback system that allows you to distinguish between hard and soft surfaces, or rough and smooth surfaces. Finally, some arcade systems use platforms that pitch, roll, or move in tandem with the view. The computer processing required to generate stereo images on the fly, and to enhance the experience through the other peripherals, is far beyond the processing power of today's desktop computer technology. Truly immersive virtual reality, such as that described by Stephenson, is at least several CPU generations away.

Stephenson is the latest to give imaginative play to the concept of cyberspace, an idea that dates back to William Gibson's *Neuromancer*, first published in 1984. Gibson's dark foreshadowing to a global network, called the matrix, inspired such pioneers as Jaron Lanier and his VPL Research company to create the technology for virtual worlds, including the tracking and display mechanisms that enhance the feeling of being immersed in a virtual world.

At the same time that Lanier laid down the first primitive attempts at creating virtual worlds in the late '80s, Tim Berners-Lee at CERN (Center for European Particle Physics) developed a hypertext system for the Internet called the World Wide Web. Lee invented his hypertext system when the information on the Internet was particularly difficult to access. You had to know where the information was and then enter a complex set of commands to navigate and retrieve the data. The invention of a hypertext system created links between related data sources, making information easier to access. These links added a layer of abstraction to the Internet. This allowed it to interconnect vast bodies of knowledge.

This eventually led to the desire to unite the trends in virtual reality technology and the hypertext system (Hypertext Markup Language, or HTML) of the World Wide Web. Virtual Reality Modeling Language (VRML) (originally called Markup Language) was conceived in 1994 at the first annual World Wide Web Conference in Geneva, Switzerland.

The opening paragraph of the draft specification for VRML makes it clear that at the heart of the authors' vision is a standard for shared, interactive, multisensory virtual worlds: "All aspects of virtual world display, interaction, and internetworking can be specified using VRML. It is the intention of its designers that VRML become the standard language for interactive simulation within the World Wide Web." (*Gavin Bell, Anthony Parisi, Mark Pesce*: VRML 1.0 Draft Specification) VRML, however, is a small step, rather than a giant leap, in this direction. The authors do not state it explicitly, but it is clear that the success of the specification does not depend on the success of immersive technology. The standard does not explicitly support such peripherals as HMDs, datagloves, and 3D tracking systems.

3D Interface

The VRML specification allows for an entirely different interface: human-centered. In the *VRML 1.0 Draft Specification*, authors Gavin Bell, Anthony Parisi, and Mark Pesce wrote "[WWW] can only tell you how to get to the VRML Forum home page by saying, "http//www.wired.com/", which is not human-centered data. In fact, I need to make an effort to remember it at all. So, while the World Wide Web provides a retrieval mechanism to complement the existing storage mechanism, it leaves a lot to be desired, particularly for human beings."

The VRML specification is positioned to become the three-dimensional front end for information systems on the Internet. It intends to present data in a form human beings can more quickly grasp and more easily understand. Right now, the Internet is structured for a generation of users taught to acquire information using the skills they learned in school: the three Rs (reading, 'riting, and 'rithmetic). The new generation of users will absorb information through the three Ls (looking, listening, and learning). In the words of the authors, "VRML is an attempt (how successful, only time and effort will tell) to place humans at the center of the Internet, ordering its universe to our whims."

In the short term, this means that specialized browsers will allow people to enter 3D environments and find information by looking for it as they would look for information on their desk, in their office, or in their town. VR can be seen as the ultimate evolution of a trend in computing to render information systems in human terms, a project that began at Xerox Parc, and was implemented on desktop computers when Apple adopted the desktop metaphor as an interface to the Macintosh.

THE DATA RATE OF THE INTERNET

The most important aspect of the VRML specification is that it allows 3D worlds to be created that can be accessed, entered, and shared among users on the Internet. The fact that it is positioned to work within the limitations of the Internet is both its strength and weakness. Its strength is that it makes the technology accessible to millions of users. Its weakness is that most of those users enter the Internet through the standard telephone system.

How fast a communications system can move data is called its *bandwidth* or *data rate*. Today's computers transfer data between mass storage (the hard drive) to the display system extraordinarily fast when compared to the transfer rate between a computer and a remote host on the standard telephone system.

The telephone system is analog, so the digital data on the computer must be converted to analog signals and converted back to digital data at the other end, by use of a modem. A modem modulates (converts digital data to analog) and demodulates (converts it back). The basic unit of information is 1 bit. The number of bits of information transferred each second is the *baud rate*. Most people have 14.4K, or 28.8K baud modems attached to their computers. This means that a 14.4K baud connection is capable of transferring 14,400 bits per second, or 1,800 bytes.

Moving pictures, such as digital video or animation made up of discrete images (frames) played back fast enough to create the illusion of motion, exacerbate the problem. For example, television has a rate of 30 frames a second. To download this onto your computer, uncompressed, the data load would have to be 30 MB per second!

USING COMPRESSION TO REDUCE THE DATA RATE

One of the methods that has been devised to overcome this problem is to send a compressed version of the image over the telephone system. Some modems do this automatically, but the most effective compression schemes are those that compress the image before transmission, and then decompress the image for display on the user's system.

Images are divided into tiny blocks of color, called *pixels,* and the color of each pixel is stored. A data compression scheme removes much of the data in the image by looking for redundancies, and replacing them with a more compact description. For example, areas of the image may have pixels of the same color. Rather than storing the color of each pixel as:

`White pixel * White pixel * White pixel * White pixel`

the four pixels are stored with a more compact description

`Four white pixels.`

A compression algorithm analyzes the image to look for these redundancies and stores the image in the compact form. The image can then be transmitted over the communications channel in the compact form and decoded upon display (see Figure 5-1).

Some compression algorithms also remove differences in the image that cannot be detected by the naked eye. For example, the eye is less sensitive to the dark areas of an image. Color differences that cannot be detected are averaged to a single color and compressed.

There are two forms of compression: intraframe and interframe. *Intraframe* compression looks for redundancies within a single image, and *interframe* compression looks for redundancies in a stream of images. JPEG (Joint Photographic

Figure 5-1
Compressing,
transmitting,
and displaying
an image

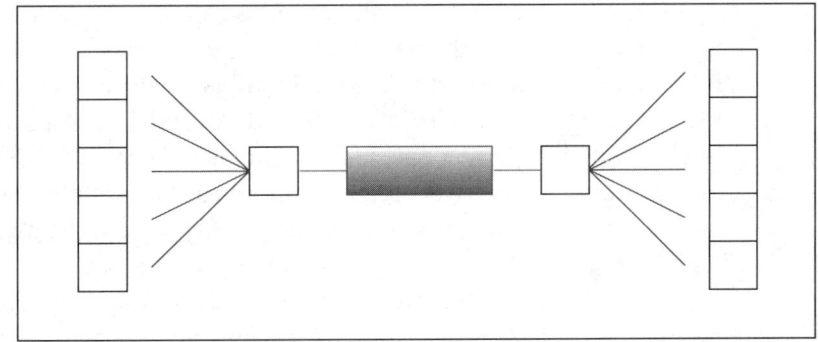

Experts Group) is a common compression format for single images. Cinepak and MPEG (Motion Picture Experts Group) are the most common standards for compressing animation and digital video. Compression standards like MPEG depend on a high degree of redundancy between one image and the next. For example, a static camera view of a bird flying from one side of the view to the other compresses very well, because the background changes little from one image to the next. But if the camera follows the bird against a rapidly changing background, the compression rate deteriorates rapidly.

Compression and the Telephone System

Because animation and digital video have a frame rate of at least 15 frames a second, they consume a lot of storage and increase the data load of communication networks. The Internet response time has slowed considerably since Web pages added graphics, digital video, and sound to them.

It will be a long time before the Internet acquires the bandwidth of a desktop PC or broadcast television. Alternatives, such as digital rather than analog telecommunications (for example, ISDN fiber optics connections), cable, or satellite transmission, are still beyond the pocketbook of most Internet users.

VRML and Telephone Bandwidth

Although VRML worlds accessed through the Internet face the same bandwidth limitations as the transmission of two-dimensional graphics, VRML uses the telecommunications link much more efficiently.

Instead of transmitting entire images, or compressed images, the instructions for building 3D objects are transmitted. (Small images called *texture maps,* which cover areas of objects, may also be transmitted.) The VRML browser residing on the user's system reads these instructions and uses the computer's internal resources to draw them on the screen.

The following analogy will help illustrate the difference between transmitting uncompressed images, compressed images, and VRML formatted files: Your friend's birthday is coming up, and you want to send her a cake. Mailing a whole cake, baked and iced, would be expensive to ship and might take a long time because of the cake's bulk, much like transmitting an uncompressed image over a telecommunications system. Now, if you were to send only the cake mix, this would greatly reduce the shipping time and cost, just as sending a compressed image would be less computationally expensive. However, this would require your friend to do some work in baking the cake, or decompressing the image. Now, imagine shipping only the recipe for the cake. Though your friend must do all of the work and will probably need a good kitchen to do it in, the recipe can be mailed for the price of a stamp. The VRML file format is like the cake recipe. The file, or a list of instructions, is quick and easy to send, but it requires a VRML browser, using the computer's resources, to do most of the work.

Figure 5-2 shows a simple representation of a cake in a 3D modeling program that has been saved as a GIF (CompuServe's graphic interchange format) compressed image.

The size of the uncompressed, full-color image is about 82K. In JPEG compressed format it is 7K.

The JPEG file stores the colors of the pixels that make up the cake shape. A VRML file stores the instructions for building the cake shape on the screen. It describes the geometry of the cake shape, its color, the light sources illuminating it, and its position in 3D space. In other words, rather than storing the colors that make up the image, it stores the three-dimensional data used to create the shape. It stores it as a standard ASCII file:

```
#VRML V1.0 ascii
Separator {
    DEF SceneInfo Info {
        string "Converted by wcvt2pov v2.6c"
    }
    PerspectiveCamera {
        position 0.000000 0.000000 -1.141893
        orientation 0 1 0 3.14
        focalDistance 5
        heightAngle 0.785398
    }
PointLight {
    on   TRUE
    intensity        1.0
    color   1.0 1.0 1.0
    location 0.000000 0.285473 1.141893

}
DEF CYLINDER_Black Separator {
```

continued on next page

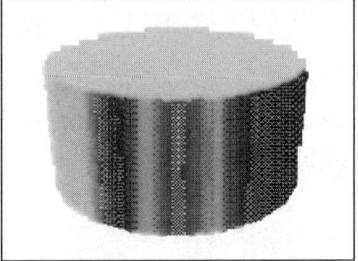

Figure 5-2
Simple cylinder
in cake shape

continued from previous page

```
Material {
    diffuseColor 0.300000 0.300000 0.300000
    ambientColor 0.030000 0.030000 0.030000
}
Coordinate3 {
    point [
            -0.158620 -0.027583 -0.547776,
            0.000000 -0.040143 -0.569531,
            0.158620 -0.027583 -0.547776,
            -0.301710 0.008872 -0.484634,
            0.301710 0.008872 -0.484634,
            -0.415270 0.065652 -0.386288,
            0.415270 0.065652 -0.386288,
            -0.488180 0.137197 -0.262369,
            0.488180 0.137197 -0.262369,
            -0.513300 0.216507 -0.125000,
            0.513300 0.216507 -0.125000,
```

The listing has been abbreviated to conserve space in the book, but the file (CAKE.WRL) is about 7K uncompressed and 1K compressed.

The file will generate an image that looks like Figure 5-2. But that's not all. The 3D VRML cake object can be interactively moved and rotated. You would not be able to do this with a JPEG file. If you wanted to see the other side of the cake, the new view would have to be downloaded as a separate image, consuming another precious 7K of storage and bandwidth.

The VRML object would not require any additional information from the source to generate a view of the other side. To see the other side of the cake, you move the mouse, spinning the cylinder on its axis. You are not restricted to a single angle of view or rotation.

Creating a cake from scratch has its advantages and disadvantages. Simple cakes place a lot less burden on the skills and time of the cook (read "computer"!) than complex cakes. The more complex the cake, the more time demands it makes on its cook. The same is true with a VRML recipe. Drawing a simple object on the screen, like the cake in Figure 5-2, and coloring it is fairly simple. Drawing a complex object such as a castle on the screen is much more complex. The more complex the scene, the greater the demand on the resources of the end-user's computer, the slower the scene will load and render.

Given that the most common computer connected to the Internet is an Intel 486, the first VRML worlds look more like Legoland than virtual reality. Desktop computers are several generations or more away from acquiring the horsepower to build more detailed worlds, and telecommunications technology is in a similar state of affairs.

VR'S SISTER ACTS

Virtual reality has risked the same fate as earlier technologies that promised too much and delivered too little. Look at how many wrecks lie at the side of the road leading to the future—pen computing, voice recognition, and to some extent artificial intelligence, to name a few.

What has saved virtual reality from drying up is the success of its sister technology: 3D modeling and simulation. Desktop VR uses the same underlying technology as workstation 3D animation programs such as Microsoft Softimage, Autodesk 3D Studio Max, Wavefront Technologies Explore, and Alias Animator.

These programs not only create scenes that look like photographs of real objects, but they also model physical properties of the world such as gravity, and physical forces such as wind currents. So-called particle systems create animated fires, falling snow, smoke, bubbling lava, and fireworks. These tools for modeling the physical properties of the world are showing up in PC-based 3D programs. The professional edition of Impulse Imagine (the "lite" version is bundled with this book) includes particle systems, a simple form of gravity, and advanced animation features, like states. The cost of entering the Metaverse is rapidly dropping to the point when the pizza delivery boy can afford to "jack" into it. Or build it.

The technology for adding interactivity to VRML worlds through programming also exists. The VRML spec is based on the object-oriented paradigm. Object-oriented programming makes it possible to create event-driven worlds that model the processes of nature, such as the variable growth rate of trees under changing climatic conditions. Although the VRML specification awaits further definition as an object-oriented programming language, such tools as MFactory MTropolis, an authoring tool dedicated to multimedia, show the way.

In MTropolis, a multimedia object is invested with "behaviors," and is able to interact with other objects through messaging and object-collision detection. For example, a bird animation attached to a MTropolis multimedia object uses object detection to avoid flying into walls and other obstructions. It flocks with other birds. It sings when the sun rises and roosts when the sun goes down. It hunts for worms and insects. And it is always on the lookout for cats.

To some degree there is an overlap between the efforts of 3D animation programmers who model natural processes in algorithms, and authoring tool programmers who use algorithms to model the interactions among multimedia objects. An example is collision detection, in which one object looks for the presence of another within its space. However, the great divide between 3D animation programs and object-oriented authoring tools is in their end result: Animation programs create movies of virtual worlds that play on the monitor. The spectator is passive. Object-oriented authoring tools create objects that interact through messaging.

The VRML specification unites these two threads by creating a world of objects that maintain dynamic relationships. The VRML specification treats each object in the 3D world as a unique entity that can be hyperlinked to other objects or users. The interactions of objects is implicit in the way objects are described by the specification. For example, child objects can inherit their color from parent objects. How these objects interact under the current specification will be treated later in this book. For now, let's discuss how 3D objects are defined.

3D MODELING

The launch of the space capsule in the movie *Apollo 13* was unremarkable except for one thing. It was entirely modeled in 3D. Few in the audience realized this. Apparently the existing footage of the historic launch was so grainy and lacking in detail that the movie's producers decided to re-create it by simulating it on the computer.

While the launch sequence required millions of dollars in resources to model and render, today's desktop computers have acquired the power to create convincingly realistic models of real and imaginary objects. Figure 5-3 shows a model of a Dimetrodon, a 300 million-year-old reptile modeled in Autodesk's 3D Studio.

Figure 5-3
Geometry for
the Dimetrodon

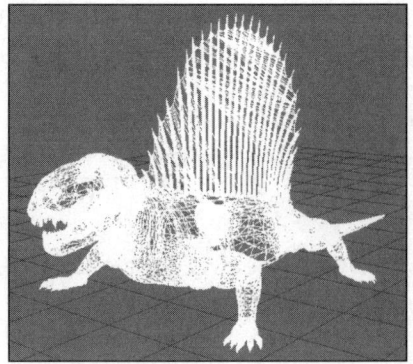

The term "modeling" can be confusing, because people normally think of a model as being something tangible. In fact, the Dimetrodon had a brief existence as a clay model before it was modeled in the computer. The clay model provided the artists at HeadSpin Studios in Columbus, Ohio with a reference for the computer simulation. The computer model is really stored geometrical 3D data represented on the screen with lines and points.

The lines and points are organized into 3- or 4-sided geometric shapes called polygons. These polygons allow the modeler to represent the shape and volume of the Dimetrodon in three dimensions. The Dimetrodon has 36,000 polygons, which makes it a complex model.

The polygons serve another purpose as well. The areas they enclose (the faces) can be colored and textured to give the surface of the Dimetrodon realistic-looking skin. Figure 5-4 shows the Dimetrodon covered with a reptilian texture.

3D models and virtual reality objects are practically identical in terms of the way they are constructed. That is, the most common way of modeling the dimension of 3D objects is by creating surfaces of interconnected polygons.

It is this surface of polygons, and the textures assigned to the polygons, that the VRML specification defines. The CAKE.WRL file shown earlier lists all the points and faces that make up the cake shape. Figure 5-5 shows the polygonal mesh for the cylinder.

Notice the four-sided polygons that ring the cylinder's shape. The VRML file lists this geometry and uses this list to build the object on the screen.

Both 3D animation programs and VR software store their worlds as three-dimensional data. The program loads the data into memory, processes it, and projects a view of the world on the screen. This process is called

Figure 5-4
Dimetrodon
rendered with
a surface

Figure 5-5
The polygonal
mesh for the
cylinder

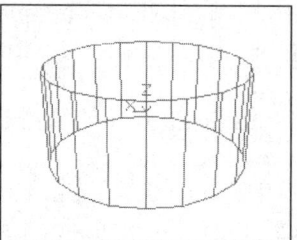

rendering. It's the same word used by architects or artists to describe drawings of three-dimensional objects or designs. 3D animators also use the word "rendering" to describe saving the current view of the world, or an animated view of the world, to a 2D graphics file or animation file.

Real-Time Rendering

Real-time 3D rendering refers to the ability of a computer's hardware and software to project a 2D view of the 3D world on the screen as quickly as the view changes. In the case of 3D animation software, real-time rendering gives the 3D artist instant feedback on changes to the model. In the case of VR worlds, real-time rendering allows the user to interactively navigate through the three-dimensional space of the world.

3D modeling programs use the metaphor of a camera to render views in the world. The virtual camera has an adjustable lens. The camera and its lens can be positioned and the scene animated, or the camera itself can be animated.

The advantage of prerendering animations is that the changing camera views can be played back comparatively quickly. A single frame in a high-resolution 3D animation can take hours to model on the computer. Using compression, the animator can reduce the time it takes to play back a rendered frame to a fraction of a second.

The disadvantage of this approach is that the camera's view must be prerendered. Ultimately, the movement of the viewer through the world is limited to predetermined paths. It's like a garden with a lot of fences and signs that say, "Keep Off the Grass."

An example is the virtual world in the game Destiny at the Royal Tyrrell Museum in Drumheller, Alberta, created by Rage Pictures. Using fossil records and a considerable body of scientific research, the animators at Rage Pictures modeled the animals and plant life in the geological period known as the Permian, 300 million years ago. It can be seen through the view window in the interface (see Figure 5-6). The player uses the paw prints at the bottom of the screen to navigate through the world, avoiding predators and searching for food.

The player is in the persona of an Eocaptorhinus, a small creature whose body is shown in profile at the top of the interface. The player's challenge is to find his or her way through the valley, avoiding predators, finding food, mating, and making it back to the nesting site within a one-year time frame. Because the world is too detailed to be built in 3D on the fly, the player's traveling view of the world had to be prerendered and then played back in the view window. Rendering saves each view in the world, or frame of an animation, as a 2D image.

Game producers are very clever at creating the illusion that the world can be freely explored. For example, in the game Myst the player always follows paths. These paths are interconnected seamlessly. When an area is explored, the player must stay on the path. However, this is not a virtual world like the Metaverse described by Stephenson. You cannot look up or down, or stray from the path. You are not free to look around at every step. Nor can you cock your head to the side and see the world at an angle, unless the designer has made this option explicitly available. In other words, the world lacks the six degrees of freedom (6DOF) that are so much a part of

Figure 5-6
Rage Pictures'
Destiny game
accurately
models the
Permian world

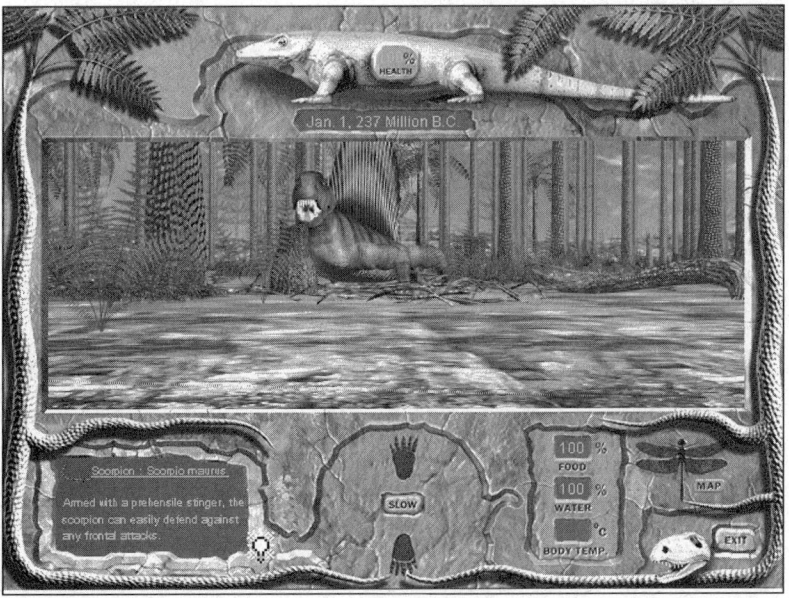

our experience of the natural world. (The six degrees of freedom are up, down, right, left, pitch, and yaw.)

2D Worlds

Although compression hardware is getting cheaper and more powerful, and CPUs are acquiring the power to encode and decode compression algorithms, playing back prerendered worlds is not the future of simulation. By definition, virtual reality worlds must be made up of 3D objects with which the viewer can randomly interact.

Certainly one of the world's most popular PC games, ID's Doom, demonstrates the extraordinary drawing power of worlds that give players greater freedom of movement. Doom does not use prerendered animations. Instead, small 2D images called *textures* are mapped onto planes. *Mapping* projects an image on a plane just as a slide projector projects an image on a wall (see Figure 5-7).

For example, instead of building a 3D wall of bricks, a picture of a brick pattern is projected on the plane, creating the illusion that the wall is composed of bricks.

Doom's world is not a true 3D world. To reduce the amount of calculations required to render the world in real time, the view (and therefore the player's movement) is restricted to a single level. You can look to the right or left, but you cannot look up or down, or look at the Doom world at an oblique angle. You can move forward or backward. But you cannot fly at an angle to the world. Imagine wandering around a bungalow with a movie camera at all times parallel to the floor. If Doom allowed six degrees of freedom within the world, the camera would be able to adopt any point of view

Figure 5-7
Projecting an
image on a
plane

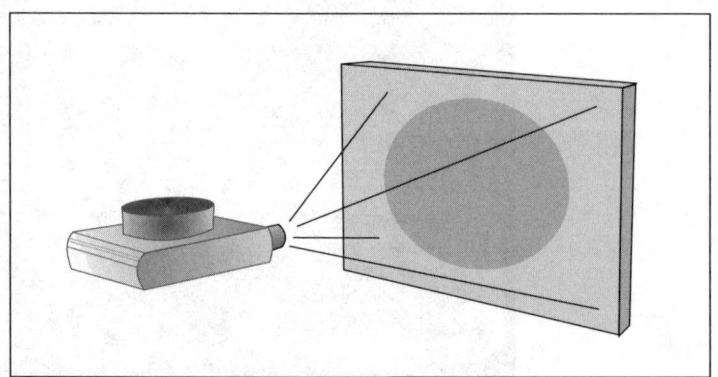

within it. Instead, the camera can only see the world along one axis (see Figure 5-8).

Doom is often referred to as a 2D world because it only allows movement along one axis of the three possible axes (up, down, and across—or x, y, and z). However, it established the appeal of worlds that provide more freedom of movement than allowed by prerendered worlds. But even at the height of Doom's success, other game companies were developing the software and hardware for creating true 3D worlds.

REAL-TIME 3D HARDWARE

The authors of the VRML specification envision a true 3D world that can be explored without restriction of movement. But the VRML spec does not specify how the world is rendered; it only specifies the objects and their links within it. Rendering is left to the VRML browser. The browser reads the list of objects and then creates them on the fly. There's the rub: How fast can the browser build the objects that make up the world?

3D animation artists wait minutes or even hours for a single frame of an animation to render. Right now the CPU is just not powerful enough to handle the millions of calculations required to create the world at 15 frames a second, the minimum acceptable frame rate of animation.

While it is conceivable that common CPUs (Intel or Motorola) will eventually have the horsepower to build detailed real-time virtual reality worlds, most people agree that it won't happen for five to ten years. Meanwhile, a number of companies have developed specialized hardware for speeding up 3D calculations.

3D acceleration chips are specialized to the task of creating 3D objects. They off-load the task of calculating 3D geometry from the CPU. Specialized

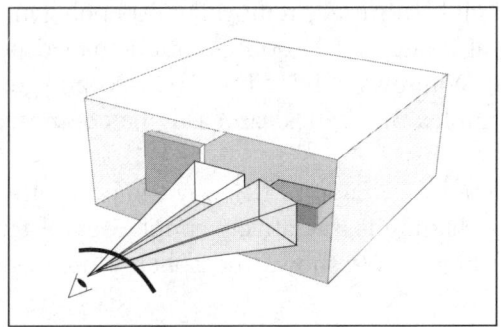

Figure 5-8
Camera and world in Doom-style world

boards have been available on high-end workstations for some time, but they are too expensive for the average user. The burgeoning interest in 3D games and 3D software has created a market for mass-produced 3D acceleration chips, driving the cost down.

A number of mass-market graphic-card makers have begun to include 3D acceleration chips on their video card, including Creative Technology, Diamond Multimedia Systems, Matrox Graphics, and STB systems. Chip makers who supply these 3D chips include 3Dlabs, Yamaha, Rendition, and Cirrus Logic.

Another development has been the support for 3D software and hardware in the dominant operating systems (Intel or Motorola). Microsoft is contributing to the rapid evolution of 3D by including support for 3D in Windows 95 and Windows NT.

Besides Microsoft, a number of software companies have developed APIs (Application Programming Interfaces) that provide specialized 3D rendering routines. These APIs look for support in the hardware for rendering. If they do not find it, they draw from their own library of routines to draw the object on the screen.

The five currently dominant APIs are as follows: Argonaut Software's BRender, Microsoft's Reality Lab, Criterion Software's RenderWare, Intel's 3DRender (3DR), and SGI's OpenGL. Microsoft provides direct support for Reality Lab and OpenGL in Windows 95.

The performance of the different APIs and chips varies widely. The most robust API is OpenGL, an open standard developed by Silicon Graphics. However, it is closely coupled with hardware and has complex features that slow rendering. The APIs are largely incompatible, although they each support a subset of the OpenGL commands.

The speed of a 3D API is often measured in terms of how many polygons it can create per second. For example, Criterion has been quoted in *Interactivity* magazine as saying that "the API running on a 60mhz can render a light-sourced, hidden surface removed 4,000 polygon teapot displayed at 320x200 pixels at a rate of 103,000 Gouraud-shaded polygons per second running under Windows 3.1." While 103,000 polygons sounds like a lot of polygons, complex 3D scenes can easily be composed of an order of magnitude more than this.

Notice that reference is made to the way the polygon's face (surface) is rendered. Gouraud shading is a relatively simple way of rendering the surface of the object. Figure 5-9 shows the sphere's polygons colored using Gouraud shading.

Figure 5-9
Gouraud
shaded sphere

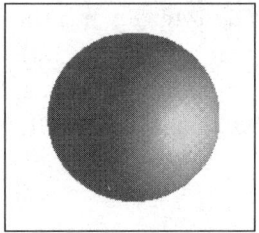

A more sophisticated type of shading, *Phong,* provides a much more realistic model. Figure 5-10 shows three spheres colored using Phong shading.

Phong shading, coupled with a type of light modeling called *ray tracing,* makes possible reflections on surfaces of objects, shadows, and detailed highlights. Although Phong shading adds realism to the scene, there is a computational cost. The additional calculations for the behavior of the light absorb CPU cycles and slow rendering.

The chapters that follow will describe polygonal modeling, shading, and lighting.

Before you plunge forward, consider this: Ivan Southerland is widely considered to be the father of virtual reality because of his early experiments with computer-generated stereoscopic viewing. On New Year's Day 1970, he put on the first HMD and viewed the first VR building block, a cube that changed perspective as he moved around. "With appropriate programming," he wrote, "such a display could literally be the Wonderland into which Alice walked."

The Wonderland has become the Internet where flame wars erupt, deadly viruses lurk, people engage in cybersex, and governments struggle to place this new world under the laws of the land. But it is still largely text-based, limiting the contact between people, and between people and ideas, to furious keyboard tapping. Desktop VR promises to raise the Internet to a new level, to a sensual reality where people look, listen, and learn in ways more naturally human-centered.

Figure 5-10
Spheres
rendered in
Phong shading

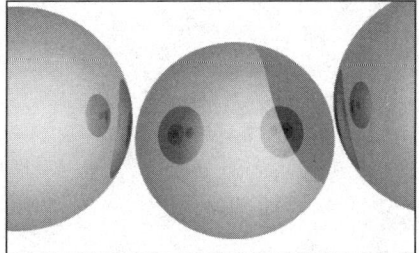

While the restricted bandwidth of the Internet and the limited power of today's CPUs push the vision of immersive VR into an indeterminate future, in the short term, VR on the desktop is growing in leaps and bounds. In the chapters that follow, you'll see how 3D worlds work and how to build them.

6

THE BASICS OF 3D MODELING

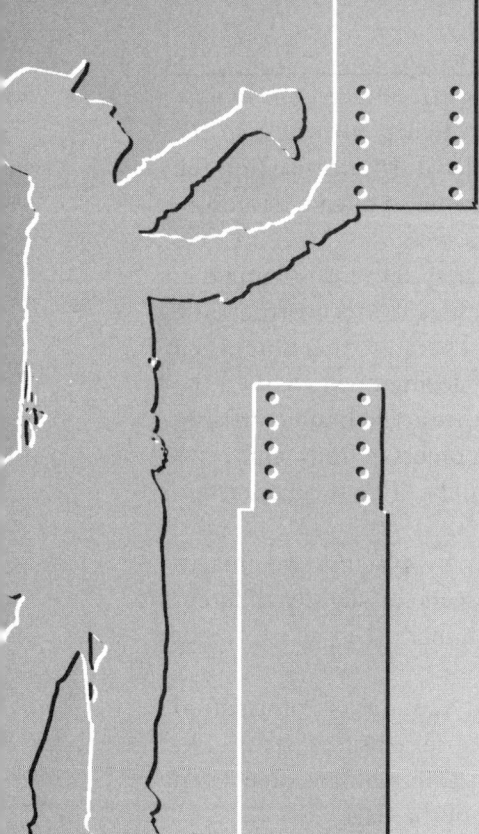

Modeling three-dimensional objects using a PC, garden-variety mouse, and standard VGA monitor is conceptually difficult. The mouse moves around on a 2D surface, and the model is displayed on the 2D surface of the monitor. There are three-dimensional mice, but few PC modeling programs support them.

The problem is that objects cannot be directly manipulated in three dimensions. The mouse supplies 2D coordinates to the program, and the program displays objects on the screen as an array of tiny dots on the screen. (The dot pitch specification lovingly reported by monitor manufacturers refers to the size of these dots, and therefore their density, on the screen.)

There's a parallel situation with the physical structure of eyes. Eyes are made up of millions of sensitive rods and cones that react to the impact of light rays arriving on their surface. When these rays strike, the rods and cones react chemically to the brightness and color of the light. This chemical reaction is encoded and sent to the brain, where these messages are interpreted. The light rays have intensity and color, but provide no other information about the scene before the eyes.

The two-dimensional image each eye sees is called its *field of view*. In Figure 6-1, the distance from the screen and the camera is the same as the size of the image, so the field of view is approximately 53°.

Figure 6-1
Field of view

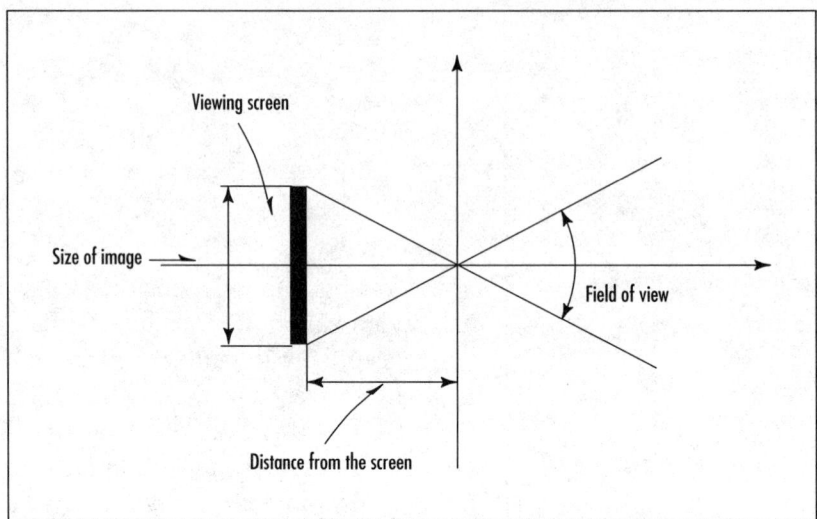

Your brain has to do a lot of detective work to figure out what's in the field of view. For example, it looks for light and color differences to find the edges of objects. Then it compares the shape to patterns already stored in memory.

The human brain does not have a built-in radar system for judging distances in space. Like a detective, it uses a lot of clues to "reconstruct" the field of view. For example, your eyes are slightly separated, therefore, each eye sees the world at slightly different angles. Try closing one eye, then the other. Notice that you see two slightly different pictures. The brain combines these views into a single view. The more distant an object is from your eyes, the larger the differences each eye's point of view will be. This is called *stereoscopic vision.*

Immersive VR reproduces stereoscopic vision by placing two images directly in front of your eyes, showing the same scene at slightly different angles. This contributes to the feeling of being immersed in space rather than observing it from a distance.

However, stereoscopic viewing is not the only source of information used by the brain to develop a mental image of three-dimensional space. For example, the Cherokee airplane in Figure 6-2 looks three-dimensional, even though it appears on the two-dimensional surface of the page.

Even though your eyes are scanning the picture as a series of dots on a two-dimensional surface, your brain "sees" the airplane as three-dimensional. This is because the image supplies clues that lead the brain to interpret the image as three-dimensional.

Figure 6-2
Cherokee
modeled in
Auto*ship* and
rendered in
Impulse
Imagine

Here are some of the clues that help the brain in its detective work:

- Objects that are near appear to be larger than distant objects.

- Objects tend to lose definition as they recede.

- The background appears darker than the foreground.

- Lines (such as train tracks) appear to converge at a vanishing point on the horizon.

- Sunlight bathes objects, revealing their shape and form by making the side facing the sun brighter, and the side facing away from the sun darker.

- Objects that obscure other objects appear to be closer.

The brain has learned to use these clues to develop a mental map of the environment. By building these clues into images (such as the Cherokee airplane), the brain can be fooled into seeing three dimensions where only two dimensions exist. This makes desktop VR possible. Desktop VR creates the illusion of three-dimensional objects on the two-dimensional surface of the screen.

If the clues to an object's dimensionality are missing, the illusion is not effective. For example, the 3D line in Figure 6-3 appears to be two-dimensional.

However, if a tube is wrapped around the line, the illusion of three dimensions is powerful (see Figure 6-4).

Figure 6-3
3D line
appears two-
dimensional

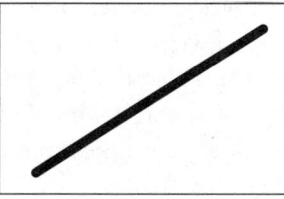

Figure 6-4
Wrapping a
tube around
a line

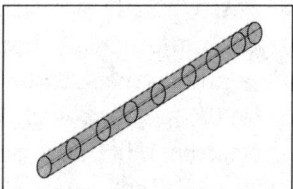

The tube's front end is much larger than its back end, and the object appears to recede into the distance, creating the illusion that it is floating in 3D space.

CREATING THE ILLUSION OF MOTION

As mentioned, when light strikes the rods and cones of the eyes, it causes a chemical reaction. Because chemical reactions take time, there is a very small lag while the rods and cones "recharge." The brain ignores this lag. If an object has moved slightly during the lag, the brain infers that the object has moved from one position in space to another.

Classical animation relies on this ability of the brain to interpret a series of discrete images of a moving object as continuous motion.

Animations are created as individual images, or frames. These frames are recorded on tape or film and are rapidly projected on the screen: 24 times a second for film animation, or 30 times a second for television animation. (Technically, each television frame has two interlaced fields. These fields are composed of alternating scan lines. When animators create for television, they create 60 images for each second of playback.) The brain's tendency to see motion in a sequence of images is so strong that only eight frames a second need be displayed for you to see an object move or rotate; however, the motion of rapidly moving objects will seem jerky.

REAL-TIME INTERACTIVE 3D

What sets VR apart from classical animation is the ability to interactively view three-dimensional renderings of objects. Rather than play back a series of frames in a predetermined manner, the viewer can reposition the point of view in 3D space, going up and around or behind objects.

Each time the user repositions the point of view in the 3D space using the mouse, the computer rebuilds the world on the screen to create the new view. For example, if the 3D world on your screen is a city block in Manhattan and you move your mouse slightly, the computer will re-create the world at the new point of view.

As with 3D animation, how smoothly the object moves from one position to another, or how smoothly the point of view changes, ultimately depends on the speed of the hardware. It takes time for the program to perform the calculations necessary to change the shape and colors of objects on the screen. The more complex the model, the longer it takes to rebuild the objects on the screen.

Complex 3D views can take minutes or hours to animate. The new desktop computer 3D acceleration software and hardware discussed in the last chapter promises to speed up animation to 30 frames a second, the minimum requirement for smooth animation. Until 3D acceleration becomes widespread among users, the VR world builder is confined to building objects with simple geometry.

3D MODELING DEFINED

The process that defines the dimensions and surface characteristics of 3D objects is called *3D modeling*. The word "modeling" is used in the same sense that a TV weather map is a model of a weather system. The weather office gathers the data about the weather (such as area temperatures, wind direction, and wind velocity), interprets the data, and displays it as colored images. The color images help you visualize the weather conditions described by the TV weatherperson.

Three-dimensional computer graphic models are used to visualize a variety of data, from financial transactions on the stock market, to natural objects such as the human heart. Instead of viewing a list of numbers, you see a 3D graph that changes over time. The data that defines the 3D object can be quite complex. In engineering and science, 3D modeling is used to explore the physical properties of objects. For example, an object created in 3D software can be exported to a scientific program where wind tunnel tests are performed on new aircraft designs. Or the model can be exported to an engineering program that uses the three-dimensional information inherent in the model to create a precise copy in the real world.

Other extremely useful information can be extracted from a 3D model. You can assign materials to the surface, and then calculate its volume or weight. A product designer can calculate the cost of materials for a product long before it is produced.

CREATING A WORLD IN A 3D MODELER

3D models are created and arranged in a volume of simulated space commonly called the *world* in 3D graphics. The world can be visualized as a cube of space, as shown in Figure 6-5.

The world is an arbitrary size. For example, the car could be reduced to a small fraction of the size shown in Figure 6-5. The 3D modeling program provides a view into this world through a window (your computer screen).

Figure 6-5
Object in a 3D
world

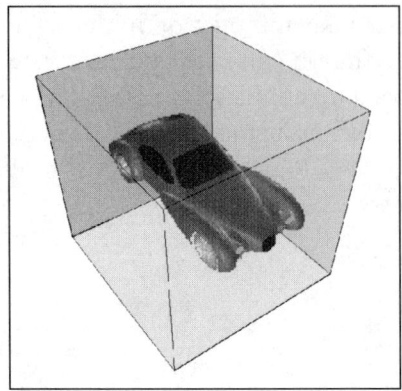

All computer graphics systems use a geometric coordinate system to situate objects in space. The most common system is the rectangular Cartesian coordinate system, named after the 17th philosopher René Descartes. Figure 6-6 shows a 2D coordinate system imposed on a plane.

The Cartesian coordinate system superimposes a set of axes on a plane—the x and y axes—which are perpendicular to each other. These axes are used as reference lines for locating a point on the plane. The grid also allows a point's position to be calculated relative to all other points on the plane.

In Figure 6-6, a point's position (the letter *P*) is specified by calculating its distance from the x and y axes. For example, the point might be two units

Figure 6-6
The Cartesian
coordinate
system

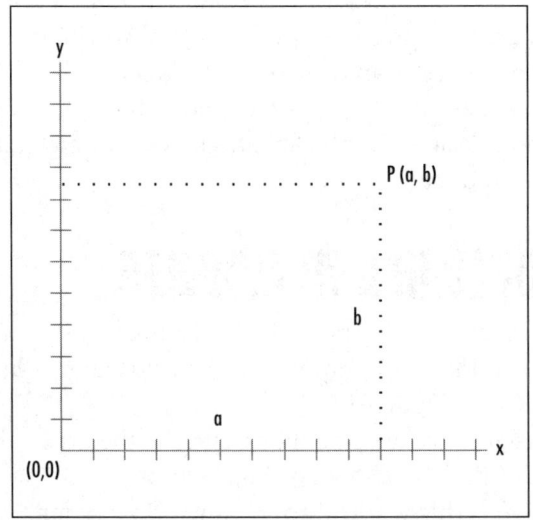

Figure 6-7
The quadrants
in a 2D
Cartesian
coordinate
system

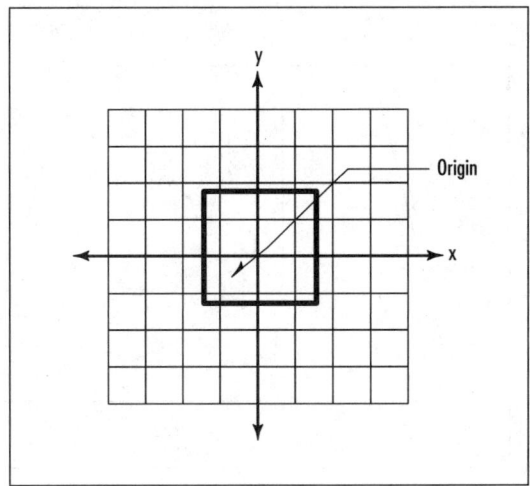

up the y axis (the rise) and one unit to the right of the x axis (the run). All the points on the plane can be plotted this way.

The point of intersection between the two axes (0) is called the origin. Figure 6-7 shows the four quadrants that make up a complete 2D Cartesian coordinate system.

Distances to the right of the origin are positive—to the left, negative. Distances along the y axis above the origin are positive. Below the origin, distances are negative.

The position of a point in a Cartesian coordinate system is usually given as a pair of numbers (its coordinates) and written as (x,y). The origin, for example, lies at (0,0) in the coordinate system.

The rectangular Cartesian coordinate system provides a way of mapping real or natural objects to a frame or reference. For example, the profile of an object like a train can be mapped to a Cartesian coordinate system by measuring the length and height of the train and translating the measurements to units on the rectangular Cartesian grid. Once the profile is created, it can then be used as a guideline for development of the picture. When an artist draws a scale model of an object on graph paper, this is the way it is done.

Adding the Third Axis

In 3D computer graphics applications, the Cartesian coordinate system is extended into the third dimension by adding a third axis at right angles to the x and y axes—the z or depth axis. The z axis intersects the x and y axes at the origin (see Figure 6-8).

123

Figure 6-8
3D coordinate system, showing the addition of the z axis

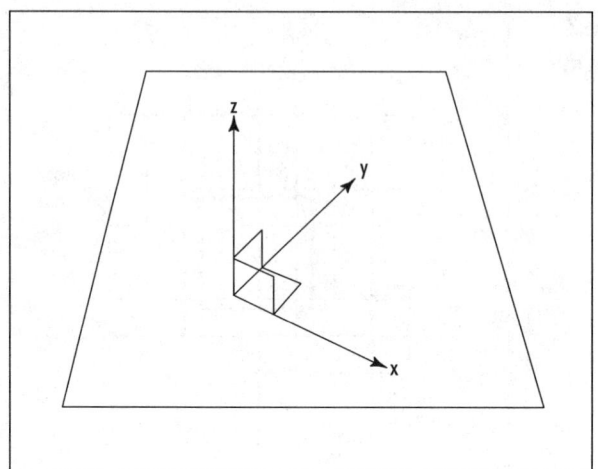

Specifying the location of a point in a 3D coordinate system is similar to that of the 2D system, only three numbers are used (x,y,z).

Notice that adding the z axis has created a second and third plane to the coordinate system. Besides the xy-plane, there are a yz-plane and a zx-plane. These planes are useful in the construction of objects, since they allow the modeler to map the profiles of objects to the three planes of three-dimensional space. For example, the front of an object such as an airplane might be mapped to the zx-plane, the top to the xy-plane, the side to the yz-plane. This allows a model to be accurately mapped to 3D space.

VRML's Coordinate System

VRML uses the 3D Cartesian coordinate system to specify locations in 3D space for objects. Figure 6-9 is an illustration of the 3D Cartesian coordinate system and the relationship of objects within it.

Objects in the VR world are stages in this coordinate system. From the point of view of the VRML specification, it does not matter if objects are created and then added to a VRML world, or if the world is created entirely in the 3D modeling coordinate system. The relationships among objects are preserved when the file is translated.

Modeling VRML Objects

The VRML specification is a data format for the 3D objects and their relationships in the 3D world. This means that you receive the VRML world as text files. These text files specify what objects are included in the world, how

Figure 6-9
Objects in
three-
dimensional
space

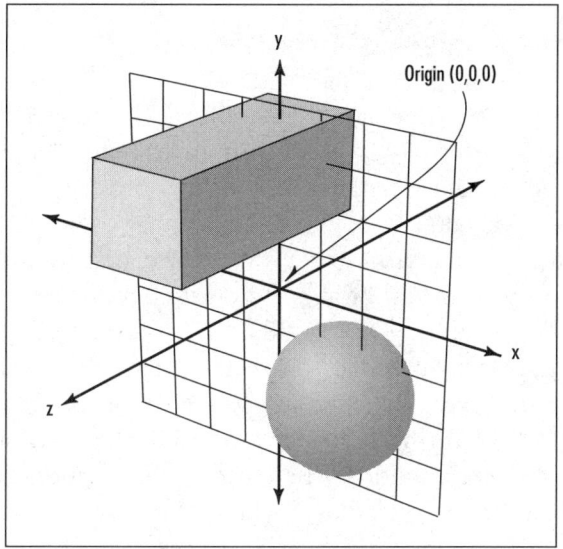

they look, and where they are situated. Then your VRML browser and your computer create the display of the world on your screen.

The current specification (1.0) does not store object attributes such as weight or material thickness. It does specify how the geometry of objects is stored in its data files. Essentially a VRML WRL file stores lists of basic 3D shapes, such as points and cubes. For example, a cube's dimensions are stored as:

```
Cube    {
                        width    5
                        height   15
                        depth    15
                        }
```

The word "Cube" specifies that a cube is about to be defined. The specifications for the cube are enclosed in curly brackets, { and }. Within the brackets, the dimensions of the cube are given.

The information about objects is stored in the VRML file in ASCII (American Standard Code for Information Interchange) format, a basic set of codes that is used to exchange information between a wide variety of hardware and software systems. ASCII files can be read and saved by most text editors.

If you open a VRML file in a word processing program, you'll see lines of text listing the object's geometry. For example, the location of a single point on a VRML model is stored as follows:

```
point [
        -0.152090 1.162290 4.545750
    ]
```

While it's possible to create the data for a VRML world in a text editor, objects can have a lot of geometric primitives. The shapes are difficult to visualize as lists of data. For these reasons it's not very practical to use a text editor to create the data.

Although there are dedicated VRML world builders, almost any VR or 3D animation program can be used to create 3D objects for VRML worlds, providing they save in the DXF standard CAD format (.DXF) or in a format that can be translated into the VRML format (.WRL). (Caligari Fountain, included with this book, will load in a variety of 3D proprietary formats and save in VRML .WRL format.) This gives the VRML world-builder wonderful versatility in designing worlds. The current specification does not limit the complexity of VRML worlds, but the limited bandwidth of the Internet and the relatively modest processing ability of the average CPU do. This situation is evolving quickly, and the VRML specification will keep pace with the new developments. By working with sophisticated 3D modeling tools now, you'll be able to respond to new creative and technical possibilities in the future.

Like VRML browsers, 3D modeling programs read 3D data into memory and convert it to two-dimensional line drawings for screen display. Figure 6-10 shows a boat cleat (the hardware used to tie a boat to a dock), as a line drawing on the screen.

The program provides a *graphical* view of the three-dimensional data. Dialog boxes and the mouse pointer working with display controls allow the viewer to see the model at different angles. For example, the cleat can be rotated around its axis for a view of the model at a different angle (see Figure 6-11).

It's much better to create and manipulate the object's data indirectly by creating and manipulating a *graphic representation* of the data on the screen. Figure 6-12 shows two screen grabs of a cup created in Auto*ship* System

Figure 6-10
Boat cleat
shown as a
line drawing

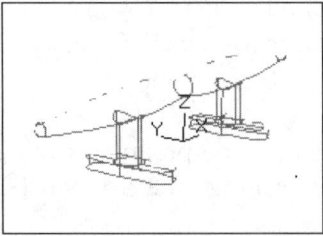

Figure 6-11
3D view of
cleat and the
display controls

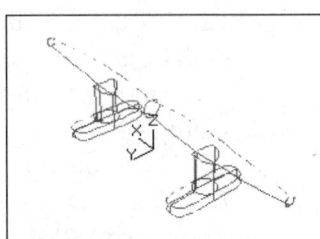

Figure 6-12
Cup created in
Auto*ship*

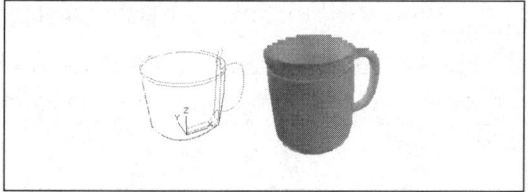

Inc.'s 3D modeling program, Auto*ship*. A "lite" version of Auto*ship* is bundled with this book.

The view on the left shows the cup as a line drawing. The modeler changes the shape of the object by manipulating the lines with a mouse or digitizing pen. The picture on the right shows the same cup with a colored surface. This view allows the modeler to view the effect of the changes on the object's surface. 3D modeling programs like Auto*ship* provide a visual interface between the artist and the computer data.

The Modeling Process

The 3D modeling process for objects that make up VRML worlds and display them on the screen is explained as follows (see Figure 6-13).

Figure 6-13
Creating 3D
objects for
VRML worlds

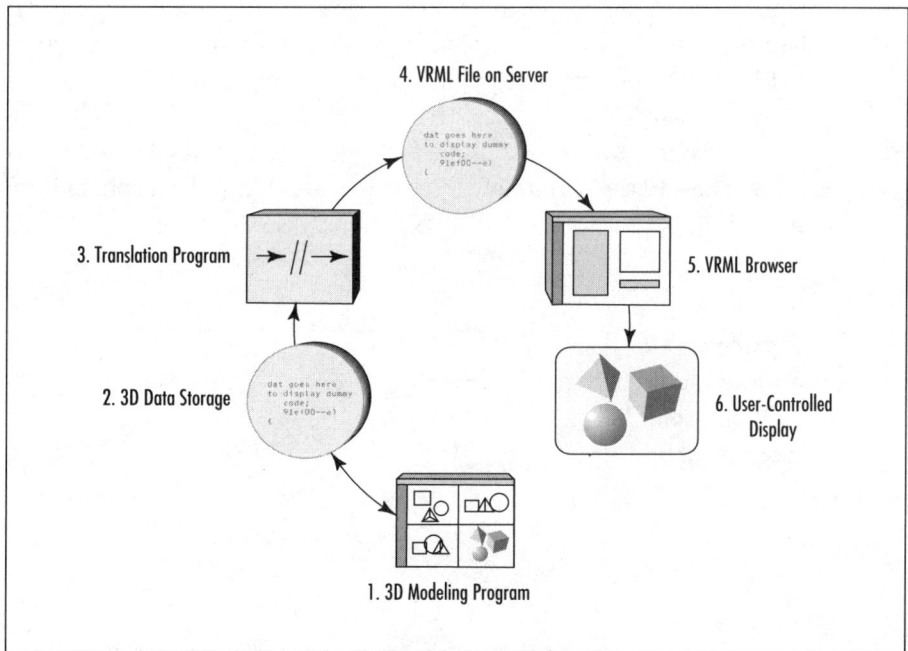

1. A modeling program is used to create the data for the 3D objects.

2. The data is usually stored in the program's proprietary binary format. It may be read back into the 3D modeling program for modification and fine-tuning.

3. A file translation utility is used to translate the proprietary data file into the VRML format. This function may be built into the 3D modeling program.

4. The VRML file is stored on a host system.

5. The file is sent to the user's system and read by a VRML browser residing on the user's system.

6. The user controls how the model is displayed on the screen.

The translation of 3D models into VRML data files and the use of VRML browsers to display 3D models are covered in later chapters. What follows is a description of how 3D models are created.

SURFACE AND SOLID MODELING

There are two basic kinds of 3D modeling: surface modeling and solid modeling. The VRML specification defines surface models. The difference between the two types can readily be seen in the objects they create. Figure 6-14 shows a hemisphere modeled with a surface modeler (left) and a solid modeler (right).

Notice that the surface modeler models the surface of an object, but not its mass. The surface is infinitely thin. When an object like a sphere is modeled, it

Figure 6-14
Surface model (left) and solid model (right)

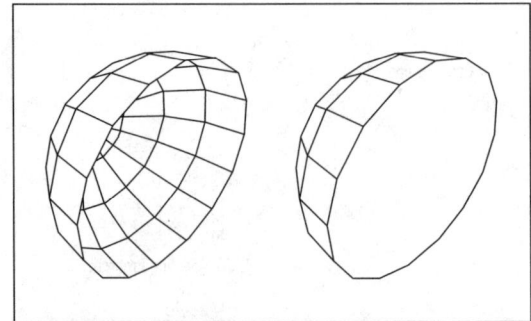

is created as an empty shell. Modeling the surface of the object rather than its mass is less calculation-intensive. This is the major advantage of surface modelers.

POLYGONAL AND SPLINE MODELING

3D surface modeling programs can also be categorized according to the basic geometry of their surfaces: polygonal versus spline surfaces.

Polygonal modelers represent the surface of objects with meshes of three- and four-sided polygons. These polygons are made up of straight lines (polylines) connected by vertices. Because polygonal modelers use simple geometric entities (straight lines and points), they can calculate and display surfaces very quickly. However, it is difficult to easily model free-form surfaces, since they incorporate irregular curves. The more curved the surfaces on a polygonal model, the more polygons must be used to approximate the curve.

Spline modelers use an entirely different method for generating curved surfaces. The curve is defined and controlled by mathematical entities called control points. These control points and their associated curves result in much more accurate representations of surfaces and smaller data files. However, because this type of curved surface generation is based on much higher-order mathematics than those used by polygonal modelers, creating and displaying spline models is much more calculation intensive, slowing program response time. Yet, considering the accuracy of spline modeling, and the greater range of shapes that can be modeled, it's well worth considering spline modelers for creating VRML objects. A spline model can be exported as a polygonal model and translated into VRML format.

The two types of modelers will be discussed next.

Polygonal Modeling

In polygonal modeling, the surface of an object is defined by a series of polygons, straight line segments (polylines) joined at vertices. The interior of the polygon is called a *face* (see Figure 6-15).

Figure 6-15
Polygon

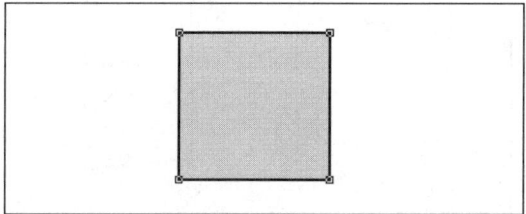

Polygonal objects are composed of a *mesh* of polygons. The polygons making up the mesh are usually three- or four-sided. For example, a cube is constructed by attaching six four-sided polygons (see Figure 6-16).

The shape of a polygonal object in a polygonal modeler is altered by editing its vertices. For example, deleting a vertex on the side of a square creates a triangle (see Figure 6-17).

Although editing polygonal objects at the level of individual vertices is quite common, in most cases the object is created, or modified, by use of tools that create the object as a whole. For example, polygonal programs include basic shapes like spheres, hexagons, and cubes that can be assembled Tinkertoy style into more complex shapes.

Polygons are very easy for the computer to calculate and display because they are linear. Straight line segments are described by relatively simple mathematical terms. For example, in a two-dimensional Cartesian coordinate system, the location of points along a line is described with such monomial (single-term) equations as $x = y$ (see Figure 6-18).

Once the starting point is known (for example, $x = -10$, $y = -10$), finding any other point along the line involves a simple calculation, for example, $x = y + 1$.

Figure 6-16
Geometry of a cube

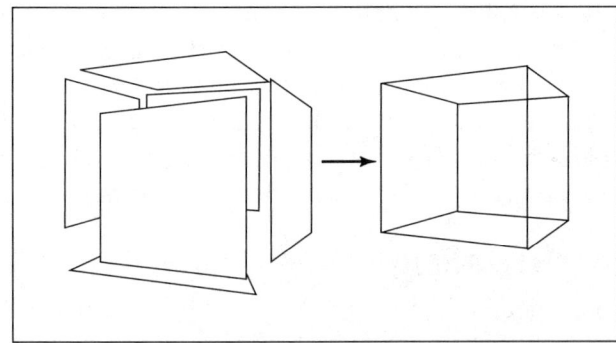

Figure 6-17
Triangle created out of a square by deleting a vertex

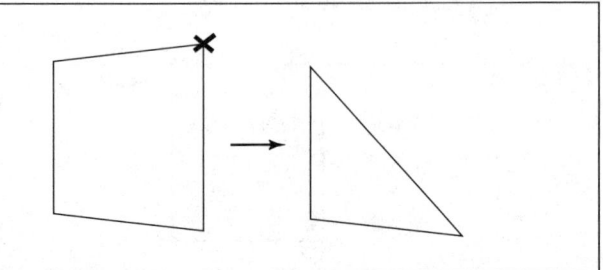

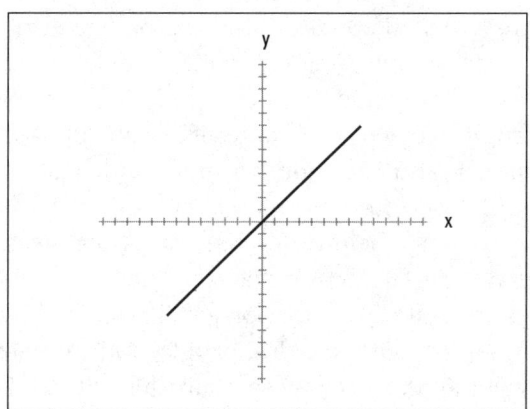

Figure 6-18
A straight line

By keeping the mathematical system simple, polygonal modelers have traditionally been well-suited to desktop PCs, which do not have the computing muscle of workstations. However, desktop 3D programs that use polygonal modeling pay a price for fast screen refreshes. Figure 6-19 shows the problem encountered when straight line segments rather than curved lines are used to describe curves.

The accuracy of the polygonal curve can be improved by increasing the density of line segments. Figure 6-20 shows the effect of creating a cylinder with four sides (left), six sides (middle), and nine sides (right).

Figure 6-19
A polygonal
shape (interior)
and the spline
curve version
(exterior)

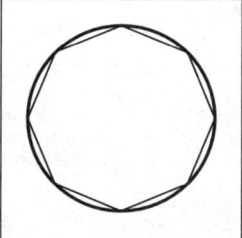

Figure 6-20
Increasing the
polygons on a
cylinder makes
it rounder

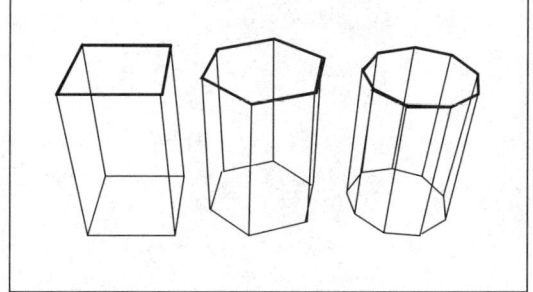

Increasing the polygon count around the perimeter of the cube creates a shape that approaches but never completely models a smooth circle.

The efficiency of polygonal modeling from the point of view of calculation has diminishing returns. The more line segments a curve is assigned, the larger the model, and the more memory and quantity of calculations required to draw it onscreen.

Polygonal objects are useful for geometric or architectural modeling. A high-rise, for example, is largely composed of straight lines. If it is seen in the distance, it makes an ideal subject for polygonal objects. However, such organic shapes as rocks, trees, bushes, sofas, people, and fruit are very difficult to model using straight lines. A face is especially difficult (see Figure 6-21).

Notice the density of polygons around the areas of the face where its curvature changes rapidly, such as the area around the mouth. It's very difficult to change the shape of the face, because deleting a vertex changes the area around the vertex, but not the overall shape of the face.

Spline Modeling

Spline modelers do a much better job of modeling objects with curved surfaces, like ships. Figure 6-22 shows a kayak modeled in Auto*ship*.

The kayak is a good example of an object that would be difficult to model with 2D polygons: it has no straight lines.

Two-dimensional and three-dimensional graphics programs that use higher-order mathematics to describe curves are computationally expensive. A simple illustration of this is a parabolic curve described by the mathematical equation $y = x^2 - 7x + 10$. It is graphically represented on a Cartesian coordinate system as in Figure 6-23.

Figure 6-21
A face
modeled with
polygons

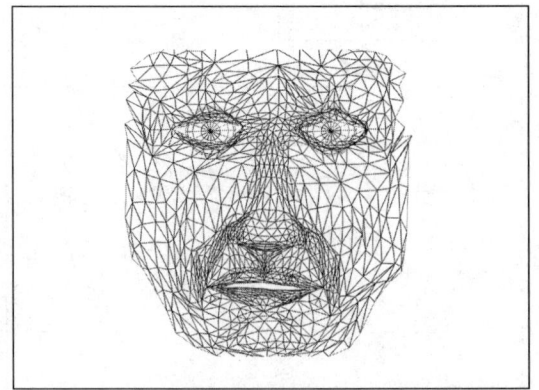

Figure 6-22
Auto*ship* kayak
model

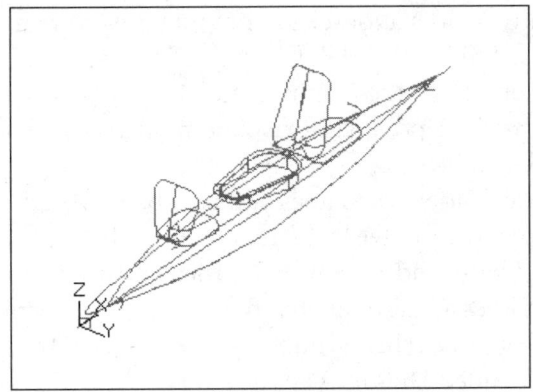

The parabolic curve is described by a second degree mathematical expression called a *quadratic polynomial*. (A monomial term in mathematics describes a quantity raised to any power, such as $y = x^2$. A polynomial has two or more such terms, such as $a^2 - 2ab + b^2$.)

Three-dimensional curves having a circular, parabolic, elliptical, or cubic form can be represented by relatively straightforward mathematical formulas. However, free-form curves that follow an arbitrary path in three-dimensional space are much more difficult to represent mathematically.

The most advanced spline modelers, like Auto*ship*, use a mathematical system called NURBS (non-uniform rational B-splines) to describe complex free-form curves. B-splines are constructed with segments described by second- and third-degree polynomials (quadratic and cubic equations), with segments joined at what are called *knots*.

Figure 6-23
Parabolic curve

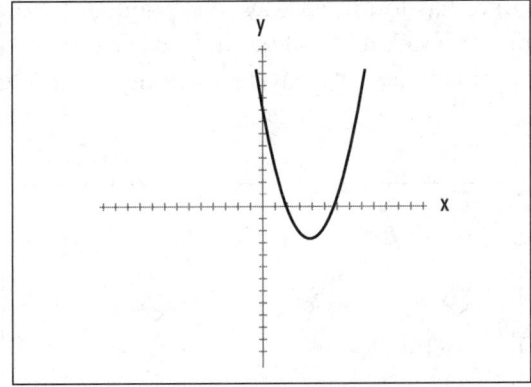

Until recently, workstation-class computers were required to calculate and display these kinds of complex curves. The advent of powerful desktop systems based on the Intel Pentium and the Motorola PowerPC microprocessors has made it possible for spline modelers to overcome this performance drawback.

A much wider variety of shapes can also be modeled by use of curved surfaces, as opposed to polygons. The complex, free-flowing lines of such shapes as cars, boats, and aircraft are easier and faster to model. Objects modeled with splines are also much more accurate representations of objects than polygonal objects. This is important for objects that are exported to CAD (Computer Aided Drafting) applications.

To understand how spline curves work, it's necessary to understand how they came about.

The Origins of Spline Curve Technology

The word "spline" has its origins in the flexible wood or metal strips used by draftspersons for drawing the curves of ships (see Figure 6-24).

The strip of wood or metal was held in place by tacks or lead weights called *ducks,* set at intervals. The curve of the wood is changed by varying the number and positions of the ducks.

In the 1960s the French mathematician Pierre Bézier developed a mathematical model for the loftsman's spline.

Bézier modeled the action of the ducks along a spline. Instead of developing mathematical formulas that directly calculated the position of points along a curve, Bézier derived the curve from a control point (see Figure 6-25).

Figure 6-25 shows a pair of quadratic Bézier curves between two end points (P_1 and P_2). The control points (P_{C1} and P_{C2}) are located at suitable positions from the curves to influence their shape.

The Bézier curve has found its way into popular 2D drawing programs such as CorelDraw from Corel Systems. If you have used the curve tool in CorelDraw, you probably already have a working knowledge of how spline

Figure 6-24
Diagram of a loftsman's spline

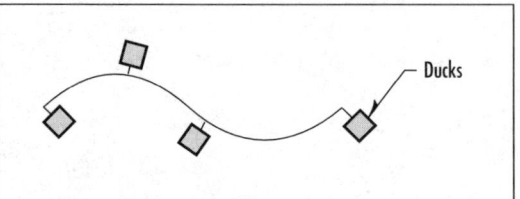

Ducks

Figure 6-25
Bézier curves

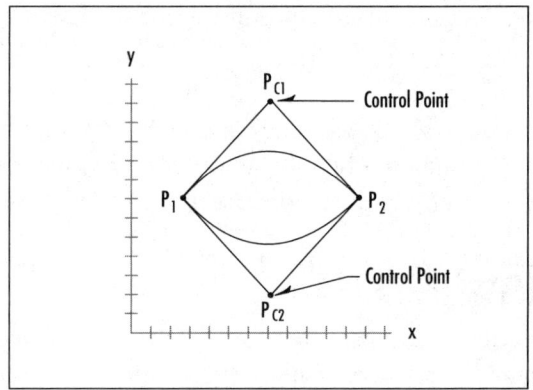

curves are used to create smooth, flowing shapes. Figure 6-26 shows a Bézier curve created in CorelDraw.

As in the case of the ducks on the physical spline, the four control points on a Bézier curve determine its shape. The curve passes through the first and fourth control points. The second and third control points determine the curve's shape. For example, moving one of these control points changes the shape of the curve (see Figure 6-27).

The spline curve overcomes several problems associated with polygonal line segments. The shape of the curve can be changed easily and smoothly. When the curve is scaled up or down, it does not lose its curve definition—and spline objects produce very small files, compared with polygonal objects.

Figure 6-26
Spline curve
with control
points, created
in CorelDraw

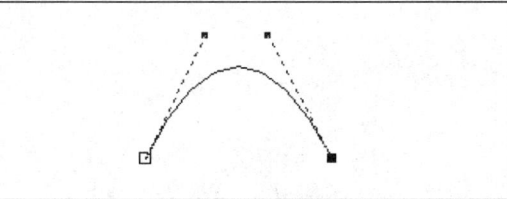

Figure 6-27
Moving a
control point
changes the
shape of the
curve

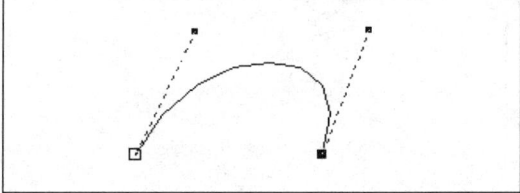

While Bézier splines allow smooth curves to be created, the control points on a Bézier affect the entire curve, limiting the complexity of the curve that can be created. They are also limited in their ability to model complex, discontinuous, free-form curves, such as those found on the hood of a car. A more complex mathematical system was invented to model such surfaces. This is the subject of the next section.

NURBS MODELING

As mentioned earlier, the most advanced mathematical system used to represent curves and surfaces is called non-uniform rational B-splines, or NURBS. B-spline curves are divided into continuous, end-to-end pieces, joined at knots, or knot vectors. The spacing between the pieces is non-uniform. Figure 6-28 shows a B-spline curve divided into pieces by knots (the black, filled dots along the curve).

Each piece of the curve is governed by a polynomial. Dividing complex free-form curves into smaller, less-complex curves allows them to be described with relatively less complicated (and therefore less computationally expensive) mathematical formulas.

The knots shown in Figure 6-28 do not normally appear in a NURBS modeler, because it is the control points (shown as unfilled squares) that are used to change the shape of the curve. Each piece of the curve is controlled by control points. This is called *local control*. Figure 6-29 shows the effect of moving a control point from position 1, to position 2, to position 3.

Figure 6-28
Control points (empty squares) and knots (filled dots) of a NURBS curve

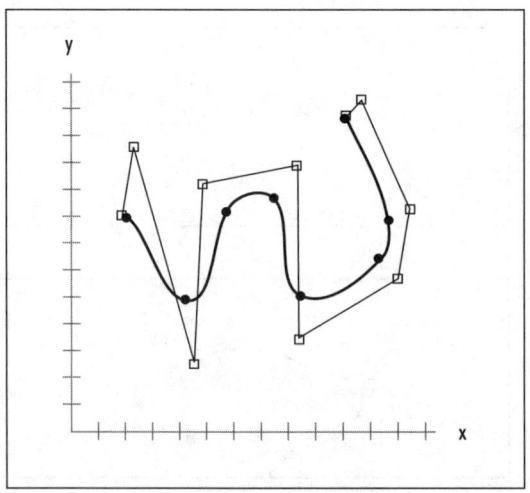

Figure 6-29
Moving a
control point

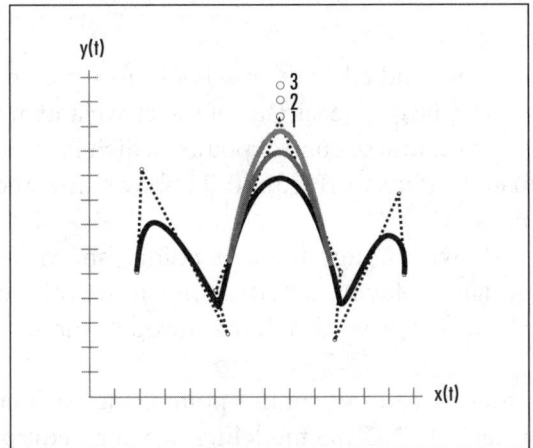

Notice that the entire curve is not affected, just the area of the curve under the influence of the control point that was moved.

NURBS programs create and store compact, efficient, and flexible formulations for both smooth and slope-discontinuous shapes, and provide exact representation of conic sections, like ellipses and cones.

Curve Control Points

Figure 6-30 shows how control points are represented on the screen.

Control points can be moved, deleted, added to a curve, and manipulated. The program bends the curve toward a control point, but does not make the curve coincide with a control point. Figure 6-31 shows the effect of moving the two control points governing the curve.

When the control points are moved, the curve is smoothly redrawn. The curve is not drawn through the control points, but rather is attracted to the new positions of the control point. This allows the curve to be smoothly deformed.

Finally, when you move a control point, you do not move the other control points attached to it.

Figure 6-30
Control points
along a curve

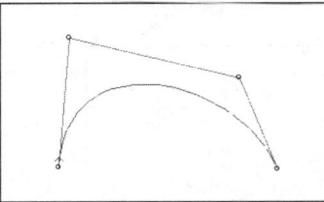

Figure 6-31
Moving a
control point

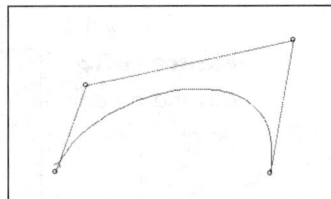

Edit Points

The NURBS modeler bundled with this book also provides *edit points* for shaping curves. These lie on the surface of the curve and are used for directly manipulating curves, unlike control points, which lie away from the curve and are manipulated indirectly. Figure 6-32 shows how they are represented on the screen.

The curve is drawn through the edit points, shown in Figure 6-33 as small, unfilled squares. Moving an edit point moves the other edit points connected to it, and the curve is redrawn through the new location of the edit points.

Edit points are *derived* from control points, and each curve contains an equal number of each. In NURBS modeling, when an edit point is moved, it is actually the corresponding control point being changed. In this sense, an edit point can be thought of as a "phantom" control point. Edit points are used to directly manipulate the curve. However, since control points can be used to create practically any shape, edit points are rarely used by Auto*ship*.

Control Points and Surfaces

Most of what has been said so far about the control points of NURBS curves also applies to surfaces.

What sets surfaces apart from curves is in the arrangement of their control and edit points. They are arranged in rows and columns, forming a control grid (see Figure 6-34).

In Figure 6-34 there are five rows and four columns of control points in the mesh. Increasing the rows and columns of control points increases the potential complexity of the surface. The surface of a round bilge hull, for

Figure 6-32
Edit points on
the curve

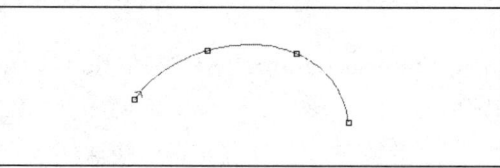

Figure 6-33
Moving an edit
point

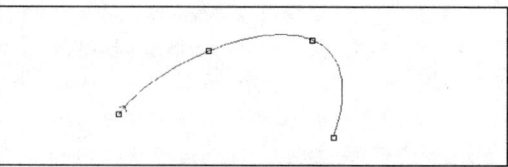

Figure 6-34
The control
point grid of a
surface

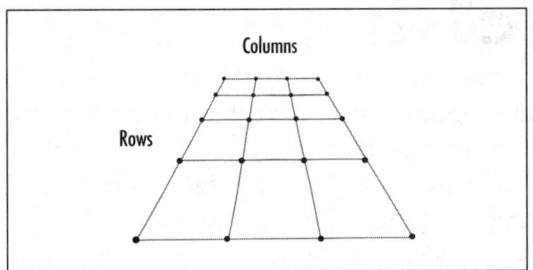

example, is created with a much higher row/column specification than that of a mast.

Individual control or edit points cannot be added to a surface. They must be added one row or column at a time. As a rule, create simple objects that can be easily edited, adding complexity to them later.

Corners

Corners are of two kinds: knuckles and chines. Knuckles are sharp discontinuities along a curve. Chines are sharp discontinuities in surfaces along complete rows or columns.

Knuckles

Control points that lie between the end points of curves do not lie on the surface of the curve. However, there is a special case where they do coincide with the surface and the corresponding edit point: knuckles (see Figure 6-35).

A knuckle is a sharp discontinuity in a curve. In Auto*ship*, the program bundled with this book, the Toggle Corner tool on the Edit Mode tool group is used to create a knuckle. When a knuckle is created, the selected control point is shown on the screen as green to indicate its status.

Chines

Corners on surfaces run the length of a row or column (see Figure 6-36). The program turns the points along the chine green to indicate their status.

Figure 6-35
A knuckle

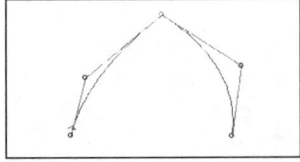

Figure 6-36
Chine along a
surface

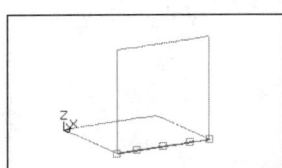

Curvature of Curves

One of the most valuable features of NURBS programs is the ability to create smooth surfaces. Smoothness describes the gradual, rather than abrupt, change in the curvature of a curve or surface. If you think of a curve as a point following a path through space, then curvature is the amount of change in the direction of the curve at any given point.

"Un-smooth" surfaces have unwanted dents or bumps in them. This is often hard to see in the line rendering of objects on the screen. NURBS programs provide a number of display options for examining the fairness of curves and surfaces. For example, Auto*ship* has a Curvature display button on the Display toolbar, which appears in edit mode. Toggling the Curvature button when a curve is selected shows a "porcupine plot" of its curvature (see Figure 6-37).

At intervals along the curve, quills are drawn perpendicular to the direction of the curve at that point. The length of the quill indicates the rate or degree of change in direction from the previous point. The longer the quill, proportional to the other quills, the more curvature there is at that point. The point at which the direction of the porcupine plot changes indicates a change in the direction of the curve.

PUTTING IT TOGETHER: MODELING AN OBJECT

The final section of this chapter illustrates how an object is created with a 3D modeling program. It uses Auto*ship*, the NURBS modeler bundled with this book—however, the principles remain the same for polygonal modelers like Impulse Imagine, also bundled with this book.

A wine glass is used because it is a simple object, and its creation is a classic demonstration of one of the most basic modeling tools: a *sweep transformation*.

Figure 6-37
Porcupine plot
of the curvature

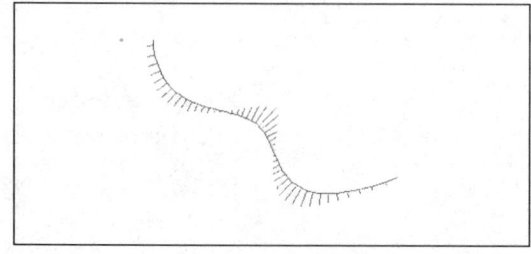

In this example, a two-dimensional profile of the wine glass will be created and then revolved around its vertical (z) axis to create the swept surface of the wine glass. The object is first imagined as a 2D profile and then as a 3D object.

Analyzing the Object

Modeling consists of developing a geometric representation of an object. This means that the modeler breaks the object down to its simplest geometric shapes. A toothbrush, for example, can be deconstructed into a long rectangular box (the handle) with an array of short cylinders at one end (the brush). Complex objects might be divided into separate modeling projects that are merged later. For example, a Cherokee airplane might be deconstructed into smaller projects (see Figure 6-38).

In pieces, the airplane is revealed as a collection of much simpler geometric shapes. The wine glass, a simple object, symmetrical around its radius, will not need to be divided into parts.

Creating the Profile

The wine glass's profile is created by use of Auto*ship*'s Draw Curve tool on the toolbar in create mode (see Figure 6-39).

The profile was drawn using a single curve. The dots along the curve show the points where "corners" were added, so that the direction of the

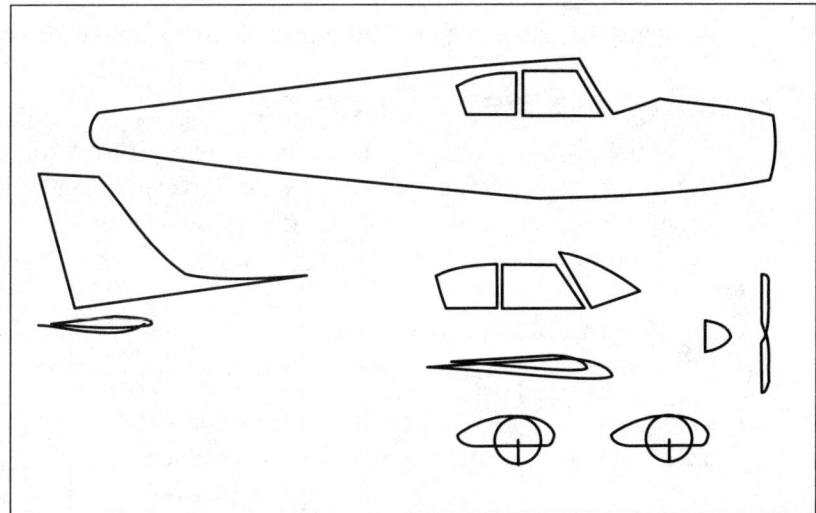

Figure 6-38
The parts to
the Cherokee
airplane

Figure 6-39
Profile of the
wine glass

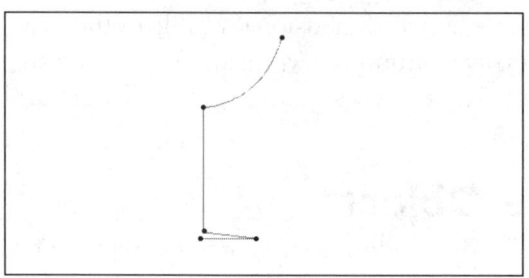

curve could be changed. For example, the point where the bowl of the wine glass meets the stem was made into a corner with the Toggle Corner tool in the toolbar's edit mode.

An alternative method for creating the profile would be to create each segment of the wine profile as a curve. As each curve is created, it is joined to the previous curve, by use of the Join Curves tool on the Create Mode toolbar.

The curve for the profile was created by placing points on the screen and then having Auto*ship* draw a curve, using the points as a guideline. For example, Figure 6-40 shows the points used to create the wine glass bowl (black dots).

Auto*ship* was told to draw a smooth curve using the construction points as a guideline. The curve that was drawn has two segments (marked by the square outline dots).

Figure 6-41 shows the control point that is automatically generated for the curve.

Moving the control point away from the curve smoothly alters its shape, allowing the modeler to be quite precise about the shape of the curve.

Creating a Swept Surface

Once the profile is created, the toolbar's Create Surface tool is used to rotate the profile on its vertical (z) axis. A 3D surface is created by sweeping the profile of the wine glass around on the object's z axis. Figure 6-42 shows the surface in mesh view mode.

Figure 6-40
Curve of the
wine glass
bowl

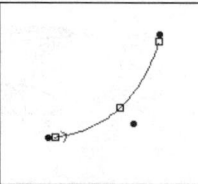

Figure 6-41
The shape of
the curve is
altered with a
control point

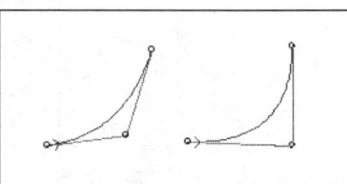

Figure 6-42
The 3D wine glass created by the sweep transformation

Creating objects by sweeping them is a very efficient modeling technique, since a 3D object can be created from a simple 2D outline, and the outline may not require a lot of work on the modeler's part. The technique works well only for objects with relatively simple geometric shapes. Further, the object is created with control points that allow its shape to be modified into much more complex shapes. See the edit mode chapters for information on tools for modifying 3D objects.

Model complexity can also be built up by adding parts to a simpler shape. A tea cup handle is added to a tea cup bowl. Or the Cherokee aircraft is assembled from disparate parts grouped by use of Auto*ship*'s group command. Auto*ship* provides tools for fitting the parts together using rotation, scaling, and positioning tools.

When the model is finished it, can be given surface characteristics and rendered (see Figure 6-43). Or it can be exported to another program for further editing or for rendering.

This has been a very brief overview of 3D modeling. 3D modeling programs allow you to create extremely detailed and accurate geometric representations of objects. The next chapters provide hands-on information on modeling objects using Impulse Imagine.

Figure 6-43
The wine glass rendered in Auto*ship*

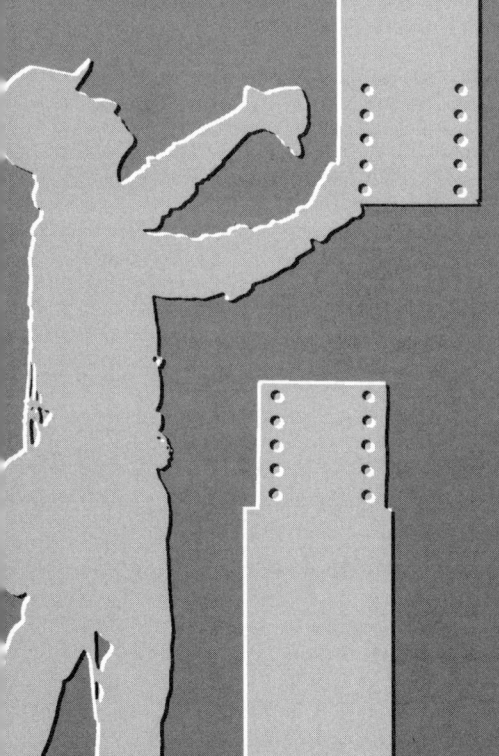

7

USING IMAGINE

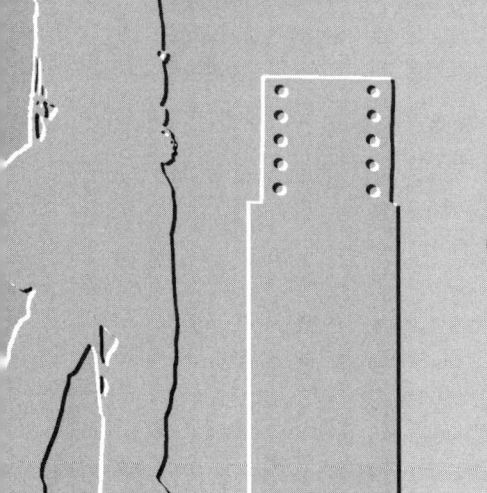

7

This chapter provides a short primer on Impulse Inc.'s Imagine Lite, the 3D program used in Chapters 8 through 12 to teach polygonal modeling. By the end of the chapter you will have a working knowledge of the program, including its organization, interface, tools, and methodology.

IMAGINE LITE

Imagine Lite is Impulse Inc.'s professional 3D modeling program. It is the younger sibling to Imagine Pro, Impulse's professional package, which includes additional animation features. A complete version of Imagine Lite is bundled with this book. This is the same version of the program shipped on Impulse's $99 Imagine Lite CD-ROM. However, the retail CD-ROM version includes additional objects, FLC-format animations, a manual, and Impulse telephone support.

NOTE: A coupon is provided in the back of the book for users who want to purchase a fully supported retail version of Imagine.

INSTALLING IMAGINE

Imagine has the following hardware and software requirements.

Hardware Requirements

Three-dimensional modeling and rendering is very CPU intensive. Although you can run Imagine on a 386 or 486 computer with a math coprocessor, a Pentium greatly speeds screen redraw and rendering. You can also run Imagine with a standard VGA card (640x480, 256 colors). However, a card capable of displaying millions of colors is recommended, since Imagine can create full-color images.

The following are the minimum requirements:

- 386 or 486 computer with a math coprocessor

- 8 MB of memory

- 12 MB of hard disk space

- 256K VGA card with a built-in VESA BIOS compatibility or a software VESA driver specific to your video card

- 100 percent Microsoft-compatible mouse

The following are the recommended requirements:

- Pentium or better

- 16 MB of system memory

- 20 MB of hard disk space

- Hi-Color or True Color VGA system (with built-in VESA BIOS compatibility or a software VESA driver specific to your video card)

- 100 percent Microsoft-compatible mouse

VESA Compatibility

The VESA standard was created by video card manufacturers to make higher color modes on video cards accessible to software. Most cards have built-in (BIOS) VESA compatibility. Not all video cards implement the VESA correctly, so one or more color modes (such as 800x600 true color mode) may not work correctly on your computer—that is, an image won't display properly on your screen. Check the manufacturer's manual to ensure your video card has VESA compatibility built into the BIOS. If not, run the software program supplied by the video card manufacturer to implement the VESA modes. (Add this to your AUTOEXEC.BAT startup file.) As a precaution, ensure that you have the most current implementation of VESA compatible with your card.

Microsoft Mouse Compatibility

Some people have experienced problems using generic mice that are not 100 percent hardware and software compatible with the Microsoft mouse—the system locks up when the mouse is moved. This is usually the case with inexpensive mice with obscure brand names.

Software Requirements

Imagine is a protected mode program with its own proprietary expanded memory manager. Its memory manager is incompatible with other expanded memory managers, including Microsoft's EMM386.SYS expanded memory driver.

Expanded Memory under MS-DOS

You cannot run Imagine with another expanded memory manager. Because Windows usually installs an expanded memory in your system by default, you must remove it from your system configuration file, CONFIG.SYS.

 WARNING: Before changing your CONFIG.SYS file, first back up your old copy onto a bootable floppy disk, or rename it CONFIG.OLD.

The file is usually found on the root directory of your computer. The offending line calls the Microsoft expanded memory manager. It will look something like this:

```
DEVICE=C:\DOS\EMM386.SYS
```

If Imagine still does not run after you remove this file, try the following bare-bones configuration file. (The recommended configuration file assumes that the DOS system files exist in a directory called C:\DOS.)

1. Edit the CONFIG.SYS file in the boot-up (root) directory, by entering

```
C:
CD \
EDIT CONFIG.SYS
```

2. Edit the CONFIG.SYS file to look like this:

```
DEVICE=C:\DOS\HIMEM.SYS
BUFFERS=10,0
FILES=20
FCBS=16,0
STACKS=9,256
```

3. From the File menu of the DOS editor, choose Save.

4. Reboot the computer.

Imagine will now run. Because the Windows extended memory manager (HIMEM.SYS) has been installed, you should be able to enter Windows before or after running Imagine. Note that you cannot shell out of Windows to run Imagine.

Windows 95

Imagine does not run under Microsoft Windows 95, not even in its DOS session mode, nor is there a work-around for users who have purchased computers preinstalled with Windows 95. You will have to install the MS-DOS operating system on your computer. For MS-DOS users who have upgraded to Windows 95, there is a work-around, but Impulse and Waite Group technical support have advised that they will *not* provide technical support for the work-around, because of the danger that inexperienced computer users may accidentally erase data on their systems. Before using the work-around, ensure that you have backed up data onto external storage media. Alternatively, find a user experienced in altering computer configurations.

The work-around consists of booting up Windows 95 in multiboot mode. In effect you will be aborting out of Windows 95 on boot-up and reverting to your old copy of MS-DOS to run Imagine. The procedure involves altering a hidden system file. Make sure that the DOS directory is in your path.

1. From Windows 95, exit to DOS.

2. Change to the root directory. For example:

```
CD C:\
```

3. The MSDOS.SYS hidden file is in the root directory. You must first make the file accessible to the DOS file editor. Enter the following command at the DOS prompt:

```
ATTRIB -R -S -H MSDOS.SYS
```

4. Now call the DOS editor:

```
EDIT MSDOS.SYS
```

5. In the editor, change the following parameters to the values shown here:

Bootmulti *1*
Boot GUI *0*
Network *0*

6. Choose Save from the File menu.

7. Now you will change the file back to a hidden file. Enter

```
ATTRIB +R +S +H MSDOS.SYS
```

From now on, whenever you want to run Imagine, switch to your old MS-DOS operating system. When you turn on your system, wait until you see the "Starting Windows 95" message at the top of the screen and press F4.

Installing and Running Imagine

Imagine is located on the CD-ROM accompanying this book, in the directory \IMAG. You should copy this directory and its subdirectories to your hard drive to run the program. It is recommended that you install Imagine under the directory name \IMAG, as the exercises in this book refer to this directory. You will require a minimum of 7 MB on your hard drive.

To run Imagine, change to the \IMAG directory and type

```
IMAGINE
```

IMAGINE TROUBLESHOOTING

Here are solutions to common problems encountered by new users of Imagine.

■ *I get memory error messages when I try to render my project.*

Check to ensure that you have at least 8 MB of RAM free when running Imagine. No objects created in the exercises in this book require more than 8 MB, but some of the sample objects do.

■ *I cannot run the program as a DOS session under IBM OS/2.*

Imagine does not run under OS/2. You must use MS-DOS. Note that Imagine does not run as a DOS session under Windows 95.

■ *The left* ALT *does not work, but the right* ALT *does.*

Imagine does not use the left ALT, because it was ported from the Amiga platform. Users of laptops that only have a left ALT must use menu commands.

■ *I changed the value in the dialog box, but nothing happened when I returned to the program.*

You must press ENTER after typing in text fields. If you forget to press ENTER and exit the dialog box by pressing the OK button, the change you made will not be activated or saved.

When I try to apply an image (brush) to an object or background, and I attempt to render the model, I get the message "unsupported or bad TIFF format."

Imagine does not support compressed TIFF (Tagged Image File Format) images. Nor does it support grayscale TIFFs. One more peculiarity: The image can be any size except 320x200 pixels. To fix the problem, load the images into a paint program and save them as uncompressed 256-color, or 16.7 million–color TIFF images. (TIFF images usually have the file extension .TIF.) Best results are accomplished with 24-bit images. Remember that images consume RAM, so be frugal in their use.

When I saved my model in the Detail Editor and later reloaded it, only one part of the model appeared to have been saved.

The Detail Editor only saves single objects, or objects that have been grouped with the Group command. Use the Pick All option on the Pick/Select menu to select all the objects in the Detail Editor. Then press F1 to pick all the objects. Finally, use the Group option on the Object menu to form a group out of the objects. Now save the group.

IMAGINE LITE EDITORS

Imagine provides tools for project management, 3D object creation, scene layout, and program configuration. The program's tools are organized into seven editors (see Figure 7-1).

Figure 7-1
Imagine Lite's editors

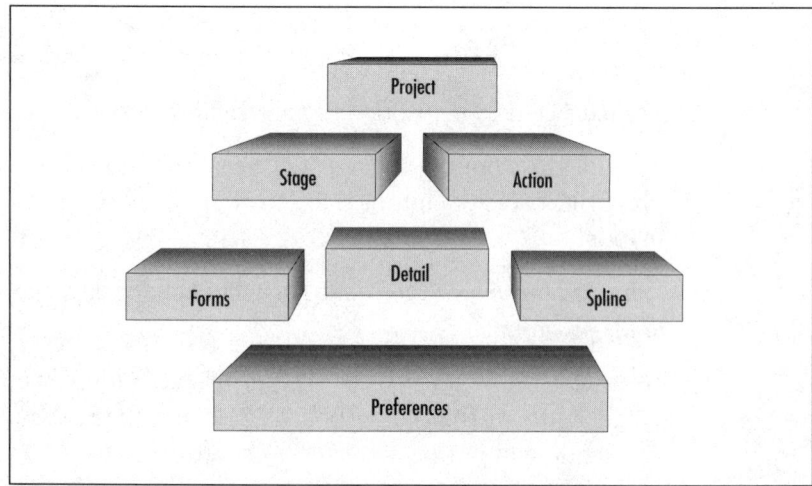

Figure 7-2

The pull-down menu for switching between editors

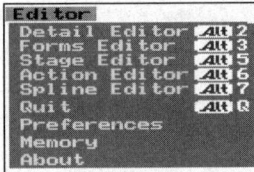

During modeling, editors are entered and exited by use of a pull-down menu at the top left of the screen (see Figure 7-2).

The following is a list of the editors and the tasks they perform:

- Project Editor—This organizes the elements of a modeling project.

- Detail Editor—This creates 3D objects, adds detail to objects imported from other editors, and assigns surface attributes (such as color) to objects.

- Stage Editor—This arranges models into scenes.

- Action Editor—This works with the Stage Editor, assigning such scene attributes as ambient light level and fog, and adjusting lights. It is also used for scripting animations.

- Forms Editor—This is a specialized editor for creating organic objects.

- Spline Editor—This is a specialized editor for importing and editing fonts, and for creating curved shapes.

- Preferences Editor—This customizes the program interface and functions.

IMAGINE'S MODELING TOOLS

The tools and commands for modeling and rendering are arranged within a modern graphical user interface. Imagine uses menu bars, drop-down menus, keyboard commands, buttons, and pop-up boxes to harness its power. The object editors (Detail, Forms, Stage, and Spline) share similar 3D viewing systems and common interface conventions. The Action, Preferences, and Project editors are specialized to the data entry tasks performed in them. Each editor will be discussed next.

NOTE: You cannot enter the Stage Editor without starting a new project. See the following section for the steps in creating a new project.

Figure 7-3
Preferences
Editor

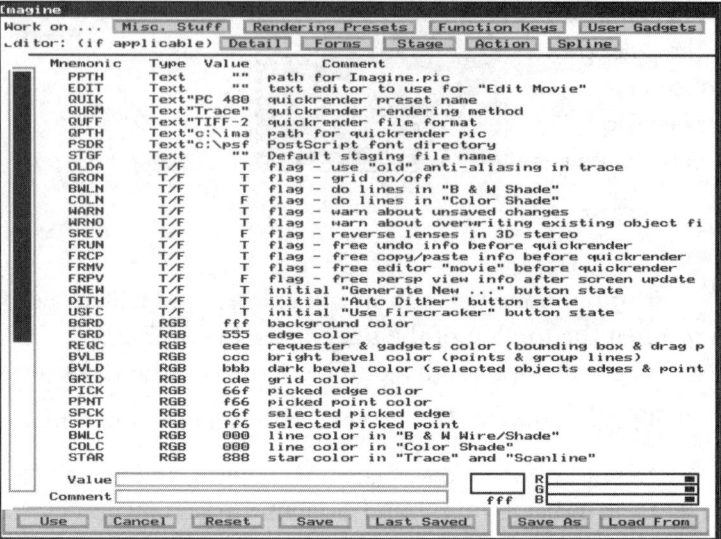

THE PREFERENCES EDITOR

The Preferences Editor is used to create a new configuration for the program. For example, the screen colors can be altered, or the default color depth and spatial resolution of the program can be changed. The Preferences Editor screen is shown in Figure 7-3.

Program parameters are changed by selecting a parameter, such as background color, from the list on the screen, and entering new values for it in the data entry fields at the bottom of the list. Here are the parts of the screen:

- Group select buttons—These are groups of parameters (shown as buttons at the top of the screen) from which you can choose.

- Parameters list—This shows a list of parameters for the currently selected group.

- Scroll bar—This scrolls through the parameters list when you click on the white area of the scroll bar.

- Data entry fields—These show the current value of a selected parameter. (These fields are editable. To edit, enter a new value, and press (ENTER).)

- Color swatch and color sliders—These change screen and rendering colors. Move the R (red), G (green), and B (blue) sliders to create a new color. The new color appears in the color swatch. To select the new color, click inside the color swatch. This updates the Value field.

154

⊞ Editing buttons—These are used as follows:

⊞ The Use button exits the Preferences Editor. The new configuration will be used by Imagine.

⊞ The Save button saves the current configuration as the new default. Imagine's configuration file is IMAGINE.CFG.

⊞ The Last Saved button restores the configuration to the last saved IMAGINE.CFG.

⊞ The Reset button returns the current configuration to the values active when you entered the Preferences Editor.

⊞ The Save As button saves the current configuration under a new name. Select the Load From button to retrieve this configuration.

Example: Changing the Quick Render Settings

Quick Render is an option on the Editor menu of the Detail and Stage editors. The option provides a quick preview of the rendered model, showing its color, shading, and lighting. For many VRML projects, a low resolution quick render may be all that's needed to visualize what the object will look like in a VRML browser. A low resolution render will render much more quickly.

The Preferences Editor includes Quick Render presets under the default Misc. (miscellaneous) group. Figure 7-4 shows how the settings appear in the editor.

Change the spatial resolution of the Quick Render:

1. Click on the QUIK line.

2. Enter the following in the data entry field at the bottom of the parameters list:

`PC Lores`

3. Press (ENTER).

Figure 7-4
The Quick
Render settings

```
Mnemonic    Type     Value          Comment
  PPTH      Text       ""     path for Imagine.pic
  EDIT      Text       ""     text editor to use for "Edit Movie"
  QUIK      Text"PC 480"      quickrender preset name
  QURM      Text"Trace"       quickrender rendering method
  QUFF      Text"TIFF-2"      quickrender file format
  QPTH      Text"c:\ima       path for quickrender pic
  PSDR      Text"c:\psf       PostScript font directory
  STGF      Text       ""     Default staging file name
  OLDA      T/F         T     flag - use "old" anti-aliasing in trace
  GRON      T/F         T     flag - grid on/off
```

NOTE: You must press ENTER after making an editing change to a data entry field. Clicking on the OK button without pressing ENTER causes Imagine to ignore the editing change.

Selecting PC640 (640x480) from the Presets pop-up box is preferred. This creates a larger image with more detail. But the time it takes to render the image increases proportionately. Here are the alternative values (enter the text marked in **bold** into the data entry field):

PC Quarterscreen	120x120 pixels
PC Lores	320x200 pixels
PC 400	640x400 pixels
PC 640	640x480 pixels

Rendering Method

Follow the same method to change the rendering method. Choose Scanline. This option is closest to the way objects will appear in a VRML browser. The Trace option refers to ray tracing, a rendering method not currently supported by the VRML specification. Ray tracing provides much more realistic treatment of the object surface than is possible with scanline rendering. Such surface attributes as reflection and refraction are rendered, and the object casts shadows. However, the rendering process will be many times slower than Scanline rendering. The options are

Scanline	Scanline rendering
Trace	Ray-tracing rendering

Color Depth

Select TIFF-24bit or TGA-24bit if you have a graphics card that can display millions of colors. If the card can display only 256 colors (8-bit), select TIFF-256 or TGA-256. The TIFF specification is a very common paint program graphic format. Imagine only supports *uncompressed*, colored TIFF images. The other common format is TGA (Targa). This format was developed by Truevision and is common in the video field. The RGB8-24bit and ILBM-24bit settings are specific to the Amiga version of Imagine and should be ignored. Follow the same method to change the color depth:

TIFF-256	256-color TIFF format (uncompressed)
TIFF-24bit	16.7 million–color TIFF (uncompressed)
TGA-256	256-color TGA format
TGA-24bit	16.7 million–color TGA format

NOTE: Rendering Display Problems
Imagine uses the VESA standard to switch the screen into the proper pixel and color depth. Determine if your card supports VESA in hardware. If it doesn't, you must load a VESA driver in memory before running Imagine. (Contact the card manufacturer for this.) Some video card manufacturers do not implement the standard correctly. If this is the case, the screen will flicker, or the computer may lock up. Try setting the screen at a lower color resolution and a lower pixel resolution to find a compatible mode.

THE PROJECT EDITOR

Imagine organizes the modeling process into projects and subprojects. A project is like a scene in a movie. When a scene from a movie is shot on film, it is usually shot over and over again: take 1, take 2, take 3, and so on. Each of these takes is stored and played back. The best take is used for the film. An Imagine subproject is like a take.

The Project Editor screen allows you to specify where on the hard drive to store projects and subprojects. It also allows you to specify the color depth and spatial resolution of individual takes.

Let's see how a project is created and defined.

Opening a Project

When Imagine is entered, it presents the Project Editor (see Figure 7-5).

Figure 7-5
Project Editor

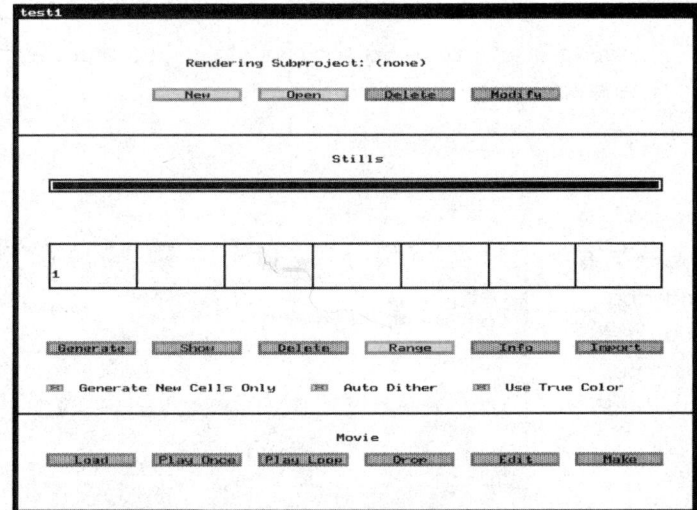

Many of the project options are grayed out, indicating they are not currently available. Opening a new project makes them active.

Open a new project:

1. Move your cursor over the drop-down menu area at the top of the screen, and press the right mouse button.
   Result: The drop-down menus appear.

2. Select New under the Project drop-down menu at the top of the screen (see Figure 7-5).
   Result: A Project Name box appears.

3. Enter the project name in the File entry box and press (ENTER).
   Result: There is a pause while Imagine sets up the directory structure on the hard drive.

   Now that the project has been named and created, set up a subproject. To set up a subproject:

4. Click on the yellow subproject button labeled "New" on the Rendering Subproject screen (see Figure 7-5).
   Result: The Rendering Subproject dialog box appears (see Figure 7-6).

5. The Rendering Subproject dialog box is used to specify how Imagine renders and saves the current scene in the Stage Editor. Only those options relevant to VRML projects will be reviewed.

▨ Rendering Method—Choose Scanline. Ignore the other options. They have a specialized use in image and video applications.

▨ Picture & Pixel Sizes—Set the spatial resolution of the rendered image. Here are the alternatives for this setting:

Figure 7-6
Rendering
Subproject
dialog box

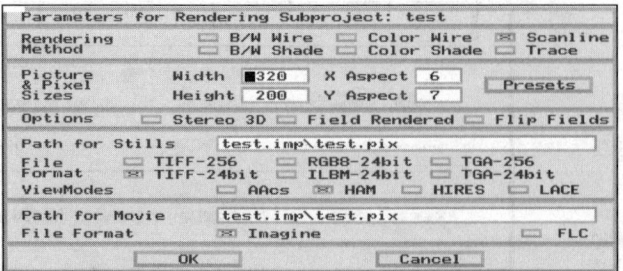

PC Quarterscreen	120x120
PC Lores	320x200
PC 400	640x400
PC 480	640x480

Normally PC480 is chosen, especially if you are creating VRML projects.

File Format—Select a color resolution and file format for the rendered image. Here are the alternatives:

TIFF-256	256-color TIFF format (uncompressed)
TIFF-24bit	16.7 million–color TIFF (uncompressed)
TGA-256	256-color TGA format
TGA-24bit	16.7 million–color TGA format

It's a good idea to choose TGA-256, since in most cases you will display graphics in a VRML world as 256 colors.

6. Click on the OK button to close the Rendering Subproject dialog box.

The project and subproject have now been set up. In the future, when Imagine is entered, you can load the project by choosing Open on the Project drop-down menu, and selecting the project by name. Once the Project is open, you can either start a new subproject, or load an existing subproject by clicking on the New or Open buttons, respectively, in the Rendering Subprojects area (see Figure 7-5).

ACTION EDITOR

The Action Editor and the Stage Editor are closely coupled. While the Stage Editor is used to arrange models into a scene, the Action Editor acts as a kind of cue sheet for actions and global conditions in the scene, such as the amount of ambient light. The animation features will not be covered, since VRML worlds are static under the present specification (1.0). Figure 7-7 shows the Action Editor screen.

The screen is arranged into a kind of spreadsheet. Here's a description of its parts, followed by a discussion of how to use them.

Object list—Objects in the current scene are listed in a column along the left side of the screen.

Frame number—The frames in the current animation are listed and numbered. Only one frame is created for a new project. It's the objects

Figure 7-7
Action Editor

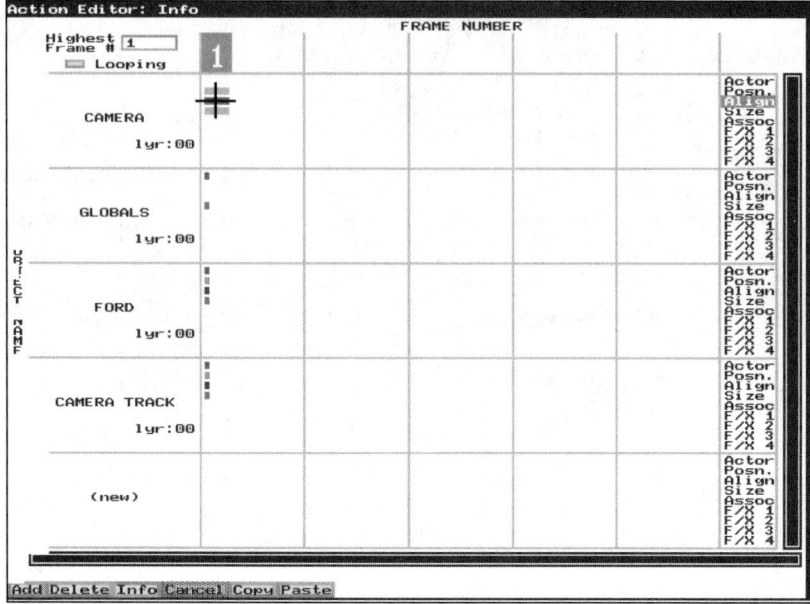

that are exported from Imagine to the VRML worlds, so one frame is all you'll need.

- Object editing options—Along the right side of the screen the editing options for each object are listed. For example, the Align option for the Camera object is currently selected (highlighted).

- Object color bars—When Imagine is used for animation, the individual frame can be given unique characteristics. The little colored bars beside the object's name are used to align the editing options at the right of the screen with a selected frame number. Clicking on a color bar brings up a dialog box where values are entered for the object option. If there is not a corresponding bar for an object option, either it has not been added, or has been deleted—thus you cannot get information about it. (See "Editing in the Action Editor," following.)

- Editing mode buttons—There are editing mode buttons along the bottom of the screen for switching the Action Editor between three editing modes—Add, Delete, and Info—plus buttons for canceling the current option, or copying one editing option from one frame and pasting it to another.

Editing in the Action Editor

The editor's three modes (Delete, Add, Info) are used for clearing a current editing option (Delete), defining a new set of values for the cleared option (Add), or redefining an existing option (Info).

Let's explore the editing process with an example.

OBJECT EDITORS: DETAIL, FORMS, STAGE, SPLINE

The object editors create and save 3D objects. They are very similar in their screen layouts. Figure 7-8 shows the screen for the Detail Editor.

The object editors have the following common features:

- Information line—This reports on program status, such as the current mode, active commands, and currently selected object.

- Menu bar—Clicking on the information line with the *right* mouse button changes it to the menu bar. The menus arranged along the menu bar contain most of the tools for constructing objects.

- View button toggle—Clicking on the bar along the left side of the window switches Imagine from four-view mode to single-view mode. For example, clicking on the Top view toggle causes the top view to fill the screen. Likewise, when one view fills the screen, clicking on the bar on the left side of the view will take you back to the four-view mode.

Figure 7-8
The Detail Editor's interface

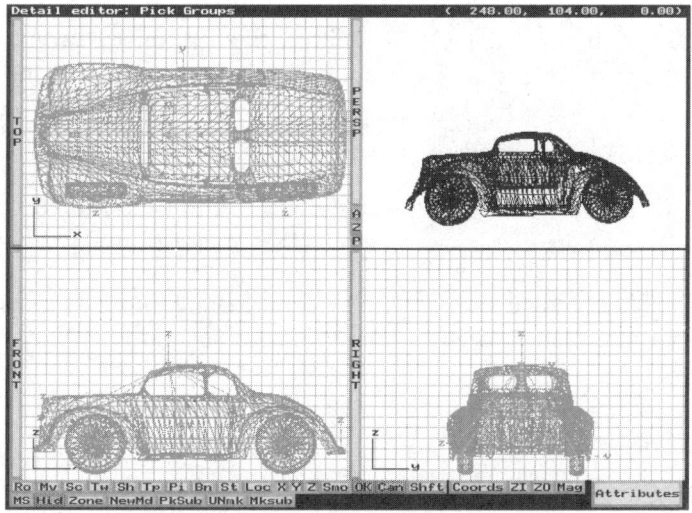

Camera controls—When the mouse pointer is placed in the 3D view and dragged, the view of the object is interactively changed. Selecting a camera control button (A, Z, P) changes the way the view of the object is affected by mouse buttons. *A* selects angle-of-view. *Z* selects zoom. *P* selects point-of-view. Changing the point-of-view is like moving a camera and changing its FOV (field of view) simultaneously.

Button bar—The buttons along the bottom of the screen provide a convenient alternative to accessing the same commands on the drop-down menus.

View windows—The 3D workspace where objects are edited is seen through four view windows. The 3D view allows the modeler to see the object in 3D perspective. The other three views (top, side, and front) are analogous to an architect's blueprints. They show a view of the model along the z, x, and y axes, respectively. Figure 7-9 shows the 3D model and its relationship to the three viewing planes.

Grid—Imagine's drawing grid appears in the top, front, and side views. It is used to precisely lay out shapes on the screen. The Grid Size option on the Display menu of the object editors allows the grid size to be changed to larger or smaller units. (A unit can represent any measurement—inches, miles, or nanometers.) In the Detail Editor, points can be restricted to intersections on the grid by selecting Lock on the Object menu's Pick Method submenu. In the Forms Editor, the Lock command is called Snap To Grid and is an option on the Object menu.

Coordinate display—By default, this option is turned off. When it is turned on, it shows the mouse pointer's position in the top, front, and side views. Three numbers appear in the top right corner of the screen (see Figure 7-10).

The three numbers represent the x, y, and z coordinates on the grid. The coordinate display is valuable when measuring objects on the screen.

This completes the overview of Imagine's interface. Next you will learn about many of the ways to manipulate objects in the object editors.

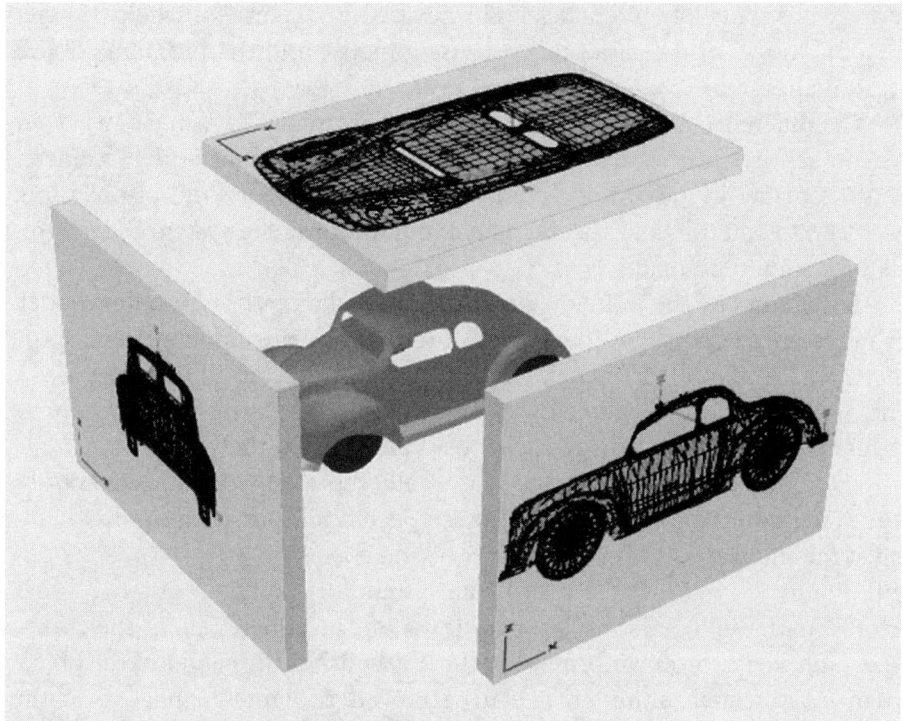

Figure 7-9 The three profiles of the Ford

NOTE: Forms and Spline Editors

The exercises in subsequent chapters (8 through 12) will not be using the Forms and Spline Editors. These editors have specialized uses for advanced users of Imagine.

IMAGINE'S OBJECT MANIPULATION TOOLS

A 3D model is usually created by putting together a number of parts. Think of building a car from a kit of parts. You can build your car using your hands

Figure 7-10
The mouse
pointer's
coordinates

(248.00, 104.00, 0.00)

and various tools like wrenches and screwdrivers. Likewise, when you create a 3D model of the same car, you use a mouse and the program's object manipulation tools.

The difference is this: When you make a car from a kit, you can use your eyes to see where the manipulations, such as attachment and placement, must be made. In a 3D modeling program, for the same kind of precision, you need to enter data to specify where in the coordinate system the manipulations should be made.

To manipulate the individual objects that make up the computer model, it's necessary to give them their own coordinate systems, independent of the coordinate system of the 3D workspace, sometimes referred to as the *world*. The world's coordinates remain fixed, while the object's internal coordinate system can be rotated, moved, or repositioned within the world.

Like other modelers, Imagine graphically represents the object's coordinate system on the screen. The object is selected for manipulation by pointing at the intersection of the object's x, y, and z axes (in other words, its origin). Figure 7-11 shows the coordinate system for a sphere.

In Figure 7-11, you are looking down on the sphere, along the z axis. By default, the coordinate system for the object lies at the center of the object when it is created, although it can be moved and rotated relative to the object. This will be discussed in the next chapter.

When an object is moved, scaled, or rotated, it is the object's coordinate system that is altered, not the world's.

Selecting Objects for Editing

A complex model can have many parts. Although Imagine allows you to point at and *pick* a single object for editing, often the object will be obscured by other parts. Sometimes it's necessary to *select* an object before you can *pick* it for manipulation.

Figure 7-11
A sphere's coordinate system

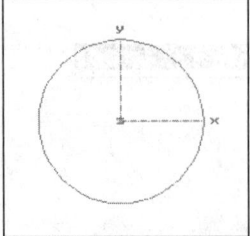

To summarize:

- Selected objects are ready for picking.

- Picked objects are ready for editing.

NOTE: To unpick an object or a group of objects, click anywhere on the screen.

Color Coding

Imagine helps you distinguish between selected and picked objects visually, through color coding. The following colors represent specific states of objects when Imagine's default screen colors are active.

- An object is black when it is unselected.

- An object is brown when it is selected and ready for picking.

- An object is purple when it has been selected and picked.

- An object is blue when it is unselected and has been picked.

Picking Objects with the Mouse

The Object menu's Pick Method submenu provides three options for picking an object with the mouse:

- Click F6   Click on the object's axes.

- Drag Box F8   Drag a box around the object or objects.

- Lasso F9   Drag the mouse around an irregular area.

NOTE: When you lasso or drag a box around several objects, only one of them will be picked. The object that was first created will be picked. See the next section for the method for selecting more than one object

Tip: Picking a Point in One View and Moving It in Another
The orthogonal views only allow a point to be moved along two of the three axes (up/down, right/left). In some cases a point that can only be seen in one view has to be moved in another. For example, a point in the middle of the top of a box may need to be moved up from the top of the box. To pick a point in one view and move it in another, take the following steps:

- Press SHIFT. Click on the point to pick it. Keeping SHIFT depressed, release the mouse button.

- Move the mouse pointer to another view. Press the mouse button and hold it.

▓ Release (SHIFT). Move the mouse pointer to move the picked point.

Selecting More Than One Object

Sometimes the same operation needs to be performed on more than one object. For example, the individual spokes of a wheel may need to be rotated as one. (SHIFT) is used in combination with any of the picking methods to form a temporary selection set.

▓ To select more than one object, press (SHIFT) while picking.

▓ To unselect objects, click anywhere on the screen.

🔩 **NOTE:** Dragging a box with (SHIFT) around vertices stacked on top of vertices selects all the vertices in the stack. To pick the vertices on top of the stack, use Click mode with the (SHIFT) multiselect option.

Grouping Objects

More permanent bonds between objects may be performed by grouping them with the Object menu's Group command. The members of the group can then be acted upon as a whole. Later they can be ungrouped by picking the group and selecting UnGroup from the Object menu.

To group objects:

1. Use (SHIFT) in combination with one of the picking methods to form the group of objects.

🔩 **NOTE:** The order in which objects are picked is important, since the first object in the group becomes the parent object for the group and will be used to select the group.

2. Select Group from the Object menu.
Result: Lines are drawn from the parent object's axes to the axes of all the other objects (see Figure 7-12).

Figure 7-12
Group formed
from objects

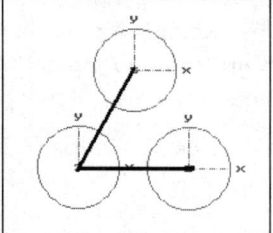

The group may now be selected by clicking on the parent object's axes.

NOTE: In Group mode, clicking on a child object picks that object for modification, not the group.

Pick Groups and Pick Objects Modes

Often you will want to give a group of objects common characteristics (such as a common color) while giving an individual object in the group its own unique attribute (such as its relative position to the group). Imagine can be switched from a mode where groups are picked (Pick Groups mode) to a mode where objects are picked (Pick Objects mode). This allows the parent object to be selected without selecting the entire group. The options are on the Mode menu.

Group Hierarchy

A hierarchical relationship may be formed among objects by making a set of objects a group, then making the group part of a larger group. In other words, a group can have child groups. This allows complex relationships to be formed among groups.

Selecting Objects by Name

Imagine keeps an internal list of the names of objects.
   To find an object by name:

1. Select the Find Requester on the Pick/Select menu.
   Result: The Object List appears.

2. Select the object from the list.
   Result: The selected object turns brown.

NOTE: When a new object is created, Imagine gives it a default name, such as CUBE02. It's good practice to immediately rename it, giving it a more descriptive name (such as GARAGE), so that it can easily be found again.

   To rename an object:

1. Pick the object and then select the Rename option on the Object menu.

Finding Objects by Name

If you know the object's name, you can select it by using the Find By Name Requester on the Pick/Select menu.

Other Options for Selecting and Picking Objects

These other options are on the Pick/Select menu:

- Pick All—This picks all the objects in the scene.

- Home—This selects the object at the top of the list.

- Select Next—This selects the next object on the list.

- Select Prev—This selects the previous object on the list.

- Pick Select—This picks the selected object.

- Unpick Select—This unpicks the selected object.

- Unpick Last—This unpicks the last object picked.

NOTE: Use F1 to pick a selected object. Use ALT-A (*right* ALT and the letter *A*) to pick all the objects in the scene.

Adjusting the View of the Object

The following tools alter the view of the object.

Zooming and Panning

Imagine allows you to move the view closer to or farther from the object in adjustable steps.

1. Click on the ZI button at the bottom of the screen to zoom in.

2. Click on the ZO button to zoom out.

3. Set the amount of zoom with the Set Zoom option on the Display menu.

Centering the View

To move the center of a view to a new location:

1. Select Re-Center on the Display menu.

2. Click in a view.

Panning the View

To pan the view up or down, or to the left or right:

1. Select a view.

2. Use the arrow keys to move the screen one half-screen in the direction of the arrow.

🔌 **NOTE:** The size of the scroll can be changed by altering the SCRL parameter in the Preferences Editor.

Redrawing the View

Imagine only redraws those objects that have changed in a view. Select Redraw on the Display menu to redraw the complete view.

SUMMARY: MODELING WITH IMAGINE

Imagine can be used not only to model VRML objects, but also to preview the look and feel of the final VRML world, using Imagine's built-in rendering capability. A typical VRML project proceeds along the following steps:

1. Open a project file in the Project Editor. This sets up directories on the hard drive for storing project files. Set the color depth and spatial resolution of the test renderings of the model.

2. Optionally set project preferences in the Preferences Editor, or load a preexisting set of preferences.

3. Enter the Detail Editor. Create objects using the Detail Editor's modeling tools. Assign surface attributes to objects by use of a special pop-up called the Attributes Requester. Save the model to the hard drive.

4. Enter the Stage Editor and import the model. Set the camera and light the model. Save the result.

5. Enter the Action Editor and adjust the lights and other scene attributes (such as the color of the background). Save the result.

6. Enter the Project Editor and render the model.

7. Enter the Detail Editor, load the model, and export it.

8
BASIC
MODELING
TOOLS

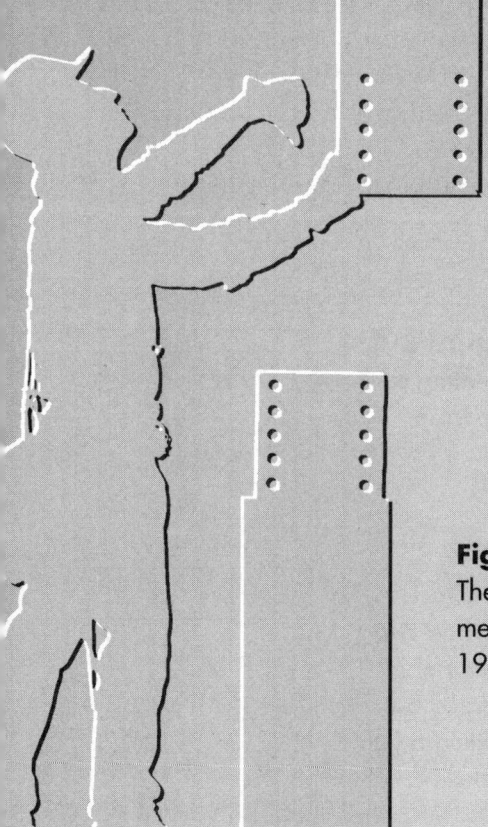

This chapter takes you into the 3D workshop and shows how to create basic objects with relatively simple tools. Even though you will build your objects in Impulse Imagine, you can apply the general principles illustrated here to most 3D modeling programs.

Let's begin by pulling together threads of ideas presented earlier.

POLYGONAL MODELING

The current VRML specification supports only polygonal models. In polygonal modeling, the object's *surface* is modeled. Figure 8-1 shows the surface geometry for a 1940 Ford model.

The surface of the car has been created as a connected series of polygons, a *polygonal mesh*. A polygon is composed of vertices (points), polylines (lines), and a face (see Figure 8-2).

Figure 8-1
The polygonal mesh for a 1940 Ford

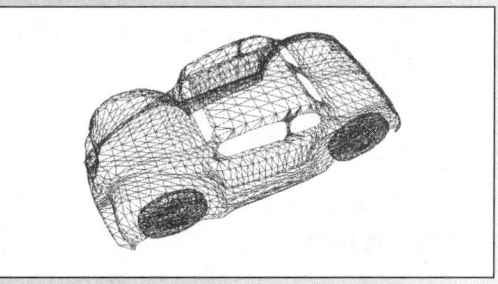

Figure 8-2
Parts of a
polygon

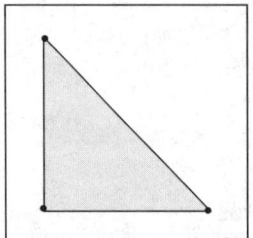

The face gives the model its surface characteristics, such as color, shading, and texture. When a polygonal object is rendered, only its face is rendered. The vertices and polylines are used in the construction of the model. For example, a triangular polygon is defined by three vertices and three polylines (see Figure 8-3).

A square may be created by adding a second triangular polygon to the first (see Figure 8-4).

When the polygons are joined, they share a side and two vertices, so the square has four vertices, instead of six (see Figure 8-5).

Adding a fifth vertex creates the geometry for an object that begins to resemble a house (see Figure 8-6).

Figure 8-3
Triangular
polygon

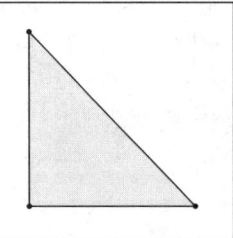

Figure 8-4
Creating a
square

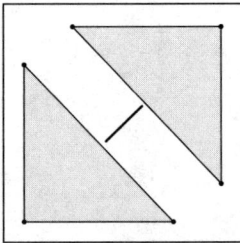

Figure 8-5
The polygonal
object

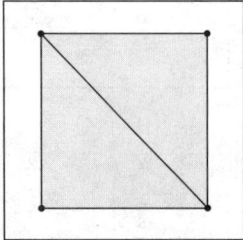

Figure 8-6
House object
created by
adding a fifth
vertex

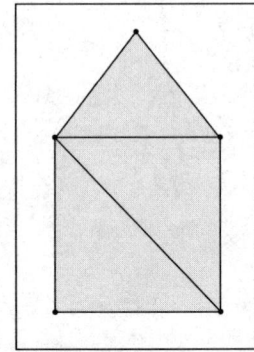

Constructing the geometry of objects from individual polygons creates very efficient models by using the fewest polygons necessary to achieve the shape.

Holes in polygonal objects can be created by deleting vertices inside a group of polygons (see Figure 8-7).

Deleting a vertex at the center of the object deletes the lines attached to it and the faces attached to the lines.

Once the basic shape is created, it can be manipulated by performing one of three types of transformations on the object or its vertices. For example, moving the vertices on the house shape creates a squat shape—or a shape that resembles an open envelope (see Figure 8-8).

You've just seen the two basic methods to polygonal modeling: changing an object's geometry and its shape. In Figures 8-5 and 8-6, where an extra polygon was added to create a house, the geometry of an object was changed. An object's geometry—its number of polygons and vertices—can be changed by adding and deleting vertices, lines, and faces. You can also change an object by changing its shape, like the preceding example (Figure 8-8), where moving an object's vertices turned a house into an envelope. When you change the shape of an object by rotating, scaling, and moving vertices, the basic geometry stays the same.

Now that you know how to create objects, let's see where they are created.

The World Coordinate System

This section recaps the description of coordinate systems from Chapter 6 and places it in a new context.

Figure 8-7
Creating a hole in a polygonal object by deleting a vertex

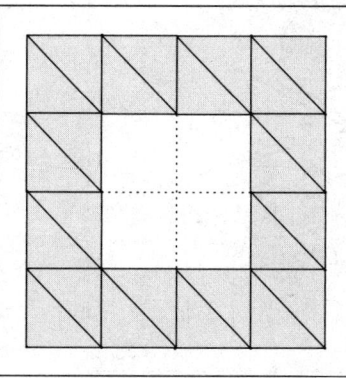

Figure 8-8
Moving the vertices of the house object

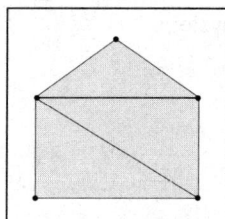

A two-dimensional triangular polygon has vertices that lie on a single plane. A three-dimensional pyramid composed of polygons has vertices located in three-dimensional space (see Figure 8-9).

The three-dimensional workspace in which the pyramid was created is called the *world coordinate system* (see Figure 8-10).

The point where the world's x, y, and z axes meet is called the *origin*. Objects that are added to the world are usually placed at the origin and then moved to a position within the world.

Most three-dimensional modeling programs provide a viewing system for the 3D workspace. There are generally three orthogonal view windows and a 3D window. The orthogonal views—which display a right-angle view of the top, side, and front—are used for constructing objects. The 3D window displays the object's *perspective,* or how the eye would see it.

Figure 8-9
Pyramid formed from four vertices

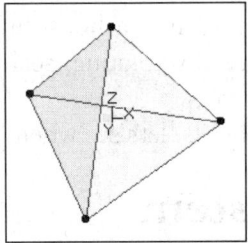

Figure 8-10
Objects in the world coordinate system

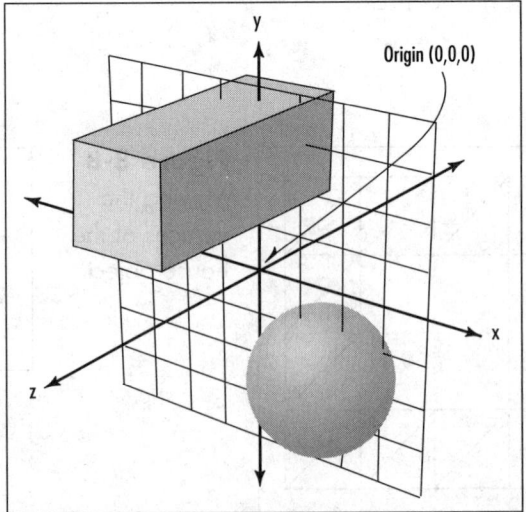

Object Coordinate System

When objects are first created, they are aligned to the world coordinate system. They can be moved from one position in the world coordinate system to another. They can also be rotated or scaled relative to the world coordinate system. However, objects have their own internal coordinate systems. This allows them to be rotated, scaled, or moved independently of the world coordinate system. The relationship of objects to worlds is analogous to a ball in a court. A ball can spin on its own axis, without reference to the world's axes. Or it can be made to move from one position to another *relative* to the court.

Polygon Count

The advantage of polygonal modeling is that the computer only needs to store relatively simple geometric objects. The basic shape of the car is stored as vertices (see Figure 8-11).

The system can load, display, and "connect the dots" between the points relatively quickly, compared with spline models. However, the disadvantage of polygonal modeling is the size of the data file, especially for objects with a lot of curves, like the Ford model. It has 4,607 polygons and 2,520 vertices (points). Since its curves must be represented with straight lines, many points and lines must be created to approximate its free-form shape. The polygon count of the car is high.

Geometric objects require far fewer polygons to represent, store, and display quickly. Objects that have large flat areas also produce relatively small data files. Figure 8-12 shows the polygonal mesh for a butterfly.

Unlike the Ford model, the butterfly model has large areas composed of flat polygons: its wings. Figure 8-13 shows a close-up view of the points and lines that make up one of the wings.

The wing is composed of 1,844 polygons and 1,040 vertices. Because polygons consume RAM and slow the screen refresh rate, the golden rule of

Figure 8-12
Butterfly mesh

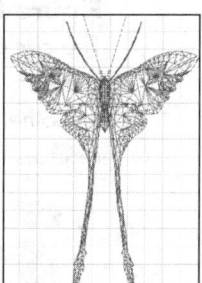

Figure 8-11
The Ford as a
cloud of points

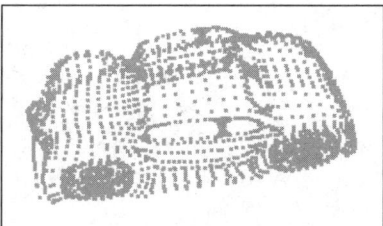

Figure 8-13
Close-up of part of the butterfly's wings, showing the lines and vertices

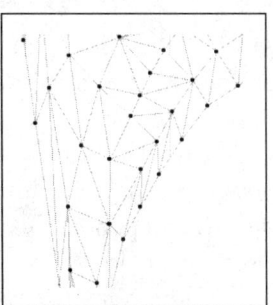

3D modeling is to create the object with as few polygons as possible. In VRML modeling, keeping down the polygon count is more than a rule; it's a law. On an average computer (a 486 or Pentium) connected to the Internet with a 28.8K baud modem, the maximum number of polygons that can be quickly processed is 10,000 polygons, and that figure drops to at least half if small images are used to texture the surface of the object. That means only two objects the size of the car can be loaded and displayed at a rate fast enough to create the illusion of motion. Three cars will slow screen refreshes to a crawl.

Until the average desktop computer is capable of displaying models with hundreds of thousands of shaded polygons per second, or until VRML supports NURBS models, the artist will have to pay strict attention to the polygon count of models. This is especially true of models that are seen at close range.

The VRML artist can take advantage of the fact that distant objects are seen at a much lower resolution than objects at close hand. For example, Figure 8-14 shows the same circle reduced at each size by 50 percent.

It's unnecessary to create a perfectly smooth circle that is really small, or distant. A circle seen in the distance can be created with a lot fewer polygons than the same circle seen at close range.

Figure 8-14
The circle seems to get smoother as it reduces in size

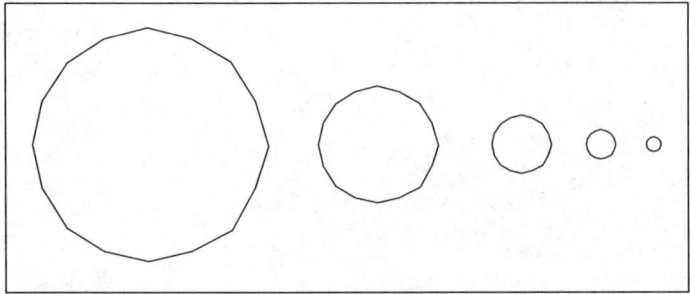

EXERCISE: BUTTERFLY WING

The butterfly wing has 304 vertices and 506 faces. In this section you'll see how to build the butterfly wing with fewer polygons. The butterfly wing could be used on a butterfly that appears at a distance from the viewer.

Figure 8-15 shows the butterfly wing laid out on the grid.

Let's draw the wing on the screen, using the grid as a guide. Install Imagine, if you have not already done so, following the installation instructions provided at the front of this book.

1. Run Imagine as instructed.

2. Since the butterfly wing will not be rendered at this time, go directly to the Detail Editor by choosing Detail Editor from the Project Editor. Result: The Detail Editor appears.

Now let's load the fully detailed butterfly wing into the Detail Editor and use it as a guideline in the creation of the low-detail butterfly wing:

1. From the Object menu, select Load.
Result: The Picture Filename dialog box appears.

Navigate to the \IMAG\OBJECTS subdirectory (the program looks in the \IMAG subdirectory by default).

2. Click on the white area of the dialog box scroll bar until the OBJECTS directory appears in the file list window.

3. Click on the OBJECTS directory.
Result: The file list window displays a list of objects in the directory.

Figure 8-15
Butterfly wing
on the grid

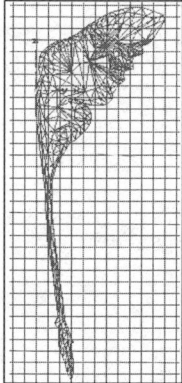

4. Either enter the file name *bflywing.obj* in the file field and press ⌈ENTER⌋, or click on the scroll bar until the file's name appears, and then select it by clicking once on the name. Select ⌈OK⌋.
Result: The butterfly wing loads into the Detail Editor.

▬ NOTE: Navigating the Directories

If you make a mistake, back out to the root directory by clicking on the Disks button on the Picture Filename dialog box, select the disk the Imagine program is located on (for example, C:\), select the \IMAG directory, and then select the OBJECTS subdirectory. Alternatively, in the dialog box's Drawer field, enter the path name \imag\objects (see Figure 8-16). The term "Drawer" is an Amiga term equivalent to the term "directory" on the MS-DOS platform.

The wing will be created in front view. Front view provides a construction plane. It's like working on the wing on a table. Let's use the view controls to get a close-up view of the wing:

1. Click on the Front button bar along the left side of the front view.
Result: The front view fills the screen.

2. On the Display menu, select Set Zoom.
Result: The Zoom Factor dialog box appears.

3. Enter *1.3* in the field.
Result: The wing is 1.3 times larger.

Now let's use the Re-center option to define a new center for the screen, moving the view to the left.

1. On the Display menu, select Re-center.

2. Click on an area to the right of the wing, halfway along its length.
Result: The screen should now look similar to Figure 8-17.

Figure 8-16
The Object
Filename
dialog box

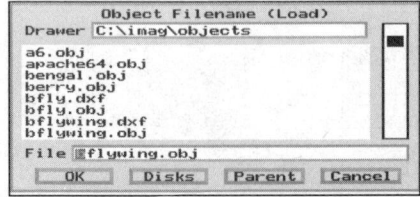

Figure 8-17
The project window adjusted and zoomed

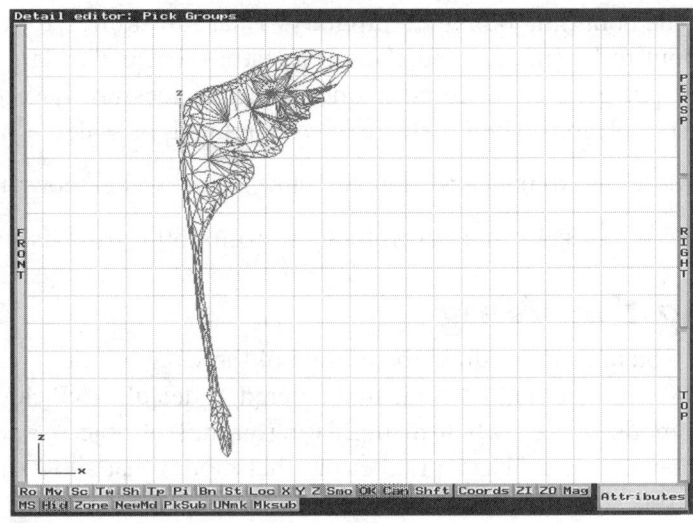

Adding the Axis for the Wing

Before a new object can be created by Imagine, it must be given an axis.

1. Create an axis:
From the Functions Add submenu, click on Axis.
Result: An axis is added at the center of the world coordinate system.

The axis is represented graphically on the screen by three lines at right angles to each other, connected by a dot. The yellow dot at the intersection of the axis is the origin. Because the view of the axes is along the y axis in the front view, the y axis is not visible.

The new wing will be created beside the detailed wing. Move the axis to a point to the right of the existing wing. The axis on the existing wing is located at the juncture between the wing and the butterfly body. This allows it to be rotated (flapped) relative to the body.

Put the new wing's axis at the equivalent position for the new wing:

1. Pick the new axis by clicking on the yellow dot or by pressing F1.

When Imagine added the axis to the Detail Editor, it automatically selected it. Picking the axis lets Imagine know that you want to perform an operation on the new object.

2. Press M or click on the MV button at the bottom of the screen to switch Imagine into move mode.
Result: A bounding box appears around the axis.

The bounding box is a temporary visual substitution for the object that is about to be transformed. This is a feature that makes large objects with many polygons easier to edit, since Imagine does not have to redraw the object's polygons when they are moved, rotated, or scaled.

3. Move the axis until it is positioned close to the location shown in Figure 8-18.

4. Press (SPACEBAR) to confirm the new position for the axis.

Drawing the Wing

Now you're ready to draw the outline of the wing on the screen.

When the Detail Editor is first entered, it defaults to Pick Groups mode. This mode is used when manipulating groups of objects or their selected members. Imagine has a number of other modes that allow the object to be edited at successively higher levels of detail. These modes appear on the Mode menu (see Figure 8-19).

The first five modes are used for selecting existing parts of objects. The next four modes are used to create selected parts of objects. The final two modes are used for editing existing parts of objects.

To create or edit an object's polylines and vertices, Imagine must be switched into a mode that allows them to be seen and edited (in the case of points).

To draw the outline of the wing, switch to Add Lines mode. Add Lines mode allows the addition of vertices and lines to the selected object (in this case, the axis) simultaneously.

1. Draw the wing:

Make sure the new axis is picked. If it is not, press (F1) or click on the dot at its center.

Figure 8-18
New position
for the axis

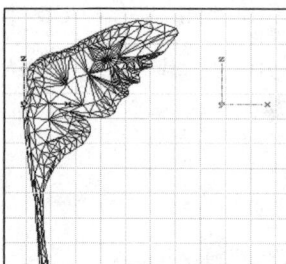

Figure 8-19
The Mode
menu

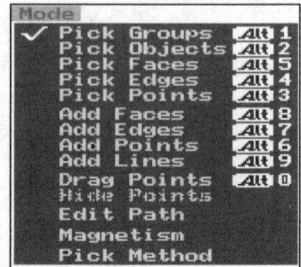

2. Select Add Lines from the Mode menu.
Result: The axis turns black, indicating it is picked.

Now, each click of the mouse will create a vertex. Lines are created between vertices. Later, faces will be attached to lines. Representing the curved shape of the wing with fewer lines will create a wing with a much lower polygon count than the detailed wing.

3. Draw the outline of the new wing on the screen. When you have drawn around the entire shape, click on the starting point to close the outline.

If you make a mistake, select Undo from the Project menu. This cancels the last operation. Don't worry about accuracy at this point. In the section that follows, you'll see how to edit the object. When you are finished, the outline should look roughly like Figure 8-20.

TIP: Redrawing the Screen
Sometimes, when you're switching between modes, the detailed butterfly wing will seem to disappear. That's because Imagine tries to keep the workspace uncluttered by only showing the current object being edited (the new wing). To restore the detailed wing to the screen, switch to Pick Groups mode, and select Redraw from the Display menu. Then select the new wing again, and enter Add Lines mode.

Saving the Model

This is a good time to save your work:

1. Switch to Pick Groups mode (Mode menu).

Figure 8-20
The finished outline of the wing

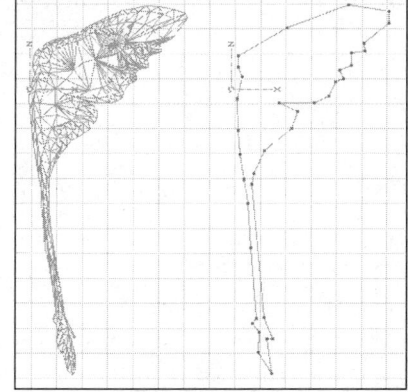

2. Select Pick All on the Pick/Select menu.

3. Select Group on the Object menu.

4. Select Save on the Object menu.

5. Save the file as *mywing.obj*.

Editing the Shape of the Wing

Object shapes can be refined by adding or deleting points from the outline, and by moving points.

Delete a point:

1. Select Pick Points from the Mode menu.

2. Click on the point to delete (see Figure 8-21, left).

3. Select Delete from the Object menu.
Result: The selected point is deleted, leaving a gap in the outline (see Figure 8-21, center).

Add a line:

4. Select Add Lines on the Mode menu.

5. Click on one end of the broken outline, and then click on the other end of the broken line.
Result: The gap is closed (Figure 8-21, right).

To increase the curve resolution, add a point between two points using Imagine's Fracture option:

1. Click on Pick Edges on the Mode menu.

2. Select the polyline between the two points by clicking on one of the points.

Figure 8-21
Deleting the point (left) creates a gap (center), and adding a line closes it (right)

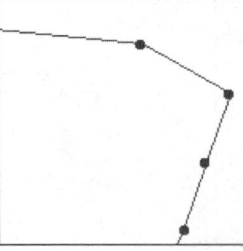 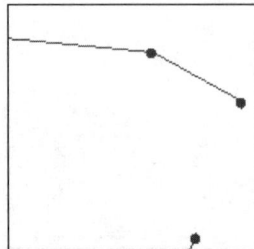 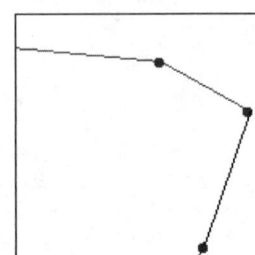

3. Select the Fracture option on the Functions menu.
Result: A new point is added between the two points.

Moving a point moves the associated lines attached to it:

1. Select Drag Points mode on the Mode menu.

2. Click on the point and move it.

To round out a curve composed of too few lines, use Fracture to add new vertices to the curve, and the Drag Points option to move the new points out to a rounder curve (see Figure 8-22).

Adding Faces to the Wing Outline

The new wing has been created out of lines. These lines will not render.

1. Check this by viewing it in Imagine's shaded mode:
Switch into Pick Objects mode by selecting it on the Mode menu.

2. Click on the PERSP (perspective) button at the right side of the screen.
Result: The view is switched to Imagine's 3D perspective view.

3. On the Display menu, select the Shaded view mode.
Result: The detailed wing is shaded, but the new wing does not appear (see Figure 8-23).

The Shaded option applies a flat gray color to the surface of the polygons and draws their edges in white.

To add polygons to the surface of the new wing, switch Imagine into Add Faces mode:

1. If the new wing is not picked, pick it.

2. Select Add Faces mode on the Mode menu.

Figure 8-22
Increasing the
resolution of
the curve

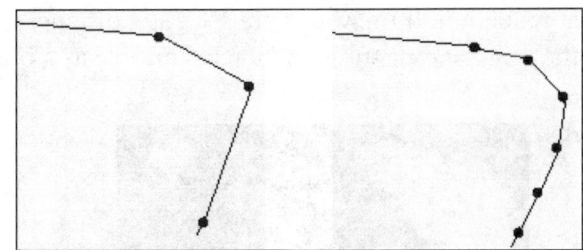

Figure 8-23
Viewing the
object in
shaded mode

Faces are added by clicking on the three defining vertices of a polygon:

3. Starting from the top of the new wing, click consecutively on the three points at the tip of the wing.
Result: As you click on each point, it turns reddish brown. After the third point is added, a line appears between two points on the wing.

Now check the perspective window to see if the face has been added to the wing (see Figure 8-24).

1. Switch back to the front view and continue adding faces.

2. Switch between front and PERSP views until the wing is complete.

3. Save mywings.obj now.

The wing has now been re-created (see Figure 8-25). The detailed wing has 304 vertices and 506 faces. The new wing has 48 vertices and 45 faces. The polygon count of the new wing is 11 times smaller than the original. This is a significant reduction. If the wings are seen at a distance, the new wing is cruder than the original, but still readily recognizable as a butterfly wing.

Figure 8-24
One face
of the new
butterfly wing

Figure 8-25
The original
and the new
wings

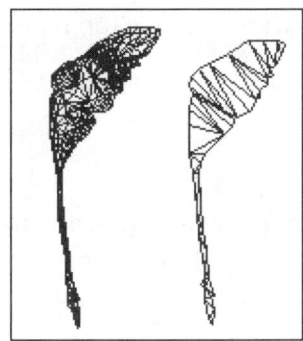

EXERCISE: MOVING AND ROTATING OBJECTS

Because the butterfly wing lies completely on a single plane, you did not need to manipulate it in three dimensions. In this section you'll see how to use Imagine's object manipulation tools to create a three-dimensional shape. In the following tutorial you'll learn how to manipulate objects both manually and with Imagine's Transformation Requester. The Transformation Requester allows objects to be moved, rotated, and scaled with precision, by use of the object and the world coordinate systems. Although you will create a cube, any type of object can be created by use of the methods illustrated.

To begin, delete the butterfly wings from the workspace, if necessary:

1. Switch to Pick Groups mode.

2. Select Pick All from the Pick/Select menu.

3. Select Delete from the Object menu.
Result: All the objects in the workspace are deleted.

Using the Grid to Create Precise Objects

First, the top of the cube will be created by aligning the sides of a square to Imagine's built-in grid system.

Begin by adding an axis to the world (all objects must have their own axes):

1. Select Axis from the Object menu's Add submenu.
Result: An axis is added at the center of the world coordinate system.

The top of a cube object will be created, so construction will occur in the top view, which looks down along the z axis.

2. Select full-screen Top view by clicking on the Top button along the left side of the top view window.

3. Press ⊑F1⊒ to pick the axis.

Now add the lines for the top:

4. Select Add Lines from the Mode menu, and roughly draw a square six grid units long and wide on the screen. Don't worry if it is crooked (see Figure 8-26).

Your rough square is a unit short along the left side.

Create a perfect square by using Lock. Lock causes object vertices to snap to the nearest grid intersection:

1. Select Lock on the Mode menu's Pick Method submenu.

2. Select Drag Points from the Mode menu.

3. Drag each of the four corners of the square close to the correct grid intersections.
Result: The points snap to the grid intersections, forming a perfect square (see Figure 8-27).

Now that the outline for the top of the cube has been created, add faces to the top:

1. Select Add Faces mode on the Mode menu, and add faces to the cube, using the method shown in the last exercise.

Check the result in the perspective window:

2. Select Pick Objects on the Mode menu.

3. Click on the PERSP button to make the perspective window active.

4. Select Shaded from the Display menu.
Result: The top of the cube appears shaded in the 3D perspective window.

Figure 8-26
Rough square

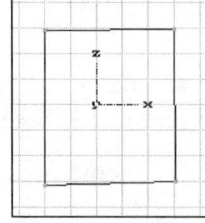

Figure 8-27
The perfect square

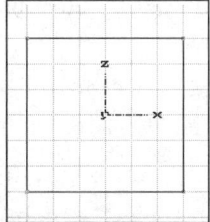

Using Copy and Paste to Add Sides to the Cube

In this part of the exercise, you'll use Imagine's Copy and Paste commands to duplicate the square you just created, and use it for the other parts of the cube. Make sure that you are still in Pick Objects mode and the square is picked. Also, make sure you are in full-screen top view.

1. Select Copy from the Object menu.

This saves the square to Imagine's hold buffer. Copy saves the selected object's current screen coordinates, so it will paste down exactly in the spot it was copied from. It also saves the object's surface characteristics, so the faces on the square will be preserved.

Let's leave the square in the copy buffer and use the square on the screen for one of the sides of the cube. It will be moved six grid units to the left, aligned so that the top and side of the cube are butted against each other, and then rotated. Figure 8-28 shows the first movement.

When an object is moved, it's really the object's axes that are moved. The axes control the position, orientation, and scale of the object geometry. In other words, moving the axes moves the object.

Figure 8-29 shows the top view and the axes of movement.

Notice the axes symbol at the bottom left of the view. In the top view, right and left movements are along the x axis. Up and down movements are along

Figure 8-28
Moving the square

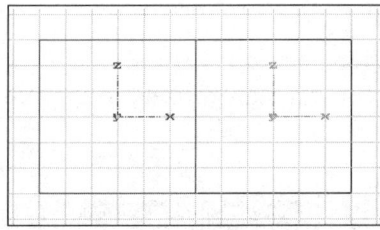

Figure 8-29
Moving objects in the top view

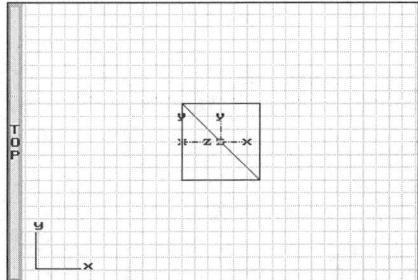

the y axis. The z axis is not represented, because you are looking straight down it toward the screen. Objects in the top, right, and side views cannot be moved toward you or away from you, only up and down, or to the right or left.

The object axes are relative to the world coordinate system. For example, when the axis for the square was added to the world, it was added at the world origin (0,0,0). The grid system is related to this world coordinate system. Each grid unit is equal to 20 units of the world coordinate system. The relative size of the grid can be changed by selecting Grid Size from the Display menu and entering a new value in the dialog box that appears.

The axes for the square will be moved six grid units along the x axis (see Figure 8-30). Since it is difficult to line up the object axes precisely by eye, Imagine allows you to turn on the world coordinate display at the top right of the screen so that you can check movements across the grid in Imagine units.

Turn on the coordinate display by clicking on the COORDS button at the bottom of the screen, and watch the top right of the screen as you move the mouse around (see Figure 8-30).

Now move the square to the left on the screen:

1. Press Ⓜ or click on the MV button at the bottom of the screen.

2. Drag the square to the left. Watch the COORDS display. Try to move the object until it is in the same position as shown in Figure 8-31. You do not have to put the object down in the exact position shown. Press ⌷SPACEBAR⌷.

Now paste down the square saved to the copy buffer earlier:

1. Select Paste from the Object menu.
Result: The copied square is placed precisely in the position just vacated (see Figure 8-31).

Figure 8-30
The coordinate
display system

`(  -122.00,    -2.00,     0.00 )`

Figure 8-31
The two copies
of the top

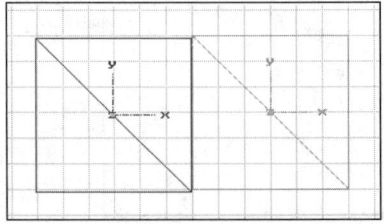

Using the Transformation Requester for Precise Alignment

The left square is misaligned with the right square, but you can align it properly using Imagine's Transformation Requester.

Align the square with the Transformation Requester:

1. Select the new side by clicking on the center of its axes.

2. Select Transformation on the Object menu.
Result: The Transformation Requester appears (see Figure 8-32).

The Transformation Requester provides a method for displaying and altering the position, orientation, and scale of objects relative to the world coordinate system. Like the coordinates display system, the Transformation Requester uses Imagine units.

1. Click on the Position option in the Transformation Requester.
Result: The object's current position in the world is displayed in the X, Y, Z data fields (see Figure 8-33).

Notice that when the Position option was clicked, the Local option beside it became grayed out. The Position option is used to display and alter the object's axes relative to the world coordinate system.

Figure 8-32
The Transformation Requester

Figure 8-33
The Transformation Requester

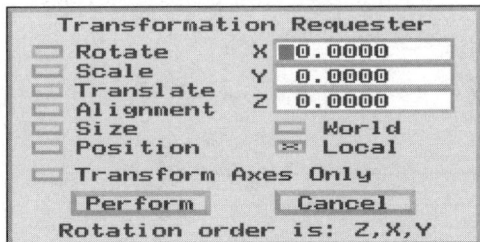

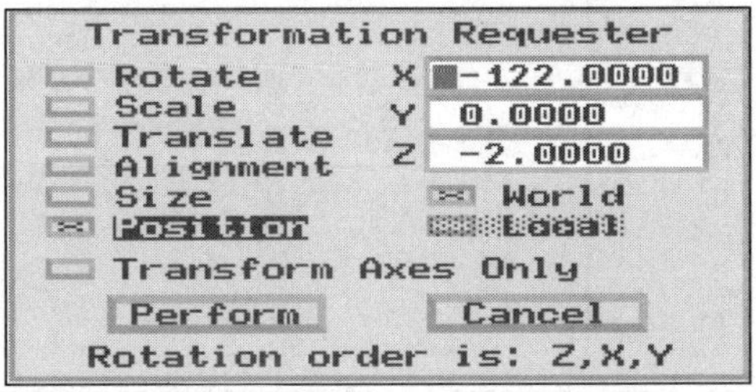

Note that in the case of the square you moved, the position of the object's axes on the x axis is -122 (122 Imagine units in the negative direction from the origin), and its position on the z axis is -2 (2 Imagine units in the negative direction from the origin). This corresponds to the numbers displayed at the top of the screen with the coordinate system turned on.

Now move the object's axes to coincide with the grid intersections:

1. Enter *-120* in the X field and press ENTER.

2. Enter *0* in the Z field and press ENTER.

Remember to press ENTER after entering values into data fields. If you don't, the transformation will not be performed.

3. Click the Perform button.

Result: The object's axes move, aligning the cube's side and top (Figure 8-34).

Rotating the Side

At this point the side and top lie on the same plane, butted up against each other. The axes for the left square lie at the middle of it, so if you rotate them, the square's edge will not match up with the top's edge. You will get a T object, where the T is on its side and the stem and top are not connected (see Figure 8-35). This happens because rotation occurs around an object's axis.

Figure 8-34
The sides now match

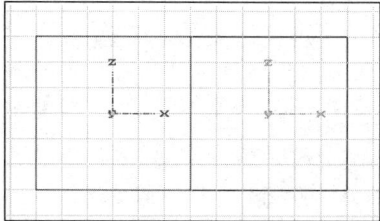

Figure 8-35
Rotating the object at its center

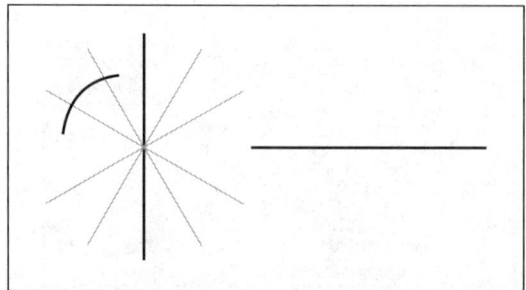

This can be corrected by moving the axes. If you move the axes of the left cube to the right edge of the cube, and then rotate them, you will get an L shape (see Figure 8-36).

Move the axes relative to the object's outer edge:

1. Make sure the left square is picked.

2. Press ⎡SHIFT⎤-⎡M⎤.

3. Move the axes to the side of the square (see Figure 8-37).

Once again let's use the Transformation Requester to adjust the position of the axes:

1. Select Transformation from the Object menu.

2. Click on the Position option to view the current position of the axes.

3. Click on the Transform Axes Only option.

The Transform Axes Only option is used to limit the object's movement to its axes.

4. Enter the values shown in Figure 8-38 in the X, Y, Z fields. Remember to press ⎡ENTER⎤ after changing data field information.

Figure 8-36
Moving the rotation point to the end of the object

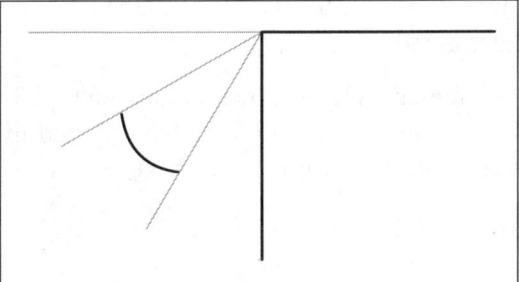

Figure 8-37
Moving the axes

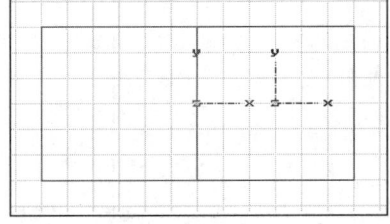

Figure 8-38
Checking the
axes position

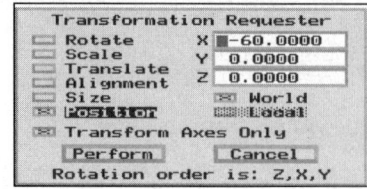

5. Click on Perform.

Result: The axes move 60 Imagine units (3 grid units) to the right. They shift to a precise position along the edge of the side.

Now that the rotation point for the side has been shifted to the edge shared with the top, you can rotate the side:

1. Call the Transformation Requester again.

2. Click on the Rotate option.

3. Enter *-90* in the Y field of the Requester and press ⌈ENTER⌋.

The -90 value will cause the side to rotate down below the top.

4. Click on Perform.

Result: The side rotates down.

Check the cube by returning to four-view display mode:

5. Click on the button along the left side of the view, and look at the front view (see Figure 8-39).

Notice that the side has rotated down below the top. The side is actually sitting below the z plane. If the side had been rotated in the other direction, what has been called the "top" would have become the bottom of the cube.

Figure 8-39
The front view

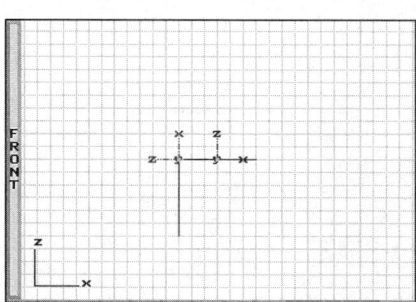

You can also view the cube in the perspective window:

1. Click on the PERSP button alongside the perspective window.

2. Select Shaded from the display window.

3. Click on the A (angle) button, and drag the mouse around to view the cube.
Result: The cube is shown in perspective.

For practice, add another side to the cube using the methods shown in the last exercise, (see Figure 8-40). You may want to try moving and rotating the square without moving the object axis. It's difficult to learn the knack of manipulating three-dimensional objects using the mouse and 3D modeling display and control systems. However, like any skill, if you practice it long enough, you'll soon learn to perform operations on objects without thinking about it. See the next section for additional information about Imagine's Transformation Requester.

OTHER FEATURES OF THE TRANSFORMATION REQUESTER

The Transformation Requester is one of Imagine's most valuable tools. You will find it available in several editors, as well as an option in other dialog boxes. Although manipulating objects is easier by use of interactive controls, the Transformation Requester provides precision and predictability. For example, when building an airplane propeller, you can create a single blade and then use the Transformation Requester in conjunction with the Copy and Paste commands to rotate copies of the blade into precise locations around the propeller's shaft. This makes learning the Transformation Requester well worth the initial effort. Figure 8-41 shows a breakdown of its features.

Figure 8-40
The two sides
of the cube

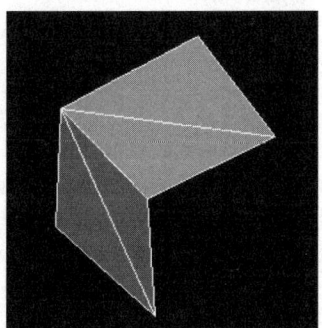

Figure 8-41
Transformation
Requester
features

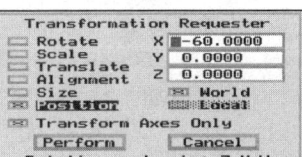

195

When objects are created, they are created at the center of the world, aligned to the world axes. This means that the x, y, and z values displayed in the data boxes are 0.

Rotate, Scale, and Translate Options

The first three options (Rotate, Scale, and Translate) allow you to change the object's orientation in space, its size, and its position relative to either the world coordinate system, or relative to its own object coordinates. To select a change relative to the world coordinate system, click on the World option. To select a change relative to the object's coordinate system, click on the Local option. For example, selecting Translate (move) and Local (object axes) moves the object along the path of its own axis. This is similar to choosing the Loc button at the bottom of the Detail Editor screen when you move objects interactively.

TIP: Mirroring Objects
Often it's useful to mirror an object. For example, you can create a duplicate copy of a butterfly's wing and then mirror it to create the opposite wing. To do this, select the Scale option and enter a negative value for one of its axes. For example, -1 entered in the X field creates a mirror image of the object along the x axis.

Alignment Option

The Alignment option allows you to move the object relative to its current orientation in the world. For example, entering *30* in the X field makes it 30 percent wider. Notice that the World option grays out when Alignment is chosen.

Size Option

The Size option allows you to change the size of an object relative to its current size. For example, entering 2 in the Size field makes the object twice as big. Notice that the World option grays out.

Transform Axes Only

Changes are always made to the object's axes. When an object is scaled up, its axes are scaled up. The axes can also be moved, scaled, or rotated independently of the object. This is useful when you want to change the geometry of the object without changing the relationship of the axes to another object, or to the world coordinate system.

This completes the brief overview of the Transformation Requester. You'll find that this is one of the most-used features of Imagine for gaining precise control over the position, orientation, and size of objects.

The last part of this chapter will look at tools that are commonly used to create complex objects out of simpler parts.

JOIN: COMBINING OBJECTS INTO SINGLE OBJECTS

Models are created out of parts, like a model airplane out of a box of plastic pieces. Although the parts can be glued together with the Object menu's Group command, the bond formed is temporary and can be broken with the Ungroup command. Sometimes it will be useful to permanently weld parts into a single object that will be easier to modify or store. The Object menu's Join option is used to do this. When two or more objects are joined, their axes are merged into one set of axes. The new axes control all the geometry of the new object (see Figure 8-42).

To join two objects:

1. Ungroup the objects if they are currently grouped.

2. Select the objects that are to be joined (using Pick All, or selecting them individually while pressing [SHIFT]).

3. Select Join from the Object menu.
Result: The two objects become one.

Figure 8-42
Two axes combined into one

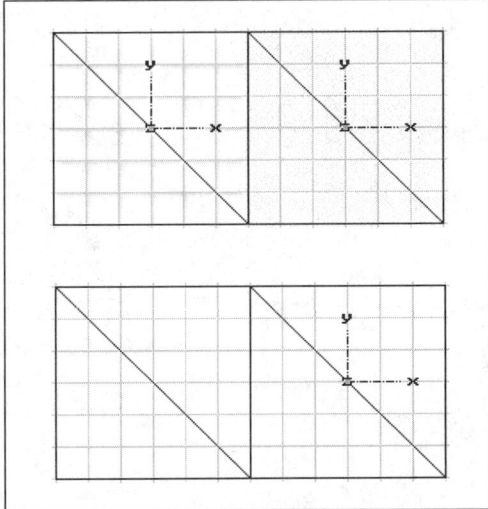

SPLIT: CARVING AN OBJECT INTO PIECES

Another useful tool is the opposite of Join. Split creates two objects out of one. Think of it as digital scissors. For example, a broken eggshell can be created from a sphere with Split.

The Split command acts on the level of vertices. To use it:

1. Switch to Pick Points mode.

2. Select the points for splitting (using SHIFT or one of the Pick/Select tools).

3. Select Split on the Object menu.

An object with new axes is created. The new axes are created on top of the old axes. Use SHIFT-M to move the axes of the new object onto the object.

In this chapter you've seen the saw, hammer, and nails of the 3D workshop. The next chapter introduces you to the power tools.

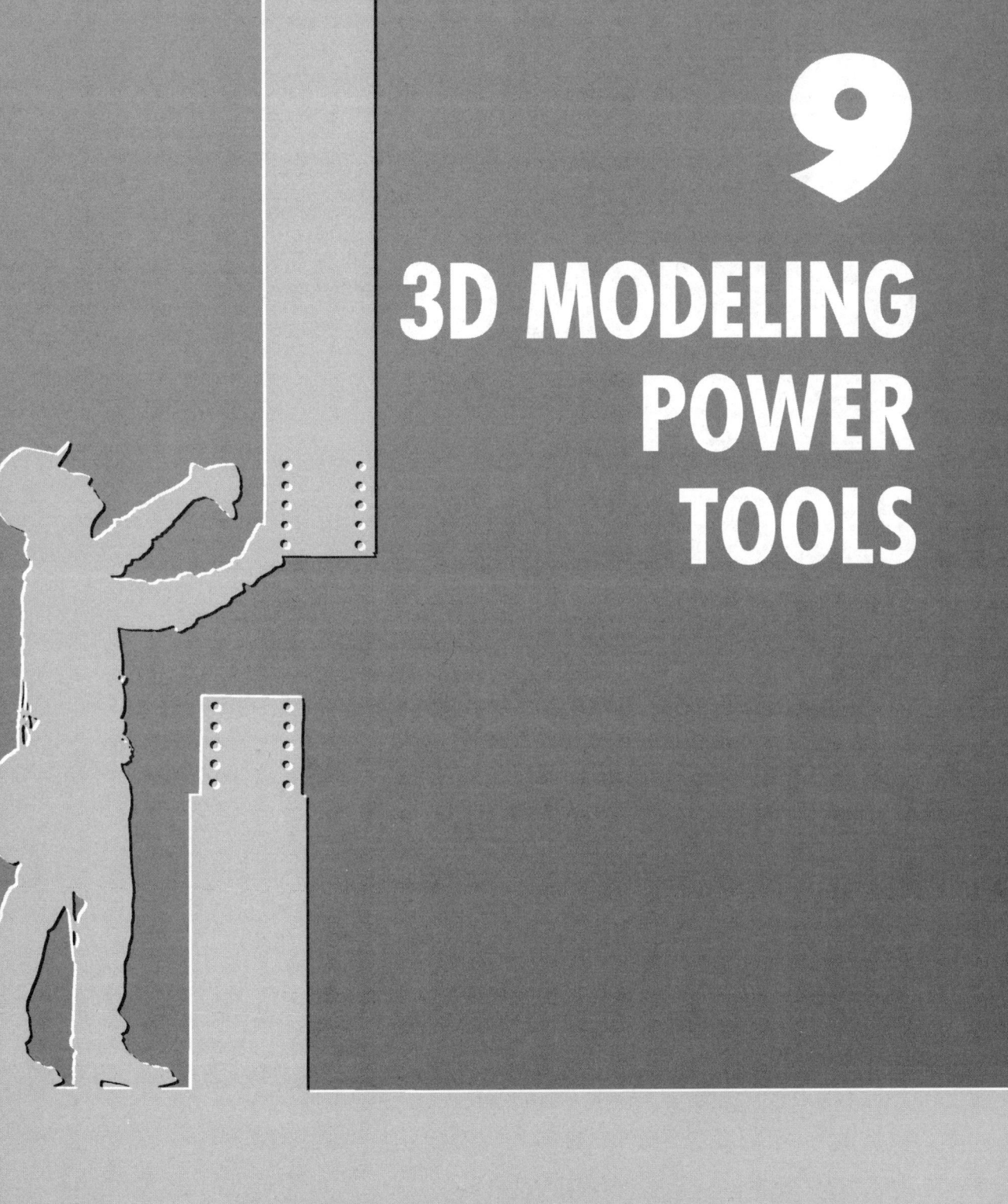

9

3D MODELING POWER TOOLS

The last chapter showed how 3D objects can be built from polygons. Creating objects out of polygons is very powerful because of the absolute control over the polygon count of the model. This is important for the VRML modeler who must "spend like Santa Claus, but save like Scrooge" when detailing a world.

The disadvantage of building models piece-by-piece out of polygons is the time it takes. Creating 10,000 polygons by hand is like building a house out of trees using a hammer and saw. Fortunately, 3D modeling software has power tools that automate the process of generating objects with tens, hundreds, even thousands of polygons. This chapter introduces you to them.

METHODS FOR AUTOMATING OBJECT CREATION

There is rarely only one correct method for creating three-dimensional objects. The trick for the 3D artist is to be able to create a great model the most efficient way with the fewest polygons. There are hundreds of tools available to do the job. The challenge is to use the right combination of tools. Here are the main categories of tools:

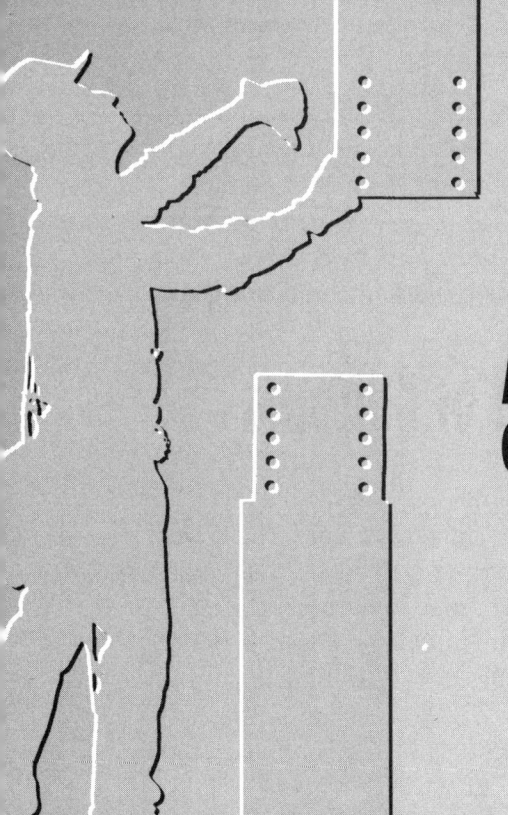

■ Primitives—3D modeling programs provide ready-made basic shapes like cones, spheres, and boxes. These can be combined and edited to create more complex shapes. Think of this as the Tinkertoy approach.

VRML Extrusion—The program generates a three-dimensional object out of a user-specified 2D outline. The 2D outline defines the profile of the final shape. For example, a wine glass is created by rotating an outline of its profile in 3D space. The analogy is to the process of plastic extrusion, where an object is created by injecting plastic into a mold.

VRML Skinning—This is a form of extrusion. Instead of projecting the shape of the object along a path, the 3D program draws a surface of polygons over user-defined shapes. For example, the modeler creates the rings on a barrel, then skins a surface over the rings.

VRML Deformation—This uses a variety of tools to deform an existing object (for example, transforming a sphere into a rock).

In the case of modelers creating objects for output to film or multimedia, there is another method for creating objects, called *procedural modeling.* The program uses mathematical models for generating objects. For example, a tree is created using fractal mathematics. Since the VRML specification does not support procedural modeling, this method won't be covered.

The balance of this chapter will explore some of these methods for generating objects using Imagine.

PRIMITIVES: CREATING OBJECTS OUT OF BUILDING BLOCKS

If you ever played with Lego building blocks or Tinkertoys when you were a kid, then you know fairly complex shapes can be created from simpler shapes. A head can be formed from a sphere; the arms, from tubes; the feet, from a box. In fact, most of the objects in the world can be reduced to basic geometric shapes: cones, spheres, tubes, and cubes. Most 3D modeling programs supply these basic three-dimensional forms, called *primitives,* that act as building blocks for more complex objects. By use of the vertex editing tools, along with such specialized tools as Split (cut an object in two) or Join (merge two objects), complex objects can be created by sculpting simple shapes and merging them.

Imagine's Primitives

Imagine's building blocks are called from the Object menu's Add submenu (see Figure 9-1).

Selecting Primitive calls a dialog box with a list of shapes: sphere, tube, cone, torus (donut-shape), disk, and plane (see Figure 9-2).

Imagine creates and places the primitives at the center of the world (see Figure 9-3).

When a primitive is chosen from Imagine's list, a parameters dialog box appears. Such factors as the size and complexity of the object can be specified

Figure 9-1
Calling the Primitive Types dialog box

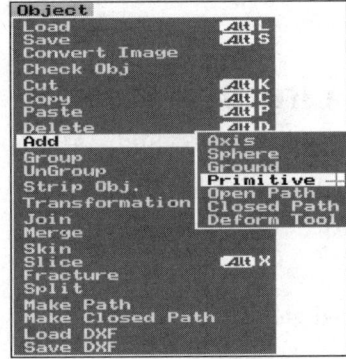

Figure 9-2
Primitive Types dialog box

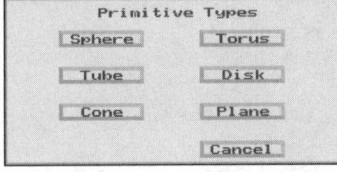

Figure 9-3
Imagine's primitives

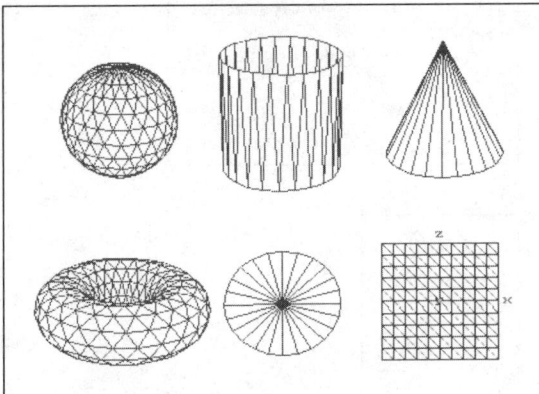

there. For example, selecting the Disk primitive calls the dialog box shown in Figure 9-4.

The radius of the disk is set in Imagine units (50 units by default). The Sections parameter (24 by default) sets how many polygons will be used to create the circle. The Sections parameter specifies how smooth the circle will be. For example, specifying 6 sections instead of 24 (the default) produces a polygonal shape rather than a circle (see Figure 9-5).

The disk and plane are especially useful in creating profiles for skinning (discussed later in the chapter) or for extruding objects, a subject covered in the next section. For example, deleting the center vertex of the disk creates an outline circle that can be extruded along a path, producing piping for a building.

Exercise: Creating an Unfilled Circle

Create an unfilled circle, used for extruding cylindrical shapes:

1. In the Detail Editor, Select Add|Primitives from the Object menu.
Result: The Primitive Types dialog box appears.

2. Select Disk.
Result: The Disk Parameters dialog box appears.

3. Enter 6 for the number of Sections, and leave the Radius at 50 (the default).
Result: The polygonal shape is created.

4. Press F1 to pick the disk.

Figure 9-4
The Disk Parameters dialog box

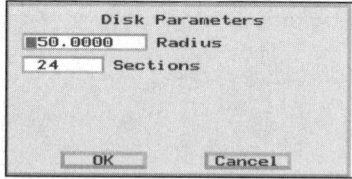

Figure 9-5
Polygon with six sides

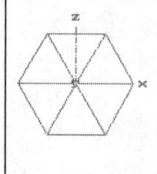

5. Select Pick Points from the Mode menu.

6. Select the vertex at the center of the disk (see Figure 9-6).

7. Delete the vertex (by selecting Object|Delete or ALT-D).
Result: The polygons attached to the vertex are deleted, leaving an outline object (see Figure 9-7).

EXTRUSION: PROJECTING SHAPES ALONG A PATH

Extrusion is one of the most basic methods for deriving a three-dimensional object from two-dimensional information. *Extrusion* projects an object along a path. The object can be a 2D outline (such as the polygon created in the last exercise), a shape drafted on the screen with Imagine's drawing tools, a shape created in Imagine's Spline Editor, or a 3D object—in fact, any Imagine object. For example, a box can be created from a filled or unfilled square by use of extrusion (see Figure 9-8).

Figure 9-6
The disk

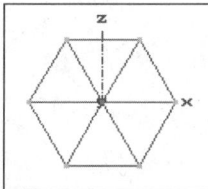

Figure 9-7
The outline shape

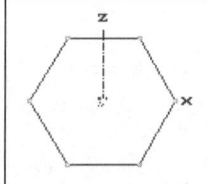

Figure 9-8
Extruding a square into a box

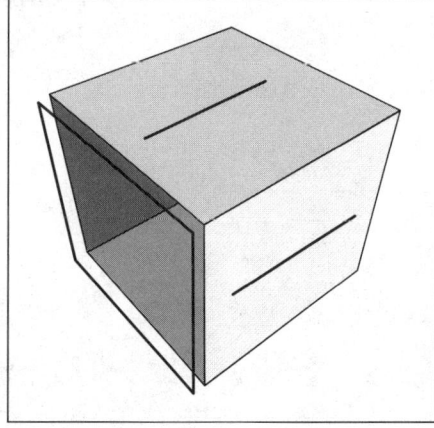

A filled square creates a front and back to the box. An unfilled square creates a box with no front and back.

Exercise: Extruding a Roof

A roof is a good candidate for extrusion because it has a simple profile: two lines attached at an angle to each other. Let's draw this shape on the screen and then extrude it:

1. Enter Imagine's Detail Editor.

Imagine extrudes objects only along the y axis. Since the y axis runs from the front to the back of Imagine's 3D space, the profile for the extrusion is created in the front view.

2. Make the front view full screen by clicking on the Front button along its left side.

3. Add an axis to the screen by selecting Add|Axis from the Object menu.

4. Using the methods learned in the last chapter, draw a triangle on the screen. When you are finished, it should resemble Figure 9-9.

5. Change back to Pick Objects mode (Mode menu).

6. Pick the triangle.

7. Select Mold from the Functions menu.
Result: A Mold Requester appears (see Figure 9-10).

Figure 9-9
Open triangle

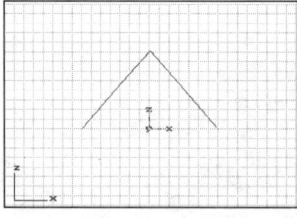

Figure 9-10
The Mold
Requester

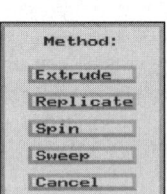

Figure 9-11
The Extrude
Data dialog
box

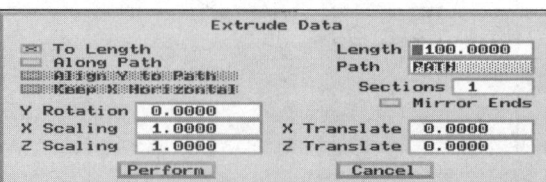

8. Select Extrude.
Result: The Extrude Data dialog box appears (see Figure 9-11).

The Extrude Data dialog box provides control over the length, complexity, and shape of the extrusion. For readers interested in experimenting with extrusions, the next section will explain what all the options in the dialog box provide. For now, the two relevant options are the length of the extrusion, and how many sections the roof will have. Since the goal of VRML modeling is to create as few polygons as possible, let's leave the Sections value at 1. This will create a roof with only one set of polygons stretched across its length. Entering a value of 2 doubles the number of polygons. Since the roof is linear, you need only one section of polygons.

By default the grid is set at 20 Imagine units per grid unit. Imagine dialog boxes use Imagine units, so assigning a value of 500 Imagine units to the length creates a roof 25 grid units long (20 x 25 = 500).

1. Enter *500* in the Length box and press [ENTER]. Then click on Perform.
Result: The roof is created.

2. Select Shaded from the Display menu, and make the perspective window full screen.
Result: A view of the shaded roof is displayed (see Figure 9-12).

Notice that Imagine created two polygons on each side of the roof. This is very efficient!

The essence of 3D modeling is seeing the basic geometry that makes up the objects you want to model. For example, a tent can also be conceived as a triangular shape. Instead of extruding an open triangle, extrude a closed triangle (see Figure 9-13).

Then add faces to the triangle, using the Add Faces option on the Mode menu. (Follow the methods discussed in Chapter 8.)

When the triangle is extruded, a solid triangular tent shape is created (see Figure 9-14).

Figure 9-12
The shaded
roof

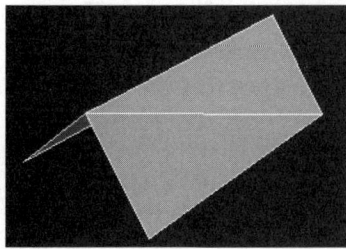

Figure 9-13
A closed
triangle

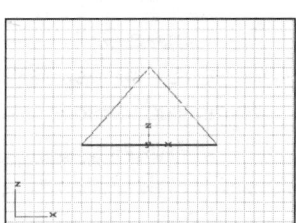

Figure 9-14
Tent shape

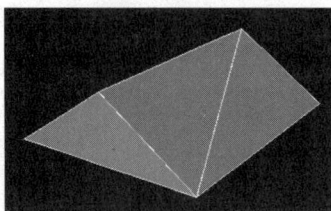

Figure 9-15
Hollow tent

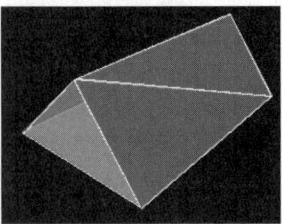

If the faces are not added to the triangle shape, then extrusion creates a hollow shape, open at both ends (see Figure 9-15).

By use of Imagine's vertex editing tools, such as Drag Point, the basic shape of the object can be elaborated into more complex shapes. For example, a window can be created at one end of the solid tent by deleting a group of faces.

The Extrude Data Dialog Box

The Extrude Data dialog box (see Figure 9-16) is an indispensable tool for creating a wide variety of shapes. Here's information on its options.

By default, Imagine extrudes shapes along a straight path between the front and back of the 3D workspace (see Figure 9-17).

The options in the Extrude Data dialog box allow you to create more complex shapes than provided by straight extrusions. The options break down to two basic activities. You can determine the *shape* of the extrusion path and how the shape *transforms* as it passes along the path.

Figure 9-16
Extrude Data
dialog box

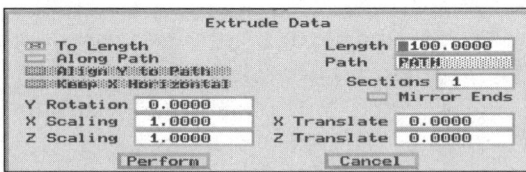

Figure 9-17
Circle shape
extruded along
a straight path

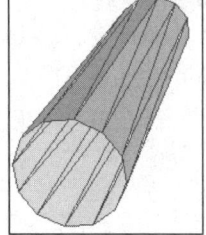

Path Shape

You can also make the object follow along a path.

▪ To Length—The shape will travel in a straight line to a length specified in the Length box. Use this setting in combination with the Path Transformations settings to rotate, scale, or offset (translate) the path. For example, rotating the cylinder around a path produces the shape in Figure 9-18.

▪ Along Path—This setting specifies a path for the extrusion. For example, a garden hose uses a twisting line as a path (see Figure 9-19).

The circle is placed at right angles to the path. When it is extruded, it follows the path (see Figure 9-20). See the exercise that follows for an example that uses this option.

▪ Align Y To Path—This option is activated when Along Path is selected. Choosing this option keeps the extruded shape's y axis parallel to the path as it travels along it. Imagine a car following a road as the road goes over hills and valleys. The car remains parallel to the road.

▪ Align Z To Path—This option is activated when Along Path is selected. This makes the shape travel "upright" relative to the path. That is, the shape follows the path as it curves and twists, but the object remains aligned to its own z axis. When you travel as a passenger in a car, you have this relative orientation to the road.

Figure 9-18
Path rotated 90
degrees

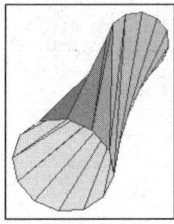

Figure 9-19
Path and disk

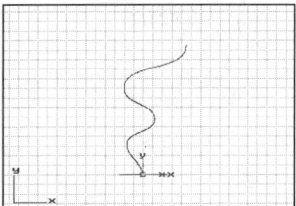

Figure 9-20
Disk extruded
along path

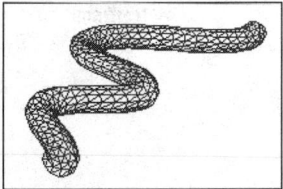

Shape Transformations

The following options transform the shape of the object as it travels down the path. Basically, you can rotate, scale, or move the shape in increments as it travels along the path.

- Mirror Ends—By default, the shape arrives at the end of the path in the same orientation as the beginning position. This option flips the shape 180 degrees at the end of the path.

- Y Rotation—The shape rotates the specified amount along its y axis as it follows the path. In Figure 9-21 the shape has been rotated 180 degrees.

- X Scaling—The object increases or decreases in size along its x axis as it travels the length of the path. In Figure 9-22 the shape is scaled down to 0.01. Notice that the cylinder looks squashed at one end.

- Z Scaling—The object increases or decreases in size along its z axis as it travels the length of the path. This is the axis at right angles to the x axis. Specifying the same X Scaling and Z Scaling values expands the shape equally from one end to the other end. In Figure 9-23 the object has been scaled by a factor of 2 along its x and z axes.

- X Translate—This moves the center of the shape along the positive or negative direction of the x axis as the object travels along the path. In Figure 9-24, the object has been translated 120 Imagine units along its x axis.

Figure 9-21
Rotation

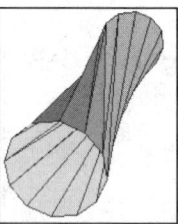

Figure 9-22
Shape
produced by
x scaling

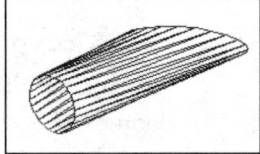

Figure 9-23
Scaling equally
along both
axes

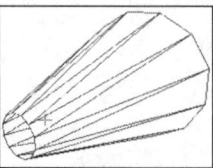

Figure 9-24
X translation

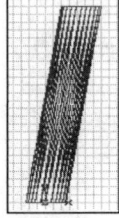

Z Translate—This moves the shape along the z axis. Specifying values for both Z Translate and X Translate moves the center to a point between the z and x axes.

Exercise: Extruding along a Path

In this exercise you'll create a path, then extrude a disk along it. The object will grow progressively smaller as it travels along the path. This produces a long, winding tube that comes to a point. This is how a lizard's tail might be created.

Creating the Cross-Section of the Tail

Create a simple circle for the cross-section of the tail:

1. Using the steps outlined earlier in the chapter ("Exercise: Creating an Unfilled Circle"), add a disk to the workspace and delete its center vertex. Use the default number of sections for the disk. This will create a tail with a lot of polygons. Using more polygons will allow you to make the surface of the tail more irregular, creating a more realistic lizard tail.

Use Drag Points to make the tail slightly irregular in shape:

2. Pick the tail if it is not already selected, and choose Drag Points mode on the Mode menu.

3. Click on a point on the perimeter of the circle to pick it.

4. Press M.

5. Drag the point slightly. Press SPACEBAR.

6. Continue making the points around the perimeter of the disk irregular until your shape looks roughly like Figure 9-25.

Creating the Path for the Tail

Create the path of the tail as seen from above:

Figure 9-25
Irregular shape
of the tail
cross-section

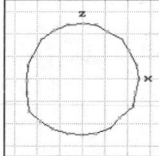

1. Switch back to Pick Objects mode on the Mode menu.

2. Switch to Top view.

A path is created in Imagine by laying down a series of axes, and then choosing the Make Path option on the Object menu.

3. Select Axis from the Object Add menu.
Result: An axis is added at the center of the world, on top of the cylinder.

4. Press F1 to pick the new axis.

5. Press M and move the axis up. Press SPACEBAR.

6. Continue adding axes and placing them in an irregularly shaped row (see Figure 9-26).

When Imagine draws the path through the axes, it draws it along the y axis. That means the direction of the y axis of each set of axes is important. Use the Move (press M) or Rotate (press R) commands to align the y axis in the direction of the path.

Often you create the axes out of order. The third axis is created first, then the fifth, then the first. Imagine creates the path in the order the axes were created. This can create a very twisted path! When you are finished creating and aligning the axes, pick them in order with the multiselect option (SHIFT-mouse click). This will tell Imagine the order in which you want the path created.

Here's how to do it for the tail:

1. Because the first axis is coincident with the axis for the disk, and therefore is hard to pick, use the Select Next option on the Pick/Select menu to isolate the first axis.

Figure 9-26
Axes added to
form path

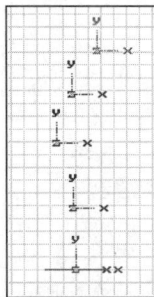

2. Press F1 to pick it.
Result: The first axis turns blue.

If the disk turned blue, then you did not select the axis. Try Select Next again, stepping through the axes, until the first axis becomes selected. Then press F1.

3. Press SHIFT and keep it depressed through the next step.

4. Pick the other axes along the path in order.
Result: The axes should turn blue as they are picked.

5. Once all the axes are picked, release SHIFT and select Make Path from the Object menu.
Result: A blue line is created in place of the axes (see Figure 9-27).

You've now created the path of the lizard's tail. If your lizard's tail looks like it is twisted around on itself, or it begins at the second axis, you've probably selected the axes in the wrong order, or you have rotated the axes in the wrong direction. Select Undo from the Project menu and multipick the axes again. You can also use the Pick/Select menu's Sort option to sort a multiselected series of objects into a sequential order.

 TIP: Imagine Is Forgiving
You don't have to place the first axis right against the disk; Imagine will automatically move the disk to the first axis and start the extrusion there.

When Imagine created the path, it gave it an arbitrary name, such as "Axis.1." Let's give the tail a more descriptive name so that it is easier to find.

1. Make sure the path is picked (blue). Select Attributes from the Functions menu.
Result: This calls the Attributes Requester.

Figure 9-27
The path

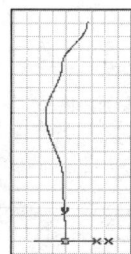

2. Enter the word *tail* in the Obj Name (object name) box (see Figure 9-28), and press ENTER. Press OK to exit the Requester.

3. Now pick the disk, deselecting the path. If you don't pick the disk, Imagine will produce an error message, since the path cannot be extruded.

4. Call the Mold Requester from the Functions menu.

5. Select Extrude on the Mold Requester.
Result: The Extrude Data dialog box appears.

6. Enter the parameters shown in Figure 9-29 for the tail.

7. Select Along Path, enter Tail in the Path box (then press ENTER), enter 30 in the Sections box (press ENTER), enter .01 in the X Scaling box (press ENTER), and enter .01 in the Z Scaling box (press ENTER).
Result: In selecting 30 sections you give the tail enough polygons to create a fairly smooth path. Leaving the default at 1 will create a straight line path between the beginning and end of the path. Entering values of 0.01 for scaling causes the disk to gradually diminish to 1/100th of its original size by the time it reaches the end of the path.

8. Click on the Perform button.
Result: The lizard's tail is created (see Figure 9-30).

9. Select the PERSP button and Shaded on the Display menu to see the tail in perspective. Click on the A (angle) button, and drag the mouse about the screen to see the tail from various angles.
Result: The tail's shape is viewed in perspective (see Figure 9-31).

Figure 9-28
Top corner of
Attributes
Requester

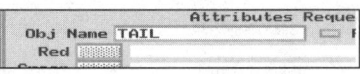

Figure 9-29
The Extrude
Data dialog
box and its
settings

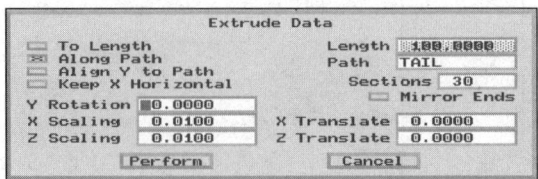

Figure 9-30
The lizard's tail

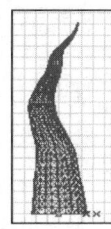

Figure 9-31
The lizard's tail
in perspective

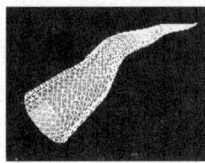

This also looks like the hat worn by Santa's helpers. Or the horn of plenty. Once you get the hang of using modeling tools, you'll soon be pouring objects from the toolbox!

Tip: Other Ways of Creating Paths
Imagine offers an alternative method for creating paths. The Object Menu's Add | Open Path and Add | Closed Path commands add small paths to the workspace that can then be shaped by use of the Edit Path mode (Mode menu). The steps are:

1. Change to Pick Objects mode.

2. From the Objects menu select Add | Open Path to create an open-ended path, or Add | Close Path to create a closed path.

3. Select Edit Path on the Mode menu to change the shape by moving the path control points (the axes). Rotate or move the axes.

4. Optionally use the Fracture command to create more control points along the path.

SPINNING: CREATING OBJECTS WITH CIRCULAR SYMMETRY

Imagine's Mold Requester includes a special form of extrusion called *spin*. Spin creates an object with circular symmetry by rotating an object around its z (up and down) axis. This is a useful tool for creating objects that have radial symmetry, like a martini glass. For example, the outline shape of a martini glass is drawn on the screen using point and line tools (see Figure 9-32).

Then the 3D object is created rotating the profile around its axis (see Figure 9-33).

There are many human-made objects with radial symmetry: lampposts, columns, table legs, to name a few. The following exercise will step you through the process.

Figure 9-32
Profile of a
martini glass

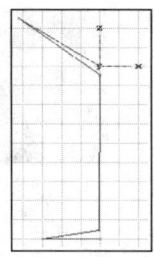

Figure 9-33
The outline
shape rotated
around its z
axis

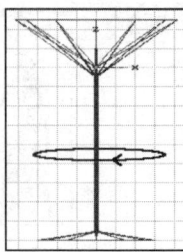

Exercise: Creating a Martini Glass

Clear the workspace of objects by picking them and using the Object menu's Delete command.

1. Change to full screen front view.

Creating the Profile

First, let's create the glass profile. Because the profile will be spun 360 degrees, you need only create half of the glass's profile.

1. Select Add from the Object menu and then Axis.

2. Pick the axis by pressing F1.

3. Switch to Add Lines mode.

4. Draw a very rough version of the profile shown in Figure 9-34.
Result: Notice where you have placed the end points (vertices) for the lines. You do not have to be precise in the placement of the vertices, because you will adjust their positions in Drag Points mode. If you make a mistake, select Undo from the Project menu.

5. Change to Drag Points mode (Mode menu).

6. Adjust the shape of the glass. Roughly align the vertices along the stem.

Figure 9-34
Drawing the
profile

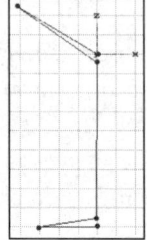

Spinning the Profile

Use extrusion to create the martini glass model.

1. Change to Pick Objects mode (Mode menu).

2. Select Mold from the Functions menu.
Result: The Mold Requester appears.

3. Select Spin on the Mold Requester.
Result: The Spin Data dialog box appears (see Figure 9-35).

NOTE: You can specify the number of polygons that will form the glass (# Of Sections). You can also create a partial rotation (Spin Angle). For the exercise, leave the Spin Data dialog box at its defaults.

4. Click on Perform.
Result: The martini glass is created (see Figure 9-36).

This martini glass has a very skinny stem, because it is spinning right on the axis. Let's make the stem thicker by moving the points that define the stem to the left of the z axis.

1. Select Undo from the Project menu.

2. With the profile picked, enter Drag Points mode on the Object menu.

3. Drag the points defining the stem to the left, along the x axis (see Figure 9-37).

Figure 9-35
The Spin Data
dialog box

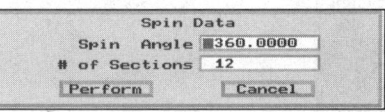

Figure 9-36
The martini
glass

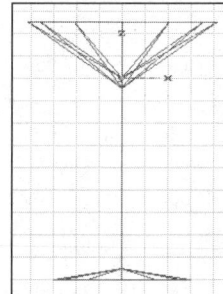

Figure 9-37
Making the
stem thicker

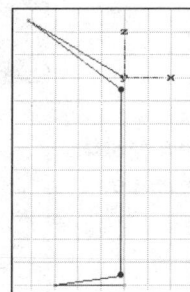

TIP: Precision
Use the Transformation Requester for precise placement of the vertices. Switch to Pick Points mode, select the vertex, and call the Transformation Requester by choosing the Transformation option on the Object menu. In the Transformation Requester, click on the Position option, enter a value for the vertex's position on the x axis, and press ENTER.

4. After placing the vertices in their new position, return to Pick Objects mode.

5. Call the Mold Requester, choose the Spin option, use the defaults in the Spin Data dialog box, and click on Perform.
Result: A martini glass with a thicker stem is created (see Figure 9-38).

The martini glass has been created with relatively few polygons, making it an ideal object for a VRML world.

Altering the Object's Axes

This exercise showed how to create an object radially symmetrical around its axis. However, the center of rotation can be changed by moving the axis away from the object. For example, the axis is moved 90 units to the right along the x axis in Figure 9-39.

When the axis is spun, it creates a torus shape (see Figure 9-40).

Figure 9-38
Martini glass seen in perspective view

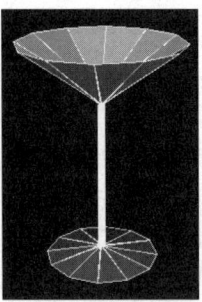

Figure 9-39
Moving the axis

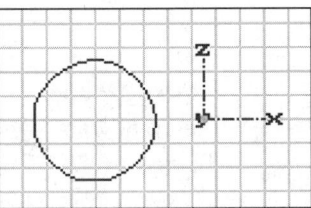

Figure 9-40
Torus shape

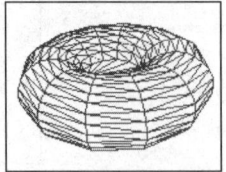

To move the axes independently of the object, use the Transform Axes Only option on the Transformation Requester (called from the Object menu), or move the axis manually using the SHIFT-M command.

This chapter showed how to use 3D modeling power tools to generate most of the basic geometric shapes that define objects in the world. The next chapter will show how to create more complex shapes by deforming existing objects.

10

SKINNING AND DEFORMATIONS

10

The last chapter showed how to use primitives and extrusion to create basic geometric shapes. A wide class of objects can be created using these techniques, including many of the human-made objects found in homes, public places, and offices. However, there are many objects in nature that are irregular in shape. Rocks, for example, do not conform to simple geometric forms. This chapter shows how to use 3D modeling tools that create more complex shapes: skinning and deformation tools.

SKINNING

Skinning draws a surface of polygons over user-defined profiles. Think of the object as composed of slices, where each slice defines a unique cross-section. An arm is such an object. Its thickness and shape changes gradually along its length. To create a skin of polygons for the arm, you draw each of its cross-sections (slices), then ask Imagine to draw a cloak of polygons over the cross-sections. A simple example will illustrate how this works. Figure 10-1 shows a hat shape created with skin.

Notice that the shape has three "slices" to it, defined by the three disks. Here's how the shape was created:

1. A primitives disk was created. Its center vertex was deleted.

Figure 10-1
Hat shape

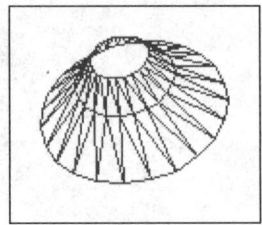

2. The disk was copied using the Object menu's Copy option.

3. In the top view, the first disk was moved up and scaled down in size.

4. The disk in the copy buffer was pasted down.

5. It was moved up above the second disk, and scaled down smaller than the second disk.

6. The disk in the copy buffer was pasted down again.

The three disks are shown in the top view in Figure 10-2.
Figure 10-3 shows the same set of disks shown from the front view.

7. The disks were picked in order, from the first, to the second, to the third, using the [SHIFT] multiselect option.

8. The Skin option was selected from the Mold Requester and executed.

The result was the hat shape. The outline shapes must have the same point count, so the easiest way to create the shapes is by copying, duplicating, and resizing the same shape.

Let's explore the use of this tool in the next exercise.

Figure 10-2
Top view of
the disks

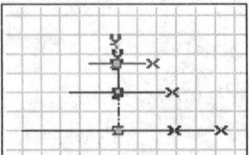

Figure 10-3
Front view of
disks

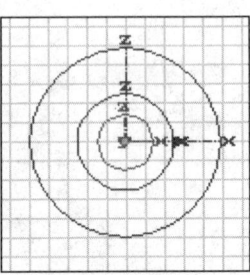

Exercise: Creating an Airplane Wing

Airplane wings are created out of foils, aerodynamic shapes that define the shape of the wing in cross-section. Figure 10-4 shows a 3D model of an airplane wing.

In the model, the shape of the wing is defined by only five cross-sections, marked 1 to 5. In this exercise, you're going to create the five cross-sections and skin them.

Enter the Detail Editor. If you are already in it, delete existing objects in it by selecting Pick All from the Pick/Select menu.

Creating the First Cross-Section

To create the first cross-section, let's create the top and bottom halves of the wings and glue them together (see Figure 10-5).

Create the top half of the profile by slicing off the top of a large disk:

1. From the Object menu Add|Primitive submenu, choose Disk.
Result: The Disk Parameters dialog box appears.

2. For Radius, enter *1500* and press ENTER.

3. For Sections, enter *100* and press ENTER.

Figure 10-4
Airplane wing

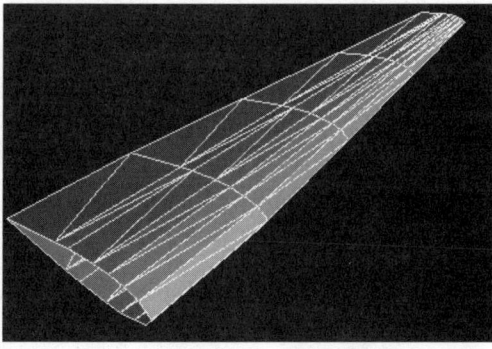

Figure 10-5
The profile of
the wing

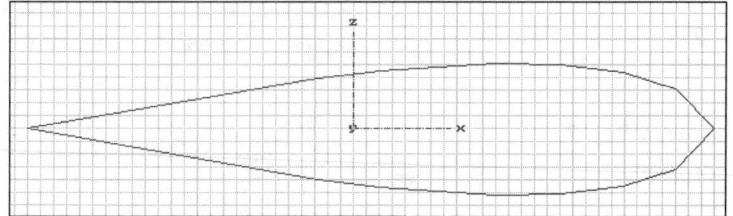

225

Figure 10-6
The disk in
points mode

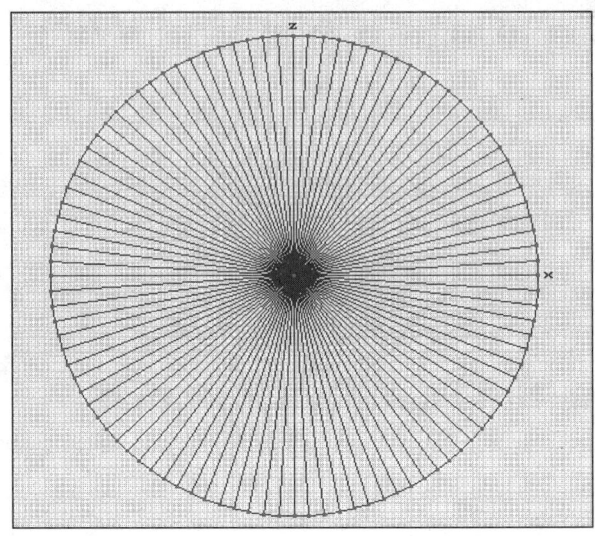

4. Click on the OK button.
Result: A large disk is created (see Figure 10-6).

The top of the disk will be used for the top half of the wing profile.
Let's delete all but the top 13 points on the disk:

1. Press F1 to pick the disk.

2. Select Pick Points mode from the Mode menu.

3. From the Mode menu, select Drag Box from the Pick Method submenu.

4. Press SHIFT and drag a box around all but the top 13 points on the disk.

5. Select Delete from the Object menu.
Result: A small, flat semicircle is left (see Figure 10-7).

The semicircle's axes are too big and unwieldy. Let's make the axes
smaller:

1. Select Pick Objects mode from the Mode menu.

2. Call the Transformation Requester from the Object menu.

Figure 10-7
Top part of
circle

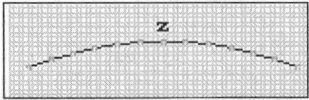

3. Select Transform Axes Only to make the change to the axes and not the semicircle.

4. Select Scale. Enter a value of *.1* in the X, Y, and Z boxes. Press (ENTER) after changing each value.
Result: This creates axes 1/10th the original size (see Figure 10-8).

Now move the axes closer to the semicircle. Try to get them as close as possible to the grid line where the two end points of the semicircle touch:

1. Press (SHIFT), press the (M) (move) key, and then drag the axes until they are in the position shown in Figure 10-9.

Now align the semicircle to the world axes:

1. Make sure the semicircle is picked. Call the Transformation Requester from the Object menu.

2. Click on Position, and enter *0* in each of the X, Y, and Z boxes. Press (ENTER) after entering each 0 in the axes fields.

3. Click on Perform.
Result: The semicircle is aligned to the world axes.

Now let's alter the semicircle to give it the aerodynamic shape of an airplane wing:

1. Using the Display menu's Re-center option, make the semicircle the center of the screen in the front view.

2. Click on the ZI button until your screen looks like Figure 10-10.

Figure 10-8
Axes reduced
in size

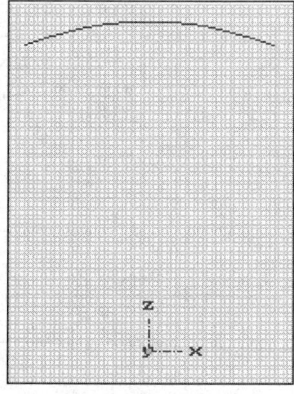

Figure 10-9
Axes moved
closer to the
semicircle

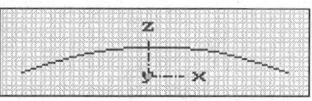

Figure 10-10
The semicircle
re-centered and
zoomed in

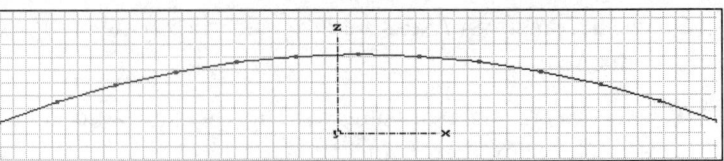

Let's get rid of some of the points along the back of the wing profile and make the front of the wing rounder. Reducing the number of points will reduce the number of polygons created for the wing. As a rule, more polygons are needed for small curves than for large curves.

1. With the semicircle picked, enter Pick Points mode on the Mode menu.

2. Select and delete points on the back of the wing profile.
Result: Your screen should look like Figure 10-11.

Now, let's reconnect the dots:

1. Select Add Lines mode from the Mode menu.

2. Connect the vertices using the Add Line tool.

3. Switch to Drag Points mode, and adjust the shape of the wing until it looks something like Figure 10-12.

Now let's copy, paste, and flip a copy of the top half of the profile to make the bottom half of the profile:

1. Switch to Pick Objects mode.

2. Select Copy from the Object menu.

3. Select Paste from the Object menu.

Figure 10-11
Deleting the
points along the
back of the
wing profile

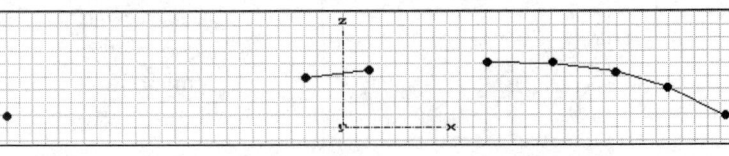

Figure 10-12
The top half of
the wing profile

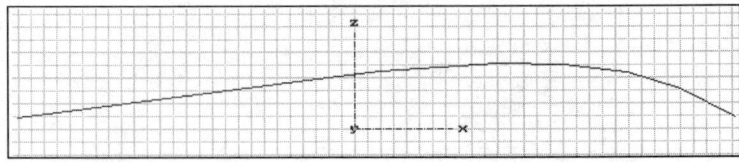

4. Press F1 to pick the copy.

5. Call the Transformation Requester by calling it from the Object menu.

6. Click on Rotate.

7. Enter *180* in the X box and press ENTER.

8. Click on Perform.

9. Select Redraw from the Display menu.
Result: The two halves face each other (see Figure 10-13).

Now let's close the gap between the two halves of the profile and make sure they lie on the same axes:

1. Switch to Pick Points mode.

2. Pick the right end point on the bottom semicircle.

3. Call the Transformation Requester.

4. Click on Position.

5. Enter the following values in the X, Y, Z boxes:

X	*560*
Y	*0*
Z	*0*

6. Click on Perform.

7. Pick the left end point on the bottom semicircle (see Figure 10-14).

8. Call the Transformation Requester.

Figure 10-13
Two wing
halves

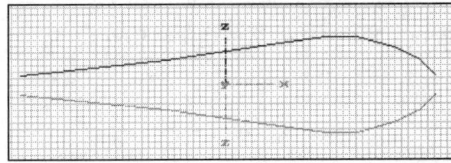

Figure 10-14
Points along
the bottom
semicircle

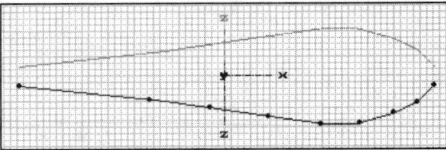

9. Click on Position.

10. Enter the following values in the X, Y, Z boxes:

X	-500
Y	0
Z	0

11. Switch to Pick Objects mode, and pick the top semicircle.

12. Switch back to Pick Objects mode.

13. Give the corresponding points on the top semicircle the same Transformation Requester values as the bottom semicircle.

14. Switch back to Pick Objects mode.
Result: This aligns the end points of the two semicircles to exactly the same spots.

Now let's join the two halves:

1. From the Pick/Select menu, select Pick All.

2. Select Join from the Object menu.
Result: The two halves are joined (see Figure 10-15).

Copying, Sizing, and Positioning the Cross-Sections

Now let's copy and lay out the other wing profiles.
First you'll make the current wing profile:

1. Make sure the wing is picked. Call the Transformation Requester.

2. Click on Scale and World.

3. Enter .3 for the object's X, Y, and Z values. Press ⒺⓃⓉⒺⓇ after each field is altered.

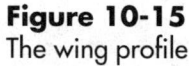

Figure 10-15
The wing profile

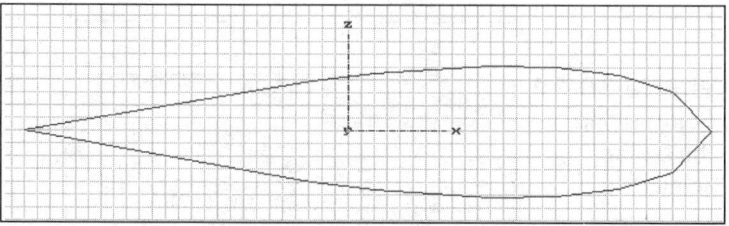

4. Click on Perform.

Result: The wing is ³/₁₀ths the size of the original.

Now let's copy, paste, and pick a copy of the cross-section:

1. Select Copy from the Object menu.

2. Select Paste from the Object menu.

3. Press F1.

Since each grid division is equal to 20 Imagine units, the wing will have a span of about 800 Imagine units (40 grid units). Let's use five profiles to define the wing, 200 Imagine units apart. You could choose more for a smooth wing, but let's assume the airplane is meant for a VRML world and economize on polygons.

Let's make the first copy of the wing profile closer in size to the original than subsequent copies, (see Figure10-16):

1. Call the Transformation Requester.

2. Select the Scale and World options.

3. Enter .9 for the x, y, and z axes values to make the second profile ⁹/₁₀ths the size of the first.

4. Click on Position and enter *200* for the y axis value of the copied profile. Result: This places the smaller copy 200 Imagine units along the y (back to front) axis.

Let's create the third profile:

1. Select Paste from the Object menu.

2. Press F1.

3. Select the Transformation Requester.

4. Select the Scale and World options.

Figure 10-16
The original wing and the smaller copy from the side and top views

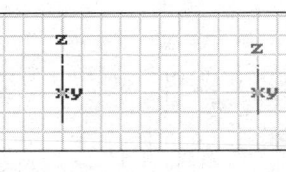 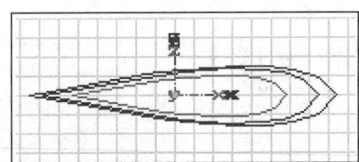

5. Enter .7 for the x, y, and z axes values to make the third profile ⁷/₁₀ths the size of the first.

6. Click on Position and enter *400* for the y axis value of the copied profile. Result: This places the smaller copy 400 Imagine units along the y (back to front) axis.

7. Switch to the Side view.

8. Select Redraw from the Display menu (see Figure 10-17). Result: The wing is beginning to take shape.

9. Switch to the Front view (see Figure 10-18).

Notice that the axes of the new profiles are slightly off center along the x axis. This makes the wing sweep slightly backwards as it moves along its span. Now create the fourth and fifth profiles:

1. Select Paste from the Object menu.

2. Press F1.

3. Select the Transformation Requester.

4. Select the Scale and World options.

5. Enter .5 for the x, y, and z axes values to make the fourth profile ⁵/₁₀ths the size of the first.

6. Click on Position and enter *600* for the y axis of the copied profile. Result: This places the smaller copy 600 Imagine units along the y (back to front) axis.

Figure 10-17
The profiles seen from the side view

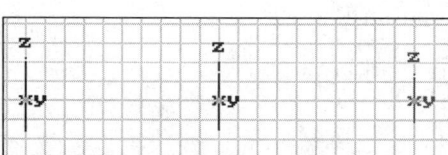

Figure 10-18
Front view

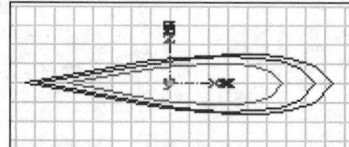

7. Select Paste from the Object menu.

8. Press F1.

9. Select the Transformation Requester.

10. Select the Scale and World options.

11. Enter .3 for the x, y, and z axes values to make the fifth profile 3/10ths the size of the first.

12. Click on Position and enter *800* for the y axis value of the copied profile. Result: This places the smaller copy 800 Imagine units along the y (back to front) axis.

You now have the five profiles in place (see Figure 10-19).

The wing that will be created from this series of profiles will have a hollow end. To prevent this, the z or depth scale of the wings could have been gradually diminished as the wing grew out to the tip. Or a cap could be created for the end of the wing after skinning.

Skinning the Wing

Now let's use the Skin option on the Object menu to draw and surface polygons over the profiles.

First pick the profiles in order:

1. Pick the first profile.

Figure 10-19
The five profiles
of the wing

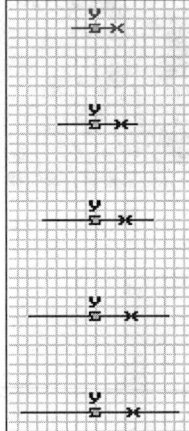

2. Press [SHIFT] and pick the second profile, and then the third, fourth, and fifth.

3. Select Skin from the Object menu.
Result: The wing is skinned (see Figure 10-20).

4. Select Shaded from the Display menu.

5. Switch to the full-screen 3D perspective window (see Figure 10-21).

You'll be using the wing object in the next exercise, so save it now:

6. Select Save from the Object menu and save the object as *wing.obj*. Make sure the object is picked when you save it.

The wing is fairly efficient from the point of view of polygon density. Get a count of the polygons in the wing:

7. Select Find Requester on the Pick/Select menu.
Result: the Object List appears (see Figure 10-22).

The wing has a default name of Disk.1. It has 80 points and 112 faces. Skinning is more labor-intensive than extrusions, but the complexity of the resulting model rewards the effort. The body of the airplane is another excellent

Figure 10-20
The wing shape

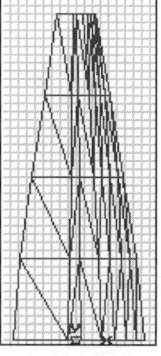

Figure 10-21
The completed wing

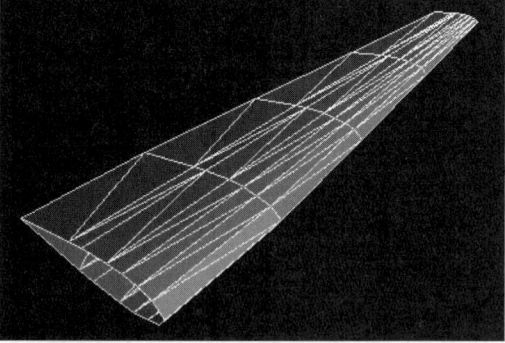

Figure 10-22
The Object List

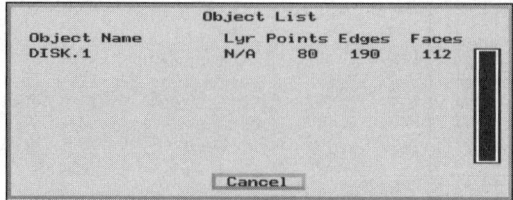

candidate for skinning, since its profile along the y axis is essentially an ellipse that changes gradually over the length, with the exception of the cockpit.

DEFORMATIONS

A popular method for creating 3D objects that are "organic" in shape is to deform existing objects. Some programs have simple twist, bend, or shear commands. The action is performed on the selected object. Other programs have advanced deformation capabilities. The most popular is the deformation grid, which surrounds the object with a grid of vertices that can be manipulated. The changes to the box translate into smooth changes to the object. Each method will be discussed next.

Simple Deformations

Simple deformations are useful when you build objects that have free-form parts. For example, a simple cylinder can be bent into the shape of a "handle" (see Figure 10-23).

Imagine's simple deformation tools are found on the Functions menu. To use them, pick an object, and then select Deformations on the Functions menu. This calls a Deformations dialog box, where the types of simple deformations are listed (see Figure 10-24).

Figure 10-23
Bending a
cylinder

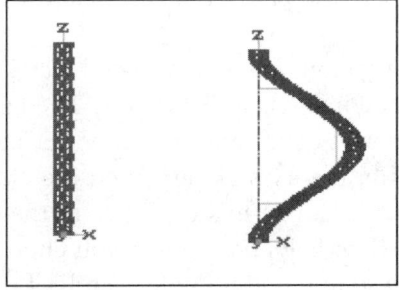

Figure 10-24
Deformations
Type dialog box

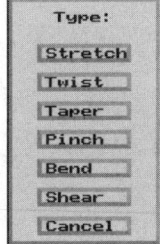

Figure 10-25
Pinching a
sphere

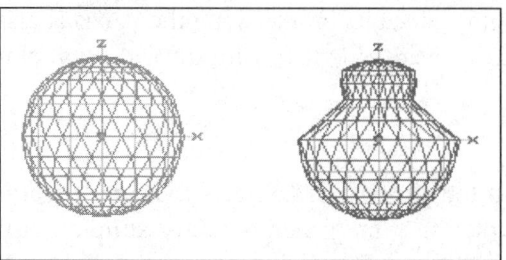

Shearing causes the object to bend over in one direction, like a tree blowing in the wind. The rest of the deformation types are self-explanatory. Any valid Imagine object (that is, a polygonal mesh with an axis) can be deformed. For example, pinching a sphere produces the shape seen in Figure 10-25.

In Figure 10-25, a sphere was created (using its defaults). Then Pinch was chosen from the Deformations Type dialog box. The Pinch Data dialog box (see Figure 10-26) appeared and its defaults were selected.

Tapering a sphere creates a slightly different shape (see Figure 10-27).

Similarly, this shape (see Figure 10-27) was created by selecting the defaults on the Taper Data dialog box.

Imagine deformations always occur along the positive axes of the object. For example, in the case of the sphere in Figure 10-27, the axes lie at the center of the object, so the taper deformation applied only to the top half of the sphere. Moving the axes to the bottom of the sphere would have created a teardrop shape.

Each of the deformation options has an associated dialog box. For example, choosing Pinch calls the Pinch Data dialog box. The Pinch Data dialog box contains typical parameters. The rate of change (Scale Factor) to the object can be set. You specify the axes along which the change will occur (Local x, y, and z). The change can be made relative to the entire axis (Use Axis) or just a portion of it (Use Beg/End). When you choose Beg/End, you specify the starting point (Beg) and ending point (End) of the change along

Figure 10-26
Pinch Data
dialog box

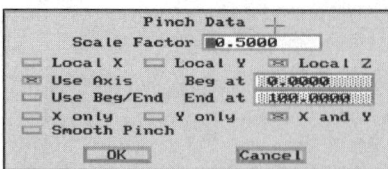

Figure 10-27
Tapering a
sphere

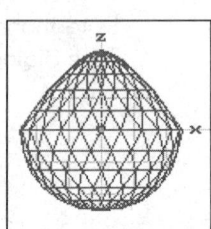

the selected axis. You can also make the change gradual or abrupt (Smooth Pinch). In the next exercise, you'll see how to use parameters to make a change to the airplane wing.

Exercise: Tapering the Airplane Wing

The wing created in the last exercise tapered to an open end (see Figure 10-28). Let's use the taper deformation tool to taper the wing to a flat edge:

1. Select Load from the Object menu.

2. Select the OBJECTS subdirectory.

3. Load the WING.OBJ created in the last exercise.

4. Press F1 to pick the object.

Since the deformation tools only alter objects along their positive x, y, and z axes, let's check the airplane wing's axes for its size.

The wing axes are very small relative to the wing. Since you want to taper the wing in the direction of the y axis, make it as long as the wing. (Remember from the last exercise that the wing is 800 units long.)

1. Call the Transformation Requester.

2. Click on Transform Axes Only.

3. Click on Size.

4. Enter a value of *800* for the y axis and press ENTER.

5. Click on Perform.
Result: The axis now stretches the length of the wing.

Figure 10-28
Wing with open end

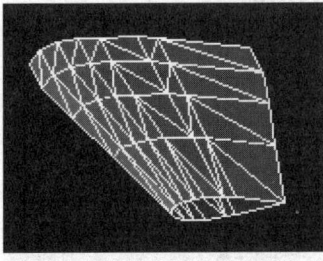

Figure 10-29
The wing axes are tiny relative to the wing

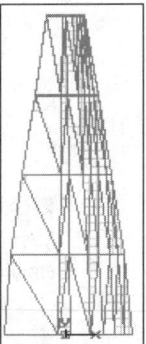

6. Now select Deformations from the Functions menu.
Result: The Type dialog box appears.

7. Select Taper from the dialog box.
Result: The Taper Data dialog box appears.

Let's taper the wing down to $1/100$th of its original size. This will effectively squeeze it to a straight line.

1. Enter *.01* for the Scale Factor.

2. Select Local Y to choose the y axis as the direction of the taper.

3. Select Z Only to confine the taper to the vertical axis of the wing.

4. Click on OK.
Result: The wing tapers to a flat edge (see Figure 10-30).

Figure 10-31 shows the wing seen from another angle.

Deformation Grids

Like simple deformations, deformation grids alter the geometry of objects. However, the deformation grids provide much more detailed control over the deformation. This is accomplished by surrounding the object with a three-dimensional grid of points. Figure 10-32 shows a flower object surrounded by a deformation grid.

Figure 10-30
Wing tapered
to end

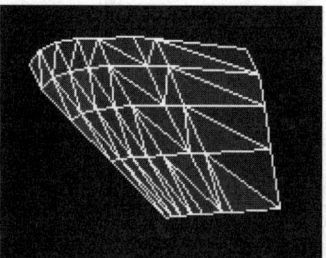

Figure 10-31
Wing seen from
another angle

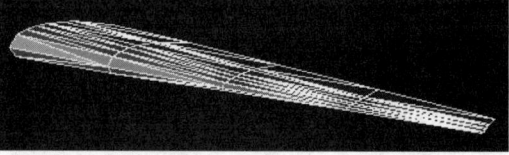

Figure 10-32
Deformation grid surrounding a flower

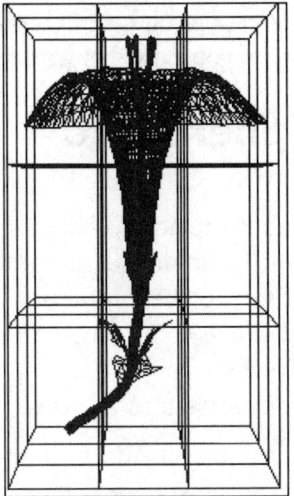

Changing the grid box changes the object it surrounds. For example, shifting part of the grid to the right deforms the shape of the flower correspondingly (see Figure 10-33).

This creates a new variation in the shape of the flower, and would be useful where several flowers with different shapes need to be created from one flower.

Most deformation grids, like Imagine's, produce smooth changes to the object. The shape of the grid box is changed by changing the individual vertices

Figure 10-33
The deformed flower

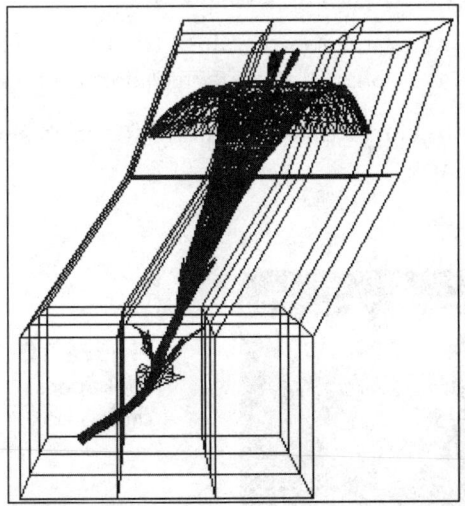

on the grid box. The vertices at the intersections of the grid box are moved, rotated, or scaled. The next exercise will show you how this works.

Exercise: Deforming a Sphere into an Acorn Shape

In this exercise you'll deform a sphere into an acorn shape (see Figure 10-34).

Notice how the object appears to be "pinched" in its top right corner. Extrusion cannot create this object, since the profile of the acorn shape changes as it spins around the vertical axis. Nor can a simple pinch deformation create the crazy tilt to the acorn shape.

Let's begin by loading a sphere primitive into the Detail Editor:

1. Load a sphere into the Detail Editor. Select Add from the Object menu, then Primitives, then Sphere. Leave the sphere at its default settings.

Imagine treats the grid box that will surround the sphere as a special kind of object. Like most objects, it has axes, vertices, and lines. It's found in the Add submenu.

1. Select Deform Tool from the Object|Add submenu.
Result: The Tool Specs dialog box appears (see Figure 10-35).

The Tool Specs dialog box specifies the size of the grid box (x, y, z sizes). Increasing the x, y, and z divisions values increases the number of divisions in the grid box. Specifying more divisions gives a finer degree of control over the surface of the object. Let's make the box slightly larger than the sphere and increase the number of divisions along each axis from 3 (the default) to 6.

1. Enter *110* for the X, Y, and Z Size values (this will make the box 110 percent the size of the sphere). Press (ENTER) after each entry.

2. Enter *6* for the number of divisions along the x, y, and z axes. Press (ENTER) after each entry.

Figure 10-34
Sphere deformed into an acorn shape

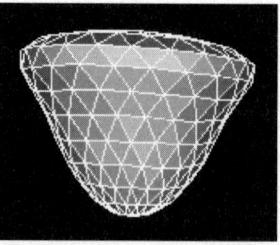

Figure 10-35
Tool Specs dialog box

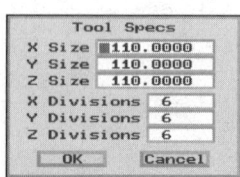

3. Click on OK.

Result: The grid box is added at the center of the world, encasing the sphere.

The grid box can be moved, scaled, or rotated, just like any other Imagine object. However, just as in the case of the deformation tools that bend and twist objects, the Deform grid tool only makes changes along its positive axes.

The deformation grid can also be saved, loaded, and then applied to another object.

Enlarging the Top of the Sphere

Let's leave the sphere's axes where they are and enlarge the top part of the sphere by switching to a vertex editing mode:

1. Pick the Deform box.

2. Select Pick Points on the Mode menu.

To move more than one point at a time, switch to drag box mode:

1. Select Drag Box from the Mode menu's Pick Method submenu.

2. In the Right view window, press ⌨SHIFT and drag a box around the top vertices of the deform grid.

Result: The vertices on the top of the deform grid are picked.

Notice that all the vertices along the row at right angles to the view were picked. In click mode, only the vertex clicked on is selected.

Let's use the Transformation Requester to scale the vertices:

1. Select Transformation from the Object menu.

2. Click on the Scale button.

3. Enter 3 in the X, Y, Z boxes. Press ⌨ENTER after each value is changed.

Figure 10-36
The sphere encased by the grid box

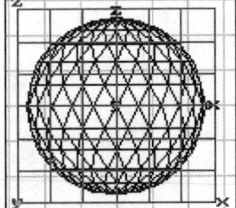

Figure 10-37
Expanded top
of the grid

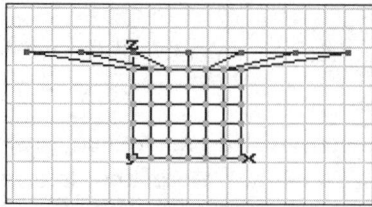

4. Click on Perform.
Result: The top grid of vertices expands to an area three times larger.

Now let's tip the top of the object to the right a little. Make sure the top vertices are still picked.

1. At the bottom of the screen, click the Ro (rotate) button, then the Loc (local) button, and then deselect the X and Z buttons.
Result: This confines rotation of the selected vertices to the y axis in local mode.

2. Using the mouse, tip the vertices to the right and press (SPACEBAR).
Result: The top of the box is tipped (see Figure 10-38).

Now perform the same operation on the vertices below the top vertices of the box, scaling them to twice their size and tipping them slightly:

1. Click on the screen to deselect the currently picked vertices.

2. Press (SHIFT) and drag a box around the second row of vertices in the Right view.
Result: The second row is selected.

3. Call the Transformation Requester and scale the picked vertices to twice their size.

4. Rotate the row slightly in the same direction as the top row of vertices.
Result: The second row of vertices is modified (see Figure 10-39).

Figure 10-38
The new shape
for the grid

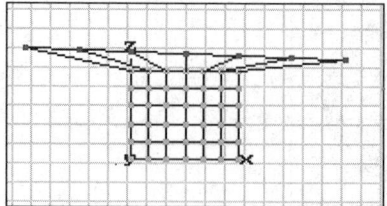

Figure 10-39
The new
shape for the
deformation
grid

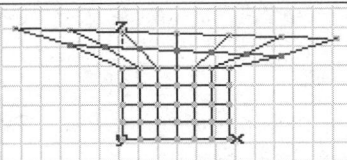

Executing the Deformation

Now let's deform the sphere:

1. Select Pick Objects mode on the Mode menu.

2. Select Redraw from the Display menu.

3. Pick the sphere, by dragging the mouse around it.

4. From the Functions menu, select Deform Tool.
Result: The Object List appears (see Figure 10-40).

It's easy to spot the Deform tool. It always begins with the keyword DTOOL_.

5. Click on the line *DTOOL_6_6_6*.
Result: Imagine places a "BUSY" message on the screen.

6. When the "BUSY" message stops, switch to the full-screen perspective window, and choose Shaded from the Display menu (see Figure 10-41).

Figure 10-40
Object List

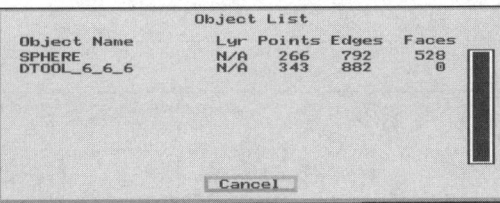

Figure 10-41
The shaded
acorn shape

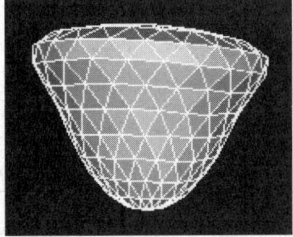

The deformation grid is extremely valuable for developing organic shapes that cannot be skinned or extruded. It is also used in animation. For example, Figure 10-42 shows a porpoise encased in a deformation grid.

Figure 10-43 shows the deformation grid twisted into a swimming shape.

When the deformation grid is applied to the porpoise, its body is deformed into a swimming shape, as in Figure 10-44.

Figure 10-42
Deformation grid encasing a porpoise

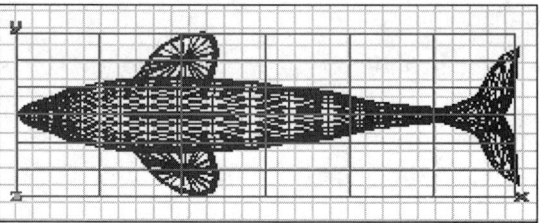

Figure 10-43
Deformation grid twisted into swimming pattern

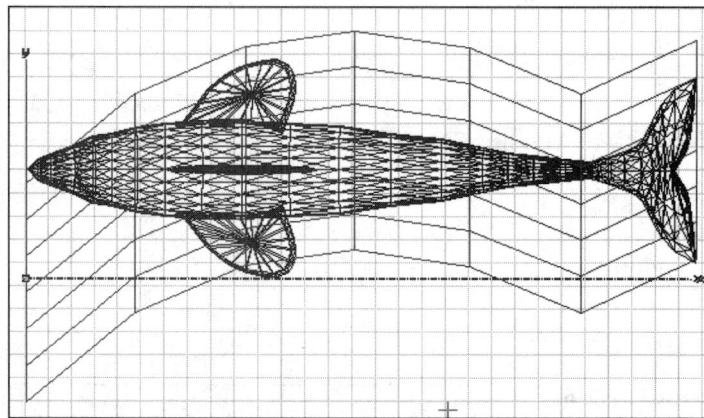

Figure 10-44
Porpoise deformed into swimming shape

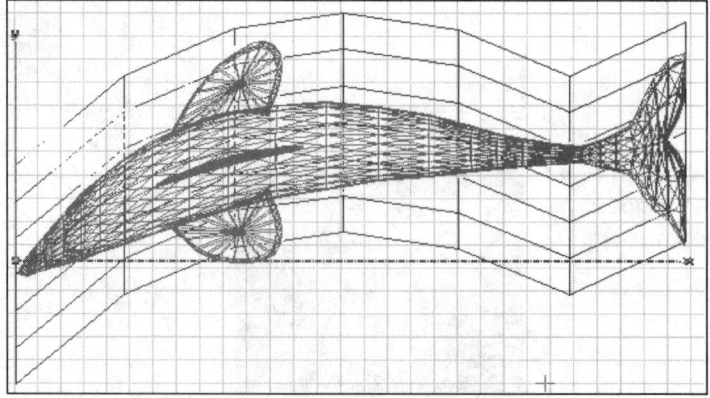

Magnetism

Magnetism turns the mouse into a magnet with a "magnetic field" that pulls a radius of points away from a surface (see Figure 10-45). Imagine's magnetism tool will be illustrated in the next exercise.

Exercise: Creating Mountains with Magnetism

Select a point at the middle of a plane and use magnetism to draw a hill up from it:

1. In the Object menu's Add submenu, choose Primitive and Plane.

2. Give the plane default parameters by clicking OK.

This is the plane from which you'll raise the hill.
Now set the parameters for the Magnetism tool and turn it on:

3. In the Mode menu, select Magnetism.
Result: A submenu pops up.

4. Select Setup.
Result: The Magnetism Parameters dialog box appears (see Figure 10-46).

The parameters dialog box specifies the shape, size, and randomness of magnetic fields. By default, a cone-, dome-, or bell-shaped bump on the surface is created with a fixed radius (50). The size of the fixed radius can be adjusted. Selecting Random Radius creates a bump that varies randomly

Figure 10-45
Magnetism

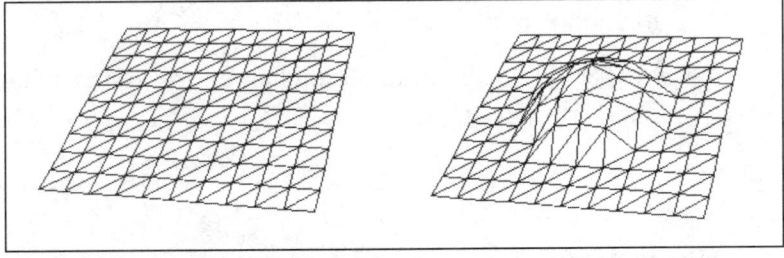

Figure 10-46
Magnetism
Parameters
dialog box

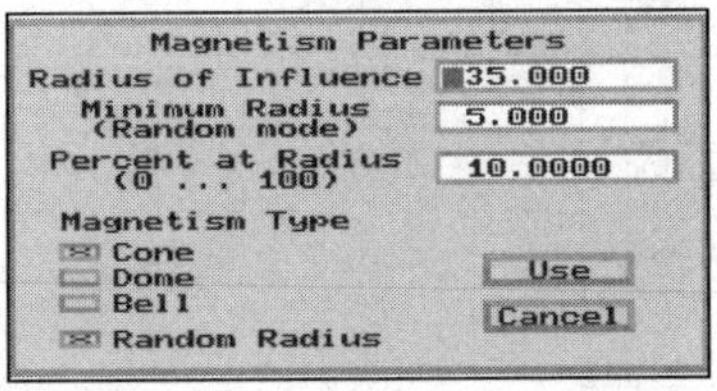

between a minimum radius and a maximum radius (Radius Of Influence). The Percent At Radius setting determines the amount of influence magnetism will have at the outer edge of the bump. In the exercise, let's choose a cone-shaped bump with a random radius between 5 and 35. The Percent At Radius value is 10.

5. Enter *35* for the Radius Of Influence.

6. Enter *5* for the Minimum Radius.

7. Enter *10* for the Percent At Radius.

8. Click on Cone.

9. Click on Random Radius.

10. Click on Perform.
Result: Magnetism's values have been set. Now turn it on.

11. On the Magnetism submenu on the Mode menu, click on the On/Off item.
Result: Magnetism has been turned on. A check mark appears beside it.

Magnetism can also be turned on and off by clicking on the Mag button on the far right of the button bar at the bottom of the screen.

The Drag Points tool on the Mode menu is used to select and drag the center point for the magnetic bulge.

12. Select Drag Points on the Mode menu.

13. Since you want to drag the center point on the plane straight up, use the (SHIFT) drag technique for selecting a point in one view and dragging it in another.

14. Press (SHIFT). In the front view, click on the center point to pick it (see Figure 10-47).

Figure 10-47
Selecting the
point

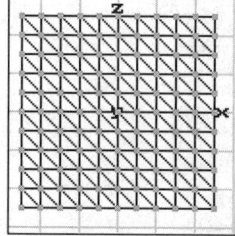

15. Keeping [SHIFT] depressed, release the mouse button.

16. Move the mouse pointer to the top view. Press the mouse button and hold it.

17. Release [SHIFT]. Move the mouse pointer up to move the picked point (see Figure 10-48).

18. Release the mouse button.

19. Select Solid from the Display menu.

20. Select full-screen 3D perspective view (see Figure 10-49).

 Tip: Creating More Dense Hills
Use the Object menu's Fracture option to fracture the finished hill into more polygons. Then pull up on parts of the hill to create peaks.

Dragging the center of magnetism down instead of up in the top view would have created a depression instead of a bump. Magnetism is often used to create terrain.

Other Deformation Tools

Imagine includes several other deformation tools that will not be detailed in this book's introduction to 3D modeling. However, they are simple enough to understand and use.

Figure 10-48
Moving the
point up

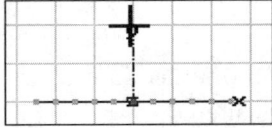

Figure 10-49
Hill created
with magnetism

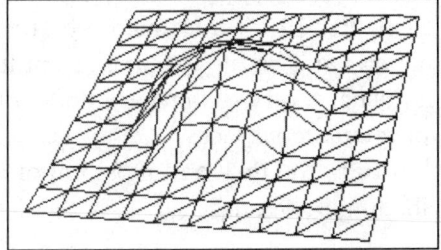

Wave

The Functions menu Wave tool creates a ripple in the surface of an object. Alter the z axis of the object to change the amplitude of the wave. Alter the x axis to change the dispersion of the wave.

Conformations: To Spheres, Cylinders, or Paths

The Functions menu Conformations option causes the selected object to conform to a sphere, cylinder, or a specified path. This is handy for creating objects that fit around other objects.

Appliqué: Creating a Surface from an Image

Appliqué uses the grayscale information in a reference image to create the protrusions and indentations of a surface. White areas of the image become the protrusions, dark areas become the indentations. Terrain, for example, might be depicted by making the tips of the mountain white, then creating darker and darker bands of color according to the contours of the mountain.

To use the option:

1. Pick the object with a surface you want to modify. For example, select a plane.

2. Choose Appliqué from the Functions menu.
Result: An image file name dialog box appears.

3. Select an image.

The image must be in TIF format and uncompressed.

A second dialog box appears when the image is loaded. The second dialog box provides a means for adjusting the size and orientation of the image relative to the object.

1. Once the image has been sized and oriented, apply it.
Result: The surface of the object is altered.

Success with this option depends on a knowledge of Imagine's image mapping techniques. See Chapter 12 for information on this.

Skinning and deformation compensate to some extent for the weakness of polygonal modelers. It's usually very difficult to model objects that have free-form curves or complex curved surfaces.

The next chapter will turn to the final and most important phase in 3D modeling: coloring and shading polygons.

11

COLORING AND SHADING OBJECTS

11

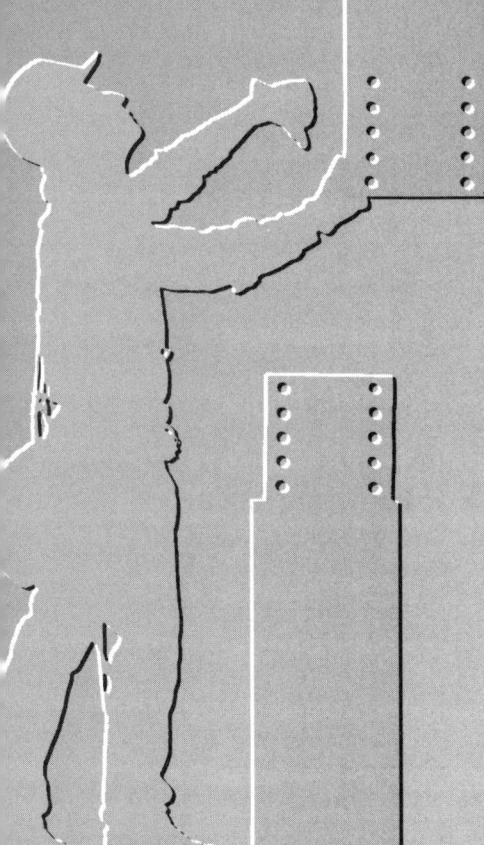

So far you've seen how surfaces of objects are constructed out of polygons. You've also seen how defining the surfaces of objects with polygons can be automated by use of primitives, extrusion, skinning, deformation, and a host of editing tools.

This chapter turns your attention away from the geometry of surfaces, to the way surfaces are colored and the way they interact with light sources in a scene.

Coloring and lighting add realism and drama to computer-generated models. A poorly lit 3D model looks drab and betrays its origin in the mathematical realm of the computer. An expertly lit scene not only looks more natural, but it also expresses the 3D modeler's artistic character.

RENDERING POLYGONAL MODELS

Rendering processes the three-dimensional model data into a two-dimensional image for display on your monitor, or for output to a file or recording device.

Polygonal models are displayed on the screen as wireframe models, solid models, flat-shaded models, Gouraud-shaded models, or Phong-shaded models. These methods of displaying three-dimensional data provide increasing levels of realism, with Phong-shaded models the most photo-realistic. However, the more realistic the image looks, the more calculations the computer has to perform. That's why in programs like Imagine, only simple renderings of objects can be viewed during editing. The more detail added to a scene, and the more detail on the surface of the object, the longer it takes the computer to process the data into an image. VRML worlds depend on the rendering to occur in real time. That's why current VRML worlds look fairly unrealistic when compared with computer-generated worlds seen in movies and television.

To understand the reason, let's review wireframe, solid, flat-shaded, Gouraud-shaded, and Phong-shaded modeling.

Wireframe Display

During construction, the lines and points that define the surfaces of objects are displayed, but not the area between the lines—the polygon's face. This is called a *wireframe* view of the object. For example, Figure 11-1 shows the wireframe view of a sphere composed of triangular polygons.

Wireframe views allow the modeler to see through to the other side of the object and provide access to its vertices. The wireframe object is displayed very quickly, because the computer only has to show lines that make up the polygons on the screen. However, the transparent polygonal faces make the object difficult to visualize, since lines in one part of the object or scene become visually confused.

Solid Models

The display of solid objects overcomes some of the problems of wireframe display. Figure 11-2 shows the sphere displayed as a solid object.

In this viewing mode, the computer removes lines that would be hidden if the polygons on the front of the object were opaque. Hidden-line removal

Figure 11-1
Wireframe
view

Figure 11-2
Solid object

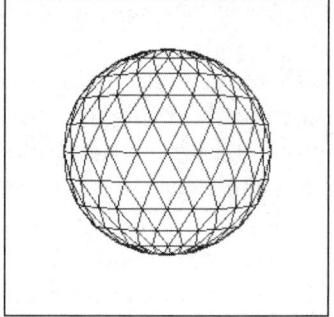

creates the illusion that the object is solid and makes the object's volume and shape easier to see. However, it takes longer to display the object, because the computer must perform the work of identifying and removing the lines invisible to the viewer.

Flat Shading

Flat shading is the first of three types of shading that assign color to the faces of polygons. In flat shading the entire face is given a single color. In a scene that is completely evenly lit, this produces objects that look entirely flat. For example, Figure 11-3 shows a sphere lit entirely by ambient lighting.

The result looks very unrealistic, since intuitively people know that flat surfaces always reflect patterns of light. The reason lies with the way 3D rendering programs try to simplify the complex interplay between surfaces and light rays in natural environments. Light rays come from a variety of sources in nature and bounce around surfaces helter-skelter. Trying to model all the possible light ray paths and interactions among surfaces in a 3D scene soon overwhelms the average computer's ability to perform the necessary calculations.

Figure 11-3
Flat-shaded
sphere

The problem is reduced by limiting the way the polygonal surface is shaded by light sources. During rendering, the polygon's face is represented by pixels, each of which is colored. In flat shading, all the points on the face of a polygon are oriented in the same direction. This greatly simplifies the kinds of interactions the polygonal surface can have with light in the scene. The direction in which the surface of the polygon is oriented is called its *surface normal*, an imaginary line at right angles to the surface. Figure 11-4 shows the surface normals for a cone composed of polygons.

It is much easier and faster to determine the color of the face's pixels when the surface has only one surface normal. A simulated light ray from a light source strikes the surface of the object at an angle, and the rendering algorithm colors the entire polygon according to the relative angles of the light source, the surface normal, and the viewer's position (see Figure 11-5).

On polygons that lie on flat surfaces, flat shading works reasonably well (see Figure 11-6).

Figure 11-4
Surface normals on a cone's polygons

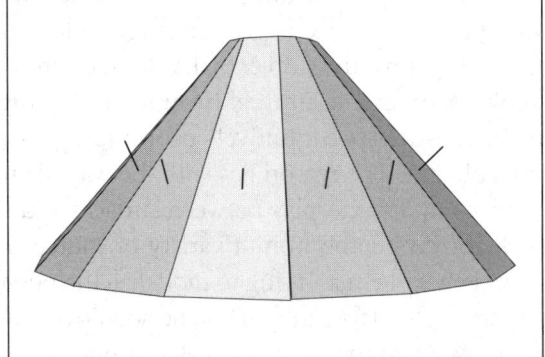

Figure 11-5
Interaction between surface and light source

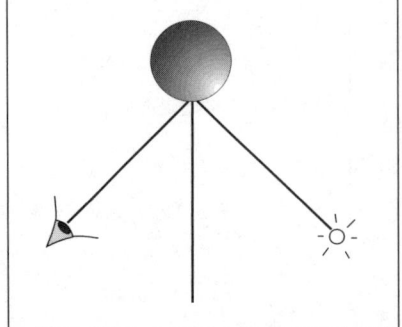

But surfaces in nature are rarely perfectly flat and often have millions of surface normals. That's because most surfaces are curved, such as Figure 11-7.

Using flat shading on a curved object, like a sphere, produces a faceted model (see Figure 11-8).

Notice how the polygons abruptly change color as the surfaces rotate away from the source of light. (You can tell the direction of the source of

Figure 11-6
Surface normal on a flat surface

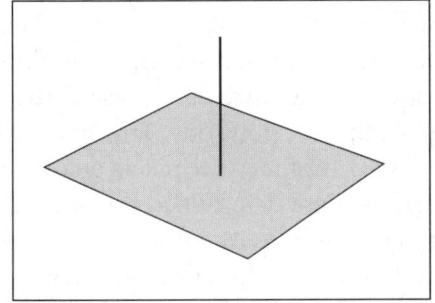

Figure 11-7
Surface normals on a curved surface

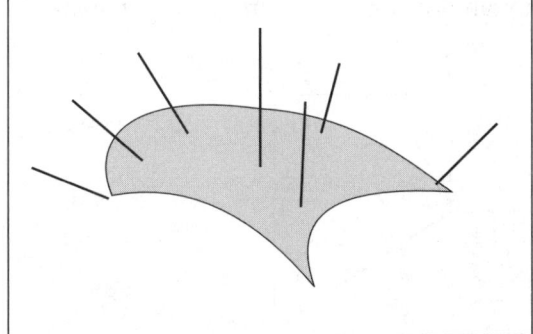

Figure 11-8
Flat shading

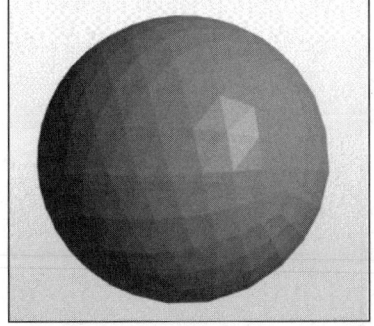

light by the placement of the highlight on the sphere.) Giving each of the polygons a single color allows flat-shaded scenes to render extremely quickly, but the result looks unrealistic.

Gouraud Shading

Gouraud shading is a major improvement to flat shading. To overcome the problem of abrupt changes in the color of polygons describing a curve, the algorithm averages the surface normals between adjacent polygons. Figure 11-9 shows a side view of three polygons describing a curve. The longer black arrows at the vertices are the surface normals as they should be: perpendicular to the surface. The shorter gray arrows represent the average between the two surface normals of adjacent polygons. This new "averaged" normal is used in the calculation that determines the pixel's color at the vertex. Once the corner colors of a polygon are determined this way, the pixels on the face of the polygon are interpolated from its corners. The smooth gradation of color across the face, and between adjacent faces, creates a much smoother-looking curved surface (see Figure 11-10).

Notice that the appearance of facets on the surface of the sphere has largely disappeared, although not completely. In the bright areas of Gouraud

Figure 11-9
Side view of three polygons joined at their vertices

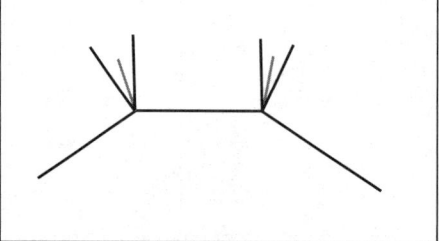

Figure 11-10
Gouraud shading

objects, the shape of the polygon can be faintly discerned, because of the slight difference in colors between adjacent polygons.

Phong Shading

Phong shading is similar to Gouraud shading in that the surface normal is calculated at the polygon's vertex and averaged. However, instead of interpolating the color of the polygonal face between these vertices, the Phong algorithm first resolves the surface normals at vertices into a single surface normal (just like Gouraud shading), but then goes the extra step of interpolating the color of pixels between them. This produces a much more accurate rendering of a curved surface, as shown in Figure 11-11.

Notice that the highlight is much rounder than in the Gouraud-shaded curve. However, the high degree of accuracy has a computational price. Phong-shaded models take substantially longer to render than Gouraud-shaded models. As a result, manufacturers of 3D acceleration hardware have chosen to implement the Gouraud algorithm in hardware, rather than the Phong algorithm. Most PC 3D software rendering programs also use Gouraud shading for real-time preview of models. At this point, VRML browsers use Gouraud shading.

Tip: A Phong Surface By Any Other Name...
Shading a flat polygon as a round surface is often referred to as "smoothing" by 3D modelers.

When you test-render a model, you often choose a lower shading setting to speed up the rendering time for the test. Many VRML browsers also allow the user to set the shading limit to a lower setting to speed up movement through the VRML world.

Figure 11-11
Phong-shaded sphere

Exercise: Creating a Smooth and a Faceted Sphere

When an object is first created in Imagine, it is by default smoothed and colored flat white. In this exercise you'll color the sphere and set its smoothing off.

Imagine's staging area for models that are placed in scenes is the Stage Editor. In this exercise you'll create a sphere in the Detail Editor, enter the Stage Editor, place the sphere in the world, and then set up the camera and lights. Finally, you'll return to the Project Editor and render the sphere.

Creating, Coloring, and Shading the Sphere

Let's begin by creating the sphere:

1. Enter the Detail Editor and use the Object menu's Add|Primitive sub-menu to call the Primitive Types dialog box.

2. From the list of primitives, select Sphere.

3. Accept the default size and polygon count for the sphere. Click on OK.

4. Press F1 to pick the sphere.

In Imagine, changes to the surface attributes of objects are made in the Attributes Requester.

1. Call the Attributes Requester by selecting Attributes from the Functions menu, or use the keyboard shortcut F1.
Result: The Attributes Requester appears (see Figure 11-12).

The Attributes Requester is used to color objects, define the reflective qualities of their surfaces, control how they are displayed in the view windows, and add brushes (images) and procedural textures to them. (Brushes and textures will be discussed in the next section.)

Figure 11-12
The Attributes Requester

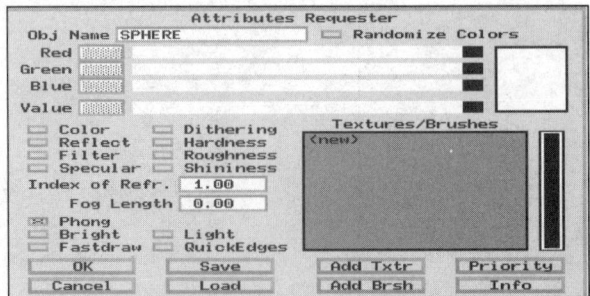

Let's use the Attributes Requester to change the color of the sphere and make it flat-shaded.

To color the sphere:

1. Click on the Color check box in the Parameters list on the Requester. Result: An *X* is placed in the box, indicating that this parameter is selected.

Above the parameters selection list are two sets of sliders used to change the value and color of selected parameters.

2. Move the sliders until a light blue appears in the color swatch at the right of the sliders (see Figure 11-13).

Now give the sphere flat shading by deselecting Imagine's Phong smoothing switch:

1. Click on the Phong check box to deselect it (see Figure 11-14).

This will create a sphere that looks faceted.

2. Click on OK to exit the Attributes Requester.

3. Select Save on the Object menu.

To move the sphere into the Stage Editor for lighting it must be saved:

4. Save the sphere as *sphere.obj* in the OBJECTS subdirectory.

Staging the Sphere

The Stage Editor cannot be entered without first creating a project in which to store the parameters of a scene and the images created when the scene is rendered.

Figure 11-13
Coloring the
sphere blue

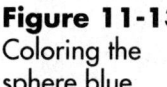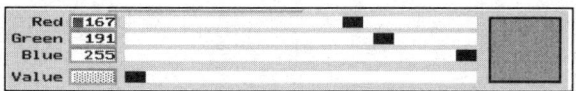

Figure 11-14
The deselected
Phong option

1. Select Project Editor from the Project drop-down menu at the top left of the screen.
Result: The Project Editor appears.

2. From the Project menu, select New.

3. In the project name dialog box, name the project *lighting*.
Result: The Rendering Subproject screen appears.

Now open a subproject, used to store the renders:

4. On the Rendering Subproject screen select the New button.
Result: The Rendering Subproject Name dialog box appears.

5. Call the subproject *flat*.
Result: The rendering parameters dialog box appears.

6. By default scanline rendering is used by Imagine as the rendering algorithm. This produces a Phong-shaded image that is close to the Gouraud shading limit used in VRML worlds. Leave the Scanline setting at its default. Note, however, that Color Shade can be selected, which renders the scene in flat shading. This is sometimes useful for quickly testing the layout of complex scenes.

7. Click on the Presets button and select PC 480.
Result: This selects the size (640x480 pixels) of the rendered image.

8. Click on the TIFF-256 button.
Result: This selects the 256-color TIF image format. This is an adequate color depth for images created in the exercise.

9. Click on OK.

The project is now set up. In the future it can be loaded by selecting the Open option on the Project menu. The subproject can then be opened by clicking on the Open button on the Rendering Subproject screen. An existing subproject's rendering parameters can be changed by clicking on the Modify button of the Rendering Subproject screen.

Now enter the Stage Editor:

10. From the Editor menu, select Stage Editor.

Loading the Object into the Scene

Now load the sphere into the Stage Editor:

1. From the Object menu, select Load.

2. If the SPHERE.OBJ file name is not already in the file, load dialog text field, navigate to the location where you saved SPHERE.OBJ and select it for loading.
Result: The Layer Number dialog box appears (see Figure 11-15).

3. This dialog box applies to a function in Imagine that won't be used. Accept the default value. The Object File Info box appears (see Figure 11-16).

4. All the parameters in this dialog box apply to advanced features that won't be used in this book. Accept the defaults.

5. Click on OK.
Result: The sphere is loaded into the Stage Editor (see Figure 11-17).

Figure 11-15
Layer Number
dialog box

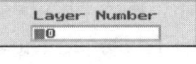

Figure 11-16
The Object File
Info box

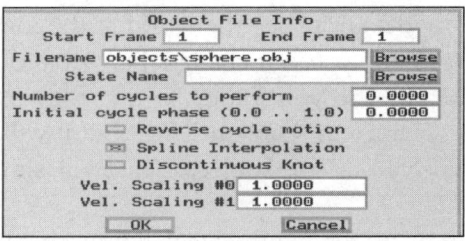

Figure 11-17
The sphere
loaded into the
Stage Editor

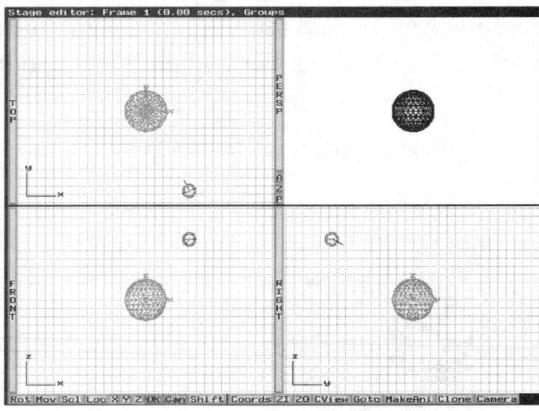

261

If the object was created at the center of the world in the Detail Editor, it usually loads at the center of the world in the Stage Editor. Also visible in the Stage Editor is a small icon, the camera (see Figure 11-18).

The camera is represented as two concentric circles with a lens barrel protruding. The lens barrel shows the direction in which the camera is pointing.

In many respects, the camera is just like any other Imagine object—it can be moved, rotated, and scaled along its axes. Changing the relative sizes of its axes changes the camera's focal length. For example, extending the y axis creates a telephoto view of the world through the camera's lens. The camera does not render, so it will not show up in the final image.

Setting Up the Camera

In 3D or VRML worlds, the model and its environment are always seen through a virtual camera. In the case of the VRML world, and in the case of 3D animation, the camera actually moves through the world, just like a movie camera.

In VRML worlds, the modeler has only two choices for the way the world appears: orthographic or perspective. These are the same as a 3D editor's orthographic (top, front, and side) and perspective views.

What distinguishes a camera view from a perspective view is that the camera is usually set by default to see the world at the same viewing angle as the eye. As with a camera, you can change the virtual camera to whatever viewing angle or focal length you want.

This book will not change the camera "lens," but it will change its angle of view and its distance from the subject. This will simulate movement through a VRML world.

When you first set up a scene in the Stage Editor, the world can be seen in the perspective window, just like in the Detail Editor. However, the perspective view does not stay aligned to the camera view. To align the perspective view to the camera view, select the Camera View option on the Display menu:

1. Select the Camera View option on the Display menu.

Figure 11-18
Camera icon

It's difficult to manually move the camera relative to the target object. Making a small change in the position or orientation of the camera often produces a large change in the view of a distant subject. The object you are trying to view often jumps out of view and is difficult to find again. It's usually a good idea to attach the camera to a camera target. Then the camera target can be placed in the middle of the subject, or near it. Moving the target automatically aligns the camera to the new position. And when the camera is moved, it keeps pointing at the target (see Figure 11-19).

A camera target is created by adding an axis to the world. Because the axis does not have polygons attached to it, it will be invisible in the rendered image. To create a target for the camera:

1. From the Object menu's Add menu, select the Axis submenu option.
Result: This adds an axis at the center of the world.

2. Press F1 to pick the axis, and move it to the center of the sphere. (Press M, drag the axis to a new position, and press SPACEBAR.)

When the axis was created, it was automatically named Track. Let's align the camera to the Track object. To do that, you must exit the Stage Editor and enter the Action Editor.

1. From the Project menu, select Save Changes.
Result: This saves the current scene in a special file in the PROJECT directory.

2. Select Action Editor on the Project menu.

To align the camera to the Track target, you must delete the camera's current alignment and create a new alignment:

1. At the bottom of the editor, click on the Delete button.
Result: This puts Imagine in delete mode.

2. Click beside "CAMERA" in the blue Align box (see Figure 11-20).

Figure 11-19
The camera's lens pointing at an object

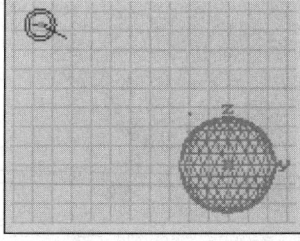

Figure 11-20
Deleting the Align box

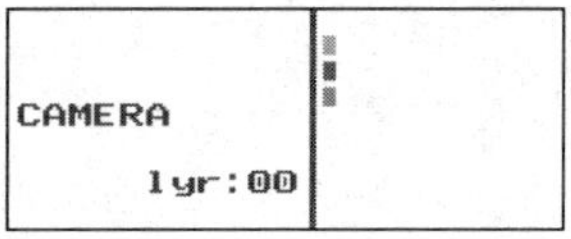

CAMERA	
1yr:00	

Now switch Imagine back to add mode:

3. Click on the Add button at the bottom of the screen.

4. In the spot vacated by the blue dot, click *twice*.
Result: The Specify Type dialog box appears (see Figure 11-21).

5. Select Track To Object from the dialog box.
Result: The Track To Object Info dialog box appears (see Figure 11-22).

6. In the Object Name box enter *Track* and press ENTER.

7. Click on OK.

8. Select Save Changes from the Project menu.

Now return to the Stage Editor to see the effect of the change:

9. Select Stage Editor from the Project menu.

The sphere appears at the center of the camera view (see Figure 11-23).

Figure 11-21
The Specify
Type dialog box

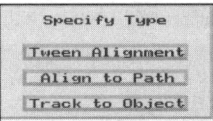

Figure 11-22
The Track To
Object Info
dialog box

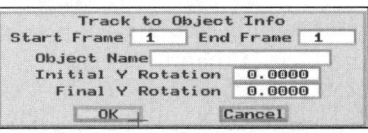

Figure 11-23
The new
camera view

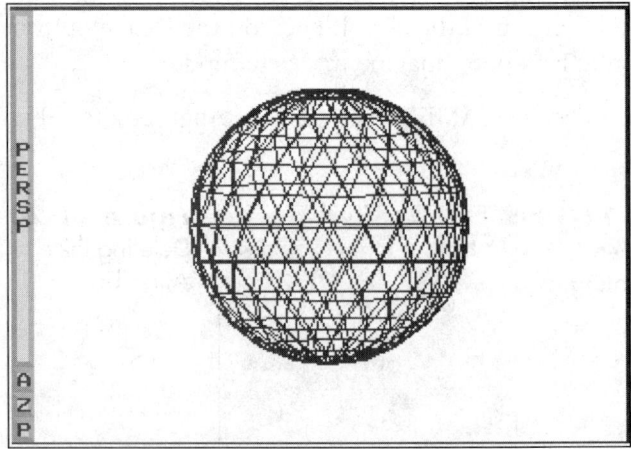

Now try moving the camera around by picking it and using the Ⓜ (move) option to move it around. Notice that the sphere remains centered in the camera view, and the camera's lens barrel remains pointing at the camera target. Try moving the camera target around using the Ⓜ option.

Adding a Light to the Scene

The final step in lighting the scene is to add a light source:

1. From the Object menu's Add option, select Light Source from the sub-menu.
Result: The Light Source Info dialog box appears (see Figure 11-24).

This dialog box allows you to set options such as the type of light (Point Source or Parallel Rays), and the shape of the light's beam when Parallel Rays is selected (round or rectangular). These options and the others will be revisited when lighting is discussed in detail. For now let's create a white light source that radiates its rays in all directions at high intensity. This is the default light.

2. Click on OK to accept the light's defaults.

The light is added at the center of the world. It appears as a round circle with a dot at its center. Let's now arrange the scene for rendering.

Arranging the Scene

The light has been added at the center of the world, inside the sphere. You need to move it to a position in front, above, and to the right of the sphere.

1. Press F1 to pick the light.

2. Press Ⓜ and drag the light until it is roughly at the position indicated in Figure 11-25 and press SPACEBAR.

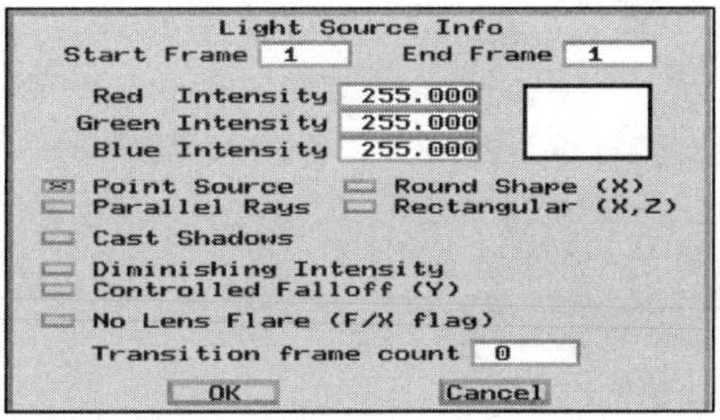

Figure 11-24
The Light Source
Info dialog box

```
              Light Source Info
   Start Frame  1      End Frame  1

   Red   Intensity  255.000
   Green Intensity  255.000        ┌──────┐
   Blue  Intensity  255.000        └──────┘

   ☒ Point Source     ☐ Round Shape (X)
   ☐ Parallel Rays    ☐ Rectangular (X,Z)
   ☐ Cast Shadows
   ☐ Diminishing Intensity
   ☐ Controlled Falloff (Y)
   ☐ No Lens Flare (F/X flag)
   Transition frame count  0
        [ OK ]          [ Cancel ]
```

Figure 11-25
Positioning the
light

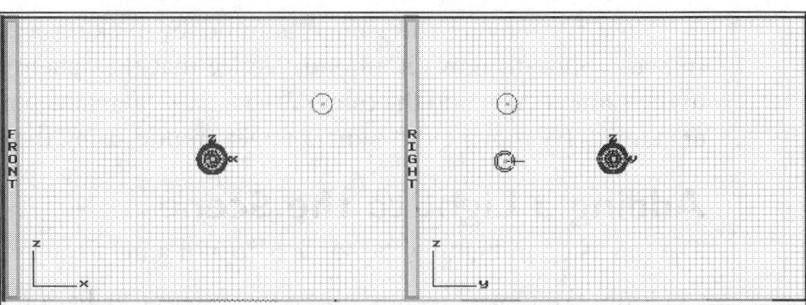

3. Move the camera until it is in front of and level with the sphere.

4. Save the changes by selecting Save Changes on the Project menu.

Rendering the Scene

Now you're ready to render the scene:

1. From the Project menu, select Project Editor.

Imagine is a 3D animation package, so it treats each image that you create as a single frame. Since this project has only one image, you just need to click on the number 1 showing on the frame display in the Project Editor.

2. Click on the number *1* in the frame display (see Figure 11-26).

3. Click on the Generate button.
Result: The Palette Method dialog box appears (see Figure 11-27).

The Palette Method dialog box appears when a rendering color depth less than True Color (16.7 million colors) is selected in the rendering parameters

Figure 11-26
Selecting the only
frame on the
frame display

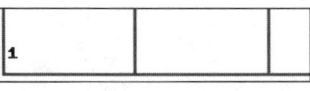

Figure 11-27
The Palette
Method dialog
box

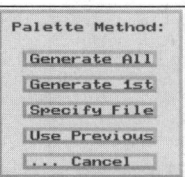

dialog box (set earlier). Internally, Imagine uses 16.7 million colors to color the scene. Selecting an 8-bit (256-color) rendering mode causes Imagine to create a 256-color palette that best matches the colors in the image. For example, a blue sphere will be created with a 256-color palette that is dominated by blue tones. You can also force Imagine to use the previously rendered palette (Use Previous) if one exists, or a user-created palette (Specify File). If you are specifying a file, it has to be a TIFF format file, uncompressed, 256-color depth.

Imagine also allows you to specify a custom palette for the image either derived from the first frame of the animation, or generated as a "best fit" palette from all the frames. Since there is only one frame in this animation, select Generate All.

4. Click on Generate All.

Imagine busies itself generating the palette. Watch the top of the screen. First the progress of the palette generation, and then the image-rendering progress will appear on the top information line. When the rendering is finished, a small asterisk (*) will appear after the number 1 in the rendering display.

5. Click on the Show button to display the rendered image.
Result: The rendered, flat-shaded sphere appears (see Figure 11-28).

6. Press ⌐ESC⌐ to return to the Project Editor.

You can press the Delete button on the Project Editor screen to rerender the image.

Try rendering the sphere as smooth-shaded by following these steps:

1. Return to the Stage Editor.

Figure 11-28
The flat-shaded
sphere

2. Pick the sphere.

3. Call the Attributes Requester from the Object menu.

4. Click on the Phong box to turn smooth shading back on.

5. Save the object.

6. Save the changes in the Stage Editor.

7. Return to the Project Editor.

8. Delete the previous render by selecting the first frame and clicking on the Delete button.

9. Click on the Generate button to rerender the image.

10. Choose to regenerate the palette, since the smooth-shaded sphere will use a different set of blue tones than the flat-shaded sphere.

When you are finished, the sphere should look like Figure 11-29. Generally, flat surfaces should have smoothing turned off; round surfaces should have smoothing turned on.

Creating Hard or Soft Edges on Objects

Many flat objects have rounded edges, and many rounded objects have "hard" edges. For example, the top of an oak desk may have rounded edges. Or a flashlight may have sharp or hard edges.

The round edge of the oak desk could be created by approximating the curve with polygons. This would be computationally expensive. It would be better to create the edge as a *hard* or straight edge, and then use Phong shading (smoothing) to round it.

Figure 11-29
The smooth-shaded sphere

The VRML specification provides a way of giving smooth objects hard edges (the creaseAngle field in the ShapeHints node). It's always a good idea to create objects with as few polygons as possible, and smoothing can be used to create a rounded surface defined with relatively few polygons. In the following exercise, you'll use Imagine's smoothing tools to create a rounded object with a smoothed surface.

Exercise: Using Smoothing to Reduce the Polygon Count

The shape you'll create is a mailbox (see Figure 11-30).

Notice that the mailbox has flat sides and a rounded top. The goal will be to assign as few polygons to the top as possible.

1. Enter the Detail Editor.

Creating the MailBox Profile

Let's create the profile of the mailbox and extrude it:

1. From the Objects|Add menu select Primitives.

2. Select Disk from the Primitive Types, give it the following parameters, and click on OK:

Radius   *50*
Sections *10*

3. Using ten sections creates a disk with ten polygons (see Figure 11-31).

4. Select full-screen Front view and zoom in.

5. Press [F1] to select the disk.

Figure 11-30
Mailbox

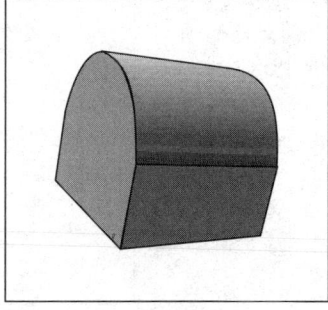

Figure 11-31
The disk

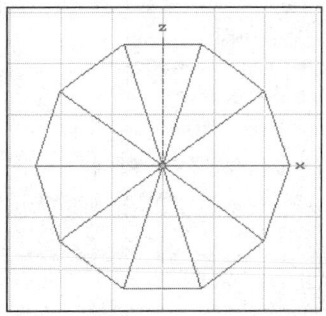

269

6. Switch to Drag Points mode on the Mode menu.

7. Drag one of the points on the circle to form a square edge (see Figure 11-32).

8. Drag the point on the other side out to form the other side of the box (see Figure 11-33).

9. Switch back to Pick Objects mode on the Mode menu.

Extruding the MailBox

Now extrude the mailbox:

1. Select Mold from the Functions menu.

2. Use the mold parameters defaults. Click on OK.
Result: The mailbox shape is created (see Figure 11-34).

Notice that there are only ten polygons defined for the curve. It is faceted. It's this curve that you will smooth.

By default, Imagine creates objects whose polygons are smoothed. Let's render the object using Imagine's quick render facility. To get a better view of the mailbox's top, let's turn it upside-down and tilt it to the side.

1. Select Shaded from the Display menu.

2. Click on the "A" (angle) button along the bottom left of the perspective window, and drag the mouse around inside the perspective window until the object is oriented like the image in Figure 11-35.

3. From the Project menu select Quick Render. When the Quick Render parameters dialog box is called, click on OK to accept the defaults.

Figure 11-32
Dragging to
form the bottom
of the mailbox

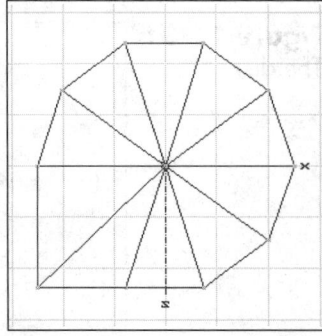

Figure 11-33
The bottom of
the box finished

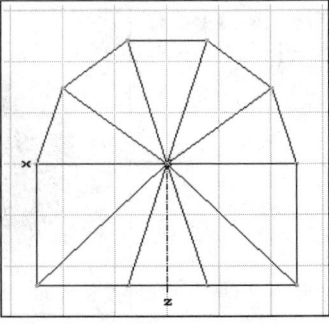

Figure 11-34
The extruded
shape

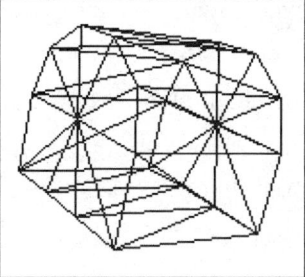

Figure 11-35
The upside-
down mailbox

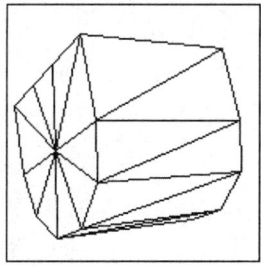

A countdown on the information line indicates the progress of the render. After a few moments, the object appears on the screen (see Figure 11-36).

4. Press ⎡ESC⎤ to return to the Detail Editor screen.

Before returning to the Detail Editor, Imagine asks if the render should be saved. Answer No. If you do want to save the image, give it a name with a .TIF extension. The file will be saved as a TIFF formatted file in the color resolution specified for Quick Render.

 Tip: Setting the Screen Resolution
Make sure that Quick Render is in a mode that your video card can display. The Quick Render color resolution mode is set in the Preferences Editor.

"Creasing" the Edges

The mailbox does not appear to have edges, because by default all its polygons have been smoothed. In this part of the exercise, you'll sharpen the edges. First you'll pick the edges along the box's bottom, then you'll use the Functions menu Make|Hard Edges command to make them sharp.

Figure 11-36
The rendered
image

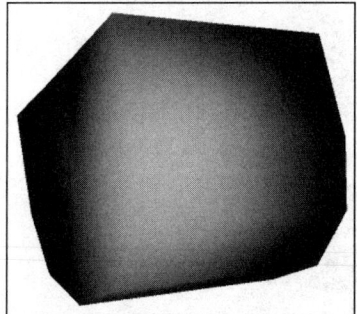

1. Make sure the mailbox is picked. Switch to Pick Edges mode on the Mode menu.

2. On the Mode menu's Pick Method submenu, choose Drag Box.

3. Press (SHIFT) and in the front view drag a box around the vertices that define the bottom of the box (see Figure 11-37).

This selects the vertices on both sides of the box.

4. From the Functions|Make submenu, choose Make Sharp Edges.

Now render the mailbox.

5. From the Project menu, select Quick Render.
Result: The box is rendered (see Figure 11-38).

The edges along the top of the box are still soft. Let's make them hard.

1. Ensure that the box is picked, and enter Pick Edges mode.

2. Press (SHIFT) and in the front view drag a box around the top part of the box.

3. From the Functions|Make submenu, choose Make Sharp Edges.

Figure 11-37
Drag a box around the bottom of the box (dotted lines)

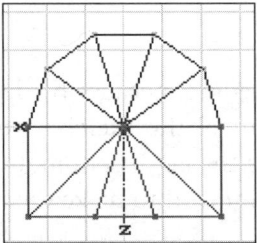

Figure 11-38
The box with hard edges

Figure 11-39
Now the sides of the box have sharp edges

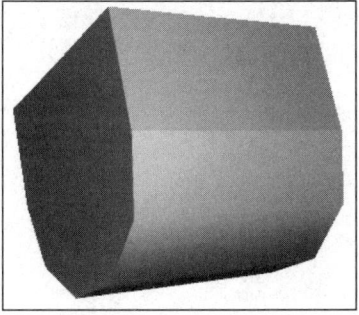

Now render the mail box:

4. From the Project menu, select Quick Render.
Result: The box is rendered (see Figure 11-39).

Coloring and shading are very basic surface attributes of objects. In the next chapter you'll see how to make simple surfaces look richer and more complex by covering them with images.

12

APPLYING SURFACE ATTRIBUTES AND TEXTURES

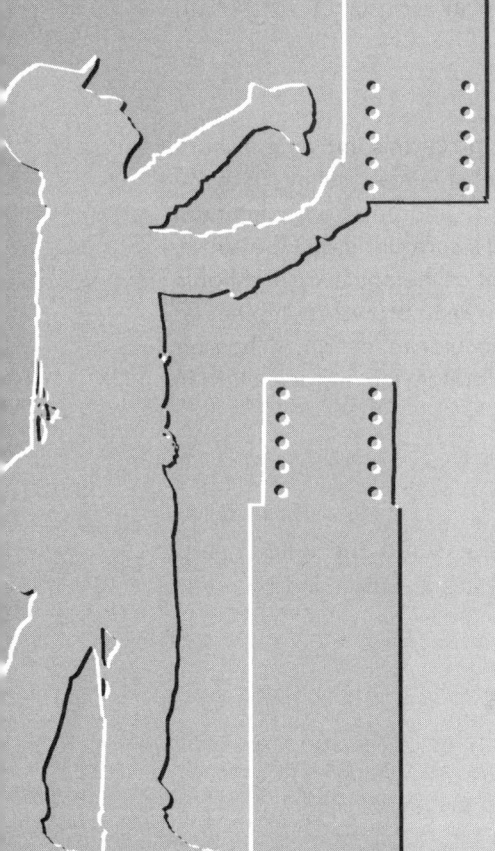

People often think of the surface attributes of objects in the tactile sense: smooth, hard, rough, or slippery. Yet they are able to judge the texture of surfaces from a distance because the way light interacts with surfaces provides visual clues. Smooth objects, like shiny wood floors, have a sheen to them, and they display bright patches of intense light. Soft, rough surfaces, like wool carpets, scatter the light and are dull and more saturated in color.

Such qualities as smoothness or hardness are inherent in the physical structure of natural objects, but must be simulated in 3D or desktop VR software. That's because a polygon is a geometric entity. It has a face that can be assigned color, but not the kind of roughness or smoothness so obvious to the caress of a hand. The computer must rely entirely on visual clues to suggest these qualities of objects.

Computers also have a limited ability to model detail. The tiny pits on an orange peel can be modeled with polygons, but the computational cost of reproducing millions or billions of polygons makes modeling the minutiae of surfaces highly inefficient, if possible at all.

This chapter shows you the techniques for shading and texturing surfaces to give them the appearance of more detail than resides simply in the geometry. It examines two basic methods:

The first method uses *shading* to simulate such surface attributes as transparency, specular highlights, and shininess. Like the shading algorithms discussed in the last chapter, these program settings use color to fool the eye into seeing surface attributes where there are none.

 Texture-mapping, the second method, projects images or pictures onto surfaces of objects, like Christmas wrapping on a dull white box. The image can be a scan of a real-world texture like skin, or a computer-generated texture.

The two methods are used to create photo-realistic images, such as the skin on the dinosaurs in the movie *Jurassic Park.* Photo-realistic objects can be built up from simple objects. For example, a sphere with relatively few polygons can be shaded and image-mapped to appear as a planet, a baseball, or an orange.

Tip: Surfaces and VRML Translators

There is incredible variance in the way 3D and VR programs implement shading and image-mapping. For example, the VRML shininess setting is completely different from the shininess setting in Imagine. Imagine treats shininess as a blurred and bleached reflection of the object's surroundings. The VRML specification treats shininess as a simple coefficient of the specular highlights on objects. There is also a variance in the way VRML browsers implement standard VRML surface settings like diffuse and specular reflection. When an object is imported from 3D software into a VRML editor, the surface attributes usually have to be reapplied (see Chapter 18).

COLORING OBJECTS WITH LIGHT

To best apply color to objects, it's helpful to understand the relationship between the physics of light and the way the physics are modeled by computer programs.

Point and Parallel Light Sources

Discrete light sources in a 3D scene, such as lamplights or the sun, are modeled as either point or parallel (directional) light sources. *Point* light sources radiate in all directions; *parallel* lights radiate light along a 3D axis (see Figure 12-1).

Point light sources are used to model lights like lamps, suns, and matches. Parallel light sources are used to model directional lights like flashlights, theatrical lights, and headlights.

Figure 12-1
Point and
parallel light
sources

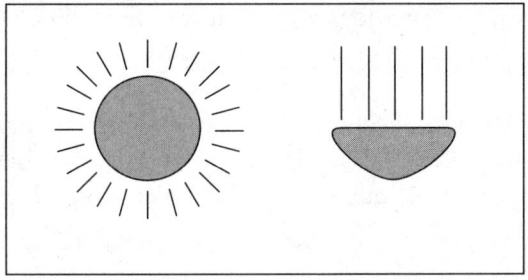

Ambient Light

In the natural world, environments are awash with a random, chaotic mixture of light rays. Billions and billions of light rays bounce endlessly around closed environments such as rooms. In the world outside, light rays are scattered by clouds, or reflected by shiny surfaces like leaves or water.

Given the finite processing capability of computers, and more importantly, the finite schedules of 3D artists in production environments, the complex soup of light in the natural world must be greatly simplified.

One of the light sources in a room or the world is the scattered light bouncing from one surface to another randomly. This is called *ambient light*. Instead of trying to model the countless rays of light casting an even level of light on all objects in an area, the 3D program merely coats all objects in a scene with the same level or color of light. Point light sources, on the other hand, do selectively add color to surfaces in their path. (In the case of ray tracing or radiosity algorithms, the light ray's path in a scene is traced.) By only accounting for the light rays of point light sources, 3D software greatly reduces the burden of tracking all the possible light rays in a natural environment. Let's look at each of these types of lights more closely.

Ambient Light Values

Ambient light values are added evenly to all objects in a scene. Adjusting ambient light levels prevents areas of a scene that are in shadow from rendering completely black. If a scene has no point sources and the ambient light level is at zero, the scene will render completely black. Gradually raising the ambient light level will gradually lighten the objects in the scene, but they become flat and one-dimensional.

In many 3D software programs, ambient light can be adjusted globally for the entire environment, or assigned to the surfaces of individual objects. The ability to assign ambient color to the sides of individual objects facing away from strong light sources provides a great deal of flexibility. For example, objects near a weak red lamp in the scene can be given a red glow in their shadow areas.

At present, the VRML specification only allows ambient light to be assigned to the surfaces of individual objects, and not globally. The ambient level is set by entering an RGB value for the ambientColor field in the Material node.

Point Light Sources

Point light sources, like the sun, or a lamp in a room, have light rays that travel in straight lines until they encounter a surface. Then they bounce back to the viewpoint in the scene. Ray-tracing rendering algorithms, used by many 3D software programs, trace the light ray's path through a scene as it bounces from one object to another. However, the ray is traced in reverse order, from the point-of-view in the scene, back to the object, and then back to the light source (see Figure 12-2).

Tracing the path of the light ray in reverse order greatly reduces the number of light rays that need to be traced. Only those rays that are seen at the point of view are calculated. However, what is lost is the complex interactions of light rays between the objects. For example, reflected light off one object may cast a colored glow on another. Radiosity rendering algorithms, which account for these kinds of secondary light rays, are rare in commercial 3D software because they are even more computationally expensive than the ray-tracing algorithms.

Ray tracing is capable of reproducing such realistic lighting effects as reflections, refraction (light bending through semitransparent media), and accurate shadows.

Figure 12-2
Ray tracing

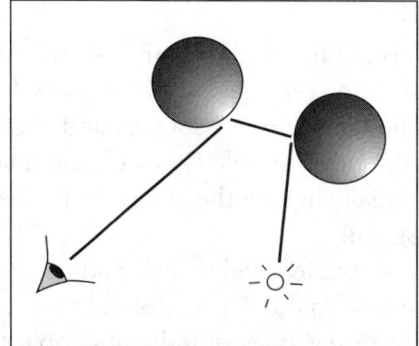

Scanline rendering—where the path of the light ray is traced from the light source to the object and back to the viewer, but not the interactions between objects—provides much faster rendering than ray-tracing. Some 3D software has compensated for some of the weaknesses of scanline rendering by "faking" shadows and reflections, or partially implementing ray-tracing algorithms.

Scanline rendering is currently the only type of rendering supported by VRML browsers. This means that reflections, shadows, and refraction cannot be reproduced.

Diffuse and Specular Reflection

Recall from the discussion of shading in the last chapter that the computer calculates the color of pixels on an object by comparing the face's normal with the angle of incidence of the light ray and the angle of view (see Figure 12-3).

When the light ray strikes the surface, some of the colors in the light's color spectrum are absorbed. The colors that are reflected give the object its basic color. For example, a blue beach ball absorbs all but the blue part of the color spectrum.

The result of the interaction of light rays between point sources and the surface of a 3D object is called its *diffuse* color. This is what is normally meant as the color of the object.

However, there are always other factors that affect the way light rays are reflected off a surface. For example, a surface that is rough will tend to scatter the light rays (see Figure 12-4).

Figure 12-3
Interaction
between surface
and light source

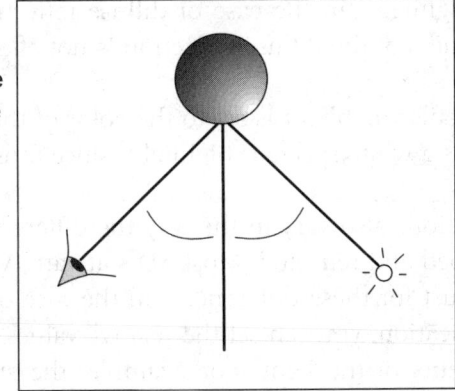

Figure 12-4
Light scattered
from the surface
of a rough
object

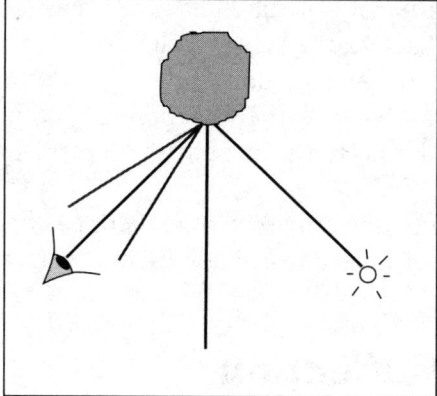

Figure 12-5
Diffuse and
specular
reflection

It will appear more evenly lit than the surface of a smooth object like an egg. It will have a very dull *specular* highlight. Most objects have these two types of light reflection. Figure 12-5 shows the relationships between diffuse and specular light. Notice that the specular highlight usually shows the location of point light sources in the environment.

Because specular reflection is highly directional, the angle of view determines the brightness of the highlight. In the case of diffuse reflection the light is scattered, so the brightness of the diffuse reflection is not affected as deeply by the point of view.

In most 3D scenes the specular highlight is set to the color of the point light source. This usually means a white specular highlight, since most environments are lit by white lights.

Diffuse and specular reflections also vary in the way the different color components of light are absorbed and reflected. Most 3D software, VR software, and VRML browsers adjust for these differences. In the case of some software, and the VRML specification, you can set the relative values for the red, green, and blue components of the light. For example, the specular highlight on an object can be made to respond more to the green component of light. This makes it appear that a green light source is shining on the surface of the object.

You should note, however, that VRML browsers will vary significantly in their implementation of ambient, diffuse, and specular reflection algorithms. The situation is analogous to the problem of color in television or computer display. Colors can shift significantly from one computer system to another. The best policy is to assign specular and diffuse settings for playback on the most common browser, and to test the settings in other popular browsers. At this point it is too early in the VRML specification's history to call a clear winner in the browser race.

In the VRML specification, RGB values can be assigned to the specularColor and diffuseColor fields in the Material node.

Shininess

Shininess is usually associated with smooth surfaces. The shinier a surface is, the smaller the specular highlight, since the light rays tend to be more directional or focused. In a lot of 3D software, shininess is adjusted by changing the size and intensity of the specular highlight (see Figure 12-6).

Some software, like Imagine, will also apply a blurred, faded image on the surface to enhance the illusion of shininess.

The VRML specification includes a shininess field in its Material node.

Emissive Color

In most 3D software programs, only light sources emit light rays. Polygonal objects do not. To create a glowing light bulb, it's necessary to place a light source near a light bulb object and then color it to look like a glowing light bulb. However, it's not good enough to simply color the object, since light sources in the environment can affect an object's color, something that wouldn't happen with a truly emissive light source. And in the case of programs that

Figure 12-6
Changing the size of the specular highlight

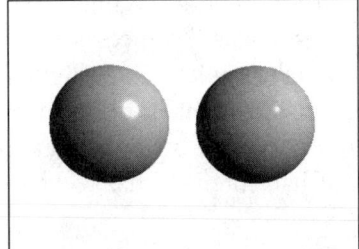

cast shadows, a colored polygon object would be partially or wholly covered with a shadow. Again, this would not happen with an emissive light source.

The VRML specification includes a field that allows you to set the RGB values for an emissive object.

Transparency

The final setting supported by the VRML specification is its transparency field in the Material node, which has a fractional value between 0 and 1. Set at 0, the surface is completely opaque. Set at 1 it is completely transparent. This will make it totally invisible.

Transparency is calculated by the software as a percentage mixture between the color of the object and the color of the background behind it. When an object is against a black background, black is combined with the color of the object, making it darker. It is more effectively used against a background that has colored detail in it.

Often the specular highlight disappears when an object is made transparent, because the color of the highlight combines with the background. To work around this, increase the intensity of the specular highlight.

Using Shading Effectively

To be effective, the computer artist must be aware of the limitations of simulated lighting. For example, a flat wall in a room in the real world is inundated by a complex interplay between light rays and surfaces. A polygonal face, on the other hand, usually has only one normal responding to a handful of light rays from a few light sources in the environment. The modeler can add more light sources to the scene to simulate natural lighting, but the render slows to a crawl. Curved objects respond more realistically to lights in the environment because they have more normals. But there is always a price: More polygons create larger and less-manageable models.

The modeler must also be aware that the artificial light rays in the computer environment are quite different from natural light rays. In the mathematical universe of the computer, light has no energy. While light loses its intensity in the natural world as it disperses over distances, or as it passes through matter, in the computer world a light ray leaves the light source at a specified color and just keeps going forever. Light intensity can only be expressed by color. For example, an intense, pure white light is expressed as pure white color. A natural white light at half intensity has to be expressed as a gray light. To make a color look more intense, you have to add more red, green, and blue to it.

Color in 3D software is usually adjusted using the RGB (red/green/blue) color system. (Some computer graphic programs also use the HSL, or hue/saturation/luminance system, but the RGB color system is favored because it is more accurate: It's the same system used by the monitor in displaying colors.)

The most common method for mixing the red, green, and blue components of a color is to use three sliders, such as those found in Imagine's Attributes Requester (see Figure 12-7).

Moving the sliders to the right increases the amount of red, green, or blue color in the mix. The swatch to the right of the sliders shows the resulting color.

Imagine's color system also includes fields for specifying the color of objects using numbers. The range is from 0 (absence of color) to 255 (fully saturated). For example, white light has the following values:

Red = 255
Green = 255
Blue = 255

Black has values of 0. A dark blue has zero values for the red and green components, and a low value for the blue component. A neon green has a high green value. Red and blue are mixed in to brighten the color.

To be effective, the 3D artist also should know about lighting conventions that have grown up around traditional photography and cinematic lighting. For example, rendering a sphere with a single light source results in the rendered image shown in Figure 12-8.

Notice how the strong, single light source placed below the object not only reveals the object's roundness through shading, but gives the image a feeling of drama. That's because lighting placed below the subject is unnatural: In the natural world the sun and artificial lights are usually located

Figure 12-7
Imagine's RGB
color sliders

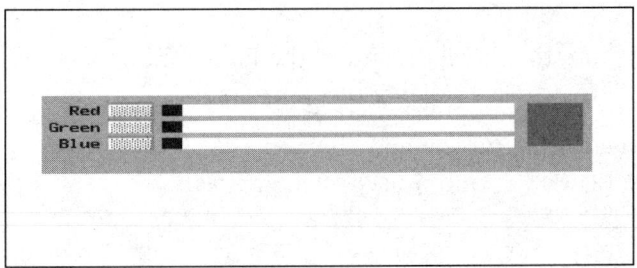

Figure 12-8
3D sphere lit by
a single light
source

above eye level. Also, this type of lighting has long been used in Hollywood to add dramatic tension to scenes—especially B-movie gangster thrillers.

Experimenting with Lighting and Shading

After constructing the object's geometry in a 3D software program like Imagine, you will probably assign the shading and lighting in a VRML authoring tool, or by editing a VRML WRL ASCII file. This is the method recommended until the VRML authoring tools and VRML browsers implement shading algorithms and lighting systems more consistently. In the latter part of this book you'll learn how to use the Material node's fields for altering the shading of objects, and the point light and directional light nodes for setting the lighting.

However, to get a better understanding of how 3D lighting and shading works, let's experiment with Imagine's shading and lighting controls.

To do this, let's set up a lighting project. Let's use Imagine's surface attributes tool (the Attributes Requester) and the lighting controls in the Stage Editor (Add Lights on the Object menu and the Global lighting controls in the Action Editor) to alter lighting and shading on a sphere. The following step-by-step exercise will get you started.

Shading and Lighting a Sphere in Imagine

Begin by setting up a project:

1. Select New from the Project menu in the Project Editor.
Result: The Project Name dialog box appears.

2. Enter a name for the project and click on OK.
Result: The Rendering Subproject screen appears.

3. Click on the Open button on the Rendering Project screen.
Result: The Rendering Project Name dialog box appears.

4. Name the subproject *ambient* and click on OK.
Result: The Rendering Parameters dialog box appears.

5. In the Rendering Parameters dialog box specify *PC640* (640x480 pixel resolution) in the Rendering Presets box, and *TGA-256* (256-color depth) for the color resolution. Click on OK.

Creating the Sphere

Now let's enter the Detail Editor and create the sphere:

1. Enter the Detail Editor and use the Add|Primitives|Sphere menu option to create a sphere with default values.

2. Press F1 to select the sphere, and save it using the Object menu's Save option. Give the sphere a descriptive name, such as *bulb01.obj*.

3. Enter the Stage Editor and load the sphere you just created. Accept the defaults for the dialog boxes that are called when you do this.
Result: The sphere is loaded at the center of the world.

4. Switch to Camera View mode on the Display menu.

Creating a Target for the Camera

Now let's align the camera to a target:

1. From the object menu, select Add|Axis.
Result: An axis called *Track* is added at the center of the world.

2. Save the scene in the Editor menu.

3. Enter the Action Editor.

4. Click on the Delete button at the bottom of the screen, and then click on the blue Align bar beside "CAMERA" (see Figure 12-9).

5. Click on the Add button.

6. Double-click on the spot vacated by the blue bar. In the dialog box that appears, select the Align To Object option. In the dialog box that follows this selection, enter the name *Track* for the target object. Press ENTER.

Figure 12-9
The camera
Align bar

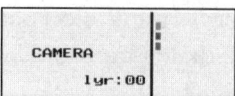

Figure 12-10
Globals
parameters
dialog box

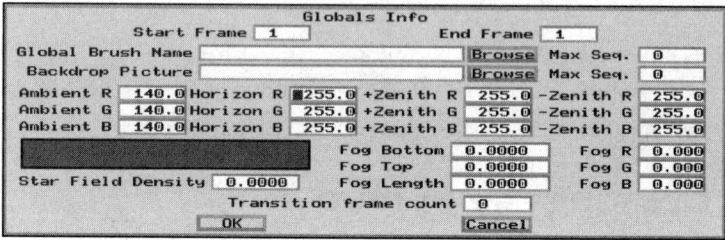

Setting the Global Ambient Color

While you are in the Action Editor, also adjust the global ambient lighting for the scene:

1. Click on the top bar beside "GLOBALS" to call the globals parameter box.
Result: The Globals Info dialog box appears (see Figure 12-10).

The global ambient light setting is on the left part of the dialog box. It has RGB values.

2. Enter a value of *140* for each of the R, G, and B boxes. (Press ⟨ENTER⟩ after each entry.)

The Horizon and Zenith settings allow you to add shading to the background scene. If you want to render the object against a white background, set the Horizon values and positive/negative Zenith values to *255*, as shown in the figure.

3. Click on OK to return to the Action Editor.

4. Select the Save option on the Editor menu.

5. Select Stage Editor on the Editor menu.

Adjusting the Camera

Adjust the camera so that the sphere is centered on the screen. As it moves, it tracks the target at the center of the sphere.

1. Use ⟨ALT⟩-⟨N⟩ to cycle through the objects until the camera is selected. (Remember to use the right ⟨ALT⟩ rather than the left ⟨ALT⟩ key.)

2. Press F1 to pick the camera.

3. Press M and move the camera until the sphere is centered in the screen.

Test Rendering the Scene

Let's see what the sphere looks like in its default color and shading:

1. Select Project Editor from the Project menu.

2. Click on the number *1* on the frame display (see Figure 12-11).

3. Click on the Generate button.
   Result: The Palette Method dialog box appears.

4. Select Generate All.
   Result: An alert dialog box appears at the top of the screen (see Figure 12-12).

Normally scenes are lit. A light has not been added to the scene. Let's look at the scene with only ambient light selected.

5. Click on No.
   Result: The progress of the render is indicated on the information line at the top of the screen. Then the object appears (see Figure 12-13).

The sphere is flat in color. Let's now add a light to the scene and adjust the shading parameters for the sphere:

1. Press ESC to exit back to the Project Editor.

2. Start a new subproject by clicking on the New button on the screen and entering a new project name (such as *specular*) in the name dialog box.

Figure 12-11
Frame display

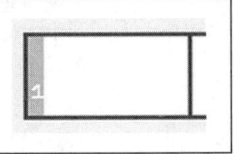

Figure 12-12
The alert dialog box

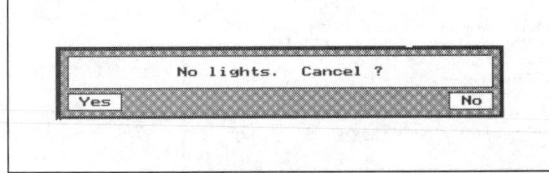

No lights. Cancel ?

Yes   No

Figure 12-13
The sphere lit
only by ambient
light

3. Accept the current parameters in the Rendering Subproject dialog box that appears.

Adding the Light

Now add a light to the scene:

1. Enter the Stage Editor.

2. From the Objects menu select Add|Light Source.
Result: The lights parameter dialog box appears (see Figure 12-14).

The dialog box allows you to specify the color (intensity) of the light, the type of light (point or parallel), and the shape of the parallel light (round or rectangular). Note that lights can be made to point at targets, but a point light source does not need one. Let's leave the light at its defaults.

1. Click on OK.
Result: The light is added at the center of the world. It is a round circle with a dot at its center.

2. Press F1 to pick the light, press M to move it, and drag it to a location in front, to the right, and above the sphere (see Figure 12-15).

Figure 12-14
The Light Source
Info dialog box

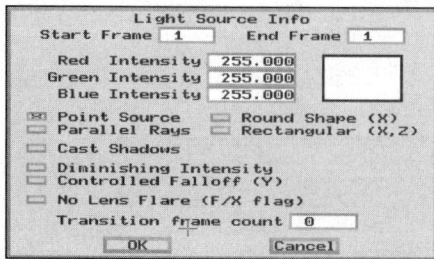

Figure 12-15
Placing the light

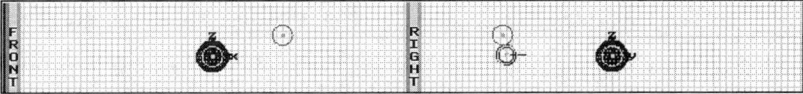

Now let's change the surface attributes of the object. This is done in Imagine's Attributes Requester, called from menus in both the Detail Editor and Stage Editor.

1. Cycle through to the sphere (right ALT-N). Press F1.

2. Select Attributes from the Object menu.
Result: The Attributes Requester appears (see Figure 12-16).

Depending on which surface attributes you choose, the objects can have either color (RGB) or value settings. Colors are changed either by entering their RGB values (0 to 255), or by dragging the color sliders and watching the swatch as the color changes.

To change a surface attribute, click on one of the attribute selector buttons, and adjust either the color or value sliders.

Here's what the attribute selectors do:

- Color—This sets the diffuse color of the object. Imagine has no ambient setting for the object.

- Reflect—This sets the reflectivity of the object. For a reflection to show up on the object, there must be something in the environment to reflect.

- Filter—This sets the transparency of the object.

- Specular—This sets the color of the specular highlight.

Figure 12-16
The Attributes
Requester

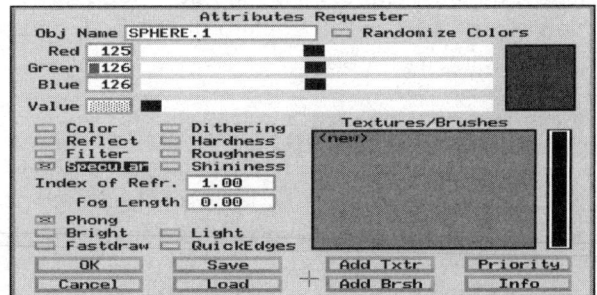

■ Hardness—This sets the size of the specular highlight.

■ Roughness—Polygons are by their nature flat. Adding color noise to a surface (such as black irregular spots) simulates a rough surface. This is a feature that is rarely used in animation because the spots tend to "crawl" when the object is animated.

■ Shininess—This creates a faded, blurred reflection on the object. Selecting this option cancels the Reflection map option.

The Dithering option is a color reduction and is not a surface attributes option.

3. Assign different values and colors for these options, and exit the Attributes Requester.
Result: The object save dialog box appears.

Surface attributes are saved with the object rather than the scene.

4. Save the object under the current object name. If you save the object under a different name, replace the sphere currently in the scene with the sphere under the new name.

5. Exit the Stage Editor, and test-render the scene in the Project Editor.

Experiment with the other settings. You may want to set the global ambient light setting back to a lower setting, about 50 or 60.

Tip: Adding a Global Reflection Map
Imagine allows an image to be used as a reflection map for the entire scene. A *reflection map* is an image projected on a reflective surface. For example, the image of the sky can be used as a global reflection map. It will appear on surfaces that are set to be reflective or shiny. To add a global reflection map to the scene, enter the Global Info dialog box in the Action Editor by following the steps shown earlier in this exercise. In the Global Brush Name box, enter the name of an uncompressed TIFF format image and its path. For example: *c:\pictures\sky.tif*. Exit the Global Info dialog box, and save the changes in the Action Editor. Then render.

TEXTURE-MAPPING A SURFACE

Many of the surfaces on objects in the real world have intricate textures that would be computationally expensive to reproduce as polygons. It's much easier to scan a photograph of the surface into the computer as a digital picture, then project the picture onto the surface of a model.

For example, a marble floor can be covered with a picture of marble. This is called *texture-mapping,* because the flat, two-dimensional digital picture is mapped (that is, projected) onto the surface of the 3D object, like a slide projected onto a surface by a slide projector.

The VRML specification describes how objects or parts of objects are texture mapped. The basic principles of texture-mapping can be demonstrated in Imagine.

Exercise: Texture-Mapping Objects

In this exercise, you will cover a flat surface with a texture map, then reduce the map so that it only covers part of the surface. Labels on bottles, or posters on walls can be created this way. The texture map is a small picture of marble scanned into the computer and saved as a TIFF-formatted image.

1. Enter the Detail Editor.

2. From the Object|Add submenu select Primitives and Plane.

3. Create a square plane at the default size, but set the number of sections to 1.
Result: This creates a small, flat tile, one polygon in width and height. Because the polygon has no depth, it is infinitely thin.

4. Press F1 to pick the square, and select Attributes from the Functions menu.
Result: The Attributes Requester (see Figure 12-17) appears.

Imagine calls texture maps *brushes.* Texture maps are added to surfaces by clicking on the Add Brsh button. Above the button is another button

Figure 12-17
The Attributes
Requester

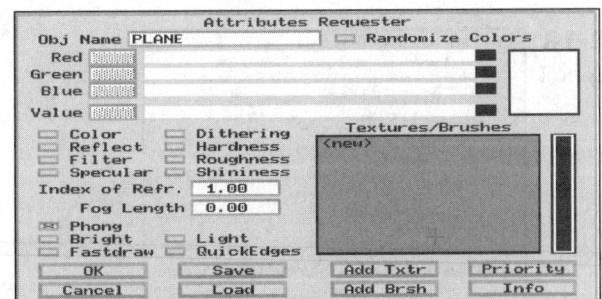

293

(Add Txtr) that is used to add procedural textures. This is a type of mathematically defined texture (such as a fractal wood grain) that is not supported by the VRML specification, so it will not be described here.

Above the buttons is a list display. You can add more than one texture to the surface of an Imagine object. For example, a small label might be placed over an orange peel map.

To add the map to the square you have created:

1. Click on the Add Brsh button.
Result: A standard Picture Filename dialog box appears.

2. Navigate to the \IMAG\PICTS subdirectory, and select the picture file named MARBLE.TIF.
Result: The map dialog box appears (see Figure 12-18).

Imagine provides a number of choices for applying maps. The two that are important here are the map Type and the Method projection used to apply the map. By default the Color type is chosen. This is an opaque map completely covering and blocking out the surface or textures below it. The other types have specialized applications. For example, the Altitude map uses the grayscale information in the image to create bumps and cavities on a surface, and is very useful for creating planets. Opaque maps are the only type currently supported by the VRML specification.

The map projection Method options are used to define how a map is projected on an object. Maps are projected along the y axis and extend in the x and z directions. By default, they project through to the other side of an object. The default is flat in the x and z axis directions. To project a map on a sphere, which is curved in both directions, choose the Wrap X, Wrap Z options. A cylinder is curved in one direction (x) and flat in another (z). Choose Wrap X, Flat Z as the mapping method for objects like these. Use the default Flat X, Flat Z option as the projection method for the square.

Figure 12-18
Map dialog box

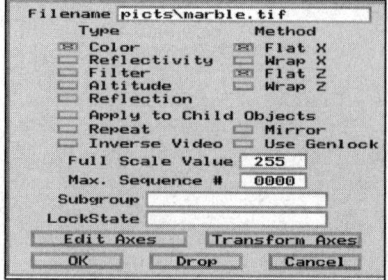

1. Click on the OK button to accept the defaults.
   Result: You return to the Attributes Requester.

2. Click on the OK button to return to the Detail Editor.
   Now do a Quick Render to test the result:

3. Choose Quick Render from the Editor menu.
   Result: The map is projected onto the square (see Figure 12-19).

If the square were extruded into a cube at this point, only the side that has been explicitly assigned texture coordinates would have the texture applied to it.

Imagine allows you to select an area of an object to apply the map to. To apply a texture to all sides of a cube, each side would have to be explicitly mapped. This is not the case for VRML texture maps. In the case of a VRML cube, the map would be applied to each of the six sides of the cube.

The way texture maps are applied to VRML objects is discussed later in this book. Mapping coordinates do not translate from one program to another easily, if at all. It's best to do mapping in a VRML authoring tool. For those who would like to explore mapping in Imagine, here's one more exercise.

Exercise: Adjusting the Image Map

Imagine provides flexibility in the way a map is applied to a surface. The map has its own set of axes, which allow it to be moved or scaled relative to the object it is attached to. In this exercise you'll make the marble map smaller than the square and apply it to the middle.

1. Ensure that the square is picked, and call the Attributes Requester from the Functions menu.

The current map is listed in the Textures/Map list. It must be removed before the map is reapplied.

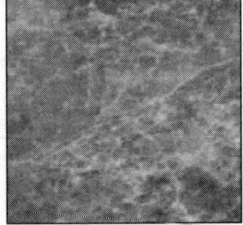

Figure 12-19
The texture-mapped square

2. Click on the map name (PICTS\MARBLE.TIF) in the list box.

3. Click on the Info button at the bottom of the Attributes Requester.
Result: The map dialog box appears (see Figure 12-20).

4. Click on the Drop button to remove the map.
Result: You are returned to the Attributes Requester.

5. Click on the Add Brsh button.
Result: The Picture Filename dialog box appears.

6. Select the map by name: *marble.tif.*
Result: The map dialog box appears again.

Now let's make the map coordinates one-fourth the size of the square and center it:

7. Click on the Edit Axes button.
Result: The map coordinates display appears (see Figure 12-21).

Imagine shows the object coordinates at the bottom left of the square and the map coordinates at the center of the box. The larger box is not meaningful, so just ignore it.

The normal transformation controls can be used to size the map axes:

1. Press the Ⓢ (scale) key, and drag the mouse until the map axes are one-fourth size (see Figure 12-22).

2. Press the Ⓜ (move) key and reposition the axes at the center of the object axes (see Figure 12-23).

3. Press SPACEBAR to confirm the changes.
Result: You are returned to the map dialog box.

Figure 12-20
The map dialog box

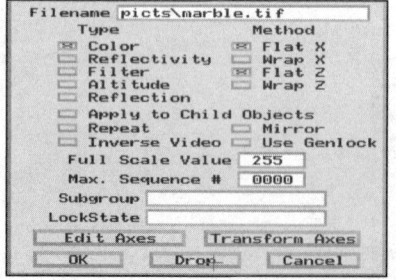

Figure 12-21
The map and object coordinates

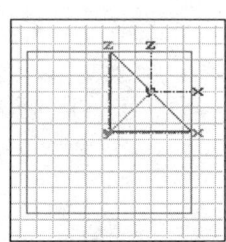

Figure 12-22
The map axes
scaled down

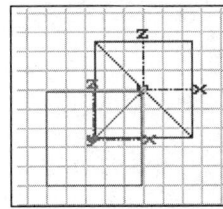

Figure 12-23
The map axes
repositioned

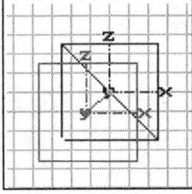

4. Click on OK to accept the changes.
Result: You are returned to the Attributes Requester.

5. Click on OK to return to the Detail Editor.

6. Select Quick Render to see the result (see Figure 12-24).

As mentioned earlier, labels can be applied to surfaces by sizing a map.

This chapter provided a brief overview of the two main ways that object surfaces are detailed by use of shading and texture mapping. Shading and mapping algorithms tend to be difficult to translate from one program to another. Here's some advice: Do the shading and mapping in a VRML authoring tool.

Figure 12-24
The map
applied to the
center of the
square

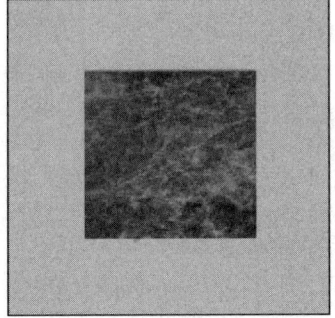

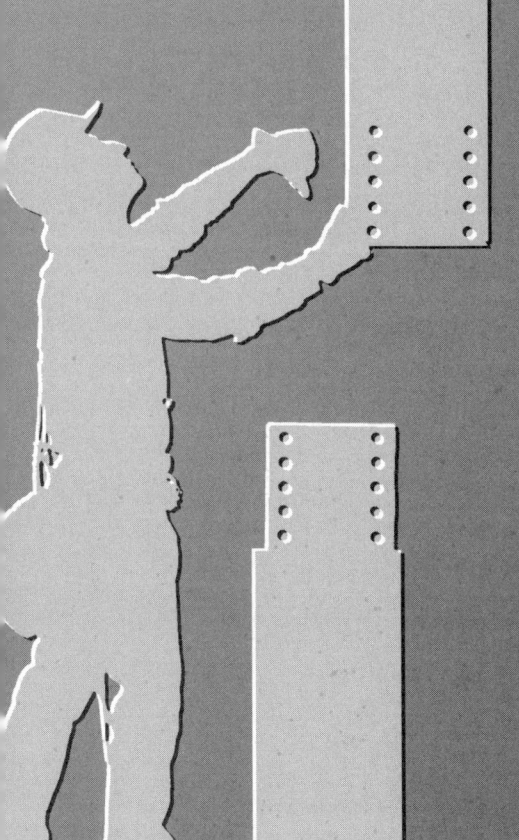

13
CREATING A SCENE IN FOUNTAIN

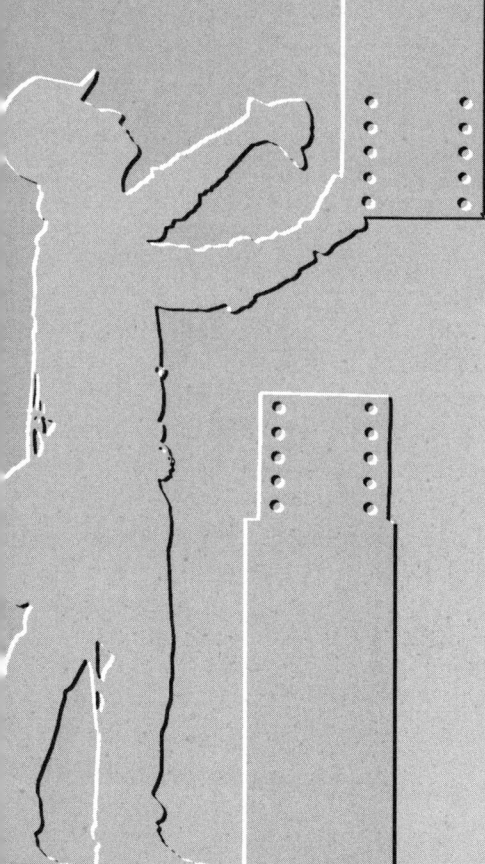

In this final chapter of the 3D section of *Web Publisher's Construction Kit with VRML/Live3D*, let's create a simple scene in a dedicated VRML creation and browsing program, Caligari Corporation's Fountain.

Fountain is a kind of Swiss Army Knife of the VRML world: a 3D creation tool, a VRML authoring tool, and a VRML browser combined into a single program.

Fountain is a subset of Caligari's TrueSpace modeling and rendering product. Its interface and tools will be familiar to users of TrueSpace, although some of the more powerful features of the animation package are missing in Fountain, such as the ability to lay out and build objects on orthogonal planes. It does include tools for creating 3D objects such as 3D primitives, 2D polygons, face editing, lathing, and sweeping, as well as the ability to extrude TrueType fonts. It supports two types of light sources: *infinite* (parallel) and *local* (spot) lights. Like its bigger sister product, it has a paint tool that allows you to dab paint on entire objects, or on individual faces and vertices.

One of the best uses for Fountain is importing and arranging 3D objects that were created in other 3D modeling programs. Fountain can import objects in formats such as DXF, Autodesk 3D Studio, Wavefront, NewTek LightWave, and Impulse Imagine. Fountain also imports a variety of 2D formats, including PostScript,

BMP, and JPG. This makes Fountain an excellent scene arrangement tool, since you can collect objects from anywhere—from sources on the Internet, from commercial 3D object libraries, or from friends. In this chapter, you'll see how to import Imagine objects into Fountain, arrange them, and export the arrangement as a VRML WRL scene file.

INSTALLING FOUNTAIN

The minimum hardware requirement for running Fountain is a 486 with 8 MB of RAM, and a 14.4 Kbps modem. To access VRML worlds on the Web, a SLIP/PPP connection and a 14.4 Kbps modem are also required. A 28.8 Kbps modem or ISDN connection is recommended for accessing larger worlds. Fountain also benefits from hardware 3D acceleration.

You must have the Internet Trumpet Winsock access program, TCPMAN.EXE, installed on your hard drive. When you first run Fountain, you have to be connected to the Internet. If you do not have Trumpet Winsock running, Fountain will complain that it did not find TCPMAN.EXE. Fountain will not thereafter run properly. However, you can disconnect your live connection to the Internet once Fountain is running.

NOTE: Beta Copy of Fountain on the CD-ROM
The version of Fountain provided on the CD-ROM (beta 6, called F09B6.EXE) was downloaded in March 1996. Because it was in beta, it had quite a few bugs. It's recommended that you download the latest version of Fountain from Caligari's Internet site: *http://caligari.com*. Look for the section on VRML or Fountain. Some of the interface conventions may have changed, so consult Fountain's online help if what is described here does not strictly apply.

Because the program on the CD-ROM is an early beta, please do not call Waite Group (the publisher of this book) for technical support.

A copy of Fountain can be found on the CD-ROM, stored in a self-extracting archive called F09B6.EXE. Follow these steps to install Fountain:

1. Exit Windows.

2. Change to the root directory of your hard drive. For example, type

```
cd C:\
```

3. Create a temporary directory for the Fountain program. For example, type

```
md TEMP
```

4. Change to the directory (cd \TEMP) and copy into it the F09B6.EXE file from the CD-ROM.

5. De-archive the file by typing

`f09b6.exe`

at the DOS prompt. A variety of files, including a Windows SETUP.EXE, will be created.

6. Make sure that Windows is in your in MS-DOS path and type

`setup`

from the directory. (Do not enter Windows at this point.)

🔩 NOTE: 3DR Installation

You can run the setup program from within Windows, rather than from the DOS prompt. However, this sometimes produces an error when you attempt to run Fountain after installation (see Figure 13-1). Run the setup program from the DOS prompt of the directory where Fountain has been installed.

7. The setup file will call Windows. Windows will load, and the Fountain installation program will automatically run. Follow the instructions for installing Fountain. A program icon will be created.

8. Before running Fountain, start up the Trumpet Winsock Internet access program (TCPMAN). Fountain will not run without it.

9. Run Fountain by double-clicking on its program icon.

INSTALLING THE WIN32S EXTENSIONS

When Fountain first ran in the authors' Windows 3.11 program, Fountain complained that the Win32s extensions were not up to date. The authors downloaded the recommended Wind32s installation zip files from the Caligari ftp site (WIN32S_125.ZIP). This file is provided on the accompanying CD-ROM.

1. Copy the WIN32S_125.ZIP file to a temporary directory.

Figure 13-1
3DR error
message

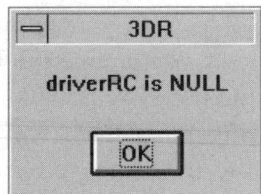

2. Using PKUNZIP, unzip the files using the -d (directory) option:

```
pkunzip -d w32s_125.zip
```

3. Enter Windows, and from the Program Manager choose the Run option.

4. Navigate to the \DISK1 subdirectory the Win32s zip created, run the SETUP.EXE file, and follow the installation instructions.

CREATION AND BROWSING MODES

Fountain has two modes: World Building (creation) mode and Walk Through World (browsing) mode. This chapter explores World Building mode, the default mode when you first enter.

World Building Mode

In World Building mode, the tools for creating and editing 3D objects become available. Objects are created, loaded from other programs, shaded or textured, and saved in WRL format. This is the mode that will be used.

Walk Through World Mode

In Walk Through World mode, the tools for creating objects disappear and are replaced by tools for navigating VRML worlds. To navigate to a location on the Internet where a WRL file is, enter its address in the URL box at the top of the screen.

INTERFACE OVERVIEW

Fountain has an interface similar to its sister modeling program, Caligari TrueSpace (see Figure 13-2).

Notice that Fountain's interface is dramatically different from Impulse Imagine's and most other 3D programs. Instead of the conventional orthogonal and perspective windows (top, front, side, and 3D perspective), it opens on a single perspective view of the 3D world. Instead of showing the objects in the scene as wireframes, the objects are shown by default as shaded. (However, Fountain can be switched to wireframe mode by clicking on the menu bar's 3DR button and selecting the Wireframe Mode button.)

Many users new to 3D prefer working interactively with objects in shaded perspective mode. Others prefer the precision and control of a more

Figure 13-2
The Fountain
interface

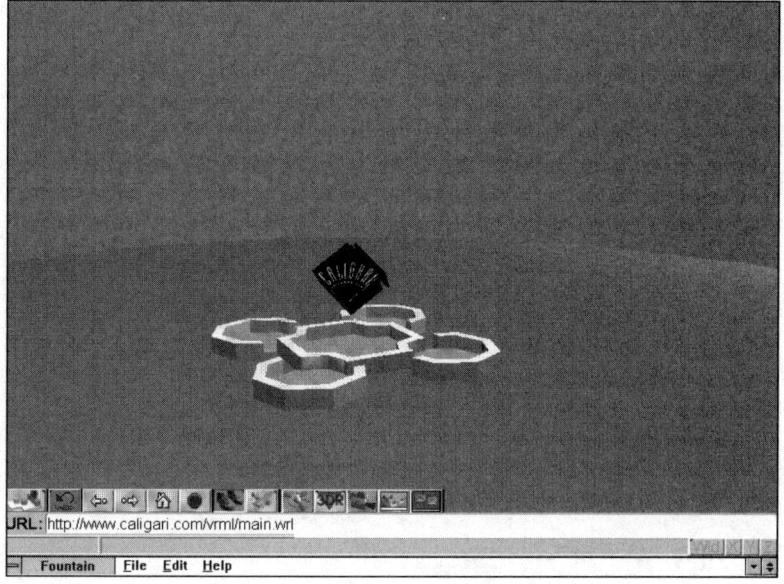

CAD-like interface with its orthogonal construction views. TrueSpace combines both.

RENDERING TECHNOLOGY

Fountain uses Intel's 3DR 3D acceleration software technology to render 3D objects. The software DLL (dynamic link library) is optimized for the Pentium processor, but it will also run on 486-class computers. If your system has 3D acceleration video hardware, Fountain will take advantage of the increased rendering speed it provides. Although 3D hardware acceleration will make Fountain's manipulation of shaded objects substantially faster, remember that if you place the VRML scene on the Web, most users will not have 3D acceleration.

PROGRAM TOOLS AND FEATURES

This chapter covers only those tools that are relevant to creating a scene, not to object building.

Fountain allows you to directly manipulate objects in a three-dimensional perspective. Since this greatly simplifies the process of choreographing objects in a scene, this makes Fountain an excellent tool for assembling and testing VRML worlds.

By default, the menus and buttons are at the bottom of the screen, although they can be shifted to the top of the screen. To do that, select Preferences from the File menu, and click on the TopMenu item in the Preferences dialog box (see Figure 13-3).

See the online help system for information on Fountain's other preference settings.

The Help On Tool

Caligari has added a Help On tool to the interface. Clicking on this button provides a short animated explanation of the function of a button or tool. The beta version included with this book does not provide help on all the buttons.

File Input/Output

Fountain loads and displays VRML scenes, or you can build a VRML scene from scratch by creating or loading objects in Fountain. Fountain saves scenes and can save parts of scenes.

As mentioned, a particularly valuable feature of Fountain is that it can import a wide variety of proprietary 3D object file formats, including Imagine objects.

Note that some problems may occur when you translate objects from one program to another. The most common is *normal flipping*. Some of the normals may become oriented in the wrong direction. This results in objects that may appear to have holes in them. Other translation problems include lost textures or lost object hierarchical relationships. For example, Fountain does not preserve Imagine's hierarchical structure, but rather attaches all objects to a single parent object. All animation information will be lost. Textures are not preserved. However, attributes such as color and shading will translate.

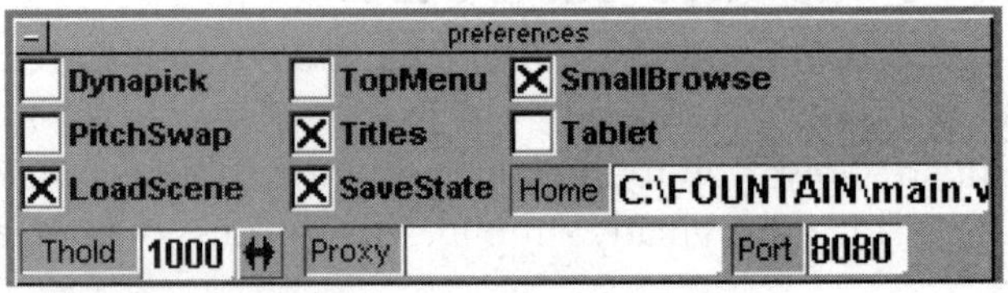

Figure 13-3
Preferences
dialog box

preferences

☐ Dynapick ☐ TopMenu ☒ SmallBrowse
☐ PitchSwap ☒ Titles ☐ Tablet
☒ LoadScene ☒ SaveState Home C:\FOUNTAIN\main.v

Thold 1000 ↔ Proxy   Port 8080

Selecting and Using Tools

Tools must be selected before they can be used. Clicking on a new tool automatically deselects the previous tool. Here are some important notes about tools.

- To select a tool, click on it with the left mouse button. If the tool uses control panels to adjust settings, they automatically open.

- Right-click on a tool to open its property panel, if it has one. These panels automatically go away when another tool is picked with the left mouse button (see Figure 13-4).

- The tool icons give indication of available mouse actions by using small triangles at the top left and top right corners of the icons. A small blue triangle in the top left corner of an icon indicates that a pop-up list of tool variants is available (see Figure 13-5).

- A small red triangle in the top right corner of an icon indicates that there is a property panel available for this tool (see Figure 13-6).

- Left-click and hold to bring up a menu of tool variant icons (see Figure 13-7).

- If you select a tool, then decide not to use it, simply move the mouse away from the tool before releasing the mouse button.

Figure 13-4
Properties for the paint tool displayed in panels

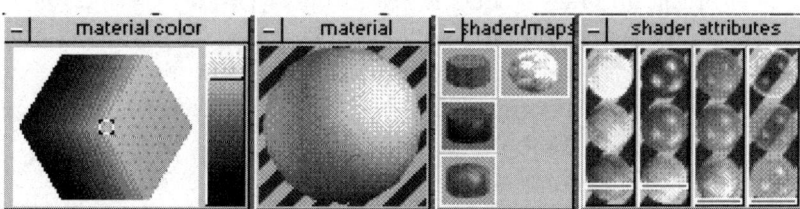

Figure 13-5
Tool icon with small triangle indicating an available pop-up list

Figure 13-6
Tool with properties

Figure 13-7
Selecting a tool

[VRML] Active, highlighted tool icons and settings buttons appear blue and "pushed in." Also, tool icons that are not currently available, for example, because no object is selected, are "grayed" and cannot be selected.

[VRML] Right-click to bring up a tool's property panel. To access a variant's property panel without invoking the variant, use the right mouse button, and drag to display the pop-up menu.

[VRML] When a tool's property or control panel is accessed, the panel itself may be moved anywhere in the workspace by clicking and dragging the panel away from the tool icons. The panel will remember its previous position when it is next opened. To close any panel manually, right-click on any gray area in the panel or on a panel button, and drag outside the panel. When an *X* appears across the entire panel, release the mouse button, and the panel will be closed.

[VRML] To select a tool variant, hold down the left mouse button until the list pops up or drops down, and then drag the mouse to the new tool and let go.

Viewing and Navigating Fountain's World

The mouse attached to your computer is probably a 2D mouse, capable of gliding along the x and y axes of your tabletop, but useless when it comes to moving along the z (up and down) dimension, as required in a 3D environment like Fountain. Navigating in Fountain is probably the most difficult aspect of the program to master.

Fountain starts up in the Fly Mode. The Fountain help section compares Fly Mode navigation to operating a video game, but the direction and type of movement is based upon which mouse button (or buttons) is pressed. as indicated in Figures 13-8a through 13-8c. The Auto-Pilot option takes this mouse-based navigation a step further, maintaining the viewer's motion continually once a direction is chosen. Auto-Pilot navigation can be a bit disorienting, so it's recommended for those already familiar with Fly Mode navigation.

View Windows

Fountain provides two views of the 3D workspace: main view and new view. The main view is the view filling the screen. New view is a small window that can be called on top of the main view to provide an additional perspective view of the world. Only one new view can be opened at a time. It's most useful as an overview of the entire world as you work close to objects.

Figure 13-8a
In Fly Mode. when the left mouse button is pressed, viewers can move backward and forward, or turn left and right within the scene

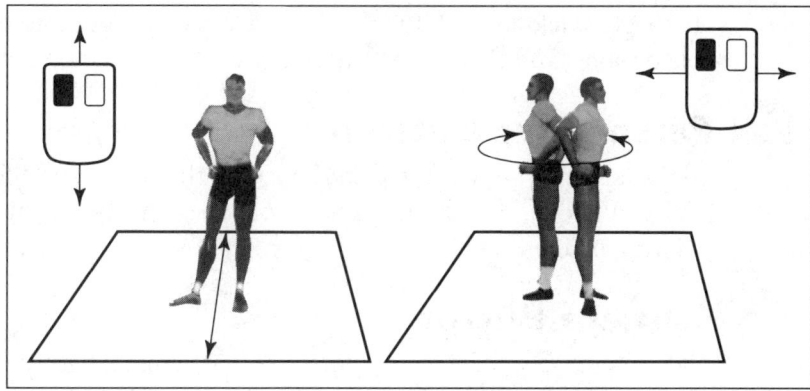

Figure 13-8b
When the right mouse button is pressed in Fly Mode, viewers can move up and down, or sidestep within the scene

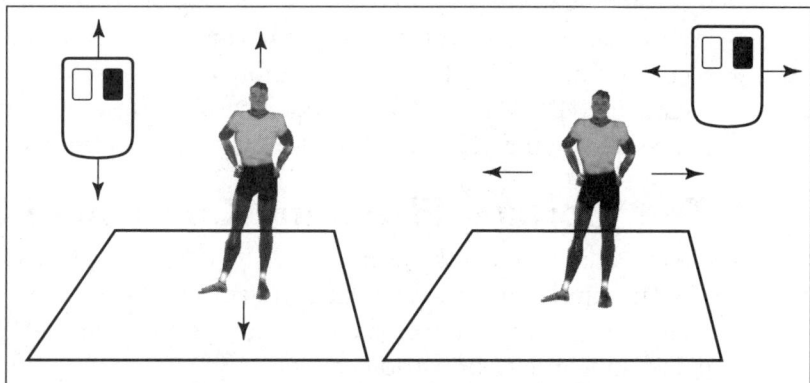

Figure 13-8c
When both mouse buttons are pressed in Fly Mode, viewers can get a slanted view of the world

Perspective View and Camera View

The main view window can be toggled between perspective view and camera view. Toggle between these two views by clicking on the following buttons.

(To toggle, click on the button with the left mouse button to pop up the available options, and then move the cursor over the selected option and click.)

Perspective Button

The perspective view is the default view of the world and the one most flexible to work in. The point of view or "eye" can be positioned anywhere, pointing in any direction.

Camera Button

The camera view is the view from a selected camera, light, or object. The orientation of the view is along the selected object's z axis. The view is altered by switching to the perspective view, clicking on a camera, then manipulating the camera icon with the object navigation tools (discussed in the next section). Then select the Camera button again. Since camera view is useful mostly for 3D animation, not VRML world navigation, it is recommended that you leave the program in its default perspective mode.

The Working Plane and Coordinate Systems

Objects are created and placed relative to a working plane (see Figure 13-9).

The aircraft in Figure 13-9 is sitting on the working plane. The working plane is aligned to the world coordinate system. The center of the working plane is the origin, or world center.

Fountain has three user-selectable coordinate systems.

World Coordinate System—This is the default when Fountain is first entered. In the world coordinate system the z axis runs up and down relative to the working plane. The y axis runs right and left, and the x axis runs from the front to the back of the working plane.

Figure 13-9
View of the working plane (no pun intended) and the axes of the world coordinate system

Object Coordinate System—Objects have their own coordinate systems. When they are first created, they are aligned to the world coordinate system. However, they can be moved, scaled, or rotated relative to themselves or relative to the world coordinate system.

Screen Coordinate System—The Screen Coordinate System is aligned to the screen plane. The x axis runs right and left. The y axis runs up and down. The z axis is perpendicular to the plane of the screen.

To select a coordinate system, click on the Coordinate System Selector button at the top left of the screen (see Figure 13-10).

When you click on the selector button, a pop-up list is presented. Click on one of the following choices:

World Coordinate System

Screen Coordinate System

Object Coordinate System

Constraining Movement to Selected Axes

Movement can be restricted to selected axes by use of the axes select buttons (see Figure 13-11).

Deselecting an axis (button up) constrains movement to the remaining axis or axes. This is useful when you want to move the point of view from one position to another along an axis. For example, deselect the y and z axes to constrain movement of the point of view to movement along the x axis.

Object Selection Tool

Click on this tool to enter object selection mode and to exit other modes. If you are performing a number of different operations on the same object, it is not necessary to reselect the object with this tool.

The currently selected object is indicated by a 3D arrow pointing at the center of the object (see Figure 13-12).

Figure 13-10
Selecting the
coordinate
system

Figure 13-11
Selecting axes

Figure 13-12
The arrow
pointing at the
object's center

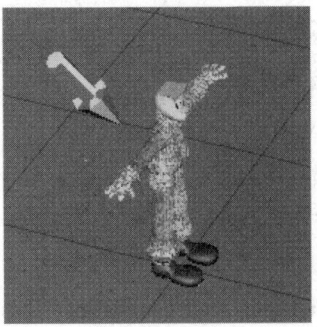

 **NOTE:** In scenes with more than one object, use [RIGHT ARROW] and [LEFT ARROW] to select objects.

Moving, Scaling, and Rotating Objects

Objects are moved, rotated, or scaled with the following tools:

Use these button in conjunction with the axes select buttons discussed earlier.

Object Move

This tool is the first one on the left in the preceding illustration. Select this tool to move an object or a group of objects in the current coordinate system. The left button controls movement along the x axis by mouse movement parallel to the x axis, and movement along the y axis by mouse movement parallel to the y axis. Using only the right mouse button controls movement along the z axis.

Object Rotate

This is the middle button in the preceding illustration. Select this tool to rotate an object or a group of glued objects in the current coordinate system. The left button controls rotation around the x axis by mouse movement perpendicular to the x axis, and rotation around the y axis by mouse movement perpendicular to the y axis. Using only the right mouse button controls rotation around the z axis by mouse movement perpendicular to the z axis.

Object Scale

This button is on the far right of the preceding illustration. Select this tool to scale an object or a group of glued objects in the current coordinate system. The left button controls scaling on the x axis by mouse movement parallel to the x axis, and scaling on the y axis by mouse movement parallel to the y axis. Using only the right mouse button controls scaling on the z axis. If both buttons are pressed, the scaling is uniform on all axes.

TUTORIAL: IMPORTING AND ARRANGING IMAGINE OBJECTS

In this short tutorial, let's import a space station made in Imagine, along with a spaceship. You'll arrange them in a scene and save the scene as a VRML scene.

World Building Button

Let's start by opening Fountain:

1. Run the Trumpet Winsock program and then run Fountain.
Result: Fountain will open in Walk Through World mode.

2. Click on the World Building button to switch to World Building mode.
Result: The construction plane appears.

3. From the File menu, select Scene|New.
Result: This clears the current default scene.

Adding Objects to a Scene

Now let's add the space station:

1. From the File menu, select Load Object.

2. In the File dialog box, navigate to the Imagine Objects directory (\IMAG\OBJECTS), and select the SPACESTA.OBJ file.
Result: The Object Import Settings dialog box appears (see Figure 13-13).

It's usually a good idea to leave the settings at their defaults. Most objects should be imported at the center of the world, with their normals aligned.

Figure 13-13
The Object
Import Settings
dialog box

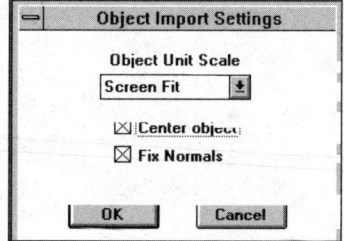

Object Import Settings

Object Unit Scale
Screen Fit ▼

☒ Center object
☒ Fix Normals

OK   Cancel

If you attempt to import an Imagine object without the Fix Normals option checked, some of the faces will appear to be transparent in the object.

3. Select OK.
Result: The space station loads (see Figure 13-14).
To see the space station, move the point of view away from the object.

4. Click with the left mouse button, and drag *down* to move the point of view away from the space station. Click and drag to the right or left to move the view to the right or left. Then click and drag with the right mouse button to move the point of view above the space station. When you are finished, the space station should look like Figure 13-15.

The space station is centered on the construction plane. Now let's add the spaceship.

5. Using the File | Load Object option, load the SPACESHP.OBJ file from Imagine's OBJECTS directory. Use the default import settings.
Result: The spaceship loads into the center of the scene, occupying the same space as the space station (see Figure 13-16).

◥ 3DR Button and Object Move Button

Let's move the ship away from the space station. It will be easier to move the ship in wireframe mode, rather than render mode, so let's switch to wireframe mode.

Figure 13-14
The space
station

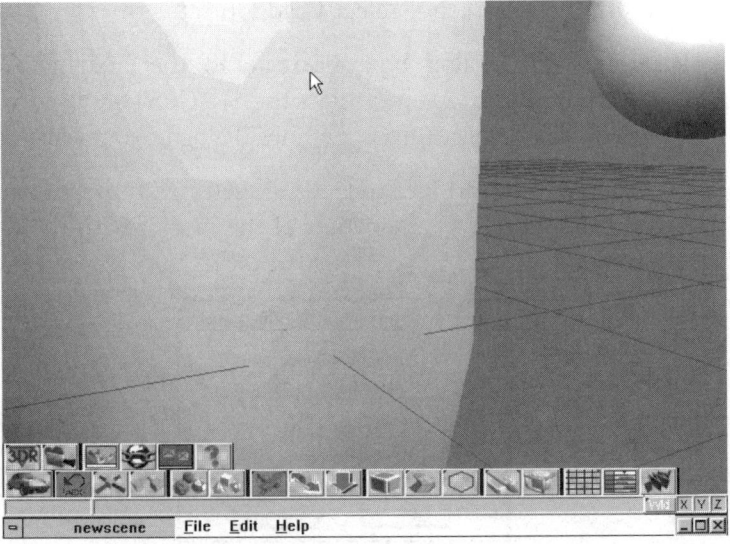

Figure 13-15
Positioning the space station

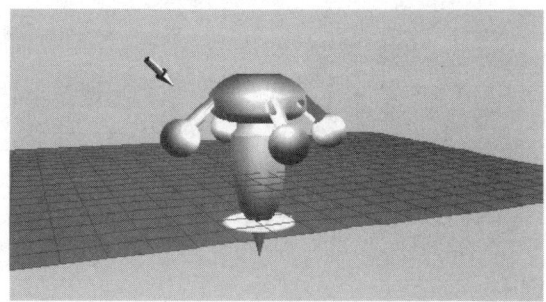

1. Select wireframe mode by clicking on the 3DR (solid rendering) button, moving the mouse cursor over the wireframe button, and clicking on it. Result: After a few moments, the objects appear as wireframe objects (see Figure 13-17).

   The spaceship appears in white because it was automatically selected when it was loaded. (If it is not, click on it with the Object Select tool, the arrow button.)

2. Click on the Object Move button.

Figure 13-16
The spaceship loads into the center of the world

Figure 13-17
The wireframe objects

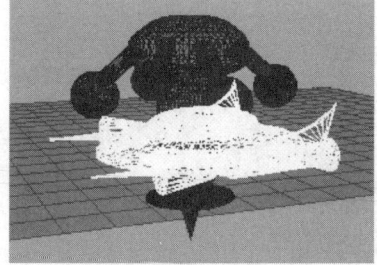

Figure 13-18
The spaceship
in its new
position

3. Using the mouse cursor, move the spaceship away from the space station (see Figure 13-18).

Object Scale Button

The spaceship is too large relative to the spaceship. Let's scale it down.

VR ML Select the Object Scale button by clicking on the Object Move button, moving the mouse cursor over the Object Scale button, and clicking.

VR ML Click on the object. Pressing both mouse buttons, scale the spaceship smaller (see Figure 13-19).

You can switch back to shaded mode by clicking on the 3DR button.

Saving the Scene in VRML Format

You're now ready to save the two objects as a VRML world scene.

1. From the File menu, select Scene|Save.
Result: The Save Scene dialog box appears.

2. From the List Files As Type list box, select "VRML scenes *.wrl."
Result: The Export VRML File dialog box appears.

Figure 13-19
The scaled-
down spaceship

Imagine supports Inlining and LOD, concepts that are explored later in this book. For now, deselect the Inlining options and click on OK.

There it is, the scene saved as a VRML WRL file! The scene can now be loaded into a VRML browser and viewed.

SUMMARY

This has been a quick introduction to creating a VRML scene with Caligari's Fountain. Building objects in Imagine and assembling them in Caligari Fountain is a valid strategy, although users who prefer TrueSpace's 3D object creation environment may prefer to create objects in Caligari's TrueSpace and import them into Fountain. You can create objects in Fountain, but it does not include the precision tools necessary to create detailed objects. Check Caligari's web site (http://www.caligari.com) for the latest version of Fountain or for new VRML tools they may have released by the time this book is published.

The VRML creation tools may be still in their infancy, but Fountain certainly is an excellent harbinger of things to come.

14

TRADING
WORLDS:
CONVERTING

The last couple of chapters showed you how to create nearly anything you can imagine. But if you want to sprinkle your world with common objects such as furniture, cars, planes, jugs, or bananas, you probably won't need to draw (or extrude) a single line. There's a wealth of spectacular 3D objects already out there.

Whether you create your objects, buy them, or borrow them, it usually won't be neat-and-trim VRML. Before you put the 3D scene on the Web, you'll need to convert it. This chapter shows you exactly how to do this.

WHERE TO GET READY-MADE OBJECTS

One of the best sources for 3D objects is, naturally, the disc that accompanies this book. You're free to use any of these lovelies to populate your 3D world. If you need more, several companies publish CD-ROM libraries full of 3D goodies. Many of these companies will custom-design complicated 3D objects for you. Some of these businesses are listed in Appendix A.

But the biggest store of 3D knickknacks is on the Internet. Table 14-1 lists a few of the largest libraries. Some of the libraries, such as Mesh Mart, will charge you a nominal price for downloading their creations. But most of the stuff is free as love in the '70s.

Table 14-1 Online 3D warehouses

3D Library	Location
VRML Models	http://www.ocnus.com/models/models.html
VRML Supermarket	http://www.dcs.ed.ac.uk/generated/package-links/objects/vrml.html
Gallery Warehouse	http://www.newcollege.edu/vrmlab/Warehouse/
Mesh Mart	http://cedar.cic.net/~rtilmann/mm/index.htm
ORC Incorporated	http://www.ocnus.com/

Most of the 3D objects you'll create, buy, borrow, or steal are not written in VRML. You'll find all sorts of different formats: DXF, BIZ, PLG, NFF, RWX, VRT, IV, and a whole lot of other acronyms. Not to worry, though. Converting a 3D object to VRML is usually a simple one-step process.

3D FILE FORMATS

There are lots of 3D formats out there. Nearly every software company, computer manufacturer, and academic institution has developed its own format to work best with its configuration. Luckily, though, most 3D formats break down into a list of carefully placed polygons. Switching from one format to another is usually only a matter of changing a few statements, juggling a few numbers, and following a few rules. VRML was carefully designed to work with nearly any existing format.

Some of the most popular graphics formats include

- DXF (Drawing Interchange File)—This is a very popular format used with AutoCAD and most other CAD packages.

- IGES (Initial Graphics Exchange Standard)—This is yet another popular format and is used with Alias and AutoCAD.

- OBJ—This is used with Wavefront animation software.

- OFF (Object File Format)—This is a mesh format used by several programs, including some public-domain ray tracers.

- NFF (Neutral File Format)—This is used with many public-domain ray tracers. A related format is ENFF (Extended Neutral File Format).

- 3DS—This is Autodesk's 3D Studio format.

- Inventor—This is SGI's Open Inventor format. The typical file extension is .IV.

- POV (Persistence of Vision)—This format is used with the POV-Ray ray tracer.

- 3D2—This is used with Stereo CAD-3D.

- ART (Another Ray Tracer)—This is the VORT ray tracer.

- AVS (Application Visualization System)—The file extensions can be .GEOM, .PROP, and .SCR.

- BYU—This format is produced by the Movie BYU software.

- DKB—This is a file from the DKB-Trace ray tracer.

- Infini-D—This is the Macintosh Infini-D modeling package.

- LightWave—This is used by the LightWave on the Amiga.

- MGF (Materials and Geometry Format)—A more obscure format.

- MSDL (Manchester Scene Description Language)—A format used at a graphics lab in Manchester.

- NURBS (Nonlinear Uniform Rational B-Splines)—This is a popular new format using splines to represent shapes.

- OOGL (Object Oriented Graphics Library)—This is used with Geomview. This format can be found with many file-name extensions, including .OOGL, .OFF, .LIST, .TLIST, .GRP, .QUAD, .MESH, .INST, .BEZ, and .VECT.

- RAD—This is the Radiance radiosity renderer.

- RIB (RenderMan Interface Bytestream)—This is used with RenderMan software.

- RWX—This is used with RenderWare and the MEME virtual reality system.

- SCN (SCeNe)—This format is used with the RTrace ray tracer.

- SDL (Scene Description Language)—This is used with Alias modeling and animation software.

- Strata—This is used with StrataVision.

- TPoly—A special format for triangulated polygons.

- VID—This is Amiga VideoScape format.

- **WLD**—This is used with several VR programs such as REND386, AVRIL, VR-386, and Gossamer.

- **X3D**—This is used with x3d 2.0 and xdart.

- **YAODL** (Yet Another Object Description Language)—This is used with the Powerflip software.

TRANSLATORS

Now that you've got your 3D file, you'll need to chop it up. Depending on the format of your file, conversion might be as easy as changing a few words around, or as complex as remodeling the geometry. Open Inventor is the easiest file structure to convert into VRML, since it's the format VRML was based on.

NOTE: Silicon Graphics has created a quick and easy converter from Open Inventor to VRML. It's called *ivtovrml*. SGI has also released two excellent utilities: *dxfTolv*, to convert any DXF file to Open Inventor, and *3dsTolv*, to handle 3D Studio files. All of the above software comes bundled with the WebSpace browser (which you can get at *http://webspace.sgi.com/Tools/index.html*).

Running converters is generally easy. Some run under Windows or Macintosh systems. Simply open the file you want to convert, and then save it under a different format. Some other conversion software must be run from the UNIX or DOS command line. This usually takes a form like

```
$ convert ball.rwx ball.wrl
```

A few converters run entirely on the Internet. Just put your 3D object in an anonymous FTP directory or public Web directory. You can then tell the converter the URL of your object. It'll download it, convert it, and store the results in an anonymous FTP site of its own.

WARNING: Be sure to keep a safe copy of your original 3D file, since some converters may warp the file.

The best VRML translator is WCVT2POV, discussed in the next section. If you have a 3D format that isn't supported by WCVT2POV and you can't find software to translate it directly into VRML, then you should have no problem converting that format into a file that is supported by WCVT2POV.

Some other useful converters include

- Syndesis' InterChange—This is commercial Windows software that transfers between most every 3D file format, including VRML. It's a must for any 3D professional.

- ORC's 3D Model to VRML—This reads a file from an Internet FTP site and returns a WRL file. You can read in most popular graphics formats including Alias wire files (.ALIAS), AutoCAD (.DXF), Autodesk 3D Studio (.3DS), IGES (.IGES or .IGS), Inventor (.IV), Softimage (.HRC or .DSC), and Wavefront (.OBJ).

- Autodesk's 3D Studio R4 to VRML—This is a plug-in module for 3D Studio Release 4 that allows you to output VRML.

- Dx2vrml—This is a plug-in module for IBM's Visualization Data Explorer (DX).

- Organic Online's dxf2wrl—Send in the address of a DXF file and it will spit out a fine-looking VRML world.

- image2wrl—This reads in an SGI image file, converting the first channel into a VRML grid.

- obj2vrml—This converts Wavefront OBJ to VRML.

- obj2wrl—This is a simpler program to convert Wavefront OBJ to VRML.

- off2vrml—This is a Perl script that converts an OFF (Object File Format) file to VRML.

- OZ, Inc.'s soft2vrml—This converts SOFTIMAGE 3.0 3D models to VRML.

- tri2wrl—This converts Alias TRI to VRML.

- Wld2vrml—This converts WLD files to VRML.

- wadtoiv—This converts a WAD file from the DOOM video game into a valid Open Inventor file.

- lwtoiv—This program converts Lightwave files to Open Inventor.

You can pick up any of the above converters on the Web. Simply refer to Table 14-2.

Table 14-2 Conversion software on the Web

Converter	Location
InterChange	http://www.webmaster.com:80/syndesis/
ORC's 3D	http://www.ocnus.com/translate.html
3DS to VRML	http://www.autodesk.com/prod/mm/vrml.htm
DX to VRML	http://www.tc.cornell.edu/Visualization/contrib/cs490-94to95/ckline/dx2vrml/dx2vrml.html
dxf2wrl	http://www.organic.com/vrml/
image2wrl	http://www.usyd.edu.au/~ghorne/VRML/software/index.html
obj2vrml	http://www.egd.igd.fhg.de:8080/~schlempp/
obj2wrl	http://www.sdsc.edu/EnablingTech/Visualization/vrml/tools/obj2wrl/help/obj2wrl.html
off2vrml	http://coney.gsfc.nasa.gov/Mathews/Objects/off2vrml.html
soft2vrml	http://www.oz.is/OZ/Products/soft2vrml
tri2wrl	http://www.sdsc.edu/EnablingTech/Visualization/vrml/tools/tri2wrl/help/tri2wrl.html
Wld2vrml	ftp://sunee.uwaterloo.ca/pub/rend386/converters/
wadtoiv	http://www-white.media.mit.edu/~kbrussel/wadtoiv.html
lwtoiv	http://amber.rc.arizona.edu/vrml.html#Converters

There are even a few programs that convert VRML to other formats. One of the coolest of these is ORC's VRML Stereograms, which warps a VRML world into one of those wacky magic-eye random-dot stereograms. Pick it up at

http://www.ocnus.com/stereogram.html

WCVT2POV

A hearty nod of thanks goes out to Keith Rule for a spectacular 3D conversion program...and it's free! You can find it on the enclosed CD-ROM. The WCVT2POV program can work with the following formats:

- AOFF (*.GEO) files
- AutoCAD (*.DXF) files
- 3D Studio (*.3DS) files
- Neutral File Format (*.NFF)
- RAW (*.RAW) files
- TPOLY (*.TPOLY) files

- TrueType fonts (*.TTF) files

- Wavefront (*.OBJ) files

- AutoCAD (*.DXF) files (output only)

- 3D Studio (*.ASC) files (output only)

- Neutral File Format (*.NFF) (output only)

- OpenGL (*.C) C program fragments (output only)

- POVRay V2.2 (*.POV, *.INC) files (output only)

- PovSB (*.PSB) files (output only)

- RAW (*.RAW) files (output only)

- TPOLY (*.TPOLY) files (output only)

- VRML V1.0 (*.WRL) files (output only)

- Wavefront (*.OBJ) files (output only)

NOTE: You can find out the latest information about WCVT2POV at *http://skexix.europa.com/~keithr/.*

Using WCVT2POV is quite simple. Simply load your object by selecting File|Open. Choose the format of the file, and then specify the Drive, Directory, and Filename. The object's wireframe will appear, as shown in Figure 14-1.

Figure 14-1
Normal lines should point outward

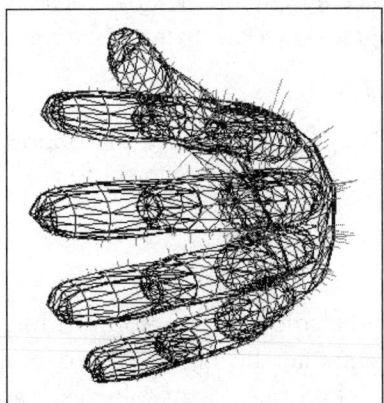

Setting It Up

For best results, you should be sure to use the following settings each time you use WCVT2POV:

- Select File|Preferences|View. Be sure the Draw Vertex Normal, Cull Backfaces, and Normal Calc Direction items are checked. Lower the smoothing angle to 50 or so.

- Select File|Preferences|DXF. Be sure the Extrude 2D item is checked. Set the Extrusion Amount to 1.0.

- Select File|Preferences|Output. Uncheck the Groups Supported In Raw Format support box. Set the Scale to *1.0* to create a VRML object that is the same size as the original object. If you want to create a smaller object, use a lower scale; use a larger scale factor to make the object bigger. For example, to create an object that is half the size of the original, set the scale to *.5*.

Making It Normal

There should be green lines jutting out from your object, making it look porcupine-like. These are the normals, discussed earlier, which let you know which way light is hitting the object. If the normals are all pointing *in* toward each other, instead of *out* toward the light (as in Figure 14-1), you will need to flip the object. Select Object|Mirror|X. Then select Mirror|Y and Mirror|Z. Alternatively, you can click the x|x, y|y, or z|z buttons in the toolbar.

Rotating

You can now rotate the object to look the way you want it. For example, you can flip the side view of the dolphins in Figure 14-2 so that they're jumping out at you. Simply select Object|Rotate or click the rotate arrow in the toolbar. Fill in the number of degrees the object should be rotated around the x, y, and z axes.

NOTE: Objects created with WCVT2POV face the opposite direction with some VRML browsers. If this happens, turn the object so it is facing away from the camera.

Color

If you'd like, you can change the color of each group within the object. Most formats will automatically separate the object into common groups. For example, a body may consist of a head, torso, some legs, and some arms.

Figure 14-2
Rotating the
scene so it
looks its best

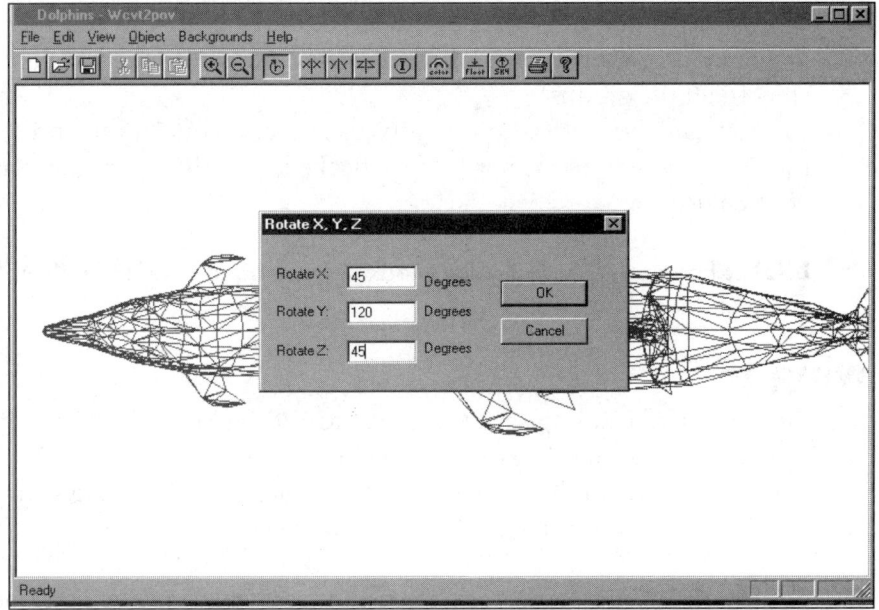

Select Object|Color or click the rainbow color icon in the toolbar. The
Color And Texture Info dialog box appears as in Figure 14-3. Click on one
of the group names. To change the name, click on the Edit Name button. If

Figure 14-3
Giving each
group its own
color and
texture

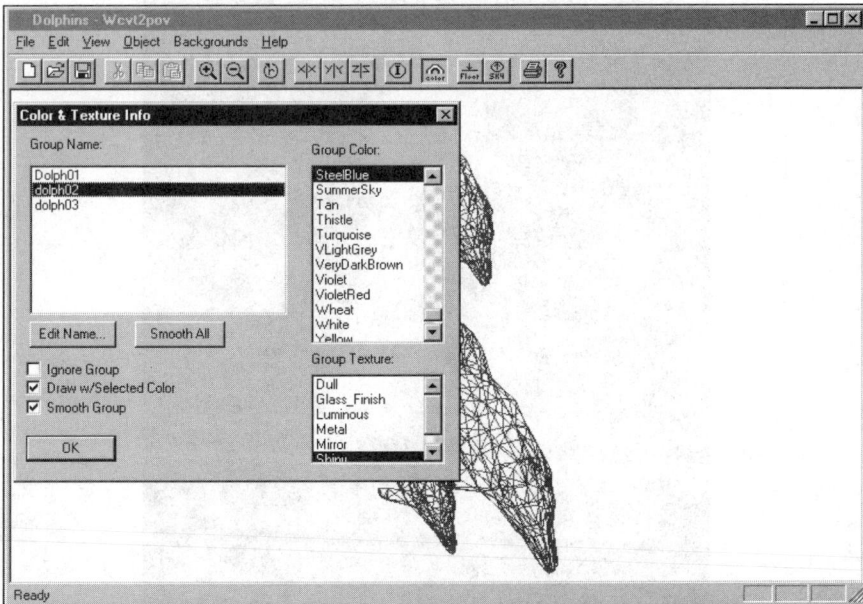

you'd like the polygons in that group to be drawn smoothly together, be sure the Smooth Group box is checked (click on the Smooth All button to smooth all the groups).

You can now select from a tasty palette of colors and textures. Be sure the Draw w/ Selected Color box is checked, and then pick the material of your choice.

NOTE: For more detailed color tweaking, you need to edit the VRML file. See Chapter 18 to learn how.

Saving It

Finally, you're ready to save the object as VRML. Select File|Save. Type in a Filename. Click on the Save As Type pop-up menu and select VRML (*.wrl). You'll now have a fully functional VRML object. Load it using your favorite VRML browser (as in Figure 14-4) and enjoy!

NOTE: POV might have done some strange things with the lights and cameras. The next section of this book shows you how to edit a WRL file and create the lighting and camera effects you desire.

Figure 14-4
The final
product

PART III
PROGRAMMING WITH VRML

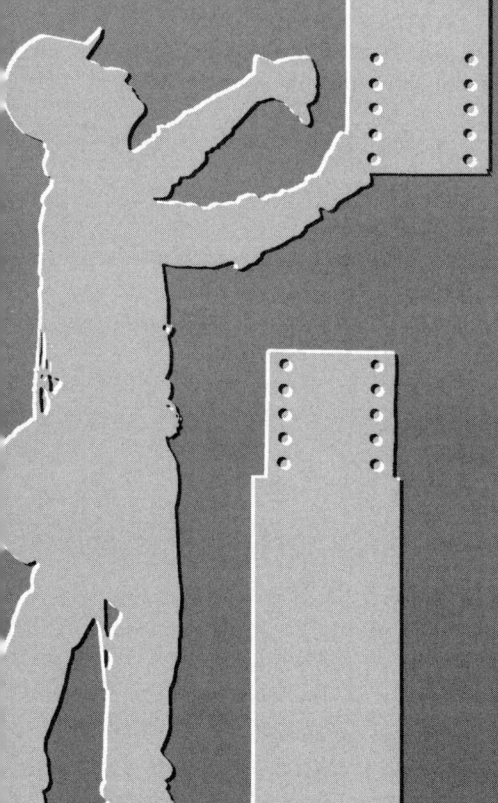

15
VERY, VERY
VRML

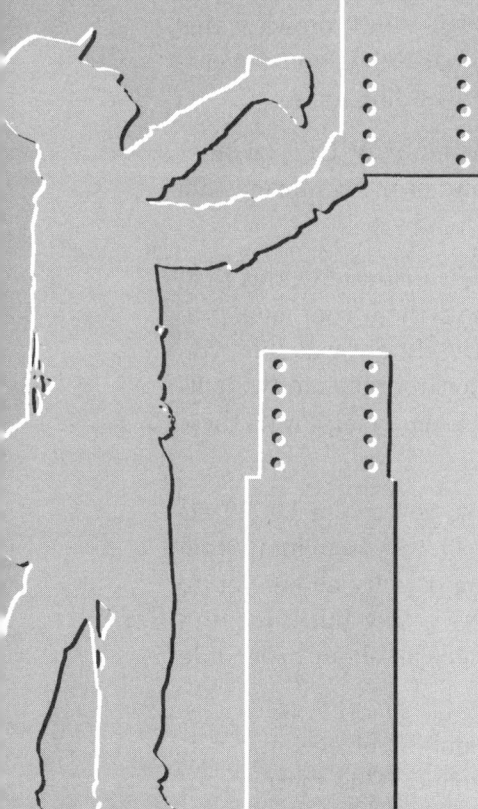

15

This chapter is an introduction to the wild and wondrous world of modeling in VRML. The Virtual Reality Modeling Language is a fascinating creation, somewhere between a simple set of routines and a multifaceted graphical power-engine. Like any advanced language, VRML uses techniques such as *object-oriented programming*. Unlike most languages, however, VRML is very intuitive and easy to learn. Although knowing markup languages (such as HTML) or programming languages (such as Pascal, C, or C++) will make learning VRML easier, it's hardly a prerequisite.

VRML is a way to describe 3D worlds by use of common words, ideas, and numbers.

WHY?

Plato asked it. Plutarch asked it. So should you. After all, you know how to create awesome-looking 3D objects on your own and convert them to VRML. So why in the world would you bother messing under the hood with the VRML commands, nodes, and formats?

In a nutshell, VRML was built to be easy to program, so you might as well take advantage of it. Here are some possible scenarios where you'll need to know the ins and outs of VRML:

- When it comes to things like lighting, textures, color, size, location, or simple shapes, it's much easier and faster to change a node than to redesign a model. For example, if you have a little red schoolhouse and you'd rather see a little purple schoolhouse, just load the VRML file with your favorite word processor, change one value, and you're done.

- Sometimes piecing together virtual scenes is the easiest way to make them. If your world is simple with lots of basic shapes, you can learn to write a VRML file in a jiffy. You'll find yourself building cool landscapes almost as easily as you can imagine them.

- VRML viewers such as WebSpace load Open Inventor files, not just VRML files. This is all well and good, but many people have made the mistake of putting non-legal Inventor commands in their VRML documents. Although such documents may look great with WebSpace, if you try using WorldView or some other strictly legal VRML browser, this document won't work. If you're familiar with legal VRML, you can easily go though an Inventor file and remove the offending lines.

- You can often convert Open Inventor, RenderWare, POV, OFF, or other 3D file formats into VRML by hand, since many of the commands are similar.

- One of the most exciting applications of VRML is to create worlds that, like the real world, change over time. You can write a computer program or *cgi script* to create virtual worlds on-the-fly. For example, you can have a city whose sky actually changes color from blue to twilight-purple to black depending on the time of day. Chapter 21 covers these dynamic worlds in more detail.

- Most importantly, you'll need to know VRML so you can make objects interactive. The whole point of VRML is that it allows you to jump from one 3D scene to another. No existing modeling package allows you to build in hyperlinks. Making these hyperobjects is easy, but it requires getting your hands a little dirty. Chapter 20 talks all about how to do this.

- Eventually VRML will be more than a way to put 3D objects in cyberspace; it'll be a full virtual programming engine. This means your objects can animate, move with true-life physical behaviors, or impede your progress (collision detection). The best way to control these complex actions will be to define them by hand.

Lastly, you may want to learn VRML for the fun of it. There's probably no better way to understand the basics of 3D graphics. Ask any mechanic—getting your hands dirty with the intricate workings of a car is more fascinating than sitting behind the driver's seat.

Building an object with VRML is like building furniture in the real world. You can just buy stuff at the furniture store, you can use power tools to quickly build basic furniture yourself, but if you want something to look perfect and elegant, it takes detailed work—a steady artisan's hand and a sopping carpenter's brow.

In most cases, you'll want to use Imagine or HomeSpace Builder to design the guts of your virtual world, and use VRML nodes to add the flourishes. For example, you might use HomeSpace Builder to design a four-story mansion. You'd then use Imagine to create chandeliers, sofas, tables, bureaus, canopy beds, bookshelves, and so on. You'd then take your many snippets of VRML code and splice them together to form a fully furnished interactive palace.

OBJECT-ORIENTED 3D GRAPHICS

"Object oriented" has become a popular catchphrase, and for good reason. Lots of computer languages, such as C++ and Smalltalk, use object-oriented ideas. This means you create small building blocks and use them to create larger structures. This saves time and energy, and makes things much easier to troubleshoot. For example, you can carefully construct one wheel and then clone it to use four of them on your car. If you want to change the size of the wheels, you don't need to do it four times—just pump up your original wheel. With VRML, this car metaphor is literal.

Figure 15-1
The skeleton in the closet is object oriented

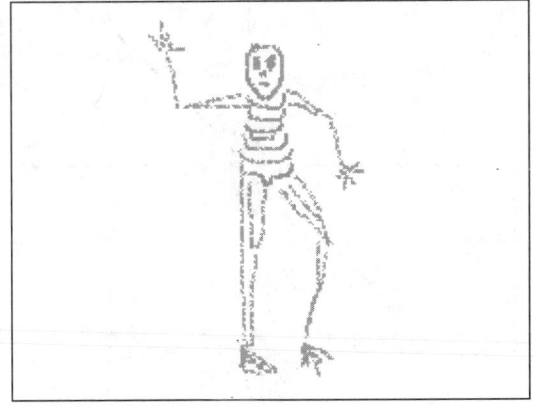

Most anything in the real world is object oriented by its nature. Figure 15-1 shows a skeleton. The arm, the leg, the torso, and the head are individual objects. The main object is the torso—everything else is connected to it. The thigh bone, for instance, is connected to the torso, the knee bone is connected to the thigh bone, and the femur to the knee bone. If you moved the torso, all of its connected bones would move as well.

If you have a background in C++ or another OOPL (object-oriented programming language), congrats...you already know the basics of structuring VRML. If not, don't despair; you'll know the basics (and more) soon enough.

When creating a graphic in VRML, start by defining the simplest elements, and then stick these objects together to draw a more complicated picture. Each of these objects is called a *node*. VRML is laid out in an object-oriented manner: The basic structures are defined first, and then you can use these for bigger and better things.

MAKING SPACE: THE SCENE GRAPH

Look at any nearby object—say, a baseball. You know the baseball is three-dimensional because you can view it from any angle, you can walk around it, and you can even drill a hole right through it. If you drew a line coming straight from the center of the baseball toward you, one line parallel to the horizon, and one line sticking through the ball vertically, you would have the axes of a graph (see Figure 15-2). All VRML objects are expressed on

Figure 15-2
Play ball!

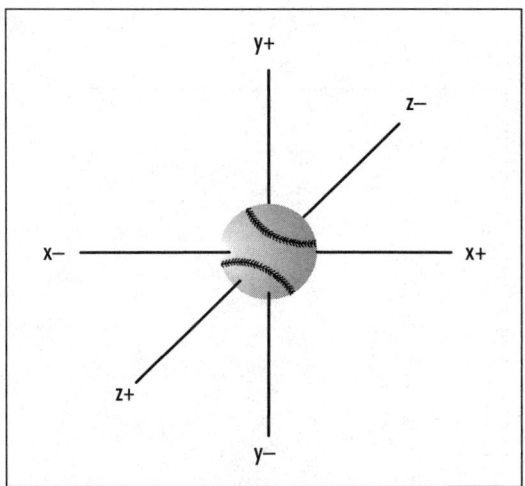

such a scene graph. (*Scene graph* is a fancy way of saying "what you actually *see*.")

Coordinate Conventions

One big question the developers of VRML had to answer was which axis should be x, which should be y, and which should get the honor of being z? These letters are very important, since every point on the scene graph is generally expressed by a trio of numbers in a matrix. Check out Chapter 8 for more information about the world coordinate system.

Open Inventor, by default, measures length in meters and angles in radians. Its coordinate system is right-handed; x is horizontal (positive to the right), y is vertical (positive up), and positive z is sticking out from your monitor straight toward you. For example, the point (3,2,1) would be 3 right on the x axis (see Figure 15-3), 2 up on the y, and 1 toward you on the z.

State of Being

When you create a node in VRML, you first need to drop it somewhere in space. The order you place each node onto the scene graph is very important. Nodes you create earlier in the scene can affect later *states* of nodes. For example, if you create a head first, you can then create a baseball cap that will rest atop the head. If you rotate the head, the visor of the cap will be smart enough to always stick forward.

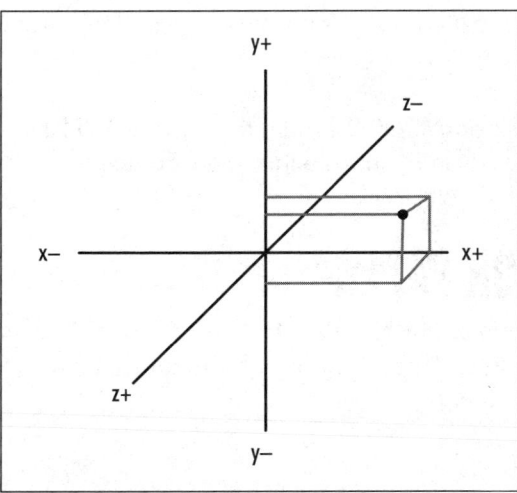

Figure 15-3
A point on the VRML scene graph

As a more complicated example, you can create a picture of a red dog and then add on a transformation node that rotates everything 45 degrees. If you then draw a cat, it will be at a different angle than the dog, but it will still be drawn in red unless you specify otherwise.

You can group objects to have them share positions, transformations, or properties. Chapter 17 teaches you how.

Transforming

Where an object is placed doesn't matter that much, since it's easy to move it around. This movement is known as *transformation*. One coordinate space can easily be transformed into another. Read more about transformation in Chapter 13.

HOW IT'S STORED

Above all else, VRML is a file format. You can know every VRML command inside and out, but unless you store the file correctly, it won't actually transfer across the World Wide Web.

THE WRL FILE

Every VRML file is stored as plain ASCII text. This means you can use your favorite word processor or editor to create or tweak a VRML scene graph. This text file must have the extension *.WRL,* which stands for "world."

Although a WRL file name can be any length, it's a good idea to make it 8 or fewer characters, so people with MS-DOS can easily reference the file. As Windows 95 becomes more popular, however, file names of any length will become more and more acceptable.

NOTE: If you use an MS-DOS system to access a WRL file more than 8 characters long, the rest of the letters are truncated. For example, FERRISWHEEL.WRL is changed to FERRISWH.WRL.

HOW IT LOOKS ON PAPER

Let's start with this simplest of VRML files—a cone. You can use this primitive object as a dunce cap, the nose of a fighter jet, the spire of a castle, or as, of course, an ice-cream cone.

```
#VRML V1.0 ascii
DEF Hat Separator {
    Cone {
```

Figure 15-4
Your first VRML
creation: a
cone

```
              parts          ALL
              bottomRadius   1
              height         3
        }
  }
```

The results are shown in Figure 15-4.

The Header

Every VRML file must begin with the following line:

```
#VRML V1.0 ascii
```

Type this line exactly as shown, paying attention to upper- and lower-case. This lets your Web browser, VRML viewer, or other Internet software immediately know what type of file it's dealing with. If you forget to include this header, or if you misspell something, your VRML viewer will probably give you an error message similar to

```
File does not have a valid header string.
```

The latest specification of VRML is 1.1. This book covers all the 1.1 nodes; however, many browsers do not yet support 1.1 commands. If your VRML file uses any 1.1 nodes or structures, you should be sure to specify this with the heading

```
#VRML V1.1 utf8
```

NOTE: UTF8 is Unicode, a file format similar to ASCII, but with wider support for multiple languages. This would allow people to name their nodes in Chinese, Swahili, and so on.

Eventually, as further versions of VRML come out, the heading will be altered. For example:

```
#VRML V2.0 utf8
```

The header lets your VRML viewer know whether it can display the current file. Most viewers will let you know if you try to load an unsupported version of VRML.

Whitespace, Capitalization, and Other Rules

Whitespace consists of blank spaces or tabs. Much as in HTML, whitespace is ignored in VRML. You can indent your VRML files any way you wish, using as many spaces or tabs as you want. For example:

```
DEF Hat Separator { Cone { parts      ALL bottomRadius 1 height 3}}
```

is perfectly legal VRML code, though it's a bit of a pain to read.

The only thing you need to ensure is putting some whitespace between each field's name and its value. For example:

```
height3
```

is illegal.

In addition, VRML is case sensitive—it distinguishes between uppercase and lowercase. As a matter of good form, nodes (and their names) are capitalized. For example, a node would look like

```
NodeName
```

Properties within nodes often begin with lowercase and then jump into uppercase within the same word (for example, textureCoordIndex). A typical property would be

```
propertyName
```

In other words,

```
cone {}
```

is illegal, since there is no node with that name. Instead, you must use

```
Cone { }
```

THE NODE

Your virtual scene is defined by use of different objects, properties, groups, and so on. Each of these instances is called a *node*. A VRML file must contain at least one node. This node may contain an infinite number of nodes which, in turn, may contain an infinite number of nodes.

A node is usually something solid like a polygon, line, cylinder, cube, or sphere. A node can often be something more ethereal, however, like a translation, a texture map, or a transformation.

Figure 15-5
The breakdown
of a node

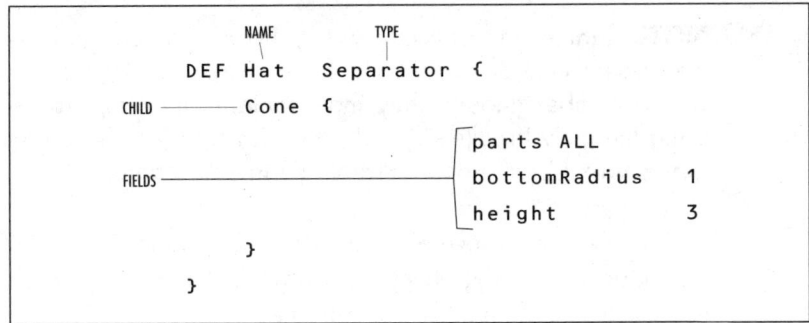

Each node has four main aspects:

- Name

- Type

- Field properties

- Children

Every node takes the following basic form, as illustrated in Figure 15-5:

```
DEF name type { fields  children }
```

The only required elements are the *type* and those cute curly brackets.

```
type { }
```

Naming A Node

A node without a name would smell as sweet. It is true, a node doesn't have to be named. However, it's nice to have the ability to use names, because then you can refer to this name anywhere in your VRML scene. Additionally, if you use names, it'll be much easier for anyone reading your VRML scene to figure out what the heck the node is.

To name a node, just use the DEF definition command. This allows you to attach an easy mnemonic to your node and refer to this node again. Simply type *DEF*, the name of the node, and the type of node. For example, if you have a cone node similar to the following:

```
Cone {}
```

you can name it DorkyHat by using the markup

```
DEF DorkyHat Cone {}
```

> **NOTE:** Names must be one word, though you can use underscores to give the appearance of two words, for example, Dorky_Hat. They cannot begin with a number (though they may contain numbers). You should also avoid using the curly brackets ({ or }), the plus sign (+), the backslash (\), a single quote mark ('), or a double quote (") in your names.

You may give several nodes the same name. If you do, however, some VRML browsers might become confused. The latest VRML specification suggests that you keep all names unique.

Node Types

There are three main types of node:

- Shape
- Property
- Group

There are several additional types of VRML nodes. The next five chapters cover each type of node.

Shapes

The most basic definition of a shape is "stuff that exists in space." The tangible stuff. Any 3D object is a shape. Even 2D objects, such as lines, are considered a shape because they exist in 3D space on the scene graph.

You can think of shape nodes as the actors. They're the good-looking talent who actually get seen.

Properties

What makes this node different from all other nodes? If you think of the shape as a noun, a property is like an adjective. A property can tell the shape what color to be, where to sit, or how to act. In some cases, these differences may be obvious; for example, one circle may be 2 inches wide and red, while another is 10 inches wide and blue. Sometimes these properties are much more complicated, letting the VRML browser know which objects should be connected to what, what order things should be drawn, and how things should act in relation to each other.

Lights and cameras are important properties. Lights, as you would imagine, let the actors actually be seen. Cameras are the perspective from which you view the actors.

Whenever you set a property, any following shape nodes are affected by the settings. You can think of property nodes as the behind-the-scenes crew: wardrobe, makeup, lighting technician, cinematographer, and director. They tell the actors exactly how and where to act.

Groups

Some nodes contain other nodes. This allows nodes to be grouped *hierarchically;* in other words, basic objects can be stacked to form more complicated drawings. This affects the order in which shapes are drawn (allowing one actor to upstage another).

Following the Hollywood analogy, groups would perhaps be the scenes of a larger film.

Other Nodes

VRML exists, above all, because it has a few important commands that make it handy to use over the World Wide Web. WWW nodes let the actors be somewhat interactive, like hypertext taken into the third dimension. You click on an actor and it performs an action, loads up another scene, or takes you someplace else on the Internet.

The Node Stands Alone

Like any real-world object, nodes can either stand alone or affect the surrounding nodes. If a node is self-contained, it is called *well-behaved.* If you try to perform an action on a well-behaved node (draw it, move it, and so on), the node has all the information it needs built in. As such, some nodes are very long and detailed.

Each node contains lots of information. These properties can be modified or tweaked at will, drastically changing the look or behavior of the node.

FIELDS OF AMBER GRAIN

The properties of an individual node are known as its *fields.* Some nodes don't have any fields; some nodes have dozens of them. Some fields are optional. A node without fields is generic—like a person without any special look or personality. Defining fields gives your nodes some character. For example, fields help set

- Rendering options—These determine how the node is drawn—its size, shape, color, texture, and material.

- Data values—This is information that can be used to draw complicated objects, normals, or textures.

- Location—This specifies where in space the node is located.

- Picking—This specifies what happens when the mouse pointer rolls over this node.

- Relationships—This specifies how this node will relate to other nodes.

The node's fields must be contained within the curly brackets. A field consists of the field's name followed by the data. This data might be a number, a word, a vector (a set of three numbers), or a long list of numbers. For example, the cone node might contain the fields *parts* and *height,* as follows:

```
Cone {
     parts   ALL
     height  3
   }
```

If you don't specify a node's fields, it usually makes an educated guess on what the value of each field should be.

NOTE: The fields within a node can be listed in any order.

Field Trips: Classes

There are two classes of fields:

- Single-value

- Multiple-value

A single-value field only contains one value, but this value can be a vector (three or four numbers) or even an entire image map taking up hundreds of pages.

Multiple-value fields can contain numerous items of data. These *data lists* are generally surrounded by square brackets, with each value separated by a comma. The basic form looks like

```
[item1, item2, item3, ..., itemN]
```

NOTE: The last item in a field list can be followed by a final comma if you so desire.

If a multiple-value field has only one value, then brackets are optional. At times, you'll want to create an empty multiple-value field to cancel out a prior list. To do this, simply use an empty pair of brackets:

[]

Table 15-1 lists the supported VRML fields. It's important to know which field contains what. If you refer to the official VRML specification (Appendix B), you'll notice each node is followed by several legal fields and their types. Each field type is preceded by either *SF* (which designates a single-value field) or *MF* (a multiple-value field). Knowing the class of a field can help you figure out what values to use.

Table 15-1 A list of legal VRML fields

Field Class	Description
Single-Value Fields	
SFBitMask	Listing of several bit flags, used as a mask
SFBool	Boolean TRUE or FALSE
SFColor	Color
SFEnum	Enumerated type field
SFFloat	Floating-point number
SFImage	Bitmap of a 2D image
SFLong	Long (32-bit) integer
SFMatrix	Transformation matrix
SFRotation	Rotation value
SFString	ASCII string (a sentence)
SFVec2f	2D vector
SFVec3f	3D vector
Multiple-Value Fields	
MFColor	RGB colors
MFLong	Long (32-bit) integers
MFVec2f	2D vectors
MFVec3f	3D vectors

Knowing the type of fields available is also important if you wish to use extended nodes, which are discussed in Chapter 21. For now, don't worry about which fields are used when. This will become apparent when specific VRML nodes are discussed.

Single-Value Fields

Most fields only take one value. Here's a detailed description of each of these fields, and the values that they take.

SFLong

This field is followed by a 32-bit integer. Each integer can be expressed in three forms:

- Decimal—A standard number

- Hexadecimal—Each number begins with 0x

- Octal—Each number begins with 0

For example, you can use the value "0x0F," "017," or "15" to represent the number 15. The SFLong field is usually used to refer to a value within a list. For example, you might want to access the fifth child of a node, or the fifth item in a list of coordinates.

SFFloat

The SFFloat field contains a single-precision floating-point number. A floating-point number is one that uses a decimal. You can represent extremely big or small numbers using standard scientific notation. For example, all of the following are valid values for SFFloat:

```
5
3.1415
-12e2
1e-1000
```

The SFFloat is used to specify the value of lots of basic properties such as width, height, depth, color intensity, rotation, distance, and so on.

SFBool

This field is like the answer to a yes-or-no question. It can only take two values: 0 (FALSE), or 1 (TRUE). This field is used most often to determine whether a light source is switched on or off.

SFString

This field holds a simple phrase, word, or sentence. This string can use any valid ASCII character and can be as many lines as you desire. Each SFString should be surrounded by quotes. To use the double-quote character itself, simply precede it with a backslash.

For example, to create the string

```
He "almost" understood VRML
```

you would use the value

```
"He \"almost\" understood VRML"
```

NOTE: Surrounding strings with quotes is optional if the string is just one word, with no spaces, tabs, or new lines in it.

Strings are used to add lines of information to VRML files, to specify the names and URLs of hyperlink anchors, and to load particular file names.

SFEnum

This field offers a list of possible values to choose from. In most cases, these values are represented by common words such as "SHINY" or "POWER-FUL." Many nodes can operate in several ways. You can use SFEnum fields to specify, for example, how a texture should map, how text should be justified, or how points should be bound to shapes.

SFVec2f

The SFVec2f field does not appear often in VRML. This field holds a two-dimensional vector, as opposed to a three-dimensional one. As you might expect, this vector is represented by two floating-point numbers (separated by some whitespace). For example, a simple vector (x is 0, y is 1) might look like

```
0 1
```

As with any floating-point number in VRML, you can use scientific notation to represent extremely big or extremely small values. For example, a vector with an x value of 10 million and a y value of pi might look like

```
[1e6 3.141 ]
```

The SFVec2f field is used to change the shape or location of 2D image maps.

SFVec3f

Much more useful and important is the SFVec3f field. This field holds a three-dimensional vector. As you know, each point in 3D space can be represented by three numbers: an x value, a y value, and a z value. The SFVec3f value takes the form of three floating-point numbers (each separated by some whitespace). For example, a point 1 unit up along the y axis might look like

`0 1 0`

Almost all VRML nodes need to know a location or center point in 3D space. The SFVec3f type of field can provide this information.

SFRotation

The SFRotation field holds a value that can be used to rotate an object in space. This is represented as four floating-point numbers (each separated by some whitespace). The first three numbers correspond to a vector, which acts as the axis of rotation. The last number is the amount of right-handed rotation about the axis, in radians.

For example, to rotate 180 degrees (pi, or roughly 3.14 radians) around the x axis [1,0,0], you would use the value

`1 0 0 3.14`

SFMatrix

This field holds a transformation matrix. This matrix can be used to flip, stretch, or otherwise alter 3D space. An SFMatrix takes the following form of 16 floating-point numbers (each separated by some whitespace). For example, to represent the following identity matrix:

```
[ 1 0 0 0
  0 1 0 0
  0 0 1 0
  0 0 0 1 ]
```

You would write

`1 0 0 0  0 1 0 0  0 0 1 0  0 0 0 1`

SFBitMask

This field holds a set of bit flags to be used as a mask. This mask sets certain options from a list of possible options. The SFBitMask field often uses a word in plain English to represent a pesky number. For example, the SFBitMask field is used to determine which parts of a basic shape to draw. If you want to specify that the sides, top, and bottom of a shape should be drawn, you'd simply use the word "ALL."

If a SFBitMask has more than one flag, it should be surrounded by parentheses.

SFColor

One of the most important aspects of a sleek-looking VRML world is setting proper colors. Colors are designated as an *RGB triplet*. As you know, any color can be designated as a mixture of red, green, and blue. To create a VRML color, specify a floating-point number between 0 and 1, indicating the percentage of red, green, and blue, respectively.

Lack of all color would be black:

0 0 0

Whereas all of each color would be white:

1 1 1

A medium dose of each color (gray) would be

.5 .5 .5

Each number in the RGB triplet is written in standard scientific notation, ranging from 0.0 to 1.0. Table 15-2 lists some common colors, along with their RGB triplet values. To use a more customized color, simply add more or less red, green, or blue—the way an artist would with a palette.

Table 15-2 Some common colors

Color	RGB Triplet
Black	0.0 0.0 0.0
Red	1.0 0.0 0.0
Yellow	1.0 1.0 0.0
Magenta	1.0 0.0 1.0
Green	0.0 1.0 0.0
Blue	0.0 0.0 1.0
Gray	0.5 0.5 0.5
White	1.0 1.0 1.0

IMPORTANT NOTE: The SFColor format will change with VRML version 1.1. The pixel values will be in a Kernighan and Ritchie style scanf format. See Appendix B for a complete draft of the VRML 1.1 specifications.

SFImage

One of the most complicated fields is SFImage, but it's also one of the most versatile. SFImage allows you to store an entire grayscale or color image. You can then use this image as a texture to wrap around any object. The value of this node begins with three integers:

- The width of the image

- The height of the image

- The number of *components* in the image

This is followed by a number of values (equal to width x height) representing each location, or *pixel,* in the image's grid. Each pixel is represented by a hexadecimal value, which always begins with *0x.* Every two hexadecimal digits represent 1 byte.

Pixels are listed opposite the way you might think they should be: Pixels run left to right, bottom to top. In other words, the bottom-left corner pixel of your image is listed first, and the last pixel in your listing represents the image's upper-right pixel.

The form each pixel takes depends on the number of components. The more components a pixel map has, the more colors and effects the image will have. However, images with more components take up much more space.

- One component—Each pixel in an image with one component is written as a hexadecimal number ranging from 0x00—which means the pixel is empty (black)—to 0xFF—which means the pixel is at its highest intensity (white). Therefore, a simple one-component checkerboard (2x2) would be represented as:

```
2 2 1 0xFF 0x00 0x00 0xFF
```

This has a width of 2, a height of 2, and 1 component. It is followed by 4 (2 x 2) values.

- Two components—Each pixel is represented by 2 bytes. The intensity of the pixel (how full it is) is stored in the first byte, and the transparency (how see-through it is) is kept in the second byte—0xFF is completely transparent and 0x00 is opaque. For example, consider the following SFImage:

```
2 2 2 0xFF00 0x00FF 0xFF80 0x0000
```

The first pixel (the bottom left of the image) is at full intensity and no transparency, the second pixel is at no intensity and full transparency, the third pixel has both full intensity and half-transparency, and the last pixel (the upper right of the image) has no intensity or transparency.

NOTE: When an image is wrapped around an object as a texture, transparent pixels will reveal the object's original color. The more transparent a pixel is, the more the object's original color will shine through.

Most VRML browsers cannot support semitransparency. Any transparency values less than 0.5 (0x80) are opaque, and any values greater than or equal to 0.5 will be transparent.

- Three components—Each pixel is stored as a 3-byte RGB color value. The red component is represented in the first (high) byte, the green component is in the second byte, and the blue is in the third (low) byte. For example, 0x0000FF is blue and 0xFF0000 is red. A blue and red checkerboard might look like

```
2 2 3 0x0000FF 0xFF0000 0xFF0000 0x0000FF
```

- Four components—Each pixel is a 4-byte value. The first three bytes represent the RGB values, as in a three-component pixel. The last byte signifies the amount of transparency. For example, 0xFF0000FF is a fully opaque red.

```
2 2 4 0xFF000080 0x00FF0000 0xFF00FF80 0x00FF0000
```

TIP: Pixels are unsigned numbers. This means you can save lots of space by chopping off any leading zeros. For example, if you have a four-component pixel that looks like 0x0000FFAB, you could shorten it to 0xFFAB. You can also refer to pixels in decimal form, if you find it easier to work that way. For example, 0xFF is 255.

NOTE: In most cases, you won't need to create these images by hand. You can take any popular 2D graphic format and convert it into an SFImage value. Techniques to do this are discussed in Chapter 19.

SFNode

VRML version 1.1 adds a new type of field called SFNode. This field can contain the description of an extended node.

Multiple-Value Fields

Fields with multiple values are used to store vast amounts of information. If you desire, you can write an MF field that stretches on for pages and pages.

MFLong

The MFLong field is a list of a bunch of 32-bit integers. Just as with SFLong, each value in MFLong can be written in decimal, hexadecimal, or octal. You can even mix and match numerical bases. For example, here's a list of three 15s:

```
[ 15, 0x0F, 017 ]
```

The MFLong field is used most often with index nodes—specifying certain values from a big list of values.

MFVec2f

The MFVec2f field holds a listing of 2D vectors. The format of each value is the same as with the SFVec2f field. This is a useful way to specify the coordinates of two-dimensional textures. For instance:

```
[ 0 1, 1 0, 1 1, 0 0 ]
```

MFVec3f

If a node needs a listing of several 3D vectors, it would have you use a MFVec3f field. This field can hold an infinite number of 3D point values. For instance, here are four valid vectors:

```
[ 0 0 0, 1e10 0 0, 1.1 2.2 3.3, -1 -2 -3]
```

MFColor

The MFColor field contains, as you might expect, a listing of any number of colors. Each color is represented as an RGB value, as in the SFColor field. For example, to specify the colors of the American flag (red, white, and blue, for any non-Americans out there), you would use

```
[ 1 0 0, 1 1 1, 0 0 1 ]
```

MFFloat

The original VRML specification forgot to allow an MFFloat field type; the 1.1 specification allows it. This type is useful for listing many floating-point numbers:

```
[5, 3.1415, -12e-2, 1.284847e100]
```

MFString

The 1.1 specification also adds an MFString field type. This allows you to list several strings, which can be useful in the WWWAnchor node, for instance, where you might want to load an alternate scene if the first scene is not available. A typical MFString field would look like

```
["http://found.cs.nyu.edu/dfox/vrml/world.wrl","http://here.there/
anywhere.wrl"]
```

CHILDREN: THE NODE NUCLEAR FAMILY

Some nodes can contain an infinite number of other nodes. This makes it easy to group related objects. These nodes-within-nodes are known as *child nodes,* and, as you might expect, the main node is called the *parent.*

The relationship of these nodes is very important. When a parent node is being drawn, it first takes care of each of its child nodes, starting from the first. The first child will be drawn first, the second child second, and so on.

Not all nodes allow children. Some are happy remaining childless. If a node is allowed children, it is known as a *group node.* These nodes are covered in Chapter 17.

HOW TO CREATE A VRML SCENE IN BRIEF

To create a typical VRML scene, you would go through the following steps:

1. Create each object in your scene using your favorite modeler—a house, each piece of furniture, each person, and so on. You may even want to break things down further into arms, legs, stairs, walls, and so on. Part 1 of this book talks about how to do this.

2. Save each object in a polygon-based 3D style. Avoid other formats such as NURBS. If possible, save to the Open Inventor format.

3. Convert each of these objects into VRML code (see Chapter 14).

4. Use a word processor or text editor to put the objects together to form a scene. Make everything the proper size so that all the objects are in scale with each other. Arrange things to your whims. Make some of the objects interactive.

5. Put your world on a properly configured World Wide Web server (see Chapter 23).

6. Get to work creating more cool virtual worlds!

THE NODE KNOWS: HOW NODES ARE PROCESSED

Most VRML renderers/browsers/viewers go through the following five steps whenever a new VRML file is encountered:

- Parsing
- Traversing
- Rendering
- Translating
- Picking

Parsing

When your VRML viewer loads your file, it starts *parsing* at the beginning. Parsing means that each node will be looked at recursively: The first node is studied; if it has any children, they are studied; if the children have children, *they* are studied; and so on. The VRML viewer will then generate a class tree based on the structure of your document.

The Class Tree

Here's where the object-oriented stuff comes into play. As you know, the beginning and end of each node are designated with curly brackets. Many nodes together look like a virtual tree of these brackets. The placement of these brackets is essential to writing correct VRML files. For example, these few lines:

```
#VRML V1.0 ascii
Separator {
    Cone { }
    Sphere { }
}
```

are vastly different from these few lines:

```
#VRML V1.0 ascii
Separator {
    Cone {
    Sphere { }
    }
}
```

The first set of routines first draws a cone and then draws a sphere. It will draw these both in the same place, since the VRML browser wasn't told to do

Figure 15-6
A cone is
hiding inside
a sphere

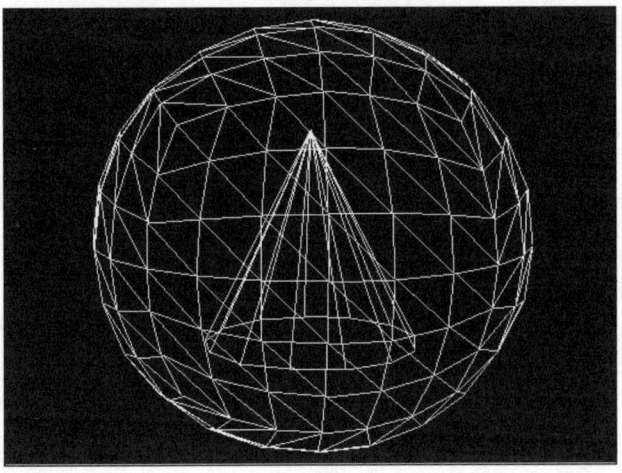

otherwise. Since spheres and cones are both 2 units tall, the result would be a generic cone inside a sphere, as shown in the wireframe in Figure 15-6.

The second example lines of VRML are illegal, since a Cone node cannot have any children.

 TIP: If you wanted to place a sphere inside a cone, you could do this by making the cone twice as big, or making the sphere twice as small. It doesn't really matter, when dealing with basic shapes, whether you draw the cone first or the sphere first.

The trick is indenting your curly brackets just right, so you know which bracket ends which nodes. A common VRML mistake is to have too many opening brackets and not enough closing ones, or vice versa.

Based on these brackets, a tree is drawn. Whenever a new opening bracket comes along, a new branch is added to the tree. Whenever a closing bracket is encountered, the process returns up the tree and continues from the previous branching point.

Children First

Whenever nodes are grouped together, children are processed before their parents, in the order they are listed. For example, if you have a VRML layout that looks similar to:

```
Group1 {
  Node1
  Group2 {
    NodeA
```

continued on next page

continued from previous page

```
        NodeB
        Group3 {
            Nodea
            Nodeb
        }
        NodeC
    }
    Node2
}
```

the nodes will be drawn in this order: Node1, NodeA, NodeB, Nodea; Nodeb, NodeC; and Node2. Note that Node1, Group2, and NodeC are *siblings,* since they are all immediate children of Group1. Although this may sound confusing at first, this process is really quite intuitive. *Nodes are drawn in the exact order in which they appear.*

A Stellar Example

Here's a sample VRML scene, shown in Figure 15-7, which simulates a moon orbiting a planet:

```
#VRML V1.0 ascii
#A moon revolving around a planet

DEF PlanetScene Separator {
  DEF Planet Separator { # The planet
    Material {
      diffuseColor 0 1 0    # Make the planet's color green
    }
  Sphere { radius 5 } # The planet
  }
  DEF Moon Separator { # The moon
    Material {
      diffuseColor 0 0 1   # Make the moon's color blue (blue moon!)
```

Figure 15-7
A typical VRML scene with several overlapping objects

```
    }
    Transform { # Move the moon's coordinates
            translation -2 0 1
            rotation 0 1 1 1
    }
    Translation { translation 3 3 15 } # Shift the moon
    Sphere {} # Draw the moon
  }
}
```

Take a moment to look over this code. If you don't understand what a node is doing, don't worry. It'll be covered in one of the following chapters. Simply pay attention to the names of the nodes, where the brackets are located, and how this all relates to the class tree:

```
PlanetScene
    /        \
  Planet    Moon
```

Traversing

The order of a group's children, as with the rest of VRML, is important. Earlier nodes will be drawn and picked first (if the mouse is rolled over them). During traversal, the state accumulated for a child is passed on to each successive child and then to the parents of the group.

The VRML browser will run through the class tree and create a *rendering display list*. This is a detailed description of what will be drawn and which functions should be used to draw them. If the node is a group, it adds that node's children to the display list. It continues. If it comes to any property nodes, the state will be changed, and future nodes will be affected. The VRML viewer takes some time to figure out the best way for each object to be drawn.

Whenever you change your point of view, the VRML browser re-traverses the scene graph and updates the display list to show any new objects. Traversal will become more and more important as VRML becomes animated and objects actually change their appearance with time.

Rendering

Once the VRML browser knows what to draw, it actually puts pen to paper (or photon gun to glass, as the case may be) and creates the objects as specified in the rendering display list.

World Transforming

You can now move through the virtual world. Most VRML viewers let you rotate the world around any axis; walk through the world; move the world left, right, forward, or back; or otherwise manipulate your perspective of the 3D scene.

Picking

You can now roll your mouse over the 3D objects. Some of these objects may be hyperlinks to VRML files or other parts of the Internet. The VRML browser will keep track of which objects are clickable and which are hidden. If you click a link, the VRML browser will take the appropriate action.

COMMENTS

Let's begin writing an honest-to-goodness VRML file. Here are some basic nodes and formats.

The only thing you'll find in a WRL file, other than nodes and the header, are comments. Comments are designated, quite simply, with the hash sign (#). Whenever your VRML browser comes across the hash sign, it ignores everything after it until the next line. You can put a comment at the beginning of a line or in the middle of a line. For example:

```
#VRML V1.0 ascii

# A simple cone.
# By David Fox.

Separator {
  Cone {
      parts   ALL
      bottomRadius 3          # The circle (6 units wide)
      height 5                # The height is five units
  }
}
```

If you use the pound sign within a string field (surrounded by quotes), it will be registered as the hash sign, not as a comment.

NOTE: Comments, like extra whitespace, may not be saved when your VRML file is downloaded. Some VRML servers may string these extraneous characters to save space or transfer time. If there's some essential information that you need to have inside your VRML document, use the Info node.

THE INFO NODE

Let's end this chapter with VRML's simplest node: Info. This node lets you attach a line or so of text to any other object. This can help you, as a world-builder, remember which object does what. You can also use the Info node to copyright an object.

The Info node has one field: *string*. For example:

```
Info {
   string  "This object copyright 1995, David Fox."
}
```

Unlike commented text, an Info node's text will always remain with the VRML file—at least until someone else edits it.

Info Hints

Info can be used for more than hidden information; it can actually affect the way your virtual world operates. The WebSpace and WebFX VRML browsers, for example, are smart enough to recognize several types of Info nodes. Using these nodes, you can customize your virtual world, letting the browser know the following:

▪ The title of your world

▪ Some basic summary information about the world

▪ The color of the background

▪ The speed to navigate through the world

▪ Whether the world is to be examined or walked-through

▪ Whether you can walk through objects or must walk around them

▪ What the background of your world will look like

 TIP: You should always put these Info hints at the beginning of any VRML file. WebSpace, and several other popular browsers, will make good use of them. Other browsers will just ignore 'em.

The Title

WebSpace and WebFX can write the title of the current world at the top of the screen, in the title bar. To give your world a specific title, simply name an Info node as *Title*. For instance, if your world is an Old West saloon, you might type the following at the beginning of your VRML file:

```
DEF Title Info {
        string "The Saloon"}
```

The Document Info

Someone looking at your world might decide to choose Document Info from WebSpace's File menu. This has all sorts of statistics about the current virtual world, such as its title and URL (location on the Web). If you wish, you can also add a bit of information. This can be a summary of the world, a copyright notice, or instructions (such as, "Look inside the green box to find a surprise").

To have WebSpace generate this information, simply name an Info node as *SceneInfo*. For example:

```
DEF SceneInfo Info {
        string "Old West Saloon scene. Copyright 1995 by David Fox."
}
```

The Background Color

In most cases, the background of your WebSpace scenes will be a delightful light blue. But perhaps the objects you designed look much better against a snowy white background, or a black night sky, or an amber field. You can tell WebSpace which background color to use by creating an Info node named *BackgroundColor*. The string should then be an RGB triplet (similar to an SFColor field). For example, to create a red background, put the following code at the beginning of your VRML file:

```
DEF BackgroundColor Info {
        string "1 0 0"
}
```

The Speed

If you were to stroll through your virtual world, how fast would you go? To move forward in WebSpace, for instance, you would hold down the forward controls (usually ⬆) for one second. You would then zoom forward into the scene.

If you like, you can control the speed of this zoom. Simply create an Info node named *ViewerSpeed*, and specify the velocity in units per second. Remember, according to the VRML specification, each unit is 1 meter. So, to have visitors to your world move 10 meters forward at a time, you would put this code at the beginning of your VRML file:

```
DEF ViewerSpeed Info {
        string "10.0"
}
```

NOTE: If you don't designate a velocity, WebSpace will pick a speed according to how large the scene is.

The Viewer Paradigm

When someone loads your scene with WebSpace, there are generally two things he or she will want to do with it:

Walk through it, like a stroll through a city

Examine it, like some sculpture at an art museum

Depending on this *viewer paradigm,* WebSpace will alter the user's controls. If you create a "walk" paradigm, the controls will move the viewer forward and back, turning left and right. If you choose the "examiner" paradigm, the viewer's controls will tilt the object. To name a paradigm, simply name an Info node as *Viewer.* You can then use the examiner paradigm:

```
DEF Viewer Info {
        string "examiner"
}
```

Or you may use the walk paradigm:

```
DEF Viewer Info {
        string "walk"
}
```

Changing the Clipping Planes

A *clipping plane* is the point at which objects can no longer be seen—similar to a horizon. This plane will cut away any object in its path, making it seem to disappear. The WebSpace browser automatically creates near and far clipping planes around each scene, based on the size of the scene and the type of camera being used. At times this clipping plane may make the scene look bad, with objects disappearing from view too soon or too late.

If you'd like to turn clipping off, make an Info node named *AutoClip,* as follows:

```
DEF AutoClip Info {
        string "off"
}
```

NOTE: If you don't let WebSpace use clipping planes, be sure that your cameras are defined with a near and far distance, so the browser knows how big the scene is. The nearDistance and farDistance fields are not part of the official VRML 1.0 specification, so use them with caution. See Chapter 19 to learn about the camera nodes.

Collision Detection

WebFX is currently the only major VRML browser that supports collision detection. This means that visitors to your world will not be able to walk through walls. If they want to enter a house, they need to find its door (or at least a window). This can greatly enhance the sense of realism.

To turn collision detection on (usually a good idea), use the Info node named *CollisionDetection*:

```
DEF CollisionDetection Info {
      string  "TRUE"
}
```

Then the WebFX browser will not let you walk through any solid objects. If you like, you can turn collision detection on and off before certain objects. Simply use the special CollisionDetection extended node (a node that only WebFX can recognize). Turn detection on and off by using the *collision* field, as follows:

```
CollisionDetection {
      fields [SFBool collision]
      collision    TRUE
}
```

For example, you might want to be able to walk through all objects *except* a wall. Use the following code:

```
#VRML V1.0 ascii
Separator {
      DEF CollisionDetection Info {
            string  "TRUE"
      }
      Separator {
            CollisionDetection {
                  fields [SFBool collision]
                  collision    FALSE
            }
            # Draw everything but the wall here.
      }
      Separator {
            CollisionDetection {
                  fields [SFBool collision]
                  collision    TRUE
```

```
        }
        # Draw the Wall Here.
    }
}
```

Background Images

The WebFX browser also supports background images. This lets you specify not only the color of your background, but also the look of it. You can have the background be a cloud-filled sky, star-filled outer space, a grassy field, or a huge brick wall.

To create a background image, simply find a good texture map in the BMP or GIF format. Chapter 19 talks some more about textures. This texture should be like bathroom tiles—small, but easy to repeat to form a clean image.

Once you have your image, use the Info node named *BackgroundImage* along with the *string* field to specify a background. For example, if you want all unfilled space in your world to be a beautiful blue sky, try

```
DEF BackgroundImage Info {
        string  "sky.bmp"
}
```

NOTE: You'll need to be sure the SKY.BMP file is stored in the same place as the VRML file for this to work.

SNEAK PREVIEW

The next chapter covers all of VRML's shape nodes. These nodes are the meat and potatoes of virtual worlds, actually telling the renderer what to draw. Future chapters cover group nodes (which let you put objects together to form bigger or more complex objects), property nodes (which tell the renderer where to draw the object), fancy property nodes (which let you define exactly what the object looks like), and World Wide Web nodes (which let you make an object clickable, leading to any other part of the Internet).

16

BUILDING
BLOCKS:
SHAPE NODES

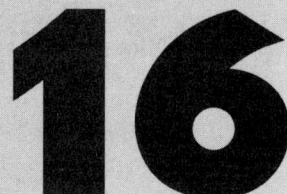

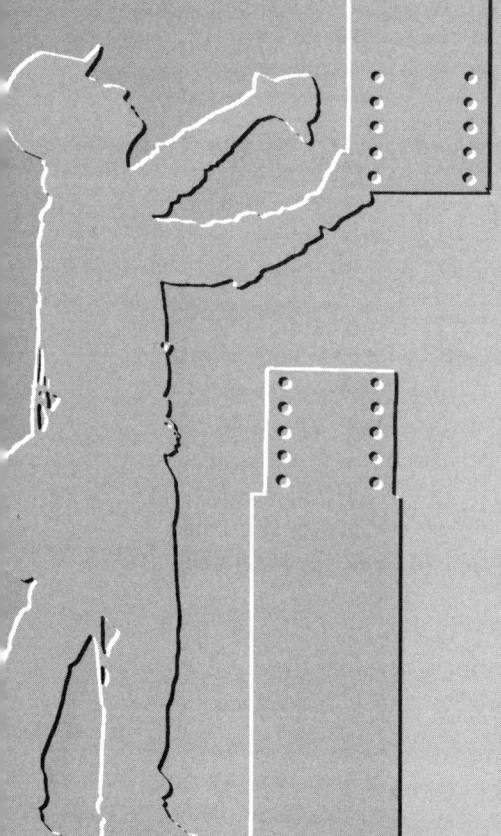

Matter matters. Without matter, space and time would be an empty void. Virtual worlds are, at their heart, built with good, solid matter. This chapter talks about geometrical nodes...nodes that actually draw something. Note, before you get rolling, that these nodes are almost useless by themselves. It's like having actors without direction, without costumes, and even without a rolling camera.

VRML deals with two main types of shapes:

- Simple—Cubes, cones, cylinders, and spheres

- Complex—Sets of polygons, lines, or points

Simple, or *primitive* shapes are simple because you don't have to do much to create them. Just tell your VRML browser you want a cone and—pow!—it exists. Complex nodes are a little trickier, as their name implies. You'll need to give the VRML browser an exact idea of what the shape looks like, and this can take lots of planning and head-scratching.

Before discussing shape nodes, however, let's cheat a little bit and talk about one very important property node: Coordinate3. Although this node is covered in more detail in Chapter 18, it's essential to the design of certain shapes.

PAINTING BY NUMBER: THE COORDINATE3 NODE

This property node is simply a list of coordinates, specified with the *point* field. This field is an MFVec3f—a list of 3D vectors; each coordinate in the point field is expressed as three numbers. The origin, for example, is "0 0 0." If you have more than one coordinate, you need to separate each point with a comma and surround the list with square brackets.

To specify one point, then, you could use a node similar to

```
Coordinate3 {
    point  0 0 0
}
```

To specify three points (perhaps to create a flat triangle), you could write something similar to

```
Coordinate3 {
    point [ 0 0 0, 1 0 0, 0 1 0]
}
```

The first point, [0,0,0], is at the origin. The second point, [1,0,0], is 1 unit to the right of the origin. The third point, [0,1,0], is 1 unit *above* the origin. If you connect these three points, you get a simple right triangle.

The corners of a basic cube (as shown in Figure 16-1) would be represented by

```
Coordinate3 {
    point [ -1  1  1,  -1 -1  1,   1 -1  1,   1  1  1,
            -1  1 -1,  -1 -1 -1,   1 -1 -1,   1  1 -1 ]
}
```

The Coordinate3 node alone will never draw anything.

NOTE: If there's an active transformation (a shifting of vertices) at the time you try to draw a point, line, or polygon, it will be applied to the Coordinate3 list. Chapter 18 discusses these transformations in more detail.

Each time you call this node, the new list of numbers becomes the current set of *working coordinates*. The PointSet, IndexedLineSet, and IndexedFaceSet

Figure 16-1
The coordinates of a cube's corners

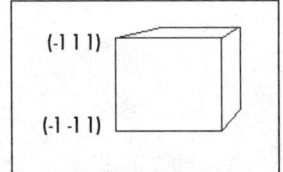
(-1 1 1)
(-1 -1 1)

nodes (covered later in this chapter) can then use these working coordinates to draw points, connect lines, or create polygons. The way the Coordinate3 node is used then, is as follows:

1. Declare your coordinates.

2. Use them to draw as many complex objects as you can.

3. Repeat step 1 with a new set of coordinates.

TIP: If you look at a typical scene, many objects wind up sharing the same points in 3D space. For example, you might be drawing a computer sitting on a desk. The bottom of the computer will have points in common with the top of the desk. The back of the desk may have similar vectors as the wall. The wall shares vectors with the ceiling...and so on. This is why just one complete listing of coordinates in the Coordinate3 node can save lots of space.

DRAWING POINTS: THE POINTSET NODE

The most basic way to fill empty 3D space with matter is to draw it, point by point. This takes lots of time, however, and a listing of all these points takes up tons of space. As such, you won't often use the PointSet node. The PointSet node can come in handy, however, if you need to touch up tiny details within a larger object. You can also draw imaginary points in space and then attach larger objects to them, spacing things out just so.

TIP: PointSets are often used to draw complex 3D mathematical equations, to show how points scatter over a given area. You'll rarely use a PointSet to draw something solid.

Before you tell a VRML browser to draw points, you need to tell it where to draw. This is done by use of the Coordinate3 node. PointSet then draws points at these coordinates in the order they were listed. This is similar to putting a checker on one square of a grid—just imagine a 3D checkerboard. For example, the following code will draw a point at the eight vertices, forming a cube-shaped constellation as shown in Figure 16-2.

```
Coordinate3 {
    point [ -1  1  1,  -1 -1  1,   1 -1  1,   1  1  1,
            -1  1 -1,  -1 -1 -1,   1 -1 -1,   1  1 -1 ]
}
PointSet { }
```

Figure 16-2
Placing points
at the corners
of a cube-
shaped area

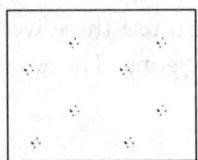

Often you'll only want to draw points at several of the current coordinates. You can use PointSet's *startIndex* field to mark which point to start drawing from. The default is 0, which means begin from the first point. If you specify 1, then PointSet will begin at the second point; 2 begins at the third point; and so on.

You can also specify the *numPoints* field, which tells PointSet how many points to draw. The default is -1, which indicates that *all* the remaining points should be drawn. For example, look at the following code:

```
#VRML V1.0 ascii
Separator {
  Coordinate3 {
        point [ -1  1  1,  -1 -1  1,   1 -1  1,   1  1  1,
        -1  1 -1,  -1 -1 -1,   1 -1 -1,   1  1 -1 ]
  }
  PointSet {
        startIndex   3
        numPoints    2
  }
}
```

Points will be drawn at two vertices, the fourth and fifth points: [1,1,1] and [-1,1,-1].

The color, style, lighting, and other properties of the drawn points depend on the most recent property settings. Read about drawing styles, materials, normal binding, textures, and other important property nodes in Chapters 18 and 19. These property nodes work hand-in-hand with PointSet to achieve remarkable effects.

DRAWING LINES: THE INDEXEDLINESET NODE

Sometimes the best way to create a 3D object is to draw a bunch of connected lines. This is similar to building a jungle gym. A LineSet is a listing of points that can be joined by straight lines to form an object.

NOTE: The IndexedLineSet node is not often used, since you'll generally want your 3D objects to have color, texture, and solidity. Even if you want to create a transparent cube, there's a difference between a glass box and one made of 12 sticks.

For example, a simple pyramid is made of six lines, as shown in Figure 16-3. The LineSet for such a pyramid would consist of the following vertices:

```
Coordinate3 {
     point [ 1 0 1, -1 0 1, 0 0 -1, 0 2 0]
}
```

To actually draw the pyramid, you'd need to connect a line from the tip of the pyramid to each of the corners of the base. You'd then need to connect the base vertices. As you can see, the same vertices are used repeatedly during this operation. Since the lines in a LineSet shape nearly *always* share the same vertices, it makes more sense to use an IndexedLineSet—simply reference a list of unique vertices.

The VRML IndexedLineSet node uses the current coordinates (as expressed in the last Coordinate3 node) as the vertices to connect with *polylines*. Recall that a polyline is a line with many twists and turns to it—in essence, a line composed of many smaller lines.

The IndexedLineSet node uses a field known as *coordIndex* to describe each line. Simply list the index values of the vertices you wish to connect. The first vertex in Coordinate3's field has an index value of 0, the second has a value of 1, and so on. Imagine a big magic marker running to each vertex and leaving a line in its wake. Whenever the current polyline has ended, use an index of -1. The VRML renderer will then begin drawing the next polyline. This is like lifting the magic marker, moving it to a new position, and then continuing to draw.

For example, to connect the first vertex to the second (whatever values they happen to be), you would use the following coordIndex field:

```
coordIndex [0,1]
```

To connect the first vertex to the second and then lift your pen and connect the third to the fourth to the fifth, you would use

```
coordIndex [0,1, -1, 2, 3, 4, -1]
```

Figure 16-3
Traveling across a desolate desert, you might see this three-sided pyramid

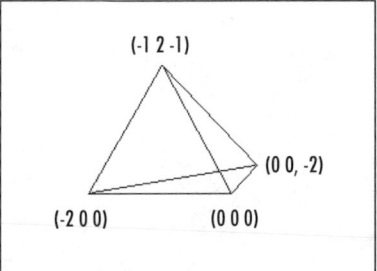

373

NOTE: If you list a vertex that isn't in the Coordinate3 node, it will be ignored. Also, if you try to create a line with fewer than two vertices, it will be ignored. All illegal vertices will be skipped, and should not mess up subsequent vertices. Ending the coordIndex list with a -1 is optional, but recommended.

List the vertices in the order you wish to connect them. Suppose you wanted to draw a simple triangle. First specify the corners of the triangle by using the Coordinate3 node:

```
Coordinate3 {
        point [ 0 0 0, 2 0 0, 1 1 0]
}
```

The vertices would then be indexed as follows:

Index Number	Coordinates
0	[0,0,0]
1	[2,0,0]
2	[1,1,0]

You could then connect vertex 0 to vertex 1, vertex 1 to vertex 2, and vertex 2 back to vertex 0 to form a closed triangle, as shown in Figure 16-4:

```
IndexedLineSet {
        coordIndex [0,1,2,0,-1]
}
```

 TIP: There's generally more than one way to draw the same shape, given a list of vertices. If you're drawing a fancy set of lines, try to start with the most isolated point and work toward the more clustered regions.

Figure 16-4
Creating a triangle with VRML

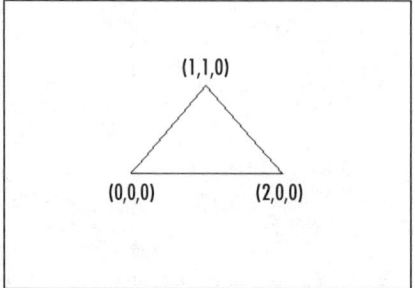

As a slightly more complicated example, to draw the pyramid in Figure 16-3, you could use the following code:

```
#VRML V1.0 ascii
Separator {
  Coordinate3 {
      point [ 1 0 1, -1 0 1, 0 0 -1, 0 2 0] # Pyramid Vertices
  }
  IndexedLineSet {
      coordIndex [0, 1, 2, 0, 3, 0, 3, 1, 3, 2] # Connect the Dots
  }
}
```

Alternatively, you could draw the pyramid without drawing any given line twice. This would be impossible to do without "lifting the pen"—using the -1 index to finish the polyline:

```
IndexedLineSet {
      coordIndex [0, 1, 2, 0, -1,       # Draw the pyramid base
                  3, 0, -1,             # Draw the right edge
                  3, 1, -1,             # Draw the left edge
                  3, 2, -1]             # Draw the rear edge
}
```

Other Fields

The IndexedLineSet node is used for more than drawing basic wireframe shapes. You can use LineSets to hold texture maps (like stretching canvas around a frame), to arrange complicated objects in a specific orientation, or to act as an invisible barrier or mark. Other important IndexedLineSet fields include

▪ materialIndex—This lets you specify what type of material each given line is made of, based on a previously created list of materials. You'll learn about the MaterialBinding node and how to use it in Chapter 18.

▪ normalIndex—The normal of a line can affect how light strikes it. Your IndexedLineSet may have many normals, which can be listed using the NormalBinding node (again, see Chapter 18 for the details). You can specify which normals to use in the normalIndex field.

▪ **NOTE:** If you don't specify any normals, an IndexedLineSet is drawn with all lighting turned off.

▪ textureCoordIndex—This field lets you describe which textures to wrap around which vertices. You'll learn all about textures in Chapter 19.

DRAWING A SOLID SHAPE: INDEXEDFACESET

The same two-dimensional shapes can be expressed in many ways. The clearest method of shape-building is to break the object into many tiny 2D shapes known as *polygons* (see Chapter 9). The IndexedFaceSet node is the easiest way to represent groups of polygons. You can use an IndexedFaceSet to draw nearly any object. The question is, how detailed should the object be? The more polygons you use, the longer your IndexedFaceSet node will be.

Polygon Gluttony

Chapter 9 explains how to build cool-looking objects using polygons. To create truly realistic things, you can go crazy with your polygons. A realistic tree, for example, might use thousands of polygons—one for each leaf, several for the twists and turns of the tree-trunk, and so on. But here's an important tip to always keep in mind:

 TIP: Polygon gluttony is the leading cause of browser slowness.

When you model an object, always try to use as few polygons as possible. In the next chapter you'll learn about the LOD node that lets you create several versions of the same object and only use the one that makes the most sense. But whether the person who walks through your scene has a clunky 486 PC or a lightning-fast reality-engine machine, objects with too many polygons throw a major wrench in the rendering machine.

The object with the most polygons defines your *scene complexity.* Table 16-1 lists several types of machines and the maximum number of polygons they can reasonably handle. Always aim to keep your scene complexity lower than these averages.

Table 16-1 The maximum number of polygons various computer platforms can handle

Platform	Maximum Number of Polygons
Pentium-90	1,300 XL (Indy/Indigo2) 1,600 XZ (Indy/Indigo2) 4,400 Extreme
(Indigo2)	10,300 RealityEngine2 30,000

When you add time-consuming things like fancy lighting and lots of textures, these maximum values are even lower.

> 🔑 **NOTE:** The VRMLINFO program, which comes with WebSpace, is a great utility that will count the number of polygons in each of your objects. This can help you determine if your objects are too complicated.

Facing the FaceSet

Almost everything you come across in virtual reality worlds is made from *FaceSets*. A FaceSet is just what it sounds like—a 3D shape that is defined by sets of polygons all glued together to form the object's faces. Specifically, a VRML FaceSet is a listing, in order, of the coordinates that define the vertices of each face. This is a very basic structure that can be used to specify nearly any other type of popular 3D object, such as:

🔲 Triangle Sets (objects made from small triangles)

🔲 A QuadMesh (objects made from small squares)

🔲 NURBS (objects made from curved lines)

Look at any object in the real world, and it's probably made of smaller 2D shapes. Let's start simple and play around with a small box. A box has six sides (faces), each made of a four-sided polygon (also known as a rectangle). A box's FaceSet is illustrated in Figure 16-5. The Coordinate3 node to represent the corners of the box, then, would be as follows:

```
Coordinate3 {
    point [-1 0 3, 1 0 3, -1 3 3, 1 3 3,
           -1 0 -3, 1 0 -3, -1 3 -3, 1 3 -3]
}
```

The IndexedFaceSet node tells your VRML renderer to take the current list of vertices and use them to draw polygons. But how does your VRML renderer know which vertices to actually join? Should it join the first three to make a triangle? The first four to make a square? Or should it take the first, third, eighth, 19th, and 15th vectors and use *those* as a pentagon?

Figure 16-5
The vectors that make up an oblong box

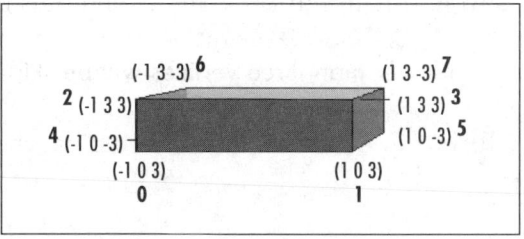

To draw the box in Figure 16-5, for instance, you'd want to connect the vertices to make five rectangles (let's leave off the top so you can put some goodies inside). If you numbered the corners of the box from 0 to 7, you'd need to make the following connections:

1. Join 1, 3, 2, and 0 to form the front of the box.

2. Join 4, 5, 7, and 6 to form the large backside of the box.

3. Join 0, 4, 6, and 2 to form the small left side.

4. Join 1, 5, 7, and 3 to form the small right side.

5. Join 0, 1, 5, and 4 to form the box's bottom.

Notice that, when forming the box, you need to use the same vertex several times. Wouldn't it save a lot of room, you may ask, to just list the vertices and have the VRML renderer connect the dots? Indeed. That is why VRML uses the IndexedFaceSet node. This node indexes the vertices, allowing you to list them in any order and reuse them. An IndexedFaceSet is similar to an IndexedLineSet, only polygons are drawn instead of open line segments. It's like the difference between a Frisbee and a hula hoop.

Much like the IndexedLineSet node, the IndexedFaceSet node uses the *coordIndex* field to specify which vertices to use. The first vertex in your Coordinate3 list is index value 0, the next is value 1, and so on. To draw a polygon, list the vertices that should be connected, in the correct order. When you've finished specifying the current polygon, use an index of -1 to let the VRML renderer know it should move on to the next set of vertices and draw a new polygon. The last vertex in each polygon list will automatically be connected to the first.

For example, the following code would create two polygons, one triangle with three vertices (values 0, 1, and 2), and one square with four vertices (values 6, 1, 2, and 3):

```
coordIndex [ 0, 1, 2, -1,
        6, 1, 2, 3, -1]
```

The above shapes would share vertices 1 and 2, and thus be connected.

NOTE: Polygons with fewer than three vertices will be skipped.

So, to create the box in Figure 16-5, you would use the following code:

```
#VRML V1.0 ascii
Separator {
```

```
Coordinate3 {
    point [-1 0 3, 1 0 3, -1 3 3, 1 3 3,
        -1 0 -3, 1 0 -3, -1 3 -3, 1 3 -3]
}
IndexedFaceSet {
    coordIndex[
        1,3,2,0,-1, # Front
        4,5,7,6,-1, # Back
        0,4,6,2,-1, # Left Side
        1,5,7,3,-1, # Right Side
        0,1,5,4,-1] # Bottom
    }
}
```

NOTE: The Separator node is discussed in the next chapter. Basically, what it does is group related nodes together.

To draw a basic shape, simply design it on graph paper. Follow these steps:

1. Mark down all the vertices.

2. Give each vertex a unique number, starting with 0.

3. List your vertices in order in the Coordinate3 node.

4. Use the IndexedFaceSet's coordIndex field to draw each flat surface.

Getting Fancier

Let's get just a little more complicated. For example, you can add a new point above the top center of the box, at [0,4,0]. You could then connect the top corners of the box to this new point to form a pyramid-shaped top. This would form a simple house, as shown in Figure 16-6. The VRML code to render this is

Figure 16-6
A modest but lovely place to call home

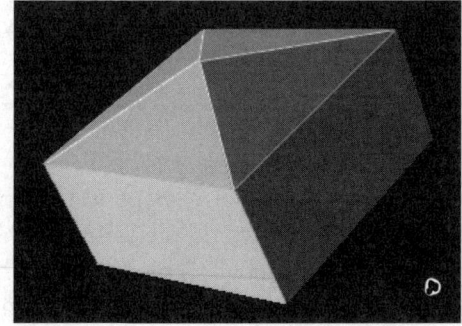

```
#VRML V1.0 ascii
Separator {
  Coordinate3 {
    point [-3 0 3, 3 0 3, -3 3 3, 3 3 3,
      -3 0 -3, 3 0 -3, -3 3 -3, 3 3 -3, 0 4 0]
  }
  IndexedFaceSet {
    coordIndex[
      1,3,2,0,-1, # Front
      4,5,7,6,-1, # Back
      0,4,6,2,-1, # Left Side
      1,5,7,3,-1, # Right Side
      0,1,5,4,-1, # Bottom
      6,8,7,-1,   # One side of the roof
      6,8,2,-1,   # Another part of the roof
      7,8,3,-1,   # The next part of the roof
      2,8,3,-1]   # The last roof face
  }
}
```

You could now easily add a chimney, some windows, a door, a walkway, and so on.

Other Fields

IndexedFaceSet takes many other fields besides coordIndex. For example, you can create a texture and then paste it against a polygon. This can be done by using the IndexedFaceSet's *textureCoordIndex* field. Textures are discussed in Chapter 19.

You can also use several materials to build your object, giving each polygon a different look. To do this, use the *materialIndex* field along with the MaterialBinding node (see Chapter 18). Lastly, you can give each polygon its own normal to change the way light hits it or to save computation time. To do this, you would use the *normalIndex* field hand in hand with the NormalBinding node (also in Chapter 18).

All in all, you can use the IndexedFaceSet node to create clusters of fully designed polygons. Used correctly, you can use these polygons to build a realistic model of nearly any object in the world.

DRAWING PRIMITIVE SHAPES

You now have the power to draw nearly any shape in the universe. But having the power and having the time are two different things. What if, for example, you wanted to draw a simple baseball? This is one of the most complicated problems in 3-D graphics—how would you do it using polygons? A true sphere doesn't have *any* flat surfaces. You could cheat, using hundreds or even millions of small triangles and piecing them together to form a sphere shape. But pity the poor soul who tries to define the vertices of each of these triangles by hand. Even if you used a computer program to define this sphere-like shape for you, it still seems like more trouble than it's worth. Not to mention that it would be built with thousands of polygons, slowing rendering to a halt on even the fastest of machines.

Luckily, VRML includes four very basic and useful primitive shapes:

■ Cube—This consists of six rectangles with all edges connected.

■ Sphere—This is a shape where each point along the surface is equally distant from some fixed point in space.

■ Cylinder—This is a shape with two circles as its top and bottom and a flat rectangle wrapped around the perimeters of the circles.

■ Cone—This is a shape with a circular base and each point along the perimeter of the circle meeting at one specified point somewhere over the center of the circle.

These shapes can be used for more than creating simple scenes. Combined wisely, primitive shapes can be used to form most any other shape. This is the theory behind some of the art of Picasso (see Figure 16-7). For example, modeler Paul Isaacs has built a simple humanoid figure entirely out of spheres, as shown in Figure 16-8.

Each primitive shape is made of several distinct parts. For example, a cylinder is made of two circles and a rectangular side. VRML allows you to omit certain parts. This lets you turn a cylinder into an open orange-juice can, or a cone into a flat disk. A shape's parts are controlled using the *parts* field.

NOTE: The look and location of each shape depend on the current state: the cumulative transformation, current materials, lighting model, drawing style, and geometric complexity. The next few chapters cover these states and how to change them.

The Cone

A cone is made of two simple parts: a bottom circle and the side.

A default cone is shown in Figure 16-9. It is centered at the origin [0,0,0] with a radius of 1 and a height of 2. This means the cone ranges from -1 to 1 along all three axes. The apex (tip) of the cone is located at [1,0,0].

Figure 16-7
Some of
Picasso's cubist
works use
basic shapes to
create scenes

To change the size of the cone's bottom, simply use the *bottomRadius* field, indicating how many units wide the radius should be. To alter the cone's height, use the *height* field.

The *parts* field can take the following values:

- SIDES—Only display the sides of the cone (the conical part). This can be used to create an open ice-cream cone.

- BOTTOM—Only display the bottom face of the cone (the circle).

Figure 16-8
A figure built
entirely out of
spheres

Figure 16-9
The default
VRML cone

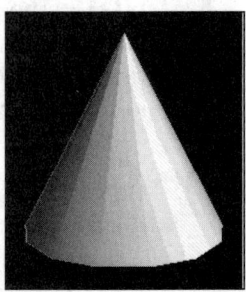

ALL—Display all parts. This is the default.

For example, to create a very flat cone that is 3 units high and 10 units wide, use the following VRML code:

```
Cone {        parts        ALL        bottomRadius  1        height 2}
```

The Cube

A VRML cube node isn't really a cube, since some sides can be longer than others. The VRML refers to this node as a *cuboid*. The default cuboid is centered at the origin [0,0,0], extending 2 units in each direction from -1 to 1, as shown in Figure 16-10.

A cube has three dimensions, each of which you can set using its associated field:

width—The x dimension

height—The y dimension

depth—The z dimension

For example, to create the cube shown in Figure 16-11 with a width of 10, a height of 5, and a depth of 3, use the following VRML code:

```
Cube {      width   10
            height  5
            depth   3
}
```

A cube doesn't have any separate parts.

The Cylinder

The cylinder node quickly creates any size cylinder you'd like. The default cylinder (in Figure 16-12) is centered around the y axis, with its center at

Figure 16-10
The default
VRML cube

Figure 16-11
A warped
brick-shaped
"cube"

Figure 16-12
The default
VRML cylinder

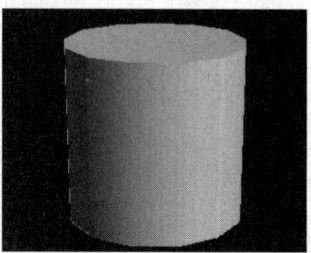

the origin [0,0,0]. It is 2 units high and wide, and therefore stretches from -1 to 1 in all three directions.

You can easily change the size or appearance of the cylinder. To make the two circular ends of the cylinder bigger or smaller, use the *radius* field. To change the height of the cylinder, use the *height* field.

You can specify the exact look of the cylinder using the *parts* field with one of the following values:

- TOP—Only draw the top face of the cylinder (a circle).

- BOTTOM—Only draw the bottom face (a circle).

- SIDES—Only draw the cylindrical sides.

- ALL—Draw the entire capped cylinder.

An open cylinder 10 units high and 3 units wide (radius of 1.5) would be expressed as follows:

```
Cylinder {        parts  SIDES       radius  1.5       height  10}
```

This cylinder is illustrated in Figure 16-13.

Figure 16-13
A more
interesting
tube, sans
bottom and top

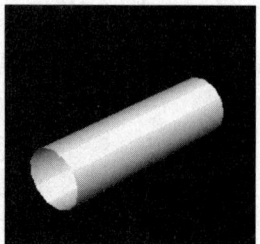

The Sphere

The sphere node draws a basic sphere, as shown in Figure 16-14. The default shape is centered at the origin [0,0,0], with a radius of 1. Like a cube, a sphere doesn't have any separate parts. The only field you can fiddle with in the sphere node is *radius*, which specifies how many unit-lengths the radius should be.

For example, to create a sphere that ranges from -10 to 10 (along all three axes), use the code:

```
Sphere {
        radius   10
}
```

TEXT: THE ASCIITEXT NODE

For those who are used to surfing the Web, VRML's lack of text may seem strange. You may be used to pages and pages of hypertextual information tossed at you from all directions. There's no reason why VRML can't have rich textual information, however. If the best way to say what you want to say is with words, then read on...

3D Text

VRML has a handy node that allows you take any ASCII character and represent it on the screen as 3D text. This node will become more popular as people transfer their home pages to VRML. Walking through worlds is lots of fun, but the real, honest-to-goodness information often comes by means of text.

The first time you use this node, the text is drawn, by default, at the origin [0,0,0]. Any additional strings are written below the first string, depending on the size of the font and the current facing. The text is created from left to right, top to bottom. The font family, size, and style can be set by calling the FontStyle node before the AsciiText node (see Chapter 18).

Figure 16-14
Your default
VRML sphere

To determine how to lay out the text, you can use the *justification* field to justify text horizontally along the x axis. Select from one of the following justifications:

- LEFT—The string begins at the origin (the default).

- RIGHT—The string ends at the origin.

- CENTER—The center of the string is at the origin.

To constrain your text within a certain space, use the *width* field. By default, width is set to 0, which means there is no constraint. Constraining is useful if you'd like all the text to be visible at a certain distance. Otherwise, the text will continue outside the field of vision. Specify the width in units.

The *spacing* field lets you specify how much of a gap should be between each new line of text. By default, spacing is 1 unit.

For example, to write the words "VRML Rules!" in the center of your screen, as shown in Figure 16-15, use the following code:

```
AsciiText {
        string          "VRML Rules!"
        spacing         1
        justification   CENTER
        width           0
}
```

2D Text

But what if you just want plain old two-dimensional text? VRML has no node allowing you to print lines of 2D words, but there are several ways to get around this limitation:

Figure 16-15
VRML rules in
3D!

Use any paint program to create the words you want to display, in whatever font, color, or style you wish. Save these words as an image map. You can then apply this text as a texture on any flat surface. This allows you to create billboards, posters, or road signs. Like real billboards, the text will disappear or be difficult to read unless you're looking at it from a head-on angle. See Chapter 19 to learn how to apply textures.

If you want some text to be associated with a particular object, you can use the WWWAnchor node. When someone rolls a mouse over that object, some text will appear at the bottom of the screen. For example, you can create an American flag. When someone touches the flag with the mouse arrow, the words "Vote Jones in 1996: He's no Kennedy, but he's the best thing we got!" can be made to flash on the screen. Check out Chapter 20 for information on how to do this.

THE ELEVATIONGRID NODE

One of the most basic objects in any scene is the ground. The ground lets you know whether things are sitting or floating. It helps you figure out where objects are relative to each other. And to land-oriented mammals such as humans, it makes things seem more real. Unfortunately, creating your own ground using an IndexedFaceSet often takes too long to render.

The VRML 1.1 specification plans to include an ElevationGrid node. This would create a rectangular graph-paper-like grid that could have various hills and valleys, helping to create terrain. You can easily drop a texture map onto this grid to create realistic surfaces.

The grid will be drawn starting from the origin [0,0,0]. The rows of the grid are aligned with the x axis. The columns are aligned with the z axis. Use the *verticesPerRow* and *verticesPerColumn* fields to specify how spaced out the grid should be. Use the stepSize field to specify how large each rectangle within the grid should be. So, to create a grid that is 100 units wide by 200 units long, with 10x20 rectangles (measuring 10x10 each) in it, you would write

```
ElevationGrid {
   verticesPerRow        10
   verticesPerColumn     20
   # Each rectangle must be 10x10 to create a 100x200 grid.
   stepSize [10,10]
}
```

You can now make various rectangles higher or lower than others by using the *heights* field. This field takes a list of numbers, one for each rectangle, specifying the y value. First, list the heights for the first row, then the second row, and so on. To figure out how many heights you should have, multiply the verticesPerRow and verticesPerColumn values.

You could create a bumpy landscape by using the following code:

```
ElevationGrid {
   verticesPerRow       3
   verticesPerColumn    3
   stepSize [100,100]
   heights [5, 2, -3, 2, -4, 3, 6, 7, 3, -4]
}
```

SHAPING UP

Shapes are quite amazing, but they're even better when you add properties to them. Properties let you position shapes around the world, color your shapes, add textures to them, light them, and draw them as fast and efficiently as possible. Chapters 18 and 19 discuss these properties.

However, there's something essential still to be covered: groups. Groups let you bundle simple shapes and properties together to form complete scenes. Groups are discussed in full in the next chapter.

17
GANGING UP: GROUPS

17

Who you are often depends on the people you hang around, and where you do the hanging. If your friends stay up dancing all night, you'll probably end up doing the same. If your friends are simple, quiet folk, you probably won't gab that much. If you and your pals enjoy chilling out at the beach, your skin will probably be tanner than it'd otherwise be.

The same is true for a virtual world. Environment plays a big role in determining how an object looks and acts. A tree standing in the shadow of several redwoods seems puny, but the same tree in an empty field seems majestic. More importantly, properties are contagious in virtual worlds. If you define the color to be beet-red, then any object you subsequently create will be red. To lay out a scene the way you want, you need a way to group like objects and separate unrelated objects. Grouping would also allow you to create a detailed hierarchy in your scene graph, drawing certain parts of the world before others.

Fortunately, VRML has several powerful group nodes:

- Separator
- TransformSeparator
- Group
- Switch
- LOD (Level of Detail)

In addition, the WWWAnchor node can be thought of as a group node. This node is discussed, however, in Chapter 20, since it relates directly to the World Wide Web.

DO YOU KNOW WHERE YOUR CHILDREN ARE?

Whenever a node contains other nodes within its curly brackets, it is known as a *parent* node. The nodes inside are known as the *children*. Group nodes can have an infinite number of children. These children are traversed and processed on a first-come, first-served basis. A typical VRML file will be a full family tree of children, grandchildren, great-grandchildren, and more.

THE SEPARATOR NODE

Think of the Separator node as a brick wall that doesn't allow any information to leak out to other nodes. Suppose, for example, you create a sphere with all sorts of fancy colors, textures, transformations, and lighting qualities. If you surround all these property sections with a Separator node, these properties won't affect any other shapes.

The purpose of separators will become much clearer once you learn about properties (in the next chapter). Each separator can contain any number of properties, such as lighting, cameras, transformations, materials, bindings, and so on. As long as they're separated, these properties won't affect any other part of the scene.

The Separator node takes the form

```
Separator {
    ...
}
```

Any nodes written between the curly brackets will be separated from any other nodes.

NOTE: A VRML file must consist of only one main node. This must be a group node, with the rest of the nodes within it. Separator is a good main node to use. Most every VRML file should begin with the Separator node, with curly brackets surrounding all the other nodes. Separator helps make your VRML scene more portable, treating the entire thing as one self-contained group.

VRML 1.1: The syntax of the Separator node is slightly more structured in VRML version 1.1. Properties come first, followed by basic shapes and coordinates. Only after all these nodes are listed may you start creating children.

Technically speaking, the Separator node uses a *stack* to work its magic. When you call the Separator node, the current state is pushed onto the stack and saved there. The node's children are then traversed and processed. When the end of the Separator node is reached, the traversal state will be popped from the stack, and all properties will be returned to their previous values.

Being a Separationist

Whenever you design a part of the scene graph that has no direct relation to any other parts, use the Separator node. For example, if you have a room with a chair, a table, and a chandelier, you probably will want to place each piece of furniture in its own Separator group. You may even want to separate each leg of the chair, or each branch of the chandelier. Here's a sample structure (the actual commands aren't legal VRML):

```
#VRML V1.0 ascii
Separator {
        Properties_Which_Affect_The_Whole_Scene_Go_Here
        Coordinates_Which_All_Subsequent_Nodes_Use_Go_Here
        Separator { Draw_Room_Here }
        Separator { Draw_Chandelier_Here }
        Separator {
            Draw_Table_Here
            Separator { Draw_Table_Top_Here }
            Separator { Draw_Table_Legs_Here }
        }
        Separator { Draw_Chair1_Here }
        Separator { Draw_Chair2_Here }
        Separator { Draw_Chair3_Here }
}
```

You can organize your VRML code in any way that makes sense to you, as long as you use separators properly and are sure to put properties before the objects you want to modify.

 TIP: It's better to err by having too many separators than too few. Whenever you're afraid of leaking a property, separate it.

Many times, the only property you'll want to separate between objects is a transformation (the way an object is warped or rotated in space). For instance, you might want to have a skeleton move its arm without it affecting the rest of the body, but otherwise you want all properties to remain the same. In this case, you would use the TransformSeparator node—one to separate the skeleton from the rest of the scene, and one to separate the arm from the torso. See the next section for further discussion.

Figure 17-1
Culling a scene

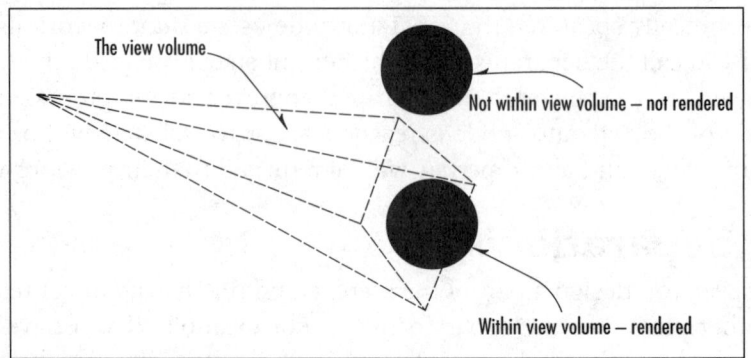

The view volume

Not within view volume — not rendered

Within view volume — rendered

Culling Time

The term *culling* isn't as violent as it sounds. Or maybe it is. Culling makes your Separator node smart, eradicating children that won't be seen. The part of the current world you can actually see is known as the *view volume*. If culling is active, the separator's *bounding box* (an invisible box that walls in all the objects in your Separator node) is kept track of. If this bounding box doesn't fit within the view volume, the node is just skipped. See Figure 17-1 for an illustration.

You can set culling by using the *renderCulling* field. You can set renderCulling to one of the following values:

▪ ON—Always cull to the view volume.

▪ OFF—Don't cull.

▪ AUTO—Let the VRML viewer decide whether the nodes should be culled.

By default, culling is set to AUTO.

You should only turn culling off if the modeler you used to create the objects explicitly requires that it be off, since culling off-screen objects saves lots of time. A Separator node with culling always turned on, for example, would look like

```
Separator {
        renderCulling        ON
        ...
}
```

Putting It to Use

A common use for the Separator node is to separate different materials. For example, suppose you want to create a sphere embedded in another (kind

Figure 17-2
A red ball with
a gray "pimple"

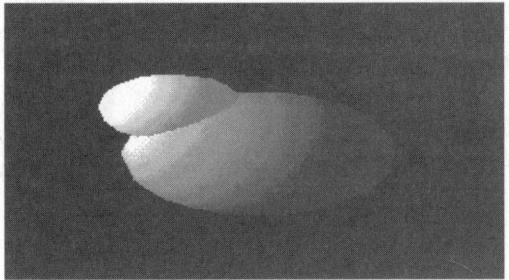

of like a ball with a wart) as shown in Figure 17-2. To change an object's color, you would use the Material node along with the diffuseColor field. Don't worry about the structure of the Material node for now (we'll cover that in Chapter 18), but instead look at how the Separator is used. Using separators, you can easily create a large red sphere and move it 3 units down. You can then end the separator and create a standard sphere, which will be the default color (gray) at the default position (the origin).

```
#VRML V1.0 ascii
Separator {
    Separator {
        Transform {
            translation 0 -3 0 # Move the ball three units down
        }
        Material {
            diffuseColor 1 0 0        # Make the ball red
        }
        Sphere {
            radius 2 # Make a big ball
        }
    }
    Separator {
        Sphere { } # Draw a small ball
    }
}
```

THE TRANSFORMSEPARATOR NODE

Much of the time, the only thing that'll change from one object to the next is where it's placed. The TransformSeparator node is like the Separator node with a twist: It separates transformations and their effects from the rest of the scene graph, but lets all the other properties flow.

Transformations are created using several nodes:

VR
ML Transform

VR
ML Scale

Rotation

Translation

You can read more about these nodes in Chapter 18. If any of these nodes is called while within a TransformSeparator node, its effects will not alter any objects beyond the current group.

The TransformSeparator node looks similar to

```
TransformSeparator {
    ...
}
```

NOTE: TransformSeparator is especially useful when used with cameras or lights. This way, you can move around a camera without messing up any of the properties of objects that the camera is shooting. Likewise, you can shift a light source without changing any of the surfaces that the light is shining upon. Read more about lights and cameras in Chapter 19.

For example, if you wanted to create a small ball budding off a larger ball (as in Figure 17-2), yet you wanted to construct both balls out of the same material (as in Figure 17-3), you could use the following code:

```
#VRML V1.0 ascii
Separator {
    TransformSeparator {
        Transform {
          translation 0 -3 0 # Move the ball three units down
        }
        Material {
            diffuseColor 1 0 0 # Make the ball red
        }
        Sphere {
            radius 2
        }
    }
    Separator {
    # Other than its position, this sphere has the same qualities
    # as the above sphere
        Sphere { }
    }
}
```

The Material from the first node leaks out into the second node, but the first node's transformation will not affect the second sphere.

Figure 17-3
The TransformSeparator node lets the attributes sneak through to subsequent nodes, letting you use the same material throughout several groups

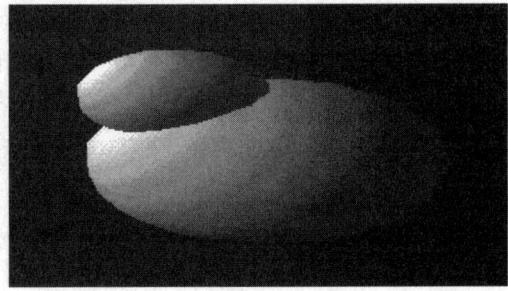

VRML 1.1: Since the TransformSeparator is not really necessary, it will probably be dropped from future versions of VRML. To simulate a TransformSeparator node, you could specify the properties for a set of objects and then place the shapes and their transformations only within the same Separator node. For example:

```
Separator {
      Put_The_Properties_Here
      Separator {
            Transform { translation 5 5 5 }
            Put_The_Translated_Object_Here
      }
      _Put_All_Other_Objects_Here
}
```

THE GROUP NODE

The most basic type of group node is aptly named the Group node. This node simply acts as a container, drawing each of its children in order, one after another. This node is generally optional, since VRML nodes are processed in order by default.

The Group node is most useful when it is named; this lets you use a given group of shapes, properties, or objects again and again. For example:

```
DEF Boxes Group {
          Separator {
             Cube    {
                     width    5
                     height   15
                     depth    15
                     }
          }
           TransformSeparator {
                  Transform {
                         translation 5 0 0
              }
```

continued on next page

continued from previous page

```
                        Cube    { }
            }
    }
```

You could now use Boxes further down in your VRML file without having to redefine the two boxes. This is called *instancing*. You can read about instancing in Chapter 22.

 TIP: Grouping and naming nodes also makes your VRML code much easier to read.

VRML 1.1: Since Group nodes are not really necessary, they will be dropped from future versions of VRML.

THE SWITCH NODE

The Switch node lets you specify objects and then ignore them. Why would you want to do this? Perhaps your VRML file has two alternate worlds in it. You'd like to be able to switch from one world to another just by changing one small value. Or perhaps you've drawn a virtual sky. Depending on the time of day, you want the sky to be either red, orange, blue, violet, or black. The Switch node makes this type of instant selection easy.

VRML 1.1: Switch nodes are automatically treated as separators. With older versions of VRML, be sure to put a separator around Switch nodes, since some browsers may not automatically do this.

You can easily tell a Switch node which children to traverse by setting the *whichChild* field. You can use whichChild to do three things:

- Traverse every node—To use every child, just give whichChild a value of -3 (this is the same thing as a Group node).

VRML 1.1: Since there is no real reason for Switch nodes to use all their children (that's what a Separator node is for), Switch no longer accepts the "Traverse every node" value of -3.

- Traverse one specific child—To use just one child node, give whichChild that node's index number. All other children will be skipped. The first child has an index number of 0, the second child is 1, the third is 2, and so on.

For example, in the following code:

```
Switch {
        whichChild 1
        Sphere { }
        Cube { }
        Cylinder { }
}
```

only the cube will be drawn.

- Traverse none of the nodes—To skip every child within the Switch node, give whichChild a value of -1 (this is the default).

TIP: While developing your VRML, you'll find the Switch node very handy to "erase" part of your world. For example, to comment out some VRML nodes, just use the following form:

```
Switch {
        whichChild -1
        Node1 { }
        Node2 { }
        Node3 { }
}
```

Node1, Node2, and Node3 will be skipped.

Remember, you can use the Group or Separator nodes to make the first child a cluster of many nodes. For example:

```
Switch {
        whichChild 1
        Separator {
            Node1 { }
            Node2 { }
            Node3 { }
        }
        Separator {
            Node4 { }
            Node5 { }
            Node6 { }
        }
    }
```

NOTE: The Switch node will take on much more importance with later implementations of VRML, when behaviors, interaction, and other instances can affect whether you want an object to be drawn.

THE LOD NODE

Look at the real world around you. Objects closest to your eye are crisp and sharp—you can see every wrinkle, every stain, every curve. Objects a little farther back are a bit less defined—similar colors blend together, small details disappear. Faraway objects lose most of their detail—they become dim, purplish, and break down into basic shapes.

The LOD node stands for "Level of Detail," letting you specify different objects depending on how far away an observer is standing. This can speed the creation of your virtual worlds a great deal. After all, why waste time drawing a complicated TV set with screen, colors, and buttons, if it looks just like a simple box from several yards away?

NOTE: Because it is a little difficult to implement, many browsers do not yet use the LOD node. These browsers will usually draw just the most complex object.

LOD can also help enhance a scene artistically. Making objects fuzzier makes them seem even farther away than they are. Using LOD to enhance the illusion of distance achieves beautiful results.

An LOD group has children that are different representations of the same object. A typical LOD node takes the form

```
LOD {
      Highest_Detailed_Object
      Medium_Detailed_Object
      Lowest_Detailed_Object
}
```

VRML 1.1: All LOD nodes will also act as separators.

Home on the Range

The LOD node uses the *range* field to figure which child should be drawn when. This field takes an array of numbers. You should have one fewer range value than you do children. For example, if you want to switch between two objects, you just need one range number, like

```
range [5]
```

When the observer is less than 5 units away, the first child will be drawn; when 5 or more units away, the second child will be drawn.

If you have more than one range value, then these are viewed as boundary marks between each level of detail. For example, if you are currently located between the first and second number in the range array, the second child will be drawn. Each number in the range array, for obvious reasons, should be bigger than the number before it. For example, if you use the following range:

```
range [3 5 15]
```

then the first child will be drawn as long as the range is less than 3; the second child is drawn if the range is 3 or more, but less than 5; the third child is drawn if the range is 5 or more, but less than 15; and the fourth child (with the least level of detail) will appear only when the observer is 15 or more units away.

NOTE: You should have one more child than you do range numbers. If your LOD node has more ranges than it does children, the last child is used for all lowest levels of detail. If you have too many children in your LOD nodes, the ones further down the list will simply be unused.

VRML 1.1: LOD will become much more important with future versions of VRML. VRML browsers will automatically adjust the ranges based on the speed of the current machine. This would allow the same scene to have a constant frame rate on any type of computer, no matter how slow. This means that LOD should not be used, in version 1.1 and on, to simulate real-life fuzzing out of objects. Instead, it should be used to create several versions of the same object. Highly detailed versions of the object will appear only on computers that are strong enough to use them.

Setting the Center

Having these ranges is great, but what do the numbers actually mean? How far away is 20 units? And how far away is 1,000?

NOTE: Remember that a VRML unit is equal to 1 meter, and the same unit measurement is used to measure the size of objects, distances, and so on.

It's important, therefore, to specify where the center of your LOD object is. This *center* field takes a 3D vector as its value. Whenever you change your point of view, the distance from your eye-point to the center of the LOD is calculated. This distance is then looked up in the range table, and the appropriate child is drawn.

VRML 1.1: Although this is not explicitly stated in the VRML 1.0 specification, the center is expressed as [0,0,0] in object coordinates.

Details, Details

A full LOD node, then, might look similar to the following:

```
LOD {
        range [3]
        center 5 0 0
        Sphere {}
        Cube {}

    }
```

If you are closer than 3 units to the center of the object (5 units along the x axis), then you'll see a sphere. Step back farther than that and you'll get a cube.

Here's a slightly more real-world example—a very simple LOD node that displays a green house as the most detailed object when you're closer than 10 units (see Figure 17-4); a green cube as the middle level of detail when you're 10 or more, but less than 20 units away (see Figure 17-5); a gray cube, at 20 or more, but less than 30 units away (in Figure 17-6); and nothing at all as the lowest level when 30 or more units away.

Figure 17-4
Coming close to a lovely green home

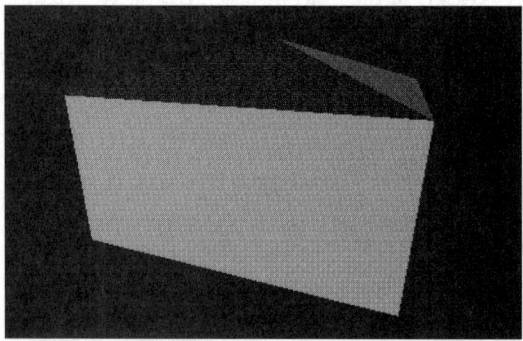

Figure 17-5
Stepping away from home, it becomes a green box

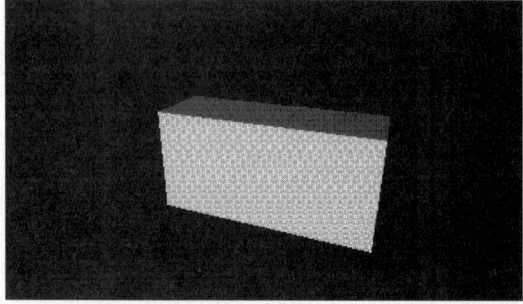

Figure 17-6
Farther away,
the home is
just a gray
shape. Walk
back farther
and the
house would
disappear
altogether

```
#VRML V1.0 ascii
LOD {
     center 0 0 0        # Center of children
     range [ 10, 20, 30 ]  # Increasing ranges
     Separator {
          Material { diffuseColor 0 1 0 }
          Coordinate3 {
              point [-3 0 3, 3 0 3, -3 3 3, 3 3 3,
              -3 0 -3, 3 0 -3, -3 3 -3, 3 3 -3, 0 4 0]
          }
          IndexedFaceSet {
              coordIndex[
              1,3,2,0,-1, # Front
              4,5,7,6,-1, # Back
              0,4,6,2,-1, # Left Side
              1,5,7,3,-1, # Right Side
              0,1,5,4,-1, # Bottom
              6,8,7,-1,   # One side of the roof
              6,8,2,-1,   # Another part of the roof
              7,8,3,-1,   # The next part of the roof
              2,8,3,-1]   # The last roof face
          }
     }
     Separator {
          Material { diffuseColor 0 1 0 }
          Cube {
              width 6
              height 3
              length 6
          }
     }
     Cube {
          width 6
          height 3
          length 6
     }
     Group { }
}
```

Notice how the LOD node has four children. The first two children are Separators. The third child is a Cube. And the last is an empty Group. The proper child will appear at the proper distances.

 TIP: It's a good idea to make complicated objects invisible when they're really far away. To "draw" this invisible object, just use a node that doesn't do anything, such as the Group or Info node. This can also be used to achieve some neat effects. For example, you might want to have hidden trapdoors or control panels that only appear when you're close enough to them. (Avoid doing this in VRML 1.1, however, since ranges may be set automatically.)

The most common way of using LOD is to create three or four versions of every object:

- One highly detailed version (1,000 polygons with texture maps and various materials).

- A less-detailed version (only 100 to 500 polygons, without any texture maps).

- A very simple version (10 polygons, no textures or multiple colors).

- A geometric primitive (a cube, sphere, or whichever simple shape most resembles the object you're simulating). Be sure to make the shape as large as the original object.

TIP: The LOD node will come in extremely handy when combined with the WWWInline node. This lets you load 3D objects only when they're close enough to be seen. This powerful technique is covered in Chapter 20.

WHAT'S NEXT?

Several of the examples in this chapter used something known as the Material node to give objects colors. You might also recall seeing a node called Transform, which moved objects. The next chapter talks about these nodes and other properties, allowing you to create more vivid and colorful scenes. You'll also learn about a number of rendering properties that can vastly cut the time it takes to draw your VRML world.

18

YOU'VE GOT THE LOOK: PROPERTIES

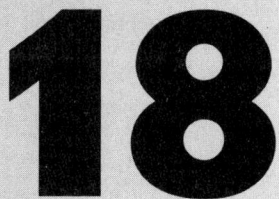

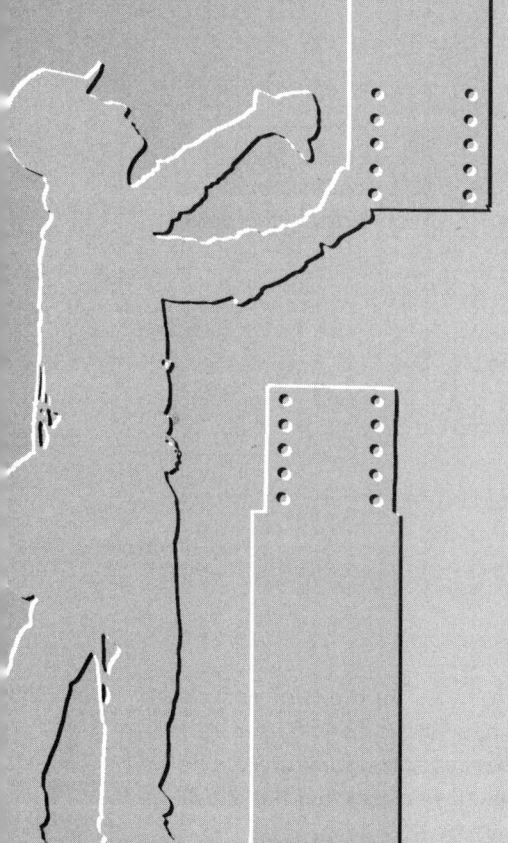

18

What is beauty? Philosophers, artists, and poets have argued this question since the dawn of humans. Many aesthetes have boldly suggested that beauty is found in uniqueness. Variety is the spice of life, and all that. If there were no colors, if light looked the same whether it hit metal or cotton, if there were no such thing as shadow, the world might still very well be beautiful in some strange way, but it would certainly be more boring. The *properties* of objects make them unique, interesting. Without properties a golden altar would be the same thing as a cardboard box.

Properties add more than flourishes to your VRML worlds, they allow them to exist. Shape nodes let you draw abstract things, but properties let you use them. Without properties, your VRML objects wouldn't know where to sit, or how to relate to each other.

There are many types of properties:

- Coordinate Sets—This is a collection of vectors that can be used to draw or help define an object.

- Materials—These determine the color, "feel," solidity, and reflectivity of objects.

- Bindings—These specify how materials and normals stick to other objects.

▦ Draw Styles—These determine how shapes are drawn.

▦ Transformations—These manipulate, stretch, or move geometry in pace.

To apply a property, just call its node. This changes the state of the entire scene. From *the current point on,* all nodes will take on the property you just called (unless, of course, the property is walled-in by a Separator node, as discussed in the previous chapter). In other words, to give a shape a property, follow these four simple steps:

1. Create a Separator node (if you want the properties to be local, not global).

2. Call the property nodes.

3. Call the shape nodes.

4. End the Separator node.

NOTE: Properties you want to apply to the entire VRML scene should be placed immediately within the first Separator node. This would apply the quality to everything in the scene.

THE COORDINATE3 NODE

We've already seen this node in action in Chapter 16. The Coordinate3 node provides the PointSet, IndexedLineSet, and IndexedFaceSet nodes a list of vertices to work with.

The values in this node are listed as a string of comma-separated vectors using the *point* field. For example:

```
Coordinate3 {
        point  0 0 0, 0 1 0, 1 1 1
}
```

NOTE: To save space, try to limit your points to four or five digits of accuracy. For example, a point as precise as 9.1234567890123456 is rarely needed; you can usually shorten this to 9.123. There is some software online called "munger" that can do this for you automatically. Check out the VRML repository at *http://www.sdsc.edu/vrml/*.

The Coordinate3 node is used to list data separately from the shapes so that future versions of VRML can represent coordinates using more compact or time-saving methods. Having separate Coordinate3 and Normal nodes makes the format more modular.

THE NORMAL NODE

In psychology as well as computer graphics, normals take time. 3D surface *normals* of an object are invisible lines that project from it perpendicularly. These normals tell the VRML browser how sloped the surface is at any given point. For example, the normals of a cube are shown in Figure 18-1.

When you create an object, normals are calculated to determine what angle each point is at. This angle determines how light hits the object—how the object is shaded and how textures are wrapped around it.

But think of it—for every point along every object a precise calculation must be made. This takes lots of time.

VRML's Normal node lets you define normals in advance. You can define a whole list of the normals all subsequent nodes will need. If you create an object with 1,000 faces, then you can also specify 1,000 normals to go along with it. This makes the job of VRML much easier—it already has much of the information it'll need.

NOTE: Granted, it's nearly impossible to apply these normals by hand. Usually you'll only need to worry about normals if you're writing a computer algorithm to create your VRML objects. Normals are usually figured automatically when software converts other 3D data formats into VRML.

Figure 18-1
Some of a
cube's normals

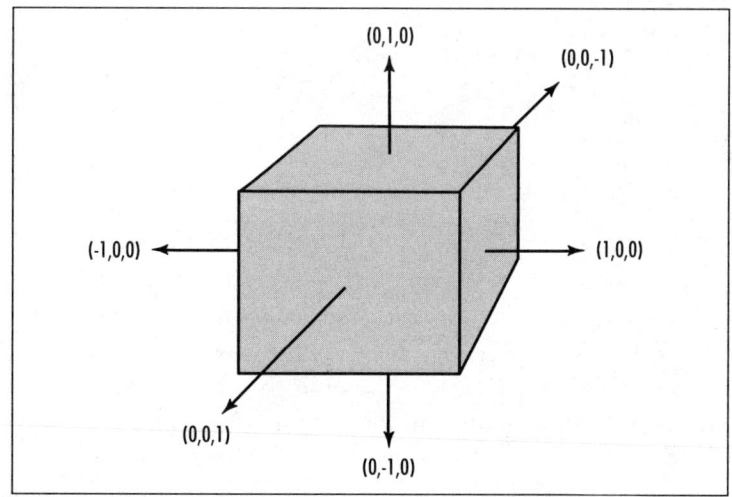

Like the Coordinate3 node, the Normal node has no visible outcome. You can list the normal vectors as values for the *vector* field. For example:

```
Normal {
        vector [0 1 -1, 0 0 0, 1 1 1, -1 -1 -1]
}
```

NOTE: Since lighting is limited in how precise it can be, you can usually keep normals as whole numbers. Having a normal like 9.1234567890123456 only wastes time and space.

Defining normals can do more than save time; you can also use them to create some groovy special effects. Suppose you have a cube centered around the origin. The top of the cube would usually have a normal along the y axis, similar to (0 1 0). If you like, you can lie to the VRML viewer and give it an awkward normal. For example, you could give the cube's top a normal value tilted to the right. Light will strike the top of the cube at a strange angle, making its top seem warped.

By creating a pattern of miscalculated normals, you can make a smooth object appear dented, bumpy, wrinkled, rippled, or wavy.

NOTE: These effects are difficult to create by hand, though most modelers can do a good job with them.

The Coordinate3 and corresponding Normal values for a typical box-shaped object would be

```
Coordinate3 {
        point [
        -1  1  1,  -1 -1  1,   1 -1  1,   1  1  1,
        -1  1 -1,  -1 -1 -1,   1 -1 -1,   1  1 -1 ]
}
Normal {
        vector [
        0 0 1, 1 0 0,     # Front and right faces
        0 0 -1, -1 0 0,   # Back and left faces
        0 1 0, 0 -1 0 ]   # Top and bottom faces
}
```

Notice that if you draw a line from each normal vector to the origin, it forms an arrow stabbing through the center of each of the box's faces, as in Figure 18-1.

Later in this chapter, you'll learn how to apply these normals to the shapes you draw by using a technique known as *binding*.

THE FONTSTYLE NODE

When you use AsciiText to print some text onto your VRML scene, what font should it be in? VRML allows you to choose from a variety of font families and styles. Simply place a FontStyle node before the AsciiText node you wish to modify.

NOTE: FontStyle only allows you to suggest what the font should look like. The actual fonts will differ from browser to browser.

The FontStyle node takes three fields:

- size—What size should the font be (in VRML units)?

- family—Which font family should the font belong to?

- style—What style, if any, should be applied to the font?

Size

The default font size for VRML text is a whopping 10 units. You can adjust this value to be any size you wish. A typical size for most types of fonts is 1. To make all subsequent fonts 1 meter high, use the following:

```
FontStyle {
        size      1
}
```

Family

VRML lets you choose from three basic font families:

- SERIF—This is a serif style. Serifs are the little flourishes at the tips of letters that make them seem fancier and more Old World. The print in this book is in the serif style. Times Roman is a popular serif font.

- SANS—This is a **sans serif** style. This type of print is bolder and more formal. **Helvetica is a typical sans serif font.**

- TYPEWRITER—This is a `fixed-width` and `fixed-pitch` style. This is good for the exact placement of text, since each letter is the same size. `Courier is a typical fixed-width font.`

The default family is SERIF. So, to make all subsequent fonts fixed-width, you would use the code

411

```
FontStyle {
        size        10
        family      TYPEWRITER
}
```

Style

Once you've decided on the family and size of text, you can get even fancier by specifying its style. You may choose from the following list:

- ☒ NONE—This is a plain style.

- ☒ BOLD—This is a **bold** style.

- ☒ ITALIC—This is an *italicized* or *slanted* style.

By default, all 3D VRML text uses no style. To print the words "VRML Rules!" in 18-point bold sans serif text, then, you could use the following code:

```
#VRML V1.0 ascii
Separator {
  FontStyle {
        size        18
        family      SANS
        style       BOLD
  }
  AsciiText {
        string              "VRML Rules!"
        spacing             1
        justification       CENTER
        width               0
  }
}
```

LIVING IN A MATERIAL NODE

When it comes to the look of an object, light is everything. The difference between red and blue, shiny and blunt, transparent and opaque, sparkling and dull, is the type of light that is reflected and the type that is absorbed. When you tell VRML to use a certain material, all subsequent nodes are drawn using that material.

VRML materials are suggestions of how light should hit the object, rather than true-life equivalents such as "steel," "leather," "polyester," or "aluminum foil." As such, each VRML browser will display a given material in a slightly different way. In general, though, you can use material to give the browser a pretty good idea of how the object should look.

Whenever light illuminates an object, some of it is reflected back. This gives your eye hints about what the object is made of. Some of this reflected light is *diffuse*—it is thrown back in all directions. And some of the light is *specular*—it is thrown back in one particular direction. The shinier an object, the more specular light it will reflect.

The mathematics behind all these reflections is incredibly complicated. VRML lets you explicitly define each type of light an object emits or reflects. You can specify the following:

- Diffuse color—This is the beginning color of the object.

- Ambient color—The amount of light that an object throws. This is how ambient light (light that shines on the whole scene) will reflect off this object.

- Specular color—What color will the highlights on this object be?

- Emissive color—This is the color of light that the object itself radiates or reflects, without light. As your object becomes more deeply shadowed, what color will it fade to?

- Shininess—This is the amount of light that will reflect off the object.

- Transparency—This is how see-through the material is.

The differences between these attributes is subtle, at best. Some browsers make little distinction between diffuse color and ambient color. Many browsers will average the red, green, and blue values and come up with a single intensity, while others browsers will actually calculate the color of the light at each point along an object. A general discussion about the color of objects, and how these colors affect the overall look of the scene, is in Chapter 12.

Diffuse Color

Diffuse light is light that bounces off an object and diffuses every which way. As long as the object is lit, it will radiate this light. The diffuse color of an object is its most basic property. Beautiful worlds can be created simply by using lots of varied, realistic colors. You can set an object's color by using the Material node along with the *diffuseColor* field. This field takes an RGB triplet as its value.

By default, the diffuseColor is a dark gray (0.8 0.8 0.8). If you'd like to make all subsequent objects blue (RGB value 0.0 0.0 1.0), you'd use the following code:

```
Material {
        diffuseColor [ 0 0 1 ]
}
```

Three cubes, one red, one green, and one blue (shown in black-and-white splendor in Figure 18-2), were created by use of the following code:

```
#VRML V1.0 ascii
Separator {
  Separator {
    Translation {
        translation  -5 0 0
    }
    Material {
        diffuseColor 1 0 0 # Red
    }
    Cube { }
  }
  Separator {
    Material {
        diffuseColor 0 1 0 # Green
    }
    Cube { }
  }
  Separator {
    Translation {
        translation  5 0 0
    }
    Material {
        diffuseColor 0 0 1 # Blue
    }
    Cube { }
  }
}
```

But what if you want to create a house with red brick walls and a green thatched roof? Will you have to create each part of the house separately, using a different Material node before each part? The answer is no. Fortunately, the Material node lets you fill in *several* diffuseColor values, as follows:

```
Material {
        diffuseColor [ 0 0 0, 1 0 0, 0 1 0, 0 0 1, 1 1 1 ]
}
```

The above node, for example, would build an index of five diffuse colors: black, red, green, blue, and white. Once you have a valid list of colors, you can bind shapes to these properties and specify the colors you want for each individual point, line, or polygon. See the binding shapes section later in this chapter.

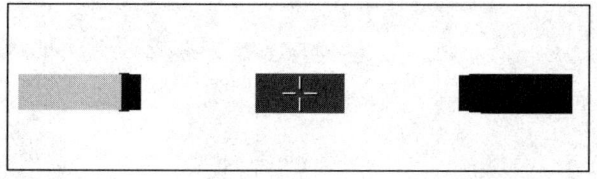

Figure 18-2
If this were in color, you'd see a red, a green, and a blue cube...honest

Ambient Color

Ambient color is the light that an object inherently gives off. Most objects in the world won't have a very strong ambient color. But things like LED lights on a control panel, radioactive gunk, and the filaments of a stove will glow with their own brightness. How well lit, in general, do you want your material to be? If the material is dull or bathed in shadow, then it will have almost no ambient color. If it is some sort of natural or man-made light source, then it will have a very clear ambient color.

NOTE: You'll really notice differences in ambient light in the shadows of your object. If ambient light is weak, shadows will be bold and dark. If ambient light is bright, shadows may not even exist.

By default, the ambient color is a light gray (RGB value 0.2 0.2 0.2), which means the material's diffuse color will generally shine through. To set a darker or lighter ambient color, use the Material node's *ambientColor* field. Figure 18-3 shows three red cubes with different levels of ambient color—almost no ambient color added (.1 .1 .1), medium (.5 .5 .5), and a bright white glow (.9 .9 .9). For example, to make the ambient color a dark red, you would type something like

```
Material {
        ambientColor [ 1 .5 .5 ]
}
```

If you want various faces of an object to have different ambient colors, you can specify an index of colors. For example:

```
Material {
        ambientColor [ 0 0 0, 1 0 0, 0 1 0, 0 0 1, 1 1 1 ]
}
```

You could then bind these colors to the faces of a solid shape (or the lines in a LineSet). Check out the Material Binding section, later in this chapter.

Figure 18-3
Notice how the
ambient light
drastically
affects the look
of a cube

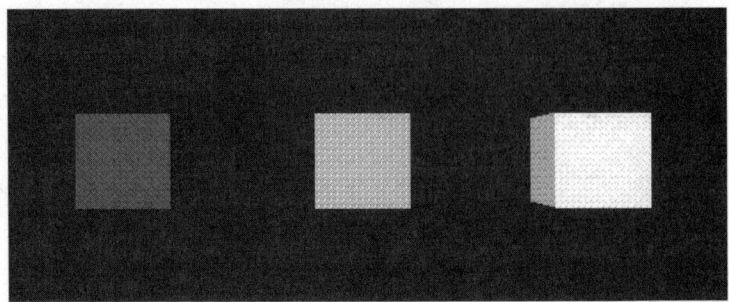

VRML 1.1: The ambient color field is not used, since its net effect can be simulated using diffuse color.

Specular Color

If you look closely at any object, you'll notice it has *specular highlights*—the highest points on the object are lit more brightly than lower ones. Depending on the shininess of the object, these highlights may be small and bright, or large and hardly visible. A pinball, for example, will generally have a small bright circle on its surface (at the point closest to the light source) that will take on the color of the light source. A tennis ball will have hardly any specular highlights.

The color of these highlights tells you a lot about the material the object is made from. VRML allows you to set the specular color of any object by using Material's *specularColor* field. The specularColor field takes an RGB triplet—the higher the numbers in the triplet, the greater the intensity of specular color.

By default, the specular color is 0 0 0—no highlights will be used. If you want a very intense white highlight, use a value of 1 1 1. Figure 18-4, for example, shows the same sphere with several different specular colors. The first sphere has no specular color (0 0 0), the second sphere has a medium value (.5 .5 .5). The rightmost sphere has a full white specular color (1 1 1). As you can see, you can use values in between to get subtle shades of highlights. For example, to give all specular colors a reddish tint, you would use

```
Material {
        specularColor [ 1 0 0 ]
}
```

NOTE: The specularColor red, green, and blue values should be equal. This way, the highlight will always be the same color as the light source.

Figure 18-4
The specular color can drastically affect an object's highlights

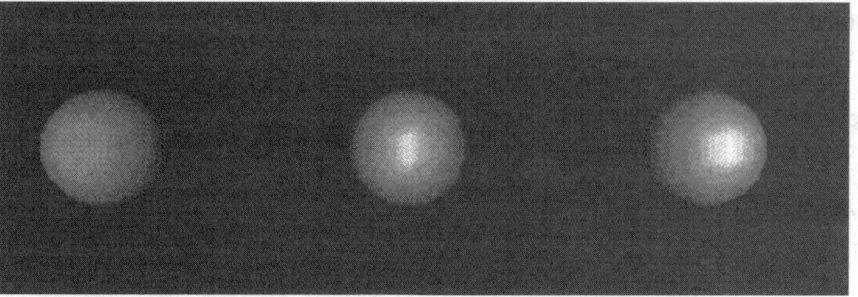

As with the ambient color, you can specify a whole list of specular colors that can then be applied to different faces of a given shape. How to use this list will be discussed shortly. An index of specular values might look like

```
Material {
        specularColor [ 0 0 0, 1 0 0, 0 1 0, 0 0 1, 1 1 1 ]
}
```

Emissive Color

A material's amount of brightness can be set using the emissive color. For example, the sun emits a vibrant full spectrum of light. At night, however, the only way we can see this light is when it's reflected off the moon—as a cheese-like, yellowish color. This yellow is the moon's *emissive color.*

By default, a VRML object's emissive color is black (0 0 0), which means that no special color is radiated. A certain type of tarnished bronze may have a green emissive color.

The Material node, as you've probably guessed by now, contains an *emissiveColor* field that can define this emissive value. To create a greenish emissive color, use the following code:

```
Material {
        emissiveColor [ 0 1 0 ]
}
```

Figure 18-5, for instance, shows three green spheres with very different emissive colors. The first sphere has a red emissive color (1 0 0), which darkens its overall green. The second sphere has no emissive color (0 0 0). The third sphere has a nearly white (.9 .9 .9) emissive color, making its shine hard.

If you plan to use several colors for each face, part, or vertex of an object, you should specify a list of emissive colors:

```
Material {
        emissiveColor [ 0 0 0, 1 0 0, 0 1 0, 0 0 1, 1 1 1 ]
}
```

Figure 18-5
Emissive colors can make your objects yell "Look at me!" or seem to cower silently in a corner

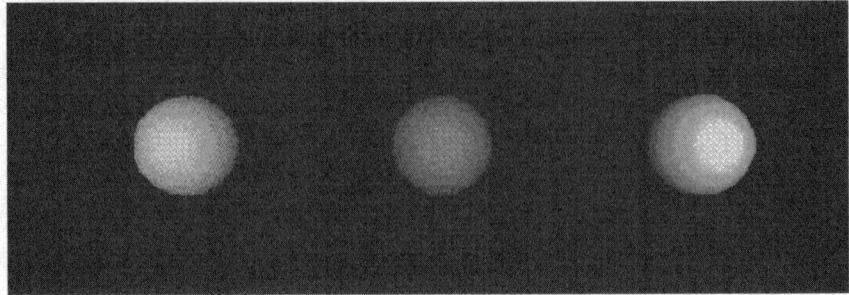

VRML 1.1: If your object has an emissive color and no diffuse or specular color, then it is considered a light source.

Shininess

Four types of material colors have now been covered. This might seem like overkill, but the values of each type of color can give the same material a vastly different look and feel. All this color is meaningless unless you know how, exactly, light behaves when it hits the material. Specifically, is the material shiny or is it dull? If it's shiny, for example, then specular highlights and emissive colors will be at their most intense.

Light may be coming from many different sources when it strikes an object. If this object is shiny, the light is reflected, causing all sorts of other effects. An extremely shiny object can provide a clear reflection of a neighboring object.

To set the shininess of a material, use the Material node's *shininess* field with a value ranging from 0 to 1. The 0 value means the material is completely dull, 1 means the material is nearly a mirror. By default, the shininess is a blunt 0.2.

To create a very shiny object, for instance, you would type

```
Material {
        shininess [ .85 ]
}
```

Figure 18-6 shows three spheres at various levels of shine (0, .5, and 1).

As with the other Material node fields, the shininess field can take multiple values. If you plan to use several materials for each face of an object, you can create a range of shine:

```
Material {
        shininess [ 0, .1, .5, .7, 1 ]
}
```

Figure 18-6
Three shines: dull, medium, and shiny

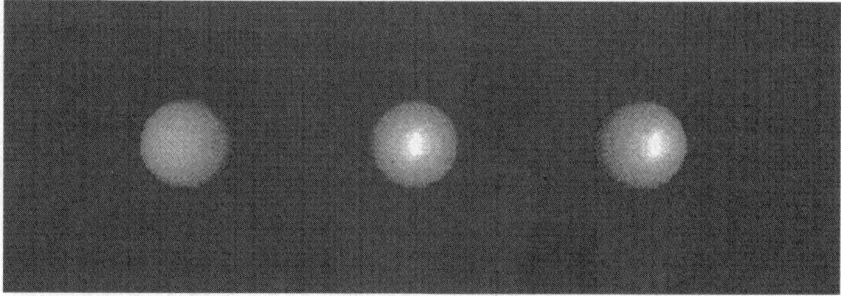

Transparency

You now have the tools to create an extremely wide range of materials. You can build with anything from gold to mud, from cloth to steel. The only attribute missing is transparency. If your object is made of some sort of glass (or plastic fiberglass), it should be somewhat see-through. A cathedral's stained glass is semitransparent, the shower curtain at the Bates motel is translucent, while a huge window overlooking the Manhattan skyline would be completely transparent (though it might have some white slicks of light).

You can set the transparency of a material by using the *transparency* field. By default, this field has a value of 0, which means the material is completely opaque. A value of 1 would be completely transparent (and thus invisible). If you wanted to make the object half-transparent, you would use the code

```
Material {
        transparency [ .5 ]
}
```

Figure 18-7 illustrates transparent materials. The three green cubes each have different levels of transparency. The farthest cube is nearly opaque at a transparency of 0.1, the middle cube has a transparency of 0.5, and the closest cube is nearly invisible with a transparency value of 0.9.

As you might come to expect, the transparency field usually takes multiple values. You can then give the various sides of an object their own levels of transparency, allowing you to create, say, a glass-topped desk:

```
Material {
        transparency [ 0, .1, .5, .7, 1 ]
}
```

Figure 18-7
Use transparency
to create
ghostlike objects

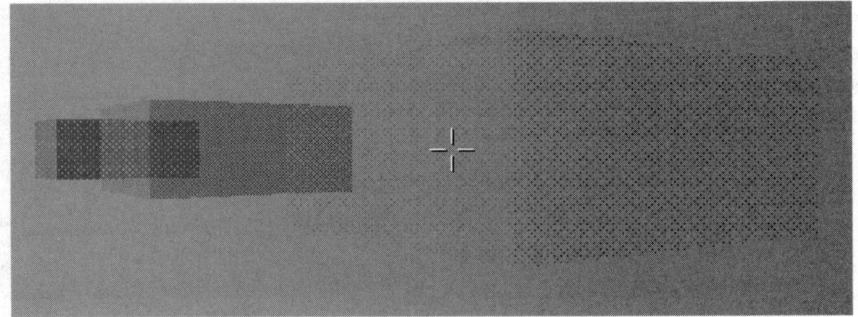

 TIP: If you set the transparency and shininess to high values, the transparency may often counteract the shininess. You can make a transparent object appear shinier by using specular light.

Sample Materials

To actually create a material to your liking, you pretty much need to make an educated guess and then experiment. This section contains some starting points for you to work with. The materials are shown (in black-and-white, unfortunately) in Figure 18-8.

 TIP: A good source of materials is other VRML files out on the Net. When you see a material you like, take a peek at the VRML code and note the Material values.

Here's a nice silvery color:

```
Material { # Silver
    ambientColor .2 .2 .2
    diffuseColor .6 .6 .6
    specularColor .5 .5 .5
    shininess .5
    transparency 0
}
```

And, for third-place winner, here's some bronze:

```
Material { # Bronze
    ambientColor .33 .22 .27
    diffuseColor .78 .57 .11
    specularColor .99 .94 .81
    shininess .28
    transparency 0
}
```

Figure 18-8
A store of
materials

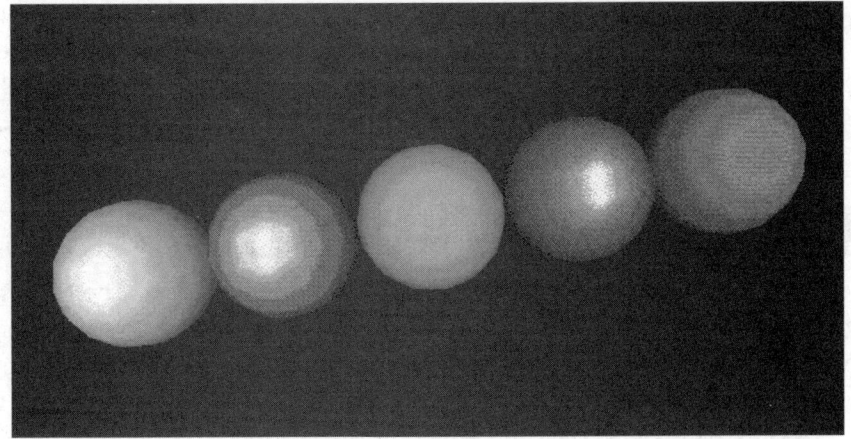

Here's a blue fabric:

```
Material { # Blue fabric
    ambientColor      0.306767 0.252662 0.311307
    diffuseColor      0.604512 0.497893 0.613458
    specularColor     0 0 0
    emissiveColor     0 0 0
    shininess         0
    transparency      0
}
```

Here's some corroded metal:

```
Material { # Corroded metal
    ambientColor      0.21 0.105 0.105
    diffuseColor      0.84 0.42 0.42
    specularColor     0.612245 0.612245 0.612245
    emissiveColor     0 0 0
    shininess         0.897959
    transparency      0
}
```

And here's a nice, solid wood:

```
Material { # Wood
    ambientColor      0.0910395 0.163265 0.151875
    diffuseColor      0.199149 0.357143 0.332226
    specularColor     0 0 0
    emissiveColor     0 0 0
    shininess         0
    transparency      0
}
```

TIP: To speed rendering time, try not to switch materials any more than you have to. For example, if you're using three materials with 100 nodes, group the first set of nodes together using a Separator node, and precede all the first group's children with the Material node. Do the same thing for the second and third groups of nodes.

BINDING NORMALS AND MATERIALS

The Normal node lets you create a list of normal vectors. The Material node lets you specify multiple values for each of its fields. But how does the VRML browser know which material or normal to bind to which surface? For example, if you create a football-shaped object made of 14 polygons, how can you specify which materials and which normals apply to which polygons?

VRML has two important nodes that let you delineate exactly how this binding occurs: NormalBinding and MaterialBinding. Both binding nodes take a *value* field. You have several choices for value:

- DEFAULT—Use the default "best" binding.

- OVERALL—The entire object uses the first material in the prior Material or Normal node.

- PER_PART—Each part of the object uses its own material or normal. What "part" actually is depends on the object being drawn. For a cylinder, the parts are the circular bases and the sides. For an IndexedFaceSet, the parts are the polygons that make up the shape.

- PER_PART_INDEXED—Each part (line, circle, polygon, whatever) in the object is made from its own material or has its own normal vector, as specified in an index field.

- PER_FACE—Each polygonal face of the object gets its own material or normal.

- PER_FACE_INDEXED—Each polygon face uses a material or normal, as indicated in an index field.

- PER_VERTEX—Each vertex of the object gets its own material or normal.

- PER_VERTEX_INDEXED—Each vertex of the object gets its own material or normal, as specified in an index field.

THE BASE VALUE

The base value of a Material or Normal node is the first value in the list. For example, when you create a material using the Material node, the first value of each of Material's fields is known as the base value. Look at the following node:

```
Material {
    ambientColor      [0 1 1, 1 1 1, 1 0 1]
    diffuseColor      [.5 .5 .5, 1 1 1, 0 .5 1]
    specularColor     [1 0 1, 1 0 0, 1 1 1]
    emissiveColor     [1 1 1, 0 .5 1, .5 .5 .5]
    shininess         [1, .5, .2]
    transparency      [0, .3, .9]
}
```

The base value would be

▪ ambientColor is 0 1 1

▪ diffuseColor is .5 .5 .5

▪ specularColor is 1 0 1

▪ emissiveColor is 1 1 1

▪ shininess is 1

▪ transparency is 0

If you don't use a MaterialBinding node (or if you use an OVERALL binding), then this base value will be used for all future shapes.

MATERIAL BINDING

Most objects aren't made of just one material. A desk may have a wood top and steel legs. A television has a shiny front screen recessed in a black box. A car is a virtual melting pot of materials with parts made of chrome, glass, plastic, leather, colored metal, and cold steel.

The way the MaterialBinding node usually works is as follows:

1. Create the materials you'll need by using the Material node.

2. Specify how materials should be bound to the shape.

3. Build the shape.

4. If the binding is indexed, be sure to use the shape's materialIndex field to let the VRML browser know which material should be used on which parts.

NOTE: Each shape node uses bindings in different ways, and not all binding applies to all shape nodes. Obviously, face bindings are only applicable to shapes with faces, and vertex bindings are only applicable to vertex shapes. An indexed binding may only be used with the IndexedLineSet and IndexedFaceSet nodes. See the following subsections for details.

For example, to bind the current set of materials to each face of all subsequent objects, use the code:

```
MaterialBinding {
        value PER_FACE
}
```

This section covers techniques for using the Material and MaterialBinding nodes along with the following shape nodes:

- PointSet
- IndexedLineSet
- IndexedFaceSet
- Cone
- Cube
- Cylinder
- Sphere
- ASCIIText

The Binding Cycle

Often, you don't care *which* side of a box gets a particular material; rather, you just want each side of the box to look different. To cycle through the list of current materials, you could use the PER_PART, PER_FACE, or PER_VERTEX value of binding.

When you create materials using the Material node, it usually makes sense to have the same number of values for each field. This way you can create a set amount of materials and know what each material looks like (all the first values form the first material, all the second values form the second material, and so on). However, if you wish, you can give different fields different numbers of values. For example:

```
Material {
    ambientColor       [0 1 1, 1 1 1, 1 0 1] # Three colors
    diffuseColor       [.5 .5 .5, 1 1 1] # Two colors
    specularColor      [1 0 1, 1 0 0] # Two colors
    emissiveColor      [1 1 1, 0 .5 1] # Two colors
    shininess          [1] # One value
    transparency       [0, .5, 1] # Three values
}
```

The ambientColor and transparency fields have three values, the other color fields have two values, and the shininess field only has one value. How are these materials bound to objects? And what will the material look like?

When a Material list is cycled through, all fields are cycled through until the last value is reached. This last value is then used repeatedly until the *maximum cycle* has finished. This maximum cycle depends on the field that has the most values. For example, if you were to cycle through the above VRML listing, ambient color and shininess would tie with a maximum cycle of three. Table 18-1 lists the values at each step of the cycle. Notice that cycle 3 is the same as cycle 0, since the entire cycle has finished its loop and is now being repeated.

Table 18-1 Cycling through the materials

Cycle	Ambient	Diffuse	Specular	Emissive	Shininess	Transparency
0	0 1 1	.5 .5 .5	1 0 1	1 1 1	1	0
1	1 1 1	1 1 1	1 0 0	0 .5 1	1	.5
2	1 0 1	1 1 1	1 0 0	0 .5 1	1	1
3 (same as 0)	0 1 1	.5 .5 .5	1 0 1	1 1 1	1	0

NOTE: These cycle numbers also correspond to index numbers that can then be called explicitly from within an IndexedFaceSet or IndexedLineSet node (read on to find out how).

VRML 1.1: Cycling is no longer used. You need to specify each material explicitly. If you want to create ten shapes using ten different colors, list all the attributes of all ten colors.

PointSet

The PointSet node is covered in Chapter 16. It allows you to draw a series of points. If you'd like to bind one material to each point, use the PER_PART, PER_FACE, or PER_VERTEX value of binding. If you'd like to use just one material for all the points, use the DEFAULT or OVERALL values of binding. Since a PointSet doesn't use an index, any indexed values for binding are ignored.

The VRML browser assumes that the first color in your Material node applies to the first point, the second color to the second point, and so on. If you'd like to use the PointSet node's startIndex field to draw only some of the listed vertices, then the same startIndex number is applied to the list of materials. For example, if you have a list of six numbers and want to draw only numbers 4 through 6, then you should also have a list of six materials—only materials numbered 4 through 6 will be used.

For example, the following code would create three points, each of which has a different color (red, green, and blue):

```
#VRML V1.0 ascii
Separator {
  Coordinate3 {
       point [ -1  1  1,  -1 -1  1,   1 -1  1,   1  1  1]
  } # Four points in space
  Material {
       diffuseColor [ 1 1 1, 1 0 0,  0 1 0,  0 0 1 ]
  } # Four colors: White, red, green, and blue
  MaterialBinding {
       value PER_PART
  } # Apply one material to each point
  PointSet {   startIndex   1
  } # Draw the points, starting from the second one in the list}
```

This code would create a set of dots as shown in Figure 18-9. Notice how the first color in the Material node (white) is skipped, since the startIndex is set to 1.

VRML 1.1: The PER_VERTEX value of binding will only be applied to the diffuseColor and transparency fields. Many browsers will not be able to apply specific colors to vertices at all.

IndexedLineSet

An IndexedLineSet is a collection of polylines connected together to form a shape. You have several binding options when it comes to IndexedLineSets:

Figure 18-9
Colorful points

To bind in order to each segment of each line, use the PER_PART value of binding.

To bind to each segment of each line using an index, use the PER_PART_INDEXED value of binding. In other words, if your polyline is made of ten segments, you'll need ten index values in the materialIndex field (see the following example).

To bind in order to each individual polyline, use the PER_FACE value.

To bind to each individual polyline using an index, use the PER_FACE_INDEXED value.

To bind in order to each vertex (connecting point), use the PER_VER-TEX value.

To bind to each vertex using an index, designate the PER_VERTEX_INDEXED value.

The DEFAULT material binding for an IndexedLineSet is equal to OVERALL; the entire shape will use only the first base material.

NOTE: When you bind materials to vertices, the materials are blended together at the vertices to appear seamless.

For example, the following VRML code will draw a pyramid, giving each vertex one of the three defined materials (these materials are delineated in Table 18-1):

```
#VRML V1.0 ascii
Separator {
  Coordinate3 {
      point [ 1 0 1, -1 0 1, 0 0 -1, 0 2 0] # Pyramid vertices
  }
  Material {
      ambientColor    [0 1 1, 1 1 1, 1 0 1]
      diffuseColor    [.5 .5 .5, 1 1 1]
      specularColor   [1 0 1, 1 0 0]
      emissiveColor   [1 1 1, 0 .5 1]
      shininess       [1]
      transparency    [0]
  }
  MaterialBinding {
      value PER_VERTEX_INDEXED
  }
  IndexedLineSet {
      coordIndex [0, 1, 2, 0, -1, 3, 1, 3, 2, 3, 0, -1 ]
      materialIndex [0, 1, 2, 1, -1, 0, 1, 2, 1, 0, 1, -1]
  }
}
```

The result is shown in Figure 18-10.

IndexedFaceSet

Things start to get interesting when you use materials along with the IndexedFaceSet node. Here are your binding options:

- To attach one material to each polygonal face, use the PER_PART or PER_FACE values of binding.

- To attach one material to each vertex, use the PER_VERTEX value.

Figure 18-10
Binding various materials to lines

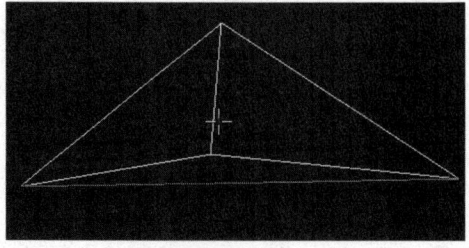

VR
ML   To attach one material to each polygonal face and specify exactly which materials to use, use the PER_PART_INDEXED or the PER_FACE_INDEXED values of binding.

VR
ML   To attach one material to each vertex, specifying which material should
go along which vertex, use the PER_VERTEX_INDEXED value (this is
also the DEFAULT binding option).

For example, to draw an open box with multicolored sides, you could
use the following code:

```
#VRML V1.0 ascii
Separator {
   Coordinate3 {
      point [-1 0 3, 1 0 3, -1 3 3, 1 3 3,
          -1 0 -3, 1 0 -3, -1 3 -3, 1 3 -3]
   } # The vertices of a box
   Material {
      diffuseColor [ 0 0 0,  1 0 0, 0 1 0,  0 0 1 ]
   } # Black, Red, Green, and Blue (Index Value 0 through 3)
   MaterialBinding {
         value PER_PART_INDEXED
   }
   IndexedFaceSet {
      coordIndex[
         1,3,2,0,-1, # Front
         4,5,7,6,-1, # Back
         0,4,6,2,-1, # Left Side
         1,5,7,3,-1, # Right Side
         0,1,5,4,-1] # Bottom
      materialIndex [
         0, 1, 2,  # Front is black, back is red, left is green
         3, 2]     # Right is blue, bottom is green.
      }
   }
}
```

This box is shown, in all its colorful (grayscale) glory, in Figure 18-11. If the
MaterialBinding in the preceding example had been OVERALL, then every
side of the box would be black (the first material). If MaterialBinding were
PER_PART or PER_FACE, then the four colors in the Material node would
be cycled between the five faces in the order the faces were created.

You can also apply a material based on the vertices (edges) of the shape,
as opposed to the faces. This alternate form of binding is illustrated in Figure
18-12. Simply use the materialIndex field and finish each vertex with a -1:

Figure 18-11
A rainbow box with a different color on every side

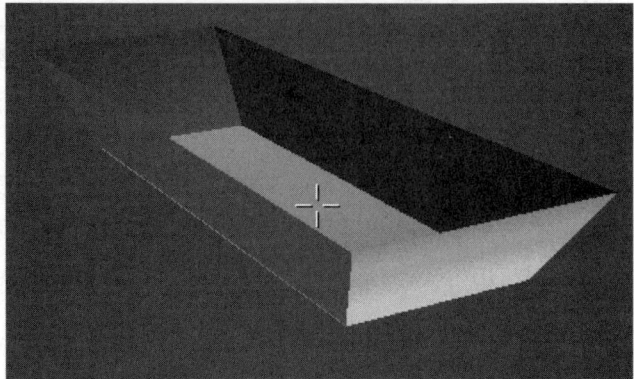

Figure 18-12
Another way of binding materials to shapes: PER_VERTEX_ INDEXED

```
#VRML V1.0 ascii
Separator {
  Coordinate3 {
    point [-1 0 3, 1 0 3, -1 3 3, 1 3 3,
        -1 0 -3, 1 0 -3, -1 3 -3, 1 3 -3]
  }
  Material {
    diffuseColor [ 0 0 0, 1 0 0, 0 1 0, 0 0 1 ]
  } # Black, Red, Green, and Blue (Index Value 0 through 3)
  MaterialBinding {
      value PER_VERTEX_INDEXED
  }
  IndexedFaceSet {
    coordIndex[
        1,3,2,0,-1, # Front
        4,5,7,6,-1, # Back
        0,4,6,2,-1, # Left Side
        1,5,7,3,-1, # Right Side
        0,1,5,4,-1] # Bottom
```

```
    materialIndex [
        0, 0, 0, 0, -1,   # Front is all black
        0, 0, 1, 1, -1,   # Back is black and red
        1, 1, 2, 2, -1,   # Left is red and green
        0, 1, 2, 3, -1,   # Right is black, red, green, and blue
        3, 3, 0, 0, -1]   # Bottom is blue and black
    }
}
```

NOTE: If you're binding by vertex, the pattern of index values in the materialIndex field should match the coordIndex field.

Depending on the shapes you now create, the various properties of the Material node will be used to give the shapes a specific look.

Cone

A cone is made of only two parts—the circular base and the sides, sloping up to a point. If you want the cone to be built from separate materials, use either the PER_PART or PER_PART_INDEXED values for the MaterialBinding. The first material will be applied to the base; the second will be applied to the sides. You can then create a multicolored cone as shown in Figure 18-13:

```
#VRML V1.0 ascii
Separator {
  Material {
        diffuseColor [ 1 0 0, 0 1 0 ]
        transparency [ .1, .6 ]
  } # Red opaque and Green translucent
  MaterialBinding {
        value PER_PART
  }
  Cone { }
}
```

If you use a type of binding other than PER_PART or PER_PART_INDEXED, then the cone will be drawn using the base material.

Figure 18-13
A cone made of two different materials: one for the base, one for the sides

Cube

A cube has six parts—the top, bottom, right, left, front, and back. If you'd like each of the cube's sides to use a different material, then designate one of the following MaterialBinding styles:

- PER_PART
- PER_PART_INDEXED
- PER_FACE
- PER_FACE_INDEXED

The material list will be applied to the cube's faces in the following order:

1. Front (positive z axis)

2. Back (negative z axis)

3. Left (negative x axis)

4. Right (positive x axis)

5. Top (positive y axis)

6. Bottom (negative y axis)

If you use any other type of MaterialBinding, then only one material will be applied to the entire cube.

So, to create a multicolored glass pedestal as in Figure 18-14, you could use the following code:

```
#VRML V1.0 ascii
Separator {
Material {
        diffuseColor [ 0 1 0, 1 0 0, 0 0 1 ] # Green, red, blue
        transparency [ .8, .8, .8, .8, 0, .8 ] # The 5th opaque
 }
 MaterialBinding {
        value PER_PART
 }
 Cube {
     width 3
     height 10
     depth 3
  }
}
```

Figure 18-14
A multicolored
primitive cube

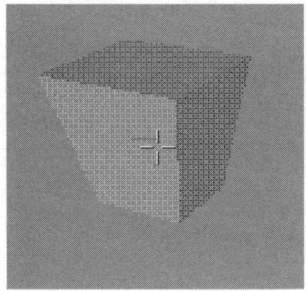

Each of the cube's faces will get a different material. The sides will cycle between green, red, and blue. Since there are six transparency values, each of the cube's faces will be given a different value. The fifth face (the top) will be solid, while the rest will be nearly transparent.

Cylinder

A cylinder is made of three parts. If you use a MaterialBinding of PER_PART or PER_PART_INDEXED, then the materials will be applied to the parts in the following order:

1. Curved sides

2. Top

3. Bottom

If you use any other value for MaterialBinding, then the first material is applied to the entire shape. For example, here's a cube trapped inside a glass-topped cylinder (see Figure 18-15):

Figure 18-15
A cube trapped
within a
cylinder

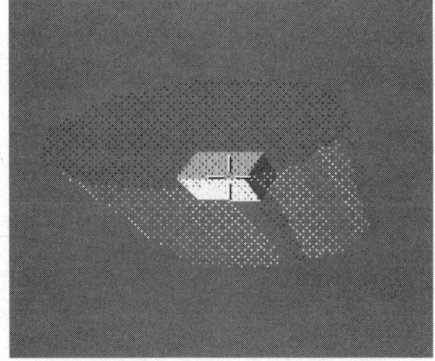

```
#VRML V1.0 ascii
Separator {
  Separator {
    Material {
        diffuseColor [ 1 1 1, 1 0 0, 0 0 1 ] # White, red, blue
        transparency [ 0, .8, 0 ] # Opaque, transparent, opaque
    }
    MaterialBinding {
        value PER_PART
    }
    Cylinder { }
  }
  Separator {
    Cube {
        width  .5
        height .5
        depth  .5
    }
  }
}
```

Sphere

Spheres don't have any sides, bases, vertices, or other parts. A sphere is continuous, and thus does not take multiple materials. The first material is always applied to the entire sphere.

ASCIIText

The ASCIIText node is also quite basic. It will be drawn using the current base material. There are no sides.

NORMAL BINDING

Specifying normals can be a great time-saver, but how does the VRML browser know which normal to apply to which element?

VRML's NormalBinding node is directly analogous to the MaterialBinding node. As with the MaterialBinding node, you can give NormalBinding's value field DEFAULT, OVERALL, PER_PART, PER_FACE, PER_VERTEX, or any of the indexed values. You can then use a normalIndex field for indexed nodes (namely, IndexedPointSet and IndexedLineSet) to delineate which normal goes with which face, vertex, line, or whatever.

Every shape uses normal bindings differently. Primitive shapes (cones, cubes, cylinders, and spheres) automatically use their own normals, and thus NormalBinding never applies to them.

NOTE: If you bind normals to shapes, be sure to have enough normals in your Normal list to cover all the parts of your most complex shape.

PointSet

The DEFAULT normal binding for a PointSet node is PER_VERTEX. This means a normal should be specified in advance for each point you draw, in the order you draw them.

IndexedLineSet

An IndexedLineSet's NormalBinding works the same way as its MaterialBinding. The only difference is that the DEFAULT value of NormalBinding is PER_VERTEX_INDEXED. See the previous section, Binding Normals And Materials, for information about how binding works.

NOTE: If you don't specify enough normals before calling the IndexedLineSet, the remaining lines or vertices will be drawn without light (that is, invisible).

If you use an indexed style of normal binding, you need to use the normalIndex field. For example, you can use PER_VERTEX_INDEXED as follows:

```
#VRML V1.0 ascii
Separator {
  Coordinate3 {
      point [ 1 0 1, -1 0 1, 0 0 -1, 0 2 0] # Pyramid Vertices
  }
  Normal {
        vector [ 1 0 1, -1 0 1, 0 0 -1, 0 1 0] # Normal Values
  NormalBinding {
        value PER_VERTEX_INDEXED
  }
  IndexedLineSet {
        coordIndex [0, 1, 2, 0, -1, 3, 1, 3, 2, 3, 0, -1 ]
        normalIndex [0, 1, 2, 0, -1, 3, 1, 3, 2, 3, 0, -1]
  }
}
```

IndexedFaceSet

Much like the IndexedLineSet, an IndexedFaceSet's normal binding works exactly the same as its material binding. The only difference is that the IndexedFaceSet's DEFAULT NormalBinding value is PER_VERTEX_ INDEXED.

NOTE: If you don't list enough normals to cover the entire IndexedFaceSet, then all remaining normals will be calculated automatically. This can take extra time, so if you're going to use normals, be sure to provide the right number of them!

So to specify the normals of a typical box using the normalIndex field, you could write the following code:

```
#VRML V1.0 ascii
Separator {
  Coordinate3 {
        point [
        -.5 1 1,  -.5 -1 1,  .5 -1 1, .5 1 1, # Front of box
        -.5 1 -1,  -.5 -1 -1, .5 -1 -1, .5 1 -1 ] # Back of box
  }
  Normal {
        vector [
        0 0 1,  1 0 0,     # Front and right face normals
        0 0 -1,  -1 0 0,   # Back and left face normals
        0 1 0,  0 -1 0 ]   # Top and bottom face normals
  }
  NormalBinding { value PER_FACE_INDEXED }
  IndexedFaceSet {
        coordIndex [
        0, 1, 2, 3, -1,  3, 2, 6, 7, -1,  # Front and right faces
        7, 6, 5, 4, -1,  4, 5, 1, 0, -1,  # Back and left faces
        0, 3, 7, 4, -1,  1, 5, 6, 2, -1 ] # Top and bottom faces
        normalIndex [
        0, 1, 2, 3, 4, 5 ]     # Apply normals to faces, in order
  }
}
```

THE SHAPEHINTS NODE

A VRML viewer takes a lot for granted. Various modelers have all sorts of rules for the way they draw shapes. Some allow you to draw million-sided polygons that fold back over on each other like taffy. Others are very strict, only allowing triangular polygons. The ShapeHints node tells your VRML browser what sort of rules to follow. As long as these rules are strictly followed, this can save lots of time.

Usually the VRML renderer does a pretty good job guessing how each shape should actually appear. If it has trouble with one type of geometry, it knows how to convert it into another type of geometry. But at times you'd like to give the renderer a couple of hints about how your shape should be created.

A few options you might want to specify are

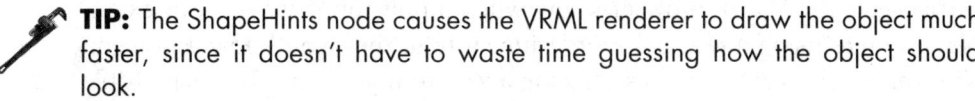 The order of vertices in the faces of the shape

Whether the polygons that make up the shape are solid

Whether all of the faces of the shape are always convex

TIP: The ShapeHints node causes the VRML renderer to draw the object much faster, since it doesn't have to waste time guessing how the object should look.

Once you give a VRML browser these little hints, it can make much better guesses about how to draw, light, and cull each object. The guesses ensure sleeker-looking graphics and faster rendering. For example, if your VRML browser knows that the following object is solid, it can cull it—that is, not draw the parts of the object that aren't facing the viewer, without affecting the object's appearance.

NOTE: ShapeHints are usually not set by hand, but by software that takes existing 3D graphics and outputs VRML.

In general, a ShapeHints node has these default values:

```
ShapeHints {
        vertexOrdering          UNKNOWN_ORDERING
        shapeType               UNKNOWN_SHAPE_TYPE
        faceType                CONVEX
        creaseAngle             0.5

}
```

VRML 1.1: ShapeHints has new defaults. The vertexOrdering field is COUNTERCLOCKWISE, and the shapeType field is SOLID.

Rock Around the Clock: VertexOrdering

As you learned in Chapter 16, when you use an IndexedFaceSet node to draw an object, you list the vertices to form each polygon. Each of these vertices is given a special number by the VRML browser so it can be referred to again and again. But how should they be numbered? Looking at each polygon from the front, there are two ways of numbering these vertices:

CLOCKWISE

COUNTERCLOCKWISE

In addition, there's a third option of ordering:

 UNKNOWN_ORDERING—It's impossible to determine which ordering is being used.

The way vertices are stored helps the VRML browser calculate normals—either pointing toward the viewer or away. As such, the ordering of vertices lets the VRML browser know when a polygon is visible. For example, if you're using a clockwise ordering system, then you know a polygon with *counter*clockwise vertices is facing away from you, and thus is invisible and shouldn't be drawn. By default, VRML browsers will never make this assumption off the bat, for fear of making the wrong polygons invisible. However, if you're sure an object's vertices are ordered one particular way, precede that object with the ShapeHints node along with the vertexOrdering field.

TIP: In general, left-handed coordinate systems will use a clockwise ordering, while right-handed will be counterclockwise.

For example, to specify all following shapes to use clockwise ordering, you would type

```
ShapeHints
{
        vertexOrdering CLOCKWISE
}
```

Concave or Convex Face Type?

In the world of 3D graphics it can make a big difference what type of angle the sides of polygons use. If any two lines forming a polygon have an external angle less than 180 degrees, then the polygon is called concave and is difficult to draw. The VRML browser will need to waste time splitting up this polygon into two or more convex polygons. Figure 18-16 illustrates several concave and convex polygons.

Whether a polygon is *concave* (indented, like a cave), or *convex* (curved outward, like a dome), can greatly affect the time it takes to render the image.

When you create a shape using an IndexedFaceSet, the VRML browser assumes the faces are convex. If you want to specify concave faces as well, use the ShapeHints faceType field.

The faceType field takes the following settings:

Figure 18-16
Concave and
convex
polygons

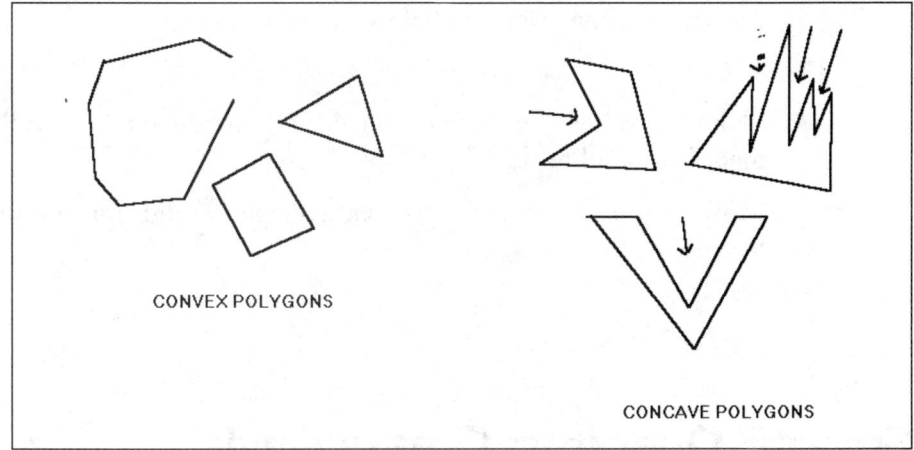

CONVEX POLYGONS

CONCAVE POLYGONS

 CONVEX—All the polygons are strictly convex.

 UNKNOWN_FACE_TYPE—The polygons may be either concave or convex.

If you plan on using any nonconvex polygons, be sure to specify an UNKNOWN_FACE_TYPE. For example:

```
ShapeHints
{
        faceType UNKNOWN_FACE_TYPE
}
```

TIP: If you know the polygons in a shape are always convex, use this node to speed rendering. For this hint to work, however, all the subsequent faces must be simple—that is, a polygon may not intersect itself at any point.

Standing Solid: ShapeType

The solidity of a shape can greatly affect the environment. An open refrigerator needs to be drawn much differently than a closed one. For one thing, VRML doesn't have to worry about lighting the inside of a closed refrigerator. For another thing, VRML doesn't have to color, texture, or otherwise deal with the inside face of a closed refrigerator. If a shape is solid, then half of it will always be facing away and won't need to be drawn.

If you're creating a shape that completely surrounds and encloses a given chunk of space, use the ShapeHints' node shapeType field to let the VRML browser know. You'll be happy you did—lots of time and computing energy will be saved.

You can give shapeType one of two values:

- SOLID—The shape is completely solid.

- UNKNOWN_SHAPE_TYPE—You don't know whether the following shapes are solid or not.

To tip off the VRML browsers that a shape is solid, for example, you would type

```
ShapeHints
{
        shapeType SOLID
}
```

Smooth Operator: Crease Angle

Whenever two polygons are drawn next to each other, there will be some sort of gap. The greater the angle between the two polygons, the greater the gap, as shown in Figure 18-17. To make objects smoother, the VRML browser uses a variety of techniques to fill in these gaps and make the shading across an object continuous. One of these techniques involves the drawing of normals at various points across the edge, filling it in the way a welder would melt two pieces of metal together.

NOTE: The way smoothing works is as follows: The dihedral angle (the angle between surface normals on neighboring polygons, as shown in Figure 18-17) is measured. If this angle is less than the set crease angle value, the normals will be smooth-shaded across the edge.

By default, the crease angle is set to .5 radian (about 30 degrees). If the dihedral angle between two adjacent faces is less than .5 radian, the edge

Figure 18-17
Ironing out creases to keep them smooth

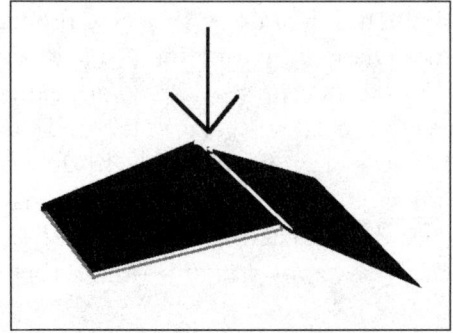

will be smoothed out during shading. If the angle is more than .5 radian, the faces will not be smooth, and the crease will be evident.

At times you may want this crease between polygons to be sharper or deeper. You can use ShapeHint's creaseAngle field to specify the angle at which normals should be created. You can give creaseAngle any radian value. For instance, to change the creaseAngle to 1 radian (about 60 degrees), you would use the following code:

```
ShapeHints {
        creaseAngle     1
}
```

THE NAVIGATIONHINTS NODE

VRML 1.1 introduces a new type of hints node: NavigationHints. This lets the VRML browser know how visitors to your world should walk through the scene. Should they fly through it? Is your world a piece of virtual sculpture that should be examined? And how fast do you want people to move through your world? When visitors navigate forward, are they moving at an easy stroll, or are they propelled like a bullet?

The NavigationHints node has two fields:

- **VRML** translationSpeed—This tells how fast people should be able to move, in meters per second. A value of IMPLIED indicates that the browser should move at its default speed.

- **VRML** navigationMode—Should users WALK, FLY, or EXAMINE the world? Or should the browser just use the DEFAULT settings?

So to create a landscape that you want visitors to fly through at breakneck speeds, you could precede your scene with the following:

```
NavigationHints {
        translationSpeed    15
        navigationMode      FLY}
```

TRANSFORMATIONS

Now that you can draw shapes and make them look pretty, let's actually put them in interesting places. VRML has several transformation nodes that let you modify the placement or look of a shape. Chapter 13 discusses different types of transformations in more detail, with lots of diagrams to help explain things.

TIP: Transformations come in very handy when you convert other 3D file formats to VRML. Often, a world created in 3D Studio may come out upside-down in VRML. Simply add a quick 180-degree rotation around the x axis, and the world is right-side-up again.

VRML's transformation nodes include

- Translation—Moving an object around in space

- Rotation—Turning an object around either the x, y, or z axis

- Scale—Making an object bigger or smaller

- Transform—Performing any combination of translation, rotation, or scaling, all at once

Unlike other property nodes, all transformations are cumulative. This means a new transformation will not replace a previous one. For example, if you move a cylinder 4 units along the x axis by first typing

```
Translation { translation 4 0 0 }
```

and then you move it 5 units up along the y axis by typing

```
Translation { translation 0 5 0 }
```

you'll have a total translation of [4, 5, 0]—4 units over and 5 units up.

Transformations have all sorts of useful purposes:

- Instead of specifying exact points for objects, relative to each other, you can just create the objects around the origin and then shift them at will. For example, you can drop a chair, a bed, and a desk in the center of the screen and then move them to different corners of a room.

- You can use objects created by someone else, stick them into your virtual world, and position and size them using transformations.

- Since primitive shapes like spheres and cubes are always drawn around the origin, transformations are the only way to move them to interesting positions.

Translation

The Translation node has one field, also named *translation,* which allows you to shift items in space. Simply define the 3D vector along which all objects should be shifted. For example, to shift all subsequent items 10 units along the x axis, 5 along the y axis, and 3 along the z axis, you would simply type

```
Translation {
        translation 10 5 3
}
```

If you created an object that was centered around [2, 3, 4] and preceded it with the following translation:

```
Translation {
        translation   5 6 7
}
```

then the object would now be centered around [7, 9, 11].

Figure 18-18 illustrates three cubes using various translations. Since the transformations are separated by TransformSeparator nodes, one translation will not affect the next.

```
#VRML V1.0 ascii
Separator {
  TransformSeparator {
    Translation {
        translation   -5 -5 -5
    }
    Cube { }
  }
  Separator {
    Cube { }
  }
  TransformSeparator {
    Translation {
        translation   5 5 5
    }
    Cube { }
  }
}
```

Figure 18-18
Toss cubes
anywhere
by using
translations

Rotation

The Rotation node allows you to spin all subsequent objects around any given axis. Simply use the rotation field to specify four numbers: The first three numbers represent the axis, and the fourth is the angle of rotation (in radians). The form is

```
Rotation {
        rotation x y z angle
}
```

NOTE: Remember, pi (3.14) radians is equal to 180 degrees. Thus, use a value of 1.5705 to specify 90 degrees; .785 is 45 degrees, and 4.71 is 270 degrees. Review Part II of this book to learn about angles of rotation.

For example, to flip all objects 90 degrees around the x axis, first type the following:

```
Rotation {
        rotation 1 0 0 1.57
}
```

The rotation is right-handed. To refresh your memory on how right-handed rotations work, read Chapter 8. You can rotate around any axis you like (just draw a line from the specified point through the origin), though the most common choices are

- X axis [1, 0, 0]

- Y axis [0, 1, 0]

- Z axis [0, 0, 1]

If you previously called any Translation or other transformation nodes, then the rotation will be added to these existing transformations.

Rotation can be used for an endless number of effects. For example, rotation can take three common cylinders and use them to form an I-beam (see Figure 18-19):

```
#VRML V1.0 ascii
Separator {
  Material { emissiveColor 0.5 0 0 }
  Cylinder {
        radius 0.5
        height 9
  }
  Translation { translation 0 4.5 0 } # Move 4.5 units up
  Rotation { rotation 0 0 1 1.5707 } # Rotate 90-deg around X-axis
```

Figure 18-19
Making a three-
dimensional
I-beam out of
cylinders

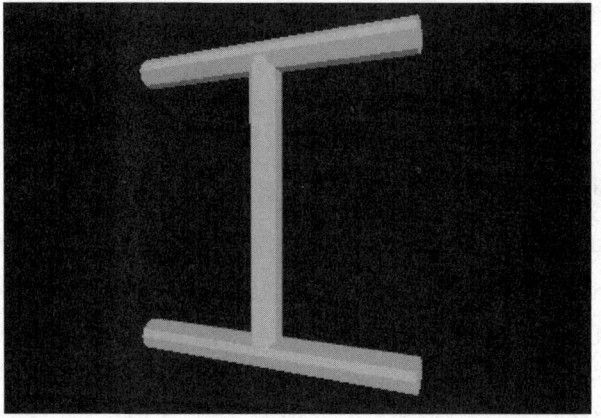

```
Cylinder {
        radius 0.5
        height 9
}
Translation { translation -9 0 0 } # Move cylinder 9 units down
Cylinder {
        radius 0.5
        height 9
   }
}
```

Let's carefully study what happened in the above VRML file (as illustrated in Figure 18-20):

Figure 18-20
Making a three-
dimensional
I-beam out of
cylinders

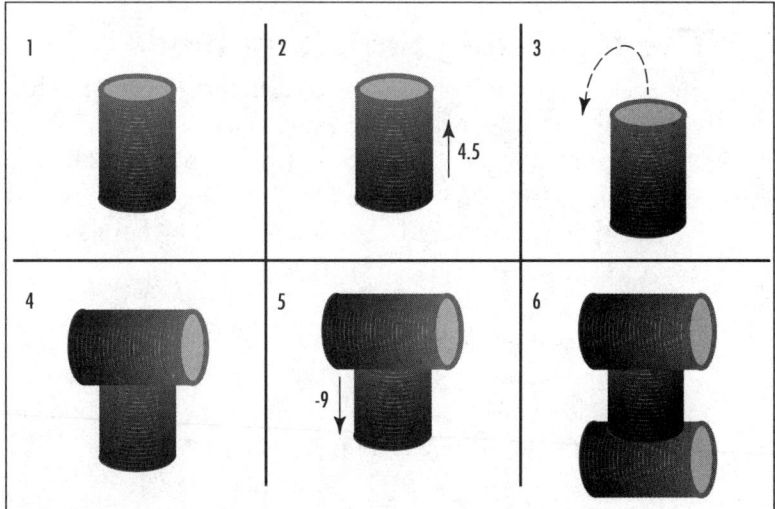

1. A default cylinder is drawn centered at the origin [0,0,0].

2. A translation causes all subsequent objects to be drawn 4.5 units higher than usual.

3. A rotation causes all subsequent objects to be rotated 90 degrees around the z axis, which is the same as laying things on their left side.

4. A default cylinder is drawn, slanted 90 degrees relative to the first cylinder (the top of the *I*).

5. A translation causes all subsequent objects to be drawn 9 units to the left (but since you already have a 90-degree rotation along the z axis, this means objects will actually be drawn 9 units down, or 4.5 units below the origin).

6. A default cylinder is drawn (the bottom of the I).

Scale

In virtual worlds, as in real worlds, things don't always come in the shapes and sizes you want. With VRML this problem is enhanced, because objects generally are converted from many sources. Suppose, for example, you're building a nice suburban park. You've managed to find some trees, some benches, a fountain, a swing-set, and some birds. The only problem is, your birds are bigger than your trees, and your benches are twice as big as your swing-set. The Scale node makes it easy to enlarge or reduce each object, helping everything fit together nicely.

The Incredible Shrinking Node

The Scale node has only one field, called scaleFactor, which takes a vector. By default, the scale is (1 1 1), which means that the object is not scaled at all. To make all objects bigger, multiply this base scale to make it bigger. If you use values less than 1, then all resulting objects will be drawn smaller. For example, if you want to create an object five times larger than all previous objects, simply use

```
Scale {
     scaleFactor 5 5 5
}
```

All objects, from now on (or until the end of the Separator or TransformSeparator node is reached) will be scaled up 5 units.

NOTE: Remember that transformations are cumulative. This means if you scale your virtual world by [5, 5, 5] and then scale it again by [5, 5, 5], all subsequent objects will end up ten times their usual size.

Totally Warped

The x, y, and z values of scaleFactor do not have to be the same. You can easily stretch or shrink an object in any direction by adjusting its values. For example, the Scale node is a terribly easy way of turning an ordinary Sphere into a cigar (see Figure 18-21). The following code stretches the sphere 5 units along the y axis:

```
#VRML V1.0 ascii
Separator {
  Scale {
        scaleFactor 1 5 1
  }
        Sphere { }
}
```

 TIP: One of the handiest ways to use Scale is to build one object and then scale it again and again to form a cluster. For example, you could scale a tree to several sizes and then translate the trees to different positions to form a forest. You could scale, color, and translate a lone figure to form a huge crowd. Chapter 22 covers the USE command, which lets you create an object and use it again and again.

Matrix Transformations

Sometimes you just wanna get mathematical. The 4x4 matrix is used all the time to transform 3D geometry. You can use VRML's MatrixTransform node

Figure 18-21
Using scaling to stretch a sphere into a cigar

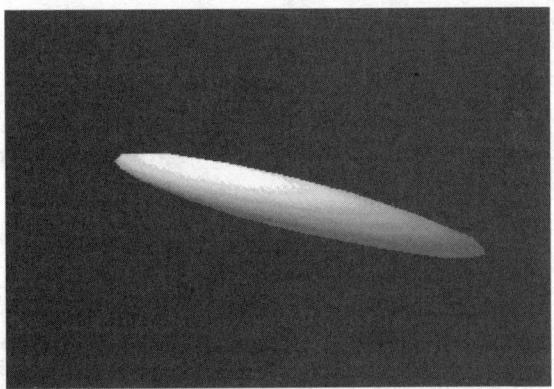

to specify a 4x4 rotation matrix, allowing you to perform a very specific rotation. This rotation will then be applied to all subsequent objects.

The 4x4 matrices represent each point using four values: [x,y,z,W]. The W value is a nonzero multiple of one of the other points and lets you rotate any direction around any axis.

The mathematics behind a transformation matrix is a little complicated. In most cases, you won't want to use a matrix when building a virtual world by hand. However, conversion software may often use MatrixTransform to adjust an entire scene.

If you are fond of matrices, however, using one couldn't be easier. Simply list the 16 numbers of the matrix after the matrix field, without commas. For example, to rotate using the following matrix:

[5 0 0 0

0 1 5 0

0 5 1 0

0 0 0 5]

you would use the following VRML code:

```
MatrixTransform {          matrix  5 0 0 0
                                   0 1 5 0
                                   0 5 1 0
                                   0 0 0 5}
```

By default, the MatrixTransform node uses the identity matrix, which means that there will be no rotation.

NOTE: Be sure to use only valid matrices. Singular matrices (matrices which have no mathematical solution, such as those with a row of all zeros) will cause errors in VRML browsers.

VRML 1.1: This latest specification of VRML clarifies the MatrixTransform node. You need only use the first three columns of the matrix to create a combination of rotation, translation, and scaling. The last column is not used. However, any matrix you use must be invertible.

Transform

VRML has one more transformation node, and what a node it is! It takes the power of the Translation, Rotation, and Scale nodes and combines them into one vast transformation. The name of the node, aptly, is Transform. The

Transform node uses the same fields as all other transformation nodes, including

▪ translation

▪ rotation

▪ scaleFactor

Having a Transform node makes transformations more convenient and customizable. When you use the Transform node, your transformations are performed in the following order:

1. The world is scaled.

2. The world is rotated.

3. The world is translated.

For example, if you load an object and want to shift it 10 units to the right, rotate it 90 degrees around the y axis, and make it half as large, you could first call the following code:

```
Transform {
        translation      10 0 0
        rotation         0 1 0 1.57
        scaleFactor      .5 .5 .5
}
```

The Transform node also has two additional fields:

▪ scaleOrientation—Along which axis should the scale be applied?

▪ center—Which point should scaling and rotation be centered around?

Scale Orientation

The *scaleOrientation* field lets you get very specific about your scaling. Normally, when you use the Scale node, the first number scales the x axis, the second number scales along the y axis, and the third number, along the z axis. But what if you'd like to stretch your objects a tad more creatively?

Simply specify a rotation vector that contains the axes the scale should be applied along. This is the same as rotating, performing the scaling operation, and then rotating back. The first three numbers represent the vector (direction) which should be scaled, and the fourth number represents the extent of the scene graph (in radians) which should be transformed. For example, to apply your scaling 45 degrees (.7854 radians) along the y axis, you might use a Transform similar to the following:

```
Transform {
        scaleFactor    1 5 1
        scaleOrientation      0 1 0   0.7854
}
```

Center

The Transform node's *center* field lets you specify the center around which your rotation and scale operations will be performed. By default, all scaling and rotation is done around the current position. If you want to shift this center, simply specify a new set of coordinates. This is the same as translating, performing the rotation and scale operations, and then translating back. For example, if you're currently at the origin and you want to center the scaling around the point [5, 6, 7], try the following code:

```
Transform {
        scaleFactor    1 1.02 1
        center         5 6 7
}
```

Combining It All

Basically, a Transform node does the work of many other nodes in a much more compact form. For example, the following set of nodes could be shortened into one Transform node:

```
Translation { translation 10 0 0 }
Translation { translation 5 6 7 }
Rotation { rotation 0 1 0 1.57 }
Rotation { rotation 0 1 0  0.7854 }
Scale { scaleFactor .5 .5 .5 }
Rotation { rotation 0 1 0  −0.7854 }
Translation { translation −5 −6 −7 }
```

is the same as

```
Transform {
        translation       10 0 0
        rotation          0 1 0 1.57
        scaleFactor       .5 .5 .5
        scaleOrientation  0 1 0  0.7854
        center            5 6 7
}
```

EXTENSIONS

Some VRML browsers support several properties not listed in the official VRML specification. It's not a good idea to use these extensions, since they may confuse or cause errors in other browsers. However, if you're designing an object that you won't be distributing over the Web, these extensions may come in handy.

BASECOLOR

WebFX offers a useful node known as BaseColor. The BaseColor node is the same thing as changing just the diffuse material. In other words, you could type

```
BaseColor { 1 1 1 }
```

instead of

```
Material {
        diffuseColor 1 1 1
}
```

PUTTING IT ALL TOGETHER

You now have a near-complete mastery of VRML. You've sorted out all the shape nodes, you've grasped the group nodes, and you've proclaimed the wonder of property nodes.

Figure 18-22 shows the wireframe of a desk, a lamp, a window, a computer, a chair, and other office supplies. Together, this doesn't look like much. The computer is bigger than anything else, and everything is the same color.

Throw in a few materials to zip up the colors, a handful of rotations to tilt things, some translations to shift things around, and a couple of scales to shrink things, and you get a full office scene (see Figure 18-23).

Figure 18-22
A bunch of objects thrown into the center of a world

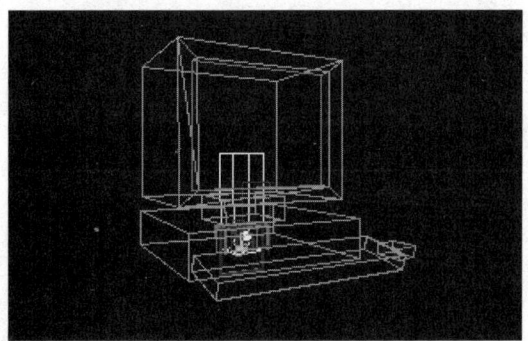

Figure 18-23
Add some
transformations,
some colors,
and you've got
yourself an
office

Transforming each object can take time. You should always grab some
graph paper and plan things out, but getting things to look just right usually takes a bit of trial and error. Luckily, modelers will usually do a great job
helping you arrange objects. Check out Part II to learn how to use powerful
modeling and other VRML authoring software.

19

LET THERE BE LIGHT (AND TEXTURES AND CAMERAS)

Shape nodes and generic property nodes let you arrange nifty-looking scenes. With enough time, patience, skill, and software, you can re-create most any scene, whether it's real or nestled in your wildest imagination. But no matter how true-to-life the objects in your world are, it still won't look its best...yet. To create truly realistic, unique, and wondrous worlds, you need to step beyond being an architect and builder. You need to harness the forces of nature: light and perspective. But before you start to put yourself in God's very large shoes, there's one more property that requires you to wear the more modest shoes of a painter or upholsterer: textures.

WRAPPING THE BOX: TEXTURES

Textures are the icing on the cake—literally. In many cases your VRML objects will seem out-and-out naked without them. Chapter 12 discussed some of the art and science behind textures. This section teaches you how to actually apply any sort of texture to your objects.

Here are some examples of where you'll want textures:

- Realism—Creating materials for things such as walls, chairs, and people. Using textures of brick, wood, skin, concrete, steel, or stucco, you can make smooth surfaces seem photo-realistic.

- **Details**—Use textures to put books on your bookshelves, to put labels on your cans of soup, to put controls on your car's dashboard.

- **Backgrounds**—Textures make a great backdrop, similar to the way a Hollywood soundstage might use a huge painting of a desert to give the appearance that it stretches for miles and miles. For example, you can make your sky a huge cloud-filled texture.

- **Quick objects**—Use textures to "draw" any distant 3D objects. This 2D version is much faster than rendering a true 3D object. As long as the viewer doesn't come too close, the illusion will hold true. For example, you can create the illusion of a row of skyscrapers and toss it into your background with some "real" 3D skyscrapers in the foreground. This can make it seem as if the city were full of buildings.

- **Posters**—Your VRML home page will usually have links to many other places. You can use textures to write 2D text on your 3D objects, giving some hint as to where they may lead. This can be great for advertisements, notices, or information superhighway road signs.

- **Variety and spice**—You can use any image you'd like as a texture. Textures don't necessarily have to be a wallpaper. Why not hang a Picasso in your virtual den (it's a lot cheaper than its real-life counterpart)? Throw in a stained-glass window. Or unfurl a kaleidoscope-like Oriental rug on the floor.

Texture Maps

No matter what your texture is, it needs to take the form of an *image map*. This is a two-dimensional grid of colors. Most any image you've ever seen on the computer can be a texture map: GIFs, JPEGs, BMPs, TIFFs, TGAs, and so on. The colors in a texture map may have various levels of transparency, allowing some parts of the texture to be completely see-through and others to "tint" your object's normal colors.

Where to Store Your Textures

A texture is a two-dimensional image map. The CD that comes with this book has a bunch of sample textures to get you started. Many textures can also be found on the Web. Table 19-1 lists some of the best places for textures. If you have a bit of the artist in you, you might want to create your own textures. Any tool such as Adobe Photoshop, Adobe Illustrator, Fractal Paint, or another 2D painting tool should do great.

Table 19-1 Vast stores of textures can be found in these places

Archive	Location
Animation Master	http//www.xmission.com/~gastown/animation/index.html
Avalon	http//www.viewpoint.com/avalon/textures.html
Backgrounds	http//www.igpp.ucla.edu/~ghyatt/icons/backgrounds/index.html
CGSD's Textures	http//www.cgsd.com/texture/1.6/texture.html
HYPE Backgrounds	http//www.phantom.com/~giant/HYPE_BACK/hypeback.html
Illuminated Gallery	http//www.yourteam.com/~jon/backgrounds.html
KPT Backgrounds	http//the-tech.mit.edu/KPT/bgs.html
Land O' Textures	http//www.primenet.com/~piglett/textures.html
Net Creations	http//www.netcreations.com/
Netscape Backgrounds	http//home.netscape.com/assist/net_sites/bg/backgrounds.html
Pattern Land	http//www.netcreations.com/patternland/
Russ' Backgrounds	http//www.issi.com/people/russ/backgrounds.html
Texture Archive	http//sunserver1.rz.uni-duesseldorf.de/~pannozzo/3dstextures.html
Texture Land!	http//www.europa.com/~yyz/textures/textures/html
Viewpoint DataLabs	http//www.viewpoint.com/

 TIP: If you want your texture to cover a large area like wallpaper, be sure to make it small enough to load quickly yet big enough so that the texture's pattern appears random. A typical size is 128x128 pixels. Use existing textures as models of how your own textures should look and act.

Once you have your image map, what should you do with it? There are two places you can store your textures:

- On the Web—One of VRML's coolest and most important features is the ability to store image maps on remote Web servers. This is similar to the way an HTML Web browser will inline images alongside text. The images may be stored in the same directory as the WRL file or at any URL (Web address) across the world.

- In memory—You can specify a list of numbers directly in your WRL file to represent the image map. This puts the image in local memory and ensures that the texture map is always available.

TIP: In most cases, you should keep your image maps separate. This allows more portability and keeps your WRL files trim and neat. Inlined textures are not compressed and can take a terribly long time to download.

The official VRML 1.0 specification says that textures should be in *RGB* style. This format usually ends in the extension .RGB, .SGI, or .IRIS. The RGB format is a common format on Silicon Graphics workstations. However, most VRML browsers accept other formats such as GIF, JPEG, and especially BMP. WebFX works with JPEGs, BMPs and GIFs; WebSpace likes RGBs, BMPs, and JPEGs. If you stick to BMP, then you should be all right.

VRML 1.1: Textures should be in the JPEG format, though PNG images are also allowed. GIFs are not recommended.

Wrapping a basic texture around an object couldn't be easier. Simply follow these steps:

1.Use the Texture2 node to specify a texture.

2.Call the proper Property nodes to position your shape.

3.Use a Shape node to draw all the objects that use the current texture.

4.Repeat this process for new textures. Be sure to turn textures off, or keep them in separators, once they're no longer needed.

TIP: Try not to call the same texture more than once within the same VRML file, since this often wastes lots of download time. In other words, if you have ten objects in your scene that use an oak texture, try to group these ten objects together preceded by an oak texture node.

Texture2

The Texture2 node is surprisingly easy to use, despite its power. Whenever you call this node, all subsequent shapes will be wrapped in the texture you specify. The Texture2 node needs to know what or where the texture is.

Separate Textures

If your texture is stored separately as an RGB, GIF, BMP, or JPEG graphic, you can call it using the *filename* field. Most every browser supports BMP, GIF, and JPEG. For example, to cover a cube with a thatched-like papyrus texture (as shown in Figure 19-1a), just use the following code:

Figure 19-1
(a) A typical papyrus texture, which would give any shape some character; (b) Wrapping a cube with the papyrus

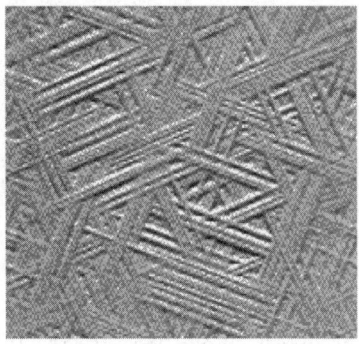
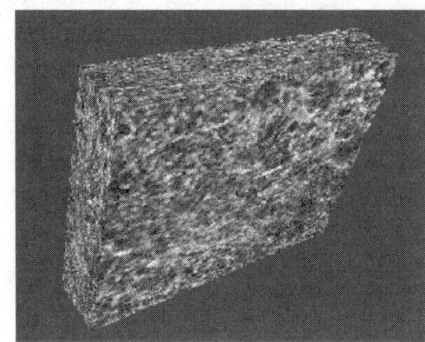

```
#VRML V1.0 ascii
Separator {
    Texture2 {
        filename "papyrus.bmp"
    }
    Cube {
        width 10
        height 8
        length 5
    }
}
```

The papyrus.bmp file contains a 128x128 image. This image is pasted to each face of the cube, as shown in Figure 19-1b.

If you provide a file name without a path, it must be stored in the same directory as the WRL file on the Web server. Otherwise you must specify a directory, such as:

```
Texture2 {
        filename "vrml/textures/wood.bmp"
}
```

NOTE: Be sure your directory is legal for the system. For instance, DOS systems use backslashes to separate directories, whereas UNIX systems (where most Web servers are running) use regular slashes.

You can also call up any image file on the Web by specifying its full URL. This is a good idea, since it will allow your VRML file to be stored anywhere. For example:

```
Texture2 {
        filename "http://found.cs.nyu.edu/dfox/wood.bmp"
}
```

TIP: If you don't want subsequent objects to have textures, use Texture2 with an empty string as its file name. For example:

```
Texture2 {
        filename ""
    }
```

VRML 1.1: You can substitute a URN instead of a URL. A URN is a Universal Resource Name—an Internet address written in plain English such as "The Library of Congress." You can use URNs anywhere where URLs are accepted, such as in the WWWInline, WWWAnchor, Texture2, and SoundEmitter nodes (covered later in this book).

Bundled Textures

If you'd like to create your image map directly within the WRL file, use Texture2 along with the *image* field. The image field takes an SFImage value. Read about how to specify an SFImage in Chapter 15. For example, to use a simple 2x2 black-and-white checkerboard as your texture map, you could use the following code:

```
#VRML V1.0 ascii
Separator {
    Texture2 {
        image 2 2 1 255 255 0 0        0 0 255 255
    }
    Cube { }
}
```

The results are shown in Figure 19-2.

NOTE: You cannot use both the Texture2 node's filename and image fields.

Figure 19-2
Bundling texture maps inside your VRML file achieves some amazing results

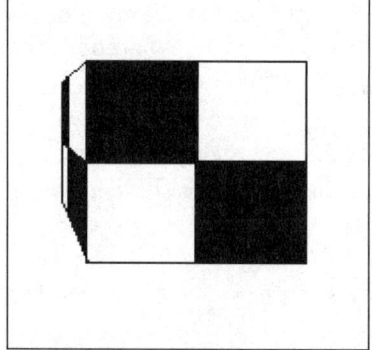

It's a Wrap!

No matter what object you're wrapping, VRML will usually use the entire texture map to cover the shape. A little later in this chapter you'll learn about the TextureCoordinate2 and Texture2Transform nodes, which allow you to customize exactly how many copies of your texture are wrapped around an object.

If you are using a customized form of texture wrapping, the Texture2 node includes two important fields that tell the VRML browser how the texture should be used. Should this texture act like wallpaper and repeat itself, or should it act more like a decal or postage stamp? There are two types of wrapping:

🔲 REPEAT—The texture map is repeated again and again.

🔲 CLAMP—The texture is not repeated.

The default wrapping is set to REPEAT. This means that, if you set a texture to be used many times within the same shape, the image map will indeed be repeated. In other words, if the texture is scaled to be smaller than the object, it repeats. You should set TextureCoordinate2 to CLAMP if you don't want this repeated wrapping to occur—this is like making your texture into a decal. Even if it is smaller than the shape, it will stay put. The edges of the texture may smear out to fill the rest of the shape, so you might want to surround your texture with a uniform-colored border.

NOTE: In VRML texture maps, the horizontal width is specified by the letter *S* and the vertical height is known as *T*.

You can set the wrap in either direction using the wrapS (horizontal) and wrapT (vertical) fields. For example, if you want to repeat the texture horizontally but not vertically, you could use the code

```
Texture2 {
        filename    "wood.bmp"
        wrapS       REPEAT
        wrapT       CLAMP
}
```

TIP: Most patterns are meant to be repeated.

These fields will make much more sense once the TextureCoordinate2 and Texure2Transform nodes are discussed.

NOTE: If a texture is clamped, the border pixel of the image is reused to fill in any remaining blank space.

How Textures Are Wrapped

Much like materials, each VRML shape deals differently with textures. In most cases, the default way the VRML browser deals with textures looks really nice, and no further tweaking is needed.

Whenever you use the Texture2 node to apply a texture, all subsequent shapes will be drawn using that texture map (until you reach the end of a Separator node, at least).

TIP: The color of a shape (as set by the Material node) often affects the texture. Depending on the VRML browser, lighter areas on a texture are often drawn transparent. The color of your objects will shine through. If you make your objects black (with a diffuseColor of 0 0 0), then textures might not appear at all. In most cases, you should make your objects white (diffuseColor 1 1 1) for best appearance.

PointSet

Individual points don't have a heck of a lot of room for textures. However, if you apply a texture before a PointSet, then each point will be drawn using that texture. Results will vary from browser to browser.

Indexed Sets

Things start to get tricky when you create an IndexedLineSet or IndexedFaceSet. This may be as simple as a large flat wall or as complex as the shape of a human. The way most VRML browsers will apply a texture is by stretching or shrinking the texture so that it can cover the shape's surface area. The image is then wrapped around the shape, curving and contouring along with the shape. For example, Figure 19-3 shows a lamp drawn with a texture—the texture is a map that has the words "VRML RULES" scrawled on it.

The way the texture is wrapped requires some intricate calculations. The *bounding box* (a 3D box neatly surrounding the shape) is drawn. The longest dimension (length, width, or height) of this box defines the length of the texture's horizontal S coordinate. The second-longest dimension defines the texture's vertical T coordinate. The length of the S coordinate is then scaled to have a value between 0 and 1. The length of the T coordinate will range

Figure 19-3
Notice the way
a flat texture
curves around
objects

Figure 19-4
The way a
texture map's
coordinates are
scaled

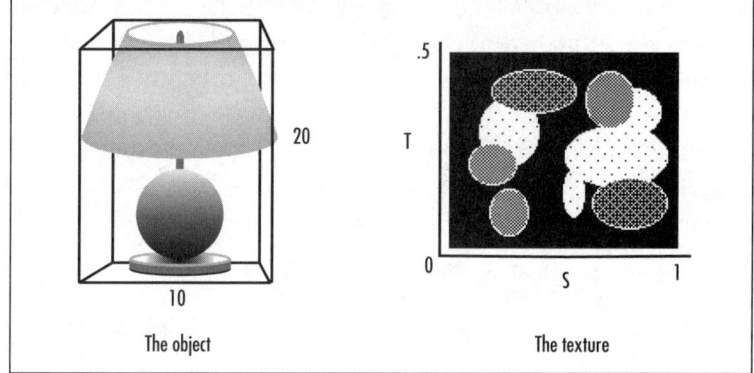

between 0 and a number slightly smaller than 1—a ratio of the second-largest dimension of the bounding box over the greatest dimension.

For example, look at Figure 19-4. The lamp has a height of 20 and a width of 10 (the depth of 5 doesn't play into the calculations since it is the smallest value). The texture's S coordinate will then be from 0 to 1, with 1 meaning all 20 units. The T coordinate is between 1 and .5, since the height over the width (10/20) has a value of .5. These S and T values will come in handy if you want to customize how a texture is wrapped using the TextureCoordinate2 node, which lets you match each vertex of your IndexedLineSet with a vertex of the texture map.

IndexedLineset

A basic texture can be applied to the lines of an IndexedLineSet as follows:

```
#VRML V1.0 ascii
Separator {
  Texture2 {
        filename "stucco1.bmp"
  }
```

continued on next page

continued from previous page

```
Coordinate3 {
    point [ 1 0 1, -1 0 1, 0 0 -1, 0 2 0] # Pyramid Vertices
}
IndexedLineSet {
    coordIndex [0, 1, 2, 0, 3, 1, 3, 2, 3, 0, -1]
}
}
```

You should note that most lines will be too thin for the texture to be clearly visible. It's something like trying to paint the roof of the Sistine Chapel with a toothpick.

IndexedFaceSet

Textures are applied to an IndexedFaceSet in exactly the same way as they are for an IndexedLineSet. The texture will be wrapped around the shape starting from the first polygon. The only difference is, since a FaceSet actually has some area to cover, textures will be much more effective. For example, here's a red brick house with a thatched bamboo roof:

```
#VRML V1.0 ascii
Separator {
  Coordinate3 {
      point [-3 0 3, 3 0 3, -3 3 3, 3 3 3,
          -3 0 -3, 3 0 -3, -3 3 -3, 3 3 -3, 0 6 0]
  }
  Texture2 {
      filename "bricks.bmp"
  }
  IndexedFaceSet {
      coordIndex[
          1,3,2,0,-1, # Front
          4,5,7,6,-1, # Back
          0,4,6,2,-1, # Left Side
          1,5,7,3,-1, # Right Side
          0,1,5,4,-1] # Bottom
  }
  Texture2 {
      filename "veggie.bmp"
  }
  IndexedFaceSet {
      coordIndex[
          6,8,7,-1,    # One side of the roof
          6,8,2,-1,    # Another part of the roof
          7,8,3,-1,    # The next part of the roof
          2,8,3,-1]    # The last roof face
  }
}
```

The results are shown in Figure 19-5.

Figure 19-5
A tropical
vacation hut

Cone

A cone is a funny-looking shape. If you had to gift-wrap a dunce cap, how would you do it? VRML does it like this:

 The texture begins at the back of the cone. It is then wrapped counter-clockwise all the way around. The texture is automatically warped into a triangular shape so that its bottom is much longer than its top. A seam will be left at the back of the cone, vertical to the y axis.

 The bottom of the cone is textured in an interesting way: A circle is cut out of the pattern, the way a cookie might be cut from a sheet of dough. This circle is then glued straight onto the cone's base. To see the texture image right-side up, just push the cone back into the screen (rotate it negatively along the y axis).

 TIP: Have your texture repeat so that the pattern on the left side continues with its right if you want the cone to be wrapped cleanly.

Here's a picture of one of the authors applied to a cone (see Figure 19-6):

```
#VRML V1.0 ascii
Separator {
    Texture2 {
        filename "david.bmp"
    }
    Cone { }
}
```

 TIP: Any nonpatterned pictures will usually be warped beyond recognition when wrapped around the sides of a cone. This effect, however, can often achieve cool-looking results.

Figure 19-6
I've been called
a conehead
many times, but
this is ridiculous

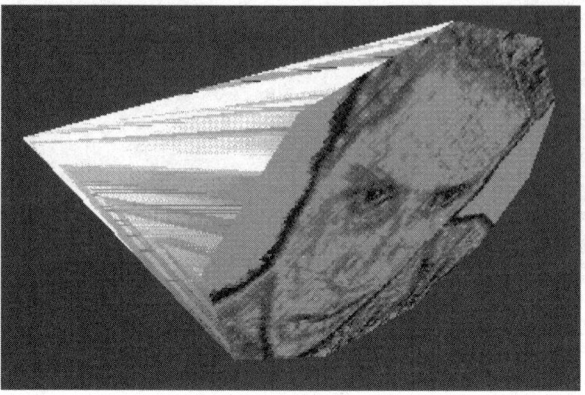

Cube

If you paste a texture to a cube, six copies of the image are made—one for each of the cube's faces. Each image map is stretched to fit on the cube's face. For example, if you have a wide cube as in Figure 19-7, the front and back textures will be warped like a fun-house mirror. The code for texturing a cube is similar to that of a cone:

```
#VRML V1.0 ascii
Separator {
    Texture2 {
        filename "david.bmp"
    }
    Cube {
        depth 2
        width 5
        height 4
    }
}
```

Figure 19-7
It's hip to be
square!

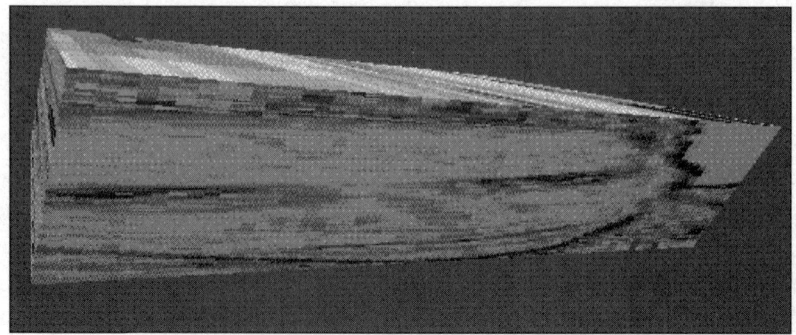

The texture is pasted right-side up on each of the cube's sides in the following orientations:

- The image is pasted as-is on the front, back, right, and left.

- The image is pasted with its bottom closest to the camera on the top of the cube. In other words, if you tilt the cube toward you so its top swings into view, then the image will be right-side up.

- The image is pasted with its bottom away from the camera on the underside of the cube. If you tilt the cube toward you so its bottom swings into view, then the image will be right-side up.

Cylinder

Things get even trickier when it comes time to wrap a texture around a cylinder. The image starts from the back, right-side up, and is wrapped counterclockwise. This will leave a vertical seam at the back of the cylinder.

The top and bottom are made with cookie-cutout circles of the image map. The top image is pasted with its bottom facing the camera, which means it'll appear right-side up if you tilt the cylinder toward you.

The bottom texture map is pasted with its bottom away from the camera. If you tilt the cylinder away from you, the image will appear right-side up. A sample texture-coated cylinder is shown in Figure 19-8. Notice how the picture is cut into a circle at the top of the shape:

```
#VRML V1.0 ascii
Separator {
    Texture2 {
        filename "renoir.bmp"
    }
    Cylinder { }
}
```

Figure 19-8
A cylinder painted with an impressionist scene

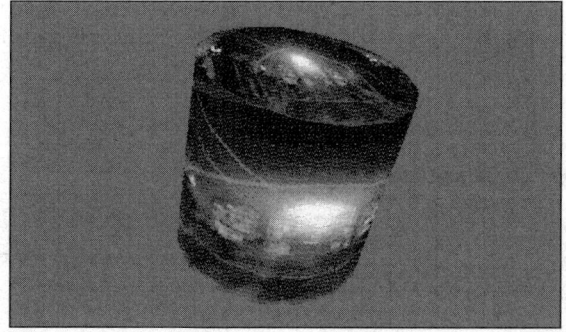

Figure 19-9
Wrapping
textures around
a sphere

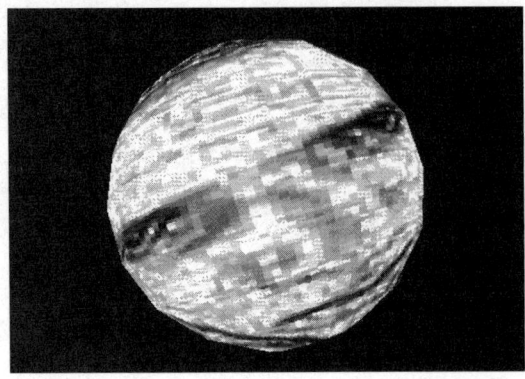

Sphere

A sphere doesn't have any faces, which makes it a tad difficult to wrap. When a texture is applied to a sphere, the texture is warped into a diamond-like shape so that it can cover the entire surface. The VRML browser starts wrapping the texture from the back of the sphere, gluing it counterclockwise until the texture meets in a vertical seam at the back again (as in Figure 19-9):

```
#VRML V1.0 ascii
Separator {
    Texture2 {
        filename "david.bmp"
    }
    Sphere { }
}
```

 TIP: Be sure textures repeat well in all directions if you plan to wrap a sphere, or else it will look strange.

ASCIIText

If you like, you can wrap your three-dimensional text with textures to make it truly eye-catching. The center of the texture is pasted at the center of the text string. The texture is stretched so that its length (S) and height (T) are equal to the height of each letter. The entire string is then wrapped with the texture.

Putting It All Together

Using these default textures, you can create some remarkably beautiful worlds. For example, the castle in Figure 19-10 is made out of simple primitives (cubes and cones), but is made to look spectacularly detailed thanks to a few textures.

Figure 19-10
Using textures
to turn simple
worlds into
vibrant ones

Wrapping Your Own Package: The TextureCoordinate2 Node

When you tell the VRML browser to wrap a texture around an object, it usually stretches the texture to fill each of the object's faces. Depending on whether you're drawing a Cube, Sphere, IndexedFaceSet, or any other type of shape node, the texture will be wrapped in some default manner.

But what if you'd like to map the texture onto your FaceSet in a more specific way? For instance, what if you'd like a texture to be upside-down on top of a shape, right-side up on the bottom of a shape, and facing right on the right side of a shape?

You can use TextureCoordinate2 along with an IndexedFaceSet to arrange the texture exactly as you want it. Just imagine that your texture is printed on both sides of a thin piece of flexible rubber. The TextureCoordinate2 node lets you cut out pieces of that rubber sheet and stretch them, in order, along the polygons of a shape.

NOTE: Use a TextureCoordinate2 node immediately after a Coordinate3 node. Each texture coordinate will automatically be glued to each 3D coordinate.

A Texture's Coordinates

When you map a texture to a polygon, the texture can be thought of as a 1x1 square. The horizontal dimension is known as *S,* and the vertical is called *T.* In reality, the texture map doesn't have to have the same height and

469

width. Rather, each dimension acts as a percentage ranging between 0 and 1. The origin (0,0) is the bottom left corner, and the top right corner is [1,1].

For instance, if your image is 200x500 pixels, then a height of 1 actually indicates 200 pixels and a width of 1 indicates 500 pixels. A height of .5 would be 100 pixels, and a width of .5 would be 250.

You can represent *any* point in the texture map, then, as a 2D vertex of two numbers. For example, the center of the map is [.5,.5]. The bottom right corner is [1,0].

Using TextureCoordinate2

Use the TextureCoordinate2 node to assign which of the texture's coordinates should be touching each polygon's vertices.

The TextureCoordinate2 node takes a list of 2D vertices as part of its *point* field. For example, to list the points shown in Figure 19-11, you would use the following TextureCoordinate2 listing:

```
TextureCoordinate2 {
    point [0 0, 1 1, .5 1, .5 0, 0 .5, 1 .5]
}
```

Much like a list in the Coordinate3 or Normal node, each value in the TextureCoordinate2 node is given an index number, starting with 0.

Extending the Texture

The vertices in a TextureCoordinate2 list, however, don't have to range between 0 and 1. After all, you might want your texture to repeat itself twice

Figure 19-11
Specific points on a texture map

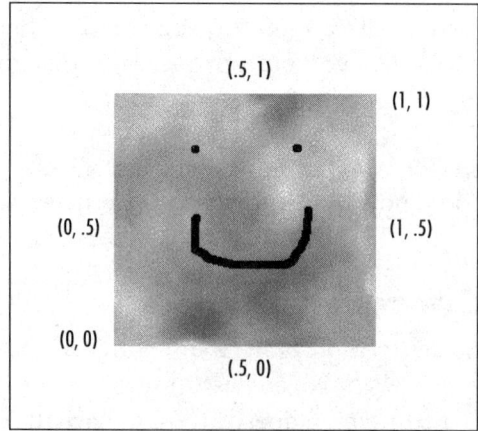

470

Figure 19-12
Points on a texture map can go beyond the bounds of the basic texture

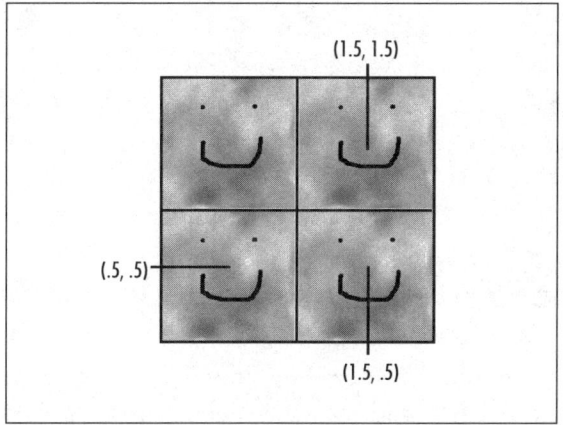

or three or a hundred times as it wraps around your object. Imagine your texture placed on a grid and then repeated, like tiling, to cover the entire grid. You could then specify points in *any* of these textures using the TextureCoordinate2 node. For example, to list the points indicated in Figure 19-12, use the following code:

```
TextureCoordinate2 {
    point [.5 .5, 1.5 .5, 1.5 1.5]
}
```

When you specify points outside the 0 to 1 range, the texture will either be repeated or clamped, depending on the wrapS and wrapT settings within your last Texture2 node. For example, the following code would repeat a wood-like texture horizontally around a shape, but would clamp it vertically.

```
Texture2 {
    filename    "wood.bmp"
    wrapS       REPEAT
    wrapT       CLAMP
}
```

Using Coordinates with a PointSet

Textures used with PointSets are usually invisible, but if you'd like to, you can use a TextureCoordinate2 node to specify exactly how these textures are applied. Simply list enough 2D texture coordinates to cover each of your points. Each point in the texture map will be applied to each point in the PointSet. For example, the following code applies each corner of a texture map to four points:

```
#VRML V1.0 ascii
Separator {
  Coordinate3 {
        point [ -1  1  1,  -1 -1  1,   1 -1  1,   1  1  1]
  }
  TextureCoordinate2 {
     point [0 0, 0 1, 1 0, 1 1]
  }
  PointSet { }}
```

Using Coordinates with an Indexed Shape

When applying specific parts of a texture to an indexed shape (IndexedLineSet or IndexedFaceSet), simply create a bunch of reference points in the texture map and then glue each of these points to each vertex of your shape.

Your IndexedFaceSet or IndexedLineSet node knows which part of the texture to apply to which vertex due to the *textureCoordIndex* field.

NOTE: There is some disparity among VRML browsers in deciding how the textureCoordIndex is interpreted. Some browsers bind each item in the textureCoordIndex field to each vertex of a particular polygon—this means you would have one textureCoordIndex item for each polygon. Most browsers, however, will glue each texture coordinate to each vertex of the object, as shown in Figure 19-13. This means you should have one textureCoordIndex item for each vertex.

For example, you can pin the four corners of an image *upside-down* to a flat plane (as illustrated in Figure 19-13) by using the following code:

Figure 19-13
Using the texture coordinates to turn everything upside-down

```
#VRML V1.0 ascii
Separator {
  Coordinate3 { # The corners of a flat plane
        point [ -1  1  0,         # Upper-left corner
          -1 -1  0,               # Lower-left corner
           1  1  0,               # Upper-right corner
           1 -1  0]               # Lower-right corner
  }
  Texture2 {
        filename "vrml.bmp"
  }
  TextureCoordinate2 { # The corners of the texture map
     point [0 1,                  # Upper-left corner
        0 0,                      # Lower-left corner
        1 1,                      # Upper-right corner
        1 0]                      # Lower-right corner
  }
  IndexedFaceSet {
     coordIndex [0, 1, 3, 2, -1] # Draw a flat plane
     textureCoordIndex [1, 0, 2, 3, -1] # Paste the image upside-down
  }
}
```

The upper-left corner of the texture is applied. This, you may notice, would turn the image inside-out. This isn't a problem. The image is printed on both sides of the virtual paper. If you like, you can even use the TextureCoordinate2 node and textureCoordIndex field to twist an image the way you'd wring out a towel. The results will vary from VRML browser to browser.

NOTE: Be sure you list enough values in the textureCoordIndex list, or else your VRML browser may generate errors.

Here's a slightly more advanced example. Let's specify some texture coordinates outside the 0 to 1 range, thereby repeating the texture.

```
#VRML V1.0 ascii
Separator {
  Coordinate3 { # The corners of a flat plane
        point [ -1  1  0,         # Upper-left corner
          -1 -1  0,               # Lower-left corner
           2  1  0,               # Upper-right corner
           2 -1  0]               # Lower-right corner
  }
  Texture2 {
        filename "renoir.bmp"
        wrapS         REPEAT
        wrapT         REPEAT
  }
```

continued on next page

continued from previous page

```
    TextureCoordinate2 { # The corners of the texture map
       point [0 2,                # The Upper-left corner
          0 0,                    # The Lower-left corner
          2 2,                    # The Upper-right corner
          2 0]                    # The Lower-right corner
    }
    IndexedFaceSet {
       coordIndex [0, 1, 3, 2, -1] # Draw a flat plane
       textureCoordIndex [1, 0, 2, 3]
    }
}
```

The results are shown in Figure 19-14.

Texture2Transform

Okay, you've got yourself a texture map. Great. You even know how to tell the VRML browser which points along the texture map should go along with which vertices. But things still might not be quite as customized as you'd like. For example, what if you want the texture map to be stretched twice as long along some of the faces, or to be tilted at 45 degrees when it's pasted along some other faces? Sure, you could use graphics manipulation software to generate a hundred different images. But wouldn't it just be easier to transform the image map live, as you need it?

The Texture2Transform node sounds like it might be the title to the next hot rap album, but actually it allows you to define a host of two-dimensional

Figure 19-14
Tiling your
bathroom wall
with Renoir

transformations to the current texture map. This way, you can specify a size and shape for your texture before you use TextureCoordinate2 and the textureCoordIndex field to wrap your shape with it. Simply transform the texture before you apply it to the shape.

The last chapter discussed the Transformation node. The Texture2Transform node is similar. It performs the following types of transformations (in the order they are listed):

1. Scaling

2. Rotation

3. Translation

NOTE: By default, the texture is going through some major transformations anyway. For example, when you wrap a texture around a cone, it is scaled into a triangular shape with a full-width bottom coming to a point at the top. The Texture2Transform node lets you take control of similar transformations.

Specifying Texture Transformations

Since Texture2Transform deals with 2D transformations, you only need to use two numbers for the *translation*, *scaleFactor*, and *center* fields, and one number for the *rotation* field. Recall that the texture map is always 1 unit by 1 unit, with (1,1) as its upper-right corner.

First, designate a center around which the transformations will occur. By default, this will be the bottom left corner of the image—the origin—at (0,0). You can now transform the image by using scaling, rotation, and translation. You can use all three types of transformations, just two, or just one. Just remember that scaling will always occur first, rotation second, with translation performed last.

NOTE: As with world transforming, all transformations are cumulative. If you rotate an image 45 degrees to the left and then rotate it another 45 degrees left, it'll end up tilted 90 degrees.

Next, designate the horizontal and vertical factors by which to scale the image. For example, if you want the texture image to be twice as wide and half as high, you would use

```
scaleFactor    .5 2
```

You can now specify a rotation. This is just one floating-point number expressed in radians. For instance, to rotate the image 90 degrees to the left (turning a portrait on its side), you would use the code

```
rotation        1.57
```

Finally, you can translate your texture map in the x or y direction (or both). For example, to move the texture .5 unit to the right and .7 unit up, use the code

```
translation    .5 .7
```

The complete node, then, would look like

```
Texture2Transform {
        translation   .5 .7
        rotation      1.57
        scaleFactor   .5 2
        center        0 0
}
```

Using Texture Transformations

You can use Texture2Transforms to change the way textures are wrapped upon any subsequent shapes. For example, you learned earlier that a texture's full image is applied to each face of a cube. But what if you want *four* copies of that texture to be tiled on each of the cube's faces? Simple! Just make the texture a quarter as large.

For example, the following code would cause four pictures to be applied to each side of the cube (as in Figure 19-15):

```
#VRML V1.0 ascii
Separator {
   Texture2 {
        filename "renoir.bmp"
   }
   Texture2Transform {
        scaleFactor   2 2
   }
   Cube {
        depth 2
        width 5
        height 4
   }
}
```

THE SPEED OF LIGHT

In the beginning They invented shapes. And They looked at shapes and They thought shapes were good. And then time passeth and They invented

Figure 19-15
Reducing the
size of your
texture to fit
more of them
onto a shape

properties. And properties were pretty darn good, too. But not quite good enough. Because no matter how groovy VRML worlds look, they won't shine without light. In a virtual world, when it's night, it's night.

Luckily, most every VRML browser throws some default *headlight* onto your scene. This is what lets you see everything you've built so far. When you first enter a virtual world, your original point of view (the camera) has a light atop it, giving things life.

But to truly customize your worlds, to make them realistic, you'll want to toss in your own lights and lighting effects. VRML includes three types of lights:

- *PointLight*—This is a light that just exists in space as a ball of illumination, like a bulb or the moon.

- *DirectionalLight*—This is light that is infinitely far off, like sunlight. You can never reach the source of this light, but it shines in one direction over the entire scene.

- *SpotLight*—This is a highly concentrated beam of light. Like real-life spotlights, these lights can be focused to shine on a particular spot, and can stop shining over a certain distance.

The way you light your scene can have a drastic effect on how the scene looks, and what sort of emotions it draws. If you have a thin, direct red light casting lots of shadows, then your scene may look haunted. If you throw many lights around your scene, then it will appear cheerful. Chapter 13 discusses some of the basics of virtual light.

You can add as many lights as you like to a VRML scene. Each Light node, like any other Property node, should be applied before the objects you want to be lit. Lights will not leak through separators. This means you can keep the light within a room by using the following structure:

```
Separator {
        PointLight { }
        Separator {
                # Everything in the room
                . . .
        }
}
```

Lights *are* affected by any previously called transformations, the same way any other object would be. If you want to transform the objects in a world but keep the light source steady, use the TransformSeparator node (see Chapter 17 for details).

 TIP: Since transformations affect lights, you can attach a light to an object without worry. This allows you to create lamps, glowing crystal balls, flashlights, and so on.

NOTE: Most VRML browsers will not stop a light even if it is a separator. For example, if you create a separator with a light and a box, then the light will illuminate not only that box, but also all surrounding objects.

VRML 1.1: You cannot currently define an ambient light in VRML—that is, a very far-off light that illuminates every object at every angle. For instance, you can't create a red glow throughout the scene, though you can drop several red directional lights around a scene to achieve roughly the same effect. VRML 1.1, however, will have an Environment node that includes an ambientColor field.

Fields of Light

Each of the three light nodes shares three important fields:

- *on*

- *intensity*

- *color*

Turned On

The *on* switch allows you to switch lights on and off. This field takes a value of TRUE or FALSE. For instance:

```
PointLight {
        on TRUE
}
```

This field is useful for testing your VRML worlds. You can create a number of lights and then manually turn them on and off. This can help you figure which combination of lighting makes your scene look its dandiest.

Intense, Dude

The *intensity* field is a sort of dimmer dial that allows you to tweak a light's intensity. This takes a number between 0 and 1. For example, Figure 19-16 shows a lamp shining on a cube with various levels of intensity (0, .5, and 1).

```
SpotLight {
        intensity  1}
```

An intensity of 1 will cast your scene in a harsh white glare. An intensity of .2 will give your scene a dim, ghostly look, much like a Rembrandt painting. An intensity of 0 will leave you in the dark.

True Colors

The *color* field lets you give a light any color. This is similar to putting a filter over a spotlight, or a colored lampshade over a bulb. The color field takes an RGB triplet as its value. For example, your standard white light would be (1 1 1). To cast your scene in an eerie red light, you could use

```
PointLight {  # upper left
    color 1 0 0
}
```

Figure 19-16
Playing around
with intensity

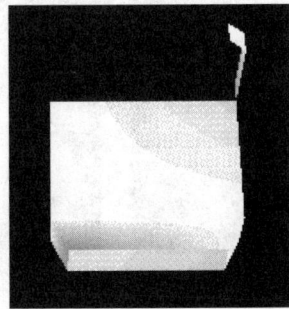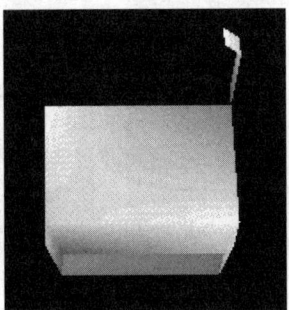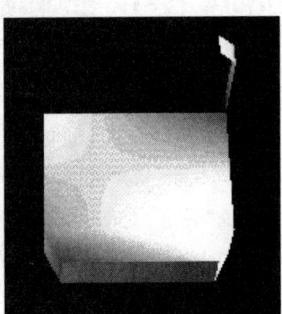

A Bright Idea: The PointLight Node

The PointLight node allows you to create a light source that shines equally in all directions. This is known as *omnidirectional* lighting. This type of light is perfect for lamps, bulbs, the tails of fireflies, and so on. Creating a PointLight couldn't be easier. Simply tell the VRML browser where the PointLight is, and define some of the light's basic properties.

Use the *location* field along with a 3D point to place the light source somewhere in your virtual world. For example, to place a light 5 units down and 10 units toward you, you could use the following code:

```
#VRML V1.0 ascii
Separator {
PointLight {
    on TRUE
    intensity 1
    color 1 1 1
    location -2.0 0.0 -2.0
}
Sphere{}
}
```

If you dropped a sphere into a world with the preceding PointLight, then it would appear as if coming from the left as in Figure 19-17a. If you changed the location of the source so that it shined from the upper right—as (10,10,10)—then the sphere appears as in Figure 19-17b. Change the location to an upper location (0,10,5), and the result in Figure 19-17c speaks for itself.

Many scenes include several point lights, coming from all directions, to make the world well-lit. For added realism, you'll probably want to throw in a PointLight whenever your virtual world has a lamp of any sort. For example, you can create an 18th century gas lamp (see Figure 19-18):

Figure 19-17
The same object seen in three different lights

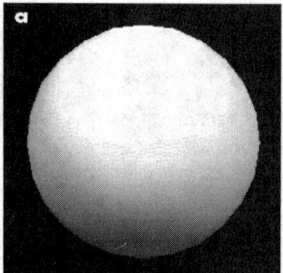
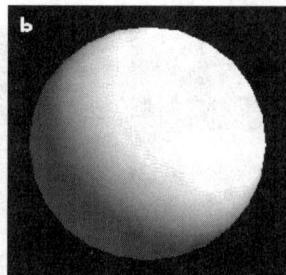
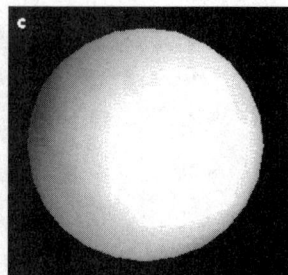

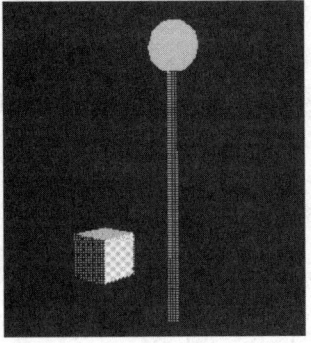

Figure 19-18
The lamp not
only looks
authentic, it
shines on all
nearby objects

```
#VRML V1.0 ascii
Separator {
    Cylinder {  # The lamppost
        parts    SIDES
        radius   .2
        height   10
    }
    Translation { translation 0 6 0 } # Move everything 10 up
    Material {
        diffuseColor 1 1 0 # Yellow
        ambientColor 1 1 1 # Bright white
        transparency .9
    } # Yellow
    Sphere { } # The lamp itself
    PointLight {  # The light
        on TRUE
        intensity 1
        color 1 1 1
        location 0 0 0 # In the center of the sphere
    }
    Translation { translation -4 -9 0 }
    Material { transparency 0 }
    Cube { }
}
```

NOTE: Some browsers will shine lights through transparent materials. Others will have problems doing this. In many cases it makes sense to put your PointLight directly *above* or *below* the physical light source.

Note that the PointLight was given a location of [0,0,0] since it is affected by the prior translation. Notice how a stray cube, thrown to the left of the lamp, is lit.

DirectionalLight

A directional light is a powerful light source that is an infinite distance away and shines its rays in one given direction. You can use VRML's DirectionalLight node to simulate this effect. Since a directional light is light-years beyond the current world coordinates, you don't need to specify a location. Instead, just use the direction field to specify a vector along which the directional light shines.

For example, to have a light shining down from straight above (draw a vector from [0 -1 0] through the origin), you could use the following code:

```
#VRML V1.0 ascii
Separator {
    DirectionalLight {      on        TRUE      intensity    .9
            color    .9 1 .7      direction    0 -1 0 }
    Sphere { }
}
```

This would light a sphere as shown in Figure 19-19a. If you substituted [1 0 0] as the direction, then the sphere would be lit on its left, as in Figure 19-19b.

SpotLight

A spotlight is like a point light and directional light mixed into one. Like a point light, you can drop a spotlight at any point in your virtual world. Like a directional light, you can point a spotlight to shine in any direction you wish. In addition, a spotlight has some bonus features, allowing you to customize exactly how long the beam of light should be. The VRML SpotLight node is almost as versatile as a real-life spotlight.

Figure 19-19
Which direction is the sunlight coming from?

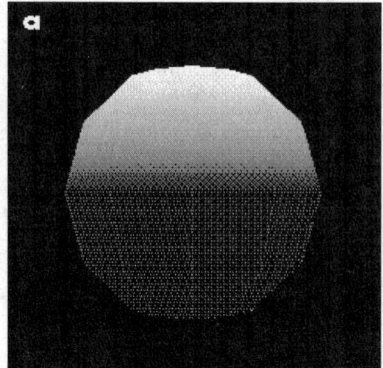
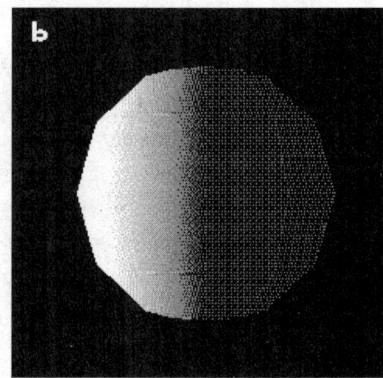

Figure 19-20
Widening a
beam of light

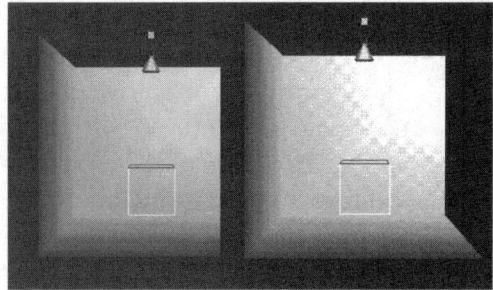

Use the *location* field along with a 3D point in space to tell the SpotLight node where to start shining. Use the *direction* field to point it in one particular direction. The spotlight will then cast a cone-shaped beam in the direction you specify. Like a real spotlight, the light is strongest at the center of the cone and becomes less and less intense at the edges of the cone. You can set the width of the beam by changing the angle of this cone. Simply specify the angle (in radians) using the *cutOffAngle* field. By default, this angle is 45 degrees (0.785398 radian). Figure 19-20 shows some track lighting with a cutOffAngle of 2, 1, and .5, respectively.

A spotlight can shine on forever or can go on only a few meters before it fades to darkness. You can set the focus of the light by using the dropOffRate. This field takes a number between 0 and 1. By default, this rate is 0, which means the light will shine on forever. If you use a rate of 1, then the light will drop off immediately. A more moderate value of .5 makes the beam half as intense for each unit it shines on. Eventually the beam will cast no light at all.

For example, to create a narrow blue spotlight that is 5 units to the left and shines directly toward the origin, fading away almost immediately, you would use the following code:

```
SpotLight {
        on              TRUE
        intensity       1
        color           0 0 1
        location        -5 0 0    # Five units left of the origin
        direction       1 0 0     # Shine to the right
        cutOffAngle     0.52359   # 30 degrees
        dropOffRate     .8        # Drop off at a rate of .8
}
```

SMILE FOR THE CAMERA

Many important Property nodes have been discussed, but the two Camera nodes have been saved for last. In a way, though, cameras are what virtual worlds are all about. What gives 3D worlds three dimensions is the ability to move around, through, and under objects. Cameras are not that important within VRML 1.0, however, since there is only one default camera position. They can be used, however, to achieve some neat effects.

When you first load a WRL file and are tossed into a virtual world, the objects are generally centered on the screen. By default, the camera is positioned at [0 0 1]—1 unit away from the origin and oriented at [0 0 1]—looking toward the negative z axis. This may put you far away from the action, or smack in the middle of an object. Many browsers will automatically pull the default camera back far enough so that you can see the whole scene.

A tourist in your virtual world can usually move around it at will. But where the tourist begins the journey is of the utmost importance. First impressions are the strongest impressions. As such, you should always be sure to use a camera at the beginning of your scene that allows people to see your world at its most strategic or beautiful point.

VRML uses two types of cameras. Indeed, it may seem strange to have more than one way of seeing the world, but virtual worlds—for all their faults—have one advantage over the real world: You can view them any way you can imagine. In fact, you don't even need to follow those pesky laws of nature. The types of VRML cameras are

- The perspective camera—This is the type of camera you're used to. You can point it in any direction. It gives you a natural eye into the virtual world. Objects that are farther will be smaller, and closer objects are large. The back face of a cube seems smaller than the front. All in all, this camera uses the laws of *perspective*.

- The orthographic camera—This camera has no natural perspective built in. Faraway objects will be just as large as close objects. This can come in handy for a variety of situations: When you're designing or laying out a world, this camera can help you place objects relative to each other. This camera can also achieve a number of special effects.

How VRML Cameras Work

It might seem strange to make cameras just another Property node. If you want to customize the camera, this should be the first node you call (after the first Separator node). Like any other Property node, a camera must come before the objects it affects.

 TIP: Any Transformation nodes applied before calling a Camera node will affect the camera. This means you can easily achieve such effects as stretching, moving, or tilting the viewpoint using transformations.

NOTE: Future versions of VRML will allow you to switch between cameras dynamically. A popular VRML extension already allows you to define several camera views (discussed later in this chapter). For now, though, only one camera can be active at any given time. If you use *several* cameras within the same scene, then only the first camera will be used.

When your VRML document is traversed, shapes will be drawn using the previously defined camera. When the browser comes across a new camera, it draws all objects—from that point on—using that camera's settings.

The *view volume* of the camera is calculated. This is the amount of space the camera can "see" at one time. This volume depends on the field of vision and the focal distance.

Any objects that don't fit into this view volume are not drawn. Why should they be?

Camera Fields

Like your handy 35 mm, pocket cam, or Polaroid, the VRML cameras have a number of built-in settings, dials, switches, and filters. These settings are discussed next.

Position

Where in the virtual world is the camera located? Use the *position* field along with a 3D point to tell the VRML browser where your camera is.

For example, Figure 19-21 shows the same object shot from four positions:

```
position 0 0 6
position 0 0 2
position -1 0 7
position 5 5 5
```

Note that the camera is pointed the same direction (forward) in each of the preceding cases. To change the camera's direction, use the orientation field.

Figure 19-21
The same object
shot from four
positions

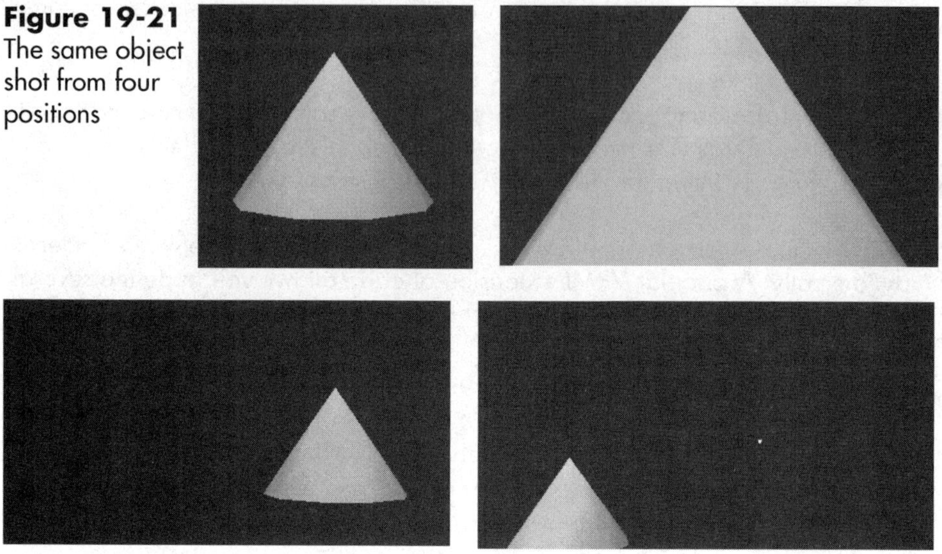

Orientation

Now that your camera is set down in space, which way should it point? The *orientation* field takes four numbers, similar to the Rotation node—a 3D vector and the degree of rotation (in radians). The first three numbers represent an axis along which to rotate. Draw a line from this vector through the origin to visualize the axis. By default the camera is angled forward (along the positive z direction [0 0 1]).

The fourth number allows you to rotate the camera along any angle. This allows you to point the camera along any axis and then tilt the camera to the angle you want. This is similar to the way a photographer might turn his or her camera on the side to take a long shot (a portrait) instead of a typical wide shot (a landscape). For example, to point your camera straight on, tilted right 45 degrees (.785 radian), you would use the code

```
orientation 0 0 1 .785
```

This would tilt everything you're looking at 45 degrees to the left, as shown in Figure 19-22—originally the biplane was drawn parallel to the "ground." An angle of 3.14 would turn your camera completely upside-down. You can tilt the camera around any axis.

Focal Distance

When you look through a camera, you're actually using two lenses—the camera's and your eye's. The VRML camera lens is usually focused to infinity,

Figure 19-22
Tilting the
camera will tilt
the world

allowing you to see objects relatively far and relatively close with equal crispness. But where does your *eye* focus? In the foreground or in the background?
When the human eye focuses on the spot, the rest of a scene is naturally
blurred away. Smart VRML browsers can use the *focalDistance* field to achieve
the same effect.

The default focal distance is 5 meters. This means you'll be focusing 5
units into the scene, from wherever the camera is located. If you want, you
can set this value to any other number. If the number is small, then you can
move around the scene much more quickly, since objects close to you seem
to move at greater lengths than objects far away. A small value will also cause
the background to be blurred out, limiting the depth of field.

For example, if you want to focus on objects that are 10 meters away, try

```
focalDistance 10
```

nearDistance and farDistance

How far can the camera see before things start getting fuzzy? And should the
camera be focused directly in front of itself, or should close-up objects disappear? VRML 1.1 adds two important fields to the camera nodes:

- *nearDistance*—This is the distance from the camera at which the scene
should begin. To simulate a zoom lens, you could make the
nearDistance quite large. It has a default value of .01 meter.

- *farDistance*—This is the maximum value the camera covers. If fog is
enabled (a VRML 1.1 feature), then it will begin at this distance by
default. The default is 5 meters.

Objects that aren't between the nearDistance and farDistance values will
be culled (not drawn), or drawn at lower complexities.

So, to create a camera that pans between 2 meters and 20 meters, use

```
PerspectiveCamera {
        nearDistance 2
        farDistance 20
}
```

The Perspective Camera

Drop a PerspectiveCamera node early on in your VRML scene. Everything will then be viewed through this camera. By default, the camera is 1 unit away from the origin, pointing toward the origin. If you want to place the camera anywhere else, be sure to set the position and orientation. You may also want to set the focalDistance. A typical VRML file might look like

```
#VRML V1.0 ascii
Separator {
    PerspectiveCamera {
        position            0 0 8
        orientation         0 0 1 .2
        focalDistance       6
    }
    Sphere { }
    Translation { translation 1 1 2 }
    Cube { }
}
```

You now have a window into the virtual world. But what if you want the shot to be extra-tight, or super-wide?

Zooming: The heightAngle Field

The PerspectiveCamera comes with an extremely useful field that lets you specify the field of vision: *heightAngle*. This allows you to explicitly set the vertical angle of the *viewing volume*.

A viewing volume is the size of the area that you can see at one time. The volume for a perspective camera is in the shape of a pyramid; the farther away objects are, the wider your field of vision. If you drew a straight line along your line of sight, you could measure an angle between the line and the walls of the pyramid (as in Figure 19-23). This angle is the height angle. By default, the angle is 0.785398 radian (or 45 degrees).

Setting the height angle is similar to zooming your camera in or out. This affects your *field of vision*—how wide an area you can see at once. A smaller angle will make the pyramid thinner, tightening in on a narrower vision field. A large angle can take sweeping panoramic shots.

Figure 19-23
The viewing volume of a perspective camera

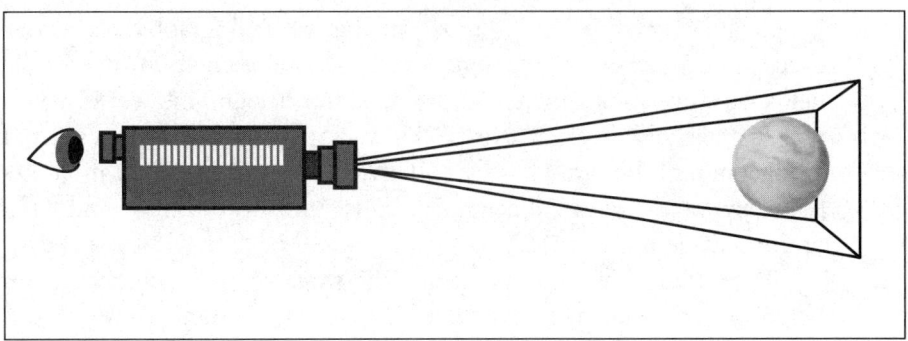

For example, to focus in on a very short span of sight (22.5 degrees), as in Figure 19-23:

```
PerspectiveCamera {        position        0 0 1
                           orientation     0 0 1  0
                           focalDistance   5
                           heightAngle     0.392699}
```

The Orthographic Camera

If you look at a long road, you'll notice how the sides of the road converge until they end together in a vanishing point at the horizon. Perspective is a natural law of optics, a law that the PerspectiveCamera captures.

Orthographic is a fancy-sounding word meaning having perpendicular lines. A road drawn orthographically would consist of two straight lines. Figure 19-24 shows a cube and a sphere arranged with an orthographic camera, as follows:

```
#VRML V1.0 ascii
Separator {
    OrthographicCamera {
        position        0 0 30
        orientation     0 0 1  0
        focalDistance   5
        height          5
    }
    Sphere { }
    Translation { translation 1 1 2 }
    Cube { }
}
```

Notice how the cube's farthest edge is the same size as the closest edge. The cube doesn't seem to have any depth. Also, the sphere is the same size as the cube, though it's several meters behind. Navigation around the world is different, as well. You can pan around all you want, but you can't zoom in or out.

Look at the above code. You'll see that an orthographic camera is almost exactly like a perspective camera. It has position, orientation, and focalDistance fields. However, since there's no depth in an orthographic world, you need no heightAngle field to specify the field of vision. An orthographic camera is like a flat diagram of the virtual world—the view volume is shaped more like a box than a pyramid. Instead of heightAngle, use the *height* field to control the height of the view volume.

The default height is 2 meters. The same scene in Figure 19-24 with a height of 2 appears as in Figure 19-25. The sphere and cube will always be the same size.

EXTENDED VRML: VANTAGE POINTS

WebSpace, WebFX, and a number of the latest VRML browsers have a handy extension that lets you, in effect, use several recommended camera-views within the same scene. This is similar to pull-offs at the side of mountain roads, vista points in tourist maps, or "Kodak moment" signposts in a theme park—places in your virtual world where you think people would want to hang out. You can even name each view, such as "Bird's Eye," "East of the City," or "Courtyard of Palace."

Figure 19-24
A depthless cube and sphere in an orthographic world

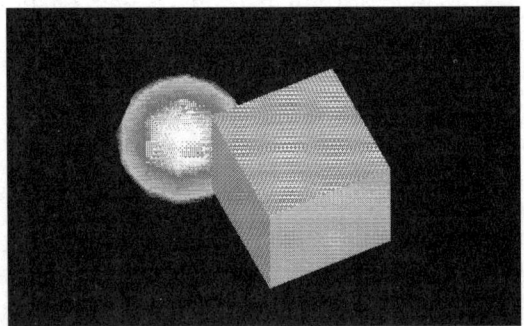

Figure 19-25
Increasing the height of the view volume

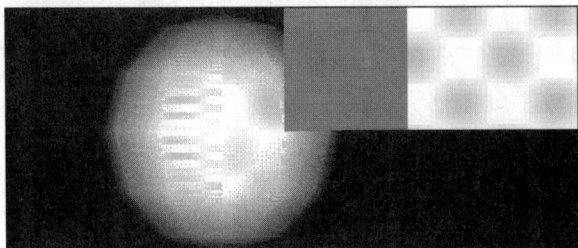

To create a vantage point, just name each of your cameras by using the DEF definition command, and then put all the cameras inside a Switch node. The Switch node needs to be named Cameras. For example:

```
DEF Cameras Switch {
  whichChild 0
  DEF Default PerspectiveCamera {
    position 20 0 -100
    orientation 0 0 1 0
  }
  DEF BirdsEye PerspectiveCamera {
    position 0 132 12
    orientation 0 1 0 .8
  }
  DEF Side PerspectiveCamera {
    position 12 0 0
    orientation 1 0 0 0
  }
}
```

NOTE: Use the whichChild field to determine the default camera view. Remember that the first child node has a child value of 0. If you don't specify a whichChild value, then the first camera in the switch list will be used as the default.

The above code will create three views to choose from:

- Default

- BirdsEye

- Side

You can then select one of the views from the WebSpace Vantage Point menu or the WebFX ViewPoints menu. The value of the whichChild field will determine the default camera.

LET'S GET MOVIN'!

You now know the ins and outs of every VRML geometrical, group, and property node. But the most exciting part of VRML is still ahead: interactivity. Building realistic and awe-inspiring worlds is one thing. Traveling between these worlds is another. The next chapter shows you how it's done.

20

JUMPING FROM WORLD TO WORLD

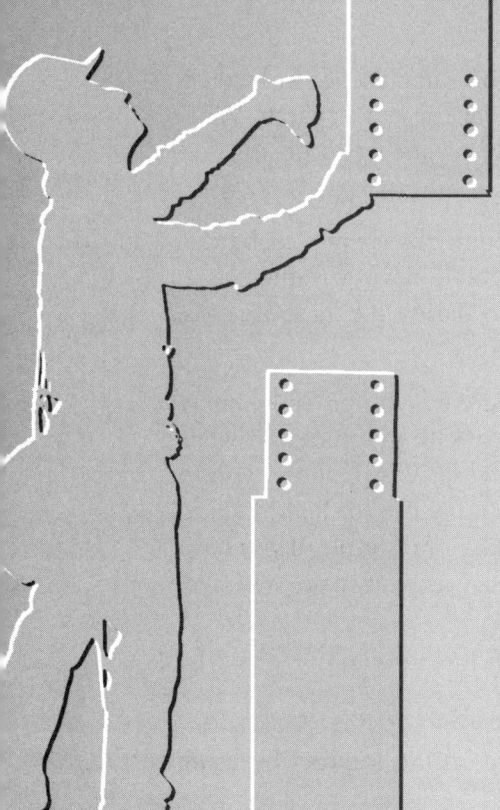

It's now time to put the standard stuff on the shelf and learn what really makes VRML exciting. The World Wide Web, at its core, is just a way of sharing material over large distances. As of now, this material is mainly HTML Web pages. But VRML will change all that, allowing your "surf" through the Web waters to feel more like real surfing. Eventually you'll see things in all directions, hear noises, react to them, and use your instincts to amble from place to place.

VRML is different from other 3D graphic formats because of its network extensions, which allow you to do the following:

- You can store other objects, scenes, or entire worlds as separate objects anywhere on the Internet.

- You can have any object be a hyperlink, leading to another VRML world, an HTML page, a graphic, a movie, a sound, a file, or any other Internet resource.

INLINED WORLDS

Since VRML is object oriented, there's no reason why all the objects need to be in the same WRL file. In fact, there are a bunch of reasons why you'd want to keep some objects separate:

- Somebody might've designed an object you're fond of. You could try to reinvent the wheel (or, say, the antique Ferris wheel), or you could just throw their object in your world simply by typing one line of code. VRML is all about sharing.

NOTE: If you use other people's creations, it's polite (and sometimes required by law) to ask their permission first.

- The VRML browser can load objects only as needed, only when visible, or only when you get close enough to them. For example, you would-n't need to waste time loading the insides of a complicated castle until your world's visitor actually crosses the moat. You might want to hide objects in boxes or in corners, and only have these objects appear when somebody stumbles onto them.

- You might want to use many trees within the same scene. Instead of redefining each object, just create one tree, save it as a separate WRL file, and call it repeatedly. (You can also use instancing to do this, as explained in Chapter 21.)

- You might want to have a world that has different objects in it each time a new visitor enters it. For example, you could have a traffic scene always be filled with different kinds of cars. Scenarios like these are covered in Chapter 22.

If you have some experience working with the Web, you probably know that HTML allows you to specify the file names of GIF graphics and *inline* these images—embed them within the text. Likewise, VRML allows you to use the WWWInline node to inline 3D objects. Simply use the *name* field to specify the file name of the object you want to load. For example, if you have an object called *moonbuggy.wrl* in the same directory as your main WRL file, you could load that buggy by using

```
WWWInline {
        name "moonbuggy.wrl"
}
```

In fact, you can call VRML objects anywhere on the Internet by using their full URL:

```
WWWInline {
        name "http://found.cs.nyu.edu/dfox/vrml/moonbuggy.wrl"
}
```

The *moonbuggy.wrl* file must be a self-contained world, a file you could open on its own by using the VRML browser. If the file you specify doesn't exist, most browsers will just ignore the WWWInline node; other browsers may give you an error.

NOTE: Different browsers use WWWInline differently. Some load the inlined objects immediately. Others wait until the WWWInline node is in the visible view volume. All browsers, however, will load the objects in the order you ask for them. Therefore, be sure to put the most important items first. For example, if you're inlining a house, a chair, a window, and a football, be sure to retrieve the house first, and then fill the house with the other objects.

VRML 1.1: You can use the WWWInline and WWWAnchor nodes to call up a URN (Universal Resource Name) as well as a URL.

An Example

A WWWInlined object acts like any other object. Any previous transformations, materials, lighting, or other attributes will be applied. This makes it easy to use several of the same objects again.

For example, you could create a pretty cool house by using the following code:

```
#VRML V1.0 ascii
Separator {
  Coordinate3 {
     point [-3 0 3, 3 0 3, -3 3 3, 3 3 3,
        -3 0 -3, 3 0 -3, -3 3 -3, 3 3 -3, 0 6 0]
  }
  Texture2 {
     filename "bricks.bmp"
  }
  IndexedFaceSet {
     coordIndex[
        1,3,2,0,-1, # Front
        4,5,7,6,-1, # Back
        0,4,6,2,-1, # Left Side
        1,5,7,3,-1, # Right Side
        0,1,5,4,-1] # Bottom
  }
  Texture2 {
     filename "veggie.bmp"
  }
  IndexedFaceSet {
     coordIndex[
```

continued on next page

continued from previous page

```
                6,8,7,-1,    # One side of the roof
                6,8,2,-1,    # Another part of the roof
                7,8,3,-1,    # The next part of the roof
                2,8,3,-1]    # The last roof face
        }
}
```

Suppose you saved the above file as *house.wrl*. You could now create a landscape that used several of these houses, as in Figure 20-1:

```
#VRML V1.0 ascii
Separator {
        PerspectiveCamera {
                position     7 20 10
                orientation 1 0 0 .785
        }
# Drop in a house
        Separator {
            WWWInline {
                name         "house.wrl"
            }
        }
# Let's build another, larger and redder house nearby
# So that the two houses merge to form a complex
        Separator {
            Material {
                diffuseColor 1 0 0
                ambientColor 1 0 0
            }
            Transform {
                translation       9 0 -5
                scaleFactor       2.5 1.5 1.5
            }
            WWWInline {
                name         "house.wrl"
            }
        }
}
```

Figure 20-1
Mixing several houses to form a whole mansion

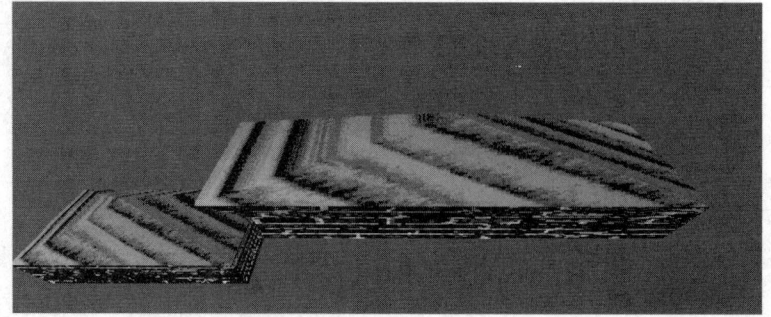

Leaps and Bounds

How does WWWInline work? Glad you asked. Basically, when the VRML browser renders your scene graph, it will go through each node, one at a time. If a WWWInline node is reached, then the specified object is loaded, as if it were part of the original scene. In this way, a WWWInline acts like a macro.

There's one small problem here. What if your browser is drawing a scene and it comes across a WWInline node. Visitors to your world have no idea what lies behind the digital curtain. Will it be a huge object, or a tiny one? Will the object appear in the current camera view, or would it normally be culled off screen?

The VRML browser could load all WWWInline objects in advance, but then you'd have to wait much longer before your scene was drawn. This defeats the whole purpose of WWWInline. So what's the deal? Does everything come to a standstill while the objects load?

Luckily, the WWWInline has a work-around: Tell it, in advance, what the *bounding box*—the volume around an object—will be. Specify the box by using two fields:

🔲 bboxSize—This is the size of each of the box's sides. For example, [1,2,3] would be a box 1 unit wide, 2 units high, and 3 units deep.

🔲 bboxCenter—This is where this box should be within the world. By default, this center is at the center of the world—[0,0,0]. However, if you're loading in a house that is translated, say, 5 units over to the right, then you would use a bboxCenter of [5,0,0], since the object's center would be 5 units to the right of the current point once the object loads.

NOTE: Some VRML browsers use a bboxCenter based on the current position. For example, if you're currently at [2,5,7], then a bboxCenter of [1,2,3] would draw the bounding box at [3,7,10]. This discrepancy will be clarified with VRML 1.1.

Once WWWInline knows the bounding box, the VRML browser can keep this space free and continue working. It'll know exactly when the object needs to be loaded and when it can stay silent and hidden off screen. Visitors to your world will see a transparent box appear. This lets them know that cool things are yet to come—it's kind of like giving somebody a gift box with the present hidden inside.

NOTE: To figure an object's bounding box size, try to imagine drawing a cube around the object. For example, a cone with a height of 10 and a radius of 5 would have a bounding box of 5x10x5. To figure out the bounding box of more complicated objects, you can use WebSpace's VRMLINFO program. Simply specify the name of your WRL file, and it'll give you all relevant statistics and information. Usually, however, you can just estimate the size of the box.

Suppose you've created a file called *cube.wrl*, as follows:

```
#VRML V1.0 ascii
Separator {
        Translation { translation 3 6 0 }
        Cube {
                width   10
                height  5
                depth   3
        }
}
```

You would specify the bounding box as follows:

```
WWWInline {
        name            "cube.wrl"
        bboxCenter      3 6 0
        bboxSize        10 5 3
}
```

Obviously, the calculations are a tad trickier if something other than a cube is involved.

3D on Demand

One of the coolest things you can do in version 1 of VRML is to have objects load only when you want them to. This can be accomplished by using the WWWInline node combined with the old favorite, LOD.

Normally, when you create objects using LOD, they will be loaded into memory so that when the time comes, they can be used. But what if you never get close enough to an LOD object to load its most advanced and complicated version? This is a waste of downloading, rendering, and computing time. If you have a very complicated world, why load objects that may never be seen?

Instead, create a series of nodes as follows:

1. Always create the simplest LOD object (the last child) within the main WRL document. This way there will always be *something* visible to begin with. If your last child is invisible, put the *second to last* child within the main VRML code.

2. Create more complicated objects separately, and use WWWInline to call them.

NOTE: Some browsers read in WWWInline objects immediately, storing them in memory. However, it's still a good idea to use WWWInlined LOD objects. You can begin seeing and navigating around a world while these hidden objects are being loaded.

For example, here's a common piece of code:

```
#VRML V1.0 ascii
DEF House LOD {
        center 0 3 0        # center of children
        range [ 100, 1000, 10000 ]  # increasing ranges
        Separator {
        # A fancy-schmancy house with lots of polygons
        # and materials and textures
                WWWInline {
                        file "house1.wrl"
                        bboxSize   6 6 6
                        bboxCenter 0 0 0
                }
        }
        Separator {
        # A less-fancy house with a few less polygons
        # but still with lots of materials and textures
                WWWInline {
                        file "house2.wrl"
                        bboxSize   6 6 6
                        bboxCenter 0  0 0
                }
        }
        # The simplest house you could imagine
        # Seen immediately
        Cube {
                width 6
                height 6
                length 6
        }
        # So far away that the house is invisible
        Group { }
}
```

TIP: Since LOD likes to know how big objects are before it can calculate your distance and cull things properly, be sure to specify bounding boxes. It'll speed things up.

You can use this node to achieve some pretty cool special effects. For example, you could create an intricate dragon and then save it in a separate

WRL file. You could then have VRnauts wander through the streets of a simple town and then, when they get close enough to a particular doorway, have the dragon appear. It might not exactly frighten your visitors, but it will make the visit more memorable.

VRML 1.1: Since LOD will use its children based on how good the browser is, a WWWInline may be read in at any time.

Fractals

A neat possibility for VRML is to build fractals. Simply create a VRML file that calls *itself*. If done craftily enough, you can achieve some fantastic results. There are some good resources on VRML fractals at: *http://www.sdsc.edu/vrml/*

WWWANCHOR

So far you've learned a lot about how you can build a scene. But what options do visitors in your virtual world have?

When tourists are first plunged into your world, they see it from the PerspectiveCamera angle you specify. They can then roam around the world using the VRML controls. This usually lets them move to any perspective they'd like—flying around, under, over, and through the virtual objects. If your world has LOD nodes, then some objects may appear when visitors get closer to them and then disappear. Fine. That's all pretty cool. But what else can VRnauts do?

The WWWAnchor node increases the VRnauts' options by a hundredfold. It allows them to click on any object and have something happen. Namely, the VRML file could perform any of the following:

- Load a new VRML world—For example, they could click on a door to see what's in the next room. Similar files linked together could form a complete house (or town, or world, or universe) for them to explore, with only one room loaded at a time.

- Load an object—For example, they could click on a 2D texture-mapped picture of a Ferrari and then have the 3D version of the Ferrari load before their eyes. Or vice versa.

- Load a sound—They click on a dog and it yaps at them.

- Load an HTML document—If they clicked on a 3D fox, it would load a home page.

502

▣ Load a movie—They click on a movie poster or on a 3D bat, and the latest preview for *Batman* appears.

▣ Go to a Telnet site—They click on a bookshelf and can log in to the Library of Congress' database.

▣ Load a gopher menu—They click on a 3D gopher and a gopher menu miraculously appears.

▣ View an FTP archive—They click on a floating floppy disk, and a list of all the files on the server appears for them to download.

▣ Read a newsgroup—They click on a picture of a beer mug to read the latest *alt.beer* articles.

The WWWAnchor node is a group node that makes all of its children hyperlinks to another part of the Internet. In essence, the WWWAnchor node acts like the <A HREF="URL"> anchor tag in HTML. The WWWAnchor node looks almost exactly like WWWInline, except it can have children.

🔑 **NOTE:** A person will know that an object is a hyperlink because the cursor arrow usually changes to a hand, as in Figure 20-2. Future versions of VRML may have other tip-offs, such as a special sound or color, or a flashing beacon. In the near future, VRML browsers may also have other ways of choosing an object. For example, you could reach out and grab the object with your powerglove, you could look directly at the object with your VR helmet, or you could say "Load!" and the link would automatically be followed. New VR hardware such as headsets could make this even more intuitive. For instance, to load a new world, you'd simply need to walk through a portal.

VRML 1.1: If you nest several overlapping WWWAnchors, then the deepest child will be the one that is loaded.

Hyperlinking

Let's get hyper. Use the *name* field to specify where the hyperlink should lead. Although this is usually another WRL file, this may be any resource on the Internet. For example, all of the following are valid name fields:

▣ name *"room12.wrl"*

▣ name *"http://found.cs.nyu.edu/dfox/vrml/room12.wrl"*

▣ name *"ftp://ftp.ncsa.uiuc.edu/"*

Figure 20-2
Using descriptions to let folks know where your links lead

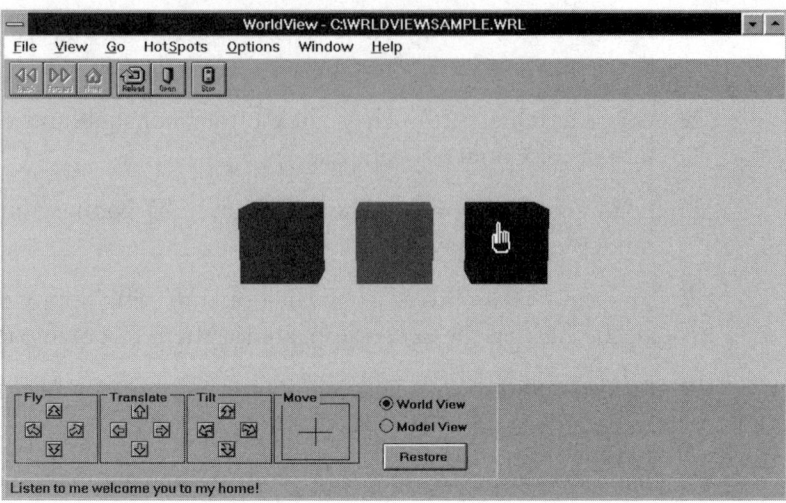

VR
ML name *"telnet:foo.edu"*

VR
ML name *"sound.au"*

VR
ML name *"video.mpg"*

The list can go on and on. As long as the name field points to a valid URL, then you may use it. For more detailed information on URLs, consult a basic book about the World Wide Web, such as the Waite Group's *HTML Web Publisher's Construction Kit.*

NOTE: For visitors in your world to access certain resources, they'll need to have the appropriate helper applications installed. For example, they'll need Netscape or some other Web browser to see HTML pages. They'll need a movie viewer to see MPEG video. They'll need a sound card and player to hear noises. Netscape and similar Web browsers usually allow you to configure these helper apps. Your VRML browser can then refer any unknown file types to your Web browser.

VRML 1.1: You can load any URN as well as any URL.

Suppose you want to have a world consisting of three cubes. You want people to click on the first cube to go to your home page, click on the second cube to load a picture of you, and click on the third cube to hear a welcome message. You could use the following code:

```
#VRML V1.0 ascii
Separator {
    WWWAnchor {
        name "http://found.cs.nyu.edu/dfox"
        Separator {
            Material { diffuseColor 1 0 0 }
            Translation { translation -3 0 0 }
            Cube { }
        }
    }
    WWWAnchor {
        name "http://found.cs.nyu.edu/dfox/dav1.gif"
        Separator {
            Material { diffuseColor 0 1 0 }
            Cube { }
        }
    }
    WWWAnchor {
        name "http://found.cs.nyu.edu/dfox/welcome.au"
        Separator {
            Material { diffuseColor 0 0 1 }
            Translation { translation 3 0 0 }
            Cube { }
        }
    }
}
```

Getting More Information

The above example is all well and good, but how will VRnauts know what to expect? They'll come into your world, see three cubes, and then what? It's much more humane to let people know where links will take them. You can use the *description* field to do just that. Simply follow the description field with a string.

If a visitor rolls the mouse over a WWWAnchor object with a description field, the description string is then printed at the bottom of the screen. This can tell people what an object is, where it leads if they click on it, or who created it.

 TIP: Use a short string (less than one line long), since many browsers only display the first few characters.

You could modify the above code to be a lot more user-friendly as follows:

```
#VRML V1.0 ascii
Separator {
```

continued on next page

continued from previous page

```
WWWAnchor {
        name "http://found.cs.nyu.edu/dfox"
        description "David Fox's Home Page"
        Separator {
                Material { diffuseColor 1 0 0 }
                Translation { translation -3 0 0 }
                Cube { }
        }
}
WWWAnchor {
        name "http://found.cs.nyu.edu/dfox/dav1.gif"
        description "A picture of me."
        Separator {
                Material { diffuseColor 0 1 0 }
                Cube { }
        }
}
WWWAnchor {
        name "http://found.cs.nyu.edu/dfox/welcome.au"
        description "Listen to me welcome you to my home!"
        Separator {
                Material { diffuseColor 0 0 1 }
                Translation { translation 3 0 0 }
                Cube { }
        }
}
}
```

If someone rolls over the third cube, then, they would see the message as
printed in the bottom left of the screen in Figure 20-2.

In fact, often you might want to have a description field that doesn't
actually link anywhere. This lets people roll over objects and have messages
appear at the bottom of their screen. For instance, you could create a maze
with hints built into the walls. For example:

```
WWWInline {
        name ""
        description "You're getting warmer!"
        Separator {
                # Draw the wall here
                ...
        }
}
```

One Image Can Take You Everywhere: The Map

HTML users will be familiar with something called a *clickable image map*—
you click on an image, and depending on where you click, you'll be whisked
to a different Web page. The WWWAnchor node has a *map* field that can
work similar wonders. The map field takes one of two values:

▣ NONE—This object leads to the same place no matter where you click on it.

▣ POINT—Different points on this object lead to different places.

By default, the map is set to NONE. If you set a map to point, then the *object-space* coordinates upon which you click will be added to the URL in the following format:

```
URL?x,y,z
```

You'll want the URL to be a cgi script that can then interpret these points and have various points whisk you to various places. Check out Chapter 22 for more details.

Recall that the object space is the local area surrounding the object, as if the object existed in its own world. For example, a cube 5 units wide, 6 units high, and 7 units deep would have object-space coordinates ranging from [0,0,0] to [5,6,7] no matter where it was located in the VRML world. You could create such a hypercube as follows:

```
WWWAnchor {
        name "http://foo.edu/cgi-bin/vrmlmap"
        map POINT
        Cube {
                width   5
                height  6
                depth   7
        }
}
```

If you clicked directly in the uppermost corner of this cube, and the cube were facing you straight on, then the following URL would be called:

```
http://foo.edu/cgi-bin/vrmlmap?5,6,7
```

☛ **NOTE:** In most cases it would be impossible to pick the point [5,6,7] exactly, unless your eyes were hawklike and you had the hands of a surgeon. More likely, you'd pick something similar to [4.89,5.91,6.79]. When you make use of the points in your cgi program, be sure to allow for a realistic range.

Probably you'd want to create a cool texture and then overlay it on an interesting shape. For example, you might want to create a 3D version of your company's logo. You could then texture a poster including a picture of your company's president, a picture of your company's best-selling product, and the word "New!" People could then click on this virtual sculpture and jump to various pages of information.

Going to a Specific View of a Scene

VRML 1.1 has a neat feature that allows you to jump not only to another world, but also to any perspective within the other world. For example, you could have several views of an Old West town—one called "General Store" and one called "Saloon." Depending on where people clicked, they could automatically be taken to the most appropriate view. For example, if they clicked on a mug, they might wind up in front of the Saloon, but if they clicked on a hammer, they'd be whisked to the General Store.

This technique works like the <A NAME="name"> and <A HREF="#name"> tags in HTML. First, name each camera node by using the DEF command (the way you would for ViewPoints):

```
DEF GeneralStore PerspectiveCamera {
    position 20 0 -100
    orientation 0 0 1 0
}
DEF Saloon PerspectiveCamera {
    position 10 23 200
    orientation 0 1 0 1.2
}
```

You can now jump to any point of view by using the WWWAnchor file name followed by a hash mark (#) followed by the camera name. So, if you wanted to make a cube that would take the user in front of the Saloon, you would write

```
WWWAnchor {
        name "#saloon"
        Cube { }
}
```

You can use this trick to jump to any perspective within *any* VRML world with named cameras:

```
WWWAnchor {
        name "http://here.there/vrml/oldwest.wrl#saloon"
        Cube { }
}
```

NOTE: The camera's focalDistance field tells the VRML browser how fast the user should be able to move through the scene.

Surprise Scenes

An old story, *The Lady and the Tiger,* talks about a guy who wants to marry a king's daughter. He is tossed into an arena and allowed to choose between two doors. Behind one is his beloved. Behind the other is a vicious tiger that will tear him to shreds. He reaches for the door, opens it, and...the story ends.

You can reenact this morbid variation of the *Let's Make a Deal* curtains by using the following code:

```
#VRML V1.0 ascii
Separator {
  Coordinate3 {
    point [-4 0 0, 4 0 0, -2 0 .1, 2 0 .1, -1 0 .1, 1 0 .1,
    -4 4 0, 4 4 0, -2 3 .1, -1 3 .1, 1 3 .1, 2 3 .1]
  }
  # Draw the wall
  IndexedFaceSet {
    coordIndex [0, 1, 7, 6, -1]
  }
  WWWAnchor {
    name "lady.wrl"
    Separator {
            # Draw the left door
            Material { diffuseColor 0 1 0 }
            IndexedFaceSet {
    coordIndex [2, 8, 9, 4, -1]
       }
    }
  }
  WWWAnchor {
    name "tiger.wrl"
    Separator {
            # Draw the right door
            Material { diffuseColor 1 0 1 }
            IndexedFaceSet {
    coordIndex [5, 10, 11, 3, -1]
       }
    }
  }
}
```

Your choices appear in Figure 20-3. Choose wisely!

Figure 20-3
The lady and
the tiger

WHAT COULD POSSIBLY BE NEXT?

The next chapter talks about extending VRML. This allows you to create one object and easily use it again. Chapter 22 will update this program to make the "Lady and Tiger" doors random. That way, even *you* won't know what you'll face when you open a door.

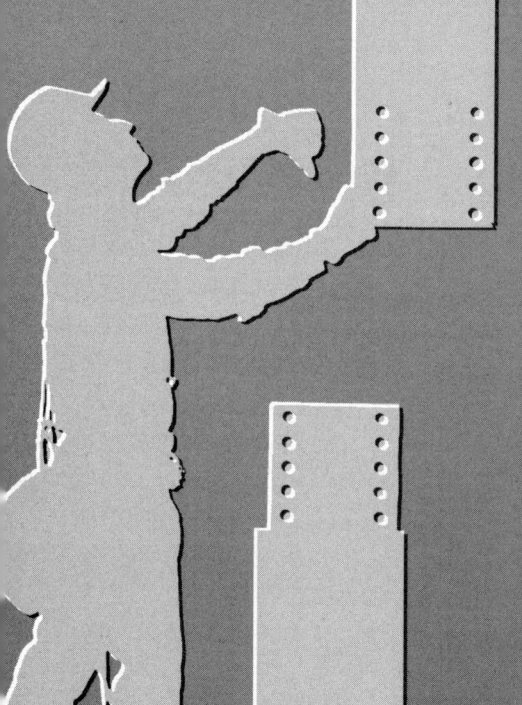

21

I WANT MORE: EXTENDING VRML

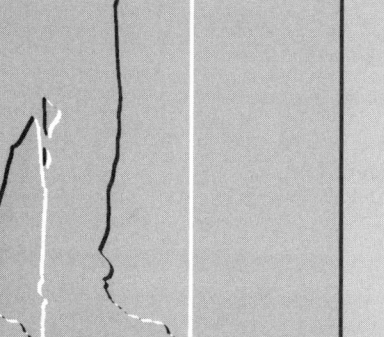

21

That's it! If you've read all the previous chapters, you now know how to use and combine the VRML nodes, fields, and techniques. But the story isn't quite over. One of VRML's most exciting features is how you can take basic collections of nodes and share them, reuse them, redefine them, or even create new nodes. This chapter covers ways to extend VRML, making it not just a 3D file format, but the basis for a full-fledged programming language.

SHARED INSTANCING

Suppose you went to a whole lot of trouble to design an intricate VRML bonsai tree. You now want to take this tree and populate a Japanese garden—some trees will be squatter, some will be darker colored, and some will be growing sideways, but the tree shape will be the same. You could, of course, just use your word processor text editor to copy the entire tree and then paste it repeatedly within the WRL file. This would save tons of time. Of course, it also would be awful messy and would make your VRML document extremely long.

VRML supports a technique known as *shared instancing* (also known in some circles as *aliasing* and *shared referencing*). In Chapter 15 you learned that you could name nodes by using the DEF marker, like so:

513

```
DEF TwoCubes Separator {
        Cube { }
        Translation { translation 5 0 0 }
        Cube { }
}
```

Once you name a node, no matter how large or complicated it is, you can easily reuse it simply by referring to its name. Just drop in the USE command whenever you'd like it. So to use the two cubes defined previously, you'd just need to type

```
USE TwoCubes
```

That's all it takes. Be sure the name you USE exactly matches the name you DEFined, or else the VRML browser will get confused. This may result in skipped objects (best case) or errors (worst case).

It works like a charm. When you define a word using the DEF command, the node is stored in memory. This allows you to use it again. You should use the DEF/USE scheme anytime your VRML file contains any repetitive code. Most of the time you'll want to define an object, perform some transformations, change some colors, use the object, do some more transformations, change some more colors, use the object again, and so on. For example, you could create a simple forest as in Figure 21-1 by using the following short sequence:

```
#VRML V1.0 ascii
#Forest Scene
Separator {
    DEF Tree Separator {
            Material {
                    diffuseColor .3 .2 0 # Brownish
            }
            Cylinder {
                    parts    SIDES
                    radius   .2
                    height   5
            }
            Translation { translation 0 3 0 }
            Material {
                    diffuseColor 0 .9 0 # Green
            }
            Sphere { }
    }
    Translation { translation 5 0 5 }
    USE Tree
    Translation { translation -8 0 -12 }
    USE Tree
    Transform {
            translation 5 2.5 13
            scaleFactor 2 2 2
```

```
    }
    USE Tree
    Translation { translation 5 0 -10 }
    USE Tree
    Translation { translation -8 0 2 }
    USE Tree
}
```

You can use one tree over and over again to form an entire orchard. You might want to continue this file by naming different types of trees or other architecture, such as bridges, one picket of a fence (used repeatedly), or a miniature shrine. You could then scatter everything around, using careful transformations to put everything on ground level.

 NOTE: If you define two nodes with the same name and then try to use one, the most recently defined node will be used. This can be useful if you decide to add a new type of tree in the middle of a scene.

You may not define a node in one file and then use it in another, though future implementations of VRML may change that limitation. This would allow easy-to-use libraries of objects that could be called by use of extremely simple commands.

TIP: You can use an inlined node simply by naming it:

```
DEF Bonzai WWWInline { name "bonzai.wrl" }
```

Clever Sharing

Sharing can do more than optimize things, though. You can use shared instancing to achieve fractal-like effects—taking one simple shape and, applying the same laws to it again and again, forming a much grander shape.

Figure 21-1
I can't see the forest for the trees, but it's all really based on one simple tree

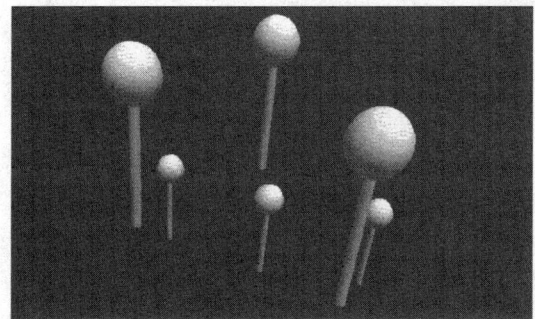

For example, carefully look over the following code (written by Rob Jagnow):

```
#VRML V1.0 ascii
Separator {
    Cylinder {
        radius .125
        height 4
    }
    Translation {translation 0 -2 0}
    DEF Step Group {
    #The definition for one step...
        Translation {translation 0 .2 0}
        Rotation {rotation 0 1 0 -.3}
        Separator {
            Translation {translation .6 0 0}
            Cube {
                height .08
                width 1.2
                depth .25
            }
        }
        Separator {
            Translation {translation 1.19 .54 -.1 }
            Cube {
                height 1
                width .04
                depth .04
            }
        }
        Separator {
            Translation {translation 1.19 1.1 0 }
            Rotation {rotation 1 0 0 -.50}
            Cube {
                height .04
                width .04
                depth .42
            }
        }
    }
    USE Step
    USE Step
    USE Step
    USE Step
    # Repeat this for as many steps as you like.
}
```

Each step of the stairway has its own transformation built in. Since transformations are cumulative, each step will be tilted at a slightly different angle than its previous incarnation. This allows you to form a marvelously easy yet intricate stairway as in Figure 21-2. To add another step, just type another "USE Step" line.

Figure 21-2
Climbing a
virtual stairway
to heaven

EXTENSIBILITY

VRML is quite basic, as 3D file formats go. As such, many software companies have created browsers that support unofficial VRML features such as collision detection, other types of primitive shapes, different lighting styles, and more materials. But what about browsers that don't support these enhanced nodes? VRML needs a way to be extended without confusing basic browsers.

VRML has two tricks that allow you to extend its features:

- Self-declaring nodes—Simply let the VRML browser know what this node expects. If it can handle the node, it'll use it. If it can't, the node will just be ignored.

- Alternate nodes (*Is-A* relationships)—If the node isn't supported, a legal VRML node can be used instead.

Using these extensions will come in most handy if you plan to write your own VRML viewer. Skip to Chapter 24 for more information about authoring custom browsers.

Self-Declaring a Node

To extend VRML, just build a node that declares *itself*. Begin by creating your node as you would any other node. Immediately after the opening curly bracket, use the *fields* field to list the type of each of your node's fields along with that field's name. Separate each field definition with a comma, and surround the field listing with square brackets.

VRML 1.1: Specialized node and field names will end with EXT, to specify that they are extended. They may also have names similar to NewNodeACMEX, if the node is made by the Acme company and only works with Acme browsers.

Suppose you know of a browser that supports a node called Fog. The Fog node fills the VRML scene with a haze that hides any faraway objects, making worlds seem somewhat more realistic (especially if your world is wintertime London, or a spooky cemetery). The fictional Fog node has two fields: *distance* (how far you can see before the fog gets too thick) and *color* (the basic color of the fog). You would use such a node as follows:

```
Fog {
    fields [ SFFloat distance, SFColor color ]
    distance 5 # 5 meters of visibility
    color 1 0 0 # A red fog
}
```

Each field must be assigned a legal SF or MF type. These types are explained in Chapter 15.

If the VRML browser supports the extended node, it'll use it. If not, the node will simply be ignored.

TIP: You need only list the fields that you'll actually be using. For example, if the extended node has 12 fields, but all you want to do is specify the value of a field called "stretchiness," then you need only define the stretchiness field:

```
fields [ SFFloat stretchiness ]
```

In essence, every VRML node was originally specified using the same layout. For instance, if the cylinder node never existed, it would be delineated using the following code:

```
Cylinder {
    fields [ SFBitMask parts, SFFloat radius, SFFloat height ]
    parts    ALL
    radius   1
    height   2
}
```

VRML 1.1: Once you've declared an extended node within a WRL file, you can use the node as normal. You don't need to specify the *isA* or *fields* fields.

Alternate Nodes (IS-A)

Lots of times the special nodes you labor so hard to create won't work with other people's VRML browsers. But that doesn't mean they should be ignored. After all, suppose you're using an extended node to, say, use a live video feed as a texture on an object. Only very fast and specialized computers with lightning-fast Internet connections will be able to use such a node. However, if this node isn't feasible, you'd still like the object to be projected with a regular 2D texture.

VRML allows you to create alternate nodes within your extended nodes, which is known as an *Is-A relationship*. These alternate nodes work like an understudy. When the main super-duper node isn't supported, the old reliable node is called in to do its stuff.

To specify an alternate node, simply create the *isA* field (of type MFString). Be sure to specify the isA field in your extended fields list. The isA field takes an entire legal VRML node as its value (you can even specify a whole group of nodes, as long as you surround them with a Separator or Group node). So, if you had an extended node that was able to create a multicolored texture map (called RainbowTexture2), then you could write something similar to

```
RainbowTexture2 {
  fields [ MFString isA, SFString filename, SFColor color ]
  isA ["Texture2"]
  filename "cool.jpg" # This will be used in either case.
  color 1 .5 .3 # This color will be used if supported.
}
```

Such nodes can become more and more useful as a VRML API (Application Programming Interface) is invented. An API is a set of common routines that can be used by browsers to perform specialized tasks. This would allow you to distribute bundles of routines that could be "plugged in" to any existing VRML browser. Using extended fields, along with properly bundled APIs, you could use the basic VRML language to perform most any task. There is no standard for a VRML API yet. But time will change that soon enough.

CAN THERE POSSIBLY BE MORE?

Oh yes. The next chapter shows you how to combine VRML with cgi scripts, achieving simple animations, behaviors, and dynamic self-building worlds. Altogether, it's some darn cool stuff.

22

VRML
MADE-TO-ORDER

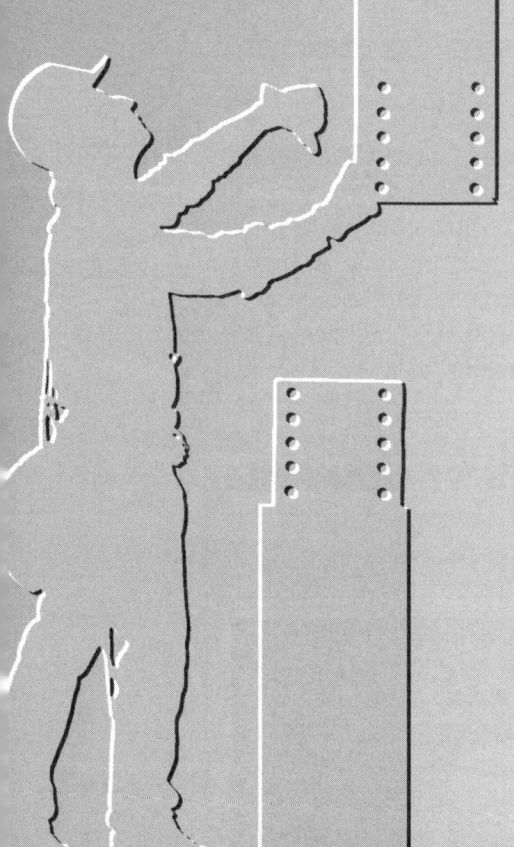

Virtual realities may never rival actual reality in its crispness, detail, or expanse. But virtual realities have some advantages over actual reality. For one thing, they don't really exist, which means you can have a virtual object change, grow, shrink, or disappear at will. This creates worlds that are, in many ways, as alive as the creatures within them. There's no reason why buildings can't walk, or why the sun can't bounce across the sky. There can even be a special house where people can push or tug at the walls, making each room as big or small as they want.

It's true, VRML has no built-in animations or behaviors. But that doesn't mean you can't program a scene that will be different each time you look at it. For instance, why not create a 3D clock that can give you the time anywhere in the world? Figure 22-1 shows the HTML front-end for the CyberClock (*http://129.217.236.254:8080/Clock/clock.html*) created by Keith Ahern at the University of Limerick. Just click on any time zone. The coordinates are then sent to a special program known as a *cgi script* or *server-side script*. This program figures out what zone you clicked on and what the current time is. This is when it starts to get interesting. The program draws a basic clock face without the hands. Using the calculated time, the hand positions are determined, and then the hands are drawn in their proper position, using a simple rotation

Figure 22-1
Where in the
world are you?
We need to
figure out your
time zone

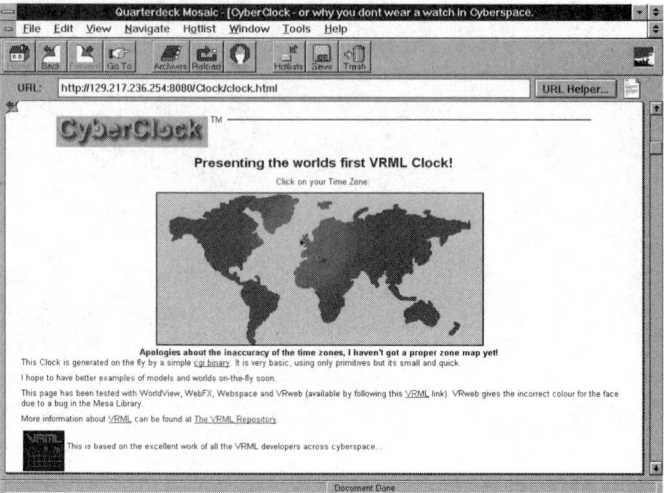

transformation (around the z axis). This achieves a full clock as shown in Figure 22-2. Click on the clock to update the time.

This is just one example of mixing VRML with a set of routines to achieve custom results. Another good example is the topographic map generator in Figure 22-3. It takes data from a number of databases to actually form a virtual world. All you do is choose the coordinates and click. It'll even take a texture and map it onto the mountains, streams, valleys, or oceans, so

Figure 22-2
An accurate
3D clock

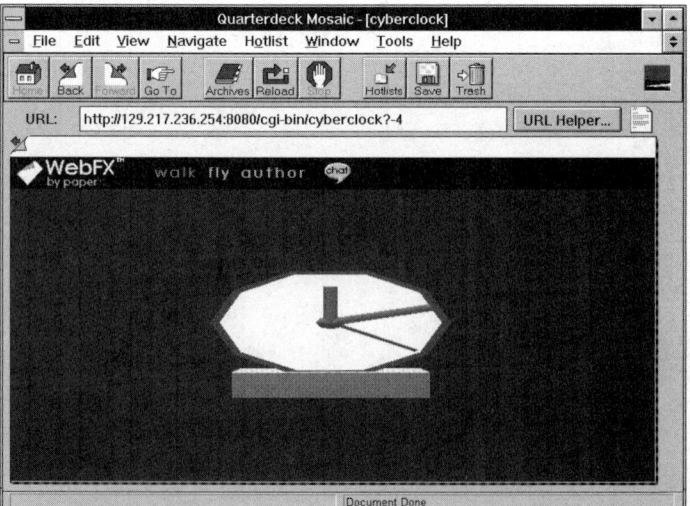

Figure 22-3
A three-dimensional topographic map builder

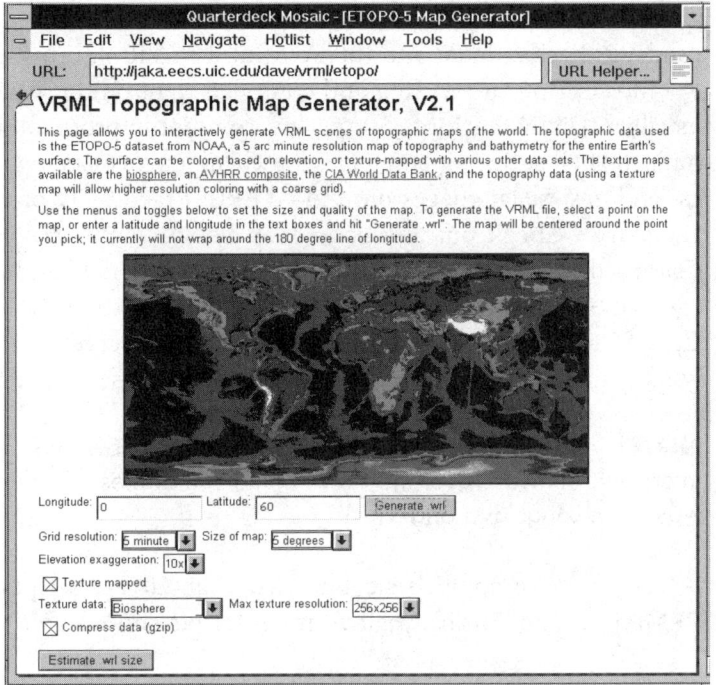

you get an accurate view of any part of the Earth, at any given moment. Flip through Chapter 2 for a magical mystery tour of some other interactive sites (and sights!).

This chapter is a primer on using the computer's processing power to create custom worlds. Certainly, entire books can (and will) be written about programs to create on-the-fly VRML. Since every person likes to use different programming languages, computer platforms, and Web servers, the code in this chapter is kept simple. You should be able, however, to use the concepts and examples in this chapter to build bigger and better 3D creations.

NOTE: The latest version of WebFX— Netscape's Live3D— allows you to link Java applets' and Javascript programs to your VRML documents. To reach more about this, visit the Netscape home page at http://www.netscape.com/

SO WHAT'S A CGI SCRIPT?

A *common gateway interface (cgi) script* is a program that can be called at any time by the Web server. It works with the Web's HyperText Transfer Protocol (HTTP), allowing you to write programs that get their input from the Web and spit their output back onto the Web. A similar program can create a valid VRML document and then output it to VRML browsers.

Most scripts are written and compiled right on the Web server, which is usually a UNIX machine. Scripts are commonly programmed using UNIX's built-in shell scripting language, the C language, or using one of the handiest and easiest languages around—PERL (Practical Expression and Report Language). Check out any good Web book such as *HTML Web Publisher's Construction Kit* (Fox and Downing 1995) for details on how to implement cgi scripts. There are many great books that talk about UNIX programming, C, and PERL in particular. If you want to create server-side scripts, it's highly recommended that you check out some of these resources.

NOTE: Java is a new network language that allows you to develop highly interactive software over the Web. Some companies are already investigating ways of mixing Java and VRML.

If you have some basic knowledge about cgi scripts, writing instant VRML is a snap. Basically, all your cgi scripts should do the following:

1. Send the following line, followed by two carriage returns:

```
Content-type: x-world/x-vrml
```

2. Send the VRML heading:

```
#VRML V1.0 ascii
```

3. Send the rest of the VRML nodes, customizing nodes, or field values where appropriate.

For instance, with PERL you would always begin your script with

```
#!/usr/bin/perl
print "Content-type: x-world/x-vrml\n\n";
print "#VRML V1.0 ascii\n";
#The rest of your VRML file goes here, preceded by print statements.
```

Using UNIX's built-in scripting language, you would begin your script as follows:

```
#! /bin/sh
echo Content-type: x-world/x-vrml
echo
echo #VRML V1.0 ascii
# The rest of the VRML document is here.
```

And using C, your script would resemble this:

```
/* Standard Input/Output Library */
#include <stdio.h>
/* NCSA's library of routines for parsing forms */
#include "util.h"

int main(void)
{
        printf("Content-type: x-world/x-vrml%c%c",10,10);
        printf("#VRML V1.0 ascii%c",10);
        /* The rest of the VRML file goes here. */
}
```

Cgi scripts usually take a basic VRML file and plug in certain variables. For example, to create a virtual maze, you could design a vertical wall using standard VRML nodes, as follows:

```
DEF Wall Separator {
        Coordinate2 { point [0 0 0, 5 0 0, 0 5 0, 5 5 0] }
        IndexedFaceSet { coordIndex [0,1,3,2] }
}
```

You could then have the VRML program figure where you were in the maze and transform these walls accordingly, making some face east-west, others face north-south. For example, you could make a straight corridor by rotating the two copies of the wall around the y axis—one to the right and one to the left. In other words, the *geometry* is usually created beforehand, and the *position* or other properties are calculated on-the-fly.

MAIL-ORDER WORLDS

A common use for VRML server scripts is to output worlds customized to the visitor's whims. This way, people can define the look, color, brightness, or perspective of your world before they step inside it.

For example, you could make an easy random generator that would output a sphere with a radius of any size the user asks for. This allows people to build custom snowballs as massive as they wish. First you'd make a quick and dirty HTML form that asked for the radius:

```
<HTML>
<HEAD>
<TITLE>The Interactive Snowball</TITLE>
</HEAD>
<BODY>
<H1>The Interactive Snowball</H1>
```

continued on next page

continued from previous page

```
<H2>A really dumb example of using a script to create on-the-fly
VRML</H2>
Type in the radius of a sphere in the input box (in meters):<BR>
<ISINDEX HREF="http://found.cs.nyu.edu/cgi-bin/snowball"
PROMPT="Sphere Radius=">
</BODY>
</HTML>
```

This form sends whatever the user typed to a program called *snowball* located in the *cgi-bin* directory at a Web server called *found.cs.nyu.edu* (as specified in the HREF field of the ISINDEX tag). You could call this file *snowball.htm* and put it in your Web home page directory.

You now need to create this snowball program. Use your favorite text editor to create this simple UNIX script:

```
#! /bin/sh
echo Content-type: x-world/x-vrml
echo
echo #VRML V1.0 ascii
echo Separator {
echo    Material { diffuseColor 1 1 1 } # A brilliant white
echo    Sphere {
echo         radius $*
echo    }
echo }
```

The *echo* command outputs the text that follows. The *$** mark indicates the value of the arguments that were sent to the program (by the *snowball.htm* index file). Basically, the snowball program outputs whatever the user typed in the ISINDEX field.

Save the script as the file *snowball*. Now all you need to do is make the snowball program executable (able to be run). Just type

```
chmod +x snowball
```

Copy this program to the *cgi-bin* directory of your Web server (or ask your system administrator to do it for you). Be sure the location of the snowball program is accurately reflected in the HREF attribute in the *snowball.htm* file.

Now, someone could call up your snowball by using their Web browser to access a URL similar to

```
http://found.cs.nyu.edu/dfox/snowball.htm
```

Anyone who accessed this page could then fill in the radius, as in Figure 22-4. Assuming the Web and VRML browsers were configured correctly, a 3D sphere of the requested size would then appear.

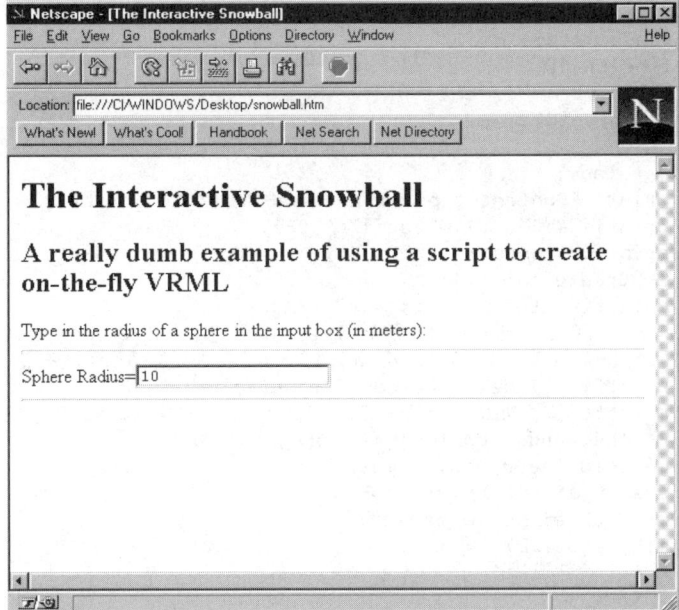

Figure 22-4
Picking the size of your snowball

THINGS CHANGE

Imagine using live photos as texture maps. This way, you could draw a Manhattan cityscape that would show the millions of lit skyscraper windows at night, the brilliant sunlight shimmering on the steel and glass during the day. Or you could create a chameleon that randomly changed its skin each time you saw it—imagine a lizard with bricks, gold leaf, or feathers as skin.

Many VRML server-side scripts are based on random numbers, the current time, stock data, or the latest image feeds from your favorite satellite. These scripts don't require any input from visitors to your world. All they need to do is access the cgi script using a VRML browser.

Such scripts will be even more complicated, amazing, and useful when VRML 2.0 comes out with simple behaviors, animations, and more multi-user interaction.

A Trickier Lady and Tiger

For example, you could create a simple C program that presented a wall with two doors. One door would lead to a lady, one to a tiger. What's behind each door would depend on the luck of the draw:

```
/* Standard Input/Output Library */
#include <stdio.h>
#define LF 10

int main(void)
{
    int lady;
    printf("Content-type: x-world/x-vrml%c%c",LF,LF);
    printf("#VRML V1.0 ascii%c",LF);
    printf("Separator {%c",LF);
    /* Create the wall */
    printf("  Coordinate3 {%c",LF);
    printf("    point [-4 0 0, 4 0 0, -2 0 .1, 2 0 .1, -1 0 .1,
1 0 .1, -4 4 0, 4 4 0, -2 3 .1, -1 3 .1, 1 3 .1, 2 3 .1] }%c",LF);
    printf("  IndexedFaceSet {%c",LF);
    printf("    coordIndex [0, 1, 7, 6, -1] }%c",LF);
    /* The random part of the program. */
    /* Seed the random number generator */
    srand(getpid());
    /* Pick either 0 or 1 */
    if (rand()%2)
    {
      lady = 1;
      printf("  WWWAnchor { name \"lady.wrl\"%c",LF);
    }
    else
    {
      lady = 0;
      printf("  WWWAnchor { name \"tiger.wrl\"%c",LF);
    }
    printf("  Separator { Material { diffuseColor 0 1 0 }%c",LF);
    printf("    IndexedFaceSet { coordIndex [2, 8, 9, 4, -1] }%c",LF);
    printf("} }%c",LF);
    if (lady)
      printf("WWWAnchor { name \"tiger.wrl\"%c",LF);
    else
      printf("WWWAnchor { name \"lady.wrl\"%c",LF);
    printf("  Separator { Material { diffuseColor 1 0 1 }%c",LF);
    printf("  IndexedFaceSet { coordIndex [5, 10, 11, 3, -1] }%c",LF);
    printf("} } }%c",LF);
}
```

The Output

If you compiled the above program and ran it, you would get the following output:

```
Content-type: x-world/x-vrml

#VRML V1.0 ascii
Separator {
  Coordinate3 {
```

```
     point [-4 0 0, 4 0 0, -2 0 .1, 2 0 .1, -1 0 .1, 1 0 .1,
-4 4 0, 4 4 0, -2 3 .1, -1 3 .1, 1 3 .1, 2 3 .1] }
  IndexedFaceSet {
   coordIndex [0, 1, 7, 6, -1] }
  WWWAnchor { name "lady.wrl"
   Separator { Material { diffuseColor 0 1 0 }
    IndexedFaceSet { coordIndex [2, 8, 9, 4, -1] }
  } }
  WWWAnchor { name "tiger.wrl"
   Separator { Material { diffuseColor 1 0 1 }
    IndexedFaceSet { coordIndex [5, 10, 11, 3, -1] }
  } } }
```

The first line tells the Web server what type of file it is. The rest of the output is good old-fashioned VRML. The lines *WWWAnchor { name "tiger.wrl"* and *WWWAnchor { name "lady.wrl"* may be switched, however, depending on the luck of the draw.

So, if you named this program *choice.wrl* and put it in the *cgi-bin* directory on your Web server (see the next chapter), anyone who accessed this page would see two doors. One holds a lady (see Figure 22-5), one a tiger. Not even you can know which fate is behind which door.

NOTE: It wouldn't be *that* difficult for you to choose correctly with most VRML browsers. If you rolled over the tiger door, the URL *tiger.wrl* would appear at the bottom of the screen!

Figure 22-5
You'll see the
lady.wrl file, if
you're lucky

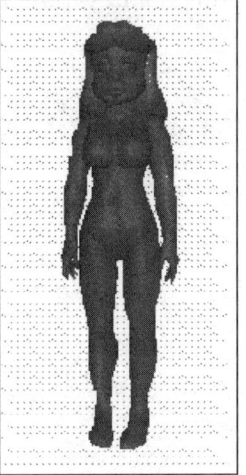

WHAT ELSE CAN YOU DO?

You can create simple interaction between two virtual people (avatars). Just keep track of their positions in 3D space, and then use cgi scripts to move these people around a virtual world.

You can create a full adventure game with precise logic, interaction, and numerous rooms. For example, you can use a script to keep track of props that players can pick up and give to each other. You can also keep track of the score, the number of monsters killed, health points, and so on. Eventually VRML will form the basis for some outlandish and outstanding video games.

Finally, you can set the MAP field of WWWAnchor to POINT. The position a user clicks will then be sent to your cgi script. You can use this 3D point to redraw the shape, load a different shape, move to a specific room, or do whatever you wish.

Future versions of VRML may also have image-mapped textures: Depending on where you click on an image, you could be transferred to various places. VRML may eventually have various input widgets, such as 3D sliders, buttons, and input boxes. This would act similarly to an HTML form. As behavior, animation, and multiuser participation become part of VRML, cgi scripts will likely become the backbone, telling the scenes how to animate and helping people to interact.

There's no limit to what you can do. Try it. If it works, your VRML site will probably be famous the very next day. Later versions of VRML will have even more behaviors, functionality, options, and geometry for you to customize with scripts.

PART IV
THE NITTY-GRITTY

23

DELIVERING REALITY: SERVER VRML

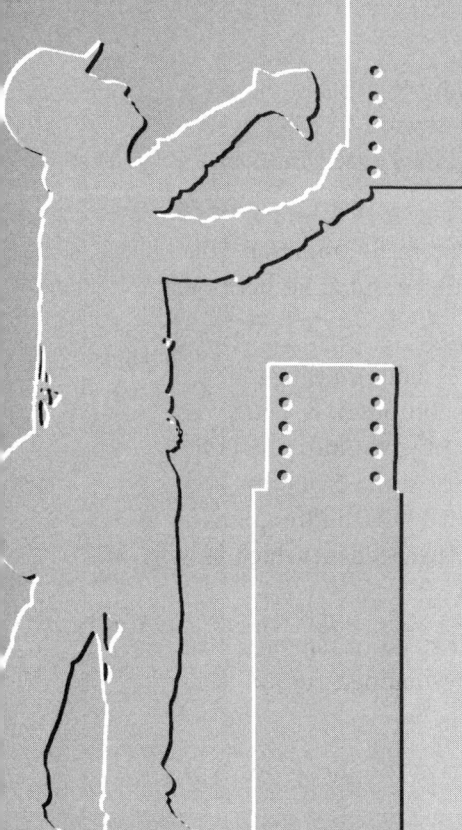

You've done a darn good job creating a world. Your world is sleek, has lots of realistic objects, yet is simple enough to move through quickly. You have lots of neat textures, and you've taken great pains with lighting and camera angles. You can't wait to throw your world onto the World Wide Web and have people visit it.

Delivering reality is easier than it sounds. Simply copy all your VRML files (WRL documents, textures, and so on) to one World Wide Web–readable directory. Here's what to do with 'em.

HOW TO OPTIMIZE 'EM

Before you drop your VRML worlds on the Internet, try them locally. Use as many VRML browsers as you can to explore your VRML scene. Textures might not appear the way you expect. It might take way too long to navigate through the scene. The scene may load much too slowly. Or maybe the file is too complicated to be drawn at all.

Here are some ways to optimize your VRML files:

- A high polygon count is usually the worst offender. Most modeling software allows you to set the complexity to any level you desire. A good rule is to make your objects as simple as possible while still retaining their meaning. For example, if you can draw a cool-looking spider as a simple sphere with 16 cylinders, then you should do it. Chapter 9 shows some examples of how to do this.

- Textures are the second-worst offenders. Textures zap lots of memory quickly. Do the math: One 128x128 bitmap means 16K of memory. These add up fast! Try to tile the same small texture again and again rather than use many unique ones. For example, an entire brick wall can consist of one many-tiled brick.

- To shorten the length of your WRL file, use lots of cones, cylinders, cubes, spheres, and AsciiText instead of defining similar objects from scratch. You can achieve many effects like this. For example, by using scale along with a sphere, you can create a cigar-like shape. Many browsers also can draw these primitives much faster than they can a set of polygons.

- Don't use any exorbitantly large objects. For example, instead of creating a detailed landscape for your scene, you may want to have everything floating in space. As long as all the objects are level, the viewer will have the impression of ground.

- Don't use a light source in vain. Calculating where illumination falls takes up lots of computing power. Cut down the number of lights if things seem to be moving too slowly.

- The LOD node is extremely important. VRML 1.1 will use this node to create customized scenes that run well on any computer system. You should create several versions of all complex objects and use LOD nodes to arrange them. Check out Chapter 17 for some LOD tips and tricks. Be sure to use lots of WWWInlines as your LOD children. Smart browsers will not load these objects unless they are needed, which can save lots of time.

- Textures are a great way to get rid of objects. Instead of having a real wagon in your Old West street, just use a texture-mapped cutout. This is similar to what Hollywood set designers do.

- Depth-complexity can kill a scene. Try not to have too many overlapping objects.

- Use as few nodes as you can. By arranging VRML files into smart groups, you can have many objects share properties, coordinate lists, textures, and so on. Switching materials takes tons of time. Instead of creating a red car, a blue horse, and a red house, create a red car and house, and then the blue horse.

- Use WWWInlines to load any objects that won't be immediately seen. This way, these objects can be loaded after the initial scene is drawn. For example, if a visitor to your world steps into a city street, you should load the *insides* of the houses with WWWInlines, since a user may never even see these objects.

- Use the ShapeHints node as often as you can. Especially be sure to specify a SOLID shapeType. This will only render the part of the object you are looking at, which is usually all that's needed.

WHERE TO PUT 'EM

You'll need to place all your WRL files, including inlined WRL objects and texture images, in the same directory on your Web server (unless, of course, you referred to textures in different directories). Many Web servers allow each user to put public files in a *public-html* directory. This is a perfect place to put all your VRML files as well.

 TIP: It's not recommended to use textures that aren't in your directory, since distant collections of textures may move or be removed. Eventually, however, some official VRML texture libraries may be developed. These libraries may even be stored locally, on each user's machine. This would allow you to create worlds with lots of common textures without inflicting any extra download time on visitors.

To access your VRML worlds, people would need to load the WRL file the same way they'd load one of your HTML Web pages. For instance, suppose your main VRML world was called *home.wrl*. If your Web home page could normally be found at *http://found.cs.nyu.edu/dfox/*, then you would copy all the WRL files to the same directory as your other Web pages. A person would then access your VRML world called *home.wrl* by using the URL

`http://found.cs.nyu.edu/dfox/home.wrl`

Alternatively, you may want to tidy up by making a subdirectory within *public-html* called *vrml*, by switching to *public-html* and typing (assuming you're using a UNIX or DOS system)

`mkdir vrml`

Copy or upload the files to the *vrml* directory. Your world could then be visited by using a URL similar to

```
http://found.cs.nyu.edu/dfox/vrml/home.wrl
```

CGI SCRIPTS

If you created any cgi scripts to serve VRML dynamically, copy or upload these programs to the server's *cgi-src* directory. Usually this directory is protected, and you'll need to ask your system administrator or Webmaster to do this for you. Here you can compile the cgi scripts (using PERL, C, or whatever language you used to write them).

NOTE: Remember that all server scripts should be made executable by using the command

```
chmod +x filename
```

If you have access to the *cgi-bin* directory, be sure to do this. Otherwise, ask your Webmistress to take care of this for you. Chapter 22 has more information about creating and compiling scripts.

Test your program by typing its name. Ideally, legal VRML source code should appear on the screen. You, or someone with enough access, should then move the ready-to-run cgi scripts to your server's *cgi-bin* directory. This is where the server stores all executable scripts.

Anyone can now access your dynamic VRML world by using a URL similar to the following (assuming your program was named *world.cgi*):

```
http://found.cs.nyu.edu/cgi-bin/world.cgi
```

HOW TO PUT 'EM THERE

If you've already put HTML files on your Web server, then you're a full-fledged expert. Just copy all the WRLs and texture BMPs, GIFs, RGBs, or JPEGs to the same directory, by using the same method.

If you're moving files between computers for the first time, check out a good Web book such as the Waite Group's *HTML Web Publisher's Construction Kit*. You can also ask your system administrator or Webmistress for help. They may even be able to move your files for you. Or, try to use one of the following two methods.

FTP

The best way to get WRL files from your home computer to your Web server is to use FTP. There are many easy-to-use FTP clients such as Fetch and WS_FTP that can make uploading a snap. Just log into your Web site, switch to your *public-html* (or equivalent) directory, and then copy the necessary files.

You can also use the old command-line FTP method, which should be available on any Internet-connected machine. Simply move to where your VRML files are stored and type

```
ftp
```

to get started. Log into the remote Web server by typing its name at the prompt. Type in your name and a legal password. Switch to the directory in which you want to put all your VRML stuff, for instance:

```
cd public-html/vrml
```

You can now transfer the files using the Put command. For example, to send over the file *world.wrl*, type

```
put world.wrl
```

Repeat this for all the necessary files.

NOTE: When sending images, be sure to set the file transfer type to binary. To do this, type the command

```
binary
```

before transferring the files.

Uploading

If you created all the VRML files on your home computer and you don't own any FTP software, you can use a regular terminal program to upload the files to your Web site.

Dial up your Web server and log onto your Web site as usual, using your name and password. Switch to the directory where you want to place the new VRML files. To receive the files using the fast and popular Zmodem protocol, just type (at your Web server's UNIX prompt)

```
rz
```

You should now tell the terminal program on your home machine to start sending the files, one at a time, using Zmodem. This command can usually be found under either the File or the Transfer menu.

HOW TO SERVE 'EM UP

When your Web server serves up a file, it tells the browser what sort of file it is. Is it HTML hypertext? A GIF graphic? A PostScript file? Or something else entirely? Every major file format has a special code that helps the server and browser communicate. This is known as its *MIME type mapping*. Each MIME type takes the form *medium/type*.

Once the browser knows the MIME code, it knows what type of file it's dealing with and can display the file appropriately, load a helper application, or whatever. Each Web browser has a list of all legal MIME types, what extension they use, and what to do with such a file. For example, if you request an MPEG video file, the server notices that the file has an extension of .MPG and tells the browser that it's using the MIME type *video/mpeg*. The browser then immediately knows it needs to call up some MPEG video playing software, and you can download the movie and watch it.

If you want to make a VRML available to the world, you need to make sure Web browsers (and VRML browsers) can recognize it. All VRML WRL files use the following MIME type:

```
x-world/x-vrml
```

The *x-world* medium refers to any virtual reality or 3D graphic format. The *x-* prefix means that the MIME type isn't officially supported yet.

People who download your VRML file are responsible for setting their browser to understand the x-world/x-vrml MIME type and to take appropriate action, such as launching a VRML browser. Read Chapter 4 for more information about how to do this.

Your Web server may already be hip to VRML. Try to access your WRL document using a Web browser. If your VRML world appears, then everything is jake. If the file appears as plain text, then your server needs to be updated.

To serve up VRML files, simply be sure your Web server knows that all WRL files are indeed the *x-world/x-vrml* MIME type. It can then relay this information to any Web or VRML browser around the world. This usually requires you (or your system administrator or Webmistress) to add a line to one of your server's configuration files. This process differs slightly depending on what server you're using.

NCSA's httpd Server

NCSA's httpd is probably the world's most popular server. Telling it to serve up VRML files is a snap. Simply switch to the *conf* directory (which should be directly beneath the server's *httpd* directory) and edit the *srm.conf* file. Add the following line to the end:

```
AddType          x-world/x-vrml   wrl
```

Save the file. Your server is now smart enough to know that WRL files are VRML. If your VRML worlds don't appear correctly (they download as text), you may need to change the *mime.types* file. This file is also in httpd's *conf* directory. Add the following line:

```
x-world/x-vrml wrl
```

The CERN Server

Find the *http.conf* file, which should be in the basic *httpd* directory. Add this line to the file:

```
# add the VRML type.
AddType .wrl    x-world/x-vrml  8bit    1.0
```

The EMWACS NT Server

Run the main HTTP server software. Click the Control Panel. A list of MIME type mappings appears. Click on the New Mapping button, and set it up so that WRL files are VRML by typing a suffix of

```
.wrl
```

and a MIME-type of

```
x-world/x-vrml
```

The NETSITE Server

Open up the */var/mc-httpd/admin/config/mime.types* file, which should be part of your NetSite directory structure. Add the following line to the end of the file:

```
type=x-world/x-vrml              exts=wrl
```

Other Servers

Simply look for where the MIME-types are matched. Do a search of all the configuration files, if need be, for other popular MIME types which should already be set up. For instance, every Web server in the world should be configured with the *text/html* MIME type with a suffix of *html* or *htm*.

Study how these MIME types are laid out. Usually the MIME type will be listed, followed by the file's suffix. Copy a previous line from the MIME map, and add it to the end of the configuration file. Change the suffix to *wrl* and the type to *x-world/x-vrml*.

Serving over FTP

Some people serve their Web pages using an FTP server instead of an HTTP server. This is perfectly acceptable, though slower and somewhat less reliable. You can, indeed, copy your WRL files and textures to an FTP directory and make these publicly available. For example, if you put everything in the */smith/vrml/* directory of the *ftp.coocoo.com* server, folks could access your VRML world called *world.wrl* by using the URL

```
ftp://ftp.coocoo.com/smith/vrml/world.wrl
```

The file would be downloaded. Some browsers may be able to display the VRML world directly, but since FTP servers do not send along the MIME type, some browsers may become confused. The user would then need to use the VRML browser to open the file from his or her hard disk.

NOTE: You cannot easily include textures or inlined WRL objects if you only offer your file over FTP.

HOW TO MAKE 'EM SMALLER

Most VRML files are relatively short. After all, that's what VRML was designed for—a quick way to share 3D graphics. Still, some VRML pages use coordinate lists that are dozens of pages long. If your VRML page is longer than 200 or so kilobytes, you may want to think about compressing it.

The only accepted form of VRML compression is the Free Software Foundation's GNU *gzip* method. Many VRML browsers, such as WebFX and WebSpace, automatically support gzip and will uncompress any gzipped files. All gzipped VRML files should have the extension .WRL.GZ. For instance:

```
world.wrl.gz
```

There are many gzip programs available—for UNIX, Mac, and Windows—that will easily compress (and decompress) your WRL files. Table 23-1 lists some of this software and where to get your hands on it.

Table 23-1 Gzip compression software

Software	Location
Windows gzip	ftp://prep.ai.mit.edu/pub/gnu
Mac gzip	http://persephone.cps.unizar.es/General/gente/spd/gzip/gzip.html
Unix gzip	ftp://www-dsed.llnl.gov/files/programs/UNIX/gzip-1.2.4.tar
Gzip Test page	http://www-dsed.llnl.gov/documents/tests/gz.html

To compress a file, you usually need only type something as simple as

```
gzip world.wrl
```

This produces a file called *world.wrl.gz*. You can then make this compressed file available over the Web. It could be uncompressed by typing something similar to

```
gzip -d world.wrl.gz
```

SERVING COMPRESSED FILES

If you do decide to compress your VRML files, you need to be aware of a whole new set of server and browser options. Just like VRML itself, gzip has its own MIME type:

```
application/x-gzip
```

You will need to add this MIME type to the content-encoding section of your Web server. With NCSA's httpd server, for example, you would need to add the following line to the *srm.conf* file, so that browsers know that gz files are encoded as gzip:

```
AddEncoding      x-gzip  gz
```

If you are using the CERN server, edit the *httpd.conf* file, and add the line

```
AddEncoding      .gz
```

The good news is, the gzip encoding method is very popular. Most Web servers should already be set up appropriately. Check with your system administrator or Webmaster if you seem to be having any problems.

 TIP: Try not to compress any WRL files that you'll be inlining within another WRL file. This can confuse some browsers.

PUTTING 'EM THROUGH THE TEST

Always test your new VRML files by using several VRML browsers before announcing them to the world. Here are some tips:

- If you get a "file not found" error, then your files must be located in the wrong place. Either you typed the wrong URL, or your files aren't where you think they are. Be sure the URL you use to access your Web pages is the same (other than the final file name) as the URL you're using to access your VRML worlds.

NOTE: The Web is a busy place. Some URLs may be busy or temporarily unavailable. If you're pretty sure everything is in the right place, try accessing your VRML file several times before pulling out your hair.

- Be sure the files are lowercase. UNIX is case-sensitive, so *WORLD.WRL* is totally different from *world.wrl*. Although it's legal to use uppercase file names, it's not common, and will probably end up confusing you and the rest of the Internet.

- If the WRL source code appears listed out instead of the actual 3D graphics, then either your Web server or Web browser isn't set up properly to handle VRML files. See the "How to Serve 'Em Up" section, earlier in this chapter. Check your browser's local MIME-mapping type (this should be automatically built into any VRML browser), which is discussed in more detail in Chapter 4.

- If your world appears without textures, be sure the VRML browser you're using supports the type of texture maps you're using. Some browsers only work with GIF images, others require JPEGs, RGBs, or BMPs. Be sure the textures are in the same directory as the WRL file and are referenced correctly. The texture files, as well, must be both called and named in lowercase.

- Be patient. Sometimes the Net runs into snags. Things like textures, inlined objects, and other external VRML objects may load slowly, or piece by piece. Complicated VRML scenes can sometimes take just a minute or two to load but a long, long time to render. You might want to try cutting down on the number of texture or polygons within your VRML files. See the "How to Optimize 'Em" section, earlier in this chapter, for more ideas about speeding up your VRML.

WHERE TO ANNOUNCE 'EM

Once everything works, you should give yourself a hearty pat on the back (if your arm is flexible enough). You've come a long way, baby. Now that you've constructed new wonders on an empty lot of cyberspace, let the world know. Here are some places to announce your new world:

- The VRML repository—This site at *http://www.sdsc.edu/vrml/* lists applications sorted by topic, such as Astronomy, Chemistry, Architecture, Entertainment, Personal Home Pages, and so on. Send a message to one of the repository's curators at *ceubanks@sdsc.edu, moreland@sdsc.edu,* or *nadeau@sdsc.edu* (Charles Eubanks, John Moreland, and Dave Nadeau).

- The VRML mailing lists and newsgroups—Check out Appendix A for specific names and places.

- Web indexes—For example, try Yahoo (*http://www.yahoo.com/*) and Global Network Navigator (*http://www.gnn.com/*).

- Any other newsgroup, mailing list, or Web page that deals with the world you've created—For example, if you've constructed a perfect 3D model of the Gettysburg battle, be sure to notify all related resources such as the many Civil War home pages or one of the Civil War newsgroups. Most places will happily include a link to your site.

VRML is very, very young. If you've created something, chances are that people have never seen anything like it before. In no time at all, your site will become legendary. As VRML grows, your little world may become outdated, but will still remain a classic, like a rustic homesteader's cabin amid air-conditioned duplex condos.

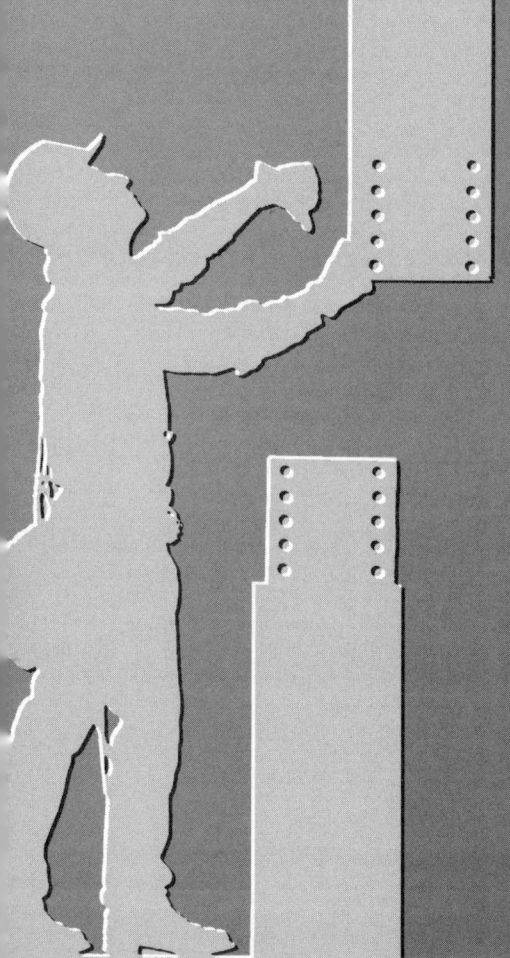

24

THE WORLD'S GEARS: CLIENT VRML

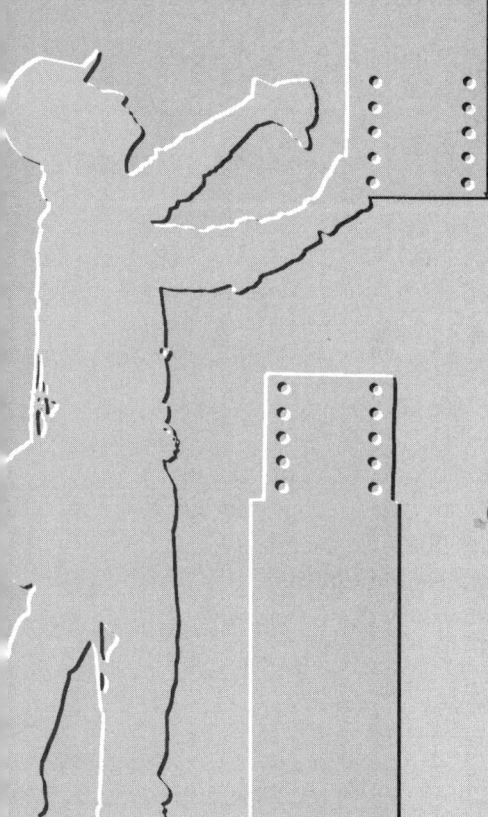

24

There are browsers and then there are browsers. Each VRML browser has its own advantages. WebSpace, for instance, can view most any VRML world, but moving around is usually quite slow. WorldView is good for fast, accurate renderings of simple worlds. WebFX is fast and full-featured, but it has problems with files that use up too much memory. And depending on the type of machine you have and the type of VRML files you want to use, you may want a stand-alone (WorldView), helper app (WebSpace), or embedded (WebFX) browser.

VRML is still young. So young, in fact, that you can write your very own VRML browser and—who knows—it might become the next Netscape. You may also be interested in using VRML as the basis for much more complex 3D software. For instance, Worlds, Inc. is planning on using VRML as the basis for a full 3D chat system.

NOTE: A good start might be to check out the source code for VRweb, which is available for UNIX and Windows. Check out Chapter 4 for information on where to obtain this.

PARSING THE VRML

The hardest part of writing a VRML browser is taking the VRML document with its tree of nodes and sub-nodes and sub-subnodes and slogging through it, figuring out what to draw and how to draw it using your particular rendering library.

Luckily, a robust set of routines known as QvLib was written by Paul Strauss and Gavin Bell of Silicon Graphics. VRML would still be on the ground if not for the easy availability of QvLib. QvLib is a full library of C++ classes to parse VRML files. It creates the parse tree, which you can then feed into your rendering library to draw your scenes. Versions of QvLib are available for most any type of computer. The enclosed CD includes many versions of QvLib, as listed in Table 24-1 (which also lists where you can find these libraries online, to help you find the latest versions or for more detailed information).

Table 24-1 Where to get QvLib

QvLib Version	Location
Original library (SGI)	http://vrml.wired.com/vrml.tech/qv.html
Windows 3.1	http://www.paperinc.com/qvlib.html
Windows 32-bit	http://www.omnicode.com/~omar/
Solaris	ftp://ftp.sdsc.edu/incoming
QvLib w/ OpenGL	http://www.ii.uib.no/~torgeir/
QvTraverse (for OpenGL)	http://vrml.wired.com/arch/1107.html
Reverse Parser	http://www.tenet.net/html/qvregen.html

YOUR OWN NODES?

Since VRML can be extended, you may want your browser to support its own special nodes. If so, you'll need to do quite a bit more programming work to parse your own nodes and use them. Some libraries, such as Open Inventor, are very open to this process. Other libraries are more rigid.

Be sure to design exactly what your VRML browser will do before you go about gathering the tools to build it.

RENDERING

The most important decision is what rendering library to use. A rendering library is what tells your computer how to actually draw 3D graphics to the screen. You can then issue simple commands like "Sphere" to draw a globe instead of defining each point yourself. Rendering libraries are all built differently. Some are fast but rigid, others are very customizable.

You can develop your own rendering library, but that would be a gargantuan job. Luckily there are a number of excellent existing libraries. You can license one of the following libraries as the basis of your VRML browser.

OpenGL

WebSpace and Open Inventor use the OpenGL library. It comes standard with Silicon Graphics workstations, and versions are available for many other platforms. OpenGL is a very full library of C routines. You can use these routines to create a *display list.* This gives you almost complete control over 3D graphics, allowing you to customize exactly how graphics will be handled. OpenGL is incredibly full-featured.

Reality Lab/Rendermorphics

Microsoft's Reality Lab and Rendermorphics is a set of routines that is slated to be included with future releases of Windows 95. WorldView uses this set of rendering routines. You can program your own *parse tree,* which is then converted to Reality Lab objects. All graphic manipulations are managed by Reality Lab. This makes graphic manipulations faster, but less flexible. You cannot customize Reality Lab quite as well as you can OpenGL.

Renderware

WebFX uses Criterion Software's RenderWare. This library is flexible and popular, very similar in operation to Reality Lab. It's also very portable. Versions are available for Windows, DOS, Mac, SunOS, and SGI.

Mesa

An alternative to OpenGL, developed by Brian Paul at the University of Wisconsin.

Amber

A basic collection of 3D graphic C++ classes by Dive Labs, based on Open GL. Amber is specially designed for creating networked virtual realities on various computer platforms. There is a shareware version of Amber for Windows NT, 3.1, and Win95, with a planned SGI version.

QuickDraw 3D

Apple Computer's QuickDraw 3D is a set of routines for rendering 3D graphics. The QuickDraw API has routines to help you create the graphics, shade them, light them, create the interface, and put it all together. There are versions of QuickDraw available for many different computer platforms.

OTHER RENDERING ISSUES

Will your browser have a default headlight (a light atop the camera that ensures that the scene is always lit), or will it leave unlit scenes in the dark? Will you render objects to their fullest and most realistic potential, or will you skimp a bit to speed things up? Should back faces of objects be rendered? And how will you handle texture maps? There are countless little issues to think about. "Smart" browsers should ideally be able to handle any type of scene, whether it's a huge city with millions of polygons or a simple cube. Most rendering libraries will have solutions to many of these problems. But how you actually implement everything depends on your ingenuity.

NAVIGATION

You now need to design the interface. Do you want a dashboard like WebSpace? Should the mouse be able to control everything like WebFX? Do you want lots of keyboard shortcuts? Maybe you want to support extended input devices like powergloves, VR goggles, or even full electronic body-suits.

When someone moves through a scene, will they have six degrees of freedom? Or should they be stuck on the ground? If they fly forward,will they keep moving once they let go of the controls, or will they stop dead in their tracks? Should there be collision detection? And how will hyperlinks work? Will the cursor change into a hand? Or maybe a link can be activated just by walking near enough to it.

Most VRML browsers provide two navigation modes: Examine and Walk. Some include a Fly or even an Authoring mode.

I'M READY!

Whether you're using VRML as the base for a new chat system, a worldwide video game, or just a better browser, good luck to you. VRML is just beginning its thing, however, so anything you do will be a worthwhile contribution.

The next chapter clues you in to what to expect with the next generation of VRML. It's already on the drawing boards, and within the year it'll be on the electronic bulletin boards. Be ready.

25

MAKING IT REALLY REAL: VRML 2.0

Nobody knows what the future will hold, but everybody's guessing. One of the likeliest candidates for VRML 2.0 is Silicon Graphics' *Moving Worlds* proposal. Over 50 major Internet companies are planning to support Moving Worlds, including the leading World Wide Web software company: Netscape. The VRML Architecture Group has recently halted work on VRML 1.1 in favor of releasing a power-packed VRML 2.0 proposal.

For VRML to be successful, it'll need to grow along with the latest hardware, video card, graphics cards, software, and telecommunications technology. Before discussing how VRML itself will change, let's try to predict how different the average desktop computer must be. Here are some possibilities in, say, a mere five years:

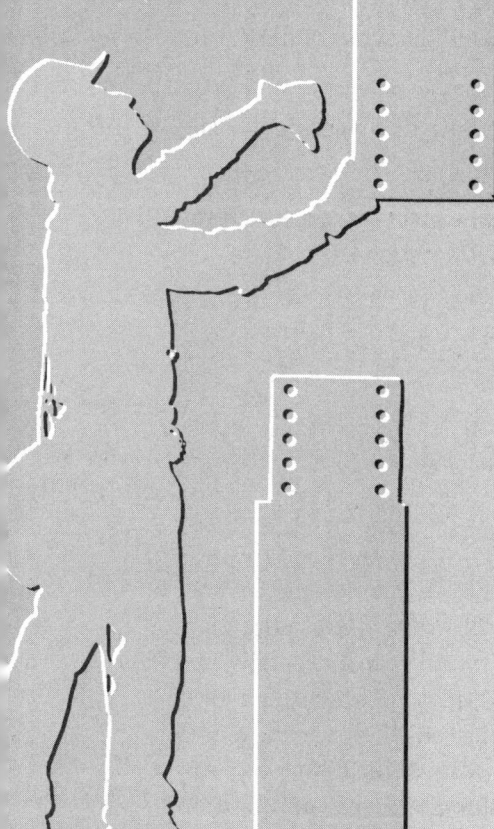

- The ubiquitous mouse will be replaced by speech and more intuitive input devices such as trackballs, powergloves, eye-trackers, and bats (flying mice).

- Everybody who's anybody will have VR goggles, visors, helmets, or other HMDs (head-mounted displays). Walking through a VR world while looking at a monitor is like being in a clumsy Sherman tank, looking at the scenery through a peephole. Exploring VR with an HMD puts the graphics all around you, as if you were a bird

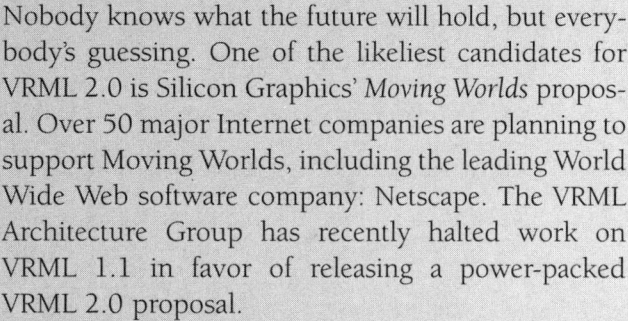

soaring through a canyon. When you turn your head to the right, you see exactly what's to the right of you. It's easy to suspend disbelief and actually feel as if you're in an alternate, albeit strange-looking, world.

- Parallel processors running at super speeds will be the norm.

- 3D graphic acceleration cards will be standard in every machine, allowing basic geometry to be drawn almost instantly.

- Texture-map cards and software will allow the realistic wrapping of images around shapes.

- Everyone who has a telephone or cable TV will be on the Internet.

How will the Internet itself be different?

- Links will be fiber optics, ISDN, cable, or satellite, which allow tons more data to flow at much faster rates.

- This increased bandwidth will be able to support real-time video, quality audio, and 3D graphics.

So how will VRML change to fit this idealized new online world? In the near future there will be important additions to VRML such as

- Three-dimensional sound

- A richer programming language

- Richer interaction

- Better graphics

- Behaviors

- Multiusers

As VRML becomes popular, some features will prove useful and some will be dropped. Is speed more important than photo-realistic detail? Is a rich set of canned animations enough, or does VRML need an entire scripting language? If several people can be in the same VRML space, how will they see each other? Countless people-hours of testing, design, programming, and brainstorming will go into VRML version 2. There's no question that VRML 2.0 will be a world of difference from VRML 1.0—quite literally.

This chapter is a technical overview of VRML 2.0. It is by no means complete. But it does provide a good idea of what to expect in the near future.

NOTE: For the latest information on Moving Worlds, check out the URL *http://webspace.sgi.com/moving-worlds/*

VRML 1.1

Many of the suggested VRML nodes are scattered throughout this book. Look for the special VRML 1.1 sidebars. What follows is a look at some additional VRML nodes, which will likely be found in VRML 1.1 and subsequent versions.

Sound

One of the most important addtions to VRML 1.1 will be the sense of sound. Sound nodes will likely include

- DirectedSound—This allows you to throw a 3D sound into your VRML scene that is coming from a certain direction. You can determine how far the sound's range extends and in what direction.

- PointSound—A sound playing from one particular spot in space.

Sound nodes can deal with the AU, AIFF, or WAV format of audio.

PointSound

The PointSound node lets you drop a sound into 3D space. Use the *name* field to specify the filename of the sound (use any valid URL). You may write a description of the sound in the *description* field which can be shown to people whose browsers don't support audio. Drop the sound into the scene by specifying a 3D point using the *location* field.

Set the *intensity* of the sound ranging from 0 (silence) to 1 (maximum volume). By default a sound is played only once. You can loop it by setting the *loop* field to true.

Imagine a sphere drawn around your sound, specified by the *minRadius* field. As long as a user is standing within this radius, the sound intensity will be at its normal maximum level. Imgaine a second, larger sphere, specified by *maxRadius*. As the user approaches the walls of this second sphere, the sound gets quieter and quieter. When the person passes the outer circle, the sound ceases to play altogether. This creates a highly realistic 3D effect.

NOTE: Live3D plans to allow for streaming sound, allowing for immediate audio whenever you approach a sound point.

So, to drop the repeated sound of a dog barking at (10,5,-5), with a maximum range of 15 meters, you would use:

```
PointSound {
name                    "woof.wav"
location                10 5 -5
description             "Dog Barking"
intensity               1
minRange                5
maxRange                15
loop                    TRUE
}
```

DirectedSound

Using the DirectedSound node you can create true 3D sounds in your virtual worlds. You can delineate exactly how the volume of a sound changes depending on where a virtual person is standing.

Use the *direction* field to specify a 3D vector pointing in the direction the sound is directed. Now imagine a cone emanating from where the sound is. Whenever somebody walks within this cone, the sound will be at its highest intensity. You can specify the angle of this cone's width by using the *minAngle* field. Imagine a second, larger cone, surrounding the first cone, specified using the *maxAngle* field. Once someone walks beyond the second cone, the sound will trail off to quiet. This allows you to create a precise region of sound. A number of other fields, similar to PointSound, let you set other particulars.

So to drop a 3D sound at (10,5,0), you might use a node similar to this:

```
DirectedSound {
        name                "speaker.wav"
        description         "Speaker Broadcast"
        intensity           1
        location            10 5 0
        direction           0 0 1
        minRange            5
        maxRange            20
        minAngle            0.785398    # SFFloat
        maxAngle            1.4
        loop                TRUE
}
```

CollideStyle

A new node called *CollideStyle* lets you define which objects you can walk through and which should not allow collision. Set the *collide* field to TRUE if you want to turn collision on, set it to FALSE if the object can be walked through. You could also define a proxy shape, to define the direction you should bounce if you try to run into an object.

Environment

The new Environment node lets you set properies that affect the entire scene, such as the ambient lighting and whether the scene should dissolve into fog at a certain distance.

Ambient lighting hits every object in the virtual world. You can set the *ambientColor* and *ambientIntensity.* You can also affect the world lighting by setting *attenuation,* a quadratic function—each value is one of the coefficients of the function. This function calculates the distance from the light source to each object. Whenever you have a point light or spot light in your scene, this attenuation function will define how far the light travels, and with what intensity.

You can also set three fog fields:

- [VRML] fogType—Choose from three styles of fog: HAZE (gradually gets thicker and thicker with distance), FOG (gets exponentially thicker and thicker), or SMOKE (thicker and thicker exponential square; pretty darn thick).

- [VRML] fogColor—What color should the haze take?

- [VRML] fogVisibility—Set this to 0 if you want the fog to begin where the camera's defined clipping plane ends. Or set it farther if you'd like.

The default values for the node are:

```
Environment {
          ambientIntensity   0.2
          ambientColor       1 1 1
          attenuation        0 0 1
          fogType            NONE
          fogColor           1 1 1
          fogVisibility      0
     }
```

HOW IT'LL LOOK

Many VRML 2.0 files will probably look similar to VRML 1.0 files. The most obvious difference will be the header. VRML 2.0 files will likely begin with the line

```
#VRML V2.0 utf8
```

The UTF8 standard allows international characters to be displayed in VRML, not just the Roman ASCII set.

The rest of the VRML file will be organized very cleanly, like a full-fledged computer program. The biggest change is that the scene can be looped, with nodes being called again and again. Also, nodes now not only accept input information, but they also can output information. For example, if a user walks into an object that has been surrounded by the new Collision node, a certain value will change. This information can then be used by the VRML program.

Node names will actually become less confusing than they currently are. For example, geometry may be simplified into a simple Shape node, and the material surrounding an object, including the texture map, may be simplified into an Appearance node.

SOUND

Ambient sound, 3D sound, and triggered sound will become an integral part of VRML. Ambient sound is a sort of soundtrack or background music that plays over a scene. This will make VRML journeys feel much more like cinema. Scary scenes can carry the *Jaws* theme, while romantic scenes can have lovely arias playing over them. This can also add realism. A virtual 42nd Street scene could be linked to an actual microphone hanging over Times Square, hearing every honk, curse, scream, wail, or wolf-whistle.

Three-dimensional sound will allow specific objects to emit specific sounds. Machinery can hum. A dog can bark. A fire can crackle. You'll hear the Doppler effect as a fire engine passes. As you walk closer to a waterfall, it'll get louder and louder until it drowns out the sound of the birds, wind, or any other sounds.

Triggered sound will play audio only at certain moments. For example, if a baseball breaks a window, you'll hear the tinkle of glass shattering.

RICHER LANGUAGE

One major proposal for VRML 2.0 is to make nodes more like full programming procedures. Each node will have its input values, its behaviors, its calculations, and its output values. This way, each node can affect any other node, depending on which variables they share.

A node may then know how to act based on the output of another node. By naming a node, recursive loops can even be created. The format might look something like this:

```
DEF Sample Node {
    input = USE Sample.output
    # Do the calculations here
    # Draw the results here
    output answer
}
```

The node named Sample will continue calling itself. These loops can make it easy to perform animations.

PROTOTYPING

Prototyping allows you to create macros or simple functions based on existing VRML nodes. This allows you to create a node that has some changeable fields. You can then call this prototype again using the USE command. This acts like a macro that you use repeatedly without having to rewrite tedious lines of VRML code.

For instance, you might create a prototype box using the PROTO command to create a prototype called *ColorBox*. This box would, by default, be blue. You could then easily create new boxes, having them be any color you wish. For example, a prototype might look like this:

```
PROTO ColorBox [ field MFColor theColor 0 0 1 ]
{
        Shape {
            # Default color is blue
            boxmaterial Material { diffuseColor IS theColor }
            Cube { ... }
        }
}
```

Now that the prototype is defined, you could easily create a red box by using

```
ColorBox{ theColor 1 0 0 }
```

A prototype's input could be any node property, or even an entire node itself. This would let you plug in entire objects. For instance, you could make a prototype that took an object, cast a spotlight on it, and put it on a beautiful pedestal. You could then throw a sphere, a cube, or a custom-created piece of sculpture into the prototype.

NOTE: Prototypes may also be defined and stored in external files. This will allow programmers to create vast libraries of prototypes while artists and world builders simply plug the values into the prototypes they wish to use.

RICHER INTERACTION

As of now, the only thing you can do while swimming in a VRML world is move around the camera or click on hyperlinked objects.

Fill-in Forms

VRML version 1.1 and higher will begin to include richer interactions. For instance, there'll be text fields, radio buttons, check boxes, and lists. These can have cool 3D widgets allowing you to turn dials, slide sliders, or push buttons. This way you can have entire 3D databases.

Collision Detection

The most basic type of interaction—in a real world or a virtual one—is one object colliding with another. Depending on how this occurs, the result might be a fight, an accident, or even a baby. Some objects disintegrate when they hit a wall, some bounce off, others break right on through. Detecting these collisions is a major task of tomorrow's VRML.

Currently, the WebFX browser allows you to turn basic collision detection on and off. This makes it impossible for you to sink beneath floors or walk through walls. This raises the question of what *you* look like. If you're a prize bull running through a crystal shop, you'll probably collide with lots of stuff. But if you're a butterfly flying through a forest, you'll seldom collide with anything. For collision to feel realistic, browsers will need to know what size and shape you are. As avatars become the norm (see the multiuser section, later in this chapter), you'll be able to be any size and shape you want.

A new group node called Collision will probably be added in VRML 2.0. If you don't want to be able to walk through an object, simply surround it with this node and set its value to TRUE. If you like, you can surround an entire world with the Collision node.

Future versions of VRML may include even richer collision detection. Detection will eventually be linked to behavior. For instance, when you collide with an object, it will perform some sort of animation. If you push a rubber ball, for instance, it might start bouncing all around the scene.

To make this even more realistic, *surrogate objects* may be created. This would be like an invisible aura or bubble around an object. This way, collisions could be handled not only when objects hit each other, but when they come close enough to each other.

Objects that can be collided with may have their own Separator node, as follows:

```
CDSeparator {
    Surrogate    Sphere {...}
    #The object goes here
    ...
}
```

This would create a surrogate sphere around the child object. If you bumped into the sphere, some sort of collision behavior would occur.

Staircases and Ramps

Eventually, it will be easy to drop staircases and ramps into your virtual worlds. This way, people wouldn't need to fly to jump to the second story of your house; they could simply walk up the rear staircase. Eventually VRML could even include elevators and escalators.

Viewpoints

Viewpoints will allow you to define special parts of your VRML scene that can be visited. It'll be easy for users to jump to various viewpoints at will. You may also have your VRML program jump to certain viewpoints depending on certain actions. Viewpoints may even be animated.

For example, you can attach a viewpoint to a moving object. This way you can hitch a ride on a moving plane, train, or automobile, for a guided tour around the VRML world. You can then hop off at any time to continue your adventures.

Grabbing the Browser by the Reins

You're used to having VRML browsers tell the 3D scene how to behave. But what about having the 3D scene tell the browser how to behave? VRML 2.0 will have an enhanced NavigationInfo node, allowing more ways for scene authors to customize the look and feel of the browser. You can set the following NavigationInfo fields:

- type—The type of navigation: "walk", "examiner", "fly", or "none"

- speed—The speed (in meters) that a user navigates through a world

- collisionRadius—How close can a user get before crashing into an object?

- headlight—Should there be a light atop the camera which always lights the scene?

A NavigationInfo node might look like:

```
NavigationInfo {
        type               "walk"
        speed              1.0
        collisionRadius    1.0
        headlight          TRUE
    }
```

You'll also be able to read in information about the VRML browser being used and then custom-tailor your scene to fit the strengths of that browser. For example, you can ask the browser for its name, its version number, its current speed settings, its frame rate, or the URL of the world currently being viewed.

Sensors

Sensors are nodes that can perform tasks whenever they're triggered. These would make a VRML scene entirely interactive. For example, walls would know when they were bumped, objects would know when they were touched, and pictures would even know when they were being looked at. A sensor will probably have several fields. An input field can turn the sensor on or off. As an output, the Sensor node can let you know whether it has been triggered. Sensors can also keep track of the last time you entered or exited the region.

There will probably be several types of *geometric sensors:*

- BoxProximitySensor—This creates a *hot region* based on an invisible cube somewhere in space. Whenever you enter this volume, the sensor will be triggered.

- PointProximitySensor—This create a hot region based on a sphere. Whenever you come within a given radius of one of these sensors, it will be triggered.

- TimeSensor—VRML 2.0 browsers will keep track of time. You can then trigger an animation or other event based on how much time has passed. The TimeSensor node reacts based on the current time. This is similar to setting an alarm clock in your VRML world. During a certain time interval, this sensor is triggered. This sensor can keep track of start times, stop times, and the number of cycles. The sensor can even be paused, similar to the button on a VCR.

- ClickSensor—Whenever you point or click on objects that are children of this sensor, the sensor is triggered. This is similar to the WWWAnchor node in VRML version 1. This sensor will keep track of more advanced information, however, such as what time the mouse button was clicked, when the mouse button was released, whether the mouse was dragged over the object, exactly where on the object the mouse was clicked, and where on the object's texture the mouse was clicked.

There will also be a number of *drag sensors*. These sensors indicate whether an object was dragged, how far, and in what direction. These sensors can be used to get information from sliders, levers, knobs, and other input devices:

- LineSensor—This sensor keeps track of the one-dimensional movement of the mouse, along the x axis. You can set a minPosition and maxPosition to limit the drag. This is useful for sliders.

- PlaneSensor—This keeps track of how an object is dragged in two dimensions, along the xy-plane.

- DiskSensor—This allows you to drag objects in a circle around the z axis. This is useful for knobs.

- CylinderSensor—This sensor tracks dragging motion as it rotates around a y axis. This allows you to twist a lever or turn a rolling pin.

- SphereSensor—This keeps track of the mouse as it drags an object freely around a certain point. This is similar to rolling a trackball.

BETTER GRAPHICS

The new VRML will include nodes that let you create fantastic 3D effects.

Fog

The proposed Fog node allows you to create a colorful smoky area where things seem to be getting denser and denser.

Textures

Textures will also be improved by leaps and bounds. Animated textures will be supported, allowing you to create running water, movie screens, sprite characters, or any other 2D sequence. You'll also be able to make transparent textures that can make a simple cube appear to be a complicated shape, such as a television set, without having to explicitly model it.

Background

The new Background mode will allow you to place a beautiful two-dimensional background behind your 3D world. This background will allow you to specify the color and size of the sky and of the ground. You can also determine where the horizon line should be placed. This creates the perfect backdrop on which to create houses, forests, space-stations, or any other real-world scene.

General Cylinders

The proposed GeneralCylinder node lets you create geometrically advanced shapes. You can create an object and then extrude it along a path, revolve various surfaces, bend it, twist it, or taper it. This gives you the ability to drop donuts, missiles, fantastic blobs, or other complex shapes into your world.

First create a 2D curve which acts as the cross-section using the *crossSection* field. The crossSection will be extruded along a second curve spelled out using the *profile* field. The new shape will then be stretched or bent so that it aligns perfectly with a third curve—in the *spine* field. That shape is then twisted around by a certain number of radians—expressed in the *angle* field— along a curve expressed in the *twist* field.

The default values for this node are

```
GeneralCylinder {
     crossSection [ -1 1, -1 -1, 1 -1, 1 1 ]
     profile [ 1 -1, 1 1 ]
     spine [ 0 0 0, 0 1 0 ]
     twist [ 0 -1, 0 1 ]
     parts    ALL
   }
```

BEHAVIOR

VRML will truly live once the worlds feel alive. Right now, you can model a busy city intersection. But it won't feel very real—no traffic lights will be blinking, no people will be moving, and, of course, no cars will be zipping by.

The question is how to make behaviors realistic, fast, rich, and yet easy to program. There are no easy answers. But the VRML community has put a lot of thought into this and come up with some possible solutions.

In general, behavior is defined as object movement. There are three ways objects can move:

■ Programmed movement—A simple computer algorithm can determine whether an object should move. This can be based on the position of other objects, the time of day, the position of avatars, or any other data.

■ Over time—This is a basic animation sequence.

■ User input—Anyone in your VRML world can cause objects to respond to their behavior. For instance, if you're visiting a world and you pick up a ball and then release it, it may bounce across the room.

One proposal is the object-oriented approach of naming each object in respect to its parent. Good naming would be the key to good behaviors. For instance, if you put a propeller on a plane, and put the plane in the sky, the propeller could be called by using *sky.plane.propeller*. You could then turn the propeller whenever the throttle was hit by using a command as simple as: *Rotate [sky.plane.propeller]*.

Client Pull and Server Push

HTML browsers like Netscape make good use of *client pull* and *server push*. The earliest VRML behaviors will be implemented by push and pull features.

Client pull allows a new Web page to be loaded every few seconds. This is useful for automatically updating stock prices, a screen capture from a video camera, or any other dynamic information. VRML can use the same client pull mechanism to update a scene based on the time of day, to animate simple characters (albeit choppily), or to bring up a slide-show of various scenes.

Server push is a similar notion. Instead of the browser continuing to ask for new information, it stays connected to the Web server. The server then pushes up the new information constantly. Server push doesn't update an entire Web page (or VRML scene), but only one object or property at a time. This is a much faster way to animate, move, or change the properties of 3D objects. Instead of loading a new frame of an elephant walking through a jungle, for example, you can just load the elephant's legs in a new position.

Camera Paths

Camera paths allow you to define a camera that can automatically move around the scene. This allows you to create simple animations.

You can take someone on a guided tour of your virtual world using camera paths. This can make objects appear to be rotating, moving closer, or changing shape.

Animation and Interpolation

The next step is to animate objects. For instance, you can create a car and have it continually move from point A to point B and back again. A visitor in your world might even be able to sit in the car and be taken on a ride.

Lights and colors can also be animated, making a scene quite dramatic. You could create a disco or even a strobe-light effect.

A special Interpolator node could perform an animation. Just tell an Interpolator what to look like at the beginning, what to look like at the end, and how long to take (the time you want each key frame to be calculated), and the node will perform the animation for you. For example, suppose you want a race car to drive from one side of the screen to another. Instead of listing every coordinate where you want the race car to be drawn, just create a loop and interpolate the position: move the race car a set distance each frame. Some Interpolator nodes may include

- OrientationInterpolator—This interpolates along a set of rotation values. It'll take a set of rotation vectors and fill in the intermediate values.

- ScalarInterpolator—Plug in a set of floating-point numbers, and this node will interpolate between them. This allows you to perform your own interpolation calculations.

- ColorInterpolator—This interpolates along a set of colors.

- PositionInterpolator—This uses linear interpolation to find the intermediate values based on a set of 3D points. This is an ideal way to move an object around the world.

- Coordinate3Interpolator—If you want to transform an object's actual shape, this node interpolates along a set of its vectors. This would let you perform some cool geometric morphing of an object's shape or size.

- NormalInterpolator—If you want to affect the way light hits an object, you can use this node to interpolate among the normal values.

Logic Scripts

A Script node would allow a full scripting language, which could change any part of the VRML scene based on any input. Script nodes may use a built-in language, or even a remote language such as C, PERL, or Java. This would make VRML itself into a full-fledged programming language.

Scripts can act as full-fledged functions. You can input a value, manipulate it, and spit out output. This can be useful for physics-based behaviors.

For instance, you can determine the acceleration of a ball based on how long it's been falling. You can easily animate an object by writing a simple loop, translating the object from one side of the world to another.

A different type of logic script could get its input from anywhere on the Internet. This would allow your VRML world to be fine-tuned based on stock prices, weather maps, time of day, and so on. Or it could get the input from other VRML scenes. This could let avatars communicate with each other, even if they're not in the same world.

Finally, Script nodes could dynamically change parts of the scene graph based on various inputs. By using prototyping along with a logic node, you can have scenes that create their own geometry based on any input.

For example, suppose you have a 3D quiz machine. It asks you the question, "Who is buried in Grant's Tomb?" The following simple script will accept a text string as its input. If you send the right answer ("Grant"), then it will return the value TRUE to indicate that you're a winner. Otherwise it'll return FALSE. Here's how the node might look:

```
DEF Trivia Script {
    # Input Variables
    eventIn SFString invalue
    # Output Variables
    eventOut SFBool outvalue
    # Which language is being used?
    scriptType "c"
    # The script
    behavior "if (invalue == "Grant") {
                outvalue = TRUE;
                else switch = FALSE;
        }"
}
```

Script nodes will be able to remember certain global variables, or states. This way, if you open a door and then turn around, the door will still be open. If you leave the room and return, the door should still be open.

NOTE: An Asynchronous Logic node may also be created. This node would wait for data from some external source. When it arrived, it would then process this input, perform any necessary tasks, and then unsynchronize from the remote source.

API

Eventually, a full VRML API (application programming interface) will be developed. This would allow people the framework to write little programs to perform specific animations or other behaviors. For example, you could create a walking man. Or a barking dog. Or a football that flies in a spiral when thrown. Or you could attach a lever to a slot machine so that when the lever was pulled, the pictures in the machine would be updated randomly.

It is unclear how detailed an API would need to be. Individual browsers might have APIs, which would allow you to program how the browser itself behaves. This would let you move the camera, change lighting, or change a scene's detail. A more complicated API would be a part of the VRML code. This would let you take any VRML object and rewrite it to act exactly the way you wanted.

VRML 2.0 will use a Code or Logic node to perform these tasks. You'll even be able to use code from anywhere on the Internet. This would allow you to borrow behaviors and use them quite painlessly in your own worlds. For an external API to work correctly, the VRML browser would need to work with the interpreter or compiler to load the program, compile it, and run it.

It might be more useful, however, to have VRML browsers include their own rich programming language. This way, everyone would be working with the same code, and any VRML document should work with any browser. You would then be able to write the code directly within your VRML documents.

Some possible API functions might be the following:

- AddNode—Insert a new node into the VRML scene.

- DeleteNode—Erase a node that is no longer needed.

- SetField—Change the value of a field.

- GetField—Get the value of a field.

- SendMessage—Send a command to the API.

- RegisterForEvent—Perform a task.

Once this code is processed, it would return some values. These values could then be studied and used to change the scene. For example, you could have some code that checks if a car has reached a dead end. If it has, you could send a command to a Trigger node that would randomly change the car's direction.

MULTIUSERS

VRML will come to fruition once it can be shared. The whole point of inter-networked worlds is to share them with other people. Cyberspace may look beautiful, but it'll be awfully lonely unless you can wander across other folk. VRML will be expanded to include the following:

- Avatars—Your avatar is your digital soul, the representation of yourself in a virtual world. What will virtual people look like? Ideally, you could look like anything you wanted…an animal, an alien, a chess piece, or just like yourself. Some 3D spaces, such as Worlds, Inc.'s WorldsChat (see Figure 25-1), give you a glimpse of what this might look like. Each person is represented by a sprite. As you walk around a person, you actually see the avatar from eight points of view. Future VRML scenes may include an Avatar node that allows you to define the size, shape, and look of your virtual self.

- Chatting—There will be a way for people to communicate with each other. This may be through a text-only chat window, or perhaps using microphones to actually speak to each other.

Figure 25-1
Chillin' out with other folks in a true 3D world. Behold Worlds Chat—a glimpse at the future of VRML

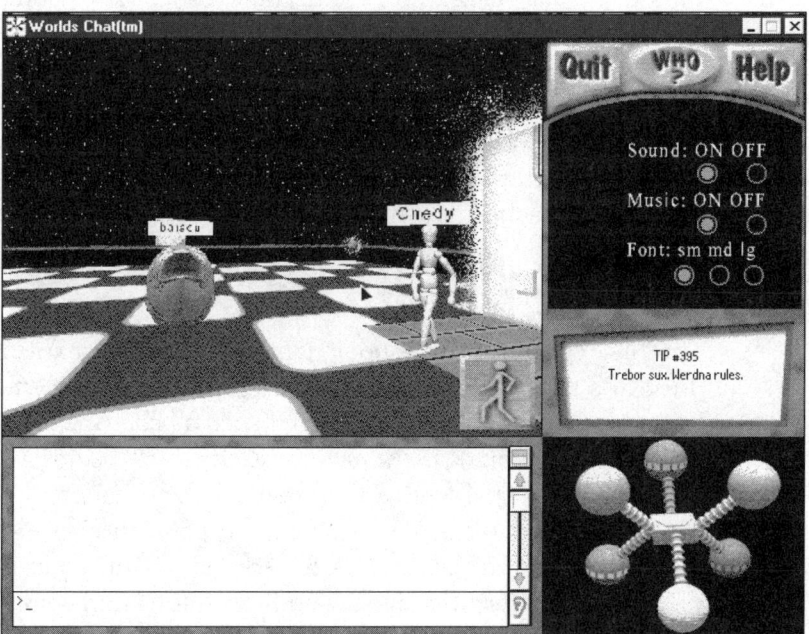

Trying to program realistic worlds is one challenge. Trying to program worlds that will act correctly while many people are inside them at once is nearly mission impossible. For example, what if two people pick up a baseball at the same time? Who gets it? Even if person A picked up the ball a fraction of a second before person B, there might be confusion. Because of a time delay, A may not see B pick up the baseball until seconds after it's been done. A and B might therefore pick up the same ball; that would be—in the real world—an impossibility. A could then throw the ball east, while B threw it west. Where would the ball land?

There are many technical and philosophical details to iron out.

It would be impossible for every user to know what's going on everywhere in cyberspace at the same time. That would be too much information to share. However, there are ways around this. You could share information only about important objects, or objects currently visible to you. Some objects might be able to be manipulated by several people at once; others may not. For example, if a room has a light-switch and you switch it off, it'll go dark only in *your* scene, but not in anybody else's.

Most likely, there will be a number of VRML servers. Each of these servers will allow a certain number of visitors to use them. A server would then relay information about its avatars to other nearby VRML servers; this process would continue until all the VRML servers had the same data. This way, any avatar across the world could conceivably bump into any other avatar.

VRML 2.0 will include multiuser capabilities that allow real people to wander in a fake world in believable ways. The idea is to share as much information as possible while wasting the least amount of time and resources. The only way to truly develop a good compromise is to experiment. Which is exactly why the next few months of VRML will be exciting ones.

WHAT WILL BE, WILL BE

The first chapter of this book talks about a girl named Jamie, walking through a virtual coffee house, meeting people, seeing amazing sights, and forgetting where she really is. Even if such a believable fantasy world is possible, many people fear the repercussions. Will people wind up spending more time in virtual worlds than they do their real one? Will VR become a 21st century opiate? Is there virtue in virtual reality?

Of course, the possibilities for entertainment, education, engineering, science, and even spirituality are endless. A fully immersive VRML will bring good along with the bad. But it cannot be denied that something truly amazing is on the horizon. Computers are on their way to becoming full-fledged windows to other parts of the world, other people, and to imaginary places that otherwise would not exist. VRML will be the blueprint for how this society of the mind is cobbled together.

Sure, today's VRML may be a far cry from a convincing escape from reality. But in this day and age, a far cry is just a whisper away.

APPENDIX A

SOFTWARE AND SOURCES

VRML is an ever-growing standard. If you've read the entire book thus far, you are ready to bring virtual reality to cyberspace. It's essential, however, that you keep up with the trends. As new versions of VRML come out, new browsers and authoring tools will appear. You can even help to define the latest standard of VRML with your own ideas and know-how.

VRML WEB PAGES

Most any VRML information you could ever want or need can be found at the VRML Repository at the San Diego Supercomputing Center (SDSC) at *http://sdsc.edu/vrml*.

The next stop in any VRML hunting you do should always be the official VRML home page at *vrml.wired.com*.

NCSA has a good VRML overview page at *www.ncsa.uiuc.edu/General/VRML /VRMLHome.html*.

Finally, you can grab the VRML FAQ (frequently asked questions) list at *http://www.virtpark.com/theme/vrmlfaq.html*.

VRML MAILING LISTS

VRML came to life on a mailing list discussion, and on a mailing list it will continue to grow. The foremost VRML list is *WIRED* magazine's unmoderated *www-vrml@wired.com*. All of the latest VRML announcements, ideas, specifications, and software are discussed on this list.

.000
.302

To subscribe to the list, send e-mail to *majordomo@wired.com*. The first line of your message should be

```
subscribe www-vrml your-email-address
```

Substitute your actual e-mail address for "your-email-address."

You can also subscribe to the digest-only version of the VRML list, *www-vrml-digest@wired.com*. This way, instead of getting dozens of letters a day, you'll just get one huge letter with the day's latest information. To subscribe, send a message to *majordomo@wired.com*. Type in the message digest:

```
subscribe www-vrml-digest
```

Most of the more technical VRML mailing lists are handled by the SDSC.

- *vrml-behaviors@sdsc.edu*—If you're interested in developing virtual behaviors, check out this group. It deals with putting animation, physics, scripting engines, and other interaction into VRML.

- *vrml-modeling@sdsc.edu*—If you want to discuss how to define 3D geometry using VRML, check out this list. You can talk about geometric primitives, implementation, performance, cross-platform converting, and other swarthy issues.

To subscribe or unsubscribe to an SDSC list, send e-mail to *listserv@sdsc.edu*. Leave the subject blank. To subscribe, type the following in the first line of the message:

```
add vrml-behaviors
```

Substitute "vrml-behaviors" with the name of the list you want to subscribe to.

To unsubscribe, type

`delete vrml-behaviors`

Substitute "vrml-behaviors" with the name of the list you want to subscribe to.

Another useful list is *worldbuilders@caligari.com*. You'll automatically be mailed information about Caligari Software's latest VRML tools. Send e-mail to *worldbuilders-request@caligari.com*. Leave the subject blank. To subscribe, simply type the following word as the first line of your message:

`subscribe`

If you're interested in the artistic or philosophic side of virtual reality, as opposed to the technical side, you might want to join *vworlds-list@netcom.com*: The Virtual Worlds Artist's mailing list. Send e-mail to *listserv@netcom.com*, and type the following as the first line of your message:

`subscribe vworlds-list`

You can also discuss virtual reality artwork in general at *vr-art@mailbase.ac.uk*. To subscribe, send mail to *mailbase@mailbase.ac.uk*, and type as your message body:

`join vr-art your name`

Substitute your first and last name for "your name."

VRML NEWS GROUPS

There are no official VRML newsgroups yet, though there is an alternate group called *alt.lang.vrml* for general VRML questions and discussions.

The following newsgroups have been proposed and may soon be created:

- *comp.vr*
- *comp.vr.vrml*
- *comp.vr.protocols*
- *comp.vr.design*

DISCUSSION GROUPS

You can sift through the *www-vrml* mailing list archives at *http://www.eit.com /www.lists/www.lists.2.html* or *http://vrml.wired.com/arch/*.

A hypermail version of the archive is also available at *http://kayak.npac.syr.edu:1963/*.

A VRML Threaded Discussion Group can be accessed at *http://www.webmaster.org/*.

You can discuss standards for an Interactive Web at *http://www.geom.umn.edu/hypernews/get/interactive/index.html*.

VRML BROWSERS

This section lists every known VRML browser and where to go to download it or find more information.

VRML Browser	Address
AmberGL VRML Browser v1.0 (Windows NT)	*http://www.divelabs.com/vrml.htm*
Caligari Fountain (Windows 3.1 and 95)	*http://www.caligari.com/ws/fount.html*
GLView (Windows NT, Windows 95)	*http://www.snafu.de/~hg/*
i3D (SGI)	*http://www.crs4.it/~3diadm/i3d-announce.html*
NAVFlyer (Windows 95, Windows NT)	*ftp://yoda.fdt.net/pub/users/m/micgreen*
Pueblo (Windows NT, Windows 3.1 and 95), a multimedia multiuser game system	*http://www.chaco.com/pueblo/*
VR Scout (Windows NT, Windows 3.1 and 95)	*http://www.chaco.com/vrscout/*
Vrweb (Windows NT, Windows 95 and 3.1, SunOS, Solaris, Irix, IBM AIX, DEC Alpha, DEC Ultrix, LINUX, Macintosh Power PC, Mac 68000)	*http://www.iicm.tu-graz.ac.at/Cvrweb*
WebFX (Windows 3.1 and 95, Windows NT; Macintosh version soon to be released)	*http://www.paperinc.com/webfx.html*
WebOOGL (SGI, Sun)	*http://www.geom.umn.edu/software/weboogl/*
WebSpace (version available for SGI, Windows NT, Windows 95, Sun Solaris ZX/TZX, IBM AIX; versions planned soon for Windows 3.1, Mac Power PC, Digital UNIX, HP/UX)	*http://www.sgi.com/Products/WebFORCE/WebSpace/*
WebView (SGI/UNIX)	*http://www.sdsc.edu/EnablingTech/Visualization/vrml/webview.html*
Whurlwind (any Macintosh with QD3D) A QuickDraw3D VRML browser	*http://www.info.apple.com/qd3d/Viewer.HTML*
WorldView (Windows 3.1 and 95, Windows NT, Mac 68000, Mac Power PC)	*http://www.webmaster.com/vrml*

VRML MODELERS

More and more browsers can now export and import VRML scenes and objects. The following table includes some of the foremost VRML authoring tools.

VRML Browser	Address
ClayWorks (PC)	http://cent1.lancs.ac.uk/tim/clay.html
Ez3d Modeler (SGI)	http://www.webcom.com/~radiance/
Fountain (Windows)	http://www.caligari.com/ws/fount.html
G Web (Windows, SGI, Sparc)	http://www.demon.co.uk/presence/gweb.html
Home Space Builder (Windows)	http://www.us.paragraph.com/whatsnew/homespce.htm
Medit (IRIX)	ftp://sgigate.sgi.com/pub/Performer/RealityCentre/Medit_dist
Spinner	http://www.3dweb.com/
STRATA StudioPro	http://www.strata3d.com:80/tools/studiopro/index.html
TriSpectives 1.0 (Windows 95)	http://www.eye.com/
WebSpace Author (SGI)	http://webspace.sgi.com/WebSpaceAuthor/index.html
World Builder	http://ruok.caligari.com:80/lvltwo/2product.html

OTHER BOOKS

If you want to learn more about the mother of VRML—Open Inventor—check out the following:

The Inventor Mentor: Programming Object-Oriented 3D Graphics with Open Inventor, Release 2, by Josie Wernecke (Addison-Wesley Publishing Company, 1994).

VRML 1.1 SPECIFICATIONS

The following information is a verbatim draft of the agreed specifications, dated December 16, 1995, for the Virtual Reality Modeling Language. You can fine the latest information at: *http://vag.vrml.org/vrml-1.1.html*

THE VIRTUAL REALITY MODELING LANGUAGE

Version 1.1 Draft

VAG: This document is a draft. Don't rely on any part of it remaining stable. The VAG now follows the IETF guideline of "Rough Consensus and Working Code", this specification will only be officially finalized when two independant implementations on different platforms are available.

16-Dec-95

Gavin Bell, Silicon Graphics, Inc.
Anthony Parisi, Intervista Software
Mark Pesce, VRML List Moderator
Mitra, WorldMaker
YON - Jan C. Hardenbergh, OKI
Tom Meyer, Brown University
Bill Martin, Headspace
Rikk Carey, SGI
Jon Marbry, Microsoft
Brian Blau, Intervista Software

REVISION HISTORY

- 1.0 first Draft - November 2, 1994
- 1.0 second Draft - May 8, 1995
- First 1.0 spec- May 26, 1995
- 1.0 clarifications - Oct 23, 1995
- 1.1 first draft - Oct 24, 1995
- 1.1 second draft - Dec 12, 1995

TABLE OF CONTENTS

- Introduction

  VRML Mission Statement

  History

  Version 1.0 Requirements

  What's New in Version 1.1

- Language Specification

  Language Basics

  Coordinate System

  Fields

Nodes

Instancing

Prototyping

Extensibility

An Example

VR Browser Considerations
ML

File Extensions

MIME Types

Acknowledgements

References

INTRODUCTION

The Virtual Reality Modeling Language (VRML) is a language for describing multi-participant interactive simulations — virtual worlds networked via the global Internet and hyperlinked with the World Wide Web. All aspects of virtual world display, interaction and internetworking can be specified using VRML. It is the intention of its designers that VRML become the standard language for interactive simulation within the World Wide Web.

The first version of VRML allows for the creation of virtual worlds with limited interactive behavior. These worlds can contain objects which have hyperlinks to other worlds, HTML documents or other valid MIME types. When the user selects an object with a hyperlink, the appropriate MIME viewer is launched. When the user selects a link to a VRML document from within a correctly configured WWW browser, a VRML viewer is launched. Thus VRML viewers are the perfect companion applications to standard WWW browsers for navigating and visualizing the Web. Future versions of VRML will allow for richer behaviors, including animations, motion physics and real-time multi-user interaction.

This document specifies the features and syntax of Version 1.1 of VRML.

VRML Mission Statement

The history of the development of the Internet has had three distinct phases; first, the development of the TCP/IP infrastructure which allowed documents and data to be stored in a proximally independent way; that is, Internet provided a layer of abstraction between data sets and the hosts which manipulated them. While this abstraction was useful, it was also confusing; without any clear sense of "what went where", access to Internet was restricted to the class of sysops/net surfers who could maintain internal cognitive maps of the data space.

Next, Tim Berners-Lee's work at CERN, where he developed the hypermedia system known as World Wide Web, added another layer of abstraction to the existing structure. This abstraction provided an "addressing" scheme, a unique identifier (the Universal Resource Locator), which could tell anyone "where to go and how to get there" for any piece of data within the Web. While useful, it lacked dimensionality; there's no there there within the web, and the only type of navigation permissible (other than surfing) is by direct reference. In other words, I can only tell you how to get to the VRML Forum home page by saying, "http://www.wired.com/", which is not human-centered data. In fact, I need to make an effort to remember it at all. So, while the World Wide Web provides a retrieval mechanism to complement the existing storage mechanism, it leaves a lot to be desired, particularly for human beings.

Finally, we move to "perceptualized" Internetworks, where the data has been sensualized, that is, rendered sensually. If something is represented sensually, it is possible to make sense of it. VRML is an attempt (how successful, only time and effort will tell) to place humans at the center of the Internet, ordering its universe to our whims. In order to do that, the most important single element is a standard that defines the particularities of perception. Virtual Reality Modeling Language is that standard, designed to be a universal description language for multi-participant simulations.

These three phases, storage, retrieval, and perceptualization are analogous to the human process of consciousness, as expressed in terms of semantics and cognitive science. Events occur and are recorded (memory); inferences are drawn from memory (associations), and from sets of related events, maps of the universe are created (cognitive perception). What is important to remember is that the map is not the territory, and we should avoid becoming trapped in any single representation or world-view. Although we need to design to avoid disorientation, we should always push the envelope in the kinds of experience we can bring into manifestation!

This document is the living proof of the success of a process that was committed to being open and flexible, responsive to the needs of a growing Web community. Rather than re-invent the wheel, we have adapted an existing specification (Open Inventor) as the basis from which our own work can grow, saving years of design work and perhaps many mistakes. Now our real work can begin; that of rendering our noospheric space.

History

VRML was conceived in the spring of 1994 at the first annual World Wide Web Conference in Geneva, Switzerland. Tim Berners-Lee and Dave Raggett organized a Birds-of-a-Feather (BOF) session to discuss Virtual Reality interfaces to the World Wide Web. Several BOF attendees described projects already underway to build three dimensional graphical visualization tools which interoperate with the Web. Attendees agreed on the need for these tools to have a common language for specifying 3D scene description and WWW hyperlinks — an analog of HTML for virtual reality. The term Virtual Reality Markup Language (VRML) was coined, and the group resolved to begin specification work after the conference. The word 'Markup' was later changed to 'Modeling' to reflect the graphical nature of VRML.

Shortly after the Geneva BOF session, the www-vrml mailing list was created to discuss the development of a specification for the first version of VRML. The response to the list invitation was overwhelming: within a week, there were over a thousand members. After an initial settling-in period, list moderator Mark Pesce of Labyrinth Group announced his intention to have a draft version of the specification ready by the WWW Fall 1994 conference, a mere five months away. There was general agreement on the list that, while this schedule was aggressive, it was achievable provided that the requirements for the first version were not too ambitious and that VRML could be adapted from an existing solution. The list quickly agreed upon a set of requirements for the first version, and began a search for technologies which could be adapted to fit the needs of VRML.

The search for existing technologies turned up a several worthwhile candidates. After much deliberation the list came to a consensus: the Open Inventor ASCII File Format from Silicon Graphics, Inc. The Inventor File Format supports complete descriptions of 3D scenes with polygonally rendered objects, lighting, materials, ambient properties and realism effects. A subset of the Inventor File Format, with extensions to support networking, forms the basis of VRML. Gavin Bell of Silicon Graphics has adapted the Inventor File Format for VRML, with design input from the mailing list. SGI has publicly stated that the file format is available for use in the open market, and have contributed a file format parser into the public domain to bootstrap VRML viewer development.

TO DO: Gavin - History of clarifications etc to be added

Version 1.0 Requirements

VRML 1.0 is designed to meet the following requirements:

- Platform independence

- Extensibility

- Ability to work well over low-bandwidth connections

As with HTML, the above are absolute requirements for a network language standard; they should need little explanation here.

Early on the designers decided that VRML would not be an extension to HTML. HTML is designed for text, not graphics. Also, VRML requires even more finely tuned network optimizations than HTML; it is expected that a typical VRML scene will be composed of many more "inline" objects and served up by many more servers than a typical HTML document. Moreover, HTML is an accepted standard, with existing implementations that depend on it. To impede the HTML design process with VRML issues and constrain the VRML design process with HTML compatibility concerns would be to do both languages a disservice. As a network language, VRML will succeed or fail independent of HTML.

It was also decided that, except for the hyperlinking feature, the first version of VRML would not support interactive behaviors. This was a practical decision intended to streamline design and implementation. Design of a language for describing interactive behaviors is a big job, especially when the language needs to express behaviors of objects communicating on a network. Such languages do exist; if we had chosen one of them, we would have risked getting into a "language war." People don't get excited about the syntax of a language for describing polygonal objects; people get very excited about the syntax of real languages for writing programs. Religious wars can extend the design process by months or years. In addition, networked inter-object operation requires brokering services such as those provided by CORBA or OLE, services which don't exist yet within WWW; we would have had to invent them. Finally, by keeping behaviors out of Version 1, we have made it a much smaller task to implement a viewer. We acknowledge that support for arbitrary interactive behaviors is critical to the long-term success of VRML; they will be included in Version 2.

What's New in Version 1.1

Changes from 1.0 to 1.1:

- Near and Far clippng planes—PerspectiveCamera and OrthographicCamera now contain nearDistance and farDistance clipping plane specifications.

- ShapeHints—field defaults have changed

- input fields—Several 1.0 nodes have input fields. These fields are dynamic fields that can be modified by other nodes.

New objects in 1.1:

- Background—describes scene background

- Cameras—now have nearDistance and farDistance fields

- CollideStyle—describes collision information

- DirectedSound and PointSound—spatial sound objects

- ElevationGrid—describes a model as heights over a regular grid

- Environment—is from Inventor to do fog and ambient lighting

- GeneralCylinder—is a new node for describing numerous families of shapes

- NavigationInfo—contains view type, speed, and headlight state

- VolumeProximitySensor and PointProximitySensor—Sensors that detect viewer proximity

- WorldInfo—contains title and other document information

New features in VRML 1.1:

- Prototyping—new node types can be defined in the VRML file

LANGUAGE SPECIFICATION

The language specification is divided into the following sections:

- Language Basics

- Coordinate System

- Fields

▣ Nodes

▣ Instancing

▣ Extensibility

▣ An Example

Language Basics

At the highest level of abstraction, VRML is just a way for objects to read and write themselves. Theoretically, the objects can contain anything—3D geometry, MIDI data, JPEG images, anything. VRML defines a set of objects useful for doing 3D graphics. These objects are called Nodes.

Nodes are arranged in hierarchical structures called scene graphs. Scene graphs are more than just a collection of nodes; the scene graph defines an ordering for the nodes. The scene graph has a notion of state—nodes earlier in the scene can affect nodes that appear later in the scene. For example, a Rotation or Material node will affect the nodes after it in the scene. A mechanism is defined to limit the effects of properties (separator nodes), allowing parts of the scene graph to be functionally isolated from other parts.

Applications that interpret VRML files need not maintain the scene graph structure internally; the scene graph is merely a convenient way of describing objects.

A node has the following characteristics:

▣ What kind of object it is. A node might be a cube, a sphere, a texture map, a transformation, etc.

▣ The parameters that distinguish this node from other nodes of the same type. For example, each Sphere node might have a different radius, and different texture maps nodes will certainly contain different images to use as the texture maps. These parameters are called Fields. A node can have 0 or more fields.

▣ A name to identify this node. Being able to name nodes and refer to them elsewhere is very powerful; it allows a scene's author to give hints to applications using the scene about what is in the scene, and creates possibilities for very powerful scripting extensions. Nodes do not have to be named, but if they are named, they can have only one name.

However, names do not have to be unique— several different nodes may be given the same name.

▣ Child nodes. Object hierarchy is implemented by allowing some types of nodes to contain other nodes. Parent nodes traverse their children in order during rendering. Nodes that may have children are referred to as group nodes. Group nodes can have zero or more children.

The syntax chosen to represent these pieces of information is straightforward:

```
DEF objectname objecttype { fields children }
```

Only the object type and curly braces are required; nodes may or may not have a name, fields, and children.

Node names must not begin with a digit, and must not contain spaces or control characters, single or double quote characters, backslashes, curly braces, the plus character or the period character.

For example, this file contains a simple scene defining a view of a red cone and a blue sphere, lit by a directional light:

```
#VRML V1.1 utf8
Separator {
    DirectionalLight {
        direction 0 0 -1  # Light shining from viewer into scene
    }
    PerspectiveCamera {
        position     -8.6 2.1 5.6
        orientation -0.1352 -0.9831 -0.1233  1.1417
        focalDistance         10.84
    }
    Separator {    # The red sphere
        Material {
            diffuseColor 1 0 0   # Red
        }
        Translation { translation 3 0 1 }
        Sphere { radius 2.3 }
    }
    Separator {  # The blue cube
        Material {
            diffuseColor 0 0 1  # Blue
        }
        Transform {
            translation -2.4 .2 1
            rotation 0 1 1  .9
        }
        Cube {}
    }
}
```

General Syntax

For easy identification of VRML files, every VRML 1.1 file must begin with the characters:

#VRML V1.1 utf8

The identifier utf8 allows for international characters to by displayed in VRML using the UTF-8 encoding of the ISO 10646 standard. Unicode is an alternate encoding of ISO 10646. UTF-8 is explained under the Text node. Any characters after these on the same line are ignored. The line is terminated by either the ASCII newline or carriage-return characters.

The '#' character begins a comment; all characters until the next newline or carriage return are ignored. The only exception to this is within double-quoted SFString and MFString fields, where the '#' character will be part of the string.

Note: Comments and whitespace may not be preserved; in particular, a VRML document server may strip comments and extraneous whitespace from a VRML file before transmitting it. Info nodes should be used for persistent information like copyrights or author information. Info nodes could also be used for object descriptions. New uses of named info nodes for conveying syntactically meaningfull information are deprecated. Use the extension nodes mechanism instead.

Blanks, tabs, newlines and carriage returns are whitespace characters wherever they appear outside of string fields. One or more whitespace characters separates the syntactical entities in VRML files, where necessary.

After the required header, a VRML file contains exactly one VRML node. That node may of course be a group node, containing any number of other nodes.

Field names start with lower case letters, Node types start with upper case. The remainder of the characters may be any printable ascii (21H-7EH) except curly braces {}, square brackets [], single ' or double " quotes, sharp #, backslash \\ plus +, period . or ampersand &.

Node names must not begin with a digit but they may begin and contain any UTF8 character except those below 21H (control characters and white space), and the characters {} [] ' " # \\ + . and &.

VRML is case-sensitive; 'Sphere' is different from 'sphere'.

Coordinate System

VRML uses a cartesian, right-handed, 3-dimensional coordinate system. By default, objects are projected onto a 2-dimensional device by projecting them in the direction of the positive Z axis, with the positive X axis to the right and the positive Y axis up. A camera or modeling transformation may be used to alter this default projection.

The standard unit for lengths and distances specified is meters. The standard unit for angles is radians.

VRML scenes may contain an arbitrary number of local (or "object-space") coordinate systems, defined by modelling transformations using Translate, Rotate, Scale, Transform, and MatrixTransform nodes. Given a vertex V and a series of transformations such as:

```
Translation { translation T }
Rotation { rotation R }
Scale { scaleFactor S }
Coordinate3 { point V } PointSet { numPoints 1 }
```

the vertex is transformed into world-space to get V' by applying the transformations in the following order:

```
V' = T R S
V (if you think of vertices as column vectors) OR
V' =
V S R T (if you think of vertices as row vectors)
```

Conceptually, VRML also has a "world" coordinate system as well as a viewing or "Camera" coordinate system. The various local coordinate transformations map objects into the world coordinate system. This is where the scene is assembled. The scene is then viewed through a camera, introducing another conceptual coordinate system. Nothing in VRML is specified using these coordinates. They are rarely found in optimized implementations where all of the steps are concatenated. However, having a clear model of the object, world and camera spaces will help authors.

Fields

There are two general classes of fields; fields that contain a single value (where a value may be a single number, a vector, or even an image), and fields that contain multiple values. Single-valued fields all have names that begin with "SF", multiple-valued fields have names that begin with "MF". Each field type defines the format for the values it writes.

Multiple-valued fields are written as a series of values separated by commas, all enclosed in square brackets. If the field has zero values then only the square brackets ("[]") are written. The last may optionally be followed by a comma. If the field has exactly one value, the brackets may be omitted and just the value written. For example, all of the following are valid for a multiple-valued field containing the single integer value 1:

```
1
[1,]
[ 1 ]
```
TODO: SYNTAX/RULES FOR INPUTS/OUTPUTS NEED TO BE FLESHED OUT HERE!

SFBitMask

A single-value field that contains a mask of bit flags. Nodes that use this field class define mnemonic names for the bit flags. SFBitMasks are written to file as one or more mnemonic enumerated type names, in this format:

```
( flag1 | flag2 | ... )
```

If only one flag is used in a mask, the parentheses are optional. These names differ among uses of this field in various node classes.

SFBool

A field containing a single boolean (true or false) value. SFBools may be written as 0 (representing FALSE), 1, TRUE, or FALSE.

SFColor/MFColor

Fields containing one (SFColor) or zero or more (MFColor) RGB colors. Each color is written to file as an RGB triple of floating point numbers in ANSI C floating point format, in the range 0.0 to 1.0. For example:

```
[ 1.0 0. 0.0, 0 1 0, 0 0 1 ]
```

is an MFColor field containing the three colors red, green, and blue.

SFEnum

A single-value field that contains an enumerated type value. Nodes that use this field class define mnemonic names for the values. SFEnums are written to file as a mnemonic enumerated type name. The name differs among uses of this field in various node classes.

SFFloat/MFFloat

Fields that contain one (SFFloat) or zero or more (MFFloat) single-precision floating point number. SFFloats are written to file in ANSI C floating point format. For example:

```
[ 3.1415926, 12.5e-3, .0001 ]
```

is an MFFloat field containing three values.

SFImage

A field that contain an uncompressed 2-dimensional color or greyscale image.

SFImages are written to file as three integers representing the width, height and number of components in the image, followed by width*height hexadecimal values representing the pixels in the image, separated by white-space. A one-component image will have one-byte hexadecimal values representing the intensity of the image. For example, 0xFF is full intensity, 0x00 is no intensity. A two-component image puts the intensity in the first (high) byte and the transparency in the second (low) byte. Pixels in a three-component image have the red component in the first (high) byte, followed by the green and blue components (so 0xFF0000 is red). Four-component images put the transparency byte after red/green/blue (so 0x0000FF80 is semi-transparent blue). A value of 1.0 is completely transparent, 0.0 is completely opaque. Note: each pixel is actually read as a single unsigned number, so a 3-component pixel with value "0x0000FF" can also be written as "0xFF" or "255" (decimal). Pixels are specified from left to right, bottom to top. The first hexadecimal value is the lower left pixel of the image, and the last value is the upper right pixel.

For example,

```
1 2 1 0xFF 0x00
```

is a 1 pixel wide by 2 pixel high greyscale image, with the bottom pixel white and the top pixel black. And:

```
2 4 3 0xFF0000 0xFF00 0 0 0 0 0xFFFFFF 0xFFFF00
```

is a 2 pixel wide by 4 pixel high RGB image, with the bottom left pixel red, the bottom right pixel green, the two middle rows of pixels black, the top left pixel white, and the top right pixel yellow.

SFLong/MFLong

Fields containing one (SFLong) or zero or more (MFLong) 32-bit integers. SFLongs are written to file as an integer in decimal, hexadecimal (beginning with '0x') or octal (beginning with '0') format. For example:

```
[ 17, -0xE20, -518820 ]
```

is an MFLong field containing three values.

SFMatrix

A field containing a transformation matrix. SFMatrices are written to file in row-major order as 16 floating point numbers separated by whitespace. For example, a matrix expressing a translation of 7.3 units along the X axis is written as:

```
1 0 0 0  0 1 0 0  0 0 1 0  7.3 0 0 1
```

NEW in I.I- SFNode/MFNode

... syntax is just node syntax, DEF/USE allowed, etc...

SFRotation

A field containing an arbitrary rotation. SFRotations are written to file as four floating point values separated by whitespace. The 4 values represent an axis of rotation followed by the amount of right-handed rotation about that axis, in radians. For example, a 180 degree rotation about the Y axis is:

```
0  1  0   3.14159265
```

SFString/MFString

Fields containing one (SFString) or zero or more (MFString) UTF-8 string (sequence of characters). Strings are written to file as a sequence of UTF-8 octets in double quotes (optional if the string doesn't contain any whitespace). Any characters (including newlines and '#') may appear within the quotes. To include a double quote character within the string, precede it with a backslash. For example:

```
Testing
"One, Two, Three"
"He said, \"Immel did it!\""
```

are all valid strings.

SFVec2f/MFVec2f

Field containing a two-dimensional vector. SFVec2fs are written to file as a pair of floating point values separated by whitespace.

SFVec3f/MFVec3f

Field containing a three-dimensional vector. SFVec3fs are written to file as three floating point values separated by whitespace.

NEW in 1.1 - SFTime

Field containing a single time value. Each time value is written to file as a double-precision floating point number in ANSI C floating point format. A absolute SFTime is the number of seconds since Jan 1, 1970 GM

NEW in 1.1 - input fields

TO DO: TBD

Nodes

VRML defines several different classes of nodes. Most of the nodes can be classified into one of three categories; shape, property or group. Shape nodes define the geometry in the scene. Conceptually, they are the only nodes that draw anything. Property nodes affect the way shapes are drawn. And grouping nodes gather other nodes together, allowing collections of nodes to be treated as a single object. Some group nodes also control whether or not their children are drawn.

Nodes may contain zero or more fields. Each node type defines the type, name, and default value for each of its fields. The default value for the field is used if a value for the field is not specified in the VRML file. The order in which the fields of a node are read is not important; for example, "Cube { width 2 height 4 depth 6 }" and "Cube { height 4 depth 6 width 2 }" are equivalent.

Here are the nodes grouped by type. The first group are the shape nodes. These specify geometry:

Cone, Cube, Cylinder, ElevationGrid, IndexedFaceSet, IndexedLineSet, PointSet, Text, Sphere

The second group are the properties. These can be further grouped into properties of the geometry and its appearance, matrix or transform properties, and cameras and lights: CollideStyle, Coordinate3, DocumentInfo, FontStyle, Info, LOD, Material, MaterialBinding, NavigationInfo, Normal, NormalBinding, TextLanguage, Texture2, Texture2Transform, TextureCoordinate2, ShapeHints

MatrixTransform, Rotation, Scale, Transform, Translation

DirectionalLight, PointLight, SpotLight

These are the group nodes:

Separator, Switch, WWWAnchor

Finally, the camera, WWWInline and Background nodes do not fit neatly into any category:

OrthographicCamera, PerspectiveCamera

Background, WWWInline

Cone

This node represents a simple cone whose central axis is aligned with the y-axis. By default, the cone is centered at (0,0,0) and has a size of -1 to +1 in all three directions. The cone has a radius of 1 at the bottom and a height of 2, with its apex at 1 and its bottom at -1. The cone has two parts: the sides and the bottom.

The cone is transformed by the current cumulative transformation and is drawn with the current texture and material.

If the current material binding is PER_PART or PER_PART_INDEXED, the first current material is used for the sides of the cone, and the second is used for the bottom. Otherwise, the first material is used for the entire cone.

When a texture is applied to a cone, it is applied differently to the sides and bottom. On the sides, the texture wraps counterclockwise (from above) starting at the back of the cone. The texture has a vertical seam at the back, intersecting the yz-plane. For the bottom, a circle is cut out of the texture square and applied to the cone's base circle. The texture appears right side up when the top of the cone is rotated towards the -Z axis.

```
PARTS
        SIDES              The conical part
        BOTTOM             The bottom circular face
        ALL                All parts
FILE FORMAT/DEFAULTS
        Cone {
                parts              ALL      # SFBitMask
                bottomRadius       1 .      # SFFloat
                height             2        # SFFloat
        }
```

MODIFIED 1.1 - Coordinate3

This node defines a set of 3D coordinates to be used by a subsequent IndexedFaceSet, IndexedLineSet, or PointSet node. This node does not produce a visible result during rendering; it simply replaces the current coordinates in the rendering state for subsequent nodes to use.

FILE FORMAT/DEFAULTS

```
Coordinate3 {
      point  0 0 0  # input MFVec3f
}
```

Cube

This node represents a cuboid aligned with the coordinate axes. By default, the cube is centered at (0,0,0) and measures 2 units in each dimension, from -1 to +1. The cube is transformed by the current cumulative transformation and is drawn with the current material and texture. A cube's width is its extent along its object-space X axis, its height is its extent along the object-space Y axis, and its depth is its extent along its object-space Z axis.

If the current material binding is PER_PART, PER_PART_INDEXED, PER_FACE, or PER_FACE_INDEXED, materials will be bound to the faces of the cube in this order: front (+Z), back (-Z), left (-X), right (+X), top (+Y), and bottom (-Y).

Textures are applied individually to each face of the cube; the entire texture goes on each face. On the front, back, right, and left sides of the cube, the texture is applied right side up. On the top, the texture appears right side up when the top of the cube is tilted toward the camera. On the bottom, the texture appears right side up when the top of the cube is tilted towards the -Z axis.

FILE FORMAT/DEFAULTS

```
Cube {
      width    2      # SFFloat
      height   2      # SFFloat
      depth    2      # SFFloat
}
```

Cylinder

This node represents a simple capped cylinder centered around the y-axis. By default, the cylinder is centered at (0,0,0) and has a default size of -1 to +1 in all three dimensions. The cylinder has three parts: the sides, the top (y = +1) and the bottom (y = -1). You can use the radius and height fields to create a cylinder with a different size.

The cylinder is transformed by the current cumulative transformation and is drawn with the current material and texture.

If the current material binding is PER_PART or PER_PART_INDEXED, the first current material is used for the sides of the cylinder, the second is used for the top, and the third is used for the bottom. Otherwise, the first material is used for the entire cylinder.

When a texture is applied to a cylinder, it is applied differently to the sides, top, and bottom. On the sides, the texture wraps counterclockwise (from above) starting at the back of the cylinder. The texture has a vertical seam at the back, intersecting the yz-plane. For the top and bottom, a circle is cut out of the texture square and applied to the top or bottom circle. The top texture appears right side up when the top of the cylinder is tilted toward the +Z axis, and the bottom texture appears right side up when the top of the cylinder is tilted toward the -Z axis.

```
PARTS
      SIDES    The cylindrical part
      TOP      The top circular face
      BOTTOM   The bottom circular face
      ALL      All parts
FILE FORMAT/DEFAULTS
      Cylinder {
           parts    ALL     # SFBitMask
           radius   1       # SFFloat
           height   2       # SFFloat
      }
```

DirectionalLight

This node defines a directional light source that illuminates along rays parallel to a given 3-dimensional vector.

A light node defines an illumination source that may affect subsequent shapes in the scene graph, depending on the current lighting style. Light sources are affected by the current transformation. A light node under a separator does not affect any objects outside that separator.

```
FILE FORMAT/DEFAULTS
      DirectionalLight {
           on           TRUE       # SFBool
           intensity    1          # SFFloat
           color        1 1 1      # SFColor
           direction    0 0 -1     # SFVec3f
      }
```

FontStyle

This node defines the current font style used for all subsequent AsciiText. Font attributes only are defined. It is up to the browser to assign specific fonts to the various attribute combinations. The size field specifies the height (in object space units) of glyphs rendered and determines the vertical spacing of adjacent lines of text.[8]

```
FAMILY

     SERIF        Serif style (such as TimesRoman)
     SANS         Sans Serif Style (such as Helvetica)
     TYPEWRITER   Fixed pitch style (such as Courier)
STYLE
     NONE         No modifications to family
     BOLD         Embolden family
     ITALIC       Italicize or Slant family
FILE FORMAT/DEFAULTS
     FontStyle {
          size      10        # SFFloat
          family    SERIF     # SFEnum
          style     NONE      # SFBitMask
     }
```

IndexedFaceSet

This node represents a 3D shape formed by constructing faces (polygons) from vertices located at the current coordinates. IndexedFaceSet uses the indices in its coordIndex field to specify the polygonal faces. An index of -1 indicates that the current face has ended and the next one begins.

The vertices of the faces are transformed by the current transformation matrix.

Treatment of the current material and normal binding is as follows: The PER_PART and PER_FACE bindings specify a material or normal for each face. PER_VERTEX specifies a material or normal for each vertex. The corresponding _INDEXED bindings are the same, but use the materialIndex or normalIndex indices. The DEFAULT material binding is equal to OVERALL. The DEFAULT normal binding is equal to PER_VERTEX_INDEXED; if insufficient normals exist in the state, vertex normals will be generated automatically.

Explicit texture coordinates (as defined by TextureCoordinate2) may be bound to vertices of an indexed shape by using the indices in the textureCoordIndex field. As with all vertex-based shapes, if there is a current texture but no texture coordinates are specified, a default texture coordinate mapping is calculated using the bounding box of the shape. The longest dimension of the bounding box defines the S coordinates, and the next longest defines the T coordinates. The value of the S coordinate ranges from 0 to 1, from one end of the bounding box to the other. The T coordinate ranges between 0 and the ratio of the second greatest dimension of the bounding box to the greatest dimension.

Be sure that the indices contained in the coordIndex, materialIndex, normalIndex, and textureCoordIndex fields are valid with respect to the current state, or errors will occur.

```
FILE FORMAT/DEFAULTS
    IndexedFaceSet {
            coordIndex          0  # MFLong
            materialIndex       -1 # MFLong
            normalIndex         -1 # MFLong
            textureCoordIndex   -1 # MFLong
    }
```

IndexedLineSet

This node represents a 3D shape formed by constructing polylines from vertices located at the current coordinates. IndexedLineSet uses the indices in its coordIndex field to specify the polylines. An index of -1 indicates that the current polyline has ended and the next one begins.

The coordinates of the line set are transformed by the current cumulative transformation.

Treatment of the current material and normal binding is as follows: The PER_PART binding specifies a material or normal for each segment of the line. The PER_FACE binding specifies a material or normal for each polyline. PER_VERTEX specifies a material or normal for each vertex. The corresponding _INDEXED bindings are the same, but use the materialIndex or normalIndex indices. The DEFAULT material binding is equal to OVERALL. The DEFAULT normal binding is equal to PER_VERTEX_INDEXED; if insufficient normals exist in the state, the lines will be drawn unlit. The same rules for texture coordinate generation as IndexedFaceSet are used.

```
FILE FORMAT/DEFAULTS
    IndexedLineSet {
            coordIndex          0  # MFLong
            materialIndex       -1 # MFLong
            normalIndex         -1 # MFLong
            textureCoordIndex   -1 # MFLong
    }
```

Info

This class defines an information node in the scene graph. This node has no effect during traversal. It is used to store information in the scene graph, typically for browser-specific purposes, copyright messages, or other strings.

```
Info {
        string   "<Undefined info>"         # SFString
    }
```

MODIFIED 1.1 - LOD

This node is used to allow browsers to switch between various representations of objects automatically. The children of this node typically represent the same object or objects at varying levels of detail, from highest detail to lowest. LOD acts as a Separator, not allowing properties underneath it to affect nodes that come after it in the scene.

The distance from the viewpoint (transformed into the local coordinate space of the LOD node) to the specified center point of the LOD is calculated. If the distance is less than the first value in the ranges array, then the first child of the LOD is drawn. If between the first and second values in the ranges array, the second child is drawn, etc. If there are N values in the ranges array, the LOD group should have N+1 children. Specifying too few children will result in the last child being used repeatedly for the lowest levels of detail; if too many children are specified, the extra children will be ignored. Each value in the ranges array should be less than the previous value, otherwise results are undefined. Not specifying any values in the ranges array (the default) is a special case that indicates that the browser may decide which child to draw to optimize rendering performance.

Authors should set LOD ranges so that the transitions from one level of detail to the next are barely noticeable. Browsers may adjust which level of detail is displayed to maintain interactive frame rates, to display an already-fetched level of detail while a higher level of detail (contained in a WWWInline node) is fetched, or might disregard the author-specified ranges for any other implementation-dependent reason. Authors should not use LOD nodes to emulate simple behaviors, because the results will be undefined. For example, using an LOD node to make a door appear to open when the user approaches probably will not work in all browsers.

For best results, specify ranges only where necessary, and nest LOD nodes with and without ranges. For example:

```
LOD {
        range [100, 1000]

        LOD {
            Separator { ... detailed version... }
            DEF LoRes Separator { ... less detailed version... }
        }
        USE LoRes
```

continued on next page

continued from previous page

```
        Info { } # Display nothing
    }
```

In this example, nothing at all will be displayed if the viewer is farther than 1,000 meters away from the object. A low-resolution version of the object will be displayed if the viewer is between 100 and 1,000 meters away, and either a low-resolution or a high-resolution version of the object will be displayed when the viewer is closer than 100 meters from the object.

FILE FORMAT/DEFAULTS

```
    LOD {
        range [ ]      # MFFloat
        center 0 0 0   # SFVec3f
    }
```

MODIFIED 1.1 - Material

This node defines the current surface material properties for all subsequent shapes. Material sets several components of the current material during traversal. Different shapes interpret materials with multiple values differently. To bind materials to shapes, use a MaterialBinding node.

The lighting parameters defined by the Material node are the same parameters defined by the OpenGL lighting model. For a rigorous mathematical description of how these parameters should be used to determine how surfaces are lit, see the description of lighting operations in the OpenGL Specification. Note that VRML 1.1 provides no mechanism for controlling the amount of ambient light in the scene, so use of the ambientColor field is browser dependent. Several other parameters (such as light attenuation factors) are also left as implementation details in VRML. Also note that OpenGL specifies the specular exponent as a non-normalized 0-128 value, which is specified as a normalized 0-1 value in VRML (simply multiplying the VRML value by 128 to translate to the OpenGL parameter).

For rendering systems that do not support the full OpenGL lighting model, the following simpler lighting model is recommended:
A transparency value of 0 is completely opaque, a value of 1 is completely transparent. Browsers need not support partial transparency, but should support at least fully transparent and fully opaque surfaces, treating transparency values >= 0.5 as fully transparent.

Specifying only emissiveColors and zero diffuse, specular, emissive, and ambient colors is the way to specify pre-computed lighting. It is expected that browsers will be able to recognize this as a special case and optimize their computations. For example:

```
Material {
    ambientColor [] diffuseColor [] specularColor []
    emissiveColor [ 0.1 0.1 0.2, 0.5 0.8 0.8 ]
}
```

Issues for Low-End Rendering Systems. Many low-end PC rendering systems are not able to support the full range of the VRML material specification. For example, many systems do not render individual red, green and blue reflected values as specified in the specularColor field. The following table describes which Material fields are typically supported in popular low-end systems and suggests actions for browser implementors to take when a field is not supported.

Field	Supported?	Suggested Action
ambientColor	No	Ignore
diffuseColor	Yes	Use
specularColor	No	Ignore
emissiveColor	No	Use in place of diffuseColor if != 0 0 0
shininess	Yes	Use
transparency	No	Ignore

It is also expected that simpler rendering systems will be unable to support both lit and unlit objects in the same scene.

```
FILE FORMAT/DEFAULTS
    Material {
        ambientColor    0.2 0.2 0.2     # input MFColor
        diffuseColor    0.8 0.8 0.8     # input MFColor
        specularColor   0 0 0           # input MFColor
        emissiveColor   0 0 0           # input MFColor
        shininess       0.2             # input MFFloat
        transparency    0               # input MFFloat
    }
```

MaterialBinding

Material nodes may contain more than one material. This node specifies how the current materials are bound to shapes that follow in the scene graph. Each shape node may interpret bindings differently. For example, a Sphere node is always drawn using the first material in the material node, no matter what the current MaterialBinding, while a Cube node may use six different materials to draw each of its six faces, depending on the MaterialBinding.

The bindings for faces and vertices are meaningful only for shapes that are made from faces and vertices. Similarly, the indexed bindings are only used by the shapes that allow indexing.

When multiple material values are needed by a shape, the previous Material node should at least as many materials as are needed, otherwise results are undefined.

Issues for low-end rendering systems. Some renderers do not support per-vertex materials, in which case the MaterialBinding values PER_VERTEX and PER_VERTEX_INDEXED will produce upredictable results in different browsers.

```
BINDINGS
     DEFAULT              Use default binding
     OVERALL              Whole object has same material
     PER_PART             One material for each part of object
     PER_PART_INDEXED     One material for each part, indexed
     PER_FACE             One material for each face of object
     PER_FACE_INDEXED     One material for each face, indexed
     PER_VERTEX            One material for each vertex of object
     PER_VERTEX_INDEXED   One material for each vertex, indexed
FILE FORMAT/DEFAULTS
     MaterialBinding {
          value  OVERALL          # SFEnum
     }
```

MatrixTransform

This node defines a geometric 3D transformation with a 4 by 4 matrix. Only matrices that are the result of rotations, translations, and non-zero (but possibly non-uniform) scales must be supported. Non-invertable matrices should be avoided.

Matrices are specified in row-major order, so, for example, a MatrixTransform representing a translation of 6.2 units along the local Z axis would be specified as:

```
MatrixTransform { matrix
     1 0 0 0
     0 1 0 0
     0 0 1 0
     0 0 6.2 1
}

FILE FORMAT/DEFAULTS
     MatrixTransform {
          matrix  1 0 0 0          # SFMatrix
                  0 1 0 0
                  0 0 1 0
                  0 0 0 1
     }
```

MODIFIED 1.1 - Normal

This node defines a set of 3D surface normal vectors to be used by vertex-based shape nodes (IndexedFaceSet, IndexedLineSet, PointSet) that follow it in the scene graph. This node does not produce a visible result during rendering; it simply replaces the current normals in the rendering state for subsequent nodes to use. This node contains one multiple-valued field that contains the normal vectors.

To save network bandwidth, it is expected that implementations will be able to automatically generate appropriate normals if none are given. However, the results will vary from implementation to implementation.

FILE FORMAT/DEFAULTS

```
Normal {
      vector   [ ] # input MFVec3f
}
```

NormalBinding

This node specifies how the current normals are bound to shapes that follow in the scene graph. Each shape node may interpret bindings differently.

The bindings for faces and vertices are meaningful only for shapes that are made from faces and vertices. Similarly, the indexed bindings are only used by the shapes that allow indexing. For bindings that require multiple normals, be sure to have at least as many normals defined as are necessary; otherwise, errors will occur.

BINDINGS

```
      DEFAULT              Use default binding
      OVERALL              Whole object has same normal
      PER_PART             One normal for each part of object
      PER_PART_INDEXED     One normal for each part, indexed
      PER_FACE             One normal for each face of object
      PER_FACE_INDEXED     One normal for each face, indexed
      PER_VERTEX           One normal for each vertex of object
      PER_VERTEX_INDEXED   One normal for each vertex, indexed
```

FILE FORMAT/DEFAULTS

```
      NormalBinding {
          value  DEFAULT          # SFEnum
      }
```

OrthographicCamera

An orthographic camera defines a parallel projection from a viewpoint. This camera does not diminish objects with distance, as a PerspectiveCamera does. The viewing volume for an orthographic camera is a rectangular parallelepiped (a box).

By default, the camera is located at (0,0,1) and looks along the negative z-axis; the position and orientation fields can be used to change these values. The height field defines the total height of the viewing volume.

A camera can be placed in a VRML world to specify the initial location of the viewer when that world is entered. VRML browsers will typically modify the camera to allow a user to move through the virtual world.

The results of traversing multiple cameras are undefined; to ensure consistent results, place multiple cameras underneath one or more Switch nodes, and set the Switch's whichChild fields so that only one is traversed. By convention, these non-traversed cameras may be used to define alternate entry points into the scene; these entry points may be named by simply giving the cameras a name (using DEF); see the specification of WWWAnchor for a conventional way of specifying an entry point in a URL.

Cameras are affected by the current transformation, so you can position a camera by placing a transformation node before it in the scene graph . The default position and orientation of a camera is at (0,0,1) looking along the negative z-axis, with the positive y-axis up.

The position and orientation fields of a camera are sufficient to place a camera anywhere in space with any orientation. The orientation field can be used to rotate the default view direction (looking down -z-, with +y up) so that it is looking in any direction, with any direction 'up'.

The focalDistance field defines the point the viewer is looking at, and may be used by a browser as a navigational hint to determine how fast the viewer should travel, which objects in the scene are most important, etc.

The nearDistance and farDistance are distances from the viewpoint (in the camera's coordinate system); objects closer to the viewpoint than nearDistance or farther from the viewpoint than farDistance should not be seen. Browsers may treat these values as hints, and may decide to adjust them as the viewer moves around the scene.

```
FILE FORMAT/DEFAULTS
    OrthographicCamera {
        position        0 0 1          # SFVec3f
        orientation     0 0 1  0       # SFRotation
        focalDistance   5              # SFFloat
        height          2              # SFFloat
        nearDistance    1              # SFFloat
        farDistance     10             # SFFloat
    }
```

Issues for low-end rendering systems. Most low-end rendering systems do not support the concept of focalDistance. Also, cameras are global to the scene; placing a camera beneath a particular Separator is equivalent to placing it at outermost scope. For broadest compatibility, cameras should only be placed at outermost scope.

MODIFIED 1.1 - PerspectiveCamera

A perspective camera defines a perspective projection from a viewpoint. The viewing volume for a perspective camera is a truncated right pyramid.

By default, the camera is located at (0,0,1) and looks along the negative z-axis; the position and orientation fields can be used to change these values. The heightAngle field defines the total vertical angle of the viewing volume.

See more on cameras in the OrthographicCamera description.

```
FILE FORMAT/DEFAULTS
     PerspectiveCamera {
          position        0 0 1            # SFVec3f
          orientation     0 0 1 0          # SFRotation
          focalDistance   5                # SFFloat
          heightAngle     0.785398         # SFFloat
          nearDistance    1                # SFFloat
          farDistance     10               # SFFloat
     }
```

PointLight

This node defines a point light source at a fixed 3D location. A point source illuminates equally in all directions; that is, it is omni- directional.

A light node defines an illumination source that may affect subsequent shapes in the scene graph, depending on the current lighting style. Light sources are affected by the current transformation. A light node under a separator should not affect any objects outside that separator (although some rendering systems do not currently support this).

```
FILE FORMAT/DEFAULTS
     PointLight {
          on            TRUE        # SFBool
          intensity     1           # SFFloat
          color         1 1 1       # SFColor
          location      0 0 1       # SFVec3f
     }
```

PointSet

This node represents a set of points located at the current coordinates. PointSet uses the current coordinates in order, starting at the index specified by the startIndex field. The number of points in the set is specified by the numPoints field. A value of -1 for this field indicates that all remaining values in the current coordinates are to be used as points.

The coordinates of the point set are transformed by the current cumulative transformation. The points are drawn with the current material and texture.

Treatment of the current material and normal binding is as follows: PER_PART, PER_FACE, and PER_VERTEX bindings bind one material or normal to each point. The DEFAULT material binding is equal to OVERALL. The DEFAULT normal binding is equal to PER_VERTEX. The startIndex is also used for materials or normals when the binding indicates that they should be used per vertex.

FILE FORMAT/DEFAULTS
```
PointSet {
    startIndex  0 # SFLong
    numPoints   -1        # SFLong
}
```

Issues for low-end rendering systems. Many low-end renderers do not support the concept of per-object lighting. This means that placing a light beneath a Separator, which implies lighting only the objects beneath the Separator with that light, is not supported in all systems. For the broadest compatibility, lights should only be placed at outermost scope.

MODIFIED 1.1 - Rotation

This node defines a 3D rotation about an arbitrary axis through the origin. The rotation is accumulated into the current transformation, which is applied to subsequent shapes.

FILE FORMAT/DEFAULTS
```
Rotation {
    rotation  0 0 1  0   # input SFRotation
}
```

See rotation field description for more information.

MODIFIED 1.1 - Scale

This node defines a 3D scaling about the origin. If the components of the scaling vector are not all the same, this produces a non-uniform scale.

FILE FORMAT/DEFAULTS
```
Scale {
    scaleFactor  1 1 1   # input SFVec3f
}
```

Separator

A proposal to replace Separator's with Frames and Leafs is at *http://earth.path.net/mitra/papers/vrml-frames.html*

This group node performs a push (save) of the traversal state before traversing its children and a pop (restore) after traversing them. This isolates the separator's children from the rest of the scene graph. A separator can include lights, cameras, coordinates, normals, bindings, and all other properties.

Separators can also perform render culling. Render culling skips over traversal of the separator's children if they are not going to be rendered, based on the comparison of the separator's bounding box with the current view volume. Culling is controlled by the renderCulling field. These are set to AUTO by default, allowing the implementation to decide whether or not to cull.

```
CULLING ENUMS
      ON     Always try to cull to the view volume
      OFF    Never try to cull to the view volume
      AUTO   Implementation-defined culling behavior

FILE FORMAT/DEFAULTS
      Separator {
            renderCulling        AUTO        # SFEnum
      }
```

ShapeHints

The ShapeHints node indicates that IndexedFaceSets are solid, contain ordered vertices, or contain convex faces.

These hints allow VRML implementations to optimize certain rendering features. Optimizations that may be performed include enabling back-face culling and disabling two-sided lighting. For example, if an object is solid and has ordered vertices, an implementation may turn on backface culling and turn off two-sided lighting. If the object is not solid but has ordered vertices, it may turn off backface culling and turn on two-sided lighting.

The ShapeHints node also affects how default normals are generated. When an IndexedFaceSet has to generate default normals, it uses the creaseAngle field to determine which edges should be smoothly shaded and which ones should have a sharp crease. The crease angle is the angle between surface normals on adjacent polygons. For example, a crease angle of .5 radians (the default value) means that an edge between two adjacent polygonal faces will be smooth shaded if the normals to the two faces form an angle that is less than .5 radians (about 30 degrees). Otherwise, it will be faceted.

Issues for low-end rendering systems. The shapeType and vertexOrdering fields are used to determine whether or not to generate back faces for each polygon in a mesh. Most low-end rendering systems do not support built-in back face generation; browsers built on these systems need to create back faces explicitly.

```
VERTEX ORDERING ENUMS
      UNKNOWN_ORDERING        Ordering of vertices is unknown
      CLOCKWISE               Face vertices are ordered clockwise
                                 (from the outside)
      COUNTERCLOCKWISE        Face vertices are ordered counterclockwise
                                 (from the outside)
SHAPE TYPE ENUMS
      UNKNOWN_SHAPE_TYPE    Nothing is known about the shape
      SOLID                   The shape encloses a volume
FACE TYPE ENUMS
      UNKNOWN_FACE_TYPE     Nothing is known about faces
      CONVEX                  All faces are convex
FILE FORMAT/DEFAULTS
      ShapeHints {
            vertexOrdering    COUNTERCLOCKWISE          # SFEnum
            shapeType         SOLID                     # SFEnum
            faceType          CONVEX                    # SFEnum
            creaseAngle       0                         # SFFloat
      }
```

Sphere

This node represents a sphere. By default, the sphere is centered at the origin and has a radius of 1. The sphere is transformed by the current cumulative transformation and is drawn with the current material and texture.

A sphere does not have faces or parts. Therefore, the sphere ignores material and normal bindings, using the first material for the entire sphere and using its own normals. When a texture is applied to a sphere, the texture covers the entire surface, wrapping counterclockwise from the back of the sphere. The texture has a seam at the back on the yz-plane.

```
FILE FORMAT/DEFAULTS
      Sphere {
            radius   1      # SFFloat
      }
```

SpotLight

This node defines a spotlight light source. A spotlight is placed at a fixed location in 3-space and illuminates in a cone along a particular direction. The intensity of the illumination drops off exponentially as a ray of light diverges from this direction toward the edges of the cone. The rate of drop-off and the angle of the cone are controlled by the dropOffRate and cutOffAngle fields.

A light node defines an illumination source that may affect subsequent shapes in the scene graph, depending on the current lighting style. Light sources are affected by the current transformation. A light node under a separator should not affect any objects outside that separator (although some rendering systems do not currently support this).

FILE FORMAT/DEFAULTS

```
SpotLight {
        on              TRUE       # SFBool
        intensity       1          # SFFloat
        color           1 1 1      # SFVec3f
        location        0 0 1      # SFVec3f
        direction       0 0 -1     # SFVec3f
        dropOffRate     0          # SFFloat
        cutOffAngle     0.785398 # SFFloat
}
```

Issues for low-end rendering systems. Many low-end renderers do not support the concept of per-object lighting. This means that placing a light beneath a Separator, which implies lighting only the objects beneath the Separator with that light, is not supported in all systems. For the broadest compatibility, lights should only be placed at outermost scope.

MODIFIED 1.1 - Switch

This group node traverses one or none of its children. One can use this node to switch on and off the effects of some properties or to switch between different properties.

The whichChild field specifies the index of the child to traverse, where the first child has index 0. This field is an input and thus can be modified by another node.

Open issue *It is expected that in a future version of VRML the Switch node will be defined to behave as a Separator node, not allowing its children to affect anything after it in the scene graph. To ensure future compatibility, it is recommended that all children of all Switch nodes be Separator nodes.*

FILE FORMAT/DEFAULTS

```
Switch {
        whichChild    -1           # input SFLong
}
```

Text

This node represents one or more text strings specified using the UTF-8 encoding of the ISO10646 character set. This is described below. An important note is that ASCII is a subset of UTF-8, so any ASCII strings are also UTF-8.

The text strings can be rendered in one of four directions: right to left (RL), left to right (LR), top to bottom (TB), or bottom to top (BT). The direction field governs this.

The justification field determines where the text will be positioned in relation to the origin (0,0,0) of the object coordinate system. The values for the justification field are BEGIN, END, CENTER. For a left to right (LR) direction, these would correspond to LEFT, RIGHT, CENTER.

For the directions RL and LR, the first line of text will be positioned with its baseline (bottom of capital letters) at y = 0. The text is positioned on the positive side of the x origin for the direction LR and justification BEGIN; the same for RL END. The text is on the negative side of X for LR END and RL BEGIN. For CENTER justification and horizontal text (RL, LR), each string will be centered at x = 0.

For the directions TB and BT, the first line of text will be positioned with the left side of the glyphs along the y = 0 axis. For TB BEGIN and BT END, the text will be positioned with the top left corner at the origin; for TB END and BT BEGIN, the bottom left will be at the origin. For TB and BT CENTER, the text will be centered vertically at x = 0.

```
LR BEGIN      LR END         LR CENTER

VRML                VRML             VRML
adds  a            adds  a          adds  a
dimension!         dimension!       dimension!

    RL BEGIN      RL END         RL CENTER

        LMRV      LMRV               LMRV
    a  sdda      a  sdda           a  sdda
 !noisnemid      !noisnemid        !noisnemid
```

```
TB BEGIN   TB END   TB CENTER      BT BEGIN   BT END   BT CENTER

  V  a  d         d            d              !       L  a  !           !
  R  d  i         i            i              n       M     n           n
  M  d  m         m         a  m              o       R  s  o        a  o
  L  s  e         e      V  d  e              i       V  d  i        L     i
        n      a  n      R  d  n           a  s          d  s        M  s  s
     a  s      d  s      M  s  s              n          a  n        R  d  n
        i   V  d  i      L     i           L  s  e          e        V  d  e
```

```
TB BEGIN    TB END   TB CENTER        BT BEGIN     BT END    BT CENTER
   o       R s o         a o          M d m          m        a m
   n       M   n           n          R d i          i          i
   !       L a !           !          V a d          d          d
```

The spacing field determines the spacing between multiple text strings. All subsequent strings advance in either x or y by -(size * spacing). See FontStyle for a description of the size field. A value of 0 for the spacing will cause the string to be in the same position. A value of -1 will cause subsequent strings to advance in the opposite direction.

The extent field will limit and scale the text string if the natural length of the string is longer than the extent. If the text string is shorter than the extent, it will not be scaled. The extent is measured horizontally for RL and LR directions; vertically for TB and BT.

UTF-8 character encodings

The 2 byte (UCS-2) encoding of ISO 10646 is identical to the Unicode standard. References for both ISO 10646 and Unicode are given in the references section at the end.

In order to avoid introducing binary data into VRML we have chosen to support the UTF-8 encoding of ISO 10646. This encoding allows ASCII text (0x0..0x7F) to appear without any changes and encodes all characters from 0x80.. 0x7FFFFFFF into a series of six or fewer bytes.

If the most significant bit of the first character is 0, then the remaining seven bits are interpretted as an ASCII character. Otherwise, the number of leading 1 bits will indicate the number of bytes following. There is always a o bit between the count bits and any data.

First byte could be one of the following. The X indicates bits available to encode the character.

```
OXXXXXXX    only one byte        0..0x7F (ASCII)
110XXXXX    two bytes            Maximum character value is 0x7FF
1110XXXX    three bytes          Maximum character value is 0xFFFF
11110XXX    four bytes           Maximum character value is 0x1FFFFF
111110XX    five bytes           Maximum character value is 0x3FFFFFF
1111110X    six bytes            Maximum character value is 0x7FFFFFFF
All following bytes have this format: 10XXXXXX
```

A two byte example. The symbol for a register trade mark is "circled R registered sign" or 174 in both ISO/Latin-1 (8859/1) and ISO 10646. In hexadecimal it is 0xAE; In HTML ¨. In UTF-8 it is has the following two byte encoding 0xC2, 0xAE.

The text is transformed by the current cumulative transformation and is drawn with the current material and texture.

Textures are applied to 3D text as follows. The texture origin is at the origin of the first string, as determined by the justification. The texture is scaled equally in both S and T dimensions, with the font height representing 1 unit. S increases to the right, T increases up.

```
DIRECTION
     LR        Character are drawn from left to right
     RL        Character are drawn from right to left
     TB        Character are drawn from top to bottom
     TB        Character are drawn from bottom to top

JUSTIFICATION
     BEGIN     Align beginning of text to origin
     CENTER    Align center of text to origin
     END       Align end of text to origin

FILE FORMAT/DEFAULTS
     Text {
            string          ""       # MFString
            direction       LR       # SFEnum
            justification   BEGIN    # SFEnum
            spacing         1        # SFFloat
            width           0        # MFFloat
     }
```

TextLanguage

There are many languages in which the proper rendering of the text requires more than just a sequence of glyphs. The TextLanguage node allows the author to specify which, if any, language specific rendering techniques to use. For simple languages, such as English, this node may be safely ignored.

The tag used to specify languages will follow RFC1766—Tags for the Identification of Languages. ftp://ftp.isi.edu/in-notes/rfc1766.txt. This RFC specifies that a language tag may simply be a two letter ISO 639 tag, for example "en" for English, "ja" for Japanese, and "sv" for Swedish. This may be optionally followed by a two letter country code from ISO 3166. So, Americans would be absolutely safe with "en-US". ISO does not have documents online, yet. They can be ordered.

```
FILE FORMAT/DEFAULTS
     TextLanguage {
            textLanguage      ""     # SFString
     }
```

Texture2

TODO: Gavin - add sentence about grey scales to Texure2

This property node defines a texture map and parameters for that map. This map is used to apply texture to subsequent shapes as they are rendered.

The texture can be read from the URL specified by the filename field. To turn off texturing, set the filename field to an empty string (""). Implementations should support at least the JPEG image file format. Also supporting GIF and PNG formats is recommended.

If multiple URLs are presented, this expresses a descending order of preference, a browser may display a lower preference URL while the higher order file is not available. See the section on URNs.

Textures can also be specified inline by setting the image field to contain the texture data. Supplying both image and filename fields will result in undefined behavior.

Texture images may be one component (greyscale), two component (greyscale plus transparency), three component (full RGB color), or four-component (full RGB color plus transparency). An ideal VRML implementation will use the texture image to modify the diffuse color and transparency of an object's material (specified in a Material node), then performing any lighting calculations using the rest of the object's material properties with the modified diffuse color to produce the final image. The texture image modifies the diffuse color and transparency depending on how many components are in the image, as follows:

1. Diffuse color is multiplied by the greyscale values in the texture image.

2. Diffuse color is multiplied by the greyscale values in the texture image, material transparency is multiplied by transparency values in texture image.

3. RGB colors in the texture image replace the material's diffuse color.

4. RGB colors in the texture image replace the material's diffuse color, transparency values in the texture image replace the material's transparency.

Browsers may approximate this ideal behavior to increase performance. One common optimization is to calculate lighting only at each vertex and combining the texture image with the color computed from lighting (performing the texturing after lighting). Another common optimization is to perform no lighting calculations at all when texturing is enabled, displaying only the colors of the texture image.

```
WRAP ENUM
     REPEAT   Repeats texture outside 0-1 texture coordinate range
     CLAMP    Clamps texture coordinates to lie within 0-1 range
FILE FORMAT/DEFAULTS
     Texture2 {
          filename      ""          # SFString
          image         0 0 0       # SFImage
          wrapS         REPEAT      # SFEnum
          wrapT         REPEAT      # SFEnum
     }
```

Texture2Transform

This node defines a 2D transformation applied to texture coordinates. This affects the way textures are applied to the surfaces of subsequent shapes. The transformation consists of (in order) a non-uniform scale about an arbitrary center point, a rotation about that same point, and a translation. This allows a user to change the size and position of the textures on shapes.

```
FILE FORMAT/DEFAULTS
     Texture2Transform {
          translation  0 0      # SFVec2f
          rotation     0        # SFFloat
          scaleFactor  1 1      # SFVec2f
          center       0 0      # SFVec2f
     }
```

TextureCoordinate2

This node defines a set of 2D coordinates to be used to map textures to the vertices of subsequent PointSet, IndexedLineSet, or IndexedFaceSet objects. It replaces the current texture coordinates in the rendering state for the shapes to use.

Texture coordinates range from 0 to 1 across the texture. The horizontal coordinate, called S, is specified first, followed by the vertical coordinate, T.

```
FILE FORMAT/DEFAULTS
     TextureCoordinate2 {
          point  0 0    # MFVec2f
     }
```

MODIFIED 1.1 - Transform

This node defines a geometric 3D transformation consisting of (in order) a (possibly) non-uniform scale about an arbitrary point, a rotation about an arbitrary point and axis, and a translation. The transform node

```
Transform {
     translation T1
     rotation R1
```

```
    scaleFactor S
    scaleOrientation R2
    center T2
}
```

is equivalent to the sequence:

```
Translation { translation T1 }
Translation { translation T2 }
Rotation { rotation R1 }
Rotation { rotation R2 }
Scale { scaleFactor S }
Rotation { rotation -R2 }
Translation { translation -T2 }
```

```
FILE FORMAT/DEFAULTS
    Transform {
            translation        0 0 0        # input SFVec3f
            rotation           0 0 1  0     # input SFRotation
            scaleFactor        1 1 1        # input SFVec3f
            scaleOrientation   0 0 1  0     # input SFRotation
            center             0 0 0        # input SFVec3f
    }
```

MODIFIED 1.1 -Translation

This node defines a translation by a 3D vector.

```
FILE FORMAT/DEFAULTS
    Translation {
            translation  0 0 0     # input SFVec3f
    }
```

WWWAnchor

The WWWAnchor group node loads a new scene into a VRML browser when one of its children is chosen. Exactly how a user "chooses" a child of the WWWAnchor is up to the VRML browser; typically, clicking on one of its children with the mouse will result in the new scene replacing the current scene. A WWWAnchor with an empty ("") name does nothing when its children are chosen. The name is an arbitrary URL.

If multiple URLs are presented, this expresses a descending order of preference, a browser may display a lower preference URL if the higher order file is not available. See the section on URNs.

WWWAnchor behaves like a Separator, pushing the traversal state before traversing its children and popping it afterwards.

The description field in the WWWAnchor allows for a friendly prompt to be displayed as an alternative to the URL in the name field. Ideally, browsers will allow the user to choose the description, the URL or both to be displayed for a candidate WWWAnchor.

The WWWAnchor's map field is an enumerated value that can be either NONE (the default) or POINT. If it is POINT then the object-space coordinates of the point on the object the user chose will be added to the URL in the name field, with the syntax "?x,y,z".

A WWWAnchor may be used to take the viewer to a particular viewpoint in a virtual world by specifying a URL ending with "#cameraName", where "cameraName" is the name of a camera defined in the world. For example:

```
WWWAnchor {
    name "http://www.school.edu/vrml/someScene.wrl#OverView"
    Cube { }
}
```

specifies an anchor that puts the viewer in the "someScene" world looking from the camera named "OverView" when the Cube is chosen. If no world is specified, then the current scene is implied; for example:

```
WWWAnchor {
    name "#Doorway"
    Sphere { }
}
```

will take the viewer to the viewpoint defined by the "Doorway" camera in the current world when the sphere is chosen.

```
MAP ENUM
     NONE  Do not add information to the URL
     POINT Add object-space coordinates to URL
FILE FORMAT/DEFAULTS
     WWWAnchor {
         name ""          # MFString
         description "" # SFString
         map NONE         # SFEnum
     }
```

WWWInline

The WWWInline node reads its children from anywhere in the World Wide Web. Exactly when its children are read is not defined; reading the children may be delayed until the WWWInline is actually displayed. A WWWInline with an empty name does nothing. The name is an arbitrary URL.

The effect of referring to a non-VRML URL in a WWWInline node is undefined.

If multiple URL's are specified then this expresses a descending order of preference, a browser may display a URL for a lower preference file while it is obtaining, or if it is unable to obtain, the higher preference file. See also the section on URNs.

If the WWWInline's bboxSize field specifies a non-empty bounding box (a bounding box is non-empty if at least one of its dimensions is greater than zero), then the WWWInline's object-space bounding box is specified by its bboxSize and bboxCenter fields. This allows an implementation to quickly determine whether or not the contents of the WWWInline might be visible. This is an optimization hint only; if the true bounding box of the contents of the WWWInline is different from the specified bounding box results will be undefined.

```
FILE FORMAT/DEFAULTS
    WWWInline {
        name ""                # MFString
        bboxSize 0 0 0         # SFVec3f
        bboxCenter 0 0 0       # SFVec3f
    }
```

NEW - New Nodes for I.I

Background

By providing a shaded ground plane, sky and scenic, textures, this node can be used to add substance to the void surrounding the scene. Only the first background node encountered is used, and it must be specified in the main file.

If groundColors are specified, then a ground plane is added to the scene-graph at Y = 0 in global coordinate space. If more than one color is specified, then the ground color is interpolates between colors from 0 degrees downward to 90 degrees at the horizon. Similarly, skyColors interpolate from the 90 degree mark to 180 degrees overhead.

A scene may describe a more precise atmosphere and include background scenery in the scenery field. This field is used to add a texture to the scene that is conceptually distant enough that it does not translate with respect to the eyepoint. The texture should be mapped wrapped around a cylinder so that it runs all the way around from Y=0 in global coordinate space.

If multiple URL's are specified then this expresses a descending order of preference, a browser may display a URL for a lower preference file while it is obtaining, or if it is unable to obtain, the higher preference file. See also the section on URNs.

```
Background{
    groundColors [ ]         # MFColor
    skyColors [ 0 0 0 ]      # MFColor
    scenery ""               # MFString
}
```

Pros:

- Resolves issue that most current scenes hover in black space.

- Implementation should make ground plane less expensive than general case.

- Geometry will provide good depth queue as closer objects move relative to the user.

- Geometry assumes nothing of what environment the author wants to portray.

- Geometry being part of scenegraph supports behaviors.

- Global coordinate space optimizes rendering of scenery.

Issues:

- Global coordinates speed up implementation. If arbitrary ground plane is absolutely needed, consider a rotation and elevation to orient the ground plane in world space.

- There has been discussion of supporting different mapping for the background texture - cylindrical, spherical, hemisphere. However current renderers do not support this functionality and simulating it would be an unacceptable performance hit.

CollideStyle

This node specifies to a browser what objects in the scene should not be navigated through. It is useful to keep viewers from walking through walls in a building, for instance. Collision response is browser defined. For example, when the camera comes sufficiently close to an object to register as a collision, the browser may have the camera bounce off the object, or simply come to a stop.

Since collision with arbitrarily complex geometry is computationally expensive, one method of increasing efficiency is to be able to define an alternate geometry that could serve as a proxy for colliding against. This collision proxy could be as crude as a simple bounding box or bounding sphere, or could be more spohisticated (for example, the convex hull of a polyhedron). This proxy volume is used ONLY to calculate the collision with the viewer and is NOT used for trivial rejection during the computation process. Efficient trivial rejection can be done using hierarchical bounding boxes or some other technique, and its implementation is not specified in the language.

VRML represents collision proxy volumes for objects through the CollideStyle property node. A CollideStyle node sets the collision proxy volume for all the geometry in the scene graph that follows it upto the next CollideStyle node. Like all other properties, the current collision style would be saved and restored by Separators. Like all other shapes, the geometry is defined in object space and is transformed by the current modeling transformation.

CollideStyle contains two fields: collide (a boolean) and proxy (a node). If the value of the collide field is FALSE, then no collision is performed with the affected geometry. If the value of the collide field is TRUE, then the proxy field defines the geometry against which collision testing is done. If the proxy value is undefined or NULL, the actual geometry is collided against. If the proxy value is not NULL, then it contains the geometry that is used in collision computations.

```
FILE FORMAT/DEFAULTS
    CollideStyle {
            collide        FALSE    # SFBool
            proxy          NULL     # SFNode
    }
```

Notes/Issues:

- Open issue - no consensus on what collides with object *The viewer must have some geometry to collide against objects in the scene. In the future, this would be an avatar geometry. For 1.1, the collisionRadius fields of the NavigationInfo node is used.*

DirectedSound

TODO: Bill ro write up minor changes; loop/start/pause probably gone

- Sound formats AU, AIFF, WAV,

- Note implication that transport system will tell you the type of the file

This node defines a sound source that is located at a specific 3D location and that emits primarily along a given direction. It adds directionality to the PointSound node. Besides the direction vector, there are minAngle and maxAngle fields that specify how the intensity of the sound changes with direction. Within the cone whose apex is the sound location, whose axis is the direction vector, and whose angle is specified by minAngle, the

DirectedSound behaves exactly like a PointSound. Moving along a constant radius (from the source location) from the surface of this cone to the surface of the similar cone whose angle is maxAngle, the intensity falls off to zero. See the PointSound node for a description of all other fields.

FILE FORMAT/DEFAULTS

```
DirectedSound {
        name                ""              # MFString
        description         ""              # SFString
        intensity           1               # SFFloat
        location            0 0 0           # SFVec3f
        direction           0 0 1           # SFVec3f
        minRange            10              # SFFloat
        maxRange            10              # SFFloat
        minAngle            0.785398        # SFFloat
        maxAngle            0.785398        # SFFloat
        loop                FALSE           # SFBool
        start               0               # input SFTime
        pause               0               # input SFTime
}
```

ElevationGrid

VAG: Accepted - no changes

This node creates a rectangular grid with varying heights, especially useful in modeling terrain and other space creating surfaces. The model is specified primarily by a scalar array of height values that describe the height of the surface above each point of the grid.

The verticesPerRow and verticesPerColumn fields define the number of grid points in the Z and X directions, respectively, defining a surface that contains (verticesPerRow-1) x (verticesPerColumn-1) rectangles.

The vertex locations for the rectangles are defined by the height field and the gridStep field. The vertex corresponding to the i th row and j th column is placed at (gridStep[0] * j, heights[i*verticesPerColumn+j], gridStep[1] * i) in object space, where 0<=i<=verticesPerRow, 0<=j<=verticesPerColumn.

The height field is an array of scalar values representing the height above the grid for each vertex. The height values are stored so that row 0 is first, followed by rows 1, 2, ... verticesPerRow. Within each row, the height values are stored so that column 0 is first, followed by columns 1, 2, ... verticesPerColumn. The rows have fixed Z values, with row 0 having the smallest Z value. The columns have fixed X values, with column 0 having the smallest X value.

The default texture coordinates will range from [0,0] at the first vertex to [1,1] at the far side of the diagonal. The S texture coordinate will be aligned with X and the T texture coordinate with Z.

Treatment of the current material and normal binding is as follows: The PER_PART binding specifies a material or normal for each row of the mesh. The PER_FACE binding specifies a material or normal for each quadrilateral. The _INDEXED bindings are equivalent to their non-indexed counterparts. The default material binding is OVERALL. The default normal binding is PER_VERTEX.

If any normals (or materials) are specified, it is assumed you provide the correct number of them, as indicated by the binding. You will see unexpected results if you specify fewer normals (or materials) than the shape requires. If no normals are specified, they will be generated automatically.

By default, the rectangles are defined with a counterclockwise ordering, so the Y component of the normal is positive. Setting the vertexOrdering field of the current ShapeHints node to CLOCKWISE reverses the normal direction. Backface culling can be turned on as for all shapes, by defining a ShapeHints node prior to the ElevationGrid node with the vertexOrdering field set to CLOCKWISE or COUNTERCLOCKWISE and the shapeType field set to SOLID.

```
FILE FORMAT/DEFAULTS
    ElevationGrid {
            verticesPerRow 0      # SFLong
            verticesPerColumn 0 # SFLong
            gridStep []           # SFVec2f
            height []             # MFFloat
    }
```

Pros:

- This is an extremely compact way to represent geometry (key for transmission times).

- There is a lot of data available that can be easily converted into this form (USGS Digital Elevation Models come to mind)

- Easy for browsers to do automatic LOD degradation to keep performance up.

Environment

This node describes global environmental attributes such as ambient lighting, light attenuation, and fog.

Ambient lighting is the amount of extra light impinging on each surface point. It is specified as an ambientColor and ambientIntensity. Light attenuation affects all subsequent lights in a scene. It is a quadratic function of distance from a light source to a surface point. The three coefficients are specified in the attenuation field. Attenuation works only for light sources with a fixed location, such as point and spot lights. The ambient lighting and attenuation calculations are defined in the OpenGL lighting model. For a description of these and other lighting calculations, see the description of lighting operations in the OpenGL Specification.

Fog has one of four types, each of which blends each surface point with the specified fog color. Each type interprets the visibility field to be the distance at which fog totally obscures objects. A visibility value of 0 (the default) causes the Environment node to set up fog so that the visibility is the distance to the far clipping plane of the current camera. For more details on the fog calculations, see the description of fog in the OpenGL Specification.

```
FOGTYPE
      NONE    No fog
      HAZE    Linear increase in opacity with distance
      FOG     Exponential increase in opacity
      SMOKE   Exponential squared increase in opacity

FILE FORMAT/DEFAULTS
      Environment {
            ambientIntensity    0.2       # SFFloat
            ambientColor        1 1 1     # SFColor
            attenuation         0 0 1     # SFVec3f
            fogType             NONE      # SFEnum
            fogColor            1 1 1     # SFColor
            fogVisibility       0         # SFFloat
      }
```

GeneralCylinder

TODO: Gavin to edit, minor changes

This is a node for parametrically describing numerous families of shapes: extrusions (along an axis or an arbitrary path), surfaces of revolution, and bend/twist/taper objects.

General Cylinders are defined by four piecewise linear curves: crossSection, profile, spine and twist. Shapes are constructed as follows. The crossSection is a 2D curve that is scaled, extruded through space, and twisted by the other curves. First, the crossSection is extruded and scaled along the path of the profile curve. Second, the shape is bent and stretched so that its central axis aligns with the spine curve. Finally, the shape is twisted about the spine by angles (in radians) given by the twist curve. The twist curve is a function of angle at given parametric distances along the spine.

Surfaces of Revolution: If the crossSection is a circle and the spine is straight, then the General Cylinder will be equivalent to a surface of revolution, where the General Cylinder profile curve maps directly to that of the surface of revolution.

Cookie-Cutter Extrusions: If both the profile and spine are straight, then the crossSection acts like a cookie-cutter, with the thickness of the cookie equal to the length of the spine.

Bend/Twist/Taper objects: Shapes like this are the result of utilizing all four curves. The spine curve bends the shape, the twist curve twists it, and the profile curve tapers it.

Planar TOP and BOTTOM surfaces will be generated when the crossSection is closed (i.e., when the first and last points of the crossSection are equal). However, if the profile is also closed, the TOP and BOTTOM are not generated; this is because a closed crossSection extruded along a closed profile creates a shape that is closed without the addition of TOP and BOTTOM parts.

The parts field determines which parts are rendered. The notion of BOTTOM versus TOP is determined by the profile curve. The end of the profile curve with a lesser y value is the BOTTOM end.

The cone is transformed by the current cumulative transformation and is drawn with the current texture and material. The first material in the state is used for the entire GeneralCylinder, regardless of the current material binding.

GeneralCylinder automatically generates its own normals. NormalBinding in the state is ignored. Orientation of the normals is determined by the vertex ordering of the triangles generated by GeneralCylinder. The vertex ordering is in turn determined by the crossSection curve. If the crossSection is drawn counterclockwise, then the polygons will have counterclockwise ordering when viewed from the 'outside' of the shape (and vice versa for clockwise ordered crossSections). The General Cylinder responds to the fields of the ShapeHints node the same way as IndexedFaceSet.

Texture coordinates are automatically generated by General Cylinders. These will map textures like the label on a soup can: the coordinates will range in the u direction from 0 to 1 along the crossSection curve and in the v direction from 0 to 1 along the spine. If the TOP and/or BOTTOM exist, textures map onto them in a planar fashion.

When a texture is applied to a General Cylinder, it is applied differently to the sides, top, and bottom. On the sides, the texture wraps [0,1] of the u-direction of the texture along the crossSection from first point to last; it wraps [0,1] of the v-direction of the texture along the direction of the spine, from first point to last. When the crossSection is closed, the texture has a seam that follows the line traced by the crossSection's start/end point as it travels along the spine. For the top and bottom, the crossSection is cut out of the texture square and applied to the top or bottom circle. The top and bottom textures' u and v directions correspond to the x and z directions in which the crossSection coordinates are defined.

```
PARTS
      SIDES    The extruded surface part
      TOP      The top cross sectional face
      BOTTOM   The bottom cross sectional face
      ALL      All parts
FILE FORMAT/DEFAULTS
      GeneralCylinder {
            spine [ 0 0 0, 0 1 0 ] # MFVec3f
            crossSection [ -1 1, -1 -1, 1 -1, 1 1 ] # MFVec2f
            profile [ 1 -1, 1 1 ] # MFVec2f
            twist [ 0 -1, 0 1 ] # MFVec2f
            parts    ALL    # SFBitMask
      }
```

Pros:

▣ This is an extremely compact way to represent geometry (key for transmission times).

▣ Easy for browsers to do automatic LOD degradation to keep performance up.

NavigationInfo

This node contains information for the viewer through several fields: type, speed, collisionRadius, and headlight.

The type field specifies a navigation paradigm to use. The types that all VRML viewers should support are "walk", "examiner", "fly", and "none". A "walk" viewer would constrain the user to a plane (x-z), suitable for architectural walkthroughs. An "examiner" viewer would let the user tumble the entire scene, suitable for examining single objects. A "fly" viewer would provide six degree of freedom movement. The "none" choice removes all viewer controls, forcing the user to navigate using only WWWAnchors linked to viewpoints. The type field is multi-valued so that authors can specify fall-backs in case a browser does not understand a given type.

The speed is the rate at which the viewer travels through a scene in meters per second. Since viewers may provide mechanisms to travel faster or slower, this should be the default or average speed of the viewer. In an examiner viewer, this only makes sense for panning and dollying - it should have no affect on the rotation speed.

Open issue - no consensus on collisionRadius - see CollideStyle node

The collisionRadius field specifies the smallest allowable distance between the camera position and any collision object (as specified by CollideStyle) before a collision is detected.

Open issue - no consensus on headlight field, relates to discussion on Avatars

The headlight field specifies whether a browser should turn a headlight on. A headlight is a directional light which always points in the direction the camera is looking. This effect can be had by adding a DirectionalLight in front of a Camera in the scene. Instead, setting this field to TRUE allows the browser to provide a headlight possibly with user interface controls to turn it on and off. Scenes that enlist precomputed lighting (e.g. radiosity solutions) can specify the headlight off here. The headlight should have intensity 1, color 1 1 1, and direction 0 0 -1. The effects of specifying headlight on in a NavigationInfo node are equivalent to an author adding a default DirectionalLight in front of a camera in the scene, except that using the NavigationInfo field allows a browser to provide user interface controlling the light.

```
FILE FORMAT/DEFAULTS
    NavigationInfo {
          type            "walk"       # input MFString
          speed           1.0          # input SFFloat
          collisionRadius 1.0          # SFFloat
          headlight       TRUE         # SFBool
    }
```

Notes/Issues:

- The following fields may be dynamic: speed, height, collisionRadius, worldUp

- How is the "knee cap" height specified? That is, at what height does the browser climb something (like stairs) as opposed to collide with it (like a table)? This is currently browser defined (probably as some percentage of the collisionRadius).

and masses could come into play here, but then browsers would be doing simulations which is beyond the scope of VRML 1.1.

▥ *Currently, most browsers automatically turn a headlight on. WebSpace only turns a headlight on if there are no lights in the scene. This means scenes are rendered with different color saturations in different browsers. Adding a headlight field forces browsers to at add headlights consistently.*

PointSound

TODO: Bill to edit, minor edits

This node defines a sound source located at a specific 3D location. The name field specifies a URL from which the sound is read. Implementations should support at least the ??? ??? sound file formats. Streaming sound files may be supported by browsers; otherwise, sounds should be loaded when the sound node is loaded. Browsers may limit the maximum number of sounds that can be played simultaneously.

If multiple URL's are specified then this expresses a descending order of preference, a browser may use a URL for a lower preference file while it is obtaining, or if it is unable to obtain, the higher preference file. See also the section on URNs.

The description field is a textual description of the sound, which may be displayed in addition to or in place of playing the sound.

The intensity field adjusts the volume of each sound source; an intensity of 0 is silence and an intensity of 1 is whatever intensity is contained in the sound file.

The sound source has a radius specified by the minRadius field. When the viewpoint is within this radius, the sound's intensity (volume) is constant, as indicated by the intensity field. Outside the minRadius, the intensity drops off to zero at a distance of maxRadius from the source location. If the two radii are equal, the drop-off is sharp and sudden. Otherwise, the drop-off should be proportional to the square of the distance of the viewpoint from the minRadius.

Browsers may also support spatial localizations of sound. However, within minRadius, localization should not occur, so intensity is constant in all channels. Between minRadius and maxRadius, the sound location should be the point on the minRadius sphere that is closest to the current viewpoint. This ensures a smooth change in location when the viewpoint leaves the minRadius sphere. Note also that an ambient sound can therefore be created by using a large minRadius value.

be the point on the minRadius sphere that is closest to the current viewpoint. This ensures a smooth change in location when the viewpoint leaves the minRadius sphere. Note also that an ambient sound can therefore be created by using a large minRadius value.

The loop field specifies whether or not the sound is constantly repeated. By default, the sound is played only once.

The start input specifies the time at which the sound should start playing. The pause input may be used to make a sound stop playing some time after it has started. If the pause time is less than the start time then it is ignored. Changing the start input while the sound is playing will result in undefined behavior; however, changing the start input after the sound is paused is well-defined and useful. If the sound is not looped, the length of time the sound plays is determined by the sound file read, and is not specified in the VRML file.

A sound's location in the scene graph determines its spatial location (the sound's location is transformed by the current transformation) and whether or not it can be heard. A sound can only be heard while it is part of the traversed scene; sound nodes underneath LOD nodes or Switch nodes will not be audible unless they are traversed. If it is later part of the traversal again, the sound picks up where it would have been had it been playing continuously.

```
FILE FORMAT/DEFAULTS
    PointSound {
        name            ""          # MFString
        description     ""          # SFString
        intensity       1           # SFFloat
        location        0 0 0       # SFVec3f
        minRange        10          # SFFloat
        maxRange        10          # SFFloat
        loop            FALSE       # SFBool
        start           0           # input SFTime
        pause           0           # input SFTime
    }
```

Issues:

What sound file formats do we want to support?

Supporting real-time effects such as frequency modulation, reverb, etc. requires too much CPU performance and is beyond the scope of this spec. Advanced browsers can always define more complicated sound sources and can use the IsA mechanism to maintain compatibility with less capable browsers.

The scene graph semantics chosen allow sounds to be easily attached to objects; putting an object underneath a Switch node is the way to make it (temporarily) disappear from the world. If the sound is part of the object, the sound should also disappear when this happens.

WorldInfo

Open issue—tied into pseudo node proposal, current proposal at *http://earth.path.net/mitra/papers/vrml-pseudo.html*, this is probably OK.

This node contains information about the world. The title of the world is stored in its own field, allowing browsers to display it for instance in their window border. Any other information about the world can be stored in the info field, for instance the scene author, copyright information, and public domain information.

```
FILE FORMAT/DEFAULTS
    WorldInfo {
        title           ""          # SFString
        info            ""          # MFString
    }
```

NEW for 1.1 - Prototyping

Prototyping is a mechanism that allows the set of node types to be extended from within a VRML file. It allows the encapsulation and parameterization of geometry, behaviors, or both.

PROTO

A prototype is defined using the PROTO keyword, as follows:

```
PROTO typename [ eventIn fieldtypename name
                    IS nodename.eventInName nodename.eventInName ... ,
                eventOut fieldtypename name
                    IS nodename.eventOutName nodename.eventOutName ...,
                field fieldtypename name IS nodename.fieldName,
                ... ]
    { node { ... } Logic and/or ROUTES }
```

A prototype is NOT a node; it merely defines a prototype (named 'typename') that can be used later in the same file as if it were a built-in node. The implementation of the prototype is contained in the scene graph rooted by node. That node may be followed by Logic and/or ROUTE declarations, as necessary to implement the prototype.

The eventIn and eventOut declarations export events inside the scene graph given by node. Specifying the type of each event in the prototype is intended to prevent errors when the implementation of prototypes are changed, and to provide consistency with external prototypes. Specifying a name for each event allows several events with the same name to be exported with unique names.

Fields hold the persistent state of VRML objects. Allowing a prototype to export fields allows the initial state of a prototyped object to be specified by prototype instances.

The node names specified in the event and field declarations must be DEF'ed inside the prototype implementation. The first node DEF'ed in lexical (not traversal) order will be exported. It is an error (and results are undefined) if there is no node with the given name, or the first node found does not contain a field of the appropriate type with the given field name. Prototype declarations have file scope, and prototype names must be unique in any given file.

Only nodes DEF'ed inside the prototype may be USE'ed inside the prototype, and nodes DEF'ed inside the prototype are not visible (may note be USE'ed) outside the prototype.

A prototype is instantiated as if typename were a built-in node. A prototype instance may be DEF'ed or USE'ed. For example, a simple chair with variable colors for the leg and seat might be prototyped as:

```
PROTO TwoColorChair [ field SFColor legColor IS leg.diffuseColor,
        field SFColor seatColor IS seat.diffuseColor ] {
      Separator {
          Separator {
              DEF seat Material { diffuseColor .6 .6 .1 }
              Cube { ... }
          }
          Separator {
              Transform { ... }
              DEF leg Material { diffuseColor .8 .4 .7 }
              Cylinder { ... }
          }
      } # End of root Separator
} # End of prototype
# Prototype is now defined.  Can be used like:
DEF redGreenChair TwoColorChair { legColor 1 0 0   seatColor 0 1 0 }

USE redGreenChair # Regular DEF/USE rules apply
```

We're making distinctions between fields, which can be given an initial value but cannot be changed except by the node that they're contained in, and events, which (at least for the built-in nodes) are requests to change fields. So, if we want our TwoColorChair to have colors that can be changed, we'd need to expose the leg.setDiffuseColor 'eventIn' and seat.diffuseColor 'eventIn' events. All of which may make for confusing and wordy prototype declarations. Are there ever cases where you might want to ONLY allow initial values to be set, and NOT allow them to be changed later?

Note: PROTO sort of gives people their non-instantiating DEF: PROTO foo [] Cube { } is roughly equal to DEF foo Cube { }, except that foo is now a type name instead of an instance name (and you say foo { } to get another cube instead of USE foo). Smart implementations will automatically share the unchanging stuff in prototype implementations, so the end result will be the same.

NodeReference

What if we wanted a prototype that could be instantiated with arbitrary geometry? For example, we might want to define a prototype chair that allowed the geometry for the legs to be defined, with the default (perhaps) being a simple cylinder.

VRML 1.1 will include the SFNode field type— a field that contains a pointer to a node. Using SFNode, it is easy to write the first part of the PROTO definition:

```
PROTO Chair [ field SFNode legGeometry IS
```

... but then we get stuck when we try to define the IS part of the prototype. We need some way of taking an SFNode field and inserting it into the scene. This can be accomplished with a new node, the NodeReference node:

```
NodeReference {
    node NULL  # SFNode field  (NULL is valid syntax for SFNode)
    # eventIn SFNode setNode
    # eventOut SFNode nodeChanged
}
```

Functionally, NodeReference is a "do-nothing" node— it just behaves exactly like whatever 'nodeToUse' points to (unless nodeToUse is NULL, of course, in which case NodeReference does nothing). For example, this would be a verbose way to add a Sphere to the scene:

```
NodeReference { nodeToUse Sphere { } }
```

NodeReference is only interesting if its nodeToUse field is exposed in a prototype (or it receives a nodeToUse event). So, for example, our Chair with arbitrary leg geometry (with a Cylinder default if none is specified) can be filled out as:

```
PROTO Chair [ field SFNode legGeometry  IS  NR.nodeToUse ] {
    Separator {
```

```
    Separator {
        Transform { ... }
        DEF NR NodeReference { nodeToUse Cylinder { } }
    }
    Separator {
        Transform { ... }
        USE NR
    }
    ... would re-use leg with a USE NR, would have
    geometry for seat/back/etc...
    }
}
```

Using the Chair prototype would look like:

```
Chair {
    legGeometry Separator { Coordinate3/IndexedFaceSet/etc }
}
```

It might also make sense to share the same geometry between several proto-type instances; for example, you might do:

```
Chair {
    legGeometry DEF LEG Separator { Coordinate3/IndexedFaceSet/etc }
}
```

... somewhere later in scene...

```
Chair {
    legGeometry USE LEG
}
```

Note that SFNode fields follow the regular DEF/USE rules, and that SFNode fields contain a pointer to a node; using DEF/USE an SFNode field may contain a pointer to a node that is also a child of some node in the scene graph, is pointed to by some other SFNode field, etc.

The NodeReference node has nice, clean semantics, and allows a lot of flexibility and power for defining prototypes. It also has some nice implementation side effects:

Browsers that want to maintain a different internal representation for the scene graph can implement NodeReference so that nodeToUse is read and the different internal representation is generated. Optimizations might also be performed at the same time:

Browsers that optimize scene graphs can implement NodeReference such that whenever nodeToUse changes an optimized scene is created. When rendering, the optimized scene will be used instead of the unotimized scene.

A really smart browser will figure out that nobody is using the unopti-mized scene and may free it from memory.

Something else to think about: should a prototype be allowed to expose the fields or events of an SFNode that is passed in? For example:

```
PROTO Foo [ field SFNode transform        IS NR.nodeToUse,
            eventIn SFVec3f setPosition IS NR.nodeToUse.translation ]
Separator { DEF NR NodeReference { nodeToUse Transform { } } Cube { } }
```

This could be pretty powerful, but might also be painful to implement, since the type-checking would have to be done at run-time when NR.nodeToUse changed.

EXTERNPROTO

A second form of the prototype syntax allows prototypes to be defined in external files:

```
EXTERNPROTO typename [ eventIn fieldtypename name,
                       eventOut fieldtypename name,
                       field fieldtypename,
                       ... ]
          URL or [ URL, URL, ... ]
```

In this case, the implementation of the prototype is found in the given URL. The file pointed to by that URL must contain ONLY a single prototype implementation (using PROTO). That prototype is then given the name typename in this file's scope (allowing possible naming clashes to be avoided). It is an error if the eventIn/eventOut declaration in the EXTERNPRO-TO is not a subset of the eventIn/eventOut declaration specified in URL.

Note: The rules about allowing exporting only from files that contain a single PROTO declaration are consistent with the WWWInline rules; until we have VRML-aware protocols that can send just one object or prototype declaration across the wire, I don't think we should encourage people to put multiple objects or prototype declarations in a single file.

We need to think about scalability when using nested EXTERNPROTO's. EXTERNPROTOS don't have bounding boxes specified like WWWInlines, and they might need them. I'm starting to think that we might need to add bboxCenter/Size fields to Separator instead of having them only on WWWInline; with animations possible, pre-specifying maximum-possible bounding boxes could save a lot of work recalculating bounding boxes as things move.

MODIFIED 1.1 - Extensibility

TODO: Jan to handle type_registry@vrml.org for new suffixes

Extensions to VRML are supported by supporting self-describing nodes. Nodes that are not part of standard VRML must write out a description of their fields first, so that all VRML implementations are able to parse and ignore the extensions.

This description is written just after the opening curly-brace for the node, and consists of the keyword 'fields' followed by a list of the types and names of fields used by that node, all enclosed in square brackets and separated by commas. For example, if Cube was not a standard VRML node, it would be written like this:

```
Cube {
  fields [ SFFloat width, SFFloat height, SFFloat depth ]
  width 10 height 4 depth 3
}
```

Specifying the fields for nodes that ARE part of standard VRML is not an error; VRML parsers must silently ignore the field[] specification. However, incorrectly specifying the fields of a built-in node is an error.

The fields specification must be written out with every non-standard node, whether or not that node type was previously encountered during parsing. For each instance of a non-standard node, only the fields written as part of that instance need to be described in the fields[] specification; that is, fields that aren't written because they contain their default value may be omitted from the fields[] specification. It is expected that future versions of VRML will relax this requirement, requiring only that the first non-standard node of a given type be given the fields[] specification.

Just like standard nodes, instances of non-standard nodes do not automatically share anything besides the default values of their fields, which are not specified in the VRML file but are considered part of the implementation of the non-standard nodes.

Is-A relationships

A new node type may also be a superset of an existing node that is part of the standard. In this case, if an implementation for the new node type cannot be found the new node type can be safely treated as as the existing node it is based on (with some loss of functionality, of course). To support this, new node types can define an MFString field called 'isA' containing the names of the types of which it is a superset. For example, a new type of Material called "ExtendedMaterial" that adds index of refraction as a material property can be written as:

```
ExtendedMaterial {
   fields [ MFString isA, MFFloat indexOfRefraction,
            MFColor diffuseColor, MFFloat transparency ]
   isA [ "Material" ]
   indexOfRefraction .34
   diffuseColor .8 .54 1
}
```

Multiple is-a relationships may be specified in order of preference; implementations are expected to use the first for which there is an implementation.

Note that IsA and PROTO are different ways to define new nodes, they should not be used together.

Nodes instantiated with isA should not copy default values or children from the first instantiation.

Alternate representations

To allow extension nodes to be handled gracefully by browsers that don't recognise them, a alternateRep field is supported. This is an SFNode field that specifies what to use if the extension node is not recognised, typically it will be a WWWInline of a more complex representation, or of a CGI script which can generate the node dynamically, for example:

```
ColoredCube {
        isA Cube
        fields [ SFColor color ]
        color 2 0 0
        alternateRep {
                WWWInline {
                        name "http://foo.com/cgi/ColoredCube/2/0/0"
                }
        }
}
```

Naming conventions

Check the General Syntax section of this standard for the rules on valid characters in names.

To avoid namespace collisions with nodes defined by other people, any of the following conventions should be followed.

1. Anyone can pick names that include a suffix of an underscore followed by a domain name that you own with the periods changed into underscores. For example a company owning foo.com could create an extension node "Cube_foo_com"

2. If you are building a product for example an authoring tool, or a browser, or defining a lot of new nodes then you can apply for a short prefix. Email type_registry@vrml.org to register for the prefix. This will normally be accepted if it is the most significant part of a .com, .org or .net address, in the above example foo.com could register the extension "_foo" and create nodes of the form "Cube_foo".

3. Extensions supported by several companies should be registered and use the "_X" extension.

This process may change as more experience is gained.

URN's

VRML1.1 browsers are not required to support URN's although if they don't then they should ignore URN's when they appear in MFString fields with URL's. URN support is specified in a seperate document at *http://earth.path.net/mitra/papers/vrml-urn.html*, which may undergo minor revisions to keep it inline with parallel work happening at the IETF.

An Example

This is a longer example of a VRML scene. It contains a simple model of a track-light consisting of primitive shapes, plus three walls (built out of polygons) and a reference to a shape defined elsewhere, both of which are illuminated by a spotlight. The shape acts as a hyperlink to some HTML text.

```
#VRML V1.1 utf8
Separator {
    Separator {          # Simple track-light geometry:
        Translation { translation 0 4 0 }
        Separator {
            Material { emissiveColor 0.1 0.3 0.3 }
            Cube {
                width   0.1
                height  0.1
                depth   4
            }
        }
        Rotation { rotation 0 1 0  1.57079 }
        Separator {
            Material { emissiveColor 0.3 0.1 0.3 }
            Cylinder {
                radius  0.1
                height  .2
            }
        }
    }
```

```
        Rotation { rotation -1 0 0  1.57079 }
        Separator {
            Material { emissiveColor 0.3 0.3 0.1 }
            Rotation { rotation 1 0 0  1.57079 }
            Translation { translation 0 -.2 0 }
            Cone {
                height   .4
                bottomRadius .2
            }
            Translation { translation 0 .4 0 }
            Cylinder {
                radius   0.02
                height   .4
            }
        }
    }
}
SpotLight {        # Light from above
    location 0 4 0
    direction 0 -1 0
    intensity       0.9
    cutOffAngle     0.7
}
Separator {        # Wall geometry; just three flat polygons
    Coordinate3 {
        point [
            -2 0 -2, -2 0 2, 2 0 2, 2 0 -2,
            -2 4 -2, -2 4 2, 2 4 2, 2 4 -2]
    }
    IndexedFaceSet {
        coordIndex [ 0, 1, 2, 3, -1,
                     0, 4, 5, 1, -1,
                     0, 3, 7, 4, -1
                   ]
    }
}
WWWAnchor {   # A hyperlinked cow:
    name "http://www.foo.edu/CowProject/AboutCows.html"
    Separator {
        Translation { translation 0 1 0 }
        WWWInline {   # Reference another object
            name "http://www.foo.edu/3DObjects/cow.wrl"
        }
    }
}
}
```

BROWSER CONSIDERATIONS

This section describes the file naming and MIME conventions to be used in building VRML browsers and configuring WWW browsers to work with them.

File Extensions

The file extension for VMRL files is .wrl (for world).

MIME

The MIME type for VRML files is defined as follows:

`x-world/x-vrml`

The MIME major type for 3D world descriptions is x-world. The MIME minor type for VRML documents is x-vrml. Other 3D world descriptions, such as oogl for The Geometry Center's Object-Oriented Geometry Language, or iv, for SGI's Open Inventor ASCII format, can be supported by using different MIME minor types.

It is anticipated that the official type will change to "model/vrml", at this time servers should present files as being of type x-world/x-vrml, browsers should recognise both x-world/x-vrml and model/vrml.

ACKNOWLEDGEMENTS

I want to thank three people who have been absolutely instrumental in the design process: Brian Behlendorf, whose drive (and disk space) made this process happen; and Tony Parisi and Gavin Bell, the final authors of this specification, who have put in a great deal of design work, ensuring that we have a satisfactory product. My hat goes off to all of them, and to all of you who have made this process a success.

Mark Pesce
I would like to add a personal note of thanks to Jan Hardenbergh of Oki Advanced Products for his diligent efforts to keep the specification process on track, and his invaluable editing assistance. I would also like to acknowledge Chris Marrin of Silicon Graphics for his timely contributions to the final design.

Tony Parisi
VRML 1.1 is a result of years of effort from the Inventor group at Silicon Graphics. All of the past and present members of the Inventor team deserve recognition and thanks for their excellent work over the last five years.

Gavin Bell
22-NOV-95

REFERENCES

The draft of the ISO UTF-8 proposal is online at:
http://www.stonehand.com/unicode/standard/wg2n1036.html

The draft for making HTML internationalized is online. We are not as constrained as HTML, since VRML will rarely be primarily text. We can be a little less efficient.

ftp://ftp.alis.com/pub/ietf/html/draft-ietf-html-i18n-00.txt

ftp://ftp.isi.edu/in-notes/rfc1766.txt

OpenGL specification and man pages are online: *http://www.sgi.com/Technology/openGL/spec.html*

Addison Wesley's "The Inventor Mentor" and "Open Inventor C++ Reference Manual" are invaluable.

TO DO

- * URN
    - Mark to write sample code
    - Mitra to revise proposal in light of IETF meeting in early December
- Gavin to spell check
- Rikk and Gavin - Input fields
- Gavin - add URL to this doc
- Gavin - deprecated features added to contents list
- Mark - specify conformance process
- VAG - check for other things which should be Input fields.
- VAG - revist NavigationInfo -
- VAG/Jan - which stings should be UTF-8, URLS? do we need a new type?

3D MODELING
IN WINDOWS 95

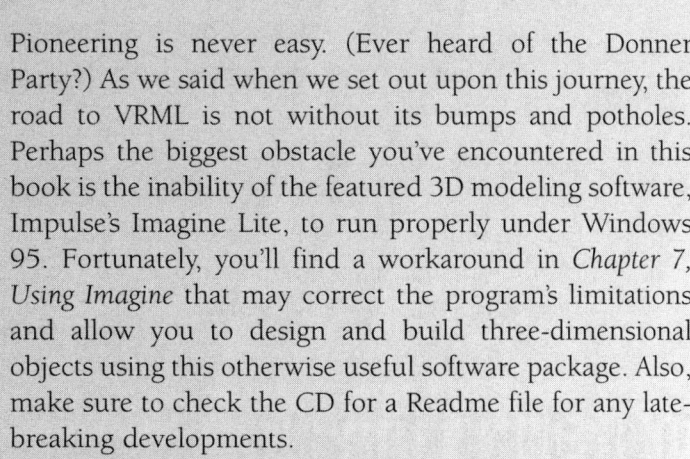

Pioneering is never easy. (Ever heard of the Donner Party?) As we said when we set out upon this journey, the road to VRML is not without its bumps and potholes. Perhaps the biggest obstacle you've encountered in this book is the inability of the featured 3D modeling software, Impulse's Imagine Lite, to run properly under Windows 95. Fortunately, you'll find a workaround in *Chapter 7, Using Imagine* that may correct the program's limitations and allow you to design and build three-dimensional objects using this otherwise useful software package. Also, make sure to check the CD for a Readme file for any late-breaking developments.

IMAGINE USING TRUESPACE2

As this book went to press, we became aware of an alternative 3D modeling program, Caligari's trueSpace2, which is not only extremely robust, but also has the added attractiveness of being fully compatible with Windows 95. If Imagine Lite is not working properly on your system (or if it is, but you'd like to try another modeling software option), we've included a demo version of trueSpace2 on the CD; it provides you with full-feature access to the program for a 30-day trial period. You can install this 3D modeler and use it to create 3D objects in Windows 95.

trueSpace2 Quick Reference

Remember those electric razor ads where the company CEO would proclaim, "I liked it so much, I bought the company"? Of course, we didn't actually purchase Caligari, but we've definitely bought into the future of trueSpace2, which is proving to be as powerful as it is reliable. Waite Group Press is so impressed by the software that they have committed to printing a book dedicated to this fast-rising star. Available as of October 1996, *3D Modeling Construction Kit* (by David Duberman, ISBN 1-576169-029-8) shows users with step-by-step projects how to create dazzling 3D objects and environments in Windows 95. The following reference is an appendix appearing in that book and is provided here courtesy of the author.

Although we cannot re-create all the lessons dedicated to Impulse's Imagine Lite in the space provided here, this reference, combined with the concepts of construction covered in this book in *Part II: Learning 3D Modeling,* will provide enough background information to design 3D objects using trueSpace2 for your VRML worlds.

TOOLS QUICK REFERENCE

Icon-based functions in trueSpace2 are known collectively as tools, even if they're used for non-tool functions such as changing the view. This is a listing of each of trueSpace2's tools with the icon, name of the tool, and associated keystroke, if any.

View Group

The View tool group is attached to the main window. It contains tools for viewpoint navigation, changing the view mode, opening new windows and view-related utilities. The Display Mode, Render, View Select and View Navigation tools are also present in the smaller auxiliary windows opened with the New Window tools.

Display Modes

 Wireframe Display (default): Redraws the objects in the workspace as wireframes. Use it after rendering, or to switch back from Solid Render Display mode. In this mode, a selected object is white, non-selected objects are dark blue, and non-selected objects in a hierarchy are orange.

 Solid Render Display (available from pop-up): Invokes the Intel 3DR library. In this mode, the selected object is always drawn as a solid when at rest, and is indicated by a 3D arrow. Depending on its complexity and Preference Panel's Threshold setting, it may switch to a bounding box when being manipulated. Other objects may be drawn as solid, wireframes or bounding boxes, depending on the Preference Panel's Scene Detail setting. Other Solid Render Display options can be set in the Render Quality panel, invoked by right-clicking the Solid Render Display tool.

Render Tools

 Render Current Object (default) (F2): Draws the current object as a textured solid, using trueSpace2's standard rendering mode. Ray-tracing, shadows, etc., are not available with this command.

 Render Scene (available from pop-up): Draws the entire scene contents, plus optional background, as textured solids, using trueSpace2's standard rendering mode. Ray-tracing, shadows, etc., are available with this command. Open Render Options panel by right-clicking this tool.

Render Scene to File (available from pop-up): Draws the entire scene contents, plus optional background, as textured solids, using trueSpace2's standard rendering mode, and saves image or animation to disk. Ray-tracing, shadows, etc., are available with this command. Open Render Options panel by right-clicking this tool.

View Select Tools

 Perspective View (default) (F3): Sets the window to a perspective view, looking at the scene from the point of view of an invisible "eye" that can be moved, rotated, and zoomed in and out.

 Front View (available from pop-up): Sets the window to an orthogonal view from the front, looking down the Y axis. The view cannot be rotated, and it can be moved only in the XZ plane.

 Left View (available from pop-up): Sets the window to an orthogonal view from the left side, looking down the X axis. The view cannot be rotated, and it can be moved only in the YZ plane.

 Top View (available from pop-up): Sets the window to an orthogonal view from the top, looking down the Z axis. The view cannot be rotated, and it can be moved only in the XY plane.

 View from Object (available from pop-up): Sets the window to a perspective view, using the currently selected object as the "camera," looking down the object's Z axis.

View Navigation Tools

 Eye Move: Enables repositioning the point of view by dragging the mouse in the window. Right-click to open Coordinates property panel, for setting coordinate system and enabling/disabling movement along specific axes.

 Eye Rotate: Enables re-orienting the point of view by dragging the mouse in the window. The orthogonal Front, Left and Top views cannot be rotated.

Right-click to open Coordinates property panel, for setting coordinate system and enabling/disabling rotation on specific axes.

 Zoom: Enables enlarging and reducing the scale of the view by dragging the mouse in the window. The view cannot be scaled along specific axes.

New Window Tools

These tools, used for opening smaller auxiliary views into the workspace, are found only in the main window View tool group. No more than three auxiliary views can be open at once.

 New Perspective View (default): Opens a new auxiliary window in perspective view mode.

 New Front View (available from pop-up): Opens a new auxiliary window in front view mode.

 New Left View (available from pop-up): Opens a new auxiliary window in left view mode.

 New Top View (available from pop-up): Opens a new auxiliary window in top view mode.

View Utilities

 Close All Panels (default): Closes any open tool property or control panels.

 Dock All Panels (available from pop-up): Lines up any open tool property or control panels above (or below) the "floating" tool groups.

 Look at Object (available from pop-up): In Perspective View mode, rotates the viewpoint to look at the selected object. In Front, Left and Top View modes, moves the viewpoint to center the selected object. Has no effect in View from Object mode.

Reset View (available from pop-up): Returns Perspective, Front, Left and Top View windows to their original positions.

Object Navigation Group

This group contains tools for selecting and manipulating specific objects, and navigating through hierarchical objects' vertical levels.

 Object Tool (space bar): Returns to object manipulation mode from use of other tools, such as point editing. Right-click to open Object Info panel, which allows renaming objects, observing their statistics, and manipulating them via numerical settings.

 Object Move (Z): Enables repositioning the selected object by dragging the mouse in the workspace. Right-click to open Coordinates property panel, for setting coordinate system and enabling/disabling movement along specific axes.

 Object Rotate (X): Enables re-orienting the selected object by dragging the mouse in the workspace. Right-click to open Coordinates property panel, for setting coordinate system and enabling/disabling rotation on specific axes.

 Object Scale (C): Enables resizing the selected object by dragging the mouse in the workspace. Right-click to open Coordinates property panel, for setting coordinate system and enabling/disabling scaling on specific axes.

Hierarchy Navigation Tools

 Navigate Down (default at topmost level) (down arrow key): Select first object in first node below the current hierarchical level. Use the left and right arrow keys to select other objects in the same node.

Navigate Up (default at all levels below topmost) (up arrow key): Select first object in first node above the current hierarchical level. Use the left and right arrow keys to select other objects in the same node.

Model Group

These tools are for creating and editing custom objects.

Point Edit Tools

The Point Edit tools allow selecting part or parts of the current object (that is, vertices, edges and/or faces) for further manipulation. Select multiple non-adjacent elements by holding the Ctrl key, and adjacent entities by holding the Shift key. Selecting any Point Edit tool opens the Point Navigation panel, with Move, Rotate and Scale tools for manipulating the selected object part or parts.

 Context (default): Enables selection of vertices by clicking on edge intersections, of edges by clicking on edges between intersections, and of faces by clicking on object away from edges and edge intersections.

 Faces (available from pop-up): Enables selection of faces only.

 Edges (available from pop-up): Enables selection of edges only.

 Vertices (available from pop-up): Enables selection of vertices only.

 Delete Face (available from pop-up): Enables deletion of all faces clicked on when the tool is active, indicated by the mouse cursor's appearance as an arrow with a small rectangular cut-out and the letter "F" attached.

Sweep Tools

These tools enable creation of three-dimensional objects from a selected face or faces, whether stand-alone or belonging to an existing object.

 Sweep (default): Causes the selected face or faces to be extruded outward. Using the Sweep tool opens the Point Navigation panel, with Move, Rotate and Scale tools for manipulating the extruded face or faces.

 Bevel (available from pop-up): Creates beveled extrusion, in which outer edges are swept inward and inner edges (that is, of holes in face) are swept outward.

 Macro/Sweep (available from pop-up): Upon initial invocation, attaches the default or most recently used sweep path to selected face(s). Rotate the path by dragging the mouse in the workspace, or select a different path from the Path library. Select the Macro/Sweep tool again to perform the path sweep.

 Lathe (available from pop-up): Upon initial invocation, attaches the default or most recently used lathe path to selected face(s). Edit the path by clicking and dragging on its various elements, then select the Lathe tool again to perform the lathe operation.

 Tip (available from pop-up): Sweeps selected face(s) to a point.

Deform/Sculpt Tools

These tools enable manipulating object surfaces like clay or putty. The first three tools are all on one pop-up, while the Sculpt tool occupies its own spot in the Model group.

 Deform Object (default): Creates a deform lattice around an object. Clicking and dragging enables moving, rotating and scaling of object surface underlying lattice intersections or cross-sections, depending on the options selected in the Deform Navigation panel.

Start Deforming by Stand-alone Deformation Object (available from pop-up): Creates connection between object and free-standing deformation object (created from Primitives panel). Used for animation; objects must be juxtaposed in space.

 Stop Deforming by Stand-alone Deformation Object (available from pop-up): Breaks connection between object and free-standing deformation object (created from Primitives panel).

 Sculpt Surface: Enables pushing/pulling of object parts with adjustable tool. Selecting tool opens panel that allows moving deformation, adjusting its scope, and copying it to other parts of the object.

Boolean Tools

These tools let you apply Boolean operations to pairs of objects. You cannot use the Boolean tools with objects imported in the DXF format.

 Object Subtraction (default): Enables sculpting of an object by subtracting other objects. First, position the two objects by overlapping their volumes. Select the object to be sculpted, then this tool, and finally the object to be subtracted. In some circumstances, can be used to eliminate unnecessary geometry in sculpted object by subtracting non-overlapping object.

 Object Intersection (available from pop-up): Creates new object consisting of overlapping volume of two objects.

 Object Union (available from pop-up): Creates new object consisting of combined volumes of two objects, which need not overlap.

Polygon Tools

These tools enable the creation of two-dimensional shapes that can be used for a variety of purposes, including as stand-alone flat objects.

Spline Polygon (default): Allows point-by-point drawing of spline-based polygons, which can be added to Path library at any point during creation. Draw Path panel options allow adjustment of splines before finishing polygon. Right-click on tool for Spline panel, which allows further modification.

 Polygon (available from pop-up): Enables point-by-point drawing of straight-edged polygons. Use Poly Modes panel options to implement Boolean operations between polygons.

 Regular Polygon (available from pop-up): Enables click-and-drag center-outward drawing of regular polygons. Use Poly Modes panel options to set the number of sides, and to implement Boolean operations between polygons.

Utilities Group

This group contains tools that don't fit into any other group, but which perform a variety of useful functions.

 Grid Snap: Toggles step-wise adjustment of view and manipulation of objects. Right-click to open Grid panel for numeric adjustment.

 Axes: Toggles object axes visibility, and enables manipulation of axes using standard object navigation tools when visible.

Normalize Tools

These variants set an object or its axes to its original status and center its axis.

 Normalize Rotation (default): Sets selected object back to its original orientation by aligning its axes with World axes.

Normalize Location (available from pop-up): Positions selected object at the center of the workspace, that is, at position X=0, Y=0, Z=0.

 Normalize Scale (available from pop-up): Resizes object to its original scale as created or loaded.

 Center Axes (available from pop-up): Positions selected object's axes at geometric center of the object, and selects axes. Click on Axes tool to return to normal.

Geometry Tools

These tools are loosely related in that their functions, for the most part, affect an object's geometry either directly or indirectly.

 Smooth Quad Divide (default): Subdivides all of an object's polygons into quadrangles and/or triangles, and adjusts new vertices' positions to smooth outline. Does not affect polygons whose angles to each other exceed Subdivision threshold (right-click on tool icon).

 Quad Divide (available from pop-up): Subdivides object's polygons without altering new vertices' positions.

 Triangulate Object (available from pop-up): Subdivides all of an object's non-triangular polygons into triangles.

 Decompose (available from pop-up): Breaks down surface groups in certain imported objects into object hierarchy.

 Mirror (available from pop-up): Reverses object geometry along Word XZ plane.

Fix Bad Geometry (available from pop-up): Attempts to resolve incorrect geometry in imported objects.

 Reverse Normals (available from pop-up): Flips all of an object's faces, so that all polygons that were facing inward now face outward, and vice versa. Useful for selecting non-accessible faces "inside" an object, or on a side not facing you.

 Dimensioning Tool (available from pop-up): Creates a non-renderable "ruler" with dynamically updated measurement between two points on an object.

Edit Group

These tools replicate functions found in the Edit menu and enable building and destroying object hierarchies.

 Undo (default) (Ctrl Z): Reverses most recent operation. In most cases, trueSpace2 remembers the most recent sequence of operations, and repeated use of the Undo function reverses each step in the chain in reverse order. Righ-click on tool icon to access options panel.

 Redo (available from pop-up): Restores most recently undone operation. Repeated use of Redo applies the operation cumulatively.

 Erase (Del): Deletes selected object from the workspace.

 Copy (Ctrl C): Makes an exact copy of the selected object in the same place as the original.

Glue Tools

 Glue as Child (default): Creates hierarchical structure, with the first object selected (before selecting the tool) as the child of the second object selected.

Glue as Sibling (available from pop-up): Combines objects at the same hierarchical level.

 Unglue (available from pop-up): Only available when sub-object(s) of a hierarchical structure is (are) selected. Detaches selected object(s) from structure.

Render Group

Despite the name of this group, its tools are actually used to create and modify textures and apply them to object surfaces.

Paint Tools

Selecting any of these tools automatically opens the four paint panels, for setting Material attributes.

 Paint Face (default): The current Material is applied to any faces clicked on when this tool is active. Objects need not be selected first. Drag the mouse to paint adjacent faces.

 Paint Object (available from pop-up): Applies the current Material to selected object(s). One-time use only.

 Paint Over (available from pop-up): Replaces the Material clicked on in the workspace wherever it exists in that object with the current Material.

 Inspect (available from pop-up): Sets the current Material to the Material clicked on in the workspace.

 Paint Vertices (available from pop-up): The current Material, sans texture mapping, is applied to any vertices, blending into the existing Material on adjacent faces.

UV Projection: Enables applying planar, cylindrical or spherical UV mapping space to an object, which determines how texture maps are "wrapped" onto its surface.

 Material Rectangle: Enables applying discrete rectangles of the current Material to object surfaces. Rectangles can be layered, repositioned and scaled.

 Plug-ins: Enables post-rendering processing of rendered scenes with up to four Adobe Photoshop-compatible plug-in filters.

Library Group

These tools give access to trueSpace2's Material and Path libraries and Primitives panel.

 Material Library: Opens the Material Library, which allows storing, naming, selection and deletion of Materials, as well as viewing of stored Materials. Also includes functions for saving and loading library files.

 Path Library: Opens the Path Library, which allows storing, naming, selection and deletion of Materials. Also includes functions for saving and loading library files.

 Primitives Panel: Opens the Primitives panel, which enables creating six geometric primitives and stand-alone deform primitives, as well as adding camera, text and light objects.

Animation Group

These tools allow animation setup and modification.

 Animation Tool: Opens the Animation panel, which gives access to basic animation functions, including moving between frames and keyframes, recording keyframes, and playing animations. Right-click on the panel's Play button to access the Animation Parameters panel, and on the Record button to access a control for toggling automatic animation recording. Right-click on any other button to access the Keyframe Monitor for editing keyframes.

 Animation Path: Enables drawing and editing spline paths along which objects move during an animation. Uses the same additional controls as the Spline Polygon tool.

 Look At (default): Forces an object to continually re-orient itself during an animation to keep its Z-axis pointed at another object. Select the "looker" object first, then this tool, then the object to be looked at.

 Look Ahead (available from pop-up): Forces an object to continually re-orient itself during an animation to keep its Z-axis pointed "forward" on the path along which it moves.

 Animation Project Window: Opens the Animation Project window, with animation editing functions.

INDEX

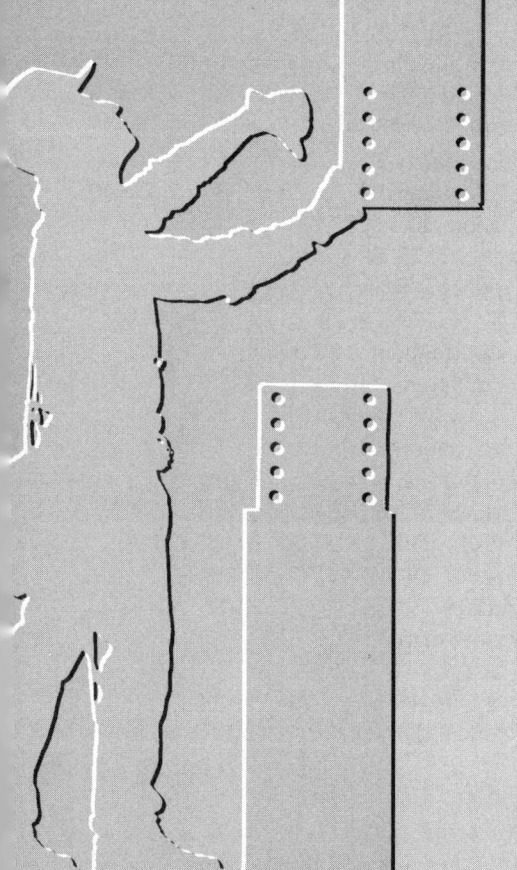